Lecture Notes in Computer Science

Edited by G. Goos, J. Hartmanis and J. van Leeuwen

Advisory Board: W. Brauer   D. Gries   J. Stoer

Springer

Berlin
Heidelberg
New York
Barcelona
Budapest
Hong Kong
London
Milan
Paris
Tokyo

Victor Malyshkin (Ed.)

Parallel Computing Technologies

Third International Conference, PaCT-95
St. Petersburg, Russia, September 12-25, 1995
Proceedings

 Springer

Series Editors

Gerhard Goos
Universität Karlsruhe
Vincenz-Priessnitz-Straße 3, D-76128 Karlsruhe, Germany

Juris Hartmanis
Department of Computer Science, Cornell University
4130 Upson Hall, Ithaca, NY 14853, USA

Jan van Leeuwen
Department of Computer Science, Utrecht University
Padualaan 14, 3584 CH Utrecht, The Netherlands

Volume Editor

Victor Malyshkin
Supercomputer Software Department, Computing Center
Siberian Division of the Russian Academy of Sciences
Lavrentiev 6, Novosibirsk, 630090 Russia

Cataloging-in-Publication data applied for

Die Deutsche Bibliothek - CIP-Einheitsaufnahme

Parallel computing technologies : third international
conference ; proceedings / PaCT-95, St. Petersburg, Russia,
September 12 - 25, 1995. Victor Malyshkin (ed.). - Berlin ;
Heidelberg ; New York ; Barcelona ; Budapest ; Hong Kong ;
London ; Milan ; Paris ; Tokyo : Springer, 1995
  (Lecture notes in computer science ; 964)
  ISBN 3-540-60222-4
NE: Malyškin, Viktor [Hrsg.]; PaCT <1995, Sankt-Peterburg>; GT

CR Subject Classification (1991): C.1-4, D.1-4, F.1-2

ISBN 3-540-60222-4 Springer-Verlag Berlin Heidelberg New York

This work is subject to copyright. All rights are reserved, whether the whole or part of the material is
concerned, specifically the rights of translation, reprinting, re-use of illustrations, recitation, broadcasting,
reproduction on microfilms or in any other way, and storage in data banks. Duplication of this publication
or parts thereof is permitted only under the provisions of the German Copyright Law of September 9, 1965,
in its current version, and permission for use must always be obtained from Springer -Verlag. Violations are
liable for prosecution under the German Copyright Law.

© Springer-Verlag Berlin Heidelberg 1995
Printed in Germany

Typesetting: Camera-ready by author
SPIN 10486622   06/3142 – 5 4 3 2 1 0   Printed on acid-free paper

Preface

PaCT 95 (Parallel Computing Technologies) conference was held in St. Petersburg during the four days September 12–15, 1995. It was the third International conference of PaCT series which are organized in Russia each odd year. The first PaCT 91 was held in Novosibirsk (Academgorodok), September 7–11. The second PaCT 93 was held in Obninsk (near Moscow), August 30 – September 4.

PaCT 95 was organized by the Computing Center of Russian Academy of Sciences (Novosibirsk) and by the Electrotechnical University of St. Petersburg.

The purpose of the conference was to bring together scientists working with theory, architecture, software, hardware, and solution of large–size problems to provide integrated discussions on Parallel Computing Technologies. This area of parallel processing gives us a chance to test our theories, models, languages and programming systems for validity and sometimes it happens that we are disappointed.

The Conference attracted more than 100 participants from around the world. Authors from over 15 countries submitted 98 papers, of which 6 were from invited speakers and 41 were contributed papers; in addition there were a number of posters presented. All the papers were internationally reviewed by at least three referees.

Many thanks to our sponsors: DRET/DS/SSR (France), IBM (USA), Parsytec (Germany), the Russian Academy of Sciences, the Russian Fund of Fundamental Research, the Russian State Committee for Higher Education for their financial support. Organizers highly appreciate the help on the part of the ACM SIGPLAN and the Association Antenne Provence (France).

June 1995

Victor Malyshkin
PaCT–95 Programm Committee Chair
Novosibirsk, Academgorodok

A.Alekseev   General Chairman

Program Committee

V. Malyshkin   Chairman
                      Computing Centre, Academy of Sciences,
                      Novosibirsk, Russia

O. Bandman   Computing Centre, Academy of Sciences,
                      Novosibirsk, Russia

H. Burkhart   Universität Basel, Switzerland

V. Burtsev   Institute for High-Performance Computer Systems,
                      Academy of Sciences (IHPCS), Moscow, Russia.

M. Cosnard   Ecole Normale Superieure de Lyon, France

J. Dongarra   University of Tennessee, USA

W. Gentzsch   GENIAS Software GmbH, Münich, Germany

W. Händler   Erlangen-Nürnberg University, Germany

V. Ivannikov   Institute of System Programming, Academy of Sciences,
                      Moscow, Russia

V. Kotov   HP, Palo Alto, USA

A. Liss   Electrotechnical University of St.-Petersburg,
                      Russia

G. Mauri   University of Milano, Italy

N. Mirenkov   University of of Aizu, Japan

E. Ozkarahan   Dokuz Eylul University, Izmir, Turkey

I. Pottosin   Institute of Informatics Systems, Academy of Sciences,
                      Novosibirsk, Russia

B. Roux   Institut de Mecanique des Fluides de Marseille, France

G. Silberman   IBM, T. Watson Research Center, New York, USA

J. Smith   Drexel University, Philadelphia, USA

H. Zima   University of Vienna, Austria

Organizing Committee

V. Malyshkin	Co-Chairman
D. Puzankov	Co-Chairman
O. Bandman	
A. Kraynikov	Vice-Chairman
N. Kuchin	
A. Liss	
V. Markova	Secretariat
V. Plusnin	
V. Rjabov	Financial director
V. Torgashov	
A. Vazhenin	Publication

List of referees

S. Achasova
H. Burkhart
M. Campbell
M. Cosnard
P. Degano
J. Dongarra
V. Evstigneev
Ya. Fet
H. Franke
J. Hulman
H. Hum
Yu. Kolosova
V. Korneev
V. Kotov
V. Malyshkin
G. Mauri
G. McNiven
N. Mirenkov
O. Monakhov

R. Mraz
M. Lucka
V. Nepomniaschy
E. Ozkarahan
S. Piskunov
I. Pottosin
C. Priami
B. Roux
N. Shilov
G. Silberman
J. Smith
I. Spillinger
M. Vajtersic
V. Valkovskii
V. Varshavsky
A. Vazhenin
V. Vshivkov
D. Yelinov
G. Zabinyako
H. Zima

Contents

Theory

S.M. Achasova
Synchronous-Asynchronous Cellular Computations 1

G.P. Agibalov
Parallel Computations and Finite Automata on Semilattices 7

A.V. Anisimov
Linear Fibonacci Forms and Parallel Algorithms
for High Dimension Arithmetic 16

O.L. Bandman
Cellular-Neural Computations. Formal Model and Possible Applications ... 21

A. Bianchi, S. Coluccini, P. Degano, C. Priami
An Efficient Verifier of Truly Concurrent Properties 36

F. Gasperoni, U. Schwiegelshohn, J. Turek
Optimal Loop Scheduling on Multiprocessors: A Pumping Lemma
for p-Processor Schedules 51

P. Hartmann
Parallel and Distributed Processing of Cellular Hypergraphs 57

V. Markova and S. Piskunov
Computer Models of 3D Cellular Structures 70

A.S. Nepomniaschaya
Comparison of Two MST Algorithms for Associative Parallel Processors .. 85

V.A. Nepomniaschy, G.I. Alekseev, A.V. Bystrov, T.G. Churina,
S.P. Mylnikov, E.V. Okunishnikova
Petri Net Modelling of Estelle-specified Communication Protocols 94

B. Schnor
Dynamic Scheduling of Parallel Applications 109

G. Vesselovski and M. Kupriyanova
A Method for Analyzing Combinatorial Properties of
Static Connecting Topologies 117

Software

A.I. Adamovich
*cT: An Imperative Language with Parallelizing Features Supporting
the Computation Model "Autotransformation of the Evaluation Network* . 127

S. Benkner
Vienna Fortran 90 - An Advanced Data Parallel Language 142

A.E. Doroshenko
*Programming Abstracts for Synchronization and Communication
in Parallel Programs* 157

V.A. Evstigneev and V.N. Kasyanov
A Program Manipulation System for Fine-grained Architectures 163

C. Hochberger, R. Hoffmann, S. Waldschmidt
Compilation of CDL for Different Target Architectures 169

A. Hondroudakis, R. Procter, K. Shanmugam
Performance Evaluation and Visualization with VISPAT 180

R. Hüsler, H.Vonder Mühll, A. Gunzinger, G. Tröster
Dataparallel Programming with Intelligent Communication 186

A.R. Hurson and B.-U. Jun
*Optimization Scheme on Execution of Logic Program
in a Dataflow Environment* 204

A.V. Borshchev, Y.G. Karpov, V.V. Roudakov
*COVERS - A Tool for the Design of Real-time
Concurrent Systems* 219

R. Klar and P. Dauphin
*Status and Prospect of ZM4/SIMPLE/PEPP: an Event-oriented
Evaluation Environment for Parallel and Distributed Programs* 234

O.V. Klimova
*The Separating Decomposition of Discrete Fourier Transform
and Vectorization of its Calculation* 241

T. Ludwig and S. Lamberts
PFSLib - A Parallel File System for Workstation Clusters 246

Y. Saad and A.V. Malevsky
*Data Structures, Computational, and Communication Kernels
for Distributed Memory Sparse Iterative Solvers* 252

A. Özerdim, M.O. Ünalir, O. Dikenelli, E. Ozkarahan
PARMA: A Multiattribute File Structure for Parallel Database Machines 258

M.M. Pic, H. Essafi, M. Viala, L. Nicolas
*T++: An Object-Oriented Language to Express Task and
Data Parallelism on Multi-SIMD Computers* 273

V. Vlassov, H. Ahmed, L.-E. Thorelli
mEDA-2: An Extension of PVM 288

A. Vazhenin and V. Morozov
*Parallel Iterative Solution of Systems of Linear Equations with
Dynamically Changed Length of Operands* 294

M. Royak, E. Shurina, Y. Soloveichik, V. Malyshkin
*Parallelization of Computer Code MASTAC Three-Dimensional
Finite Elements Method Implementing* 304

Hardware and Architecture

L. Barriga and R. Ayani
New Trends in Simulation of Distributed Shared Memory Architectures ... 314

D. Etiemble and C. Germain
*Standard Microprocessors Versus Custom Processing Elements
for Massively Parallel Architectures* 320

B. Goossens and D.T. Vu
*Further Pipelining and Multithreading to Improve RISC Processor Speed.
A Proposed Architecture and Simulation Results* 326

A.V. Zabrodin, V.K. Levin, V.V. Korneev
The Massively Parallel Computer System MBC-100 341

V.P. Srini
*DFS-SuperMPx: Low-cost Parallel Processing System
for Machine Vision and Image Processing* 356

C. Bussler, S. Jablonski, T. Kirsche, H. Schuster, H. Wedekind
Architectural Issues of Distributed Workflow Management Systems 370

Applications

O. Bessonov, V. Brailovskaya, V. Polezhaev, B. Roux
*Parallelization of the Solution of 3D Navier-Stokes Equations
for Fluid Flow in a Cavity with Moving Covers* 385

P. Ciancarini and P. Mancini
Distributing Search and Knowledge Using a Coordination Language 400

F. Caudal and B. Lecussan
*Design and Evaluation of a Multi-Threaded Architecture for
Parallel Graph Reduction* 411

I.G. Mamedova
*Implementation of the Multigrid Method for Solving the Boundary-Value
Problems for the Poisson and Helmholtz Equations
on the Massively Parallel Computers* 427

A. Kremlev, O. Monakhov, T. Thiel
*Parallel Seismic Data Processing Method for MEMSY
Multiprocessor System* 434

E. Ozkarahan
Hardware and Software Platform for Information Processing 439

Last papers

E. Kessy, A. Stoukov, D. Vandromme
*Numerical Simulation of Reacting Mixing Layer with
a Parallel Implementation* 453

Y.I. Fet and D.A. Pospelov
Parallel Computing in Russia 464

W. Händler
*Early Approaches to Parallel Processing: Increasing Performance and
Dependability* 477

Author Index 497

Synchronous–Asynchronous Cellular Computations*

S.M. Achasova

Computing Center of Siberian Branch of
Russian Academy of Sciences
Pr. Lavrentieva, 6, Novosibirsk, 630090, Russia
E-mail: achasova@comcen.nsk.su

Abstract. Operation of parallel substitutions over cellular arrays in synchronous–asynchronous mode is studied. Correctness conditions for parallel substitution systems in this mode of execution are stated.

1 Introduction

This paper discusses the problem of correctness of cellular computations in the context of the Parallel Substitution Algorithm theory. The Parallel Substitution Algorithm (PSA) is an abstract model of distributed (cellular) computations [1]. A PSA is specified by a set of parallel substitutions which operate over a cellular array in parallel (everywhere and at the same time).

Attractive for the practical applications is the class of systems of stationary parallel substitutions. Unlike general–type parallel substitutions, which may either decrease or increase the cardinality of a cellular array at hand, stationary substitutions result in no change of the cardinality of the array.

The paper only concerns with systems of stationary parallel substitutions. In [2, 3] termination, determinacy and correctness conditions of stationary parallel substitution systems in synchronous and asynchronous modes of execution are studied. Considering these modes as the pure ones this paper focuses on a mixed mode, which combines the features of the synchronous and the asynchronous modes. In this mode, at each computation step one from the applicable substitutions or any group of them can be executed. It is just how applicable substitutions can be executed in a cellular array (in a net of automata which interprets systems of parallel substitutions in one or other mode) without clock pulses. In other words, in transient regime can occur such a situation when some automata of a net change their states for a fixed time domain and thus, effect of synchronous execution of some substitutions appears.

2 Basic Concepts

A cellular array under processing is represented by a set of pairs (a_i, m_i) where a_i is a data item from an alphabet A and m_i is a place of the data item,

---

* This work was supported by Russian Fund of Fundamental Research 93–01–01000

$\{m_i,\ i = 1, 2, \ldots\} = M$. The sets A and M are finite. A pair (a_i, m_i) is termed a cell, a_i is a state of the cell, m_i is a name of the cell. The name of a cell is specified by integer coordinates $m_i = m_i^1, \ldots, m_i^n$ and a cellular array is viewed as an integer grid of any dimensionality in theory, and of 2D, 3D in practice. *A cellular array is a finite set of cells* with no pair of cells having one and the same name.

An expression

$$S_1 * S_2 \rightarrow S_3$$

is an elementary substitution, where S_1, S_2, S_3 are cellular arrays, S_1 is *the base*, S_2 is *the context* of a substitution. The base and the right–hand side S_3 of a substitution are of the same cardinality and contain cells with the same set of names. This is the condition for a substitution to be stationary.

A substitution is applicable to a cellular array W if the left–hand side $S_1 * S_2$ is contained in W, i.e., $S_1 \cup S_2 \subseteq W$. The substitution is executed by substituting S_3 for S_1, i.e., $W' = (W \setminus S_1) \cup S_3$.

To represent the execution of the same operation in different places of a cellular array by an unified expression, a substitution is generalized to *a parallel substitution*

$$\Theta(m) : S_1(m) * S_2(m) \rightarrow S_3(m),$$

here m is a variable name from M, and

$$S_1(m) = \{(a_1, \varphi_1(m)), (a_2, \varphi_2(m)), \ldots, (a_p, \varphi_p(m))\},$$

$$S_2(m) = \{(b_1, \psi_1(m)), (b_2, \psi_2(m)), \ldots, (b_q, \psi_q(m))\},$$

$$S_3(m) = \{(c_1, \varphi_1(m)), (c_2, \varphi_2(m)), \ldots, (c_p, \varphi_p(m))\},$$

where φ_i, ψ_j, $(i = 1, \ldots, p, \ j = 1, \ldots, q)$ are *naming functions* such that for any m $\varphi_i(m) \neq \varphi_j(m)$, $\psi_i(m) \neq \psi_j(m)$, $i \neq j$, and $\varphi_i(m) \neq \psi_j(m)$ for all i, j. $S_1(m)$ is the base and $S_2(m)$ is the context of a parallel substitution.

In this paper coordinate shift functions are taken as the naming functions. One of the naming functions is convenient to be taken equal to the trivial function $f(m) = m$, it is agreed that this is a function of the base.

When fixing $m = m_t$, the expression

$$\vartheta(m_t) : \ S_1(m_t) * S_2(m_t) \rightarrow S_3(m_t)$$

is an elementary substitution, which is further called a microoperation. The cell with the name m_t of the base $S_1(m_t)$ is called the central cell.

A parallel substitution $\theta_i(m) : S_{i1}(m) * S_{i2}(m) \rightarrow S_{i3}(m)$ (in what follows it is merely a substitution) is applicable to a cellular array W if in W there is a cell with a name m_q such that $S_{i1}(m_q) \cup S_{i2}(m_q) \subseteq W$ (i.e., the microoperation $\vartheta_i(m_q)$ is applicable to W). If in W there is more than one such a cell (let there be a set of such cells with names $\{m_1, \ldots, m_q\}$), then to execute the applicable substitution $\theta_i(m)$ is to execute the microoperations $\vartheta(m_1), \ldots, \vartheta(m_q)$.

A finite set of substitutions $\Phi = \{\theta_1, \ldots, \theta_v\}$ is called *a Parallel Substitution System* (a PSS).

Example 1. A PSS Φ_1 realizing a parallel binary adder for an arbitrary number of summands comprises two substitutions [1, 4].

$$\theta_1 : \{(1, \langle i,j \rangle)(1, \langle i+1,j \rangle)(0, \langle i,j-1 \rangle)\} * \{(0, \langle i-1,j-1 \rangle)(0, \langle i-1,j \rangle)\} \rightarrow$$
$$\{(0, \langle i,j \rangle)(0, \langle i+1,j \rangle)(1, \langle i,j-1 \rangle)\},$$

$$\theta_2 : \{(1, \langle i,j \rangle)(0, \langle i+1,j \rangle)\} * (0, \langle i-1,j \rangle) \rightarrow \{(0, \langle i,j \rangle)(1, \langle i+1,j \rangle)\}.$$

In Fig. 1 there is a visual representation of the substitutions.

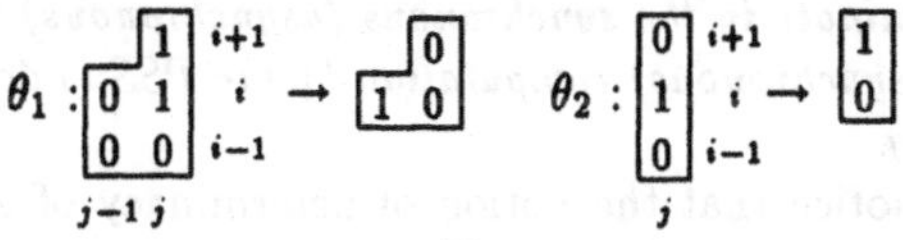

Fig. 1

A PSS may be executed in the synchronous and the asynchronous modes.

The synchronous mode of execution of a PSS Φ in a cellular array W is the following iterative procedure. Let a cellular array W_i be the result of the ith step of the procedure, then:

1) if no substitution of Φ is applicable to W_i, then W_i is the result,
2) if a number of substitutions of Φ are applicable to W_i, then W_i is transformed to W_{i+1} by executing all applicable substitutions simultaneously (all applicable microoperations).
3) if W_{i+1} is not a cellular array (i.e., there are cells with the same name in it), then the procedure is stopped without a result.

A PSS Φ is called *contradictory* if the synchronous execution of Φ mets the condition of Item 3 of the above procedure at least for one cellular array W. In other words, this is the case when in Φ there is at least two substitutions which being simultaneously executed change the state of one and the same cell to different ones.

The asynchronous mode of execution of a PSS Φ in a cellular array W is the following iterative procedure. Let a cellular array W_i be a result of the ith step of the procedure, then:

1) if no substitution of Φ is applicable to W_i, then W_i is a result,
2) if a number of substitutions of Φ are applicable to W_i, then W_i is transformed to W_{i+1} by executing a single microoperation, anyone from the set of microoperations applicable to W_i.

A set of cellular arrays, which can be produced from an initial cellular array W by executing a PSS in the asynchronous (synchronous, in this case a PSS is assumed to be non–contradictory) mode, together with the succession relation of cellular arrays is called *an asynchronous (synchronous) computation* and is denoted by $\tilde{\Phi}(W)$ ($\bar{\Phi}(W)$). The succession relation graph is referred to as *an asynchronous (synchronous) computation graph*. A sequence of cellular arrays, which forms a path from an initial vertex of a graph to a terminal one is termed *a computation realization*.

A *computation (asynchronous or synchronous)* is *terminating* if its graph contains no loop. A *PSS is terminating in the asynchronous (synchronous) mode* if an asynchronous (synchronous) computation by the PSS is terminating for any initial cellular array.

A *terminating computation (asynchronous or synchronous)* whose graph has a single terminal vertex (it is a vertex corresponding to a cellular array to which no substitution is applicable) is called *determinate*.

A *PSS is determinate in the synchronous (asynchronous) mode of execution if a synchronous (asynchronous) computation by the PSS is determinate for any initial cellular array*.

It is worth to notice that the notion of determinacy of a PSS in the synchronous mode is exhausted by the notion of non–contradictoriness.

A key notion for finding the determinacy conditions of a PSS is a concept of intersection of substitutions. Two substitutions θ_i and θ_j intersect if there exists at least one pair of microoperations $\vartheta_i(m')$ and $\vartheta_j(m'')$ such that their left–hand sides $S_{i1}(m') * S_{i2}(m')$ and $S_{j1}(m'') * S_{j2}(m'')$ have common cells and $S_{i1}(m') \cup S_{i2}(m') \cup S_{j1}(m'') \cup S_{j2}(m'')$ is a cellular array (i.e., there are no cells with the same names in it). Considering that the naming functions are shifts, all pairs of microoperations $\vartheta_i(m_t)$ and $\vartheta_j(m_g)$ such that the difference of the names of the central cells $m_g - m_t = k$, where $k = m'' - m'$, intersect. Fig. 2 shows the intersections (and self–intersections) of the binary adder substitutions with the associated values of the vector k.

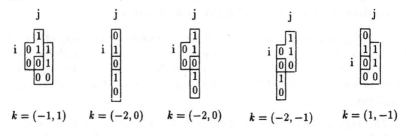

$$k = (-1, 1) \qquad k = (-2, 0) \qquad k = (-2, 0) \qquad k = (-2, -1) \qquad k = (1, -1)$$

Fig. 2

Certain types of the intersections may be a reason for arising non–determinate synchronous and asynchronous computations. They are termed critical intersections. For synchronous computations only base–base intersections can be critical. If two microoperations $\vartheta_i(m')$ and $\vartheta_j(m'')$ have a base–base intersection (the common cells of the intersected microoperations belong to their bases) and $S_{i3}(m') \cup S_{i2}(m') \cup S_{j3}(m'') \cup S_{j2}(m'')$ is not a cellular array (i.e., there are at least two cells with the same names and different states in it), then such a intersection is critical and it is called contradictory.

For asynchronous computations, among critical intersections are base–base ones and base–context intersections (common cells belong to the base of one microoperation and to the context of the other). When two microoperations intersect critically, in the asynchronous computation the applicability condition of one of the microoperations is broken after the other has been executed and, as a result, being branched the computation does not have a common end for all its realizations. Context–context intersections are called safe.

In [2, 3] the determinacy conditions are stated. *A PSS in the synchronous (asynchronous) mode of execution is determinate iff the synchronous (asynchronous) computations by the PSS are determinate for all critical words* (these are cellular arrays which are made up from the left–hand sides of critically intersecting microoperations, for example, the critical words for the binary adder PSS are shown in Fig. 2).

A determinate asynchronous computation by a PSS for a cellular array W is correct if its result is equal to that of the synchronous computation by this PSS for the same cellular array. A PSS is correct in the asynchronous mode if an asynchronous computation by the PSS is correct for any initial cellular array.

3   Synchronous–Asynchronous Mode

We define *the synchronous–asynchronous mode of execution of a non–contradictory PSS* (in short, SA–mode) as an iterative procedure, whose ith step is the transformation of a cellular array W^{i-1} to W^i by simultaneous executing some applicable microoperations, but not necessarily all applicable ones at once. It may be any group of applicable microoperations, including a group consisting of one microoperation or the group of all applicable microoperations.

Like the asynchronous computation by a PSS, *an SA–computation* is defined as a set of cellular arrays, which are produced from an initial cellular array W by executing a PSS Φ in the SA–mode, together with the succession relation of the cellular arrays. The SA–computation is denoted by $\hat{\Phi}(W)$. In Fig. 3 the graph of an SA–computation by the substitution system Φ_1 is shown.

In an SA–computation graph all realizations of the asynchronous and the synchronous computations for the one and same initial cellular array are contained as the realizations of the SA–computation for the same cellular array.

By analogy with the asynchronous computation, we define a terminating, determinate and correct SA–computation.

An SA–computation $\hat{\Phi}(W)$ is terminating if its graph contains no loop. A PSS Φ is non–terminating in the SA–mode if there exists at least one cellular array W such that the SA–computation $\hat{\Phi}(W)$ is non–terminating.

A terminating SA–computation $\hat{\Phi}(W)$ is determinate if the graph of the SA–computation has only one terminal vertex, and the determinate SA–computation is correct if the cellular array of the terminal vertex is equal to the result of the synchronous computation $\bar{\Phi}(W)$. For instance, the SA–computation of Fig. 3 is terminating, determinate and correct.

Note that a determinate SA–computation $\hat{\Phi}(W)$ is always correct, since among the realizations of $\hat{\Phi}(W)$ there is always the realization of the synchronous computation $\bar{\Phi}(W)$. In the context of the fact we define only the

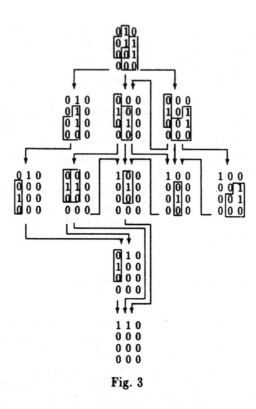

Fig. 3

notion of correctness of a PSS in the SA–mode. *A PSS is correct in the SA–mode* if an SA–computation by the PSS is correct for any initial cellular array.

In closing, the condition of correctness of a PSS in the SA–mode is formulated through the same condition in the synchronous and the asynchronous modes.

Theorem 1. *A non–contradictory PSS Φ is correct in the SA–mode iff it is correct in the asynchronous mode.*

References

1. Bandman, O., Piskunov, S.: Parallel Substitution Algorithms as a Model for Distributed Computations. J. New Gener. Comput. Syst. **4**(1991)1, 3-18.
2. Achasova, S.: Correctness of Interpretations of Parallel Substitution Systems. J. New Gener. Comput. Syst. **4**(1991)1, 19-27.
3. Achasova, S., Bandman, O.: Correctness of Parallel Computation Processes (Nauka, Novosibirsk 1990, 252 p., in Russian).
4. Bandman, O., Piskunov, S.: Parallel Microprogramming as a Tool for Multi-Microprocessor System Design. Lect. Notes in Comp. Sci. **342**(1989), 57-68.

Parallel Computations and Finite Automata on Semilattices

Gennady P. Agibalov

Radiophysical Department of
Tomsk State University
Pr. Lenina, 36, Tomsk, 634050, Russia

Abstract. First, we outline a possibility to associate with parallel computations on a semilattice a finite automaton defined on semilattices which models the computations, and then we study three problems concerning the design of finite automata on semilattices – synthesis, minimization, and decomposition.

1 Introduction

We consider finite automata defined on upper semilattices. We call them *SL-automata*. Unlike an abstract automaton whose alphabets (of inputs, of states, of outputs) are all abstract sets, in any *SL*-automaton each of the alphabets is an upper semilattice that is a partially ordered set in which each pair of elements has the least upper bound called the sum of the elements. In *SL*-automaton modelling a parallel computing system, the ordering relation compares the values of data according to the degree of their inderterminance obliged to hazards which appear between them when they are asynchronously changed, and the semilattice sum of values models this change as an intermediate value. So, in contrast with abstract automata, by applying *SL*-automata one may describe not only the synchronous and static (under input data fixed) behaviour of a computing system but also the asynchronous and dynamic (under input data changed) behaviour of the system.

This paper is intended to provide an English reader with some ideas, methods, and results of the theory of automata on semilattices developed by the author and published in Russian in the monograph [1]. The limited scope of the paper excluded automatically many aspects of the theory; the choice was largely biased by the conference's interests. First, we outline how one can associate with a parallel computing system a *SL*-automaton which models the system, and then we study three problems concerning the design of *SL*-automata – synthesis,minimization, and decomposition. The results related to the coding problem for *SL*-automata have been given in English before [2].

Throughout the paper, all the semilattices under consideration are assumed to be finite upper semilattices, and $m(A)$ denotes the set of all the minimal elements of a semilattice A. A function is called a *SL-function* if it maps a semilattice into a semilattice. A *SL*-function is *additive* if it is a homomorphism of semilattices. A *SL*-function $f : A \rightarrow B$ is *monotonic* if $a \leq b \Rightarrow f(a) \leq f(b)$;

it is *realized by a function* $g : A \to B$ if $g(a) \leq f(a)$ for all a in A. A SL-function is *quasimonotonic* if it is realized by a monotonic SL-function. A SL-automaton is *additive* (*monotonic* or *quasimonotonic*) if its transition and output functions are both additive (respectively, monotonic or quasimonotonic). Note that all the additive and monotonic SL-automata are quasimonotonic; the quasimonotonic SL-automata are of great interest because of their physical realizability.

2 Parallel Computations

A parallel computing system on a semilattice L is defined by a system of equations

$$z_i = f_i(Z_i), \quad i = 1, \ldots, k,$$

where, for every i, z_i is a variable ranging over L and $f_i(Z_i)$ is a monotonic SL-function with values in L depending on a finite set Z_i of variables ranging over L.

If $Z = \{z_1, \ldots, z_s\} = \{z_1, \ldots, z_k\} \cup Z_1 \cup \ldots \cup Z_k$, then, for any $a_1, \ldots, a_s$ in L, the sequence $\alpha = a_1 \ldots a_s$ is called a state of the system, and, for $A = \{z_{i_1}, \ldots, z_{i_r}\} \subseteq Z$, the sequence $a_{i_1} \ldots a_{i_r}$ is denoted by $\alpha(A)$. The state α is *a stability point* if $a_i = f_i(\alpha(Z_i))$ for every $i = 1, \ldots, k$; it is *a monotony point* if $a_i \leq f_i(\alpha(Z_i))$, or $a_i \geq f_i(\alpha(Z_i))$ for all i. For states $\alpha = a_1 \ldots a_s$ and $\beta = b_1 \ldots b_s$, it is said that β *results from* α if $b_i = a_i$ or $b_i = f_i(\alpha(Z_i))$ for every $i = 1, \ldots, s$. A sequence of states $\pi = \alpha_1 \alpha_2 \ldots$ is *a computational process* if α_{i+1} results from α_i for every $i \geq 1$. The process π is *convergent* if there is a natural n such that α_n is a stability point; in this case, we say that π *terminates* at the state α_n.

Theorem 1. *All the convergent computational processes beginning with one and the same monotony point terminate at one and the same stability point.*

This theorem makes it possible to associate with a parallel computing system on a semilattice a monotonic SL-automaton S which models the system as follows: if a convergent process in the system begins with a monotony point p and terminates at a stability point q, then the automaton S passes from the state p to the state q.

3 Synthesis

At the beginning, we outline necessary preliminaries and define the appropriate notation.

A binary relation $\rho \subseteq A \times B$ is a SL-*relation* if A and B are both semilattices. A SL-relation $\rho \subseteq A \times B$ is *realized* by a SL-function $f : A \to B$ if, for any a in A and b in B, the proposition $a\rho b$ implies that $f(a) \leq b$. A SL-relation is *quasimonotonic* if it is realized by a monotonic SL-function.

Theorem 2 (quasimonotony test). *A SL-relation $\rho \subseteq A \times B$ is quasimonotonic if and only if, for any $(a_1, b_1), \ldots, (a_m, b_m)$ in ρ where $2 \le m \le |m(B)|$, the existence of a common lower bound for $a_1, \ldots, a_m$ in A implies the existence of a common lower bound for $b_1, \ldots, b_m$ in B.*

The same theorem takes place for a SL-function $f : A \to B$ to be quasimonotonic.

Let $S = (X, Q, Y, \psi, \varphi)$ be a SL-automaton that is an automaton whose the set of inputs X, the set of states Q, and the set of outputs Y are all semilattices and the transition function $\psi : X \times Q \to Q$ and the output function $\varphi : X \times Q \to Y$ are both SL-functions. The function ψ is *monotonic at a point* ar in $X \times Q$ if $\psi(a, r) \le r$ or $\psi(a, r) \ge r$; in this case, ar is called a *monotony point* of ψ. The set of all the monotony points of ψ is denoted by M_ψ. If $\psi(a, r) = r$, then ψ is *stable at* ar and ar is a *stability point* of ψ. The set of all the stability points of ψ is denoted by S_ψ.

In the case of the monotonic automaton S, functions

$$\psi^\varepsilon : M_\psi \to Q, \quad \varphi^\varepsilon : M_\psi \to Y$$

are defined as follows:

$$\varphi^\varepsilon(a, r) = \varphi(a, \psi^\varepsilon(a, r)), \qquad \psi^\varepsilon(a, r) = q(m)$$

where $q(1) = r$, $q(t + 1) = \psi(a, q(t))$ for $t = 1, 2, \ldots, m$ and m satisfies the condition $q(m) = q(m + 1)$.

A *dynamic transition* in the monotonic automaton S is a 7-tuple $T = (ab, rts, uv)$ where $ar \in S_\psi$, $b \in X$, $t = \psi^\varepsilon(a + b, r)$, $s = \psi^\varepsilon(b, t)$, $u = \varphi^\varepsilon(a + b, r)$, $v = \varphi^\varepsilon(b, t)$. It can be interpreted in the following way: if, at a time, the state of a computing system modelled by the automaton S is contained in r and the input of the system changes asynchronously from a into b, then the system goes asynchronously into a state contained in s and produces the output in v having, for the transition time, the state in t and the output in u.

A sequence of dynamic transitions $\tau = (T_1, \ldots, T_n)$ is *a transition chain* if $T_i = (a_i a_{i+1}, r_i t_i r_{i+1}, u_i v_i)$ for $i = 1, 2, \ldots, n$. A *command* over semilattices X, Q, Y is a 6-tuple $C = (ab, rp, wz)$ where $a \in X$, $b \in X$, $r \in Q$, $p \in Q$, $w \in Y$, $z \in Y$. The pair ar in it is *the initial point*. A sequence of commands $\sigma = (C_1, \ldots, C_n)$ is a *command chain* if $C_i = (a_i a_{i+1}, p_i p_{i+1}, w_i z_i)$ for $i = 1, 2, \ldots, n$. The command C *is realized by the transition* T if $s \le p$, $u \le w$, $v \le z$. The command chain σ *is realized by the transition chain* τ if $r_1 = p_1$, $r_{i+1} \le p_{i+1}$, $u_i \le w_i$, $v_i \le z_i$ for $i = 1, 2, \ldots, n$. A system of commands SC over X, Q, Y *is realized by the monotonic automaton* S if every command in SC is realized by a dynamic transition in S; the system SC *is strongly realised by* S if every command chain consisting of commands in SC is realized by a transition chain in S. The system SC *is (strongly) automated* if it is (strongly) realized by a monotonic SL-automaton.

Theorem 3. *The system of commands SC is strongly automated if and only if it is automated.*

Theorem 4 (synthesis theorem). *The system of commands SC is automated if and only if, for every command $C = (ab,\ rp,\ wz)$ in SC, there exist t_C and p_C in Q such that $r \leq t_C$, $p_C = inf(p, t_C)$ and binary relations $\gamma \subseteq (X \times Q) \times Y$ and $\delta \subseteq (X \times Q) \times Q$ which are defined by the propositions $(b, t_C)\gamma z, (a + b, t_C)\gamma w, (b, t_C)\delta p_C, (a+b, t_C)\delta t_C$ taken for all the commands C in SC, are both quasimonotonic and the relation δ is realized by a monotonic function which is stable at the initial points of all the commands in SC.*

4   Minimization

There are many different minimization problems for SL-automata; some of them are put as follows: given a SL-automaton S belonging to a certain family A of SL-automata, find a SL-automaton in A with the minimum number of states realizing the automaton S. Here, we consider this problem for the family A being the set of all the additive, monotonic or quasimonotonic SL-automata and for the following two notions of the realization relation between SL-automata. First, a SL-automaton $S = (X,\ Q,\ Y,\ \psi,\ \varphi)$ is *realized on outputs* by a SL-automaton $L = (X,\ P,\ Y,\ \lambda,\ \delta)$ if, for any q in Q, there exists a p in P such that $\delta(\alpha, p) \leq \varphi(\alpha, q)$ for every α in X^*. Second, S is *realized on transitions and outputs* by L if there exists an epimorphism of semilattices $h : Q \to P$ such that $h\psi(x, q) = \lambda(x, hq)$ and $\delta(x, hq) \leq \varphi(x, q)$ for all x in X and q in Q.

To state the results define necessary auxiliary notions.

A *cover on a set* Q is a set of subsets of Q whose union equels Q; the subsets in it are called *blocks* of the cover. A *cover on a semilattice* Q is a cover on the set Q where all the blocks are non–empty and different subsemilattices of Q and, for any blocks A and B, there exists a block C which is the least upper bound of the set

$$A + B = \{a + b \mid a \in A,\ b \in\}$$

in the ordered set $(2^Q, \subseteq)$. The block C having this property is called the *sum* of blocks A and B and is denoted by $A \oplus B$ defining an addition operation $\oplus$ on the cover considered. A cover P on a semilattice is a $\cap - -cover$ if $A \oplus B = A \cap B$; the cover P is *associative* if the addition operation $\oplus$ on it is associative. A $\cap--cover$ and the set Q/σ of all the cosets of a congruence σ on the semilattice Q are examples of associative covers. An associative cover P on the semilattice Q is *agreeable* to the additive (monotonic or quasimonotonic) SL-automaton $S = (X,\ Q,\ Y,\ \psi,\ \varphi)$ if there exist additive (respectively, monotonic or quasimonotonic) functions $\psi' : X \times P \to P$ and $\varphi' : X \times P \to Y$ such that, for x in X and A in P, the value $\varphi'(x, A)$ is a lower bound of the subset $\varphi(x, A)$ of Y and $\psi(x, A) \subseteq \psi'(x, A)$; in this case, if $P = Q/\sigma$ for a congruence σ on Q, then we say that σ is *agreeable* to S.

Theorem 5. *If an additive SL-automaton S is realized on outputs by an additive SL-automaton with m states, then there exists a $\cap--cover$ on the semilattice of states in S which has not more than m blocks and is agreeable to S. Conversely,* *if S is an additive SL-automaton and there exists a ∩——cover on the semilattice of states in S which has m blocks and is agreeable to S, then S is realized on outputs by an additive SL-automaton with m states.*

Thus, to minimize an additive SL-automaton S under the realization on outputs it suffies to find, on the semilattice of states in S, an agreeable ∩——*cover* with the minimum number of blocks.

Theorem 6. *An additive (monotonic or quasimonotonic) SL-automaton S is realized on transitions and outputs by an additive (respectively, monotonic or quasimonotonic) SL-automaton with m states if and only if there exists a congruence of index m on the semilattice of states in S which is agreeable to S.*

Thus, to minimize an additive, monotonic or quasimonotonic SL-automaton S under the realization on transitions and outputs it suffies to find, on the semilattice of states in S, an agreeable congruence of the minimum index.

5 Decomposition

In this section, we characterize all the exact decompositions of a quasimonotonic SL-automaton into quasimonotonic components, and state conditions for it to have a nontrivial cascade, serial or parallel decomposition into quasimonotonic components. For the beginning, appropriate definitions are introduced.

A *semiautomaton* is defined by a triplet (X, Q, ψ) where X is the set of inputs, Q is the set of states, and ψ is the transition function, $\psi : X \times Q \to Q$. In a *SL-semiautomaton*, the sets X and Q are both semilattices, and ψ is a SL-function.

A *SL-automata network* is a finite sequence

$$N = Q_0 z_1 S_1 z_2 S_2 \ldots z_l S_l z_{l+1} X_{l+1},$$

where Q_0 and X_{l+1} are semilattices called, respectively, the set of *inputs* and the set of *outputs*;

$$S_j = (X_j, Q_j, \psi_j)$$

for $j = 1, 2, \ldots, l$ is a SL-semiautomaton called a *component*; and $z_j : Q_0 \times Q_1 \times \ldots \times Q_l \to X_j$ for $j = 1, 2, \ldots, l+1$ is a homomorphism of semilattices called a *connection*. The network N is *in standard form* if $X_j = X_{0j} \times X_{1j} \times \ldots \times X_{lj}$ for some semilattices X_{ij} and $z_j = z_{0j} z_{1j} \ldots z_{lj}$ for some homomorphisms $z_{ij} : Q_i \to X_j$ $(i = 0, 1, \ldots, l; \ j = 1, 2, \ldots, l)$. The network is *quasimonotonic* if any component in it is a quasimonotonic SL-semiautomaton.

The *automaton of the network N* is the SL-automaton

$$S_N = (Q_0, \ Q_1 \times \ldots \times Q_l, \ Q_{l+1}, \ \psi_N, \ \varphi_N)$$

where, for x in Q_0 and for $q = q_1 q_2 \ldots q_l$ in $Q_1 \times \ldots \times Q_l$,

$$\psi_N(x, q) = (\psi_1(z_1(x, q), q_1), \ \psi_2(z_2(x, q), q_2), \ldots, \psi_l(z_l(x, q), q_l)),$$

$$\varphi_N(x,q) = z_{l+1}(x,q).$$

A subautomaton of a SL-automaton S is an *exact subautomaton* if its sets of inputs, states and outputs are subsemilattices of the corresponding semilattices in S.

A SL-automaton $S = (X,\ Q,\ Y,\ \psi,\ \varphi)$ is a *homomorphic (isomorphic) image* of a SL-automaton $L = (U,\ P,\ V,\ \lambda,\ \delta)$, if there exist epimorphisms (respectively, isomorphisms) of semilattices $h_1 : U \to X$, $h_2 : P \to Q$, $h_3 : V \to Y$ such that, for all up in $U \times P$,

$$h_2\lambda(u,p) = \psi(h_1 u, h_2 p), \ \ h_3\delta(u,p) = \varphi(h_1 u, h_2 p);$$

in this case, $h_1 h_2 h_3$ is called the *homomorphism* (respectively, *isomorphism*) of L onto S. The automaton S is (*exactly*) *realized* by the automaton L if there exist an (exact) subautomaton $L' = (U',\ P',\ V',\ \lambda',\ \delta')$ of L and a homomorphism (respectively, isomorphism) $h_1 h_2 h_3$ of L' onto S such that, for any subset W' of $U' \times P'$, the existence of a lower bound of $\lambda'(W')$ in P or of $\delta'(W')$ in V implies the existence of a lower bound, respectively, of $h_2\lambda'(W')$ in Q or of $h_3\delta'(W')$ in Y.

Let for $i = 1,\ldots,l$ the homomorphism

$$\pi_i : Q_1 \times \ldots \times Q_l \to Q_i$$

is defined by $\pi_i(q_1 \ldots q_l) = q_i$. If the network N is in standard form, and $h_1 h_2 h_3$ is an isomorphism of an exact subautomaton of S_N onto S, then we can, for all i and j in $\{1,\ldots,l\}$, define binary relations τ_i and ρ_{ij} on the semilattice Q and μ_j on the semilattice X being core congruences of homomorphisms

$$\pi_i h_2^{-1} : Q \to Q_1 \times \ldots \times Q_l, \ \ z_{ij}\pi_i h_2^{-1} : Q \to X_j, \ \ z_{0j}h_1^{-1} : X \to X_j,$$

respectively. We call them *congruences induced in S* by N (under isomorphism $h_1 h_2 h_3$). A system of congruences on a semilattice is *complete* if their intersection is the identity. A pair of congruences (σ, ρ) on the semilattice Q is *preserved* by the SL-function $\psi : X \times Q \to Q$ if $p\sigma q \Rightarrow \psi(x,p)\rho\psi(x,q)$ for all x in X and p and q in Q. If (σ, σ) is preserved by ψ, then we say that σ is *preserved* by ψ.

The next theorem is the analogy to Theorem 3.5 in [3].

Theorem 7 (characterization theorem). *Given a SL-automaton $S = (X,$ $Q,\ Y,\ \psi,\ \varphi)$ and congruences τ_i and ρ_{ij} on Q and μ_j on X for $1 \leq i,\ j \leq l$; then there exists a quasimonotonic SL-automata network N in standard form such that S is exactly realized by S_N, and τ_i, ρ_{ij}, μ_j are induced in S by N if and only if the following conditions are satisfied:*

(i) $\tau_i \subseteq \rho_{ij}$ for all i and j;

(ii) the system of congruences $\tau_1,\ldots,\tau_l$ is complete;

(iii) for every j, the pair of congruences $(\mu_j \times (\rho_{1j} \cap \ldots \cap \rho_{lj} \cap \tau_j),\ \tau_j)$ is preserved by ψ;

(iv) for all j and $U_j \subseteq D_j$ where $D_j = X/\mu_j \times Q/\rho_{1j} \times \ldots \times Q/\rho_{lj} \times Q/\tau_j$,

$$U_j = \{[x_m]_{\mu_j}[q_m]_{\rho_{1j}} \ldots [q_m]_{\rho_{lj}}[q_m]_{\tau_j} \mid m = 1, \ldots, k_j\}$$

and $2 \leq k_j \leq \mid m(Q/\tau_j) \mid$, the existence of a lower bound of U_j in D_j implies the existence of a lower bound of $V_j = \{[\psi(x_m, q_m)]_{\tau_j} \mid m = 1, \ldots, k_j\}$ in Q/τ_j;

(v) for any $A \subseteq D$ where $D = X \times Q/\tau_1 \times \ldots \times Q/\tau_l$,

$$A = \{x_m[q_m]_{\tau_1} \ldots [q_m]_{\tau_l} \mid m = 1, \ldots, k\}$$

and $2 \leq k \leq \mid m(Y) \mid$, the existence of a lower bound of A in D implies the existence of a lower bound of $\{\varphi(x_m, q_m) \mid m = 1, \ldots, k\}$ in Y;

(vi) for any $W \subseteq X \times Q$ where $W = \{x_m q_m \mid m = 1, \ldots, k\}$ and $2 \leq k \leq \mid m(Q) \mid$, the existence of a lower bound of $V = \{[\psi(x_m, q_m)]_{\tau_1} \ldots [\psi(x_m, q_m)]_{\tau_l} \mid m = 1, \ldots, k\}$ in $Q/\tau_1 \times \ldots \times Q/\tau_l$ implies the existence of a lower bound of $\psi(W) = \{\psi(x_m, q_m) \mid m = 1, \ldots, k\}$ in Q.

In the SL-automata network N, a component S_j does *not depend* on a component S_i or on the input of the network if the connection $z_j(q_0, q_1, \ldots, q_l)$ does not essentially depend on q_j or on q_0 respectively. The network N is said to be *cascade, parallel-serial* or *parallel* if S_i does not depend on S_j, respectively, for $j \geq i$, for $j \neq i - 1$ or for all j. The parallel-serial network N is *serial* if each its component S_j for $j > 1$ does not depend on the input of N. The network N is the *(exact)decomposition* of a SL-automaton S if S is (exactly) realized by the automaton S_N. The decomposition is *cascade* if it is a cascade network. The *parallel-serial, parallel, serial* and *quasimonotonic* decompositions are defined in the same way.

The least and the greatest congruences on a semilattice A are denoted by 0_A and 1_A respectively. A congruence on A is *nontrivial* if it differs from 0_A and 1_A. The number of states of the automaton S is called the *order* of S.

Theorem 8. *A quasimonotonic SL-automaton $S = (X, Q, Y, \psi, \varphi)$ has an exact parallel quasimonotonic decomposition into components of fewer orders if and only if there exists a complete system of nontrivial congruences $\tau_1, \ldots, \tau_l$ on Q such that every τ_i is preserved by ψ, and the conditions (v) and (vi) of Theorem 7 hold.*

Theorem 9. *A quasimonotonic SL-automaton $S = (X, Q, Y, \psi, \varphi)$ has an exact cascade quasimonotonic decomposition into components of fewer orders if and only if there exists a complete pair of nontrivial congruences τ_1, τ_2 on Q such that τ_1 is preserved by ψ, and the conditions (v) and (vi) of Theorem 7 under $l = 2$ and the following condition hold:*
(iv') for $U \subseteq D$ where

$$U = \{x_m[q_m]_{\tau_1}[q_m]_{\tau_2} \mid m = 1, \ldots, k\}, \quad 2 \leq k \leq \mid m(Q/\tau_2) \mid$$

and $D = X \times Q/\tau_1 \times Q/\tau_2$, the existence of a lower bound of U in D implies the existence of a lower bound of $\{[\psi(x_m, q_m)]_{\tau_2} \mid m = 1, \ldots, k\}$ in Q/τ_2.

Theorem 10. *A SL-automaton $S = (X, Q, \dot{Y}, \psi, \varphi)$ has an exact parallel-serial quasimonotonic decomposition of length $l \geq 2$ if and only if there exists a complete system of congruences $\tau_1, \ldots, \tau_l$ on Q such that the congruence τ_1 and the pairs of congruences $(0_X \times (\tau_{i-1} \cap \tau_i), \tau_i)$ for $i = 2, \ldots, l$ are preserved by ψ, and the conditions (iv), (v), and (vi) of Theorem 7 hold.*

Theorem 11. *A SL-automaton $S = (X, Q, Y, \psi, \varphi)$ has an exact serial quasi-monotonic decomposition of length $l \geq 2$ if and only if there exists a complete system of congruences $\tau_1, \ldots, \tau_l$ on Q such that the congruence τ_1 and the pairs of congruences $(0_X \times (\tau_{i-1} \cap \tau_i), \tau_i)$ and $(1_X \times \tau_i, \tau_i)$ for $i = 2, \ldots, l$ are preserved by ψ, and the conditions (iv), (v), and (vi) of Theorem 7 hold.*

An associative cover P on a semilattice Q is *regular* if for any its blocks A and B the condition $\exists a \in A \exists b \in B(a \leq b)$ implies that $A \leq B$. The cover P is *preserved* in the automaton $S = (X, Q, Y, \psi, \varphi)$ if, for any x in X and A in P, there exists B in P such that $\psi(x, A) \subseteq B$. A system of covers $P_1, \ldots, P_l$ on Q is *complete* if $\mid A_1 \cap \ldots \cap A_l \mid \leq 1$ for all A_1 in $P_1, \ldots, A_l$ in P_l.

Theorem 12. *Let $S = (X, Q, Y, \psi, \varphi)$ be a quasimonotonic SL-automaton and $Q' = P_1 \times \ldots \times P_l$ where $\{P_1, \ldots, P_l\}$ is a complete system of associative and regular covers on Q each preserved by S such that, for any $W = \{a_1q_1, \ldots, a_kq_k\} \subseteq X \times Q$ and $(A_{1m} \ldots A_{lm}) \in Q'$ where $m = 1, \ldots, k$ and $A_{1m} \cap \ldots \cap A_{lm} = \{q_m\}$, the following conditions are satisfied:*
(i) if $2 \leq k \leq \mid m(Y) \mid$ and there exists a lower bound of $\{a_m A_{1m} \ldots A_{lm} \mid m = 1, \ldots, k\}$ in $X \times Q'$, then there exists a lower bound of $\varphi(W)$ in Y;
(ii) if $2 \leq k \leq \mid m(Q) \mid$, $V = \{B_{1m} \ldots B_{lm} \mid m = 1, \ldots, k\} \subseteq Q'$ where, for $i = 1, \ldots, l$ and $m = 1, \ldots, k$, the block B_{im} is a minimal (under ordering relation in P_i) element in the set of those blocks B_i in P_i for which $\psi(a_m, A_{im}) \subseteq B_i$, and there exists a lower bound of V in Q', then there exists a lower bound of $\psi(W)$ in Q.
Let also S_i and z_i for $i = 1, \ldots, l$ and z_{l+1} be defined as follows: $S_i = (X_i, P_i, \psi_i)$ where, for all x in X and A_i in P_i, the block $\psi(a, A_i)$ is a minimal (under ordering relation in P_i) element in the set of those blocks B_i in P_i for which $\psi(a, A_i) \subseteq B_i$, $z_i(aA_1 \ldots A_l) = a$, and $z_{l+1}(aA_1 \ldots A_l) = y$ where $y = \varphi(a, q)$ if $q \in A_1 \cap \ldots \cap A_l$ or $y = \sup Y$ if $A_1 \cap \ldots \cap A_l = \emptyset$.
Then the SL-automata network $N = X z_1 S_1 z_2 S_2 \ldots z_l S_l z_{l+1} Y$ is a parallel quasimonotonic decomposition of the automaton S.

Theorem 13. *Let $S = (X, Q, Y, \psi, \varphi)$ be a quasimonotonic SL-automaton, $Q' = P_1 \times P_2$ where P_1 and P_2 are both associative covers on Q, the cover P_1 is regular and is preserved by ψ, the pair $\{P_1, P_2\}$ is a complete system, and, for any $W = \{a_1q_1, \ldots, a_kq_k\} \subseteq X \times Q$ and $A_{1m}A_{2m} \in Q'$ where $m \in \{1, \ldots, k\}$ and $A_{1m} \cap A_{2m} = \{q_m\}$, the condition (i) of Theorem 12 under $l = 2$ and the following conditions are satisfied:*

(ii') if $2 \leq k \leq \mid m(Q) \mid$, $V = \{B_{1m}B_{2m} \mid m = 1,\ldots,k\} \subseteq Q'$ where, for $m = 1,\ldots,k$, the block B_{1m} is a minimal (under ordering relation in P_1) element in the set of those blocks B_1 in P_1 for which $\psi(a_m, A_m) \subseteq B_1$, the block B_{2m} is the greatest (under ordering relation in P_2) element in the set of those blocks B_2 in P_2 for which $\psi(a_m, q_m) \in B_2$, and there exists a lower bound of V in Q', then there exists a lower bound of $\psi(W)$ in Q;

(iii) if $2 \leq k \leq \mid m(P_2) \mid$, $U = \{a_m A_{1m} A_{2m} \mid m = 1,\ldots,k\} \subseteq X \times Q'$, $T = \{B_{21},\ldots,B_{2k}\} \subseteq P_2$ where, for $m = 1,\ldots,k$, the block B_{2m} is the greatest (under ordering relation in P_2) element in the set of those blocks B_2 in P_2 for which $\psi(a_m, q_m) \in B_2$, and there exists a lower bound of U in $X \times Q'$, then there exists a lower bound of T in P_2.

Let also $S_1 = (X, P_1, \psi_1)$, $S_2 = (X \times P_1, P_2, \psi_2)$ where, for all a in X, A_1 in P_1 and A_2 in P_2, the block $\psi_1(a, A_1)$ is a minimal (under ordering relation in P_1) element in the set of those blocks B_1 in P_1 for which $\psi(a, A_1) \subseteq B_1$, the block $\psi_2(aA_1, A_2)$ is the greatest (under ordering relation in P_2) element in the set of those blocks B_2 in P_2 for which $\psi(a, A_1 \cap A_2) \subseteq B_2$, $z_1(aA_1A_2) = a$, $z_2(aA_1A_2) = aA_1$, and $z_3(aA_1A_2) = y$ where $y = \varphi(a, q)$ if $q \in A_1 \cap A_2$ or $y = supY$ if $A_1 \cap A_2 = \emptyset$.

Then the SL-automata network $N = Xz_1S_1z_2S_2z_3Y$ is a cascade quasi-monotonic decomposition of the automaton S.

References

1. Agibalov,G.P.: Discrete automata on semilattices. Tomsk, Tomsk University (1993) (in Russian)
2. Agibalov,G.P.: Finite automata on partially ordered sets. 11th IFAC World Congress Proceedings **3** (1991)
3. Hartmanis,J., Stearns,R.E.: Algebraic Structure Theory of Sequential Machines. Prentice-Hall, Englewood Cliffs (1966).

Linear Fibonacci Forms and Parallel Algorithms for High Dimension Arithmetic

Anisimov A.V.

Glushkov Institute of Cybernetics,
pr. Akademika Glushkova-40, 252650, Kiev, Ukraine

E-mail: vig@gicrtc.kiev.ua

Abstract. Applications of special representation of natural numbers as linear forms of the type $x F_{t-1} + y F_t$, where F_{t-1} and F_t are adjacent Fibonacci numbers, for constructing effective parallel algorithms of modular exponentiation and factorization are considered in this report. These operations over large numbers are ones of the main in design and analysis of well-known public-key cryptosystems like RSA-schemes. Proofs of two important theorems are shown also.

Define Fibonacci numbers as usual by $F_0 = 0; F_1 = 1; F_n = F_{n-2} + F_{n-1}$ for $n \geq 2$. Application of Fibonacci numbers for constructing effective sequential arithmetic algorithms are well known. For instance, in the paper [1] the fact of representing any natural integer as a sum of Fibonacci numbers was intensively exploited. For addition machines (using finite number of registers and only operations of input-output, copy, addition, subtraction and comparison) it was possible for operation $x^y \bmod z$ to obtain evaluation $O((\log y)(\log z) + \log(x/z))$ for the number of operations. Nevertheless algorithms obtained on this idea are strictly sequential in nature and can not give advantage on parallel computing devices.

In spite of huge studies of Fibonacci numbers the linear Fibonacci representation is not well known. It was firstly introduced in [2] with the purpose to compress digital information. But further study of such representation yields more interesting algorithmic results and in particular, for parallelization of integer algorithms.

The linear Fibonacci form of a range t is defined as a linear combination of the form: $x F_{t-1} + y F_t$, where x and y are integers and $y \neq 0$.

We call the linear form $x F_{t-1} + y F_t$ to be positively defined linear Fibonacci form if it is different from the null and coefficients x and y are natural numbers.

For any natural number n there exists a representation of this number as positively defined linear Fibonacci form. For instance any trivial partition $n = x + y = xF_1 + xF_2$ could be considered as the representation of the range 2. The representation of the maximum range is of interest for us because in such representation there is possibility to use maximally the optimization effects of Fibonacci numbers .

Theorem 1. If n - any natural number (not equal to the null) then there exists the unique representation of this number as a positively defined linear Fibonacci form of the maximal range t, $n = aF_{t-1} + bF_t$. At that inequalities hold true: *if* $a \neq 0$, *then* $0 < b < a < F_t$; *if* $a = 0$ *then* $0 < b < F_{t+1}$; $a + b < c\sqrt{n}$; $(\log_\alpha n)/2 + c_1 < t < \log_\alpha n$; $\alpha = (1 + \sqrt{5})/2$; $c > 0$; $c_1 > 0$, c and c_1 are small constants.

The proof is based on the idea of using sequentially two possible transformations which do not change the value of an integer. If $n = xF_{t-1} + yF_t$ and $y \geq x$ then it is possible to increase a current range, $n = (y - x)F_t + xF_{t+1}$. If $y < x$ but $x \geq sF_t$ for some s then one can try to reduce x and increase y using the following transformation: $n = (x - sF_t)F_{t-1} + (y + sF_{t-1})F_t$. The purpose of the transformation of this type is to reach, if possible, the first considered above case when a range is increased. The time of obtaining the linear Fibonacci form of the maximal range is $O(\log n)$. It is interesting that under more restricted conditions there exists an algorithm on an addition machine constructing the maximal linear Fibonacci representation of the number n and using $O(\log n)$ operations.

In some other form this assertion was proved in [2].

If $n = aF_{t-1} + bF_t$ is represented as the maximum linear Fibonacci form then numbers a and b also have the same representation. Corresponding coefficients for linear forms of a and b in the same way have the similar representation and so on. In this manner we naturally get the notion of the linear Fibonacci tree for the number n.

The linear Fibonacci tree is constructed in the following way.

1. The starting vertex is marked by n.

2. If a formed vertex is marked by a number z and $z \neq 1$, then firstly we construct the linear Fibonacci representation for z of the maximum range, $z = xF_{t-1} + yF_t$. Then we form two (or one the right if $x = 0$) vertices - sons for the vertex z. The left edge of z is marked by F_{t-1}, the right edge - by F_t. The corresponding vertices of the lower level are marked respectively by x and y.

3. Repeat the step 2 on all vertices having marks distinguished from 1.

The following fact is important.

Theorem 2. The depth of the linear Fibonacci tree of any number n is bounded by a value $O(\log \log n)$.

The idea of the proof of this theorem consists in the following. From the Theorem 1 one can get the fact that if $n = aF_{i-1} + bF_i$ is the linear Fibonacci representation of the maximal range then numbers a and b are less than $c\sqrt{n}$ with the small constant c. Therefore, on the next level below vertices marked by a and b the corresponding coefficients do not exceed $c\sqrt{c\sqrt{n}} = c^{1+1/2} n^{1/4}$. On the k level coefficients-marks of vertices do not exceed $c^{1+1/2+1/4+...+1/2^k} n^{1/2^{k+1}}$.

Taking into account that the sequence $1+1/2+1/4+...$ is converged to 2 one can easily derive the theorem assertion.

The obtained above optimistic evaluation displays that linear Fibonacci trees are good objects to represent large and even superlarge numbers. Let us consider for instance the modular exponentiation problem, $x^y \bmod z$.

It is evident that exponentiation into power equal to some Fibonacci number is a convenient and effective operation. Exponentiation $x^{F_i} \bmod z$ demands computation of $x \bmod z$ and t times cyclic modular multiplication only on two registers. That is why we try the computation of $x^y \bmod z$ to reduce to the series of computations of a simple type $u^{F_i} \bmod z$. If $y = aF_{i-1} + bF_i$ -is the linear Fibonacci partition of y of the maximum range then $x^y \bmod z = (x^{F_{i-1}})^a * (x^{F_i})^b \bmod z$.

Thus the problem is recursively reduced to the similar problem but with numbers of $O(\sqrt{y})$ degree.

A linear Fibonacci tree is a base for constructing the parallel algorithm. Input x is given to the root of the Fibonacci tree for y. The value $x^{F_{i-1}} \bmod z$ is transmitted down to the left son. Similarly the value $x^{F_i} \bmod z$ is transmitted by the right channel. Computed results are transformed by the same way under decent on the next level. After reaching leaves the process changes its direction - results from vertices - sons are multiplied and transmitted up to a vertex-father. This algorithms demands $O(\log\log y)$ level passes with simple homogeneous computations on each level. If to take into account time spending by the process on each level computing powers which are Fibonacci numbers then the total running time is $O(\log y + \log(x/z))$.

In the considered above problem the computing tree is dynamically generated with data transmission along channels and with modification of computing functions in vertices during running up and down. Such problems are well described in PARCS-technology of programming [3],[4],[5].

It is interesting to note that in cryptographic schemes such as RSA or digital signature, in computing $x^y \bmod z$, values y and z are given constants and x - is a variable. That is why the necessity to build a Fibonacci tree arises only once and the process of obtaining modular exponentiation is reduced to runs over the fixed Fibonacci tree.

Let's consider the factorization problem of large numbers. This problem often arises in different aspects of the open cryptology. There exist special computing factorization machines, for example, the sifting machine of C.Pomerance. The importance of finding concurrent homogeneous algorithms for this problem was also stressed by many authors.

Let $n = pq$, where q is a greater factor. For q there exists a linear Fibonacci representation of the maximum range t, $q = aF_{t-1} + bF_t$. If $n = A_0 F_{t-1} + A_1 F_t$ is some representation of the integer n as a linear Fibonacci form of the range t then for some parameter i the following equalities hold true: $ap = A_0 + iF_t$, $bp = A_1 - iF_{t-1}$.

From this using some properties of linear Fibonacci forms the factorization of n could be reduced to the sorting out problem $p=GCD(n,d+i)$, where d is a computing constant and i is a sorting out parameter. It is possible to prove that for i the following inequality holds true: $\dfrac{m}{F_i F_{i+1}} < i < \dfrac{m}{F_i F_{i-1}} < p$ where t is a range of the maximal linear Fibonacci form of q.

The sequential algorithm computing p by this formula gives time evaluation $O(\dfrac{m}{F_i F_{i+1}})$. This method works well if the number n has large (or small) factors or factors with large Fibonacci degrees. In this case the value F_i is large and therefore $\dfrac{m}{F_i F_{i+1}}$ is of computable degree. When p and q are of the same degree the sequential search becomes quite exhaustive.

It is evident that this case also defines the possible parallel implementation like "processor farms" using partition of the diapason for i.

Taking into account the fact that all computations in the process of finding $GCD(n,d+i)$ are similar to each other and based on the operation $x \bmod y$ it is possible to suggest a pipe-line architecture for this considered task.

The basic computing module fulfills computation: *input* (x,y); *if* $y \neq 1$ *then* {z:=xmody; (x,y)=(y,z)}; *output* (x,y).

Connecting $\lfloor \log_2 n \rfloor$ of such elements into a ring and choosing a control point for data loading and checking the second field in pairs (x,y) one can assemble ring computing structure having $\log n$ modules of the same type. The number $\lfloor \log_2 n \rfloor$ is taken from consideration that the number of steps in computing GCD according to the Euclid's scheme does not exceed $\log_2 n$. That is why under passing the control point if the second field is equal to 1 then loading of a next corresponding portion of data could be done, or if it is different from 1 then it is equal to the corresponding divisor of n.

It is not difficult to modify the basic module adding possibility to memorize, to change, to add a constant, and to transmit to the next neighboring element the current value of i. Then it is possible to use the input loading only once. In this variant the computation speed depends only on time frequency of the ring structure.

The computing time on addition machines of the operation $x \bmod z$ is $O(\log(x/z))$ [1]. It is interesting to note that Fibonacci numbers are also play important role in the algorithm from [1]. This operation could be also parallelized if necessary.

It is possible to develop the introduced above idea on multiring structure. As first computations under large numbers are quite slow then it is desirable to separate the beginning stage in one slow ring and the ending stage in some other fast ring.

The simplicity and homogeneity of basic computing elements gives a hint on the realization of the ring structure by of optocomputing means. The detailed delineation of the presented results could be found in the paper [6].

References

1. R.W.Floyd, D.E.Knuth Addition Machiens, SIAM J.Comput.Vol. 19, No 2, 1990, pp.329-340.
2. A.V.Anisimov, Y.P.Ryndin, S.E.Redko The Riverse Fibonacci Transformation, Kibernetika , N 3, 1983, pp.9-11.
3. A.V.Anisimov, P.P.Kulyabko Programming Parallel Computation in Controlling Spaces, Kibernetika , N 3, 1984, pp.79-88.
4. A.V.Anisimov, Y.E.Boreisha, P.P.Kulyabko The Programming System PARCS, Programming , N 6, 1991, pp.91-102.
5. A.V.Anisimov, P.P.Kulyabko The picularities of PARCS-technology of rogramming , Cybernetics and System Analysis, N 3, 1993, pp.128-137.
6. A.V.Anisimov Linear Fibonacci Forms Cybernetics and System Analysis, N3, 1995.

Cellular-Neural Computations.
Formal Model and Possible Applications *

O.L.Bandman

Computer center
Siberian Department of Russian Academy of Sciences
Pr. Acad. Lavrentieva, 6, Novosibirsk, 90, 630090, Russia
Tel.: (8 3832) 35 09 94, e-mail: Bandman@comcen.nsk.su

Abstract. A formal model of fine-grained parallel computations is presented, in which the connectionist method of Artificial Neural Networks is combined with the cellular-like structure of interneuron communication. The model is based on the concepts and formalisms of Parallel Substitution Algorithm, which is considered be the most theoretically advanced generalization of Cellular Automaton. Some fields of application are discussed and computer simulation results are given.

1 Introduction

There are two different approaches to fine-grained parallel computations. The first ascends to von-Neumann's Cellular Automaton [1]. The second – to Mc-Calloch' and Pitts' Logical Calculus [2]. The two approaches are progressing rapidly both in formal methods sophistication and in looking for a proper hardware implementation.

The first approach has gained greatest advancement in the theory of Parallel Substitution Algorithm (PSA) [3], which is directed to the investigation and design of cellular algorithmically oriented architecture. The following fundamental concepts form the background of the PSA.

1. The PSA processes cellular arrays which are sets of cells, characterized by a state and a name. The set of states form the PSA alphabet. The set of names represents a discrete space, in which interaction patterns are defined by means of naming functions.

2. Operations over a cellular array are specified by a set of substitutions. All substitutions are applied in parallel (at once) at every cell of the array. The substitution is applicable to an array at a certain cell if the left-hand side containing this cell is included in it. The execution of an applicable substitution is in replacing the subarray of its left-hand side to that of its right-hand side.

3. The computation is an iterative procedure. At each step all applicable substitutions are executed resulting in a new cellular array. The computation terminates when the array is obtained to which no single substitution is applicable.

* The research is supported by Russian Foundation for Basic Research grant (93-01-01000)

4. Each PSA has an explicit interpretation by an automata net, transition function of net automata being determined by the substitution set.

5. Due to the context in the left-hand side of substitutions similar constructs are used to represent both processing and control. This fact underlines PSA composition and decomposition techniques as well as the methods for control synthesis.

The second approach is under intensive elaboration for creating the Artificial Neural Networks (ANN), the interest being concentrated on two paradigms: Hopfield's Associative Memory [4] and Boltzmann's Machine [5]. The ANN is a model of fine-grained parallel computation belonging to connectionist type. The main difference of this model from other massively parallel computations is in that the results are not computed under the program control, but are obtained when the network is settled in a stable state. The implicit and redundant form of storing data as connection weight values provides the ability of restoring the lost information. So, the main field of ANN application is as follows: pattern restoring, pattern classification, searching for optimal solution.

The following features characterize the ANN computational model.

1. The ANN processes a data array which represents the states of bistable elements, called *neurons*. Each neuron is connected to all others, the connections being characterized by real non-negative numbers, referred to as *connection weights*.

2. The algorithm for ANN to solve a given problem is specified by the nonlinear function and the values of connection weights – *the weight matrix*. Constructing the weight matrix and choosing the non-linear function constitute the process of ANN programming or *learning*. It is the most complicated stage of problem solving by the ANN, which requires much skill and time.

3. Two modes of computation are admitted in the ANN theory. Originally, a continuous variant of computation was proposed, and its implementation as an asynchronous transition from a given initial state to a stable one, characterized by the (possibly, local) minimum of the *energy function* was studied [4]. Later on, the discrete time synchronous mode of ANN operation has become more popular. In this case the iterative procedure starting from the initial state at each step brings the network closer and closer to a stable state, where the computation stops, because no single neuron changes its state.

4. There are two ways of implementing the ANN. The first is widely used nowadays. It consists in simulation the ANN algorithm on a conventional computer, sometimes augmented by special-purpose processor for fast computing sum-of-products. The second way is associated with the direct implementation of neural network architecture. Much investigations are done to find the technologies (optics, opto-electronics, holography) which would provide the effective realization of ANN, the global connections being the most difficult task.

5. The ANN model of computation has no special means for composing, decomposing, and making equivalent transformations of the algorithm.

In spite of the fact, that the two above models have some opposite features, we here make an attempt to cross them hoping that the resulting hybrid would possess some merits of both. Particularly, we want it to inherit the interaction boundedness from PSA and the connectionist mode of computation from ANN. However, since parents disadvantages should also be inherited, the problem arises to study them and determine the limits of the new model capabilities. Speaking more specifically, the aim of the paper is to construct a formal representation and a set of tools for studying the computation process in cellular arrays, whose cells perform neural functions. The Table bellow shows, what properties cellular-neural computations inherit from what of its parents.

	PSA	ANN	cellular-neural computation
Process	discrete	continuous	discrete
Mode	synchronous	asynchronous	synchronous
Connections	bounded unweighted	each with all weighted	bounded weighted
Cell function	finite automaton	sigmoid	sigmoid

The proposed model may be considered formally both as ANN with local connections and as PSA with sigmoid (threshold) cell functions. The first approach has already been explored when studies ANN of Hopfield type. There are three lines of inquiries in this studying. The first is associated with the ANN implementation in a form of asynchronous cellular system with amplifiers [6]. The main theoretical result is stability conditions expressed in terms of circuit parameters. The applications are confined to pattern classification problems. The second line [7] is concerned to the investigation of the capability of Hopfield's ANN, in which cell connections outside the given neighborhood are cut off, the loss of connections being paid by the decrease of memory capacity. The third direction of investigations seems to be the most fruitful [8]. It introduces the method of construction a sparse weight matrix with the predetermined locations of zeroes, which provides the correspondence of stable states to the given set of stored patterns.

Here we introduce an alternative representation of cellular-neural algorithm. It is regarded as a PSA with sigmoid (neuron-like) cell functions. There are two reasons for that. Firstly, we hope that the wide expressive ability of PSA (naming functions, context, operation on subsets of cells, equivalent transformations, etc.) would compensate the constraints imposed on connection structure. Secondly, PSA is a model born and bred in our staff, and we have in our possession all the facilities to deal with.

The paper consists of five sections. The second section introduces the cellular-neural algorithm as a computational model and all formal definition are presented here. In the third section the problem of cellular-neural synthesis is stated in a general form and possible methods and tools for its solution are discussed. The fourth section deals with some applications, which are illustrated by simple example and simulation results. In the last section some conclusions are made about the directions of future investigations.

2 Formal Representation of a Cellular-Neural Algorithm

When constructing the formal representation of cellular-neural algorithm the priority is given to "cellular" notation, which is as close as possible to that of PSA. Sometimes, if necessary, the ANN concepts are also used.

Definition 1. A triple (a, m, v), where $a \in A$, A – a finite *alphabet*, $m \in M$, M – *a naming set*, and $v \in V$, V –*a weight vector set*, is called *a neuron*. A pair (a, m) is referred to as *a cell*, a being interpreted as *a state*, m – as *a name*.

Definition 2. A set of neural cells $N = \{(a_i, m_i, v_i) : i = 1, \ldots, q\}$ with no pair of elements in N having equal names, is called *a cellular-neural array*. The set of cells, obtained by omitting he vectors v_i from the triples in N

$$C(N) = \{(a_i, m_i) : (a_i, m_i . v_i) \in N\} \tag{1}$$

is called *a cellular array, generated by* N and denoted as $C(N)$.

The alphabet A consists of three parts: $A = A_0 \cup A_x \cup A_c$, where $A_0 \in \mathbb{R}$ is a state alphabet, $A_x = \{x_1, x_2, \ldots, x_n\}$ is an alphabet of variables with the domain in A_0, $A_c = \{\alpha, \beta, \ldots\}$ is a control alphabet. The naming set M may consist of any kind of symbols or tuples of symbols. The set V of weight vectors has the same cardinality as that of the naming set, the length of vectors being not more than this value, the component being from $\mathbb{R}$.

The set of all finite cellular-neural arrays, generated by an alphabet A, a naming set M, and a set of weight vectors V isomorphic to M, is denoted as $K(A, M, V)$. The set of cellular arrays, generated by A and M is referred to as $K(A, M)$.

Definition 3. . A function $\phi(m)$ determined on a naming set M is called *a naming function*. A finite set of naming functions

$$T(m) = \{m, \phi_1(m), \ldots, \phi_n(m)\}, \tag{2}$$

in which for any $m \in M$ $\phi_i(m) \neq \phi_j(m)$, $i, j \in \{1, \ldots, n\}$, $i \neq j$, is called *a template*. A set of names $T(m_i) = \{m_i, \phi_1(m_i), \ldots, \phi_n(m_i)\}$ is referred to as *a template element* for the cell named m_i.

Each template element $T(m_i)$ is characterized by a *weight vector* $v_i \in V$,

$$v_i = \{w(m_i, \phi_1(m_i)), \ldots, w(m_i, \phi_n(m_i))\}, \tag{3}$$

whose components are interpreted as weights of the connections between the cells named m_i and $\phi_j(m) \in T(m)$.

Definition 4. A mapping $S(m) \Rightarrow K(A, M)$, expressed by the equation

$$S(m) = \{(a_0, m)(a_1, \phi_1(m)), \ldots, (a_n, \phi_n(m))\}, \tag{4}$$

in which the set of naming functions constitute a template, is called *a configuration*, the vector $S_A(m) = (a_0, a_1, \ldots, a_n)$ being referred to as *a state configuration vector*.

A configuration is called *k-bounded* if each name m_i appears not more than in k elements of it. A bounded configuration is called *local* if a metric is given on a set of names, and within this metric a sphere of a finite radius may be constructed such, that for each $m_i \in M$ all cell names appearing in $S(m_i)$ are inside this sphere.

Definition 5. . The expression of the form

$$\theta : S'(m) \Rightarrow S''(m), \tag{5}$$

where S' и S'' are configurations, is called *a parallel substitution* (*substitution* for short).

$S'(m)$ contains two parts separated by the sign $*$, $S'(m) = S'_1(m) * S'_2)m)$. The first part

$$S'_1(m) = \{(a_0, m), (a_1, \phi_1(m)), \ldots, (a_n, \phi_n(m))\}, \quad a_i \in A_0 \cup A_x,$$

is referred to as *a base* , and the second part

$$S'_2(m) = \{(b_1, \psi_1(m)), \ldots, (b_l, \psi_l(m))\}, \quad a_i \in A_0 \cup A_c$$

– as *a context*. In the right-hand side of (5)

$$S''(m) = \{(f_0, m), (f_1, \phi_1(m)), \ldots, (f_n, \phi_n(m))\},$$

$f_j, j = 1, \ldots, n$, are nonlinear (sigmoid or threshold) functions of the inner product of the state configuration vector by the weight vector. The most oftenly used is the function

$$f_j = \begin{cases} a, & \text{if } \sum_{j=1}^{n} a_j w_j \geq 0 \\ b, & \text{otherwise} \end{cases} \tag{6}$$

where a_j, w_j are components of $S_A(m_i)$ and v_i respectively, $a, b \in A_0$. It is worth to take attention that we use here *stationary substitutions* which have configurations S'_1 and S'' generated by the same template.

A substitution is considered to be *applicable* to a cellular-neural array $N \in K(A, M, V)$, if there exists $M' \subset M$ such, that for any $m_i \in M'$ the following holds

$$S'_1(m_i) \cup S'_2(m_i) \subseteq C(N). \tag{7}$$

If $S'_1(m)$ contains variable symbols, then the substitution θ is applicable at any $m_i \in M$ where all components of $S_A(m_i)$ are in A_0. An application of θ to an array N results in substituting the states a_i in the cells of $S'_1 \subseteq C(N)$ for the values of f_i in the equally named cells of the right-hand side of (5). This is done simultaneously all over the array.

The set of substitutions $\Phi = \{\theta_1, \ldots, \theta_k\}$ constitute a *parallel substitution system or a PSS*. A PSS is applied to a cellular-neuron array in accordance to the following procedure.

Procedure 1. Let $N \in K(A, M, V)$ be a cellular neural array to be processed by Φ, $C(N)_t$ – an array at the t-th step of computation, $C(N)_0 = C(N)$. Then

1) if there exists a nonempty subset of substitutions $\Phi' \subset \Phi$, applicable to $C(N)_t$, then all of them are applied simultaneously, the obtained array being $C(N)_{t-1}$;
2) if the application of Φ does not change the array or no substitution is applicable to $C(t)$, then $C(N)_t$ is the result of the computation, denoted as $\Phi(N)$.

The determinacy of computations generated by a given PSS Φ is provided by its noncontradictoriness [3]. This property guarantees that the application of Φ to any $N \in K(A, M, V)$ results in a cellular-neuron array, i.e. such one which contains no equally named neurons.

Definition 6. A noncontradictory substitution set Φ, applied to $N \in K(A, M, V)$ in accordance with Procedure 1 is called *a cellular-neuron algorithm* which is represented by a pair $\langle \Phi, K(A, M, V) \rangle$

For each cellular-neural algorithm an artificial neural net may be constructed. This net consists of a set of processing elements, $P = p_1, \ldots, p_q$, $q = |M|$, which corresponds to the set of neurons. Each processing element should be capable to perform the following:

1) to be in any state from a state alphabet,
2) to perform the non-linear functions indicated in the right-hand sides of all substitutions , and
3) to store the connection weight vector.

The connections between processing elements are predetermined by the substitution system Φ. If Φ consists of a single substitution, then the weight vector contains the names from $T'(m_i)$, T' being the template generating the configuration of the left-hand side of the substitution. In general case the connection vector of p_i corresponds to the union of template elements generating the left-hand sides $S'(m)$ from(5) of all substitutions $\theta \in \Phi$.

Definition 7. Let $T'_j(m)$ be the template, generating the substitution $S'_j(m)$, which constitutes the left-hand side of $\theta \in \Phi$. Then the set of names

$$Q'(m_i) = \bigcup_{j=1}^{k} T'_j(m_i), \quad k = |\Phi|, \tag{8}$$

is called *a neighborhood* of a cell named $m_i \in M$.

The neighborhood is represented, sometimes, as a vector

$$Q(m_i) = (m_i, m'_1, \ldots, m'_r),$$

where the neighbors are ordered in an arbitrary way, but, once chosen, the order is kept when forming the *neighborhood weight vector*,

$$v_i = (w(m_i, m_i), w(m_i, m'_1), \ldots, w(m_i, m'r)) = (w_0.w_1, \ldots, w_r),$$

and *neighborhood state vector*

$$S'(m_i) = (a_0, a_1, \ldots, a_r),$$

which characterize the neuron named m_i.

Example 1. Let $N \in K(A, M, V)$ be given such, that $A = \{-1, 1\} \cup \{x, y, z, u, v\} \cup \{\alpha, \beta\}$. $M = \{\langle i, j \rangle : i = 0, 1, 2, 3; \ j = 0, 1, 2, 3, 4\}$. The initial cellular array is

$$C(N)_0 = \{(1, \langle 1, 1 \rangle)(1, \langle 0, 2 \rangle)(1, \langle 0, 3 \rangle)(\alpha, \langle 0, 4 \rangle)(\alpha, \langle 1, 4 \rangle)(\alpha, \langle 2, 4 \rangle)(\beta, \langle 3, 4 \rangle)\},$$

the state of other cells being equal to -1 (Fig.1 a)).

The following templates are used:

$$T_1 = \{\langle i, j \rangle\},$$
$$T_2 = \{\langle i-1, j \rangle, \langle i, j+1 \rangle, \langle i+1, j \rangle, \langle i, j-1 \rangle \langle i, 4 \rangle\},$$
$$T_3 = \{\langle i-1, j \rangle, \langle i, j+1 \rangle, \langle i, j-1 \rangle, \langle i, 4 \rangle\},$$

The neighborhood of cells whose names have $i = 0, 1, 2$ corresponds to the template $T_1 \cup T_2$, the neighborhood of cells whose names have $i = 3$ – to the template $T_2 \cup T_3$. Neighbor numbering corresponds to that of naming functions in the template. The weight vectors $w(\langle i, j \rangle) = (w_1, \ldots, w_5) : \langle i, j \rangle \in M\}$ are computed according to the formula: $w_k = a_{ij} a_{ij}^k + b_{ij} b_{ij}^k$, where a_{ij}^k and b_{ij}^k are the states of k-th neighbors of the cells $(a_{ij}, \langle i, j \rangle)$ and $(b_{ij}, \langle ij \rangle)$ in the two given stored patterns, respectively (Fig.1 b). The weight vectors are given in the table below.

j i	0	1	2	3
0	(1,0,2,0,0)	(1,0,2,-2,0)	(1,0,2,-2,2)	(1,0,0,0,2)
1	(1,0,0,2,0)	(1,-2,2,-2,0)	(1,-2,0,-2,0)	(1,2,0,2,0)
2	(1,2,0,2,0)	(1,-2,2,2,0)	(1,-2,0,2,2)	(1,2,0,2,0)
3	(1,2,0,0)	(1,2,2,0)	(1,2,0,2)	(1,2,0,0)

The set of substitutions $\Phi = \{\theta_1, \theta_2\}$:

$$\theta_1 = \{(v, \langle i, j \rangle)\} * \{(x, \langle i-1, j \rangle)(y, \langle i, j+1 \rangle)(z, \langle i+1, j \rangle)(u, \langle i, j-1 \rangle)$$
$$(\alpha, \langle i, 4 \rangle)\} \Rightarrow \{(f_1, \langle i, j \rangle)\},$$
$$\theta_2 = \{(v, \langle i, j \rangle)\} * \{(x, \langle i-1, j \rangle)(y, \langle i, j+1 \rangle)(u, \langle i, j-1 \rangle)\}$$
$$(\beta, \langle i, j \rangle)\} \Rightarrow \{(f_2, \langle i, j \rangle)\}.$$

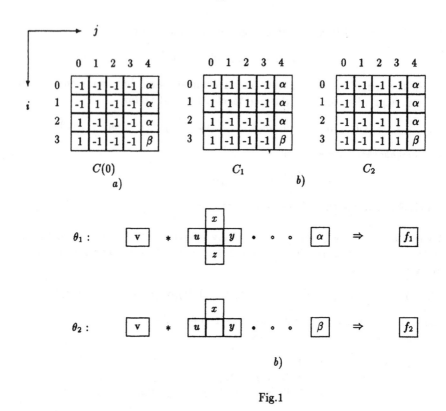

Fig.1

where

$$f_1 = \begin{cases} 1 & \text{if } w_1 v + w_2 x + w_3 y + w_4 z + w_5 u \geq 0, \\ -1 & \text{otherwise} \end{cases}$$

$$f_2 = \begin{cases} 1 & \text{if } w_1 v + w_2 x + w_3 y + w_4 u \geq 0, \\ -1 & \text{otherwise} \end{cases}$$

The application of Φ to the cellular-neuron $\langle C, W \rangle$ after one iteration results in the stored pattern $C(N)_1 = C_1$.

3 Methods for Cellular-Neural Algorithm Synthesis

Synthesis procedure of a cellular-neural algorithm for solving a given problem consists in the following: 1) choosing the alphabet, 2) choosing the naming set, 3) determining the set of weight vectors and 4) writing the substitutions.

The alphabet is determined by data representation in the problem to be solved. The state alphabet A_0 is a one-to-one mapping of data to be processed. For example, in the problems of pattern retrieval $A_0 = \{0, 1\}$ or $A_0 = \{1, -1\}$ for bistable patterns and $A_0 = \mathbf{R}$, if the patterns are in multigraduated grey or colored. The variable alphabet A_x contains as many symbols as is the cardinality of a neuron neighborhood. If the computation process requires controlling actions, then a set $A_c = \{\alpha, \beta, \ldots\}$ should be added.

The neural naming set is chosen according to data representation of the problem to be solved, and the way of mapping the given parameters to the set of neurons. Thus, in the optimization problems the neuron naming set is in correspondence with the set of parameters forming the domain where the objective function is determined. When the optimization problems on graphs are to be solved, the naming set may be put in one-to-one correspondence with the set of vertices, circuits, edges or other parameters. If some kind of activity is to be optimized, the naming set is chosen isomorphic to the set of actors or subjects the actors are dealing with. The names in this algorithms are symbols or digits, the naming functions are constant or in the form of shifts $\phi_i(m) = m + d$, where $d \in \mathbf{N}$. When the initial data are represented as a picture in the space (image processing, pattern retrieval), the most oftenly used is the set of coordinate in Euclidean space, $M = \{\langle i, j, k \rangle : i = 0, \ldots, n_i, \ j = 0, \ldots, n_j, \ k = 0, \ldots, n_k\}$. The templates may contain any kinds of naming functions defined on M, but the most usable are also shifts and constants. The neighborhood or at least its admissible size should also be chosen at this stage of synthesis. It is done according to the requirements imposed by the implementation conditions. The naming set may consist of several subsets, $M = \{M_i : i = 1, \ldots, q\}$, each M_i being peculiar to its own cellular-neuron algorithm Φ_i. The interactions of Φ_i with any other Φ_j is represented by means of context configurations in substitutions of Φ_i containing naming functions defined on M_j.

Weight vector set determining is the most important and the most labor consuming stage in cellular-neural algorithm synthesis. This part of synthesis constitutes the "learning process" and should exploit the same approaches, than those of the ANN theory adapted to cellular-neural arrays. Though the methods of determining the weights strongly depend on the problem to be solved, there is a fundamental concept forming the basis for all of them, which in its turn is based on the dynamic properties of cellular-neural algorithm operation. The point is that the cellular-neural array is an autonomous system, such that its dynamic characteristics depend on the weight vectors on the one hand, and on the other hand the computation results are in correspondence with its stable states. Hence, the weight may be determined starting from the dynamic stability condition of the array, which is characterized by the extremum of the following function.

$$E = - \sum_{m_i \in M} a_i \sum_{m_j \in Q(m_i)} w_j a_j, \tag{9}$$

where w_j and a_j are the equally indexed neighborhood weight vector and state neighborhood vector components respectively. In the ANN theory the expression (9) is called *Liapunov's function* or *energy function* [4]. Its inverse $B = -E$ is used in Boltzmann machine theory being called there as the *consensus function* [5]. The minimal value of E (the maximum of B) indicates that the cellular-neural array is in a stable state, i.e. being left to perform the cellular-neural functions without the outer intervention, it does not change neuron states. From above it follows that the strategy for weight vector synthesis should be grounded on the following requirements.

1) . The result of computation should be represented by a stable state of the array. Formally it is expressed as follows. Let the result of applying a cellular-neural algorithm to an array $N \in K(A, M, V)$ be $\overline{N}$ with the cellular array $C(\overline{N})$, corresponding to the result of the computation. Then for the resulting array the following condition is to be met.

$$\Phi(\overline{N}) = \overline{N}. \tag{10}$$

2) Starting at any initial cellular array $C(N) \in K(A, M)$ the algorithm should reach a stable state, i.e. no oscillation should occur in the array.
3) There should be no spurious stable states, which do not represent any result in the problem.

It follows from above that the methods of weight vector synthesis are based on solving the set of equations of the form (10), or comparing the given parameters of the problem with the condition (10). This is not always possible to perform precisely, therefore some approximate and iterative methods are developed and studied. Sometimes, the expression for energy function increment caused by a state change in a single neuron $(a_i, m_i, v_i) \in N$

$$\Delta E_i = -2a_i \sum_{m_j \in Q(m_i)} w(m_i, m_j) a_j. \tag{11}$$

may be used as well. Till now in the ANN theory there are no methods of determining the connection weights, which provide all three above requirements to be met completely. Though some approaches are developed which succeeded to come close to the aim. As for weight vector determining in cellular-neural synthesis, the problem is only touched. We hope, that the capabilities of celullar-neural model would help to develop proper synthesis techniques.

Moreover, the learning algorithms are essentially cellular, because the connection weights are computed as the functions of neighbor neuron states of the prototypes (examples of neuron nets to be processed), the computations being independent for each neuron and, hence, may be executed in parallel.

The substitution system is formed according to the rules of PSA theory [3]. The main peculiarity is as follows. The cellular-neural algorithm is represented by a PSS containing functional substitutions performing sigmoid function of the inner product of two vectors. These functional substitutions are structurally similar to the class of Neumann substitutions (the cardinality of the base is equal to 1).

The PSS should contain also substitutions which makes the algorithm to stop and to generate a signal of termination when the result is obtained. Some general techniques for that are described in [3], but in any particular algorithm this is to be done taking into account the peculiarities of the problem.

The PSS for weight vector set determining is formed according to the methods of PSS theory. This "learning" algorithm belongs to a class of functional PSA's, operating on the same cellular-neural array, the weight vector components being considered as cell states.

4 Examples of Cellular-Neural Algorithm Application

The expressive capability of cellular-neural algorithm is displayed here by three simple examples chosen as representatives of three following classes of problems: 1) optimization on graphs, 2) retrieval of patterns, and 3) identification of figures. Some considerations based on the experience of study and computer simulation are suggested.

4.1 Optimization on graphs

The synthesis of cellular-neural algorithm for solving these problems consists of direct mapping the graph representation onto the cellular-neural array, the weight vector determination being reduced to the direct comparison of the objective function expression to that of the energy function (9).

Let a weighted graph $G = \langle V, E \rangle$, where $V = \{v_1, \ldots, v_{10}\}$ is the set of vertices, $E = \{e_{ij} : i, j = 1, \ldots, 10\}$ is a set of integers, interpreting the weights of edges, be given (Fig.2). A path between two given vertices v_1 and v_{10} is to be found such, that the total weight of its edges is minimal. The problem is reduced to the problem of searching a circuit of minimal weight. The circuit is formed by adding an edge between v_1 and v_{10} with $e_{1,10} = 0$. The solution is sought as a stable state of a cellular-neural array corresponding to the minimum of the inverse of the energy function $B = -E$ (9). So, the set of neural cells are taken isomorphic to the set of simple circuits, representing the graph, the set of neurons in the state equal to 1 corresponding to the set of circuits forming the sought circuit. The algorithm is based on the calculation of the increment ΔB_i caused by the change of the state of the neuron named m_i (11), and then changing the states of those neurons whose increments are minimal. The result is obtained when for all neurons the increments are positive, indicating that B has reached its minimum. The synthesis procedure according to Section 3, is as follows.

1. The alphabet $A = A_0 \cup A_x \cup A_c$, $A_0 = \{0, 1\}$, $A_x = \{x_0, x_1, x_2, x_3, k\}$, $A_c \subset \mathbf{N}$.

2. The naming set is the union of two subsets: $M \cup M'$, $M = \{m_1, \ldots, m_9\}$, $M' = \{m'_1, \ldots, m'_9\}$. Both are isomorphic to the set of simple circuits $L = \{l_1, \ldots, l_9\}$ of the graph. The naming functions used are constants. The templates are defined for each neuron separately, so that $T(m_i)$ contains m_i together with the names corresponding to the circuits adjacent to l_i. For example,

$$T(m_1) = (m_1, m_2, m_3, m_9), \quad T(m_2) = (m_2, m_1, m_4, m_9).$$

3. The weight vectors are computed according to the following assumptions:

a) The weight of any circuit l is the sum of weights of its edges. The weight of a simple circuit l_i is $e(l_i) = e_i^1 + \ldots + e_i^r$, where e_i^j is the weight of edge shared by l_i and l_j.

b) The weight of a circuit l composed of a subset $L' = \{l_i^1, \ldots, l_i^r\}$ of the simple circuits is as follows.

$$e(l) = \sum_{l_i \in L'} e(l_i) - 2 \sum_{l_i, l_j \in L'} e_i^j. \tag{12}$$

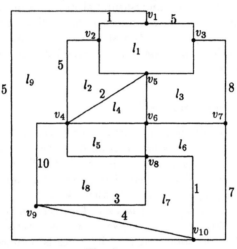

Fig. 2

Comparing (12) with (9) it is easy to obtain the expression for computing the weight vectors.

$$w(m_i, m_i) = e(l_i), \quad w(m_i, m_j) = -2e_i^j, \quad m_i, m_j \in T(m_i).$$

For example,

$$v_1 = (13, -4, -10, -2), \quad v_2 = (9, -4, -4, -10).$$

3) The substitution set is represented here by two substitutions: θ_1, which performs the cellular-neural computation, and a θ_2, which performs a controlling function, changing the threshold at each step of iteration.

$$\theta_1 : \{(x_0, m_i)\} * \{(x_i^1, m_i^1), \ldots, (x_i^4, m_i^4)(k, m_i')\} \Rightarrow \{(f_i, m_i)\},$$
$$\theta_2 : \{(k, m_i')\} \Rightarrow \{(f, m_i')\},$$

where

$$f_i = \begin{cases} \bar{x} & \text{if } \sum_{j=1}^4 x_i^j v_i^j \geq k \\ x & \text{otherwise} \end{cases}$$

$$f = \min_{i=1} \sum_{j=1}^4 x_i^j v_i^j.$$

The initial cellular state is chosen arbitrarily, in our case it is $C(N)_0 = \{(1, m_1),$ $(0, m_2), (1, m_3), (0, m_4), (1, m_5), (0, m_6), (1, m_7)(0, m_8)(1, m_9)\}$. The results of computations are given in the table bellow.

t	neuron states	energy decrements	k	B
0	1,0,1,0,1,0,1,0,1	-1,-5,-5,-3,-12, 3, 0,-19, 10	-19	33
1	1,0,1,0,1,0,1,1,1	-1,-5,-5,-3, 0, 3, 6, 19, 10	-5	26
2	1,1,0,0,1,0,1,1,1	-7, 5, 5,-5, 0, 5, 6, 19, 20	-7	19
3	0,1,0,0,1,0,1,1,1	7, 1,15,-5, 0, 5, 6, 19, 20	-5	12
4	0,1,0,1,1,0,1,1,1	7, 5,13, 5, 8, 5, 6, 19, 20	0	7

As it is seen from the table the result is obtained after the fourth iteration. The sought circuit is the composition of the subset $L = \{l_2, l_4, l_5, l_7, l_8, l_9\}$, which yields the minimal weight path from v_1 to v_{10} going via the vertices: v_2, v_5, v_6, v_8, and having the weight equal to 7.

4.2 Pattern Retrieval

The cellular-neuron algorithm for pattern retrieval descends from Hopfield's neural associative memory [4]. The problem is as follows. A number of patterns (prototypes) are given to be stored in the array, weight vector values providing the correspondence of each prototype to a stable state. So, if the initial cellular array is set to represent an arbitrary pattern, the algorithm should start the computations and terminate in a stable state corresponding to a prototype with closest resemblance to the initial pattern. This class of problems presents a good illustration of synthesis procedure, where a cellular algorithm (PSA) is used for weight vector determining, which gives the possibility to combine the learning and the processing stages.

Let a set of patterns $P = \{p_1, \ldots, p_s\}$, represented by two-dimensional white-black pictures, be stored in the array. Then the synthesis procedure is as follows.

1) Following Hopfield's model, A_0 is taken as $\{1, -1\} \cup N$, $A_x = \{x, x_0, x_1, \ldots, x_r, v_0, \ldots, v_s\}$, $r + 1$ is the cardinality of the neighborhood, s –the number of prototypes.

2) The naming set consists of two subsets M and M', both being taken as sets of coordinates in a 3D Eucledian space. The first is the naming set for cellular-neuron array, where the main computations are performed, $M = \{\langle i, j, k \rangle\}$. The ranges of i and j are defined according to the size of the patterns, $k = 0, 1, \ldots, r+1$. The plane $\{\langle i, j, r+1 \rangle\}$ is dedicated for pattern representation, the cells named $\{\langle i, j, 0 \rangle, \ldots, \langle i, j, r \rangle\}$ are for storing the weight vector $v_{ij} = (w_{ij}^0, \ldots, w_{ij}^r)$. The second subset $M' = \{\langle i', j', h \rangle\}$, i', j' ranging as i, j in M, $h = 1, \ldots, s$ is dedicated for storing the prototypes.

3) The method used for weight vector synthesis is based on a well-known itarative algorithm of perceptron learning [9]. Here it is presented in the form of a PSA. The initial array is composed of N and N', where $N \in K(A, M, V)$ all cell states being equal to 0, $N' \in K(A, M')$ whose planes represent the

prototypes. The substitution set is $\Phi = \{\theta_1, \theta_2\}$, θ_1 performs the calculation of weights, θ_2 transfers the prototypes from N to N'. The geometrical representation of the configuration S' with $(r = 9)$, used in θ_1 is shown in Fig.3.

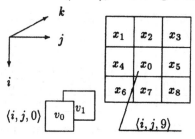

Fig.3

$\theta_1 : \{(v_k, \langle i, j, k \rangle)\} * \{(x_0 \langle i, j, 9 \rangle), (x_1, \langle i-1, j-1, 9 \rangle) \ldots, (x_8, \langle i+1, j+1, 9 \rangle)$
$(v_0, \langle i, j, 0 \rangle), \ldots, (v_8, \langle i, j, 8 \rangle)\} \Rightarrow \{(f, \langle i, j, k \rangle)\}$,
$\theta_2 : \{(v, \langle i', j', h \rangle)\} \Rightarrow \{(v, \langle i, j, 9 \rangle)\}$,

where

$$f = \begin{cases} v & \text{if } v \sum_{j=1}^{r} x_j v_j > 0 \\ v + x_i x_j & \text{otherwise} \end{cases}$$

These two substitutions show only the main operations of the algorithm. Some substitutions should be added to make them be applied alternatively, and to transfer the prototypes in turn until the weight become stable.

4). The main algorithm for the retrieval of a stored pattern consists of a single substitution, in which the same configuration S is used.

$\theta : \{(x, \langle i, j, 9 \rangle)\} * \{(x_1 \langle i-1, j-1, 9 \rangle) \ldots, (x_8, \langle i+1, j+1, 9 \rangle)$
$(v_0, \langle i, j, 0 \rangle), \ldots, (v_8, \langle i, j, 8 \rangle)\} \Rightarrow \{(f, \langle i, j, 9 \rangle)\}$,

where

$$f = \begin{cases} 1, & \text{if } \sum_{j=0}^{j=8} x_j v_j \geq 0 \\ -1, & \text{otherwise} \end{cases}$$

The simulation of the algorithm shows that all prototypes correspond to stable states and more than r patterns may be stored.

4.3 Image Processing

Here the problem of making some transformation on images is briefly considered. The image is given in a colored or in a multigraduated gray form. The most typical problems are the following: to classify the cells or the areas by colors, to determine the locations of some given symbols or figures, to clean the image from the noise, to distinguish contours, edges, angles, etc. The peculiarity of cellular-neural algorithms for these problems is in that the weights are associated with the configurations (cloning templates in [6]) of the substitution rather than with the cellular-neural array. In the neural-cellular algorithm synthesis the alphabet is the set of codes of the colors, representing the image. The naming set is a set of coordinates of a 2D plane, the size being determined by the size of the image. The templates are usually taken in the form of squares or a crosses. The main difficulty is to determine the weight vector. There is no regular methods for doing this, except the intuitive choice with subsequent simulation. The substitution set consists of functional substitutions, the function being in the form of (6).

5 Conclusion

A formal model for fine-grained parallel computations is presented. The model combines the features of Parallel Substitution System and Artificial Neural Nets. It is shown that such combination provides new, useful possibilities in representation, synthesis, and simulation of neural-net algorithms with bounded number of each neuron connections. The future investigations are to be directed to develop method of cellular-neuron algorithms synthesis which provide satisfactory quality of problem solution and to define the field of model application.

References

1. von-Neumann J.: Theory of Self-Reproducing Automata, ed. A.W.Burks. University of Illinois Press, Urbana and London, 1966, 382p.
2. Mc-Culloch W.S., W.Pitts W.: A Logical Calculus of the Ideas Immanent in Nervous Activity. Bull.of Math.Biophysics. 5, p.115.
3. Achasova S., Bandman O., Markova V., Piskunov S.: Parallel Substitution Algorithm. Theory and Application. World Scientific, Singapore (1995) 240 p.
4. Hopfield J.J., Tank D.W.: Computing with Neural Circuits: a Model. Science. 233 (1986) p. 625.
5. Korst J.H.M. Aarts E.H.L.: Combinatorial Optimization on Boltzmann Machine..Journ. of Parallel and Distributed Computing. 6 (1989) p.331.
6. Chua L.O, Yang I.: Cellular Neural Networks: Theory amd Application. IEEE Transactions, CS-35, N 10 (1988) p.1257.
7. Zhang J., Zhang I., Yan D., He A., Liu L.: Local Interconnection Neural Network and its Optical Implementation. Optics Communication. 102 (1993) p.13.
8. Liu D., Michel A.: Sparsely Interconnected Artificial Neuron Networks for Associative Memories. Lecture Notes in Comp. Sci.. 606 p.155.
9. Rosenblatt F.: Principles of Neurodumamics. Washington, Spartan. (1959).

An Efficient Verifier of Truly Concurrent Properties *

Alessandro Bianchi, Stefano Coluccini, Pierpaolo Degano and Corrado Priami

Dipartimento di Informatica, Università di Pisa
Corso Italia 40, I-56125 Pisa, Italy - {degano,priami}@di.unipi.it

Abstract. We present a parametric tool for the analysis of distributed concurrent systems. Processes are internally represented as proved transition systems. Actually, we use a fragment of them, in which only one transition exits from a node among those mutually concurrent. This permits to have compact representations that are linear in average with the number of actions in the term of the language that describes the system. Another important property of these compact transition systems is that they preserve truly concurrent bisimulations, that can be checked in average in polynomial time. Parametricity is achieved by resorting to the rich labelling of the transitions encoding the parallel structure of processes. These labels are then "observed" for retrieving the interleaving, causal and locational semantics.

1 Introduction

In the last years, an increasing interest has been addressed to the development of automatic tools for the verification of distributed concurrent systems described through the so-called *process algebras*, e.g., [18, 13]. The first implementations in this area, such as *CWB* [3], *AUTO* [6], *TAV* [12], are based on the *interleaving* semantics [18]. The designers of systems, i.e., the potential users of these tools, may be interested also in aspects like causality among actions or distribution in space of resources, especially when they proceed towards a real implementation of the system. Instead of having many different tools, a single one would be appreciable, provided that it can be tuned to deal with different aspects. A first example of parametric tool, based also on truly concurrent semantics, is the *PisaTool* described in [14] (see last section for a comparison with our present implementation).

The major limitation to the practical usage of process verifiers is the so-called *state explosion problem*. It is essentially due to the assumption that concurrent transitions (= system activities) are represented in transition systems through their interleavings. Some attempts to overcome this problem have been presented

* Work partially supported by ESPRIT Basic Research Action n. 8130 - LOMAPS, by Progetto Finalizzato CNR "Sistemi Informatici e Calcolo Parallelo - Obiettivo Lambrusco" and by Progetto Speciale CNR "Specifica ad Alto Livello e Verifica Formale di Sistemi Digitali".

in the literature. All of them exploit a relation of concurrency ($=$ temporal and causal independence) among the transitions enabled in a given state. The basic idea is to give an ordering in which concurrent transitions are sequentially fired [4, 11, 23, 21, 9]. Indeed, when some of these are enabled, say $\theta_1, \theta_2, \ldots, \theta_n$, fire only one of them, e.g., θ_1. The delayed transitions will be surely enabled in the state reached through θ_1 because they are independent. Often a single computation (sequence of transitions) is sufficient to represent all those obtained by permutation of concurrent transitions, especially when non-time dependent aspects of processes (e.g., causality, distribution in space, etc.) are to be studied. Among the mentioned approaches, the compact transition systems by [9] preserve truly concurrent bisimulations and we base on it our representation of processes.

We recall the basic ideas of [9], and the way compact representations of processes are obtained. The first step is the identification of computations that differ only in the ordering in which concurrent events occur, i.e., of equivalent paths in the transition system generated by the term that specifies the concurrent system at hand. As an example, the term $t = \alpha.\beta|(\delta + \gamma)$ originates two sets of maximal paths, one with δ and the other with γ, that are equivalent when any sensible truly concurrent aspect is of interest, e.g., causality.

The next step consists in choosing a representative for each of these equivalence classes. In the example above, the selected computations are those in which α precedes β which in turn precedes δ, and the one with α before β before γ. In this way, only one transition of term t is kept out of the initial three, namely $t = \alpha.\beta|(\delta+\gamma) \xrightarrow{\alpha} t' = \beta|(\delta+\gamma)$; similarly, out of the three transitions of t', only $\beta|(\delta + \gamma) \xrightarrow{\beta} nil|(\delta + \gamma)$ is kept; finally, two more transitions are possible, i.e., $nil|(\delta+\gamma) \xrightarrow{\delta} nil|nil$ and $nil|(\delta+\gamma) \xrightarrow{\gamma} nil|nil$, leading to the same final state. In order to preserve bisimulations, a unique way is imposed in the selection of the transitions to be kept among those outgoing from a given node.

Another aspect we are particularly interested in is the *parametricity* of verifiers. Indeed, their users should switch easily from one semantic model to another, for receiving support in all the life-cycle phases of a distributed system. For instance, when the designer has to debug a system, causality helps in reducing the event history of a computation that has to be examined when a bug shows up. Instead, if one wants to check whether the external behaviour of the system meets the commitments, an interleaving semantics is quite enough. Parametricity is made easy by resorting to proved transition systems [1], where transitions are labelled by encodings of their proofs [8]. This rich labelling permits to derive automatically the relations of concurrency, conflict and causal dependency among transitions. Then, relabelling functions called *observation functions* can be defined, in order to retrieve the aspects under investigation, e.g., causality [5], locality [2], global-local cause [16], read write causality [22]. The neat result is that two processes are equivalent (according to a selected truly concurrent bisimulation) if and only if their observed compact transition systems are such.

The internal representations of processes in our tool are (finite state) compact transition systems in which the dependencies between transitions are made explicit through "real" pointers. Thus, we have a loop-insensitive mechanism, i.e., it does not produce labels which grow with the lenght of computations as happens, e.g., for the causal [5] or the locational transition systems [2].

If n is the number of occurrences of actions in a process, the generation of its compact transition system is $O(n^3)$, its observation is inductively done in $O(n)$, bisimulation can be checked in $O(n \times \log n)$ [19]; finally, each step in the check requires to compare two strings, which is made in linear time (rather than two pomsets or the like, made in exponential time). Thus, truly concurrent bisimulations can be checked in $O(n^3)$ time in average, instead of in exponential time.

We have designed and implemented a prototype of a tool called *YAPV* (Yet Another Property Verifier) that supports the designer of distributed and concurrent systems in various activities. It provides the standard editing facilities for the input of processes, specified up to now in restriction-free *CCS*. The graphical representation of the transition system is also displayed and animated. The semantical features of *YAPV* concern the equivalence checking of two processes according to a selected semantic model, the detection of deadlock states, the study of reachability properties and some simulation operations.

In this paper, we assume the reader familiar with the notions of process algebras, transition systems and true concurrency.

2 Background

We briefly recall the basic notions of *proved transition system* (PTS) [1], using *CCS* [18] without the restriction operator as a test bed.

Definition 1 CCS. Let Δ be a set of *names* (ranged over by $\alpha, \beta, \ldots$). Let $\bar{\ }$ be an involution on Δ, and call *complementary names* the elements of the set $\bar{\Delta}$. Then, $\Lambda = \Delta \cup \bar{\Delta}$ is the set of *labels* (ranged over by λ) and $A = \Lambda \cup \{\tau\}$ is the set of *actions* (ranged over by μ). A CCS *term* is expressed by the following BNF-like grammar:

$$t ::= nil \mid x \mid \mu.t \mid t|t \mid t+t \mid t[\phi] \mid rec\,x\,t$$

where ϕ is a relabelling function preserving τ and $\bar{\ }$, and the term rec x.t is guarded. The variable x is guarded in t if each occurrence of x is within some subexpression $\lambda.t'$ of t. A recursive expression $rec\,x\,t$ is guarded if x is guarded in t. The set of *closed* CCS terms is denoted by T. In the sequel, we will often omit nil's when irrelevant.

The operational semantics of *CCS* is defined by the axiom and rules reported in Tab. 1.

We now define the set of labels of transitions and an auxiliary function which extracts from them the action name. For the sake of brevity, here the labels are simpler than the original proof terms. Indeed, we retain only the markers of the application of parallel composition and summation like in [7] because we are interested mainly in truly concurrent aspects. Full proof terms can be used when

Table 1. Transition system of CCS

$$Act : \mu.t \xrightarrow{\mu} t \qquad\qquad Rel : \dfrac{t_1 \xrightarrow{\mu} t_2}{t_1[\phi] \xrightarrow{\phi(\mu)} t_2[\phi]}$$

$$Sum_1 : \dfrac{t_1 \xrightarrow{\mu} t_2}{t_1 + t \xrightarrow{\mu} t_2} \qquad\qquad Sum_2 : \dfrac{t_1 \xrightarrow{\mu} t_2}{t + t_1 \xrightarrow{\mu} t_2}$$

$$Par_1 : \dfrac{t_1 \xrightarrow{\mu} t_2}{t_1|t \xrightarrow{\mu} t_2|t} \qquad\qquad Par_2 : \dfrac{t_1 \xrightarrow{\mu} t_2}{t|t_1 \xrightarrow{\mu} t|t_2}$$

$$Syn : \dfrac{t_1 \xrightarrow{\lambda} t_2, t_1' \xrightarrow{\bar{\lambda}} t_2'}{t_1|t_1' \xrightarrow{\tau} t_2|t_2'} \qquad\qquad Rec : \dfrac{t_1[rec\,x.\,t_1/x] \xrightarrow{\mu} t_2}{rec\,x.\,t_1 \xrightarrow{\mu} t_2}$$

other aspects are of interest, by a simple tuning of what follows. We still call our labels proof terms.

Definition 2 Proof terms. Let $\{+_1, +_0, ||_1, ||_0\}$ be the set of labels constructors ranged over by φ, and let $\vartheta \in \{+_1, +_0, ||_1, ||_0\}^*$. Then, the set of *proof terms* is $\Theta = \{\vartheta\mu\} \cup \{\vartheta\langle||_0\vartheta_0\lambda, ||_1\vartheta_1\bar{\lambda}\rangle\} \ni \theta$. The function $\mathcal{L} : \Theta \to A$ that extracts the action name from a proof term is defined by structural induction as follows:

$$\mathcal{L}(\mu) = \mu \qquad \mathcal{L}(\langle\theta, \theta'\rangle) = \tau \qquad \mathcal{L}(\varphi\theta) = \mathcal{L}(\theta)$$

The intuitive meaning of the labels Θ of the proved transition system is as follows. The symbol $||_0$ ($||_1$) denotes that an event has been performed by the left (right) component of a parallel composition. Synchronizations are expressed as pairs of complementary labels. Tag $+_0$ ($+_1$) means that a nondeterministic choice is resolved in favour of the left (right) summand.

The operational semantics is obtained by the classical CCS semantics by prefixing to the action name an encoding of the proof of the transition.

Definition 3 Proved Transition System. The *proved transition system* is the triple $PTS = \langle T, \Theta, \xrightarrow{\theta}\rangle$, where T is the set of CCS terms, Θ is the set of proof terms and $\xrightarrow{\theta}$ is the transition relation defined by the axiom and rules of Table 2.
In the sequel,

- the *proved transition system of t* ($[t]$) is the portion of the *PTS* originated from t;
- the set of transitions outgoing from t is $Ts(t)$.

Table 2. Proved transition system of CCS

$$Act : \mu.t \xrightarrow{\mu} t \qquad\qquad Rel : \frac{t_1 \xrightarrow{\theta} t_2}{t_1[\phi] \xrightarrow{\phi(\theta)} t_2[\phi]}$$

$$Sum_1 : \frac{t_1 \xrightarrow{\theta} t_2}{t_1 + t \xrightarrow{+_0 \theta} t_2} \qquad\qquad Sum_2 : \frac{t_1 \xrightarrow{\theta} t_2}{t + t_1 \xrightarrow{+_1 \theta} t_2}$$

$$Par_1 : \frac{t_1 \xrightarrow{\theta} t_2}{t_1 | t \xrightarrow{\|_0 \theta} t_2 | t} \qquad\qquad Par_2 : \frac{t_1 \xrightarrow{\theta} t_2}{t | t_1 \xrightarrow{\|_1 \theta} t | t_2}$$

$$Syn : \frac{t_1 \xrightarrow{\theta} t_2, \; t_1' \xrightarrow{\theta'} t_2'}{t_1 | t_1' \xrightarrow{\langle \|_0 \theta, \|_1 \theta' \rangle} t_2 | t_2'}, \; \mathcal{L}(\theta) = \overline{\mathcal{L}(\theta')} \quad Rec : \frac{t_1[rec\, x.\, t_1 / x] \xrightarrow{\theta} t_2}{rec\, x.\, t_1 \xrightarrow{\theta} t_2}$$

Note that more than one arc exits from a node t if and only if the transitions from t are obtained by applying the rules for summation or asynchrony/synchrony of the operational semantics. Moreover, the transitions of a PTS outgoing from a node t can be identified with their labels. Indeed, the labels of the transitions generated by asynchronous moves are distinguished by the $\|_0$ and $\|_1$ constructors, while the ones due to summation are made different by the tags $+_0$ and $+_1$. As a matter of fact, the proved transition system is deterministic.

Since the labels of the transitions record the concurrent structure of processes, it is easy to define a conflict, or mutual exclusion ($\#$), and a concurrency relation ($\smile$) between those originated by a term. Then, a new SOS operational semantics is defined that yields compact representation of processes [9].

The basic idea is to fix a total ordering $\preceq$ in which concurrent events are sequentially fired. Essentially, it is used to select in an unique way a single transition among the ones mutually concurrent outgoing from a node of the PTS. The total ordering extends the lexicographic ordering on the labels of transitions. If two visible transitions θ_1 and θ_2 of the same term are concurrent and $\theta_1 \preceq \theta_2$, θ_2 is removed from the whole transition system, togheter with the sub-graph G reached only through it. Indeed, θ_2 (and also all the transitions $\theta \neq \theta_1$ of G) will occur after θ_1, due to the obvious "proved" variant of the expansion theorem (see [8]). Obviously, the transitions of the term reached through θ_1 are processed in the same manner. Instead, all the conflicting transitions are present in the compact transition system. Some problems may be caused by autoconcurrency. Roughly two transitions are said autoconcurrent if they have the same action label and are concurrent. Indeed, if two transitions exiting from a given node have the same action, we do not now which branches discard. In this case, we keep them all.

This pathological case has also an impact on the worst-case complexity in time and space of our method, because it may make the compact and the complete transition systems coincide.

The method discussed so far cannot be applied to recursive terms as it is. Indeed, the recursive term $t = recx \ \alpha.x | recx \ \beta.x$ originates the compact transition system with the single transition $\|_0\alpha$ leading to t again, because $\|_0\alpha \preceq \|_1\beta$ and thus $\|_1\beta$ is always discarded. Therefore a recursive transition is less than the non-recursive ones in $\preceq$. To this aim, $\theta_r \in A_r (\theta \in A)$ are used as proof terms labelling transitions of recursive nodes (μ ranges over $A \cup A_r$).

The SOS semantics that generates compact proved transition systems is obtained by adding to the rules of Tab. 2 the following one

$$Red : \frac{t \overset{\theta}{\longrightarrow} t', t \overset{\beta'}{\not\longrightarrow}, \theta' \smile \theta, \theta' \prec \theta}{t \overset{\theta}{\longrightarrow}_c t'}$$

Some comments are in order. If a transition θ has some concurrent transition, a rule Par is used at least once in its derivation. Actually, the application of the rule is possible if there is no transition θ_i concurrent with θ, non-recursive, and such that $\theta_i \preceq \theta$ that can be derived from the same subterm t_1 of t or from subterms in parallel with t_1. Since the recursive transitions outgoing from the same node are not pruned, even if mutually concurrent, we need only to delay as much as possible their selection. This is accomplished by the ordering $\preceq$ which sets any recursive transition larger than all the non-recursive ones. Thus, a recursive transition θ_r may be derived only if the considered subterm t_1 (or subterms in parallel with it) cannot fire non-recursive transitions $\theta_i \in \Lambda$ concurrent with θ_r.

The soundness of the reduction strategy is ensured by a result of [9] stating that it is possible to retrieve the complete proved transition system from the compact one. The same paper proves also that given a term t, its compact PTS maintains full information on its truly concurrent behaviour. Recall from [9] that the $O(n)$ transitions of the compact PTS is generated in $O(n^3)$ and that the compact representation preserves truly concurrent bisimulations.

3   Observing proved transition systems

This section describes the mechanism that allows us to discard unwanted details from the labels of the transitions according to the aspects under investigation. This task is accomplished by relabelling functions called *observation functions* by extending the technique of [8] to work on graphs. This abstraction step is the core of parametricity. The models that can be recovered in the present prototype are, among the others, the classical interleaving [18], the causal [5] and the locational [2] ones.

Various extensions of calculi for expressing truly concurrent properties lead to transition systems that are not finite state, even if the classical and its proved

42

version are such. E.g., consider the process $rec\ x\ \alpha.\beta.x$ which have a finite classical and proved transition system, but infinite causal and locational ones. Also the labels of causal and locatioal transition systems have no upper bound to their size. The main cause of these expensive representations is the dynamic change of the states due to the updating of the auxiliary information recorded after the occurrence of a transition. Instead, the states in PTS are exactly the terms of the language. Thus, any process with a finite state representation in the classical interleaving semantics has the same states also in the PTS (see Fig. 1). More formally, we have the following proposition.

Proposition 4 Interleaving and proved transition system. *Given a CCS term t, its interleaving transition system is finite if and only if its PTS is such.*

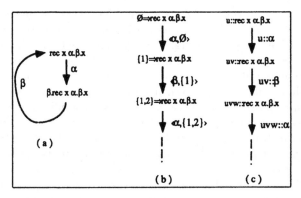

Fig. 1. (a) Proved, (b) causal and (c) locational transition system of $rec\ x\ \alpha.\beta.x$.

The compactness of PTS is mainly due to single-arc representation of different occurrences of transitions, but this may rise some ambiguities when associating dependencies to transitions. For instance, consider the process $\alpha.\beta+\alpha.\gamma.\beta$. Its proved and causal transition system are depicted in Fig. 2(a-b). If we want to associate dependencies to β in the PTS, we need a way of distinguishing the two different paths that enable β and of keeping them distinct in the causal graph. Our proposal is to associate to any transition a set of dependencies for any path leading to it. We represent dependencies through encodings of the triple (source node, target node, transition label) represented by the gray pointers in Fig. 2(c). In this way, all the dependencies due to different instances of the same transition of a loop are represented by a single pointer. Therefore, this encoding is suitable also for recursive definition of processes.

We now define the pointers and the structure of the observed labels of the PTS.

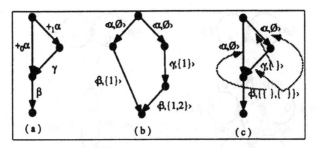

Fig. 2. (a) Proved, (b) causal and (c) causally observed transition system of $\alpha.\beta+\alpha.\gamma.\beta$.

Definition 5 Pointers and observed labels.

A *pointer* is a triple ⟨source node, target node, proof term⟩.

An *observed label* is an element of $A \times 2^{Point}$, where A is the set of actions and *Point* is the set of pointers.

An *observed transition system* is obtained from proved transition systems by substituting observed labels for proof terms according to an observation function defined below.

In order to simplify the definition of the bisimulation given in the next section, we unwind of all the loops in the PTS exactly once (we call this operation Unf_1), i.e, the parser replaces any occurrence of $rec\,x\,\,t''$ in a term with $t''[rec\,x\,\,t''/x]$.

Note that isomorphic proved transition systems may have different Unf_1. Consider the two CCS terms $t = (rec\,x\,\,\alpha.x)|(rec\,x\beta.x)$ and $t' = rec\,x(\alpha.x + \beta.x)$. Their corresponding PTS are depicted in Figure 3(a) and (b), respectively, have the same shape and their labels are isomorphic under $f(\|_0\alpha) = +_0\alpha$ and $f(\|_1\beta) = +_1\beta$. Figure 3(c) and (d) show the PTS of $Unf_1(t) = (\alpha.rec\,x\,\,\alpha.x)|(\beta.rec\,x\beta.x)$ and $Unf_1(t') = (\alpha.rec\,x(\alpha.x + \beta.x)) + (\beta.rec\,x(\alpha.x + \beta.x))$, respectively. They have no more the same shape.

As mentioned above, the observation functions relabel the transitions of a PTS maintaining only the information relevant to the aspects that the user wants to investigate. This abstraction step provides us with the parametricity wanted. Here, we adapt three observation functions presented in [8] to work on proved transition systems. We define the classical interleaving transition system [18] and the causal [5] and the locational [2] ones. The interleaving semantics is obtained by discarding from a proof term all but the action name.

Definition 6 Interleaving observation function. Given a CCS term t, let $t' \xrightarrow{\theta} t''$ be a transition of $[t]$. Then $\mathcal{O}_i(t' \xrightarrow{\theta} t'') = t' \xrightarrow{\mathcal{L}(\theta)} t''$.

In order to define the causal and locational observation functions we need the auxiliary definition of the set of paths ending with a given transition.

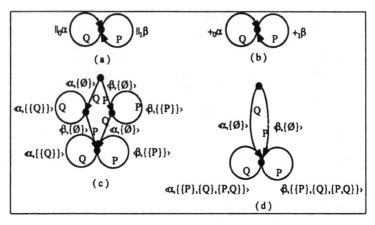

Fig. 3. PTS of (a) $t = (rec\,x\ \alpha.x)|(rec\,x\beta.x)$, (b) $t' = rec\,x(\alpha.x + \beta.x)$, (c) $Unf_1(t)$, (d) $Unf_1(t')$.

Definition 7 Set of paths ending with a fixed transition. Let t be a *CCS* term, and let A be a transition of $[t]$. The *set of paths* or *computations* in $[t]$ ending with A is $C(t, A) = \{(t = t_0 \xrightarrow{\theta_1} t_1, t_1 \xrightarrow{\theta_2} t_2, \dots, t_{n-1} \xrightarrow{\theta_n} t_n)|\forall i \in \{1, \dots, n\}\ (t_{i-1} \xrightarrow{\theta_i} t_i) \in [t]\ and\ (t_{n-1} \xrightarrow{\theta_n} t_n) = A\}$.

Before defining the causal observation function, we define the notion of dependency of transitions according to the causal semantics. In the sequel, we use a function F that erases from a proof term the action names and the $+_i$ constructors. Intuitively, a proof term θ' depends on another one, say θ, if $F(\theta)$ is a prefix of $F(\theta')$. As an example, consider the term $t = \alpha.(\gamma|(\beta+\delta))|\beta+\alpha$ where the leftmost β depends on the leftmost α. The labels of the arcs corresponding to these actions in the proved transtion system of t are $||_0 +_0 ||_1\beta$ and $+_0||_0\alpha$, and indeed $||_0 = F(+_0||_0\alpha)$ is a prefix of $||_0||_1 = F(||_0 +_0 ||_1\beta)$. Particular care has to be taken when θ records a synchronization, i.e., when it has the form $\vartheta\langle||_0\theta_0, ||_1\theta_1\rangle$. In this case, the synchronization is de-coupled in $\vartheta||_0\theta_0$ and $\vartheta||_1\theta_1$. Then, the proof term θ' depends on θ if either $F(\vartheta||_0\theta_0)$ or $F(\vartheta||_1\theta_1)$ is a prefix of $F(\theta')$. The dependency between two synchronizations is defined componentwise.

Definition 8 Causal dependency of transitions. Let $\theta_0\theta_1 \dots \theta_n$ be a path in *PTS*. Then, θ_j *causally depends* on θ_i (written $\theta_i \sqsubset_c \theta_j$) if and only if $i < j$ and one of the following conditions holds:

1. $\theta_i = \vartheta\mu$, $\theta_j = \vartheta'\theta$ and $F(\theta_i) = F(\vartheta')$;
2. $\theta_i = \vartheta\langle\vartheta_0\lambda, \vartheta_1\bar{\lambda}\rangle$, $\theta_j = \vartheta'\theta$ and either $\vartheta||_0\vartheta_0 \sqsubset_c \theta_j$ or $\vartheta||_1\vartheta_1 \sqsubset_c \theta_j$;
3. Symmetric of 2.;
4. $\theta_i = \vartheta'\langle\theta'_0, \theta'_1\rangle$, $\theta_j = \vartheta''\langle\theta''_0, \theta''_1\rangle$ and $\exists h, k \in \{0, 1\}\ .\ \vartheta'||_k\theta'_k \sqsubset_c \vartheta''||_h\theta''_h$.

The causal observation function is the following.

Definition 9 Causal observation function. Given a CCS term t_0, let $A = t \xrightarrow{\theta} t'$ and $A_i = t_{i-1} \xrightarrow{\theta_i} t_i$ be two transitions of $[Unf_1(t_0)]$. Also, let the set of computations be $C(Unf_1(t_0), A) = \{c_0, \ldots, c_n\}$. Then,

$$\mathcal{O}_c(A) = \begin{cases} t \xrightarrow{\tau} t' & \text{if } \mathcal{L}(\theta) = \tau \\ t \xrightarrow{(\lambda, K_c)} t' & \text{if } \mathcal{L}(\theta) = \lambda \end{cases}$$

with $K_c = \{k_0, \ldots, k_n\}$, where $k_i = \{A_j | \theta_j \sqsubset_c^+ \theta, A_j \in c_i\}$, for $i = 1, \ldots, n$, is the set of the dependencies of the path c_i ($\sqsubset_c^+$ is the transitive closure of $\sqsubset_c$.)

Also for the definition of the locational observation function we need the notion of dependency of proof terms to take locations into account. Since locational semantics completely ignores invisible transitions, we have only the first item of Definition 8.

Definition 10 Locational dependency of transitions. Let $\theta_0 \theta_1 \ldots \theta_n \ldots$ be a path in PTS. Then, θ_j *locally depends* on θ_i (written $\theta_i \sqsubset_l \theta_j$) if and only if $i < j$ and $\theta_i = \vartheta\mu$, $\theta_j = \vartheta'\theta$ and $F(\theta_i) = F(\vartheta')$.

The locational observation function is defined as follows.

Definition 11 Locational observation function. Given a CCS term t_0, let $A = t \xrightarrow{\theta} t'$ and $A_i = t_{i-1} \xrightarrow{\theta_i} t_i$ be two transitions of $[Unf_1(t_0)]$. Moreover, let the set of computations be $C(Unf_1(t_0), A) = \{c_0, \ldots, c_n\}$. Then,

$$\mathcal{O}_l(A) = \begin{cases} t \xrightarrow{\tau} t' & \text{if } \mathcal{L}(\theta) = \tau \\ t \xrightarrow{(\lambda, K_l)} t' & \text{if } \mathcal{L}(\theta) = \lambda \end{cases}$$

with $K_l = \{k_0, \ldots, k_n\}$, where $k_i = \{A_j | \theta_j \sqsubset_l^+ \theta, A_j \in c_i\}$, for $i = 1, \ldots, n$, is the set of the dependencies of the path c_i ($\sqsubset_l^+$ is the transitive closure of $\sqsubset_l$.)

Presently, two further observation functions, therefore two further semantics are supported by our tool. One is the global-local cause semantics by [16] that takes into account both causes and locations. Its observation functions is easily obtained as composition of the two described above. The other model that it is possible to retrieve is the one based on read-write causality [22]. It distinguishes the kind of operation performed in the synchronizations (read or write). The inheritance of causes in the synchronizations is then made only when a process reads a value, while the process that offers the value does not inherit any dependency from the reader. As a matter of fact, this semantics consider the *flow of information* in place of of the flow of control as in usual causality models. The observation function is obtained by a slightly modification of the causal one. It is enough to distinguish in exchanging causes within a communication which is the reader and which is the writer.

4   Generalizing bisimulation

Each semantic model of concurrent processes comes with its own equivalences. In this respect, we speak of *interleaving, causal, locational* bisimulations, and so on. The definition of bisimulation on observed *PTS*, from which the above others follows, needs extensions for considering pointers. This is done in several steps. First, we define when two pointers and two sets of pointers are equivalent. Second, we say when two classes of dependencies (= of sets of pointers) are such. Third, we establish when two transitions are equivalent. The last step is the definition of the wanted relation, called ↑-*bisimulation*.

The following example shows that different pointers, as well as different sets of pointers, should sometimes be considered equivalent during a bisimulation check. Consider the process *rec x α.x* and the bisimilar one *α.(rec x α.x)*. Their *PTS* observed in the causal semantics (after Unf_1) are depicted in Fig. 4(a-b), where arcs are given a capital letter as a name. When the causes of the arcs B and R are compared for bisimilarity, the pointer P must be considered equivalent to the pointer A. Similarly, the pointer B must be considered equivalent to the pointers R and Q. Therefore, the set $\{A, B\}$ is equivalent both to $\{P, Q\}$ and to $\{P, Q, R\}$.

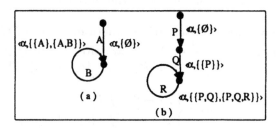

Fig. 4. Causally observed PTS of (a) *rec x α.x* and of (b) *α.(rec x α.x)* after their Unf_1. Capital letters denote names of arcs.

We consider two pointers as equivalent if they point to two transitions that have the same action name and that have equivalent dependencies. The dependencies of two transitions are equivalent if the pointed transitions lead to ↑-bisimilar states. Two sets of pointers are equivalent if for each element of one of them there exists an equivalent pointer in the other set, and *vice versa*. We formalize these intuitions below.

Definition 12 Equivalence of pointers, ≡, and of sets of pointers, ≐.
Let $p_0 = \langle t_0, t'_0, \theta_0 \rangle$ and $p_1 = \langle t_1, t'_1, \theta_1 \rangle$ be two pointers. Then, $p_0 \equiv p_1$ if and only if $\mathcal{L}(\theta_0) = \mathcal{L}(\theta_1)$ and t'_0 is bisimilar to t'_1.
Let $I_0 = \{p_0, \ldots, p_n\}$ and $I_1 = \{p'_0, \ldots, p'_m\}$ be two sets of pointers. Then, $I_0 \doteq I_1$ if and only if $\forall i \in \{0, \ldots, n\} \, \exists j \in \{0, \ldots, m\}$ such that $p_i \equiv p'_j$ and *vice versa*.

The condition for considering equivalent two classes of dependencies is: for each set of the first one there is an equivalent set in the other class (even if the *vice versa* does not hold). Roughly, we impose that a node of the transition system may simulate the other. The arcs B and R in Fig. 4 are clearly equivalent, so the classes $\{\{A\}, \{A, B\}\}$ and $\{\{P, Q\}, \{P, Q, R\}\}$ must be equivalent.

Definition 13 Inclusions between classes of dependencies, $\subset$. Let $C_0 = \{I_0, \ldots, I_n\}$ and $C_1 = \{I'_0, \ldots, I'_m\}$ be two classes of sets of pointers. Then, $C_0 \subset C_1$ if and only if $\forall i \in \{0, \ldots, n\}\ \exists j \in \{0, \ldots, m\}$ such that $I_i \doteq I'_j$.

Third, we define the equivalence between the arcs of the PTS, once observed.

Definition 14 Equivalence of arcs of the observed PTS, $\simeq$.
Let $e_0 = \langle \lambda_0, C_0 \rangle$ and $e_1 = \langle \lambda_1, C_1 \rangle$ be the labels of two arcs of two observed PTS. Then, $e_0 \simeq e_1$ if and only if $\lambda_0 = \lambda_1$ and $C_0 \subset C_1$ or $C_1 \subset C_0$.

As noted above, pointers make more economic the representation of transition systems by collapsing transition and states that are usually kept distinct in the original versions (see, e.g., transitions β and their sources in Fig. 2). Thus, a node may be related *via* $\uparrow$-bisimulation to a set of nodes t_i, because its class of dependencies is covered by the union of the classes of t_i. The actual definition of $\uparrow$-bisimulation follows.

Definition 15 Pointer bisimulation, $\uparrow$. Given two processes t and t' and an observation function $\mathcal{O}$, let $[t]_O$ and $[t']_O$ be their corresponding observed proved transition systems. Then t is pointer bisimilar to t' ($t \sim_\uparrow t'$) if and only if whenever $t \xrightarrow{(\lambda, C)} t_0$ then, for some t_1, $t' \xrightarrow{(\lambda', C')} t_1$, $\langle \lambda, C \rangle \simeq \langle \lambda', C' \rangle$, $t_0 \sim_\uparrow t_1$, and for any arc A of $[t]_O$, $(\bigcup_{B \simeq A} \ell(B)) \subset \ell(A)$, and symmetrically, where $\ell(A) = C$ if $A = t_i \xrightarrow{(\lambda, C)} t_j$.

Note that the symmetric conditions above do ensure that all the sets in a class of a transition have been compared in some bisimulation step, possibly with sets belonging to different classes of different transitions. As a matter of fact, $\uparrow$-bisimulation extends the classical one [20] only in checking the "semantic" inclusion of the causes of a label in another, and viceversa.

The soundness of the pointer bisimulation is expressed by the following theorem. It states that two causally (locationally,..) observed processes are pointer bisimilar if and only if their causal (local,..) transition systems are causally (locationally,..) bisimilar.

Theorem 16 Soundeness of the pointer bisimulation. *Let $\sim_i$ and $\approx_i$ be the strong and weak interleaving congruences of [18]; let $\sim_c$ and $\approx_c$ be the strong and weak causal congruences of [5]; let $\sim_l$ and $\approx_l$ be the strong and weak locational congruences of [2]; let $\sim_{gl}$ and $\approx_{gl}$ be the strong and weak global local cause congruences of [16].*
Let $x \in \{i, c, l, gl\}$, then given two processes t and t',

- $\mathcal{O}_x([t]) \sim_\uparrow \mathcal{O}_x([t'])$ *iff $t \sim_x t'$; and*
- $\mathcal{O}_x([t]) \approx_\uparrow \mathcal{O}_x([t'])$ *iff $t \approx_x t'$.*

5 Implementation of YAPV

The prototype of our parametric tool $YAPV$ is implemented in the *Caml Light* [17] dialect of SML and runs on Macintosh machines.

The logical design of the tool is divided in phases. First, we have a *parser* that checks the syntactic correctness of the input process, and that possibly applies Unf_1. The standard functionalities of program editors are supported (cut-and-paste, paretheses balance checking, constant definition,..).

The second phase generates in compact or in complete form the PTS, starting from the parse tree obtained in the previous phase. Note that the PTS constitutes the internal representation of processes. It is generated only once, independently of the models one is interested in. This avoids many different generations when passing from one model to another, e.g., from an interleaving to a causal one. Furthermore, the parametricity of PTS makes our tool higly modular and thus easily extendible.

The task of the third phase is to observe the proved transition system. Some built-in observation functions are provided. In particular, the interleaving semantics [18] can be retrieved if the whole PTS has been generated. Otherwise, the tool provides the observation functions for causality [5], locality [2], global-local cause [16], and the read/write causality [22]. Indeed, it suffices to define only one function for implementing a new semantic model that is retrieved from the PTS. Note also that the definition of such observation functions is very easy.

In the last phase properties of systems can be verified. Among these properties, the most important concerns equivalence checking. Two systems can be checked for bisimilarity in the selected model, using a slight modification of the algorithm in [15]. Actually, the main algorithm implements the strong version of the equivalence. The weak bisimulation which abstracts from internal moves is obtained by τ-saturation. Other functionalities are present for detecting deadlocks, for visualizing the structures of the proved transition system in a graphical form, for studying reachability properties, for animation of specifications.

We now give some rough information on the storing space and the time performance of our implementation. Consider a process t made of n occurrences of actions (note that $Unf_1(t)$ may have $2 \times O(n)$ occurrences of actions). Its compact representation has in average $O(n)$ transitions and $O(n)$ states. States are internally represented as numbers, and arcs as tuples ⟨unique name, source state, target state, label⟩. Since each arc has at most $n-1$ pointers, the class of dependencies of t is encoded by at most $O(n)$ integers. We have only few experimental data on the actual space needed by our prototype for storing terms. A very preliminary estimate is that a term t with 10 actions requires $32K$ bytes, and the growth of the space is quadratic. Additional space is also needed for auxiliary structures, that is almost constant.

As for time performance, the generation of a compact transition system and its observation are linear and require about $1''$ per 10 actions. Instead, bisimulation is quadratic and requires about $2''$ for comparing terms with 10 actions each.

Of course, the more are the processes in parallel in a system, the better is the performance of our tool with respect to other existing tools. We have chosen "carefully" a term made of about 30 actions without τ's nor communications and with about 20 "|". Then, we have transformed it into a bisimilar one by inserting appropriately about 7 τ's. The generation and the observation of the compact transition systems required on a Macintosh Quadra 950 less than 4′ and $8M$ bytes. The bisimilarity has been checked in about an hour. Note that the number of states of both compact transition system is a bit less than 200, while that of the complete transition system is about 2^{200}.

We end this section with a comparison of *YAPV* and *PisaTool* [14]. In the present implementation of *YAPV* we need no information on the states of transition systems and we simply compare the labels of transitions, while *PisaTool* requires decomposition of regular expressions to be matched. Moreover, the construction of the dependencies of each transition is made in linear time during the observation step once and for all, while in *PisaTool* the decomposition of regular expressions must be computed and observed at each comparison step.

The extension of the above approach described above for CCS to other calculi, among which π-calculus [10] is under investigation.

References

1. G. Boudol and I. Castellani. A non-interleaving semantics for CCS based on proved transitions. *Foundamenta Informaticae*, XI(4):433–452, 1988.
2. G. Boudol, I. Castellani, M. Hennessy, and A. Kiehn. A theory of processes with localities. In *Proceedings of CONCUR'92, LNCS 630*, pages 108–122. Springer-Verlag, 1992.
3. R. Cleaveland, J. Parrow, and B. Steffen. The concurrency workbench: A semantics-based tool for the verification of concurrent systems. *ACM Transaction on Programming Languages and Systems*, pages 36–72, 1993.
4. M. Clegg and A. Valmari. Reduced labelled transition systems save verification effort. In *Proceedings of CONCUR'91, LNCS 527*. Springer-Verlag, 1991.
5. Ph. Darondeau and P. Degano. Causal trees. In *Proceedings of ICALP'89, LNCS 372*, pages 234–248. Springer-Verlag, 1989.
6. R. de Simone and D. Vergamini. Aboard AUTO. Technical Report 111, INRIA Sophia-Antipolis, 1989.
7. P. Degano, R. De Nicola, and U. Montanari. Partial ordering derivations for CCS. In *Proceedings of FCT, LNCS 199*, pages 520–533. Springer-Verlag, 1985.
8. P. Degano and C. Priami. Proved trees. In *Proceedings of ICALP'92, LNCS 623*, pages 629–640. Springer-Verlag, 1992.
9. P. Degano and C. Priami. A compact representation of finite-state processes. Technical Report LOMAPSDIPISA2, LOMAPS Project, 1993.
10. P. Degano and C. Priami. Causality for mobile processes. In *Proceedings of ICALP'95, LNCS*. Springer-Verlag, 1995. To appear.
11. P. Godefroid and P. Wolper. Using partial orders for the efficient verification of deadlock freedom and safety properties. In *Proceedings of CAV'91, LNCS 575*, pages 332–342. Springer-Verlag, 1991.

12. J.C. Godskesen, K.G. Larsen, and M. Zeeberg. TAV users manual. Technical report, Aalborg University Center, Denmark, 1989.

13. C.A.R. Hoare. *Communicating Sequential Processes*. Prentice-Hall, 1985.

14. P. Inverardi, C. Priami, and D. Yankelevich. Automatizing parametric reasoning on distributed concurrent systems. *Formal Aspects of Computing*, 6(6):676–695, 1994.

15. P. C. Kanellakis and S. C. Smolka. CCS expressions, finite state processes and three problems of equivalence. In *Proceedings of the Second ACM Symposium on Principles of Distributed Computing*, 1983.

16. A. Kiehn. Local and global causes. Technical report, TUM 342/23/91, 1991.

17. X. Leroy and M. Mauny. *The Caml Light System, Release 0.5. Documentation and User's Manual.*, 1992.

18. R. Milner. *Communication and Concurrency*. Prentice-Hall, London, 1989.

19. R. Paige and R. Tarjan. Three partition refinement algorithms. *SIAM Journal on Computing*, 16(6):973–989, 1987.

20. D. Park. Concurrency and automata on infinite sequences. In *Proceedings of GI, LNCS 104*, pages 167–183. Springer-Verlag, 1981.

21. D. Peled. All from one, one from all: On model checking using representatives. In *Proceedings of CAV'93, LNCS 697*, pages 409–423. Springer-Verlag, 1993.

22. C. Priami and D. Yankelevich. Read-write causality. In *Proceedings of MFCS'94, LNCS 841*, pages 567–576. Springer-Verlag, 1994.

23. A. Valmari and M. Tienari. An improved failure equivalence for finite-state systems with a reduction algorithm. In *Proceedings of IFIP WG6.1 Protocol Specification, Testing and Verification*, Stockholm, June 1991.

Optimal Loop Scheduling on Multiprocessors: A Pumping Lemma for p-Processor Schedules

Franco Gasperoni[1], Uwe Schwiegelshohn[2], John Turek[3]

[1] Télécom Paris-ENST, Dépt. Informatique, 75634 Paris, Cedex 13, France
[2] Inst. for Information Tech., University Dortmund, 44221 Dortmund, Germany
[3] IBM T.J. Watson Research Center, Yorktown Heights, NY 10598, USA

Abstract. This paper addresses the problem of optimally scheduling a cyclic set of interdependent operations (or tasks), representing for instance a program loop. While the existence of optimum *periodic* schedules has been demonstrated when processors are plentiful, the corresponding problem when the number of available processors is fixed, remains unanswered. In this work we show that if the operations' dependence graph is strongly connected, then there exists a p-processor optimum schedule, for any p, which is expressible in the form of a loop. To prove this result we have established a general pumping lemma for p-processor schedules akin to the classical pumping lemma for regular languages.

1 Introduction

Consider the problem of executing a cyclic set of activities or tasks, such as the operations contained in a computer loop (see figure 2), by $p \geq 1$ processors. If some of the activities can be executed in parallel, the issue of scheduling them on the p processors has to be resolved.

In general, it is desirable to devise schedules which can be encoded in a finite amount of space, independently of the number of iterations that will be executed. Put it in other words, schedules which exhibit some sort of periodic behavior. This is precisely the problem that is investigated in this work. Previous work in this area has been conducted by a number of researchers in the realm of machines with an unlimited number of processors [1, 2, 5, 7]. Their conclusions were that an optimum periodic schedule always exists when the number of processors is unlimited. Furthermore this schedule can be computed in polynomial time.

If the number of processors is finite then [8, 4] have provided heuristics to compute good but not necessarily optimum periodic schedules. The heuristic given in [4] formally guarantees a worst case performance behavior of at most twice the optimum performance. No one, however, proved or disproved the existence of optimum p-processor schedules exhibiting a periodic behavior. This is the problem that we address in this work. Computing such a schedule, if it existed, would be an NP-hard problem [4].

The practical significance of this work is the following. If a p-processor schedule for a cyclic set of tasks has to be executed over and over, for instance if it is to be cast in silicon, it may be worthwhile employing computationally expensive algorithms to generate the best possible solution. Such an approach is possible only if there exists a p-processor periodic optimum schedule. In this work we show that if the dependence graph which embodies cyclic task dependences is strongly connected, then there always exists a p-processor periodic optimum schedule for any p. In the general case where the cyclic dependence graph contains several non trivial strong-components, the problem remains unresolved.

To prove the main theorem of this paper we have established an independently interesting result. We show that all p-processor schedules respecting some set of cyclic dependences, contains a bounded-size pattern which can be replicated (pumped) without affecting the validity of cyclic dependences. This result is akin to the pumping lemma for regular languages [6].

The pumping lemma is schematically illustrated in figure 1. μ is some schedule which is valid for the execution of a finite number of cycles (or iterations) of some cyclic set of tasks. The pumping lemma states that there always exists a sub-schedule β of μ whose size is bounded a priori, such that its arbitrary replication, as shown in the figure, yields a longer schedule which still respects cyclic task dependences.

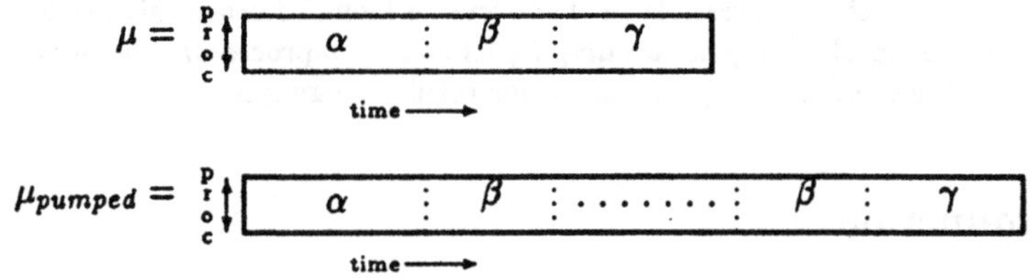

Fig. 1. The pumping lemma.

2 Modeling Cyclic Tasks

A cyclic set of activities (from here on loop), is modeled by a weighted directed graph $G = (O, E, d)$, called cyclic dependence graph, where the vertex set O is the set of operations to execute, E is the edge set of G and d a mapping from E into $\mathbb{N}$, the set of non-negative integers. E and d specify operation dependences. More specifically an edge $e = (op, op') \in E$ with weight $d(e)$ states that for every iteration $i \geq d(e)$ of the loop, operation op' depends on the outcome of operation op in iteration $i - d(e)$ and cannot be initiated until its completion. If $0 \leq i < d(e)$, then op' does not depend on op. For the dependence graph to have any meaning, i.e. embody the dependences of a program loop, every cycle in G must contain at least one edge with positive weight, or else two operations in the same iteration would be circularly depending on each other. An example of a program loop and the corresponding cyclic dependence graph is given in Figure 2.

```
FOR i IN 0..n LOOP
  a[i] := a[i]+d[i-2]; -- op₁
  b[i] := a[i]/e[i-2]; -- op₂
  c[i] := a[i]*e[i-2]; -- op₃
  d[i] := c[i]+b[i-1]; -- op₄
  e[i] := e[i]+b[i]  ; -- op₅
END LOOP;
```

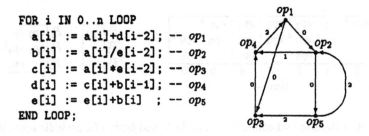

Fig. 2. Some loop and its cyclic dependence graph.

3 p-Processor Schedules

In this work time is viewed as a discrete entity. Thus a time instant is an element of $\mathbb{N}$ the set of natural integers. Given a cyclic dependence graph $G = (O, E, d)$, a *partial schedule* σ for G is a mapping from $O \times \mathbb{N}$ into $\mathbb{N} \cup \{\bot\}$ where either $\sigma(op, i) = \bot$ ($\sigma(op, i)$ is undefined) or $\sigma(op, i) \in \mathbb{N}$ denotes the time in which the instance of operation op in iteration i is initiated. If σ maps $O \times \mathbb{N}$ into $\mathbb{N}$ (rather then $\mathbb{N} \cup \{\bot\}$), σ is said to be a *full schedule* for G. In the remainder of the paper all partial schedules σ are such that:

$$\sigma(op, i + 1) \in \mathbb{N} \Rightarrow \sigma(op, i) \in \mathbb{N} \tag{1}$$

An n-iteration schedule σ_n for G is a partial schedule such that

$$\forall\, op \in O \quad \sigma(op, n) \in \mathbb{N} \quad \text{and} \quad \sigma(op, n + 1) = \bot \tag{2}$$

Finally a full or partial schedule σ is a *p-processor* schedule iff there are at most p operations executing in σ at any point in time.

In this work operations require one unit of time to execute. The results presented here extend to arbitrary operation durations (see [3]).

A full or partial schedule σ is said to respect G's dependences if and only if for all $(op, op') \in E$ and for all $i \geq d(e)$ we have:

$$\sigma(op', i) \in \mathbb{N} \Rightarrow \sigma(op, i - d(e)) \in \mathbb{N} \text{ and } \sigma(op, i - d(e)) + 1 \leq \sigma(op', i) \tag{3}$$

As an example the left of figure 3 portrays a 3-processor 2-iteration schedule σ_2 valid for the cyclic dependence graph given in figure 2.

Let α and β be two partial schedules for G such that the length of α, $|\alpha| = \max_{op, i} \alpha(op, i) + 1$ is defined. Then the concatenation of α and β, denoted $\alpha \odot \beta$, is defined as follows.

$$\forall\, op \in O \quad k_{op} = \min\{i \mid \alpha(op, i) = \bot\} \quad (k_{op} \text{ must exists since } |\alpha| \text{ is defined})$$

$$\alpha \odot \beta(op, i) = \begin{cases} \alpha(op, i) & \text{if } i < k_{op} \\ \beta(op, i - k_{op}) + |\alpha| & k_{op} \leq i \end{cases} \tag{4}$$

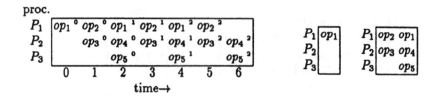

proc.

P_1	$op_1{}^0$	$op_2{}^0$	$op_1{}^1$	$op_2{}^1$	$op_1{}^2$	$op_2{}^2$
P_2		$op_3{}^0$	$op_4{}^0$	$op_3{}^1$	$op_4{}^1$	$op_3{}^2$	$op_4{}^2$
P_3			$op_5{}^0$		$op_5{}^1$		$op_5{}^2$

P_1	op_1
P_2	
P_3	

P_1	$op_2\ op_1$
P_2	$op_3\ op_4$
P_3	op_5

Fig. 3. Left: 2-iteration schedule. Right: prelude and body of a periodic schedule.

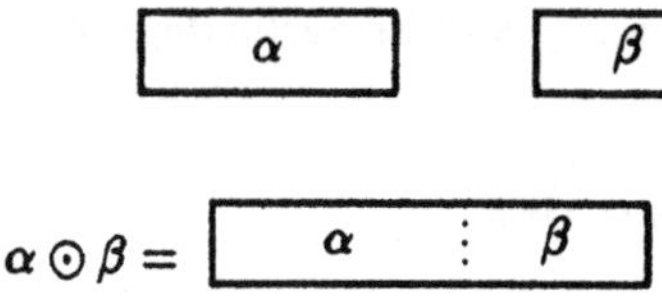

Fig. 4. $\alpha \odot \beta$.

Note that if $|\beta|$ is defined then $|\alpha \odot \beta| = |\alpha| + |\beta|$. Figure 4 portrays the intuitive result of the concatenation operator: $\alpha \odot \beta$.

The $\odot$ operator, will be used in the remainder of the paper to analyze the periodic behavior of optimum schedules.

4 Periodic Schedules

As we mentioned in the introduction, it is important that p-processor schedules for cyclic task systems possess a repetitive behavior so that they be encoded in a finite amount of space. The simplest form of repetitiveness is periodicity. Periodicity is portrayed in figure 5.

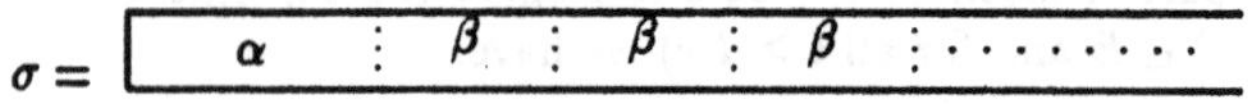

Fig. 5. A periodic schedule.

Definition 1 (Periodicity). Let G be a cyclic dependence graph and σ a full schedule for G. σ is said to be periodic iff there exist two schedules α and β, respectively called the prelude and body, such that

$$\sigma = \alpha \odot \underbrace{\beta \odot \beta \odot \beta \odot \cdots}_{\text{infinitely many times}} \tag{5}$$

As an example, the right of figure 3 shows the prelude and body of a periodic schedule respecting the dependences the loop of figure 2 on a 3 processor machine.

5 Optimality

The notion of performance and optimality is well defined in the finite case. Namely, let G be some cyclic dependence graph and μ_n some p-processor n-iteration schedule that satisfies G's dependences. Then the ratio $|\mu_n|/n$ is the average time μ_n needs to execute 1 iteration of G.

Let σ be a full schedule for G and σ_n the n-iteration sub-schedule of σ. If σ is periodic with prelude α and body β, then $|\sigma_n| = |\alpha| + |\beta|/u \cdot n + \mathcal{O}(1)$, where u is the number of iterations of G executed in the body β and therefore

$$\lim_{n \to \infty} \frac{|\sigma_n|}{n} = \frac{|\beta|}{u} \tag{6}$$

is a natural estimator of σ's performance. Let opt_n be a shortest p-processor n-iteration schedule respecting G's dependences. Clearly $|opt_n| \leq |\sigma_n|$ and therefore $|opt_n|/n \leq |\sigma_n|/n$ thus if $\lim |opt_n|/n$ existed, such value would be the best possible performance that any periodic schedule for G could hope to achieve. The following result proves the existence of such limit.

Theorem 2 (Optimum Performance). Let G be some cyclic dependence graph, $n \geq 0$ some integer, and opt_n an optimum n-iteration schedule respecting G's dependences on a p processor machine. Then

$$\lim_{n \to \infty} \frac{|opt_n|}{n} \quad \text{exists.} \tag{7}$$

Proof. All the proofs in this article can be found in [3]. □

6 Optimality and Periodicity

Given the previous result the obvious question is whether an optimum periodic p-processor schedule always exists. In the important special case where the dependence graph G is strongly connected we will show that there always exists an optimum periodic p-processor schedule for G.

To prove this result we show that in any p-processor *partial* schedule respecting G's dependences, one can always extract a bounded-size sub-schedule which can be replicated while preserving cyclic dependences.

In some sense this lemma is akin to the pumping lemma for regular languages [6], as one can always extract from any schedule, a bounded size pattern, that can be concatenated (pumped) to yield a longer valid schedule.

In the following β^n will denote the schedule obtained by concatenating a finite partial schedule β n times. β^0 is the empty schedule.

Lemma 3 (Pumping lemma). Let $G = (O, E, d)$ be an arbitrary cyclic dependence graph. Then there exists a constant Δ depending solely on G and the number of available processors p, such that any full or partial p-processor schedule respecting G's dependences, can be written in the form $\alpha \odot \beta \odot \gamma$, where $|\alpha \odot \beta| \le \Delta$ and such that

$$\forall k \ge 0 \quad \alpha \odot \beta^k \odot \gamma \text{ respects } G\text{'s dependences} \tag{8}$$

Theorem 4 (Periodic Optimum). Let G be a cyclic dependence graph. If G is strongly connected then there always exist an optimum periodic p-processor schedule for G, for any $p \ge 1$.

7 Conclusion and Open Problems

In this paper we have addressed the problem of optimally scheduling a cyclic set of interdependent operations when a finite number of processors are available. We have shown that if the cyclic dependence graph is strongly connected then there always exist an optimum p-processor periodic schedule which is expressible in the form of a loop.

The major open question is whether the result of theorem 4 can be generalized to the general case where the cyclic dependence graph comprises several strong components.

References

[1] A. AIKEN AND A. NICOLAU, *Optimal loop parallelization*, Proceedings of the SIGPLAN 1988 Conference on Programming Language Design and Implementation (Atlanta, Georgia), pp. 308–317.

[2] P. CHRETIENNE, *The basic cyclic scheduling problem with deadlines*, Discrete Applied Mathematics, 30, 1991, pp. 109–123.

[3] F. GASPERONI, *Scheduling for Horizontal Systems: The VLIW Paradigm in Perspective*, PhD thesis, New York University, New York, New York, July 1991.

[4] F. GASPERONI AND U. SCHWIEGELSHOHN, *Generating Close to Optimim Loop Schedules on Parallel Processors*, Parallel Processing Letters, 4(4), 1994, pp. 391–403.

[5] N. S. GRIGOR'YEVA, I. S. LATYPOV, AND I. V. ROMANOVSKII, *Cyclic problems of scheduling theory*, Tekhnicheskaya Kibernetika, 1988, pp. 3–11. English translation.

[6] J. HOPCROFT AND J. ULLMAN, *Introduction to Automata Theory, Languages and Computation*, Addison Wesley, 1979.

[7] K. IWANO AND S. YEH, *An efficient algorithm for optimal loop parallelization*, in International Symposium on Algorithms, Springer-Verlag, Aug. 1990, pp. 201–210. Lecture Notes in Computer Science 450.

[8] M. LAM, *Software pipelining: An effective scheduling technique for VLIW machines*, Proceedings of the SIGPLAN'88 Conference on Programming Language Design and Implementation, June 1988, pp. 318–328.

Parallel and Distributed Processing of Cellular Hypergraphs

Peter Hartmann

Fachgebiet Mikroprogrammierung
Fachbereich Informatik
TH Darmstadt
Alexanderstraße 10, D-64283 Darmstadt, Germany
Tel.: [+49] 6151 / 16-3474   Fax: [+49] 6151 / 16-5410
E.-Mail: hartmann@isa.informatik.th-darmstadt.de

Abstract. In this paper it will be explained how *cellular hypergraphs* (CHG) can be easily distributed to a network of processor nodes. *Replacement systems* (CHGRS) can be used to describe the dynamics of a CHG. A CHGRS can operate in a conflict-free and synchronous-parallel manner and it can be implemented in a multiprocessor system with little overhead. As a consequence CHGRS can be used as abstract models for many natural phenomena and can support the efficient simulation on a multiprocessor system.

The two major questions will be discussed: How a CHGRS can be implemented distributively, even if it contains complex replacement rules. And how load balancing can be performed using a non-supervised algorithm.

1 Introduction

In natural sciences great interest on the simulation of natural phenomena can be observed. Many interesting effects like biological cellular tissues can be interpreted as dynamic cellular structures. Since for the simulation of cellular structures high computational performance is required, parallel computer systems should be used.

In order to simulate a natural phenomenon it is convenient to use an abstract model which can be implemented efficiently on a parallel computer system. Easily implementable models like that of *cellular automata* [4, 5] have the disadvantage that they cannot be used to imitate dynamically changing structures.

In the articles [1] and [2] the concept of *cellular hypergraphs* (CHG) and synchronous-parallel replacement systems (CHGRS) has been introduced[1]. One of the important advantages of this concept are the versatile relative addressing mechanisms that can be used within a CHG model. And a replacement system can be used to describe the dynamic behaviour of a model CHG: Sections of a CHG may grow, shrink, migrate or they can change their shape in an arbitrary way. Another feature of the CHG concept results from the possibility to dissect a given CHG into *partitions* and to distribute the partitions to a multiprocessor system.

---

[1] In these earlier articles the graphs have been called *geometric* hypergraphs.

This alltogether allows to implement the simulation of a natural phenomenon efficiently if its behaviour can be described in a CHGRS model.

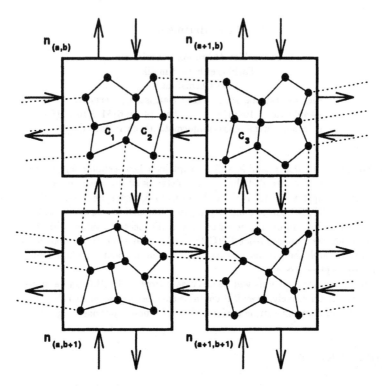

Fig. 1. Distribution of the sample CHGRS among a multiprocessor array.

In an efficient implementation dynamic load balancing must be performed: Partitions of the graph may grow or shrink with different rates. As a consequence the load will not be equally distributed to the processor network. A method will be sketched out that allows the load balancing for a distributively implemented CHG model. It will be shown that, when parts of a CHG are shifted between processor nodes, the resulting change in communication costs can be estimated locally.

In the first section a simple example is used to explain how a cellular hypergraph with 2 dimensions can be implemented in a multiprocessor network (see figure 1). In section 3 it is explained how a CHGRS can be implemented on a parallel computer system. It is shown how one of the major problems can be solved: The distributed implementation of complex replacement operations. Finally in section 4 it is demonstrated that dynamic load balancing can be done by shifting cells of the graph from one processor node to another.

Some assumptions will be made which refer to the imaginated multiprocessor systems that consist of a network of processor nodes:

1. A multiprocessor system with the set of processor nodes $N = \{n_1, n_2, \ldots\}$ will be considered where every processor n_i has an identical computational power. Since no assumptions about the specific structure of the network shall be made, it is assumed that communication is possible between every pair of processors n_i and n_j. The costs for communicating between two nodes n_i and n_j should be independent from the direction and will be assumed to be proportional to the constants $w(n_i, n_j)$. Within a single node the costs for communication should be equal to zero so that $\forall n_i \in N : w(n_i, n_i) = 0$

2. All processors have identical knowledge about the whole replacement system and the structure of the multiprocessor network.

3. When the graph will be dissected into cells, each cell of the graph gives rise to identical computational costs. That means, the load of a processor node is approximately proportional to the number of cells stored in it.

2   A Simple Example

The following example will help to sketch out the fundamental ideas about the presented concept[2]. In figure 1 the section of a cellular hypergraph is displayed. The boxes that are labeled $n_{(a,b)}, n_{(a+1,b)}, \ldots$ symbolize the nodes of a multiprocessor system and how the sample CHG can be distributed among these processor nodes. The arrows connecting the boxes stand for the direct communication paths between the processors.

Like for conventional hypergraphs, a *cellular hypergraph* consists of edges that can contain an arbitrary number of vertices. Each of the individual edges is associated with a specific number of dimensions. In figure 1 the 0-dimensional edges are drawn as dots, and the 1-dimensional edges are drawn as line segments. The 2-dimensional edges are not drawn explicitly, but whenever a couple of 1-dimensional edges encloses an area segment, this area segment will denote a 2-dimensional edge. In the same way 3-dimensional edges could be used to symbolize volume elements.

In figure 2 the graphical representation of the sample replacement system $P_{sample} = \{p_1^1, p_2^1, p_3^2, p_4^2\}$ is shown. Each production consists of a *left-hand* side and a *right-hand* side[3]. This symbolizes that replacing the left- by the right-hand side constitutes a valid operation on the graph.

The replacement system P_{sample} illustrates the variety of types of productions that may be contained in a replacement system. It consists of two 1-dimensional

---

[2] The example is of an artificial type and has been designed to be easily understandable.

[3] In practical applications the productions will be associated with more components which can enhance their flexibility. For instance, a *application condition* can be used to test the applicability of the productions, and a *marker description* can be used to manipulate marker symbols that are stored within the graph. But this paper will focus on the pure struture of the productions.

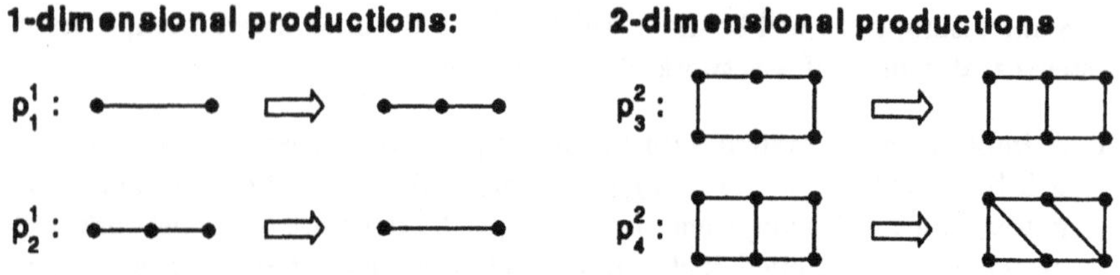

1-dimensional productions: **2-dimensional productions**

$p_1^1:$ $\Rightarrow$

$p_2^1:$ $\Rightarrow$

$p_3^2:$ $\Rightarrow$

$p_4^2:$ $\Rightarrow$

Fig. 2. A sample parallel replacement system for cellular hypergraphs.

productions p_1^1 and p_2^1 as well as two 2-dimensional productions p_3^2 and p_4^2. The number of dimensions of some production is identical to the dimensions of those components of the graph that can be altered by this production. The productions can be classified according to their type. The productions p_1^1 and p_3^2 are called *simple expanding*, because they introduce new components to the graph. The production p_2^1 is called *simple reducing*, because it eliminates components from the graph. The *complex* production p_4^2 can be synthesized as a combination of a *reducing* and an *expanding* production.

When a production shall be applied to the graph, it must be searched for the occurance of the left-hand side. If an appropriate subgraph can be found, this subgraph can be replaced by the right-hand side of the production. The application of *complex* and *reducing* productions constitutes the most complicated case, because different parts of the left-hand side may be located within different processor nodes. In figure 3 the necessary steps are sketched out that realize the application of the complex production p_4^2 to the sample CHG under these conditions:

(A) the cell c_3 is shifted from node $n_{(a,b+1)}$ to node $n_{(a,b)}$,
(B) the complex production p_4^2 can be applied to the graph, and
(C) the new cell c_4 is shifted from $n_{(a,b)}$ to the node $n_{(a,b+1)}$ (load balancing).

From this example it can be observed that as a result of step (B) the distribution of the graph may be suboptimal. This demonstrates the importance of mechanisms for performing *dynamic load balancing* that is symbolized by step (C): The new cell c_4 is shifted from node $n_{(a,b)}$ to node $n_{(a+1,b)}$.

3 Distributed Implementation of a CHGRS

In this section the fundamentals about the distributed implementation of CHGRS are explained.

Cellular hypergraphs (CHG) are a versatile instrument that can be used to describe inhomogeneous cellular structures with an arbitrary number of dimensions. A cellular hypergraph g^D consists of a set of edges $e^d \in g^D$, where each

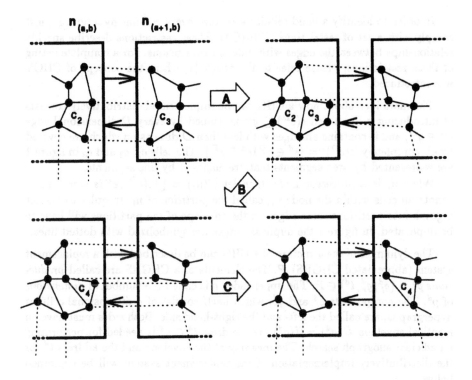

Fig. 3. Steps for applying the production p_4^2 and the subsequent load balancing.

of its edges is associated with a specific number of dimensions d; $0 \le d \le D$, and where an edge can contain any subset from a set of vertices V. Each of the edges $e^d \in g^D$ is interpreted as a component of the cellular structure, and the vertices $v_i \in e^d$ constitute the corners of this component. The dimensions of each edge are identical with the number of dimensions of that structural component it stands for.

The integer number D which is noted as an upper index of the graph g^D is called the number of dimensions of this graph. In the case of a CHG the set of all vertices $V(g^D)$ needs not to be mentioned explicitly since it is always defined as the union of all vertices of the graph: $V := \bigcup e^d \in g^D$.

A hypergraph can be written down in the notation of sets. The dimensions d are noted as an upper index with the brackets: $\{\dots\}^d$. For instance the structure of the 3-dimensional tetrahedron with its 4 corners named a, b, c and d can be described with the CHG

$$
\begin{aligned}
g_{tetrahedron}^3 = \{\; & \{a\}^0, \{b\}^0, \{c\}^0, \{d\}^0, \\
& \{a,b\}^1, \{a,c\}^1, \{a,d\}^1, \{b,c\}^1, \{b,d\}^1, \{c,d\}^1, \\
& \{a,b,c\}^2, \{a,b,d\}^2, \{a,c,d\}^2, \{b,c,d\}^2, \\
& \{a,b,c,d\}^3 \;\}^3 .
\end{aligned}
$$

In order to identify a valid cellular structure every cellular hypergraph must comply with a set of restrictions (G0)-(G4). These restrictions describe specific relationships between the edges with different dimensions. For a complete listing of these restrictions, please refer to the article [1] where the concept of CHG's was introduced.

The main idea about how a CHG can be implemented distributively consists of introducing *cells*. A cell $c(e^D) \subseteq g^D$ is defined by every D-dimensional edge $e^D \in g^D$, and it contains all edges with less than D dimension which are covered by e^D completely: $c(e^D) := \{\hat{e}^d \in g^D \,|\, \hat{e}^d \subseteq e^D\}$. The cells c_1, c_2 and c_3 in figure 1 are represented by area segments that are enclosed by line segments.

When n_i is a processor node, then let $C(n_i) = \bigcup c(e^D)$; e^D *is stored in* n_i denote all cells within the node n_i, called the *partition* of n_i. In order to dissect a graph into partitions some edges on the envelope of the partitions will have to be duplicated. In figure 1 the duplicate edges are symbolized with dotted lines.

The dynamics of the structure of a CHG can be described with a replacement system (abbreviated CHGRS) P. The elements of a CHGRS are called *productions* $p^d = (g_l^d, g_r^d, t^d) \in P$. The upper index d is called the number of *dimensions* of p^d. The components g_l^d and g_r^d, which itself consist of d-dimensional cellular hypergraphs, are called the left- and the right-hand side. Both sides must have an identical envelope: $U(g_l^d) = U(g_r^d)$. The address $t^d \subset g_l^d$ is needed for performing an efficient subgraph search. The meaning of the envelope and the address t^d for the distributively implementation of the replacement system will be explained below.

Productions can have different dimensions and are of different type. In the list P they are sorted according to their characteristics: $P = (P^0, P^1, \ldots, P^D, \hat{P}^D, \hat{P}^{D-1}, \ldots, \hat{P}^1)$. The sets P^d; $0 \le d \le D$ contain all *expanding* d-dimensional productions (they introduce new components to a graph), while all *reducing* d-dimensional productions (which can eliminate components from a graph) are contained in the sets $\hat{P}^d$. The complex productions which can be seen as a combination of a reducing and an expanding production will be handled like the reducing productions.

The dimensions of a production describe the types of componentes on which they operate: 1-dimensional productions are used to manipulate the 1-dimensional line segments, 2-dimensional productions can be used to alter area segments, and 3-dimensional productions can be used to operate on volume elements[4].

The replacement system P is structured in this way because a maximum level of parallelism shall be obtained. When a CHGRS is implemented on a multiprocessor system, the following list of steps (called *global schedule*) has to be executed repeatedly according to this structuring of the rule set:

---

[4] The 0-dimensional productions play a special role since they can never alter the structure of a CHG. In applications where computations shall be performed on the level of marker symbols the 0-dimensional productions are used to formalize these computations.

1. Perform all computations on the status information stored in the CHG. For instance, if the CHG represents the mesh used in a finite element application, the forces on the finite elements will be computed in this step.

2. Modify the structure of the graph according to the replacement rules (macroscopic replacement step): Sequentially select a set of productions $P^d :=$ $P^0, P^1, \ldots, P^D$. Apply P^d to the graph in parallel according to the following two steps. Do the same for $P^d := \hat{P}^D, \hat{P}^{D-1}, \ldots, \hat{P}^0$ with decreasing dimensions.

   (a) Apply the set of productions P^d in parallel to the graph (microscopic replacement step).

   (b) Synchronize all processor nodes.

3. Perform load balancing.

The sequential processing of the set of productions P^d (or $\hat{P}^d$) in step 2 is necessary because a maximal level of parallelism shall be obtained: Step 2a can be performed in a synchronous-parallel manner if only productions with identical dimensions are used simultaneously (see [1]).

The importance of a load balancing mechanism is demonstrated by step 2b: The next microscopic replacement step cannot be started before all processor nodes have finished the previous step[5].

In the listing above the step 2a summarizes the parallel application of a set of productions. This process can be further subdivided into the application of the individual productions. If a production p^d shall be applied to a CHG g^D the following steps must be performed:

1. **Subgraph search.** A subgraph of g^D has to be searched which is isomorphic to the left-hand side of the production p^d and that complies with some specific restrictions.

2. **Resolving conflicts.** In the case of reducing and complex productions the left-hand sides of different productions may overlap. The way how these conflicts are resolved will depend on the distinct application and the formulation of the related rules will be subject of a specific programming language.

3. **Elimination of inner edges.** All edges that are located within the interior of the left-hand side have to be eliminated from the graph.

4. **Insertion of new edges.** All edges that are contained in the interior of the right-hand side have to be inserted into the graph.

The implementation of the step 1 requires a quite complex algorithm[6]. And it must be possible to handle the complicated case where the left-hand side of a production is not located within a single processor node, but where instead it

---

[5] An enhanced implementation is imaginable where processor nodes must only wait for neighbouring nodes. But nevertheless the balanced distribution of the graph will be desirable.

[6] For most types of graph replacement systems the subgraph search is the initial and most time consuming step.

is distributed among a number of nodes (see production p_4^2 in the example). In the following it will be demonstrated that only the D-dimensional reducing and complex productions must be handled specifically. The necessary mechanisms for implementing the D-dimensional complex productions will be explained below with the help of the example p_4^2.

The application of the productions must be restricted according to further conditions, because it must be ensured that only legal modifications can be performed on the graph, so that every CHGRS shows the property of *closure*. The necessary restrictions are listed in [1], and the most important one reads:

Embedding: For every applicable production $p^d = (g_l^d, g_r^d, t^d)$ there exists no edge $e^{d+1} \in g^D$ that covers only parts of the left-hand side, but not the whole left-hand side of p^d: $\forall e^{d+1} \in g^D; e^d \in g_l^d : e^d \not\subseteq e^{d+1} \lor (\forall \hat{e}^d \in g_l^d : \hat{e}^d \subseteq e^{d+1})$.

Figure 4 illustrates two different situations where in one case the application of the production p_2^1 is forbidden while in the other case its application can be allowed. This production codes the operation where two line segments are combined to form a single one. In both cases the affected edges have been drawn emphasized. All covering edges e_i^2 (some edge e^{d+1} in the formula above) are visualized in the form of set diagrams.

Application forbidden: **Application allowed:**

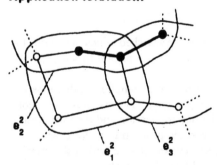 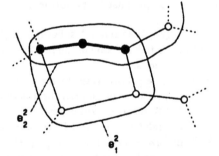

Fig. 4. Two different situations for the occurance of the left-hand side of p_2^1.

This condition has an important influence on the locations where productions p^d with less than D dimensions can be applied to the graph: It is only allowed that some applicable production p^d is covered *completely* by $d+1$-dimensional edge, and these edges itself can only be located completely within an edge with D dimensions. As a consequence the complete left-hand side must be located within a single cell of the graph. And since only complete cells are distributed among the processor nodes, any production $p^d; d < D$ can allways be applied locally within a single processor node.

Even if the production is applied to the outer part of a partition which is shared by a number of processor nodes, no communication will be necessary in the case of deterministic replacement systems: All nodes realize an identical replacement system, and therefore all shared edges will be manipulated in the same way. Only if non-deterministic rules shall be used synchronization between the processors will be necessary.

The most difficult case of D-dimensional non-expanding productions p^D (like p_4^2 in the example) that involves more than one processor node can be handled as follows. Both steps, the subgraph search and the process of applying the production, require specific support.

The algorithm for the subgraph search is presented in [3] and will be explained in short form with the help of figure 5. Let there be given the production $p^d = (g_l^d, g_r^d, t^d)$. In a first step a valid pairing of addresses $(t^d, \hat{t}^d)$, called an *anchor*, will be determined. The address t^d is part of a production and it must be located within the left-hand side: $t^d \subseteq g_l^d$. The corresponding address $\hat{t}^D$ must be located in the graph g^D. This anchor contains enough information for defining unequivocally the position where a production can be applied to the graph g^D. The address $\hat{t}^D$ will allways be located completely within a single cell, and therefore it can be assigned to a specific processor node n_{master}.

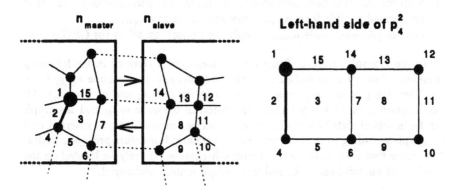

Fig. 5. Sequence of edges in the search strategy for the production p_4^2.

After having selected an anchor, this anchor must be verified. All edges of the left-hand side g_l^d must be inspected sequentially according to a pre-compiled *search strategy*. Whenever a one-to-one correspondence between the left-hand side and the graph is observed, the productions is classified to be applicable to the graph. Otherwise its application must be refused.

In figure 5 all corresponding edges of the graph and the left-hand side of p_4^2

are labeled with numbers 1 to 15. The addresses t^D and $\hat{t}^D$ which consist of the edges with numbers 1, 2 and 3 have been drawn emphasized. It can be seen that the tests for the edges numbered with 1 to 7 and 15 can be performed by the processor n_{master}, while the tests for the edges 8 to 14 must be performed by the processor n_{slave}. Since all processor nodes use the identical set of rules, the communication turns out to be quite simple:

The subgraph search starts with the edges addressed by $\hat{t}^D$ and it is performed as long as possible within the processor node n_{master}. If it is determined that an edge shall be addressed which is located in a neighbouring node, the search process is paused. A message is sent to the node n_{slave} that contains information about the actual address and the actual step in the search strategy. The node n_{slave} will process the search strategy starting from the given step. If n_{slave} determines an invalid matching between a pair of edges, it passes back the result *not applicable*. Otherwise, if the search strategy leads back to the node n_{master} (in the example because of the inspection of edge number 15), the node n_{slave} sends a message to n_{master} that contains the result *applicable* as well as the actual address and the actual step in the search strategy. Then the rest of the search strategy is processed within n_{master}. A production will be qualified to be *applicable* if all tests performed by the node n_{master} reveal a valid matching, and if each node n_{slave} sends back the signal *applicable* to n_{master}.

If the production can be applied to the graph, the remaining steps for modifying the graph can be executed according to the following sequence:

1. Shift all cells that have been identified with the left-hand side of p^D and that are located outside from n_{master} towards the node n_{master}.
2. Let the processor node n_{master} apply the production p^D to the CHG g^D.

In the example shown in figure 3 these steps are performed in the following sequence: The cell c_3 is shifted from the node $n_{(a,b+1)}$ to the node $n_{(a,b)}$ (step A). Then the production p_4^2 can be applied to the cells c_2 and c_3 (step B). All cells contained in the left-hand side are stored in the node $n_{(a,b)}$ and the graph can be modified distributively: Any edges can be removed from or inserted into the graph according to the production independently from other processor nodes. Any edges that may be in common with other nodes can only be located on the envelope of the left-hand side, and these edges remain unchanged.

4 Load Balancing

Load balancing is an important task when handling a CHG because of the specific structuring of the rule system: In order to perform synchronous parallel replacement operations within a CHG it is necessary to dissect the rule system according to the dimensions and the type of the rules (see step 2 of the *global schedule* from above). A macroscopic derivative step consists of a sequence of synchronous parallel microscopic derivative steps, where in each step all productions with identical dimension and of identical type are applied to the graph (step 2a of the global schedule). This leads to the necessity to synchronize the processors between different microscopic derivative steps: All processors that have finished this step have to wait for their direct neighbours until they have finished the identical microscopic step. If the computational load was distributed unbalanced among the processors, this would lead to a great amount of wasted processor time.

In step C of figure 3 the process of *load balancing* is symbolized: The new cell c_4 is shifted from $n_{(a,b)}$ to $n_{(a,b+1)}$, so that a better balanced distribution of the graph is achieved. This cell is selected because a favourable change in communication costs result from this choice. In this section it will be explained how load balancing can be performed using a non-supervised algorithm.

When doing load balancing two different subtopics are of interest:

1. The *computational* costs shall be equally distributed.
2. The *communication* costs between the different nodes shall be minimized.

An imaginable algorithm for doing load balancing can be described as follows:

1. Compute the number of cells S_{total} across the whole processor field. Broadcast the value $S_{avg} := S_{total}/|N|$ to all nodes.
2. Compute the number of cells to be shifted: $S_{shift}(n_i) := S_{actual}(n_i) - S_{avg}$.
3. For every processor node n_i where the number of cells to be shifted is above some given limit ($S_{shift}(n_i) > S_{min}$), repeat the following sequence:

   (a) From all processor nodes n_k that have some edge in common with n_i, select a target node n_j so that $S_{shift}(n_j) = min_{n_k} S_{shift}(n_k)$. Select a cell $c \in C(n_i)$ from the partition stored in n_i, so that the estimation of the change in communication costs is maximal for c in comparison to all other cells c': $\forall c, c' \in C(n_i); c \neq c' : \Delta \hat{t}_c(n_i, n_j) > \Delta \hat{t}_{c'}(n_i, n_j)$.

   (b) Shift the cell c from the node n_i to node n_j: $C(n_i) := C(n_i) \backslash c$ and $C(n_j) := C(n_j) \cup c$.

In step 3a a cell has to be selected which will be shifted between two neighbouring processor nodes. The decision is based on the change in communication costs $\Delta \hat{t}_c(n_i, n_j)$. In the rest of this section it will be shown how this function can be computed efficiently.

The average costs $t_c(n_i)$ that arise from a cell c that is located in the outer region of a partition[7] $C(n_i)$ can be estimated as:

$$t_c(n_i) = \sum_{e^d} \sum_{n_k} k_d \cdot w(n_i, n_k) \text{ with } e^d \in c; C(n_k) \ni e^d$$

The expected costs compute as the sum over all shared edges e^d, weighted with constants k_d and $w(n_i, n_k)$. The constants k_d denote the average costs that arise from a shared d-dimensional edge, while the weights $w(n_i, n_k)$ reflect how the network topology influences the communication costs.

---

[7] This formula is true for the interior of a partition, too. But then it is constantly 0.

The expression $t_c(n_j)$ approximates the communication costs arising from the cell c for the case that it is stored in the node n_i. When this cell is shifted to the node n_j the change in costs can be estimated as:

$$\Delta t_c(n_i, n_j) := t_c(n_j) - t_c(n_i)$$

If the function $\Delta t_c(n_i, n_j)$ shall be computed locally, the following information must be available to each node n_i:

1. Each node must have knowledge about all weights $w(n_i, n_k)$.
2. With every edge that is contained in more that one partition, a list of all of these partitions must be associated with the edge.

Part one can be accomplished easily if the nodes are organized within a regular grid and if the weights $w(n_i, n_j)$ can be computed from the relative distance between the nodes n_i and n_j. For instance if an orthogonal grid is used, the weights will be proportional to the *Manhattan*-distance between the coordinates of the processor nodes.

Part two demonstrates that the knowledge about the edges and their replicates within other processor nodes is of great importance. The space for storing this information as well as the time for computing the communication costs shall be as low as possible. Therefore the estimation will be restricted to the edges with $D-1$ dimensions. The shared edges with $D-1$ dimensions have the greatest influence on the communication costs, and the costs that arise from edges with less dimensions can be estimated from the size of the $D-1$-dimensional edges. The function $t_c(n_i)$ from above can be approximated as:

$$\hat{t}_c(n_i) = \sum_{e^{D-1}} \sum_{n_k} \hat{k}(|e^{D-1}|) \cdot w(n_i, n_k) \text{ with } e^{D-1} \in c; \ C(n_k) \ni e^{D-1}$$

The constants k are replaced by the constants $\hat{k}$ that reflect the influence of the size of the actual edge e^{D-1} on $\hat{t}_c(n_i)$.

In section 3 it is mentioned that a CHG must comply with the restrictions (G0)-(G4). Especially the condition (G4) expresses that for each edge $e^{D-1} \in g^D$ with $D-1$ dimensions there can exist at most 2 edges $e^D \in g^D$ so that $e^{D-1} \subseteq e^D$. As a consequence if there is given some edge e^{D-1} stored in the partition $C(n_i)$ there can be at most one further partition $C(n_j)$ in which this edge is contained, too. That means it is sufficient to store the index $J(e^{D-1})$ of the neighbouring processor node with every edge e^{D-1} that is located on the surface of a partition. Then the change in the communiational costs can be estimated efficiently:

$$\Delta \hat{t}_c(n_i, n_j) = \sum_{e^{D-1} \in c} \hat{k}(|e^{D-1}|) \cdot (w(n_j, J(e^{D-1})) - w(n_i, J(e^{D-1})))$$

It can be deduced from this equation that the change in communication costs can be estimated efficiently and locally within the processor nodes.

5 Summary and Conclusions

It has been sketched out how a *cellular hypergraph* can be implemented on a parallel computer system. A cellular hypergraph can be dissected into partitions and each partition can be stored within a distinct processor node. It has been explained how productions can be applied to the graph even if a production acts simultaneously on partitions that are stored in different processor nodes. In order to ensure the balanced distribution of the graph to the processor nodes a heuristic algorithm for performing *dynamic load balancing* has been sketched out. These are necessary preconditions for using CHGRS as abstract models for natural phenomena and for simulating these models on a multiprocessor system.

In the future CHGRS for sample applications and the load balancing algorithm will be implemented on a parallel computer system. Tests will have to be performed in order to determine how the topology of the processor network and several parameters influence the efficiency of the load balancing algorithm.

References

1. P. Hartmann. Parallel Replacement Systems on Geometric Hypergraphs: A Mathematical Tool for Handling Dynamic Geometric Sceneries. *Proceedings of the VIth International Workshop on Parallel Processing by Cellular Automata and Arrays, PARCELLA Workshop Potsdam*, 12:81–90, September 1994.
2. P. Hartmann. *Parallel Replacement Systems on Hierarchically Structured Hypergraphs: A new Method for Modelling Dynamic Geometric Sceneries*, pages 235–240. Proceedings of the 5th International Workshop on Graph Grammars and their Application to Computer Science, Williamsburg Virginia, November 1994.
3. P. Hartmann. Efficient Subgraph Matching within Cellular Hypergraphs. *Accepted for: Second International Conference on Developments in Language Theory, Magdeburg, Germany*, 1995.
4. T. Toffoli and N. Margolus. *Cellular Automata Machines*. MIT Press, 1987.
5. R. Vollmar. *Algorithmen in Zellularautomaten*. Teubner-Verlag, 1979.

Computer Models of 3D Cellular Structures*

V. Markova, S. Piskunov

Supercomputer Software Department, Computing Center
The Siberian Division of the Russian Academy of Sciences
Pr. Lavrentieva, 6, 630090, Novosibirsk, RUSSIA
E-mail: mark@comcen.nsk.su, E-mail: grey@comcen.nsk.su

Abstract. A computer technology of 3D cellular structure design based on the model of distributed computations (Parallel Substitution Algorithm) is presented. This technology is demonstrated on the example of two original 3D structures (universal and algorithm–oriented). It is shown that the structures can be converted into electrooptical devices with a simple topology of each layer and massive data exchanges between layers.

1   Introduction

A fairly stable interest is manifested in the investigation and the design of computer devices with an essentially homogeneous structure which consists of large sets of low–power calculators (functional cells). Bellow such a structure is referred to as *cellular*. This interest is attributed by high performance and manufacturability. Cellular structures can be both universal (homogeneous computing media), i.e., capable to imitate the work of digital logic, and algorithm–oriented, i.e., intended for performing algorithms for image recognition, fast arithmetic, matrix algebra, signal processing, etc.

It is known that the currently used VLSI technology has reached the level at which further advancement is restrained by the problem of connections. It has two aspects. Firstly, the limited number of inputs/outputs of a chip. Secondly, the connections between the switching elements which occupy most of the chip area (near 90%). At our sight, one possible solution of the connection problem is the use of optics. Let us distinguish the electrooptical circuitry (see [1], for example) among numerous methods of designing devices using optics for data processing. There are two reasons for this. On the one hand, it allows one to combine optics and microelectronics in a natural way unlike the pure optical methods of designing devices for which VLSI implementation is hardly possible. On the other hand, the electrooptical circuitry opens up the way to design a 3D (multilayer) VLSI. It is organized in the following manner. Inside the layers the connections are made with metallized strips like those in solid–state chips. Between the layers the switching elements are connected by light signals.

* This work was supported Russian Foundation for Basic Research grant No. 93–01–0100

The goal of this paper is to elaborate a computer technology of 3D cellular structure design which is done on the basis of the previously known 2D structure (prototype). *The design criteria* is the transfer of the greater part of interconnections of 2D cellular structure into interlayer connections of 3D cellular structure. It allows one to construct the electrooptical VLSI with a simple topology of each layer and massive data exchanges between layers using the light signal.

2 Computer Technology of 3D cellular structure design

Let a 2D cellular structure be given. Transformation 2D⇒3D is based on the following two strategies, which may be used individually and in combination.

1. *Partition* of the initial 2D structure into a number of substructures. The obtained substructures are distributed among layers of a 3D structure.
2. *Decomposition* of a cell functioning algorithm (logical or operator scheme) into a number of subalgorithms, according to which a cell is divided into a set of cells. Decomposed cells are distributed among layers of a 3D structure.

There are known several formal procedures of the transformation 2D⇒3D [2], based on the above strategies. 3D structure design, using both formal and informal procedures, requires constructing a set of 3D structures and then choosing the best suited to electrooptical implementation. It means, that we have to seek a trade-off between a number of layers, cell complexity, the number of neighbours of a cell in each layer (i.e. the cells which directly exchange information) and a share of interconnections of 2D prototype transferred into interlayer connections of 3D structure. In addition, in the design of 3D structure, we have to be sure that the result of date processing in 3D structure is the same as in 2D prototype. In fact, we should try to reduce the time, required for obtaining the result in 3D structure, due to the introduction of additional operations into the decomposition of a cell functioning algorithm in terms of the chosen variant of 3D structure.

As you can see, the design process of 3D cellular structure is a multivariant and rather a difficult task, especially, for structures of a sufficient large size. That is why, the computer simulation becomes a necessity.

The technology of 3D cellular structure design, using a computer, is based on the original model of distributed computations called Parallel Substitution Algorithm (PSA) [2,3]. In this model, a cellular structure is put in correspondence *a cellular array*, consisting of cells. Each cell has *the name* from a set of names M (as a rule, the name is the coordinates of cell in a cellular array) and *the state* from a given finite alphabet A. Structure functioning is distributed by an algorithm, which is represented by a list of commands (*parallel substitutions*). A parallel substitution (is further referred to as substitution) consists of *the left-hand* side and *right-hand* side. Each side is a pattern, which associates a set of cells (they are called *neighbours*) with each name from the array. If a cellular array being processed contains a set of cells associated with the left–hand side, the substitution is applicable to this array. Its application means performing two actions: 1) removing the subset of neighbouring cells associated with the left–hand side and 2) adding the set of neighbouring cells associated with the same name by the right–hand side. This replacement is performed simultaneously for all sets of neighbouring cells which meet readiness conditions. The step is repeated iteratively. In practice, a composition of cellular arrays is most often used, and left–hand and right–hand sides of substitutions are composed from a few patterns (they are separated by the symbol ∗). The following features of PSA make it a powerful tool for description of cellular structures: 1) all applicable substitutions are executed in parallel (at the same time and everywhere), 2) space relations between data are contained in a substitution.

PSA is embodied in an experimental computer simulating system [3, 4]. As distinct from the system [5], in our system there is graphical representation not only of cellular arrays but of patterns as well.

Bellow we consider two original 3D structures (universal and algorithm–oriented). Design of these structures are performed according to the second strategy, since it uses to a considerable extent the characteristic features of algorithms, which describe functioning of 2D structures.

2.1   Computer Model of 3D Universal Cellular Structure

The 2D universal structure [5] is used as the prototype for designing a 3D cellular universal structure. The reason is that the 2D structure provides direct simulation of digit logic and compact representation of a digit scheme [5].

Computer Model of the 2D structure. Let us represent this structure as a computer model. Two cellular arrays sr and gr are put in correspondence with the structure. The alphabet A of cell states contains the symbols ◦, •, ⋆, and "neutral" symbol, which is not a sign. The array sr contains image of a digital schema (IDS), which is constructed of one–, two–input gates connected by binary transmitting channels. The IDS is "drawn" by cells in the state ◦, gates are marked by cells in the state ⋆, background is formed by cells in the neutral state. In the IDS, the unit signal is displayed by a cell in the state •. The array gr allows to realize two partitions (the even and the odd) of the array sr on elements – squares, composed of four cells. The partition is considered as active, if each cell belonging to the array gr and being put in correspondence to the left–top cell of each square of this partition is in the state ◦. In Fig. 1 fragments of the sr and gr are shown in the initial state. In Fig. 2 a set of the patterns is presented. It is used for constructing the substitutions of the algorithm which describes functioning the 2D structure (2D PSA). To simplify Fig. 2, only a subset of the patterns is shown, the other are built in the same way. The cellular arrays and the patterns are displayed on the monitor screen, each symbol of the alphabet is put correspondence to a fixed colour.

The substitutions of the 2D PSA realize moving the signals along channels, crossing, branching and transformating the signals. In computer model, the 2D

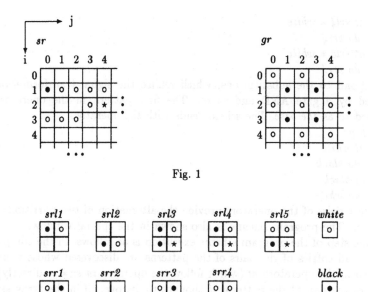

Fig. 1

Fig. 2

PSA is specified by the program scheme. In this scheme, the synchronous and the iterative execution of the PSA is given by the operator *ex*. The operator *in* with the name of the cellular array (or several arrays separated by the symbol *) specifies the space, where the substitutions are to be executed. The substitution is given by two operators *at* and *do*. After the reserved word *at*, the pattern name from the left–hand side of the substitution (or the list of the pattern names separated by the symbol * and located as well as the names of the arrays in the operator *in*) follows. After the reserved word *do* – from the right–hand side of the substitution. So, the program scheme is started by the rows:

    ex

    *in sr * gr*

Then the pairs of the operators *at, do* follows. Each pair of the operators corresponds to one substitution. For example, two pairs of the operators:

    *at srl1 * white*

      do srr1

    *at srl2 * white*

      do srr2

correspond to two substitutions, which realize motion of the signal along a horizontal channel. Three pairs of operators:

    *at srl3 * white*

      do srr3

*at srl4 * white*
do srr4
*at srl5 * white*
do srr4

correspond to the substitutions, which realize the signal transformation performed by a gate AND and so on. The first pattern in the operator *at* is referred to as *the base*. The scheme ends with the operators:

in gr
at white
do black
at black
do white

Two last pairs of the operators provide the alternation of two partitions of the array *sr*. The program scheme is also shown in the special window.

One step of the program scheme execution is as follows. In the composition *sr * gr*, all entries of the pairs of the patterns are discovered whose names are pointed in the operators *at* (which follow the operator *in sr * gr* directly). The entry of the pair of the patterns is thought to discover, if in the array **sr** there is the entry of the base, and in the array *gr* there is the entry of the pattern with the name *white*, and moreover the coordinates of the left–top cells of the both entries coincided. All entries of the bases are replaced by the patterns from the corresponding operators *do*. For the operators, which directly follow the operator *in gr*, the search and the replacement of the entries are performed in the single array *gr*. The step of the program scheme execution is repeated iteratively.

Representation of the base as a square predetermines a view of the partition element. Choice of the positions of the cells, which take the states o or • in the array *gr*, provides superposition of elements of two partitions. Alternation of the cell states in the array *gr* provides alternation of activity of the even and the odd partitions. Taken together they provide the possibility of motion and transformation of signals. For example, the even partition is active in the initial state of the arrays *sr* and *gr*. Hence, at the first step of the program scheme execution, the first pair of the operators *at, do* moves signal to a neighbouring cell on the left. At the second step, the odd partition is active. Hence, the second pair of the operators *at, do* performs similar shift of the signal and so on.

In the prototype, a cell is a "black box", which carries out some actions. Let us unpack it. Based on the above 2D PSA (which is given as the program scheme), a logical scheme of a cell may be constructed. The logical scheme is represented in Fig. 3.

Now we give the observations which were taken into consideration when constructing the logical scheme.

1. The 2D PSA does not change an IDS, it provides only motion and transformation of the signals. Therefore, the same substitutions are applicable to the same parts of the IDS corresponding to elements of the even and

the odd partitions. A number of these substitutions are equal or less to three (by a number of the substitutions which imitate a gate or crossing the signals).

2. Each cell, excepting the borderline ones, enters into an element of the even partition and into an element of the odd partition, and occupies the appointed position in either of the two elements.

3. Each substitution is shared by four cells. It means that in accordance with its position, a cell must store only quarter of the base (one symbol) and only quarter of the right–hand side (one symbol) of every of the three substitutions for the even and the odd partitions.

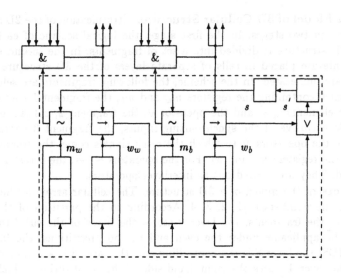

Fig. 3

Let us describe the cell construction and the cell functioning in detail. Each cell contains the basic storage element s, the buffer storage element s' and the storage elements forming four three–digit ring registers $m_w[0 : 2]$, $w_w[0 : 2]$, $m_b[0 : 2]$, $w_b[0 : 2]$. The storage element states belong to the alphabet A. The basic storage element s of a cell with coordinates i, j stores the state of the cell with the same coordinates from the array sr. The buffer storage element is a delay component. A symbol from the base and a symbol from the right–hand side of the gth substitution, $g = 0, 1, 2$, for the even (odd) partition are stored in gth digits of the registers m_w (m_b) and w_w (w_b).

To realize one step of the 2D PSA, each cell performs three times the actions i), ii) and iii) being listed below, and then it duplicates a state of the buffer storage element s' in the basic storage element s.

i) The operator $\sim$ compares a state of the element s with states of the upper digits of registers m_w and m_b. The comparison result is fed to the inputs of the two operators &. The left (right) operator & is common for four cells involved in an element of the even (odd) partition. The right upper input of the operators & serves to supply one of two clock signals. The array gr shows what clock signal must be fed to each operator &.

ii) Let in this step a cell be in an element of the even (odd) partition, and the comparison be successful for all four cells which perform a substitution in common. In this case, the left (right) operator & allows the operator $\rightarrow$ to duplicate a symbol from the top digit of the register w_w (w_b) in the buffer storage element s'.

iii) The registers m_w, w_w, m_b, w_b are shifted one digit along a ring.

Computer Model of 3D Cellular Structure. Stratification of the 2D structure consists in two stages. In the first stage, the logical scheme of each cell from the 2D structure is divided into a set of fragments. In the second stage, the fragments are placed in cells of separate layers of the 3D structure. The fragments are numerated. In the scheme, the following fragments are selected: the fragment 0 containing the registers m_w and m_b, the fragment 1 containing the storage elements s, s' and the operator $\vee$, the fragment 2, containing the operators & exclusive of the synchronizing inputs; the fragment 3 containing the parts of the operators & to which the clock signals come, the fragment 4 containing the registers w_w and w_b. For the operators $\sim$, $\rightarrow$, the fragments are not selected. They are carried out as interlayer operators.

Let us design the model of a 3D structure. The cellular array srd has five layers with the numbers 0, 1, 2, 3, 4. According to the partition of the cell into a set of the fragments, the layer 0 stores the bases of the substitutions which can be applicable under the even and the odd partitions, the layer 1 stores the IDS, the layer 2 is the controlling one, the layer 3 is a analog of the array gr, the layer 4 stores the right-hand side of the substitutions which can be applicable under the even and the odd partitions.

The alphabet of states of cells belonging to the array srd is the alphabet A $\bigcup$ ×, where × – "don't care" symbol. This symbol plays the service role and is used in the model only.

A column consisting from the symbols × is placed to the right (left) of each column of the pattern specifying the base (right-hand side) of the substitution. This column is further referred to as *empty*. It is made to use the layer 2 when executing both the operator $\sim$ and the operator $\rightarrow$. In a separate element of the even (odd) partition, the empty column is placed to the right of each column. The partition of the layer 3 is constructed from such elements. In this layer, the elements of the even and the odd subpartitions are made unoverlapping, i.e., the layer 3 consists of alternating strips of width two cells. The even (odd) strips contain elements of the even (odd) subpartition. The elements of the odd subpartition are shifted on four cells on the right about the elements of the even subpartition. It is made to provide joint storage of the bases of the substitutions (which can be applied under conditions as the even and so odd subpartitions) in the only layer. The bases of the substitutions, which can be applied under conditions of the even (odd) subpartition, are stored in the even (odd) strips of the layer 0. These even (odd) strips have as the arrangement as the strips of the even (odd) subpartition have in the layer 3. The right–hand sides is stored in the layer 4 in the similar way.

As distinct from the array sr, in the layer 1 each cell is divided into two neighbouring cells. They are arranged along the axe j. One cell stores the state of the element s, another cell stores the state of the element s'. Since the subpartitions are not intersected, each pair of the cells corresponding to the elements s, s' is duplicated along axe i in order to provide motion and transformation of the signals in the IDS. These actions lead to the double size of all layers of the array srd in comparison with the arrays of the prototype. The cell states of the layer 3 of the array srd are neutral. In Fig. 4, the fragments of the layers 0, 1 of the array srd are shown side by side and marked by numbers instead of the stairs form as they are on the monitor screen. In the layer 1 the semi–adder is drown. Its upper gate is the gate AND, its lower gate is gate MOD 2. The inputs of the semi–adder are on the left. The signal is fed to the top input of the semi–adder (here the signal is drawn by four symbols •). In the layer 0, the bases of the substitutions are represented. In the layer 4 (it is not drawn in Fig. 4), each right–hand side is arranged under the corresponding base, the empty columns are shifted one position to the left.

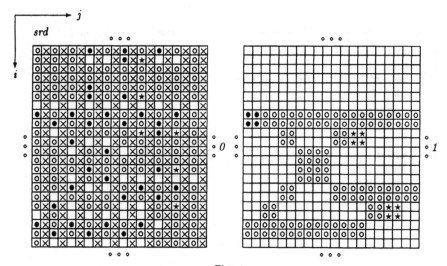

Fig. 4

Before we go to the description of the cellular structure functioning, let us supplement our knowledge about simulating means. The first remark concerns to pairs of the operators which represent functional substitutions [2,3], i.e., the substitutions which in addition to the symbols from the given alphabet of cell states contain variable symbols in their left–hand sides and functional symbols in their right–hand sides. Values of the symbols are calculated when the substitutions are executed. In the computer representation the functional substitution is given by the pair of the operators *ab* (instead of the operator *at*) and *do*. Variable symbols are written in the corresponding cells of the patterns. The operator *do* is followed by the functional symbol which identifies the function. The function points what new values are assigned to variable symbols and under what conditions. Each function is the notation of a single C–language operator. It is shown in the special window. The second remark concerns the rules of execution of operators. One step of the program scheme execution can consist of a sequence of substeps. A substep is given by the operator *ch*, which precedes the operator *in*. Data changes in the cellular arrays are performed after each substep. The third remark regards the use of 3D cellular arrays and patterns. The operator *on* with the number is used to point out a layer of an array. The closest (to the observer) layer of the pattern slides along the pointed layer of the cellular array. A 3D pattern is displayed as a set of 2D patterns arranged on the stairs. The lowest 2D pattern of the stairs form is the closest to the observer. The operator *on* follows the operator *in*.

The 3D PSA is fully specified by the actions i), ii), iii), which are performed by the cells of the 2D structure. In Fig. 5 are shown the fragment of the program scheme, the function being used in it, and all needed patterns. It is

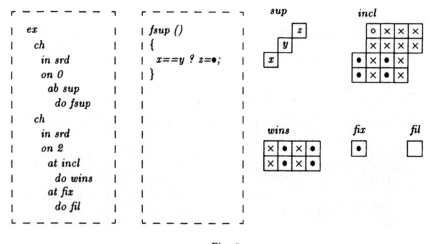

Fig. 5

easy to verify that the fragment using the layers 0, 1, 2 of the array *srd* carries out the action i). Indeed, the first pair of the operators *ab*, *do* marks in the controlling layer all coincidence of the cell states in the layers 0, 1. For the active partition, the second and the third pairs of operators mark only those bases which coincide with the parts of the IDS arranged under them. This fragment of the program scheme is the most complexity, and in fact, it specifies logical (and hence optical) schemes of cells for all layers of the 3D structure. Therefore, the full scheme of the program is not shown here.

We notice the following.

1. For reasons of rendezvous of the fragment of the IDS with the bases and the right–hand sides of the substitutions, shifting the cell states of the layer 1 is performed along the axe i. Let us recall that in the 2D structure such rendezvous is performed by shift of digits of the registers m_w, w_w, m_b, w_b.
2. Replacing the IDS by another in the layer 1 requires a new arrangement of the patterns in the layers 0, 4 in the order corresponding to fragments of new IDS. It is profitable to perform introducing new IDS and the patterns in combination so that a number of shifts along the axe i would be minimal (for example, no more than three). Solving this task is one of the main purposes of the computer model of the 3D structure.

The analysis of the 3D structure model allows one to make the following conclusions about the 3D structure itself.

1. All layers of the structure except for the controlling layer are memories. The requirements to these memories are standard: data writing (rewriting), date storage and, in addition, data shifting for the controlling layer. The controlling layer is simple. It consists of an coincidence scheme being repeated iteratively.
2. A comparison of the 2D and the 3D structures shows that the overwhelming part of interconnections for the 2D structure turns into interlayer connections for the 3D structure.

The further elaboration of the model includes conversion to boolean coding of symbols which are the states of the cells. Now one can say about a possibility of construction of the electrooptical device. It consists of four layers (the layers 2, 3 from the 3D model merge together forming the controlling layer of the device). Three of these layers are the boolean storage elements with optical inputs (photodetectors) and outputs (modulators). The controlling layer is formed of the coincidence schemes constructed from photodetectors and modulators.

2.2 Computer model of 3D Cellular Complex Number Multiplier

In this section, a 2D cellular complex number multiplier [6] is used as a prototype. The multiplier realizes an algorithm of complex number multiplication in the Knuth number system (NS) [7], which has attracted our attention due to the possibility of representing a complex number as a single vector.

The Knuth Number System. The Knuth (or the quaterimaginary) number system is defined as a positional NS with the image radix $r = 2i$ and with the base $B = \{0, 1, 2, 3\}$. Any Gaussian integer $G = A + Ci$ (both its parts are integer) can be represented in the Knuth NS as the following sequence of the coefficients a *quaterimaginary number*

$$\mathbf{G} = g_{m-1} \ldots g_0.g_{-1}, \tag{1}$$

where $g_j \in B$ for all $j \neq -1$, and $g_{-1} \in \{0, 2\}$. The digits with the even indices in the sequence (1) specify the real part of a Gaussian integer G, the digits with the odd indices – the imaginary ones. The length of a quaterimaginary number is equal or one digit greater than the length of the greatest part of its associated Gaussian integer in two's complement form, if it is positive or negative, respectively.

Let $\mathbf{G} = g_{m-1} \ldots g_0.g_{-1}$ and $\mathbf{H} = h_{m-1} \ldots h_0.h_{-1}$ be two n–digit quaterimaginary numbers, $n = m + 1$.

The quaterimaginary product $\mathbf{P} = p_{2m-1} \ldots p_0.p_{-1}$ is calculated in a classic manner by first obtaining n partial products (PP) and then summation of them.

Each *ith* partial product $\mathbf{P_i} = (p_{i,m+1} \ldots p_{i,0}.p_{i,-1})$, $i = -1, 0, \ldots, m - 1$, is obtained in two steps. At the first step, for each pair (g_i, h_j), $j = -1, 0, \ldots,$ $m + 1$, the product modulo (-4) is obtained

$$(g_j \cdot h_i)_{mod(-4)} = d_{i,j+2} + p'_{i,j},$$

where $d_{i,j+2} \in \{0, -1, -2\}$ and $p'_{i,j} \in D$ are *the intermediate carry* digit and *the intermediate product* digit, respectively. Distinctly from other NS, the carry is transferred to two positions ahead of the current intermediate product digit.

At the second step, the partial product digit $p''_{i,j}$ is calculated by usual arithmetic addition

$$p'_{i,j} + d_{i,j} = p''_{i,j} \quad \text{for all} \quad j = -1, 0, \ldots, m+1.$$

It is clear that the obtained result P'' may be not a quaterimaginary number, i.e., among the digits which belong to the base (*the staff* digits) there exists at least one digit, which doesn't belong to the base (*the unstaff* digit). In order that the result P'' becomes the quaterimaginary number $\mathbf{P}$, the modification of all unstaff digits should be performed according to Rule 1.

Rule 1. Let P'' be an intermediate result. Then for each pair of the digits (p''_j, p''_{j+2}), $j = -1, 0, \ldots, m + 1$, the following computation is done beginning with the least significant digit.

1. If $p''_j < 0$, then $p''_j = p''_j + 4$ and $p''_{j+2} = p''_{j+2} + 1$.
2. If $p''_j \geq 4$, then $p''_j = p''_j - 4$ and $p''_{j+2} = p''_{j+2} - 1$.

The calculation of new values of the intermediate result digits (*the reduction*) is similar to the carry propagation along the number. The time required for reduction of n–digit intermediate result is n/2 steps.

The final result $\mathbf{P}$ is calculated by summation of all PP with the use of *the quaterimaginary addition*. It is carried out in two steps like the quaterimaginary multiplication. At the first step, for each pair of the digits of quaterimaginary numbers the sum modulo (-4) is defined. The obtained *intermediate carry* digits take the values from the set $\{-1, 0\}$, *intermediate sum* digits – from the base. At the second step, the sum digit is calculated by usual arithmetic addition. If the obtained sum is not a quaterimaginary number, the reduction should be done according to Rule 1.

Computer Model of 2D multiplier. Four cellular arrays: the multiplier, the multiplicand, the processing field, and the controlling register are put in correspondence with the 2D cellular complex number multiplier [6]. The cell states are from the alphabet $A = \{-2, -1, 0, 1, 2, 3, 4, 5\}$. The multiplier and the multiplicand store the initial dates. The processing field is dedicated for partial product generation and then their summation. The functional cell performs three operators: data shift, parallel reduction and quaterimaginary summation. The purpose of the controlling register consists in the following. It checks whether the intermediate results are quaterimaginary numbers, generates the signals for performing above enumerated operators, and moreover, plays the role of a mask, which distinguishes the even and the odd rows in the array.

The computation process is distributed in the 2D cellular space as follows.

1. Generation of intermediate results (partial products and their sums) and reduction are performed concurrently.
2. Reduction of the unstaff digits is executed in parallel according to Rule 2.
3. Pairwise addition of quaterimaginary numbers starts without waiting for all intermediate results to be reduced.
4. Intermediate results shift in the direction of the smaller values of i, so that the result is obtained in the 0th row of the array.

Rule 2. Let P'' be an intermediate result. For all pairs (p''_j, p''_{j+2}), $j = -1, 0, \ldots, n+1$, the following computations are performed in parallel

1. If $p''_j < 0$, then $p''_{j+2} = \mathbf{p}_{j+2} + 1$, where

$$\mathbf{p}_{j+2} = \begin{cases} p''_{j+2}, & if\ p''_{j+2} \in B, \\ p''_{j+2} + 4, & if\ p''_{j+2} < 0, \\ p''_{j+2} - 4, & if\ p''_{j+2} > 3. \end{cases} \tag{2}$$

2. If $p''_j > 3$, then $p''_{j+2} = \mathbf{p}_{j+2} - 1$, where $\mathbf{p}_{j+2}$ is calculated according to (2).
3. If $p''_j \in B$, then $p''_{j+2} = \mathbf{p}_{j+2}$, where $\mathbf{p}_{j+2}$ is calculated according to (2).

The computer model of the 2D multiplier has been investigated for the certain values of n (from 8 to 32). This investigation allows to draw the following conclusions about the 2D multiplier corresponding to this model. The structural complexity of the functional cell (the number of its inputs and outputs) is 11. The upper time complexity (the number of steps needed for calculate of the quaterimaginary product) of the 2D multiplier is $3,5n$ As would be expected, it computes the product of two n–digit quaterimaginary numbers with the speed less than that of multiplication of two binary numbers of the same length. In other words, the reduction of intermediate results preceding their summation has been and still remains the bottleneck which limits the multiplication speed.

To overcome this bottleneck, the processing of the. staff and the unstaff digits should be done in parallel during the summation of intermediate results. It may be done by means of the decomposition of the operator scheme of the functional cell of the prototype, and distributing the cells associated with the obtained subschemes among the layers of the 3D array.

Computer Model of 3D multiplier. A number of computer models of 3D multipliers have been constructed and investigated for the certain values of n (from 8 to 32). 3D multipliers corresponding to these models differ in the number of layers, the structural complexity of the functional cells in each layer, the number of interlayer connections, the alphabet, the number of simple operations (shift of digit, summation of two digits and so on) and the time complexity.

One variant of a computer model of 3D multiplier has been considered in [3]. It is constructed relying on the decomposition of the operator scheme of the functional cell into three subscheme: data shift, summation of the staff digits and reduction of the unstaff digits. In the decomposed scheme, the additional operator (transmission of the digits among layers) is introduced. The first subscheme is realized in the layer 0, the second subscheme – in the layers 0 and 1, the third subscheme – in the layer 2. By this decomposition, the staff digits are summed up in the layers 0 and 1, the unstaff digits are transmitted from the layer 0 into the layer 2, and are returned back in the layer 0 or (and) 1 after their reduction according to Rule 2.

The analysis of this computer model shows that the structural complexity of the most complex layer of the 3D multiplier is (7,5), where the first digit in the parenthesis denotes the number of connections in the layer, the second digit – the number of interlayer connections. The upper time complexity of the 3D multiplier is $3n$.

A new computer model of 3D multiplier is presented in this paper. As distinct from the model in [3], this model doesn't require a separate layer for reduction of the unstaff digits. Here, the operator scheme of the functional cell of the 2D prototype is decomposed into two subscheme: data shift together with reduction of the unstaff digits and summation of the staff digits. Moreover, the second subscheme is modified by introducing an additional operator, which adds up the unstaff digits in each pair of the neighboring results, i.e., the results located in the neighboring rows, from which the first has the even index and the second — the odd one. The first subscheme is realized in the layers 0 and 1, the second subscheme – in the layers 0 and 1.

So, this computer model of the 3D multiplier is the four–layer cellular array m and the alphabet $A = \{-2, -1, 0, 1, 2, 3, 4, 5\}$. The layers 0 and 1 are the pure processing field. The layers 2 and 3 are the controlling ones. They are destined for realization of the controlling functions of the prototype excepting the first function. Here, only the result loaded in the zeroth row of the layer 0 is checked if it is the quaterimaginary number or not.

Let a set of the partial products be obtained and located in the layers 0 and 1. Then the following processes take place during the summation of these products.

1. *The two–layer summation* of the staff digits in each pair of the neighboring results is carried out in two steps. At the first step, the intermediate sum and carry are calculated and placed in the layer 1. At the same time, the unstaff digits corresponding to the summed results from the odd row of the layer 0 are added to the unstaff digits in the even row of the same layer. At the second step, the arithmetic sum of the unstaff digits and the sum of the staff ones is calculated and loaded in the layer 0. Both steps are accompanied by the change of the cell states in the layer 2.
2. *The shift* of the obtained results together with *the two–layer reduction* of the unstaff digits, based on Rule. 2.
3. *The one–layer reduction* of the intermediate result written in the zeroth row of the layer 0 according to Rule. 2. It is carried out when this intermediate result does not participate in the summation.

Those processes are repeated until the last sum is calculated. Then the obtained sum is reduced to the quaterimaginary number.

Using the patterns *s1* and *s2* (Fig. 6), Fig. 7 shows the fragment of the program scheme realizing the modified summation of the intermediate results with some simplification.

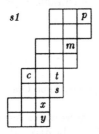
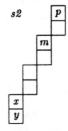

Fig. 6

The 3D multiplier corresponding to this model has the following characteristics. The structure complexity of the functional cell of the most complex layer is $(7,5)$. The upper time complexity of this multiplier is $2,5n$. Increasing of the multiplication speed is achieved by the reduction of the unstaff digits of the result loaded in the zeroth row of the zeroth layer, when it does not participate in summation. Hence, when the last sum is calculated, n least significant digits of this result are the staff ones. So, only the remaining n digits of the result should be reduced. In the worst case, this time is $n/2$. Moreover, the results of the simulation show that time needed for the reduction of n–digit number is less or equal to $logn/2$ for the certain values of n (from 8 to 32).

```
┌ ─ ─ ─ ─ ─ ┐   ┌ ─ ─ ─ ─ ─ ─ ─ ─ ─ ─ ─ ─ ─ ─ ┐
│ in m      │   │ cs1 ()                       │
│ on 0      │   │  {(p==1 && m==1 && x≥0        │
│  ab s1    │   │   && x<4 && y≥0 && y<4)?      │
│  do cs1   │   │   c = -(x+y+t+s-(x+y+t+s)%4)/4,│
│  do cs2   │   │   s =  (x+y+t+s)%4, x = 0, y = 0;}│
└  cs3 ─ ─ ─┘   └ ─ ─ ─ ─ ─ ─ ─ ─ ─ ─ ─ ─ ─ ─ ┘

┌ ─ ─ ─ ─ ─ ┐   ┌ ─ ─ ─ ─ ─ ─ ─ ─ ─ ─ ─ ─ ─ ─ ┐
│ in m      │   │ cft1 ()                      │
│ on 0      │   │  {(p==1 && m==1 && x≥0        │
│  ab s2    │   │   && x<4 && (y<0 !! y>3))?    │
│  do sft1  │   │   x = y, y = 0;}              │
└  do sft2 ─┘   └ ─ ─ ─ ─ ─ ─ ─ ─ ─ ─ ─ ─ ─ ─ ┘

┌ ─ ─ ─ ─ ─ ┐   ┌ ─ ─ ─ ─ ─ ─ ─ ─ ─ ─ ─ ─ ─ ─ ┐
│ in m      │   │ sum ()                       │
│ on 0      │   │  {(m==2)?                     │
│  ab s1    │   │   x = x+t+s, s = 0, t = 0;}   │
└  do sum ─ ┘   └ ─ ─ ─ ─ ─ ─ ─ ─ ─ ─ ─ ─ ─ ─ ┘
```

Fig. 7

So, the stratification of the 2D prototype allows us to multiply two complex numbers with the speed close to the multiplication speed of conventional binary numbers of the same length, on the one hand, and to transfer a half or so of the connections of a layer into the interlayer connections, on the other hand. Now we can conclude that this 3D multiplier will be suitable to electrooptic implementation.

References

1. Egorov, V., Koszov, E,.: Integral Optical Digital Computers. Appl. Optics. 8 (1990) 29, 1178
2. Anishev, P., Achasova, S., Bandman, O., Piskunov, S., Sergeev, S.: Parallel Microprogramming Methods. Nauka, Novosibirsk (1981) 180 p. (In Russian)
3. Achasova, S., Bandman, O., Markova, V., Piskunov, S.: Parallel Substitution Algorithm. World Scientific, Singapore (1994) 220 p.
4. Pogudin, Yu.: ALT – a Graphical System for Parallel Microprogramming. Parallel Algorithms and Structures. Computer Center, Novosibirsk (1991) 77–88 (in Russian)
5. Toffoli, T., Margolus, N.: Cellular Automata Machines. Massachusetts Institute of Technology (1987). Russian Translation: Mir, Moscow (1991) 278 p.
6. Markova, V.: The Cellular Knuth Algorithm for Complex Number Multiplication. Parcella'94, Mathematical Research 81, Akademie Verlag, Berlin (1994) 91–98
7. Knuth, D.: An imaginary number system. ACM 4 (1960) 3, 245–247

Comparison of Two MST Algorithms for Associative Parallel Processors

Ann Sh. Nepomniaschaya

Computing Center, Siberian Division
of Russian Academy of Sciences,
Supercomputer Software Department
pr. Lavrentieva, 6, Novosibirsk, 630090, Russia

Abstract. In this paper, we analyze procedures for finding a minimal spanning tree of a graph for an abstract associative STAR–machine with bit–serial processing. We compare the implementations of the Prim–Dijkstra algorithm and the Baase algorithm on the STAR–machine for the same graph representation. Then we briefly describe our STAR–system.

1 Introduction

The revived interest in associative (content-addressable) architectures is caused by declining hardware prices due to modern technology achievements [5]. We will analyze algorithms for STARAN-like associative parallel processors (APP's) belonging to fine–grain SIMD–systems with bit–serial (vertical) processing and simple single-bit processor elements. For such computers algorithms are represented by means of languages ASC [12], Apple [7] or some special tools, for example, [4,6,8]). In order to carry out massive associative searching for the tabular data written in binary code and to investigate new vertical processing algorithms, a high–level language STAR was proposed in [9]. Its operational semantics is given by means of an abstract STAR–machine. This language resembles Pascal, but has special data types and corresponding operations for them allowing one to simulate easily the run of associative architecture.

In this paper, we consider an approach to analyzing algorithms of associative processing. Its novelty lies in the fact that for a group of parallel architectures we define a formal semantic model (the STAR–machine) which is used both for programmed modeling and for theoretical analysis of algorithms. We will use our approach for comparing the implementations of the Prim–Dijkstra algorithm [2,14] and the Baase algorithm [1] on the STAR–machine for the same graph representation.

For finding a minimal spanning tree of a graph on sequential computers there are different well–known algorithms, however for APP's the mentioned above two algorithms are best suited [3, 12]. In [12], for graphs represented as a set of triples (edge nodes and their weight) the effective program MST was considered. It was written in the language ASC with time $0(n)$ for a graph having n nodes and based on the Baase algorithm. In [3], for graphs represented as a distance matrix the implementation of the Prim–Dijkstra algorithm on the associative array processor LUCAS was briefly described and its time was evaluated as $0(n)$.

Here, for graphs represented as a set of triples we analyze STAR procedures MST1 and MSTP and evaluate their complexity in terms of the access number to the matrix memory [4] of the model employed. We prove that complexity of the examined procedures is $0(n \log n)$, and this estimation is essential for the considered problem if we use associative parallel processors with bit-serial processing. Moreover, we briefly describe our STAR– system on IBM PC which allows us to verify STAR procedures and to define the time of the computation.

2   Model of Associative Parallel Machine

We define our model as an abstract STAR–machine of the SIMD–type with vertical data processing. It consists of the following components:

- a sequential common control unit (CU) where the programs and scalar constants are stored;
- associative processor consisting of m single–digit processor elements (PE's);
- matrix memory for the associative processor.

Data are loaded in the matrix memory in the form of two–dimensional array written in binary code. Each array element occupies an individual row and all elements have the same length (coinciding with the length of the maximal element). The rows are numbered from top to bottom and the columns from left to right. A row (word) or a column (slice) may be accessed equally easy. Some arrays may be loaded in the matrix memory. In the CU a rendition table should be located allowing one to associate with each array identifier its number of columns.

The associative processor is represented as h vertical registers each of m bits. The bit columns of the data array are stored in the registers which perform the necessary Boolean operations, record the search results and ensure the word selection capability. We assume that the STAR–machine processor has a sufficient number of vertical registers to store intermediate results of data processing without using the matrix memory.

By analogy with [11,13], we define a STAR–machine program to be a finite directed graph with one start vertex and a set of accepting vertices and with edges each labeled with one assignment instruction or predicate. If the program uses k registers then a configuration consists of a node of the graph and the current contents of the k registers. A computation of the machine is a path in the graph.

3   Review of the Language STAR

In this section, we briefly consider STAR constructions from [9] needed for the paper. To simulate data processing in the matrix memory we use the following data types: **integer, boolean, word, slice, table** and **array.** Data types are introduced in the same manner as in Pascal. Constants for the types **slice** and **word** are represented as a sequence of symbols from $\{0,1\}$ enclosed within single apostrophes. We use the types **slice** and **word** for bit column access and bit row access, respectively and the type **table** for defining the tabular data. Assume that any variable of the type **slice** consists of m components which belong to $\{0,1\}$.

Consider operations and predicates for slices.

Let X, Y be variables of the type **slice** and i, k be variables of the type **integer.** Define the following operations:

SET(Y) sets all components of Y to $'1'$;

CLR(Y) sets all components of Y to $'0'$;

$Y(i)$ selects the i-th component of Y;

FND(Y) yields the ordinal number i of the first component '1' in the slice Y, $i \geq 0$.

The following bitwise logical operations are executed simultaneously by all corresponding components of X and Y. We introduce them in the usual way:

$X \wedge Y$ is conjunction, $X \vee Y$ is disjunction, $\neg X$ is componentwise negation, $X \oplus Y$ is exclusive OR.

We use two predicates ZERO(Y) and SOME(Y) which are introduced in the usual way.

Let T be a variable of the type **table.** We utilize the following two operations:

$T(i)$ yields the i-th row in the matrix T ($1 \leq i \leq m$);

col(i, T) yields the i-th column in T ($1 \leq i \leq m$).

It should be noted that STAR statements resemble those of Pascal.

Remark 1. When we define a variable of the type **slice** we put in brackets the name of the matrix which uses it. Therefore if the matrix consists of n rows where $n < m$ then only first n components of the corresponding slice (column) will be used in the vertical processing.

4 Preliminary Notions

In this paper, we represent algorithms in the form of STAR procedures. To analyze implementations of the Prim–Dijkstra algorithm and the Baase algorithm on associative parallel processors we use the procedures MATCH and MIN from [10]. The procedure MATCH(T, X, w, Z) defines the row positions in the matrix T coinciding with the given row w. Its result is the slice Z in which $Z(i) =' 1'$ if $T(i)=w$. The procedure MIN(T, X, Z) defines the row positions in T where the minimal element is located. Its result is the slice Z in which $Z(i) =' 1'$ if $T(i)$ is the minimal matrix element. Recall that these procedures realize the search only among the matrix rows which correspond to positions $'1'$ in the slice X.

In [13], the time of a computation is defined as its length, that is, by assigning unit cost to each instruction (including predicates). However, in real associative computers different elementary operations take different times. Moreover, according to [4], one can assume that definition of the response existence among PE's does not take the additional time. Therefore following [4], we evaluate complexity of the algorithm P by means of the *access number $N(P)$* to the STAR–machine *matrix memory* during its execution. We agree that the execution of any STAR statement takes only one access to the matrix memory of our model.

Let $G=(V, E, w)$ represent an *undirected weighted graph* with the node (vertex) set $V = \{1, 2, \ldots, n\}$, the edge set $E \subseteq V \times V$ and the weight function w correlating each edge $(i, j) \in E$ with an integer $w(i, j)$.

A *minimal spanning tree T_S* of the graph $G = (V, E, w)$ is defined as a connected graph without loops containing all nodes from V where the sum of weights of the corresponding edges is minimal.

In this paper, we represent a graph $G=(V, E, w)$ in the form of association of the matrices *left*, *right* and *weight* in which each edge $(i, j) \in E$ is matched with the triple $< i, j, w(i, j) >$, where $i \in left$, $j \in right$, $w(i, j) \in weight$.

Note that all logarithms in the paper are taken to the base 2.

5 Representation of the Prim–Dijkstra Algorithm

Let us briefly explain the Prim–Dijkstra algorithm. It constructs a minimal spanning tree of a graph by means of extension of a subtree of T_S. As initial edge of T_S an arbitrary edge of the graph with minimal weight is selected. Let there be k edges in T_S where $k \geq 1$. Then the $(k + 1)$-th edge is selected in the following way. It is necessary to define all edges having only one node which belongs to T_S and among them to select an edge with the minimal weight. The extension process of T_S is finished as soon as the number of edges is equal to $n - 1$.

Before considering the procedure MST1 let us informally explain the meaning of its variables: node1 and node2 of the type **word** and $S, N1$ and $N2$ of the type **slice**. The variables node1 and node2 are used for storing the left and the right nodes of the current edge which is added to the fragment of T_S. The variable S points by '1' the triple positions where the search is realized by means of the procedure MATCH. The variables $N1$ and $N2$ are used for accumulation of triple positions which are potential candidates for adding to the fragment of T_S. Other variables are used for storing intermediate results.

Now consider the procedure MST1.

```
proc MST1(left, right, weight: table; n: integer; var R: slice(left));
label 1; var i, r: integer; node1, node2: word;
S, N1, N2, X, Y, Z: slice(left);
begin CLR(R); CLR(N1); CLR(N2); SET(Z); SET(S);
  for r := 1 to n − 1 do
    begin MIN(weight,Z,X); i:=FND(X); R(i):='1';
      if r = n − 1 then goto 1;
```

node1:=$left(i)$; node2:=$right(i)$; $S(i) :=' 0'$;
/* The i-th edge position is deleted from S. */
  MATCH($left$, S, node1, Z); $N1 := N1 \vee Z$;
  MATCH($left$, S, node2, Z); $N1 := N1 \vee Z$;
  MATCH($right$, S, node1, Z); $N2 := N2 \vee Z$;
  MATCH($right$, S, node2, Z); $N2 := N2 \vee Z$;
/* Positions of potential candidates are accumulated in $N1$ and $N2$. */
  $Y := N1 \wedge N2$; **if** SOME(Y) **then** $S := S \wedge \neg Y$;
/* We delete from S positions of edges which do not
  belong to T_S but both their nodes are in T_S. */
  $Z := N1 \vee N2$; $Z := Z \wedge S$
  end;
1: **end**

To prove the correctness of this procedure we will utilize the following lemma which is verified by contradiction.

Lemma 1. *Let a graph G be represented as a matrix M_G being an association of matrices left, right and weight. Let by means of the procedure MST1(left, right, weight, n, R) a minimal spanning tree be constructed where q is the last added node. Let a graph G' be obtained from the graph G by deleting the node q together with all edges incident to it and respectively $M_{G'}$ be obtained from M_G by deleting all triples containing q. Then MST1 constructs for M_G and $M_{G'}$ minimal spanning trees having the same first $n - 2$ edges.*

Theorem 1. *Let a graph G be represented as an association of matrices left, right and weight. Then the procedure MST1(left, right, weight, n, R) constructs a minimal spanning tree whose edges are indicated by positions of '1' in the slice R.*

Proof. We will prove the theorem by induction on the number of edges in the minimal spanning tree T_S of the graph G.
  Basis is directly checked.
  Step of induction. Assume the claim is true for graphs having no more than k nodes ($k \leq n - 1$). We prove it for graphs with $k + 1$ nodes. In view of inductive assumption by lemma 1 the procedure MST1($left$, $right$, $weight$, $k + 1, R$) selects positions of the first $k - 1$ edges of M_G which belong to T_S. Since $r = k - 1$ then the statement **if** $r = k$ **then goto** 1 is not realized. For finding the k-th edge for T_S we carry out the following three steps:

- define positions of new edges (candidates) which appear after adding the $(k - 1)$-th edge to T_S;
- define positions of edges which should be deleted from further analysis;
- choose the k-th edge for T_S.

At the first step, after executing the statement i:=FND(X), we define the row position in which the $(k-1)$-th edge for T_S is located. To store its nodes we carry out the statements node1:=$left(i)$ and node2:=$right(i)$ and after using the statement $S(i) :=' 0'$ we delete the $(k-1)$-th edge from the further analysis. After executing the procedure MATCH($left$, S, node$j$, Z) row positions of the matrix $left$ coinciding with the node$j$ for $j = 1, 2$ are stored in the slice Z. We add these positions to the slice $N1$ by the statement $N1 := N1 \vee Z$. Similarly by means of the statement $N2 := N2 \vee Z$ we add row positions of the matrix $right$ coinciding with node1 and node2.

At the second step, by analogy with [12] using the statement $Y := N1 \wedge N2$ we define edge positions whose both nodes belong to T_S, but they are not in T_S. For eliminating loops such edges should be deleted from the further analysis by using the statement **if** SOME(Y) **then** $S := S \wedge \neg Y$. Then by means of the statement $Z := N1 \vee N2$ we determine the set of potential candidates. We can prove that for defining the proper candidates it is necessary to delete from Z the positions of edges included in Y and the row position where the $(k-1)$-th edge is located. Therefore we carry out the statement $Z := Z \wedge S$ and then jump to the end of the statement **for** $r := 1$ **to** $k - 1$ **do**.

At the third step, after executing the procedure MIN($weight$, Z, X) we select the candidates with the minimal weight among candidates whose positions are marked by $'1'$ in the slice Z. By the statement i:=FND(X) we define the position of the next (that is, k-th) edge and add it to T_S using the statement $R(i) :=' 1'$. After executing the statement **if** $r = k$ **then goto** 1 we jump to the procedure exit. This completes the proof. □

The following theorem can be immediately proved.

Theorem 2. *Each statement in the procedure MST1(left, right, weight, n, R) is essential.*

For evaluating the complexity of the procedure MST1 at first we estimate the complexity of procedures MATCH and MIN. Let m be a maximal number in the matrix $weight$. In view of [10] we obtain $N(MATCH) \leq 1 + 2\log n$ and $N(MIN) \leq 1 + 3\log m$, where n is the number of graph nodes. Therefore

$$N(\text{MST1}) \leq 8 + 3\log m + (18 + 3\log m + 8\log n)(n - 2). \tag{1}$$

6 Representation of the Baase Algorithm

In [12], an effective program MST for finding the minimal spanning tree of a graph has been written by using the associative computing language ASC. This program is based on the Baase algorithm and utilizes the same graph representation as the procedure MST1. For comparing MST1 and the program MST we have written the STAR procedure MSTP for the Potter's MST program and then compare the corresponding STAR procedures.

At first, we briefly consider the Baase algorithm being a modification of the Prim–Dijkstra one. It separates all graph edges into four states. Edges belong to state 1 (respectively state 4) if they are included in (respectively excluded from) the fragment of the minimal spanning tree. State 3 consists of edges which have not been considered yet. State 2 contains edges which connect a node in state 1 with a node in state 3. The algorithm iteration includes the location of the minimal weight edge in state 2, setting it to state 1 and changing the edge states which take part in this selection. The process is iterated while there are edges having state 2.

Note that the STAR procedure MSTP utilizes all variable names from the Potter's MST program and for the similar purposes. Other variables are used for intermediate results.

Now consider the procedure MSTP.

```
proc MSTP(nodel, noder, weight: table; var state1: slice(nodel));
var graph, reachl, reachr, state2, state3, state4,
X, Y, Z: slice(nodel); node1, node2: word; i: integer;
begin CLR(reachl); CLR(reachr); CLR(state1); CLR(state2);
   CLR(state4); SET(graph); MIN(weight, graph, X);
   i:=FND(X); state2(i):='1'; state3:= ¬state2;
   while SOME(state2) do
   begin MIN(weight, state2, X); i:=FND(X);
      state1(i):='1'; state2(i):='0'; node1:=nodel(i);
      node2:=noder(i); graph:=state2∨state3;
      MATCH(nodel, graph, node1, Z); reachl:=reachl∨Z;
      MATCH(nodel, graph, node2, Z); reachl:=reachl∨Z;
      MATCH(noder, graph, node1, Z); reachr:=reachr∨Z;
      MATCH(noder, graph, node2, Z); reachr:=reachr∨Z;
      X:=reachl∧reachr; graph:=graph∧X;
      if SOME(graph) then
         begin state2:=state2∧¬X; state3:=state3∧¬X;
            state4:=state4∨X
         end;
      Y:=reachl∨reachr; Y := Y∧state3;
      if SOME(Y) then
         begin state2:=state2∨Y; state3:=state3∧¬Y
         end;
   end;
end
```

It is not difficult to verify that

$$N(\text{MSTP}) \leq 10 + 3\log m + (24 + 3\log m + 8\log n)(n - 1). \qquad (2)$$

Correctness of the procedure MSTP follows from the correctness of the Potter's program MST. From comparing the complexity of the procedures MST1 and MSTP we obtain $N(\text{MST1}) < N(\text{MSTP})$.

Remark 2. Due to the implementation of the procedure MST1 on the STAR–machine at any iteration it is sufficient to store the following three sets (instead of four sets in the Baase algorithm): (1) positions of edges which have been included in the minimal spanning tree fragment; (2) positions of *potential candidates* for adding to the fragment which have a node belonging to the matrix *left*; (3) positions of *potential candidates* for adding to the fragment which have a node belonging to the matrix *right*.

7 Modeling of the STAR–machine Run

In parallel with proving the correctness of the procedures considered, we have verified them using our STAR–system on IBM PC. Though, for the time being, we have not at hand an associative parallel computer with bit–serial processing nor an emulator, we can verify vertical processing algorithms using our system. It translates any STAR procedure written in the ASCII code in a corresponding program written in Pascal. In order to obtain the ASCII code of the STAR procedure, we replace all occurrences of the bitwise logical operation symbols $\wedge$, $\vee$, $\neg$ and $\oplus$ by the symbols $*$, $+$, $\sim$ and @, correspondingly. Note that the translation result of any auxiliary procedure is written to the library, whereas any main procedure is translated in the Pascal program and then executed.

The translator is implemented in Turbo–Pascal of version 6.0. For convenient debugging the STAR–system includes an auxiliary module where for any STAR construction there is its equivalent in Pascal. At first, the translator initializes the vocabulary of reserved words. Then, if necessary, it parses the STAR program using the auxiliary module. Note that the STAR–system includes a shell allowing one to edit the STAR program, to create libraries and to execute the program immediately after its translation.

The run time of any STAR procedure is defined as the run time of the resulting Pascal program. For defining the time we use two standard Pascal procedures SetTime and GetTime. Note that before we start the translation, the data type **word** is to be renamed. We have made sure that for the same graph the procedures MST1 and MSTP yield the same minimal spanning tree. By means of the STAR–system we have analyzed a number of different graphs. The experiments corroborate that $t(\text{MST1}) < t(\text{MSTP})$.

8 Conclusions

We have considered the abstract STAR–machine which simulates in detail the associative bit-serial processing. We have analyzed the STAR procedure MST1 of implementing the Prim–Dijkstra algorithm and the procedure MSTP of implementing the Baase algorithm. From comparing these procedures we have obtained that $N(\text{MST1}) < N(\text{MSTP})$.

At last, we have briefly described the STAR–system which allows us to verify the STAR procedures on IBM PC.

References

1. Baase, S.: Computer algorithms: Introduction to design and analysis. Addison-Wesley Reading MA 1978.
2. Dijkstra, E. W.: A note on two problems in connection with graphs. Numerische Math. **1** (1959) 269–271.
3. Fernstrom, C., Kruzela, J., Svensson, B.: LUCAS associative array processor. Design, programming and application studies. Lecture Notes in Computer Science Berlin: Springer-Verlag **216** 1986.
4. Foster, C. C.: Content addressable parallel processors. Van Nostrand Reinhold Company, New York 1976.
5. Grosspietsch, K. E.: Associative processors and memories: A survey. IEEE, Micro (June, 1992) 12–19.
6. Huebler, A., Sykora, O.: Image processing and recognition algorithms for an orthogonal computer. Computers and Artificial Intelligence **6** N2 (1987) 131–149.
7. Lange, R. G.: High level language for associative and parallel computation with Staran. Proc. of Intl. Conf. on Parallel Processing (1976) 170–176.
8. Miklosko, J., Klette, R., Vajtersic, M., Vrto, J.: Fast algorithms and their implementation on specialized parallel computers. Special Topics in Supercomputing North-Holland **5** 1989.
9. Nepomniaschaya, A. Sh.: Language STAR for associative and parallel computation with vertical data processing. Proc. of the Intern. Conf. "Parallel Computing Technologies". Novosibirsk USSR (1991) 258–265.
10. Nepomniaschaya, A. Sh.: Investigation of associative search algorithms in vertical processing systems. Proc. of the Intern. Conf. "Parallel Computing Technologies". Obninsk Russia (1993) 631–641.
11. Otrubova, B., Sykora O.: Orthogonal computer and its application to some graph problems. Parcella'86. Berlin Academie Verlag (1986) 259–266.
12. Potter, J. L.: Associative computing: A programming paradigm for massively parallel computers. Kent State University, Plenum Press, New York and London 1992.
13. Pratt, V. R., Stockmeyer, L.J.: A characterization of the power of vector machines. J. of Computer and System Sciences. **12** N2 (1976) 198–221.
14. Prim, R. C.: Shortest connection networks and some generalizations. Bell System Tech. J. **36**, (1957) 1389–1401.

Petri Net Modelling of Estelle-specified Communication Protocols *

V.A.Nepomniaschy, G.I.Alekseev, A.V.Bystrov,
T.G.Churina, S.P.Mylnikov, E.V.Okunishnikova

Institute of Informatics Systems
Russian Academy of Sciences, Siberian Division
6, Lavrentiev ave., Novosibirsk 630090, Russia
e-mail: vnep@isi.itfs.nsk.su

Abstract. In order to use net models for communication protocol verification, a method intended for automatic translation of Estelle protocol specifications in coloured Petri nets is proposed. A tool for simulation and analysis of the net models is outlined. For explanation of the method the Stenning protocol is used.

1 Introduction

Verification and specification of communication protocols are one of the fast-growing scope of formal methods and techniques in computer science. Despite of some progress, the acceptable solution of the protocol verification problem is yet to be achieved [7, 10].

Two principal approaches are used in practical applications. The first one consists in the use of such formal description techniques as Estelle, SDL, LOTOS, ISO international standards. The advantage of Estelle [4] is its expressive power for describing communication protocols and services, but the power increases difficulties of protocol analysis and verification. Nevertheless, some useful tools have been developed for Estelle [2, 5, 11].

The second approach consists in modelling of protocols by finite state machines, Petri nets or their modifications, and then in verifying these models. Petri net model can be naturally extended by temporal constraints. Automatic translation of time Petri net in Estelle is described in [3]. Among the models coloured Petri nets (CPN) [8] could be distinguished because of enlarged expressive power.

Although the models are more useful for analysis and verification, their expressive power is essentially decreased with respect to formal description techniques mentioned above. The modelling is mostly carried out by hand. As notable exception the method in [11] uses exhaustive simulation to obtain finite

* This work is supported by Russian Basic Research Fund (Project 93-01-00986) and Intern. Association for the Promotion of Cooperation with Scientists from the Independent States of the Former Soviet Union (INTAS) under contract 1010-CT93-0048.

state models. A gap between protocol specification and verification methods is noticed in [10].

A problem of combining the advantages of the approaches is of considerable importance. The paper [9] examined the problem for LOTOS and extended Petri nets using a new LOTOS semantics related to net one.

An approach to the problem is proposed in our paper. It consists of a protocol-oriented method for translation of Estelle specifications in CPN, and a tool for simulation and analysis of the net models. The rest of the paper contains five sections. In Section 2 such basic notions as protocols, Estelle constructions and CPN are shortly reminded. In Section 3 the translation method is explained with the help of Stenning protocol [13]. In Section 4 the tool and an experiment with the protocol model are shortly described. In conclusion perspectives of the approach are considered. Appendix contains Estelle specification of the protocol.

2 Basic Notions

Let us remind basic notions of the protocol theory, specification language Estelle and coloured Petri nets.

2.1 Protocols

Usually *sender* and *receiver* operate in a protocol. They communicate over a medium which may lose, duplicate or reorder messages. We illustrate our method by the Stenning protocol [13] as an example of the sliding window protocol. This protocol supports unidirectional flow of data with a positive handshake on each transfer and uses an acknowledgement window for flow control (see Fig.1).

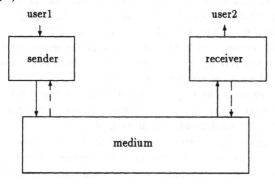

Fig. 1. General protocol diagram

Sender is a producer of data blocks, and *receiver* is a consumer of data blocks. We want data blocks to be consumed in the same order as they were produced and within a finite time of being produced. We consider a sliding window protocol that uses modulo-N sequence numbers to achieve this objective. Let us review the basic features found in all sliding window protocols.

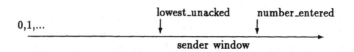

Fig. 2. Sender processing diagram

At any time at *sender* (see Fig.2), the data blocks from 0 to *lowest_unacked* − 1 have been sent and acknowledged, while data blocks from *lowest_unacked* to *number_entered* − 1 are unacknowledged. The *sender* maintains a window containing the sequence numbers from *lowest_unacked* to (*lowest_unacked* + *number_entered* − 1) *mod N* included, i.e. the numbers of the messages transmitted and not acknowledged. Its size is limited by a value TWS (Transmitter Window Size), $TWS \leq N$.

At any time at *receiver*, data blocks from 0 to *next_required* − 1 have been received and consumed in a sequence, while data blocks from *next_required* to *next_required..next_required* + *RWS* − 1 may have been received (perhaps out of sequence) and are temporarily buffered. The numbers from *next_required* to *next_required* + *RWS* − 1 constitute the *receiver window*; RWS (Receiver Window Size) is its constant size.

Sender sends *n*-th datum in the form *n mod N*. We use $\bar{n}$ to denote *n mod N* for any integer value *n*. Receiver receives a data block $\bar{n}$. If there is a number *i* in the receiver window such that $\bar{i} = \bar{n}$, then the received data block is interpreted as being produced *i*-th block. Receiver sends acknowledgment messages containing $\bar{n}$, where *n* is a current value of *next_required*.

If the received message lies within the maximum receiver window (defined by *next_required* and *RWS*) then all the messages from *next_required* up to the first unreceived message are delivered to the user.

When Sender receives the sequence number $\bar{n}$, and there exists a number *i* in the range *lowest_unacked* + 1 to *number_entered* such that $\bar{i} = \bar{n}$, $\bar{n}$ is interpreted as an acknowledgment to *i*-th data block.

When a message is sent, a timer is started for that message; if a time-out occurs, then the timers for all the messages transmitted after the time-outed one are cancelled. All these time-outed messages are retransmitted in the order of their transmission and have timers started for them.

2.2 The Estelle Language

A distributed system specified in Estelle is composed of several communicating components. Each component is specified in Estelle by a *module definition*.

There may be more than one component in a system defined (textually) by the same module definition - *module instances.*

In Estelle a particular care is taken to specify the communication interface of a module. Such an interface is defined using *interaction points* and *channels.*

Each module has a number of input/output access points called *interaction points.* There are two categories of interaction points: *external* and *internal.* The interaction points refer to channels in a specific way.

Module instances may exchange messages. A module instance can send an interaction to another module through a communication link between their two interaction points. A message sent by the module instance at its interaction point is appended to an *unbounded* FIFO queue associated with this interaction point. The FIFO queue either exclusively belongs to the single interaction point (so called *individual queue*) or it is shared with some other interaction points of module (so called *common queue*).

A module may have one of the following class attributes: *systemprocess, systemactivity, process* or *activity.* The modules attributed by *systemprocess* or *systemactivity* are called *system* modules.

Estelle provides means to create instances of child modules defined within the module definition. Within a specified system, a fixed number of *subsystems* is distinguished. Each system is a subtree of modules' instances rooted in a system modules' instance.

Some modules of an Estelle specification may dynamically create, release children instance and change the structure of links between them. Note that a number of instances of the same module may change *dynamically* since they may be created and destroyed.

The internal dynamic behavior of an Estelle module is characterized in terms of a state transition system whose *control states* are defined by enumeration of their names, the actions of a module instance is defined by a set of transitions. To define transitions' actions the Pascal compound statements are used. The well known model of a finite state automaton is a particular case of the state transition system. Each transition declaration is composed of two parts: a transition condition and transition action. The *transition condition* is composed of one or more clauses of the following categories: *from*-clause (*from* $a_1, ..., a_n$, where a_i is a control state); *when*-clause (*when* p.m, where p is an interaction point and m is a message); *provided*-clause (*provided B*, where B is a boolean expression); *priority*-clause (*priority n*, where n is a non-negative constant); *delay*-clause (*delay* (e_1, e_2), where e_1, e_2 are non-negative integer expressions). Transitions with a *when*-clause in their condition are called *input transitions.* The transition action is composed of a *to*-clause (*to a*, where a is a control state identifier) and a transition block, i.e. a sequence of Pascal statements.

The main restrictions for Estelle in our approach are the absence of dynamic structuring features such as activities and creation of processes. Also files and pointers are not used.

Let us illustrate the Estelle constructions by the module *receiver* of well-known Stenning protocol (its text can be found in Appendix).

Receiver is modelled by two states: *wait, deliver*. From the initialization part we see that the module begins in its *wait* control state. The definition of the *receiver* has declarations of two interaction points *mr* and *rm*. In the first case, the set of messages which can be received from *medium* to *mr* contains all messages specified for role R1 in the channel definition, and the set of messages which can be sent by *rm* to *medium* contains all message specified for role R2.

Receiver maintains a window containing sequence numbers with "lowest" edge defined by an integer *next_required* and *size* limited by a value RWS. The integer *next_required* is the sequence number following (modulo N) the sequence number of the message the most recently acknowledged. The function defining whether the message lies within the receiver window is implemented in the module.

The transition part of the *reception* body consists of three transitions. The first transition is the *input* transition, the third transition is the *output* one. If a *message(i)* message arrives to the interaction point *mr* and the module is in the *wait* state, then the first transition (* *message received* *) of the module is firing. If the *message(i)* (module N) belongs to the receiver window and this message has not been received yet, then the tag of receiving is set and the module change into *deliver* state. If the *message(i)* does not belong to the receiver window or has been already received, then the module sénd requirement on a message following the most recently acknowledged message.

The second transition (* *deliver to the user* *) fires in the *deliver* state. If a message is received which lies within the maximum receiver window, then all the messages from *next_required* up to the first unreceived message are delivered to the user.

The third transition fires in the *deliver* state too. An acknowledgement giving the last delivered sequence number is sent to the interaction point *rm*.

The protocol initialization part creates four module instances referenced by the module variables *s, r, s_to_r, r_to_s*. The initialization also establishes bindings between appropriate interaction points of the four newly created module instances. Two bound interaction points *sm, min* of two modules *s, s_to_r* are connected. Similarly the points *ms, mout* are connected. So, a message which can be sent via *sm* can be received via *min*, i.e. the message can go out from *sender* to *medium*. And a message sent via *mout* arrives to the *ms*. Similarly, the communication link can be created between *medium* and *receiver*. A message sent through the interaction point *rm* that is an end-point of a communication link, directly arrives at the other end-point *min* of this link and is always accepted by the receiving module *medium*. A message sent via *mout* can be received via *ms*.

2.3 Coloured Petri Nets

A coloured Petri net model is an extension of the basic Petri net model. It consists of three different parts: *the net structure, the declarations* and *the net inscriptions.*

The net structure is a directed graph with two kinds of nodes, *places* and *transitions*, interconnected by *arcs* in such a way that each arc connects two different kinds of nodes. Places and their *tokens* represent states, while transitions represent state changes. An arc represents an input or output relationship between a place and transition.

The declarations contain definitions of *colour sets* and declarations of variables which can be bound by colours. The declarations can also contain definitions of new operations and functions which can be applied to the colours. Moreover, a colour set definition often implicitly introduces operations and functions which can be applied to its members.

Each *net inscription* is attached to a place, a transition or an arc. In the CP-net each place has three different kinds of inscriptions: *name, colour set* and *initialization expression*. *The colour set* determines the type of tokens which may reside on that place. *The initialization expression* must evaluate to a multiset over the corresponding colour set which determines *the initial marking* of the place. Transitions have two kinds of inscriptions: *names* and *guards*. *The guard* of a transition is a boolean expression which must be fulfilled before a transition can occur. Arcs have one kind of inscriptions: *arc expressions*. They may contain variables, constants, functions and operations which are defined in the declarations. When the variables of an arc expression are bound (i.e. replaced by colours), the arc expression must evaluate to a colour which belongs to the colour set attached to the place of the arc.

Transitions are active components of the CPN's. If transition is *enabled*, it may occur. Before a transition may occur all the variables of the guard of the transition and the arc expressions on its surrounding arcs have to be bound to the colours of the corresponding types. The transition is *enabled* for this binding if the guard evaluates to true and each of the input places contains at least the tokens to which the corresponding arc expression evaluates. *The occurrence* of the transition removes the tokens from its input places and adds tokens to its output places. The number of removed/added tokens and the colours of these tokens are determined by the value of the arc expressions evaluated with respect to the binding.

3 Translation of Estelle Specifications in CP-nets

As it has been mentioned above, we consider only specifications describing systems with structure which does not change over lifetime. Moreover, we assume here that there exists exactly one level in the hierarchy of modules and leave out of consideration that some transitions may have priority or be delayed. In the future we are going to consider priority and time aspects too.

Translation of an Estelle specification in CP-net is made in several steps. The net is constructed by stepwise refinement. At each step some transitions and their surrounding arcs of the net which has been built at the previous steps are replaced by more complex CP-nets. These CP-nets give a more detailed description of the activity represented by the substituted transition.

At the first step, a CP-net is built which represents the general structure of the system described by an Estelle specification and contains one transition for each module instance. Each couple of interaction points connected by a channel is represented in this net either by one place, if messages may be sent through this channel in a single direction, or by two places, if there exists a bidirectional message interchange. The arcs connect each of these places with the transitions corresponding to the module interaction points of which determine these places. The direction of the arcs is the same as that of the messages interchanged through these interaction points. The colour sets of these places are determined by the messages which may be received and sent through the interaction points.

At the second step, each transition corresponding to a module instance is replaced by a CP-net which represents the inner structure of the module. Such the net contains one place for each variable, one place for each array and one transition for each Estelle-transition of the specification. In order to distinguish the transitions of the CP-net and transitions of the Estelle specification we will call them N- and E-transitions, respectively. The colour set of a place which represents a variable is equal to a type of the variable. The colour set of a place representing an array is a set of pairs which consist of an index and value of corresponding array element. The number of tokens at such a place is equal to the dimension of the array. If a module has a set of local states, then in the net there is a place *State* with the local state set defining a colour set. Otherwise in the net there is a place *Manager*. The initial marking of all the places (except *Manager*) is determined from the initialization part in the module body definition. *Manager* contains a token carrying no information ("uncoloured" token).

The interconnection of places and transitions is determined as follows. If some variable or array is referred in an E-transition, then the corresponding place is the input and output place for the corresponding N-transition. If some E-transition is an *input* transition, then there is an arc from a place which represents the interaction point referred in when-clause of the E-transition to the N-transition associated with this E-transition. If the E-transition is an *output* transition, then there is an arc from the corresponding N-transition to a place associated with the interaction point. If there exists the place *State*, then it is the input and output place for all the transitions of the CP-net, otherwise the place *Manager* is the input and output place for all the transitions.

The execution of some E-transitions may be modelled by a single N-transition. At the next step for such E-transitions the guards of the corresponding N-transitions and the expressions on their surrounding arcs are determined. The guard is determined from *when-*, *from-* and *provided-*clauses, while *to-*clause and a transition block (a sequence of Pascal statements) determine the arc expressions. The refinement process is completed.

If an E-transition contains some *provided-*clauses, loops or calls of procedures and functions, the process of refinement is continued. The procedure/function definition is translated into the net by the same way. Note that its parameters are translated into places. The resulted net is substituted for the call operator. In this net the names of places (formal parameters) are replaced by names of actual parameters specified in the call operator. A transition may contains some control statements such as loops, *any* -statements, and such data structures as arrays and queues. The library of the CP-nets is used for modelling these language constructions.

Let us illustrate the translation of an Estelle specification of Stenning protocol (see *Appendix*) in CP-net. The most of the net inscriptions will be omitted, since we are focussing more on the net structure than on the details of colour sets. For more transparency we will use some identifiers of the Estelle specification as names of places and transitions of the CP-net.

Fig. 3 gives a CP-net which represents the structure of the Stenning specification. It follows from the initialization part of this specification that the net contains four transitions: the transitions *s* and *r* which correspond to the instances of the modules *sender* and *receiver*, respectively, and the transitions *s_to_r* and *r_to_s* which represent the instances of the *medium* module. For each statement which connects two interaction points the corresponding place is constructed, for example: the statement "connect r.mr to s_to_r.mout;" gives the place *mout_to_mr*. This place is an input place for the transition *r* since the interaction point *mr* belongs to the module *receiver*, and output place for the transition *s_to_r* since the interaction point *mout* belongs to the instance *s_to_r* of the *medium* module.

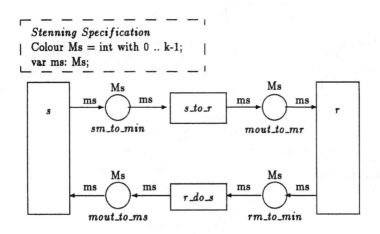

Fig. 3. Net structure of Stenning specification

Let us give more details for the net which models *receiver*. For more clearness, we represent it as a separate net in Fig. 4. This net has three transitions: *trans1*, *trans2* and *trans3*.

The place *next_required* corresponds to the variable of the same name and has the colour set *Inter*. An array is represented by the place *received* which is both input and output place of all transitions in the net.

Initially the place *next_required* contains the token with the value 0. The place *received* contains N tokens which initially have the values $(i, false)$. Since *receiver* has the set of local states, there is a place *State* in the net which is also input and output place for all its transitions. The token residing on *State* may have the colour *wait* or *deliver* (initially *wait*). Moreover, the net contains the places *mout_to_mr* and *rm_to_min*. Since the first transition of *receiver* is both input and output, the place *mout_to_mr* is an input and the place *rm_to_min* is an output for the transition *trans1*. The place *rm_to_min* is also an output for the transition *trans3* which corresponds to the output transition of *receiver*.

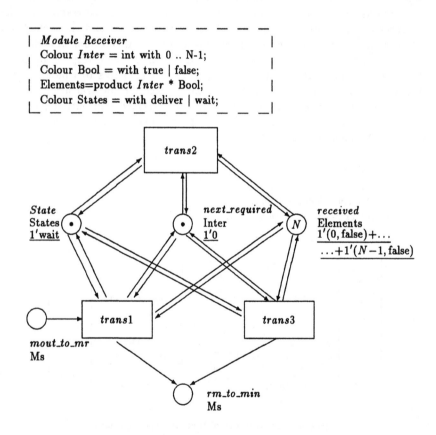

Fig. 4. Net structure of *receiver*

The second and third transitions of *receiver* may be modelled by corresponding transitions of CP-net. We consider the translation of the second transition *trans2* to demonstrate the construction of guards and arc expressions.

Fig. 5 shows the net for the second transition of *receiver*. The enabling condition of its occurrence is such that:

- the module is in the *deliver* state (the place *State* contains the *deliver*-token);
- the message with the number *i* has been received, where *i* is the value of the token at the place *next_required*. This means that there is $(i, true)$-token at the place *received*.

If these conditions are satisfied, *trans2* may occur.

The occurrence removes:

- *deliver*-token from *State* and adds a token with the same value to it;
- *i*-token from *next_required* and adds a token with the value $(i + 1) mod N$ to it;
- $(i, true)$-token from *received* and adds $(i, false)$-token to it.

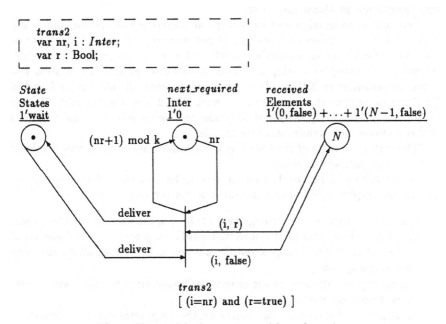

trans2
[(i=nr) and (r=true)]

Fig. 5. Net model of *trans2* transition of *receiver*

Note that the translation of the first transition of *receiver* is rather difficult since it contains the call of the function and two provided-clauses.

This approach has been applied to a number of protocols including Stenning protocol [13].

Let us suppose Estelle-module to contain:

- M variables including *var* local variables, *arr* arrays, *ip* interaction points, *par* parameters;
- N statements including k_1 *for* cycles, k_2 *while* cycles, k_3 *repeat* cycles, k_4 *if* statements;
- D procedure and function definitions;
- C call statements of procedure and function.

Then the resulting net has at most $TN = N*F+12*k*F$ transitions and $PM = att*F+13*k*F+M*F$ places, where $F = C*D+1$, $k = max(k_1, k_2, k_3, k_4)$, $att = var + arr + par + 4*ip + 1$. For example for *receiver* module of Stenning protocol (see *Appendix*) $TN = 50$, $PM = 68$. But, in fact, the resulting net has 11 transitions and 19 places.

4 A Petri Net Tool

Over the past several years a number of Petri net tools have been appeared [6]. These tools differ in types of net models, analysis and simulation methods, implementation platform and so on.

Our aim is to develop and implement an experimental system supporting construction, simulation and analysis of net models of communication protocols. The orientation on protocols restricts a class of corresponding net models. Therefore we intend to develop a more efficient Petri net tool. The system was being implemented in MS-Windows environment, some details can be found in [1]. The tool provide the opportunity to work with different net models. We can create and modify nets, analyze their properties, perform their transformations and reductions and, finally, simulate models.

The system consists of the following main components: interactive graphical editor, simulator, and analyser.

Editor allows hierarchical coloured nets to be created and modified in an interactive graphic mode. The main functions of the editor are:

- dynamic creation and of arrangement of the graphic windows on the screen;
- creation and deletion of the objects: transitions, places or arcs (deletion of a place or transition brings about the automatic deletion of all its incoming and outgoing arcs).
- setting and modification of the object attributes: place marking, arc expressions, transition names, etc.;
- movement and alignment of objects on the page retaining the connection between transitions and places;
- selection of a group of objects to perform the same operations as for a single object;
- creation or modification of the net hierarchy;
- saving or loading of a net as a binary file or a plain text file.

The user can also fix some class of net models (e.g. finite automata, marked graphs, free-choice nets). During the construction and modification of the net the editor performs the check-up of the syntax of the resulting model, thus erroneous modifications will be rejected.

Simulator is integrated with the editor and enables immediate simulation of the constructed net. The fired transitions are highlighted on the screen and occurrence of the simulation step can be animated. The operating mode of the simulator can be both manual (stepwise) and automatic. The manual simulation mode allows a user to see the current state of the model at each step and, if desired, to select explicitly the transition for firing. This selection in automatic mode is random.

The simulator also provides special tools for model debugging: breakpoints and simulation tracing.

Breakpoint allows a user to stop automatic simulation whenever any pre-defined condition is satisfied. These conditions can be defined by the formula which contains variables, arithmetic and logical operations and built-in functions. Built-in functions reflect the current state of a model and some of its auxiliary characteristics, such as a number of tokens added to the place during the simulation, number of tokens extracted from the place, number of firings of the transition, etc.

Simulation tracing gives to a net designer the opportunities to reproduce any stages of simulation, to check the net node states, to change them and to continue the simulation. The trace can be saved and used later for the simulation repetition or further analysis.

The trace feature allows a user:

- to repeat the simulation as a whole or partly, forwards or backwards, using the breakpoints or step-by-step, with optional animation;
- to gather the net simulation statistics.

Analyser was developed and implemented as a separate system module to perform automatic analysis of some properties of net models. We can get structural information about the model, place and transition invariants and build a coverability and reachability graph to analyze behavioral properties.

As an example of application of the tool we consider its use for testing of Stenning protocol. Estelle specification of the protocol was transformed to a net model (CP-net with restrictions mentioned in section 2.3). For the correct net model of Stenning protocol (see Fig.5) the following assumption have to be valid: $E(t_2) \bmod N = nr$, where $E(t_2)$ is the number of firings of *trans2* transition in the net. This condition was used as a break condition for net simulation. The net model of an incorrect protocol have been simulated. The incorrectness consists in absence of incrementation of the number of transmitted messages. The statement $next_r equired := next_r equired \bmod N$ was used instead $(*1*)$ of *trans2* of the *receiver* module. Then, the occurrence of *trans2* removes i-token from *next_required* place and adds a token with the same value to it. So, the message was erroneously retransmited. The simulation demonstrated that the given assumption becomes not valid.

5 Conclusion

The paper represents a new method of constructing CPN models for protocols specified in Estelle. The main features of the tool for net model simulation and analysis are also outlined. This method can be automated and it allows us to develop an useful tool for protocol verification. For increasing efficiency of the tool we intend to use the hierarchical structure of CPN and restrictions of the problem domain. In future the approach will be extended on temporal constraints. To verify properties expressed in a temporal logic, protocols could be annotated like in [12] and a model-checking method could be used.

References

1. Alekseev, G.I. et al.: Petri-net based environment for the specification, analysis and simulation of concurrent systems. In: Specification, verification and net models of concurrent systems. Novosibirsk, 1994, 116-127.
2. Algayres, B. et al.: VESAR: a progmatic approach to formal specification and verification. Computer Networks 25 (1993) 779-790.
3. Alkhechi, A.B., Budkowski, S.: Automatic translation of time Petri nets into Estelle description. In: Proc. Intern. Conf. on Formal Description Techniques III. North-Holland 1991, 369-376.
4. Budkowski, S., Dembinski, P.: An introduction to Estelle: a specification language for distributed systems. Computer Networks 14 (1988) 3-23.
5. Courtiat, J.P., de Saqui-Sannes, P.: ESTIM: an integrated environment for the simulation and verification of OSI protocols specified in Estelle. Computer Networks 25 (1992) 83-98.
6. Feldbrugge, F.: Petri net tool pvervier 1992. Lecture Notes in Computer Science 674 (1993) 169-209.
7. Holzmann, G.J.: Design and validation of computer protocols. 1991.
8. Jensen, K.: An introduction to the theoretical aspects of coloured Petri nets. Lecture Notes in Computer Science 803 (1994) 230-272.
9. Marchena, S., Leon, G.: Transformation from LOTOS specs to Galileo nets. In: Intern.Conf. on Formal Description Techniques I. North-Holland 1989, 217-230.
10. Miller, R.E.: Protocol verification: the first ten years, the next ten years; some personal observations. Proc. IFIP Intern. Symposium on Protocol Specification, Testing and Verification X. North-Holland 1990, 199-225.
11. Richier, J.L., Rodriguz, C., Sifakis, J., Voiron, J.: Verification in Xesar of the sliding window protocol. In : Proc. IFIP Inter. Symposium on Protocol Specification, Testing and Verification VII. North-Holland 1987, 235-248.
12. Shankar, A.U., Lam, S.S.: A stepwise refinement heuristic for protocol construction. ACM Transactions on Programming Languages and Systems 14 (1992) 417-461.
13. Stenning, N.V.: A data transfer protocol. Computer Networks 1 (1976) 99-110.

Appendix

Estelle specification of Stenning Protocol

```
_specification stenning;
_const
   N = 3;               (* an numbers are modulo N *)
   RWS = 1;             (* Receiver Window Size *)
   TOE = 1;             (* Transmit Time Out *)
_type inter = 0 .. N-1;
_channel data(R1, R2);
   _by R1, R2: message(val: inter);
_module sender  _process ... _end;

_module receiver  _process;
   _ip mr : data(R1) _individual queue;
       rm : data(R2) _individual queue;
   _body reception _for receiver;
(* test if i is in the interval base <= i < base + width(mod N) *)
   _function in_window (i, base, width: integer): boolean;
       _begin
           _if (base + width) <= N _then
               in_window:= (base <= i) _and (i < base + width)
                                    _else
               in_window:= (base <= i) _or (i < base + width - N)
       _end;
   _state: (wait, deliver);
   _var
     next_required: inter;   (* first message not received *)
     received: _packed _array [inter] _of _boolean;
   _initialize _to wait
   _var i: _integer;
   _begin
     _for i:= 0 _to N-1  _do received[i]:= false;
     next_required:= 0;
   _end;

_trans  (* trans1  *    message received *)
     _from wait _when mr.message(i)
       _provided in_window(i, next_required, RWS) _and _not received[i]
     _to deliver
               _begin  received[i]:= true; _end;
     _provided _otherwise   (* the message is out of sequence *)
     _to wait
       _begin output rm.message ((next_required - 1 + N) mod N) _end;
```

```
_trans { : mess_out }   (* trans2   *   deliver to the user*)
    _from deliver _provided received[next_required]  _to deliver
      _begin
        received[next_required]:= false;
        next_required:= (next_required +1) mod N;  (* 1 *)
      _end;
_trans   (* trans3   *   end of deliver, send an acknowledge*)
    _from deliver _provided _not received[next_required] _to wait
      _begin
        _output rm.message((next_required - 1 + N) mod N)
      _end;
_end;

_module medium _process .... _end;
_var s : sender;
    r : receiver;
    s_to_r, r_to_s : medium;
_initialize _begin
    _init s _with ....;
    _init r _with reception;
    _init s_to_r _with ...;
    _init r_to_s _with ...;
    _connect s.sm _to s_to_r.min;
    _connect s.ms _to r_to_s.mout;
    _connect r.rm _to r_to_s.min;
    _connect r.mr _to s_to_r.mout;
_end;
_end.
```

Dynamic Scheduling of Parallel Applications

Bettina Schnor

TU Braunschweig, Germany
Bültenweg 74/75, 38106 Braunschweig
schnor@ibr.cs.tu-bs.de

Abstract. This paper is concerned with dynamic strategies for group scheduling. We present preemptive and non preemptive strategies which are suitable for scheduling parallel applications on large workstation-clusters and investigate their performance behavior.

1 Introduction

A parallel application consists of a group of communicating processes which have to be assigned to the processors of the given parallel system. The concept of group scheduling is to schedule all processes of a group in parallel. Other common terms for group scheduling are gang scheduling [2] and co-scheduling [7].

A lot of papers are concerned with deterministic group scheduling algorithms which suppose for each process group a given execution time and a given process group size (see for example [1], [8]). This paper discusses dynamic strategies for group scheduling, i.e., only the parallel degree of an application is known, but nothing is known about its execution time in advance.

A well-known example of a dynamic scheduling strategy is the matrix algorithm [7] which is a preemptive algorithm. A simulation study in [4] for the Hypercube [10] shows that a simple non preemptive strategy which mapps only onto buddy subcubes, but orders arriving process groups in a runqueue due to their size, performs better than more sophisticated allocation strategies. Further examples and performance investigations of dynamic group scheduling on 2-dimensional grid architectures like the Intel Paragon are given in [6] and in [9] where a timesharing policy is tested.

A workstation-cluster may also be considered as a parallel computer. A number of recent research activities have tried to exploit the computing power of such environments ([11],[12]). All these systems lack failure transparency and support for group scheduling. We study dynamic group scheduling strategies which are suitable for workstation-clusters.

In a workstation-cluster, all processors are connected by a broadcast medium and any free processors are suitable for mapping. Hence we have a simpler mapping problem compared to hypercubes and grids, where we have to find free subcubes resp. rectangles.

In the next section we give a short overview over the SPAWN system which supports parallel applications on workstation-clusters. Algorithms of the scheduler component of SPAWN are presented in section 3. The aspects of modelling an adequate workload are given in section 4. Section 5 presents the results of our simulations. The paper finishs with conclusions and further remarks.

2 Support for Parallel Applications on Workstation– Cluster (SPAWN)

Our aim is to develop a system for scheduling parallel applications on workstation-cluster (SPAWN) on top of UNIX [1]. SPAWN supports process migration to improve fault tolerance, by evacuating hosts prior to regular shutdown, or through checkpointing. One of our interests is to decide whether migration is also a useful technique for performance improvement.

To make migration transparent we use a modified system library similar to the Condor approach [13]. Further, we build a system wide virtual name space for process identifiers, transport addresses, and file names. The applications work with objects in a common, location independent name space.

The freeze and restart of a process requires an expensive overhead. Condor writes the (large) core dump and executable files via NFS which is the main performance killer. We avoid this by exploiting the installer's knowledge about the network topology. On diskless clients, the dispatcher is configured to provide the freeze procedure with a TCP address instead of a name for the new executable file, and then the address space contents are saved through a TCP connection instead of a regular file. The dispatcher process on the file server accepts incoming checkpoint data and writes onto the local disk. With a bit of socket buffer tuning we were able to obtain transfer rates up to 6Mbit/s across a lightly loaded Ethernet. More details are given in [14].

To decide which group scheduling strategy will be best for our system we implemented different strategies, preemptive and non preemptive, and have tested them by simulation.

3 Dynamic Group Scheduling Algorithms on Workstation–Cluster

We consider a non–preemptive algorithm LS, a preemptive algorithm LS_TS, and its modification LS_TS_MIG which uses process group migration. For comparison we also implemented a simple FIFO algorithm. All algorithms are central, i.e., there is only one central runqueue.

LS stands for "Largest Size" which means that arriving process groups are ordered due to their size. If a process group terminates the scheduler looks for the first process group in the runqueue which will fit on the free processors. We use priorities to save jobs from starvation. Arriving process groups get priority 0. This priority is increased each time a group is not assigned during a scheduling round. The order of the LS-runqueue is given by

---

[1] UNIX is trademark of AT&T

$$P_1 > P_2 :\Longleftrightarrow (prio\,(P_1) > prio\,(P_2)$$
$$\text{or}\quad (prio\,(P_1) = prio\,(P_2)\ \text{and}\ size\,(P_1) > size\,(P_2)).$$

If the priority of a process group reaches the value *maxprio* the process group moves to a FIFO-runqueue which is considered before the LS-queue each time the scheduler gets active. The groups in the *maxprio*-runqueue have to be assigned in FIFO order. Hence, if the next job in the *maxprio*-queue is bigger than the number of idle processors these processors will be kept idle until more processors get free and the waiting process group can be assigned. The value of the parameter *maxprio* has big influence on the behavior of the LS-algorithm which we will see in the next section.

Further, we tested a preemptive algorithm called LS_TS which uses time slices. Arriving groups are ordered in the LS-runqueue due to their priority and their size. Since all processors are free at the beginning of a time slice, the biggest high-priority group always fits and no group can starve. If the size of the first process group is less than the numbers of processors in the system, there are still processors free. Now the scheduler will assign the next process group which fits. Different from the matrix algorithm we don't use fix packed time slots. If a group terminates and half of the time slice is left we use an alternate selection. In this case the scheduler assigns the next group in the LS-runqueue which fits. Introducing time slices also favours groups with shorter runtime. Of course, for this algorithm the size of the time slice is the important parameter and its optimal value depends on the expected runtime of the applications.

LS_TS is based on processor preference which means that a process group is assigned to the same processors each scheduling time. Since the SPAWN system supports migration of process groups, we investigate a algorithm LS_TS_MIG which migrates a process group when its first placement is already assigned and there are still enough processors free. We introduce a migration constant which gives an estimation for the migration overhead, i.e., the maximal time needed for migration. In our simulation, a process group gets in case of migration only time slice – migration constant time units. By varying the migration constant, we are able to investigate how much time we can afford for migration to be still better than LS_TS. The parameters of the LS_TS_MIG-algorithm are the size of the time slice and the migration constant.

4 Workload

For the interpretation of a simulation study, two aspects are important: First, the simulation software has to be correct, and second, the input workload should be realistic.

Random arrival processes are modeled by a Poisson process. Little is known about realistic distributions of process group sizes and execution times. Therefore, the investigation of different workloads by varying the distributions (exponential or hyperexponential for example) is recommended.

To take into account that there might be a correlation between the parallel degree of the applications and its execution time, earlier studies ([4],[5]) propose to consider correlated and uncorrelated workloads based on Gustafson's Fixed–Time– resp. Fixed–Load–Model [3]. Gustafson proposes to distinguish two different classes of parallel applications. Fixed–Time–applications have to be solved in restricted time. An example are weather forecasts. Here the problem is sized up by taking the finest grid of measure points which can be solved within the given time and with given parallel degree. Hence, execution time and parallel degree of the application are independent. This motivates uncorrelated workload.

Correlated workload appears when a problem has fixed size and its execution time depends on the parallel degree of the implementation. In the optimal case there will be a speed up of k when the application runs on k processors. Hence, given a random execution time x for the sequential problem the parallel execution time on k processors is set to $\frac{x}{k}$.

For our simulations we have chosen the uncorrelated workload model where the user submits his parallel application to the system and specifies its fixed parallel degree.

5 Simulation Results

Our main objective is to determine the benefits and limitations of the different algorithms as a function of system load. The system load is given by

$$\rho = \frac{\lambda \cdot size}{\mu \cdot n},$$

where λ is the mean arrival rate (Poisson process), μ is the expected execution rate (exponentially distributed), $n = 100$ is the number of processors, and $size$ is the expected process group size (exponentially or uniform distributed).

The performance measure of interest is the mean waiting time. The following figures give the mean waiting time as a function of the system load. If not stated otherwise $\mu^{-1} = 50$, and $size = 20$ (both exponentially distributed). The parameter $maxprio$ is set to 10, and the size of the time slice is 50 time units. We have observed similar results for different distributions of the group size and execution times.

Figure 1 shows the performance of the algorithms compared with FIFO under low system load. All three LS-algorithms show better performance than FIFO. Up to $\rho = 0.5$ LS behaves as good as LS_TS_MIG, but for bigger ρ the mean waiting time of LS starts to increase rapidly.

Since the time slice is equal to the mean execution time, most process groups terminate within one time slice and LS_TS_MIG has less benefits. To investigate the influence of the time slice size, we variied this parameter (see Fig. 2, and 3). The influence on LS_TS_MIG is light for low load and only for system load equal to 0.9 the smaller time slice is more efficient. Figure 3 shows the performance of LS_TS_MIG without alternate selection. In this case the mean waiting times

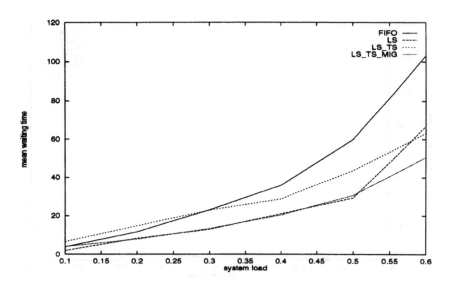

Fig. 1. Performance under low system load.

increase rapidly and differ much. Hence, alternate selection is a very strong method to balance the influence of a wrong chosen time slice size.

Figure 4 shows results for LS_TS_MIG for different values of the migration constant. For all values $k = 0, 1, 3, 5$ of the migration constant the LS_TS_MIG algorithms behave better than LS_TS. Our experiences with the SPAWN system

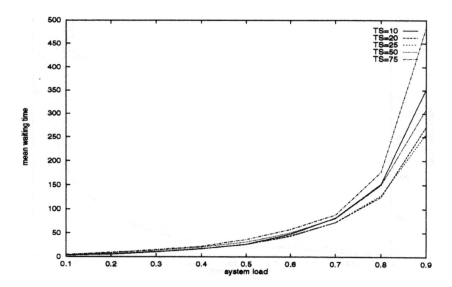

Fig. 2. Varying time slice size for LS_TS_MIG.

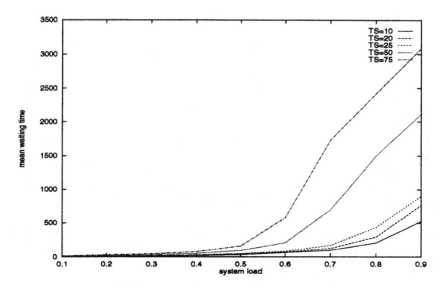

Fig. 3. Varying time slice size for LS_TS_MIG without alternate selection.

show that the migration costs will be in the order of some minutes depending on the group size. Expecting runtimes of some hours for the parallel applications, the migration constant will be less than 1 in our model. In this case LS_TS_MIG will behave nearly like the optimal LS_TS_MIG. It is interesting that even for

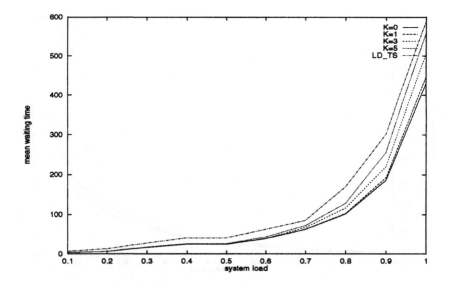

Fig. 4. Varying the migration constant.

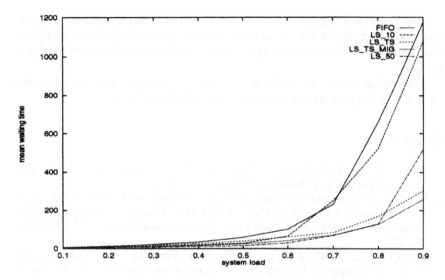

Fig. 5. Performance under high system load.

$\rho = 0.9$ only in 7 % of all assignments there occurs migration, but the achieved improvement by LS_TS_MIG is about 30 %.

Figure 5 shows the behavior of the algorithms under high system load. Here, the time slice is 25 time units. The parameter *maxprio* of LS determines how quick the LS algorithm changes to FIFO. Figure 5 shows simulation runs with *maxprio* 10 and 50. For system load $\rho > 0.7$ waiting times under both FIFO and LS_10 increase rapidly where the time sharing algorithms behave modest. It is astonishing that for the higher value of *maxprio*, LS_50 performs up to $\rho = 0.8$ as good as the time sharing algorithms. But this effect was not the same for uniform distributions, for example.

6 Conclusions

Our simulations show that in a homogeneous environment simple strategies like LS, LS_TS, and LS_TS_MIG have much benefits compared to FIFO. In special for higher system load, the time sharing algorithms have a better performance and their behavior was stable under the considered workloads.

Workstation–cluster are normally used by interactive users for program development, text processing, and net applications like electronic mail. Additionally, workstation–cluster get used as parallel machines where the parallel applications run concurrent to the user applications. The user applications can be seen as a background load which will slowdown a parallel application. Since nothing is known about the future load of interactive users, migration may be an effective tool to react on these load changes.

The benefits of migration strategies will be even stronger in the case of heterogeneous systems. In case of an heterogeneous system it may be advisable to start on slower machines and migrate onto the faster ones when these machines get idle.

Our current work concentrates on extending our simulation software for modeling also heterogeneous environments with background load.

References

1. Chen, G.I., Lai, T.H.: Scheduling Independent Jobs on Partitionable Hypercubes. Journal of Parallel and Distributed Computing **12** (1991) 74–78
2. Feitelson, D.G., Rudolph, L.: Gang Scheduling Performance Benefits for Fine-Grain Synchronization. Journal of Parallel and Distributed Computing **16** (1992) 306–318
3. Gustafson,J.: Reevaluating Amdahl's Law. Communications of the ACM **31** 5 (1988) 532–533
4. Krueger, P., Lai, T.-H., Radiya, V.A.: Processor Allocation vs. Job Scheduling on Hypercube Computers. Proc. of the 1991 International Conference on Distributed Computer Systems (1991) 394–401
5. Leutenegger, S.T., Vernon, M.K.: Performance of Multiprogrammed Multiprocessor Scheduling Policies. Proc. of the 1990 ACM SIGMETRICS Conference on Measurements & Modeling of Computer Systems (1990), 226–236
6. Min, D., Mutka, M.W.: Effects of Job Size Irregularity on the Dynamic Resource Scheduling of a 2-D Mesh Multicomputer. 5th International PARLE Conference (1993), 476–487
7. Ousterhout, J.K.: Scheduling techniques for concurrent systems. 3rd Intl. Conf. Distributed Computing Systems (1982) 22–30
8. Schnor, B.: Architectures and Algorithms for Group Scheduling. 3th International Conference Parallel Computing Technologies (1993) 225–233
9. Setia, S.K., Squillante, M.S., Tripathi, S.K.: Processor Scheduling on Multiprogrammed, Distributed Memory Parallel Computers. Performance Evaluation Review **21**, 1 (1993) 158–170
10. Trew, A., Wilson, G. (Eds.): Past, Present, Parallel: A Survey of Available Parallel Computing Systems. Springer, London, 1991
11. Cap, C.H., Strumpen, V.: Efficient Parallel Computing in Distributed Workstation Environments. Parallel Computing **19**, 11 (1993) 1221–1234
12. Sunderam, V.S.: PVM: A framework for parallel distributed computing. Concurrency: Practice and Experience **2**, 4 (1990) 315–339
13. Litzkow, M., Solomon, M.: Supporting Checkpointing and Process Migration Outside the UNIX Kernel. USENIX Conference Proceedings, San Francisco (1992) 283–290
14. Petri, S.: Migrating Communicating Processes in Workstation Clusters. Technical Report, TU Braunschweig (1995)

A Method for Analyzing Combinatorial Properties of Static Connecting Topologies*

Guennadi Vesselovski and Marina Kupriyanova

Institute of Control Sciences
Profsoyuznaya 65, 117806 Moscow, Russia

Abstract. The mathematical method which allows examining the possibility of a conflict - free realization of a given permutation by a static interconnection network has been developed. The method is based on the use of the congruence notion of the number theory. The method was used to examine the possibility of a conflict-free realization of such well- known permutations as perfect shuffle, cyclic shift, bit reversal and flip permutation by a binary hypercube and by a two-dimensional mesh with the use of common routing algorithms. Moreover a hypercube combinatorial properties were explored under two modes of the same routing algorithm: synchronous and asynchronous. It was shown that using of an asynchronous mode of routing in a hypercube enhances its permutation capabilities.

1   Introduction

There are two main classes of connecting topologies used in parallel computers: dynamic and static. A dynamic topology arranges connections between the network inputs and outputs according to the requests. Crossbars and all kinds of multistage networks belong to this class of connecting topologies. An interconnection network is said to be static if its neighbour nodes are connected in accordance with a strict rule. A two-dimensional mesh and a binary hypercube are examples of such kind of a network. There are also two main types of request patterns. A parallel request pattern in which destination addresses are formed in a random way is defined as a random request. In such a request pattern for some input-output pairs destination addresses may coincide. But if there is a set of requests issued in parallel and every destination node in this set is addressed by at most one source node, then we refer to this type of a request pattern as a permutation request. Random requests are more typical for MIMD systems and permutation requests are typical feature of SIMD systems. In spite of static interconnection networks being applied not only in MIMD systems but also in SIMD systems their permutation capability or in other words, combinatorial properties remain scantily investigated. The papers devoted to the issue are few in number. An example of such a paper may be found in [3]. Now, a mathematical method has been developed which allows to examine the possibility of the

---

* Supported by Russian Foundation for Basic Research, Project No. 94-01-01650

conflict-free realization of a permutation by a static interconnection network . The method is based on the use of the congruence notion of the number theory. It is the extension of the known approach for examining the possibility of a conflict-free realization of some permutations by a one-path dynamic multistage network [1] to static networks. When analyzing the topological features of a network and its routing algorithm are taken into account and the conditions of a blocking occurence are formulated, then for a given permutation it can be found out whether this permutation does cause blockings in the network or not. The method was used to examine the possibility of a conflict-free realization of frequently used permutations from the classification given in [2] by a binary hypercube and by a two-dimensional mesh with common routing algorithms.

2 Definitions

We define a permutation P_N as a set of the integer pairs $P_N = \{(S_i, D_i), 0 \le i < N\}$ which represent a mapping of sources to destinations $S_0 \to D_0, S_1 \to D_1, ..., S_{N-1} \to D_{N-1}$. Its components will be considered as n–dimensional vectors whose elements are either 0 or 1 : the vector $(s_{n-1}s_{n-2}...s_0)$ is identified with the integer S_i, s_{n-1} being the most significant bit. According to the accepted classification, permutations frequently used in parallel computing are grouped in several families. These families are based on such well-known permutations as perfect shuffle, bit reversal, cyclic shift and flip permutation. The definitions and rules of formation for above–mentioned regular permutations are listed further on:

Perfect shuffle $\sigma^n : (s_{n-1}s_{n-2}...s_0) \to (s_{n-2}...s_0s_{n-1})$
Bit reversal $\rho^n : (s_{n-1}s_{n-2}...s_0) \to (s_0...s_{n-2}s_{n-1})$
Cyclic shift $\pi^n : S \to (S + h)mod N$
Flip permutation $\tau^n : S \to S \oplus \lambda$

In the following some definitions and methods of the number theory are being used [1].

Definition 1. Let $a = a^*m + \alpha$ and $b = b^*m + \beta$ where $\alpha, \beta < m$ and a, b, α, β, a^*, b^* and m are all nonnegative integers. We say $a \equiv_m b$ if and only if $\alpha = \beta$. This is the common definition of "a is congruent to b modulo m".

Definition 2. Assume m is a factor of N. With a and b as above, we say $a \equiv_N^m b$ if and only if $a^*m \equiv_N b^*m$, i.e. $m\lfloor a/m \rfloor mod N = m\lfloor b/m \rfloor mod N$.

Example 1. Let $a = 11010$(binary), $b = 01010$ and $c = 10010$. Then $a \equiv_4 b \equiv_4 c$, $a \equiv_{16}^2 b$ (since 101=101) and $a \not\equiv_{16}^2 c$ (since 101 ≠ 001).

3 An Investigation of Some Combinatorial Properties of a Binary Hypercube under a Synchronous Mode of Routing

The direct binary n–cube or hypercube network consists of $N = 2^n$ nodes interconnected by links in accordance with the following rule: two nodes whose binary

addresses differ in exactly one bit position are connected by a link i.e. Hamming
distance between them is equal to 1. An example of a binary 4-cube with 16
nodes is shown in Fig.1(a). The structure of a node consists of a processing
element (PE) and means to communicate with its neighbours Fig.1(b).

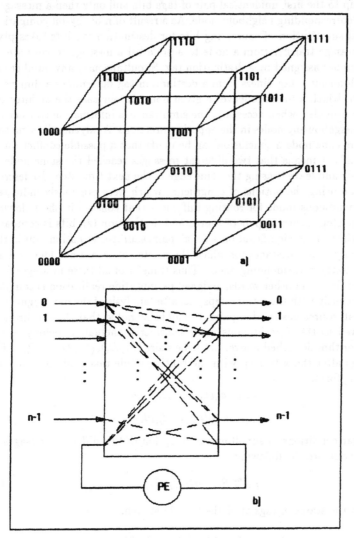

Fig. 1. (a) Structure of the direct binary 4-cube network (b) Architecture of a node

The cube routing algorithm is as follows [4]. Let a message be transferred
from one node with a binary number $(s_{n-1}s_{n-2}...s_0)$ to a node with the number
$(d_{n-1}d_{n-2}...d_0)$. The number of a source node S is to be referred as a source tag

while the number of a destination node D is to be called a destination tag. In routing comparison starts with the least significant digits s_0 and d_0 of the source tags and destination tags respectively. With $s_0 \neq d_0$ a message is sent from the node $(s_{n-1}s_{n-2}...s_0)$ to the node $(s_{n-1}s_{n-2}...d_0)$. With $s_0 = d_0$ comparing is continued up to the first unidentical pair of tags bits and only then a message is sent to the corresponding neighbour node. As a result of n bit-by-bit comparison a sequential substitution of source tag bits for destination tag bits takes place with the message transfer from a node to a node till a message reaches a node with the number assigned by a destination tag. Simultaneously any number of a bit in which a source tag differs from a destination tag determines a dimension according to which a message leaves a given node. In our case the architecture of the node provides, when necessary, the simultaneous information transfer between two neighbouring nodes in the opposite directions. Analyzing the structure of a direct n-cube node a conclusion can be made that a possible conflict might exist. Actually it means that two different messages reached the same node simultaneously and leave it using the same edge in the next time step. To describe this situation using the notions of congruence which were previously indicated, define a synchronous mode for routing fulfilment that consists in the following: in each time step a current pair of source and destination tag bits is compared starting with the least significant ones for all pairs source-destination, but in this time step only those messages for which these bits values are not identical are transferred to the corresponding nodes. Thus transfer of all these messages from the assigned list or, in other words, assigned permutation realization is completed simultaneously with the n time steps, i.e. after analysis of the most significant tag bits of all source-destination pairs. It should be noted that the synchronous mode, as well as the asynchronous mode considered thereafter, belong to the routing algorithm described above. Let it be pairs $(S_i, D_i), (S_j, D_j) \in P_N$. The state of tags after the k-th step with the routing mode taken into account has the following form:

$$s_{i,n-1}...s_{i,k}d_{i,k-1}...d_{i,1}d_{i,0}$$

$$s_{j,n-1}...s_{j,k}d_{j,k-1}...d_{j,1}d_{i,0}.$$

Note that conditions of simultaneous reception of two different messages in a common node are the following:

$$S_i \equiv_N^m S_j, \quad D_i \equiv_m Dj . \tag{1}$$

Write down the states of tags after the $(k+1)$-st step:

$$s_{i,n-1}...s_{i,k+1}d_{i,k}d_{i,k-1}...d_{i,1}d_{i,0}$$

$$s_{j,n-1}...s_{j,k+1}d_{j,k}d_{j,k-1}...d_{j,1}d_{i,0}.$$

Then conditions of transfers along the same edge have the following form:

$$S_i \not\equiv_N S_j, \quad S_i \equiv_N^{2m} S_j, \quad D_i \equiv_{2m} D_j, \text{where} \quad m = 2^{k+1}(0 < k < n-1) . \tag{2}$$

Thus, taking into account conditions (1) we have the following theorem.

Theorem 3. *For a direct n-cube in the synchronous routing mode a conflict takes place iff there exists such $k(0 \leq k \leq n - 1)$, that for $m = 2^{k+1}$ the following conditions are fulfilled:*

$$S_i \not\equiv_N S_j, \quad D_i \equiv_{2m} D_j, \quad S_i \equiv_N^m S_j . \tag{3}$$

Now we will begin to examine the possibility of a conflict–free realization of above–mentioned frequently used permutations by a binary hypercube.

Theorem 4. *The permutation of the π^n type, the cyclic shift with an amplitude h does not cause blockings in a binary hypercube under the synchronous routing mode.*

Proof. By contradiction assume, that a conflict exists, then conditions (3) of Theorem 3 should be fulfilled. Since $D_i = S_j + h; D_j = S_j + h$, then $S_i + h \equiv_{2m} S_j + h \rightarrow S_i \equiv_{2m} S_j$, but $S_i \equiv_N^m S_j$, then $S_i \equiv_N S_j$ contradicts the initial condition. □

Theorem 5. *The permutation of the type $\tau^n(S \rightarrow S \oplus \lambda)$, called flip permutation does not cause blockings in a binary hypercube under the synchronous routing mode.*

The proof is evident and similar to that of Theorem 4 and therefore, its presentation is not necessary.

Theorem 6. *The permutation of the σ^n type , $(s_{n-1}s_{n-2}...s_0) \rightarrow (s_{n-2}...s_0s_{n-1})$, called the perfect shuffle does not cause blockings in a binary hypercube under the synchronous routing mode.*

Proof. By contradiction assume that conflict exists and it is equal to conditions (3) of Theorem 3. Thus $D_i \equiv_{2m} D_j$, then $S_i \equiv_m S_j$, since D_i , D_j is obtained from S_i, S_j by one bit cyclic shift to the left. Then from $S_i \equiv_m S_j$ and $S_i \equiv_N^m S_j$ it follows that $S_i \equiv_N Sj$, which contradicts the initial condition. □

Theorem 7. *The permutation of the ρ^n type, the bit reversal $(s_{n-1}s_{n-2}...s_0) \rightarrow (s_0...s_{n-2}s_{n-1})$, causes conflicts in a binary hypercube under the synchronous routing mode.*

Proof. Let $S_i \not\equiv_N S_j$ then choose such $k + 2 \geq \lceil n/2 \rceil$,that for $m = 2^{k+1}$ the condition $S_i \equiv_N^{2^{n-(k+2)}} S_j$ is fulfilled, i.e. $k + 2$ of the most significant bits of the source tags S_i and S_j are identical, then $D_i \equiv_{2m} D_j$, i.e. $k + 2$ of the least significant bits of the destination tags are also identical. However from $S_i \equiv_N^{2^{n-(k+2)}} S_j$ follows $S_i \equiv_N^m S_j$, i.e. all conditions of Theorem 3 are fulfilled. □

4 An Investigation of Some Combinatorial Properties of a Binary Hypercube under an Asynchronous Mode of Routing

Now consider the asynchronous mode to control information exchange in a binary hypercube, which is as follows . The realization of a given permutation for all source - destination pairs starts simultaneously. However, unlike the above considered synchronous mode the bits of source and destination tags are being analyzed independently in each pair (S_i, D_j) till the first unidentity with the consequent transfer of a message corresponding with this pair to one of the neighboring nodes according to the route formed by this pair. Then in the next time step all pair analysis is carried out independently up to the next unidentity, etc. In this way the transfer of various messages in this mode can proceed in various number of time steps, in a general case less than n. Thus let there be the pairs $(S_i, D_i), (S_j, D_j) \in P_N$. Introduce the notations: $l_1(k)$ - a set of dimensions where bits of the S_i source tag are not identical to the bits of the D_i destination tag; $l_2(k)$ - a set of dimensions where the bits of the S_j source tag are not identical to the bits of the D_j destination tag $(0 \le k \le n-1,\ 0 \le l_1(k), l_2(k) \le n-1)$. Assume that there exist $l_1(k)$ and $l_2(k)$ such that $l_2(k) \ge l_1(k)$. Then for two messages to reach the same node after the k-th time step, it is necessary to fulfill the following conditions:

$$D_i \equiv_{2^{l_1(k)+1}} D_j, \quad S_i \equiv_N^{2^{l_2(k)+1}} S_j, \quad S_i \equiv_{2^{l_2(k)+1}}^{2^{l_1(k)+1}} D_j \qquad (4)$$

For two messages to leave the node along one and the same edge it is necessary to have identity of tags intermediate states in the $(k+1)$-st time step. Since the condition $S_i \equiv_N^{2^{l_2(k)+1}} S_j$ should be fulfilled in the k-th time step it causes the necessity of identity of the values $l_2(k+1)$ and $l_1(k+1)$ in the $(k+1)$-st time step since only in this case switching-over takes place simultaneously in one and the same dimension. Therefore conditions of transfer along one and the same edge in the $(k+1)$-st time step have the following form:

$$l_2(k+1) = l_1(k+1), \quad D_i \equiv_{2^{l_2(k+1)+1}} D_j, \quad S_i \equiv_N^{2^{l_2(k+1)+1}} S_j \ . \qquad (5)$$

To simplify further conclusions and make writing convenient we shall redenote $2^{l_1(k)+1},\ 2^{l_2(k)+1},\ 2^{l_1(k+1)+1},\ 2^{l_2(k+1)+1}$ by $L_1(k),\ L_2(k),\ L_1(k+1),\ L_2(k+1)$ respectively. Thus we have the following theorem.

Theorem 8. *For a binary hypercube in the asynchronous routing mode a conflict will take place iff there exists such k and $l_1(k),\ l_2(k),\ l_1(k+1),\ l_2(k+1),\ (0 \le k \le n-1),\ (1 \le l_1(k), l_2(k) \le n)$, with $l_1(k+1) = l_2(k+1)$ that the following conditions are fulfilled:*

$$S_i \not\equiv_N S_j, \quad S_i \equiv_{L_2(k)}^{L_1(k)} D_j, \quad S_i \equiv_N^{L_2(k)} S_j, \quad D_i \equiv_{L_2(k+1)} D_j \ . \qquad (6)$$

Now explore some combinatorial properties of a binary hypercube under the asynchronous mode of routing.

Theorem 9. *The permutation of the σ^n type, i.e. the perfect shuffle is conflict-free in a binary hypercube under the asynchronous routing mode.*

Proof. By contradiction assume that a conflict exists, then conditions (6) of Theorem 8 should be fulfilled. So $S_i \equiv_N^{2^{l_2(k)}} S_j$, $D_i \equiv_{2^{l_2(k+1)}} D_j$. From the above it might be assumed that $S_i \equiv_{2^{l_2(k+1)-1}} S_j$ since for the perfect shuffle D_i and D_j are derived from S_i and S_j accordingly by the one-bit leftward cyclic shift. But then $S_i \equiv_{2^{l_2(k)}} S_j$ because $l_2(k+1) \geq l_2(k)$. Then from conditions $S_i \equiv_N^{2^{l_2(k)}} S_j$ and $S_i \equiv_{2^{l_2(k)}} S_j$ we have $S_i \equiv_N S_j$ which contradicts the initial condition. $\square$

Theorem 10. *The permutation of the ρ^n type, the bit reversal, in a binary hypercube under the asynchronous routing mode is realized without conflicts.*

Proof. Let there be such $l_1(k)$, $l_2(k)$, $l_1(k+1) = l_2(k+1)$ that all conflict conditions (6) are fulfilled. In addition note that from the idea of bit reversal it follows that $l_1(k) = l_2(k)$. Since $S_i \equiv_{L_1(k)} D_i$, then $D_i \equiv_{L_1(k)} D_j$, but $S_j \equiv_{L_1(k)} D_j$, then $S_i \equiv_{L_1(k)} S_j$. Thus, if $S_i \equiv_N^{L_1(k)} S_j$ then Theorem 8 is valid only if conditions $S_i \equiv_N S_j$, $D_i \equiv_N D_j$ are fulfilled. $\square$

Using Theorem 8 it is not diifficult to prove that the cyclic shift π^n and the flip permutation τ^n are also conflict-free in a binary hypercube under the routing mode discussed above. Note one important property for this permutation which is useful in its applications. If $\lambda = 2^i (0 \leq i \leq n-1)$ then the permutation τ^n on a direct n–cube is realized for one time step. Thus, we have that all main permutations from the accepted classification are conflict-free in a binary hypercube under the asynchronous routing mode.

Theorem 11. *If a permutation causes conflicts in a binary hypercube under the asynchronous routing mode then this permutation will also cause conflicts in it under the synchronous routing mode.*

Proof. Let $l_2(k+1) = l_2(k)+\gamma (0 \leq \gamma < n-1)$, $l_2(k) \geq k$, i.e. $l_2(k) = k+\mu (0 \leq \mu < n-1)$, then $L_2(k+1) = m2^{\gamma+\mu}$, $L_2(k) = m2^\mu$. If $D_i \equiv_{L_2(k+1)} D_j$ then $D_i \equiv_{2L_2(k)} D_j (\gamma = 1)$ under the synchronous routing mode, i.e. all conditions of Theorem 3 are fulfilled. $\square$

5 An Investigation of Some Combinatorial Properties of a Two- Dimensional Mesh

A two-dimensional mesh was applied as an interconnection topology in a series of parallel computer systems from Illiac IV to the present-day Touchstone DELTA System [5]. Here the combinatorial capabilities of a two-dimensional mesh were investigated with the use of the proposed technique. An example of a two-dimensional mesh of 16 nodes is shown in Fig.2 (more exactly this topology may be referred as a two-dimensional torus).

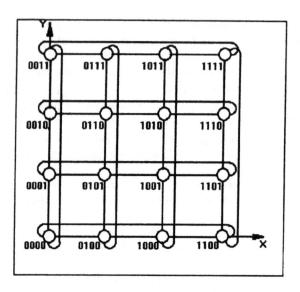

Fig. 2. The two-dimensional mesh 4 × 4

It is easily seen that for the numbering of nodes accepted in Fig.2 two most significant bits define the X coordinate of a node whereas two least significant bits define its Y coordinate. Accordingly for a square two-dimensional mesh of N nodes $(\log N)/2$ most significant bits define the coordinate X of a node and $(\log N)/2$ least significant bits define its Y coordinate. Routing in a two-dimensional mesh may be effected by moving along the first dimension and then along the second dimension. When a permutation is realized in such a manner that the moving along the Y coordinate begins only after completion of the moving along the X coordinate for all source-destination pairs, then a mode of routing is defined as a synchronous. Suppose that the moving along a dimension is always effected by sequential adding of one to the most significant (or to the least significant) half of a node number modulo $\sqrt{N}$. Then two different messages arrive at one and the same node if the most significant halves of their destinations tags and the least significant halves of the source tags coincide. A blocking occurs when this node is not terminal for neither message and the moving along the second dimension is necessary. (Recall that in our case the moving along dimensions is always unidirectional for the sake of simplicity). Thus, we have the following theorem.

Theorem 12. *For a two-dimensional mesh under the synchronous routing mode a blocking takes place iff the following conditions are fulfilled:*

$$S_i \not\equiv_N S_j, \quad S_i \equiv_{\sqrt{N}} S_j, \quad D_i \equiv_N^{\sqrt{N}} D_j, \quad S_i \not\equiv_{\sqrt{N}} D_i, \quad S_j \not\equiv_{\sqrt{N}} D_j \ . \quad (7)$$

Now explore some combinatorial capabilities of a two-dimensional mesh under the above described routing algorithm.

Theorem 13. *The permutation of the π^n type, the cyclic shift, does not cause blockings in a two-dimensional mesh under the synchronous routing mode.*

Proof. By contradiction assume that a conflict exists, then conditions (7) of Theorem 12 should be fulfilled. Since $D_i = S_i + h; D_j = S_j + h$, then $(S_i + h) \equiv_N^{\sqrt{N}} (S_j + h) \rightarrow S_i \equiv_N^{\sqrt{N}} S_j$, but in accordance with conditions (7) $S_i \equiv_{\sqrt{N}} S_j$, then $S_i \equiv_N S_j$ contradicts the initial condition. □

In a similar manner it can be shown that the flip permutation τ^n is conflict-free on a two-dimensional mesh. As to the perfect shuffle σ^n, it can be shown that conditions (7) are fulfilled if S_i and S_j differ only in the most significant bits.

Example 2. Let, for example, $S_i = 0001$ and $S_j = 1001$ then D_i and D_j are 0010 and 0011 respectively. These two source-destinations pairs will conflict in the network.

For the bit reversal ρ^n conditions (7) are fulfilled when the least significant halves of the source tags S_i and S_j coincide because the most significant halves of the destination tags D_i and D_j in this case will also coincide.

Example 3. Let, for example, $S_i = 0001$ and $S_j = 1101$, then $D_i = 1000$ and $D_j = 1011$. In this case we also will have a conflict.

Thus permutations of the σ^n and ρ^n types cause blockings in a two-dimensional mesh under the above routing algorithm and need a special routing.

6   Conclusion

The combinatorial capabilities of static connecting topologies now in use are poorly explored. This paper has presented a technique to investigate the possibility of a conflict-free realization of regular permutations by such topologies. The technique is based on the use of congruence notion from number theory. It is applicable to a variety of static topologies with distinct routing algorithms. We have applied the approach for exploring some combinatorial properties of a binary hypercube. It has been shown that such frequently used permutations as perfect shuffle, bit reversal, cyclic shift and flip permutation are conflict-free in a binary hypercube under the asynchronous mode of the common routing algorithm. The approach has been used also for exploring some permutation capabilities of a two-dimensional mesh.

References

1. Lawrie, D.: Access and alingment of data in an array processor. IEEE Trans. on Computers. Vol. C-24 (1975) **12** 1145–1155
2. Lenfant, J.: A versatile mechanism to move data in an array processor. IEEE Trans. on Computers. Vol. C-34 (1985) **6** 506–522
3. Orcutt, S.: Implementation of permutation functions in Illiac IV-type computers. IEEE Trans. on Computers. Vol. C-25 (1976)**9** 929–935
4. Padmanabhan, K.: Cube structures for multiprocessors. Commun. of the ACM. Vol. 33 (1990) **1** 45–52
5. Rattner, J.: The new age of supercomputing. Lecture Notes in Computer Science. (1991) **487** 1–6

cT: an Imperative Language with Parallelizing Features
Supporting the Computation Model "Autotransformation of the Evaluation Network"

Alexey I. Adamovich

Research Centre for Multiprocessor Systems
Program Systems Institute of the Russian Academy of Sciences
Pereslavl-Zalessky, Russia

Abstract. In this paper we present the programming language cT, intended for the development of portable software for multiprocessors in the environment supporting the computation model "autotransformation of evaluation network". The language was designed as an extension of C programming language with the new language primitives that represent the notions of the computation model. As a result, there was produced an imperative language with functional features.

1 Introduction

It's a common knowledge that programming for multiprocessors[1] is very tiresome and time consuming. Besides, the software for multiprocessors is hardly portable. One of the ways to eliminate these drawbacks is to make a computer-independent system for the development of the parallel software, that provides automatic parallelizing of programs.

Now there are available many implementations of functional languages with parallelizing features [2]. But their syntax usually repels those programmers, who are used to imperative languages.

In this paper we discuss an approach to the development of parallel software, that allows one to combine syntactical and semantic paradigms of well-known imperative languages, C in particular, with the possibilities of parallelizing, provided by functional languages. The approach is based on the use of a computation model called "autotransformation of evaluation network" [1].

Section 2 of the paper provides a short description of the computation model and some peculiarities of its implementing by run-time support system. Section 3 contains an introduction to cT programming language. Finally, we present a sample program to give an illustration to the preceding summary of the language and conclude with some prospective comments on future work.

---

[1] By a multiprocessor we mean a network built of conventional Von Neuman style monoprocessor elements.

2 Computation Model and its Implementation

Our approach is based on the following principles:

1. The whole computation process is an autotransformation of a network, the nodes of which are data and processes. Data and processes are situated in cells, i.e. in tagged parts of memory of different size. The arcs connecting the cells into a network are specially organized pointers. At the start of computation the network consists of a single root process.

2. Processes are active parts of a network and are responsible for its transformation. During its work the process can generate new data and modify or even delete its own existing data. Moreover, any process can generate another process or a network of processes to which the fragments of the network can be transferred as inputs.

3. Every process is linked by one or several arcs to the cells-consumers outside the process. The process sends returned values to the cells-consumers via these links. When one of the returned values is sent to the consumers, the corresponding link is destroyed. The process terminates when all its links are destroyed, i.e. all the returned values are sent. Sending of the returned values is the only way the process can change the part of the network to which it is linked.

4. The cells-consumers contain the so called "unevaluated values". If a process tries to use such a value in its own computations, it is announced to be not ready and is suspended. The process is announced to be ready again when this cell-consumer receives the evaluated value and becomes an ordinary cell. Thus, the inter-process synchronization is implicit.

In more detail this computation model is described in [1]. Since the process modifies the evaluation network only by sending the returned values, it has no side effect. That allows to run all the ready processes in parallel. To provide paralellizing the process may be transferred from one monoprocessor to another, and run-time support system can do this automatically.

The available run-time system, implementing the computation model, is based on vector representation of lists and garbage collection.

In vector representation a list is a sequence of cells situated in the memory successively. If the list has a regular structure there can be provided the direct access to any cell, i.e. indexing. To connect the list with the rest part of the computation network and to prevent it from being deleted by garbage collection, a cell containing a reference to this list is used. This cell is called a holder. The holder also contains the number of the cells in the list. As an example you can look at Fig. 1 where is shown a list consisting of 11 cells 'information', and its holder.

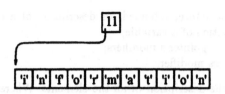

Fig. 1. A sample list in vector representation.

Apart from holding the list in memory, the holder may be used to provide the access to the list. The cell, containing a holder also can be an element of a list. Thus a list with any number of nesting levels can be built.

So far we have not discussed an important issue – the internal structure of a process. Generally speaking, in terms of the computation model it's irrelevant, if the rules described above and specifying the characteristics of the model are followed.

The processes used in the available implementation of the computation model are very similar to processes as they are used in operating systems. A process has a code, data and a stack. Inside the process the computation is being performed in the traditional von Neuman manner. Thus for a process the memory is divided into two unequal parts: inner world and outer space, and the rules of behaviour in this two parts are very different.

3 cT language

Below we give a brief description of a programming language called cT. cT is intended for the description of processes' behaviour, i.e. for writing programs for the processes. The language was constructed as an extension of C language, and C is an intermediate level language for the cT compiler. This approach allows to use C-compilers available for monoprocessor elements, such as Intel microprocessors, DSP's or transputers, that are parts of multiprocessors. This feature together with the use of run-time support system provides the portability of the software written in cT. C language was extended by adding the structures for representing the notions of the computation model. The extensions are described below.

3.1 Data description

All the objects situated in the cells in the outer space will be correspondingly called outer objects (outer variables, outer values).

To work with outer objects in cT the following new elements of data description is used:

- **"outer"**, **"packed"** – modifiers of the base type;

- **typeof** – the structure, intended for description of a complex base type within the definition of a variable;
- **"rack"**, **"safe"** – pointer's modifiers;
- **"holder"** – access modifiers.

Below there is the description of all the elements. Where necessary, we use EBNF notation to describe the syntax.

"outer". This base type modifier is intended for the description of outer variables and other objects used to get access to the outer values.

Example (1):

```
outer int oi,               // integer outer variable
     oai[ 10 ] ;            // homogeneous list (vector)
                            //    of integer outer values

outer struct {              // heterogeneous list (structure)
     int i, char c ; } nl ; //    of outer values

static outer void * ovp ;   // static pointer at
                            //    an arbitrary outer object
```

We'd like to draw your attention to the definitions of the variables **oai** and **nl**. These are definitions of lists. Due to the vector representation of lists in the implementation of this computation model, the lists are represented in the language by outer arrays and outer structures.

Outer variables can be defined only as results, arguments or local variables of the network functions (processes).

"packed". As it was specified above, the cells with outer objects can have different length. The minimal length allows to place there a small portion of information – an integer, a symbol, a holder. To define the cells of extended size containing packed information, the keyword **"packed"** is used. This keyword is a modifier of the base type. Thus, we have to define first the complex base type, so that then, while defining an outer object we would be able to pack it into the cell.

Example (2):

```
typedef int t_ia[ 16 ] ; // we define the type
                         //    "integer array"

outer packed t_ia pia;   // definition of a "packed array"
                         // outer variable

typedef struct {
    real re, im;         // we define the type "complex"
```

```
} t_complex;
outer packed t_complex pcs ;   // definition of a "packed
                               // structure" outer variable
```

In this example the outer variable pia is defined as a large cell, into which there is packed an array of 16 integers. The variable pcs is defined as a cell containing the structure consisting of two real numbers.

"typeof". This primitive allows to describe a complex base type without the use of a separate typedef-sentence. This extension to C was originally introduced in the well-known gcc C compiler. Syntactically this structure looks like an abstract declaration (the identifier is not specified), put in brackets and preceded by the **"typeof"** keyword:

```
"typeof" "(" <abstract-declaration> ")"
```

Let's rewrite the Example 2 with the use of this facility.
Example (3):

```
    outer packed typeof (int[ 16 ]) pia;

    outer packed typeof (struct {real re, im;}) pcs ;
```

"rack", "safe" and "holder". In the Example 1 we've shown that lists are represented in the language cT as arrays and structures. Now we proceed to the representation of the holder, the cell that provides access to the list and protects it from garbage collection.

We can regard holder as a special pointer. To define such pointers we use two modifiers: **"rack"** and **"safe"**.

Pointer modifier **"rack"** is used to define variables and outer values, that are cells holding a single outer value.

Pointer modifier **"safe"** is used to define variables and outer values that are cells holding a homogeneous array of a certain outer type. We introduced this modifier to provide for a programmer an outer pointer that has the same features as a common pointer in C language. In particular, an ordinary pointer in C may be regarded as a pointer to a homogeneous array, and you can index it.
Example (4):

```
outer struct {int r, i;}
   rack * hcomplex, // holder, holding one outer structure
   safe * hca ;     // holder, of an array of outer structures
```

On the other hand, a holder may be regarded as part and parcel of the data structure it is holding. To define a data structure with a holder in this case we use the keyword **"holder"**. This keyword can be used in data definition as a modifier of the access to outer arrays and outer structures (even to the packed ones). Although in operations with such data this keyword is not used, in data definition it may be regarded as a symbol of operation, that has the same priority as the operation of dereferencing "*".

Example (5):

```
outer struct { int r, i; }
  holder ach [ ]; // the array of held outer structures
```

3.2   Network functions

The notion of a network function in ¢T corresponds to the notion of a process in the evaluation model. Thus the network functions are the grains of parallelism. They coexist in the language with the ordinary functions and differ from them with the following peculiarities:

- a network function can return several results;
- a network function must return at least one result;
- the network functions may accept outer objects as parameters and use them as local variables and return them as results.

The definition of a network function, similar to the definition of an ordinary function, consists of a header and the function body and the header of a network function is similar to the header of an ordinary function:

```
"[" <results description> "]" <identifier>
                    "(" <arguments description> ")"
```

Example (6):

```
[int r, i] f (int a, b, long l)
```

In this example there is presented the header of the network function f, that has three arguments (two of them are integers, the third one is a long integer) and two integer results.

The pointers to the network functions are described in the same style.
Example (7):

```
[ ] (* fp1) ( ) ;
[int r, i] (* fp2) (int a, b, long l) ;
```

In this example there are described two pointers to the network functions:

- fp1 – the pointer to a network function;
- fp2 – the pointer to a network function of the same type as the function f from the Example 6.

3.3   New operations and control structures

As we have mentioned above, outer objects can be defined in cT only as parameters, results and local variables of network functions. Thus, the transformation of evaluation network is mainly performed in the bodies of network functions.

To perform calls of network functions and to manipulate with outer objects, the language was extended with outer oriented operations and new cotrol structures.

Evaluation of the attributes of outer values. The language is extended with the notion of an attribute of outer value. Any outer value has a set of attributes, which includes at least a readiness attribute "R" and an error attribute "E". The names of the attributes are the keywords. Syntactically the operation of evaluation of an attribute is similar to the operation of access to a field of a structure or a union:

<outer variable name> "." <attribute name>

Example (8):
Let variable oi be defined as follows

```
outer int oi ;
```

Then execution of the program part containing the sentences

```
if( ! oi.R )
        printf( "Not ready\n" ) ;
else if( oi.E )
        printf( "Error\n" ) ;
else
        printf( "%d,\n", oi ) ;
```

– will result in "Not ready", if the variable contains an unevaluated value;
– will result in "Error", if the variable contains an error value;
– will result in printing the value itself if it's ready and is not an error one.

Apart from the attributes specified above some outer values may have attribute "L", that designates the number of the cells in an outer data structure, i.e. in an array, a structure or a union. For the data that have constant length that is computable in compile time, the value of this attribute is a constant. If the number of the cells in the data structures varies during the program execution and cannot be computed in compile time, the attribute "L" can be evaluated with the use of the cell holding this array, structure or union.

Example (9):
Let variables foo, bar and foobar be defined as follows:

```
outer int (holder foo) [16] ;
outer struct { int tag, float fa [ ] } rack * bar ;
outer struct { int r, i } safe * foobar ;
```

Then the value of the expression

    foo.L

is equal 16; the value of the expression

    bar -> fa.L

is equal to the number of the cells in the field (array) **fa** of the corresponding structure, while the value of the expression

    foobar.L

is equal to the number of the cells held by the pointer **foobar**.

Outer arrays for which the value of the attribute "L" can be evaluated, have two more attributes – "**N**" and "**H**". The value of the attribute "**N**" is equal to the number of the elements in the array, while the value of the attribute "**H**" is equal to the number of its last element (**N** - 1). Thus, for the array foo, defined in Example 9, the value of the expression

    (foo.N == foo.L) && (foo.H == foo.L - 1)

will always be true.

If an array or a **"safe"** pointer is indexed by its own attribute, the expression may be written in an abbreviated form. Thus, the expression

    foobar[foobar.H - 2]

can be rewritten as follows:

    foobar[H - 2]

Evaluation of a sub-array. In cT language there is introduced an operation of evaluation of a sub-array. It is written down as follows:

    <expression, specifying the
                array> "[" <low boundary> .. <high boundary> "]"

This operation results in "safe" pointer, holding a part of the array.

Example (10): for the variable foobar, defined in Example 9, the operator

    foobar = foobar [1 .. H - 1] ;

casts out the first and the last elements of the array, held by the pointer foobar.

Network call. The operation of a network function call, the network call, has the following syntax:

```
"[" <the list of the results> "]" "<-" <identifier>
                    "(" <the list of the expressions> ")"
```

If we do not need some results of a network function, their names can be dropped out of the list of the results.

Example (11): Let the definition of the function angabs, that returns the angle and the module of a complex number, have the following header:

```
[packed double angle, abs] angabs (struct complex v)
{ ...
```

Then the network call

```
[ , ar_v[ 0 ]] <- angabs( cmpx_v )
```

will result in the initial element of the array ar_v becoming a consumer of the second result of the function angabs. The first result will not be used at all.

The execution of a network call results in an ordered set (tuple) of values. In the current implementation of the compiler the tuples may be used as operands only in the operations of the network call. We plan to provide an option to use the tuples as operands of the operation of assignment, etc.

Combined network call - spark. The combined network call (spark) provides an opportunity to build a network of processes consisting of more then one element with one call to the run-time system. The combined network call is organized to make evident in compile time the interprocess information flow between the network functions, that are the arguments of the network call.

The syntax of combined network call is as follows:

```
"spark" "(" <the list of liaison names> ")"
                    "{" <spark-sentence>* "}"
```

Example (12):

```
spark( s, c ) {
  s <- sin( x ) ; // 1
  c <- cos( x ) ; // 2
  v = s / c ;      // 3
}
```

The execution of this network call results in three processes. Two of them (sin and cos) are explicitly specified. The third process will be a network call built out of the last sentence "v = s / c ;" in braces. The compiler will generate a network function (let's call it div for now), that can be defined as follows:

```
[packed double divres] div (packed double value, divider) {
    divres = value / divider ;
}
```

Taking into consideration this additional definition we can rewrite Example 12 as follows:

Example (13):

```
spark ( s, c ) {
  [ s ] <- sin ( x ) ;    // 1
  [ c ] <- cos ( x ) ;    // 2
  [ v ] <- div ( s, c ) ; // 3
}
```

The evaluation network, generated after the execution of the system call as it is defined above, is shown at the Fig. 2.

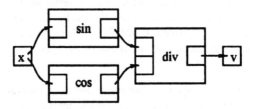

Fig. 2. The evaluation network, generated after the execution of the combined network call in the Example 13.

4 Modularity

In C by program module is meant that part of a program, which text is situated in one file. In cT language every module is compiled and linked separately and thus is turned into an independent executable file. The notion of module in cT terms is very similar to the notion of dynamically linked library (DLL).

The text of a module is an unordered sequence of descriptions and definitions of static data, network functions and ordinary C functions. Besides, the module may contain the import-export statements that are included into the language to support the modularity. These statements are intended to match the interfaces during the inter-module calls to different network functions.

Export description. The export statements allow to describe the interfaces of
the functions of a particular module to provide correct access to these functions
from the other modules.

These statements may be:

- situated in the file containing the text of the module;
- put into a separate file of the export description similar to definition module
  in Modula programming language.

If the export statements are put into a separate file, they are as follows:

> "export" \<export sequence\>, ["," \<export sequence\>]* ";"

The export sequence consists of full descriptions of network functions types
(prototypes), which are optionally ended with the indication of the export type.
There exist three types of export:

- "by" "name" – by name;
- "by" "ordinal" – by number in the export file;
- "at" \<integer\> – by specified number.

By default the functions are exported by name. The network call of such
a function will be slightly less effective then a network call of a function exported by number. But the export by name is more reliable, since the number
of the network function is calculated automatically during the execution of the
program.

Example (14):

```
export [int] foo (int, long), bar (int,),
        [packed typeof (char[ ]) holder] foobar (int,,) at 1;
```

In the example above

- functions foo and bar are described as exported by name. They both return
  one result of the int type. The function foo is described as a function of two
  arguments, that are of int and long types, while function bar is described
  as a function with two arguments of int type;
- function foobar is described as a function exported by specific number (1),
  returning one result of the "held packed array of characters" type and accepting three arguments of int type.

Import description. The import section must be situated in the file before
other declarations. The import sentences have the following format:

> "from" \<import file specification\> ["named" \<identifier\>]
>   "import" [\<the sequence of import names descriptions\>] ";"

In the simplest case the sequence of import names descriptions is a list of names of functions imported from the specified module. If the sequence of the import names is absent, then all the accessible network functions are imported from the module.

Example (15):

```
from "io.xpr" named io import ;
from <sys.tlx> import connect ;
```

These lines import from the export description file **io.xpr**, situated in the current directory, all accessible network functions, and from the executed module **sys.tlx**, situated in one of the standard directories, function **connect**. The second line of this example shows that information about the export of the module is placed into the executable file. This can be performed by the compiler during linking of the executable module.

5 A sample program

Below you will find an example of a simple program in cT that provides an illustration of how the primitives described in Section 3 work with each other and with C statements. The program implements the merge-sort algorithm and uses it to sort an array of random numbers.

The program lines are numbered to make the commenting easier. The numbers aren't part of the program and must not be included into the source file.

```
01    from <rtsio.idf> import Tfprintf ;
02
03    #include <rts.h>
04
05    extern void rand_sequence( outer int *, int ) ;
06
```

The program starts with an import sentence (line 1). The network function **Tfprintf** is imported from the module **rtsio**, the interface of which is described in the system file **rtsio.idf**. Then the header file **rts.h** with C prototypes of ordinary system functions is included into the program. The fifth line contains the prototype of C function **rand_sequence**, that is situated in a separate file and is integrated into the executable module during linking.

```
07    [int oU] main (packed typeof (char[ ]) holder safe *vArgs) {
08        int i, size ;
09        outer int
10            safe * v ;
11            oFile = stdOut ;
12
13        if( vArgs.L != 2 ) {
```

the computation model, since the array is created by operation **new** in line 21 and becomes a part of evaluation network only after it is transferred as a parameter of the network function **sort**, called in line 23.

```
30
31    [ int safe * vDst ] sort( int safe * vSrc ) {
32         if( vSrc.L ) == 1 )
33              vDst = vSrc ;
34         else
35              spark( lft, rht ) {
36                   [ lft ] <- sort( vSrc[ 0 .. L/2 - 1 ]) ;
37                   [ rht ] <- sort( vSrc[ L/2 .. H ]) ;
38                   [ vDst ] <- merge( lft, rht ) ;
39                   }
40    }
```

The function **sort** is the main function of the sorting algorithm. In lines 35-39 it halves the array received as an argument. The resulting sub-arrays become the arguments of two recursive network calls. The results of these network calls are transferred as arguments to the network function **merge**. The result of this last network call is returned as the result of the function **sort**. This whole operation is performed by the complex network call **spark**. After **spark** execution the function **sort** is terminated, and the network of processes, shown at Fig. 4, is linked to the consumer of the function **sort** results.

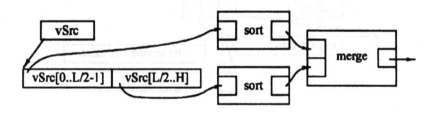

Fig. 4. Network of processes built as a result of execution of the function **sort**.

Line 33 processes the trivial case of the length of the input array being equal 1. Such an array is already sorted.

```
41
42    [ int safe * vDst ] merge (int safe * vLft, vRht) {
43         outer int
44              safe * vSorted = new (int [vLft.L + vRht.L]) ;
45              * pSorted = vSorted,
46              safe * vW ;
```

```
14              [ oFile ] <- Tfprintf( oFile,
15                              "Usage: sort <size>\n" ) ;
16              wait( & oFile ) ;
17              exit( -1 ) ;
18          }
19
20          size = atoi( vArgs[ 1 ]) ;
21          v = new( outer int[ size ]) ;
22          rand_sequence( v, size ) ;
23          [ v ] <- sort( v ) ;
24
25          while( v.L )
26              [ oFile ] <- Tfprintf( oFile, "%05d ", * v ++) ;
27          wait( & oFile ) ;
28          exit( 0 ) ;
29      }
```

Lines 7 to 29 contain the definition of the head function of the program. This function must be called **main** and must have one result of **int** type. Its only argument allows to analyze the command line which started the execution of the program (lines 13, 20). The data structure held by this argument is shown at Fig. 3.

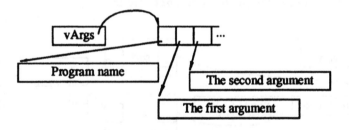

Fig. 3. Standard data structure passed as the only argument to the function **main**.

Lines 13-18 and 25-27 illustrate synchronization of sequential input-output with peripherals by token-passing. The network function **Tfprintf** receives as an argument and returns as a result the outer variable **oFile**, which is used as token and is linked to an outer file **stdOut**. This variable stays unevaluated till the end of i/o operation and thus sequences all the outputs to this file.

The ordinary function **wait** (lines 16 and 27) called before the end of the program prevents termination of the program before the completion of all the i/o operations.

We want to draw your attention to lines 21-23. In line 22 the function **rand_sequence** modifies the outer array, held by **v**. But this does not contradict

```
47
48        while( vLft.L && vRht.L )
49             if ( * vLft >= * vRht )
50                  * pSorted ++ = * vLft ++ ;
51             else
52                  * pSorted ++ = * vRht ++ ;
53
54        while( vRht.L ) ;
55             * pSorted ++ = * vRht ++ ;
56        while( vLft.L )
58             * pSorted ++ = * vLft ++ ;
59        vDst = vSorted ;
60   }
```

The function **merge** merges two sorted arrays into one. Outer array held by vSorted is modified, since it is created in line 44 and is not yet included a part of evaluation network until the result is returned (line 59). To access the element of this array the pointer pSorted is used.

Lines 49-52 are executed till the length of both arrays differs from 0. This condition is checked in line 48. Since vLft and vRht are safe pointers, their incrementation (lines 50, 52, 55, 58) casts out the head elements of the arrays held by these pointers. When the length of one of the arrays equals 0, the other one is appended to the sorted array (lines 54-58).

6 Conclusion

We described the exciting new parallel programming language cT and showed how its primitives represent the notions of the computation model "autotransformation of the evaluation network".

The optimization techniques, which must be used to compile effectively the programs written in cT, are now under development. At the same time an advanced versions of the run-time system for the variety of parallel architectures is developed. The combination of the optimizing compiler and these run-time systems will provide a promising programming environment for the extensive development of software for multiprocessors.

References

1. Abramov, S. M., Adamovitch, A. I., Nesterov, I. A., Pimenov, S. P., Shevchuck, Yu. V.: Autotransformation of evaluation network as a basis for automatic dynamic parallelizing. In Proceedings of of the Sixth Conference of NATUG, IOS Press, 1993, pp.333-344.
2. S. L. Peyton Jones. Parallel Implementations of Functional Programming Languages. The Computer Journal, Vol.32, No.2, 1989, pp.175-186

Vienna Fortran 90 - An Advanced Data Parallel Language

Siegfried Benkner

Institute for Software Technology and Parallel Systems
University of Vienna, Liechtenstein Strasse 22, A-1090 VIENNA, AUSTRIA
E-Mail: sigi@par.univie.ac.at

Abstract. This paper describes Vienna Fortran 90, an advanced data parallel language based on Fortran 90 and Vienna Fortran, that enables the user to program distributed memory parallel computers almost as easily as sequential computers using global addresses only. Vienna Fortran offers a variety of high level features for data distribution and thus combines the advantages of a shared memory programming paradigm with mechanisms for explicit user control of those aspects that have the greatest impact on efficiency. Vienna Fortran 90 provides a number of new features not found in any other comparable language such as HPF or Fortran D. This includes concepts for distributing user defined data structures, distribution of pointer objects, and a general framework for specifying arbitrary data and work distribution.

1 Introduction

Massively parallel architectures, scalable to a large number of processors and offering spectacular peak performance ratios, have become increasingly important for solving large scale scientific and engineering problems. However, because of the lack of a shared memory, these machines are difficult to program usually forcing the user to distribute the data across the processors and to insert message passing operations for communicating non-local data. Currently, most scientific and numerical applications on distributed memory parallel computers (DMPCs) are based on the single program multiple data (SPMD) model using conventional programming languages like Fortran and C with extensions for explicit message passing. With this approach the user has full control of the underlying hardware but is forced to cope with a number of low level details, which can become surprisingly complex. Several issues arise which do not have their counterpart in sequential programming. New types of errors, such as deadlock and livelock, must be avoided. As a consequence, the use of explicit message passing languages results in a programming style which can be likened to assembly programming on a sequential machine.

Over the last years a number of data parallel languages have been developed that enable users to design programs for DMPCs in much the same way as they are accustomed to on sequential machines. Most of these approaches are based on sequential languages like Fortran or C with extensions for data distribution.

This work includes Blaze [14], extensions to CM Fortran [19], CRAFT [16], Fortran D [10], the Yale Extensions [8], Kali [15], Vienna Fortran [20], and HPF [12]. All these languages offer the user a global address space, assume a single thread of control, and provide high level constructs that enable the user to specify the distribution of the data across the local memories of the target machine. Furthermore, some of these languages enable the user to indicate parallel computations and to control the distribution of loop iterations across the processors. Using a data-parallel language, the user writes a sequential program and specifies at a high level how the data space of the program should be distributed. Usually the data distribution is specified by means of compiler directives or annotations added to the declaration of arrays. Based on the user specified data distribution the compiler automatically derives an explicitly parallel SPMD program, i.e., it decides how to partition the control, sets up the necessary communication and generates the target code. This style of programming hides the machine specific details inside the compiler and enables the user to concentrate on the algorithmic issues. As a consequence, programs written in this way are not only much simpler than message passing programs but also more flexible. Changing the data layout requires only minor program changes. Furthermore, it eases the migration of existing sequential programs to distributed memory machines and the porting of codes between various different architectures.

In this paper we give an overview of Vienna Fortran 90, a machine independent, data parallel language based on Fortran 90 and Vienna Fortran[1] [20]. Since the distribution of data is crucial for performance, Vienna Fortran 90 extends Fortran 90 by a variety of methods to distribute data. This includes direct specification of distributions to processor array sections, distribution by alignment or by referring to the distribution of another array, and the use of mapping arrays to support indirect and irregular distributions. Whereas many language features of Vienna Fortran 90 have been taken over from Vienna Fortran a number of language constructs and mechanisms have been redesigned, extended or clarified. In the following we describe the main language concepts and focus our discussion on new features not found in any other comparable language like High Performance Fortran (HPF) [12] or Fortran D [10], such as distribution of user defined data structures, distribution of pointer objects, and a general concept for specifying arbitrary data and work distribution. We assume that the reader is familiar with the basic data distribution mechanism of HPF. A detailed language specification of Vienna Fortran 90 can be found in [3].

2   Processor Arrays

Processor arrays are declared by means of the **PROCESSORS** statement and establish an abstraction from the actual underlying machine topology, and thus provide a suitable means for achieving machine independence. The mapping of

---

[1] Vienna Fortran is based on FORTRAN 77.

processor arrays to the physical machine is hidden in the compiler. More than one processor declaration is permitted in order to provide different *views* of the available set of processors. The textually first is called the *primary processor array*; all others are *secondary processor arrays* or reshapes of the primary processor array. Correspondence between different processor arrays is established by means of the Fortran element order. The number of processors on which the program executes may be accessed by the intrinsic function $NP. A one-dimensional processor array, $P(1:$NP), is always implicitly declared and may be referred to. In the absence of an explicit processor array declaration it is also the primary processor array. The processor arrays of the main program define the set of processors on which the program will execute. The number of processors is either fixed at compile time or is determined at link- or runtime. All processor arrays refer to the same set of processors and thus the size of any two explicitly declared processor arrays in a program unit must be the same. As a consequence, the size of processor arrays occurring in internal procedures must match the size of the processor array of the host program unit. The size of a processor array of an external procedure must be equal or less $NP. A globally accessible processor arrays has to be declared within a module which must be *use-associated* [13] by all program units that access this processor array.

The data objects of a program may be distributed to arbitrary subsets of the available processors. Subsets of processor arrays may be referenced by means of Fortran 90 array sections. For example rows, columns, rectilinear blocks and regular discontiguous regions of a two-dimensional processor array can be described by means of subscript triplets and, in addition, irregular subsets of a processor array may be referenced using vector subscripts. The dimensions of a processor array (section) may be permuted by supplying a *dimension permutation* after a processor reference.

3   Data Distribution Features

In Vienna Fortran data distribution is modeled as a mapping of array elements to (non-empty) subsets of processors, including total as well as partial replication of data. Distributions may be specified either directly, or implicitly by referring to the distribution of another array. For the most common regular distributions intrinsic functions are provided. Arbitrary new distribution functions may be specified by the user.

3.1   Basic Concepts

In Vienna Fortran there are two classes of distributed arrays, *statically distributed* and *dynamically distributed* arrays. The distribution of a statically distributed array may not change within the scope of its declaration. An array whose distribution may be modified within the scope of its declaration is called a dynamically distributed array and must be declared with the DYNAMIC attribute.

145

```
INTEGER, PARAMETER :: N=2, SB=(/10,40,40,10/), MAP=(/1,3,2,1,4,4,2,1/)
PROCESSORS :: R1(N*N), R2(N,N)

REAL, DISTRIBUTED(BLOCK)              :: A(0:101)
REAL, DISTRIBUTED(CYCLIC(5)) TO R2(1,:) :: B(100)
REAL, DISTRIBUTED(S_BLOCK(SB))        :: C(100)
REAL, DISTRIBUTED(INDIRECT(MAP),:)    :: D(8,100)
```

In this example $R1$ is the primary processor array and $R2$ is the secondary processor
array. Array A is distributed in the first dimension in a block-wise fashion with respect
to the primary processor array. Array B is split into contiguous segments of length 5
which are mapped in a round-robin fashion to the first row of the processor array $R2$.
The third declaration specifies a general block distribution of array C which partitions
the array into four blocks of lengths 10, 40, 40 and 10 with respect to the primary
processor array R1. The first dimension of D is distributed indirectly using a mapping
array, while the second dimension stays undistributed. For example, the second row of
D is mapped to processor R1(3).

Fig. 1. Direct Distributions

The distribution of statically distributed arrays is specified within their declaration by means of the **DISTRIBUTED** or **ALIGNED** attribute. Alignment and
distribution extraction allows specifying the distribution of an array implicitly by referring to the distribution of another array. An alignment relationship
between two statically distributed arrays is valid throughout the scope of the
declaration as long as none of them is reallocated.

Dynamically distributed arrays are usually associated with a distribution by
execution of a **DISTRIBUTE** statement, an **ALIGN** statement or as the result of a
procedure call. The **CONNECT** attribute is provided to specify a run-time invariant relationship between the distributions of groups of dynamically distributed
arrays, and can be used to specify either a direct distribution or an implicit
distribution. Furthermore, an initial distribution may be specified within the
declaration of dynamically distributed arrays.

The distribution of data objects for which a distribution has not been specified by the programmer is automatically determined by the compiler[2].

3.2 Direct Data Distribution

A direct distribution is a one-level mapping of array elements to non-empty
sets of processors and is specified by means of distribution functions. In case
of multidimensional arrays either each array dimension may be distributed separately by means of a *dimensional distribution function* or the array may be
distributed as a whole using a *general distribution function*. The intrinsic distribution functions **BLOCK(M)** and **CYCLIC(M)**, and the symbol ":" which indicates

---

[2] The compiler for example may choose to replicate (i.e. allocate on each processor)
such objects.

that the corresponding dimension is not distributed, may be used. Furthermore, intrinsic functions for specifying *generalized block distributions* and *indirect* distributions are provided. Mapping procedures, as discussed in Section 3.7, enable the user to define arbitrary new distributions.

Generalized block distributions are important in the context of load balancing problems, since they enable the user to explicitly vary the sizes of blocks mapped to different processors. Vienna Fortran 90 provides two intrinsic functions for specifying such distributions, B_BLOCK(arr), and S_BLOCK(arr), which both take a one-dimensional integer array, as argument. The i-th element of the argument array determines the upper bound of the i-th block or the the size of the i-th block, respectively.

Indirect distributions are important for applications that are characterized by irregular data distribution and access patterns. They are defined by means of the intrinsic function INDIRECT which takes a mapping array as argument. This mechanism allows defining arbitrary mappings of array elements to processors. However, since each array element must be mapped to exactly one processor replication is not possible. In case of multidimensional arrays, the distribution function INDIRECT may either be used to specify the distribution of the array as a whole, as defined in [20], or to specify the distribution of a single array dimension.

3.3 Implicit Data Distribution

Implicit data distribution enables the user to specify that an array should be distributed in the same way as another already distributed array, or to specify that certain elements of two or more arrays should be placed on the same processors.

The first form of implicit distribution is *distribution extraction*, which states that an array (or array dimension) should be distributed using the same distribution function as another array.

The second form of implicit distribution is known as alignment and enables the programmer to specify for each element of one array, called *alignee*, that it should be distributed to the same processor(s) as a certain element (or section) of another array, called *alignment-source array*. This allows the user to enforce that elements which are used in a common context are allocated on the same abstract processor(s). Vienna Fortran 90 distinguishes three forms of alignment specifications: *element-based alignment*, *section-based alignment*, and *functional alignment*. Element-based alignment specifies for each element of the alignee to which element (or section) of the source array it should be mapped. This includes collapsing and permutation of dimensions and replication. By means of section-based alignment, it is only possible to align the alignee with a conformable section of the source array. This allows for embedding the alignee into the source array, possibly using offsets and strides, but without allowing any replication, collapsing, or permutation of dimensions. Arbitrary alignments can be specified by means of functional alignment using mapping procedures as explained in Section 3.7.

```
REAL, ALIGNED(A(1:100))          :: E(100)   ! section based alignment
REAL, ALIGNED(F(I) WITH A(2*I-1)) :: F(50)    ! element based alignment
REAL, DISTRIBUTED(=A)             :: G(100)   ! distribution extraction
```

The alignment attribute for array E specifies that array E is distributed to the same processors as the interior section of array A of Figure 1. As a consequence, element E(I) is placed on the same processor(s) as element A(I), $1 \leq I \leq 100$. The meaning of the second alignment attribute is that element F(I) is co-located with element A(2*I-1), $1 \leq I \leq 50$. Array G is distributed by means of distribution extraction which specifies that the same distribution function as for array A will be used. However, since the shapes of A and G are not conform, some elements A(I) and G(I) may reside on different processors.

Fig. 2. Implicit Distributions

An alignment relationship between two statically distributed and statically allocated arrays, which has been established at the time of declaration by means of the **ALIGNED** attribute, remains invariant within the scope of declaration. However, in the context of dynamically allocated arrays the alignment relationship may be broken, since their shapes may be modified as the result of the execution of an allocate statement. In order to enable the user to specify sets of dynamically distributed arrays that have a run-time invariant alignment relationship, the **CONNECT** attribute may be used.

3.4 Control of Dynamic Redistribution

Dynamic redistribution allows defining or changing the distribution (or alignment) of an array by means of executable statements. Dynamically distributed arrays are useful for applications in which the distribution of an array needs to be changed dynamically according to different computation phases, or in order to support applications for which an efficient distribution is dependent on run-time data. However, unrestricted use of dynamic data distribution significantly complicates the compiler's task to generate an efficient parallel program. In those cases where the compiler cannot determine the distribution of an array at a certain point in the program, worst case assumptions have to be made. Because of the significant impact of dynamic data distributions on the complexity of the compilation and optimization process, language features that enable the user to supply the compiler with additional information are provided.

By means of the **RANGE** attribute the user is able to specify the *range of possible distributions* an array may be associated with at runtime. Moreover, the **CONNECT** attribute allows to specify a run-time invariant relationship between the distributions of groups of dynamically distributed arrays.

3.5 Distribution of Derived Types

In Vienna Fortran 90 an object of derived type may be distributed in the same way as objects of intrinsic types as long as no component at any level of compo-

```
PROCESSORS R(4),R2(2,2)

TYPE VECTOR
   REAL, DISTRIBUTED(BLOCK) :: V(N)
END TYPE VECTOR

TYPE T
  REAL, DISTRIBUTED(BLOCK,BLOCK) TO R2 :: MAT(N,N)
  TYPE(VECTOR)                         :: VEC(M)
END TYPE T

TYPE(T)      :: A,B
TYPE(VECTOR) :: X
```

A, B and X are objects of a statically distributed derived type. Note that forall $I, J, 1 \leq I, J \leq M$, the arrays $A\%VEC(I)$, $B\%VEC(J)$, and X always have identical distributions.

Fig. 3. Distribution of components of derived type

nent selection has a distribution associated with it. Furthermore, under certain restrictions, components of derived types may be associated with a distribution. This is important for applications that use derived data types to store several arrays in a single data structure.

A derived type is called *distributed derived type* iff there exists a component at any level of component selection for which a distribution has been specified. For objects of distributed derived type a distribution must not be specified. If in a distributed derived type *all* components, at any level of component selection, for which a distribution has been specified, are statically distributed, then it is called a *statically distributed derived type*, otherwise a *dynamically distributed derived type*.

Corresponding subobjects of different objects of a statically distributed derived type have the same distribution type associated with them at any point in the program. Note that this usually will not be the case for objects of a dynamically distributed derived type.

The concept of statically distributed derived types is somehow restrictive since all objects of the same derived type always are distributed in the same way. It may, however, often be necessary that different objects of the same derived type are statically distributed to different subsets of processors. To achieve this, we have modified the derived type definition of Fortran 90 such that derived types may be parameterized with a processor array. Parameterization of derived types is achieved by specifying a dummy processor array within the derived type definition statement. The dummy processor array is associated with an actual processor array section by means of the LOCATION attribute, which has to be provided within the type declaration statement. It has the effect that the speci-

```
PROCESSORS R(1:100)

TYPE T, PROCESSORS Q(:)                    ! parameterized type definition
   REAL, DISTRIBUTED(BLOCK) TO Q(1:SIZE(Q)/2) :: X(M)
   TYPE(T2), LOCATION(Q(SIZE(Q)/2+1:))         :: Y
END TYPE

TYPE(T), LOCATION(R(1:50))   :: A
TYPE(T), LOCATION(R(51:100)) :: B
TYPE(T)                      :: C
```

Array $A\%X$ is distributed to the first 25 processors of R whereas $B\%X$ is distributed
to processors $R(51:75)$. Since C is declared without a LOCATION attribute, $C\%X$ is
distributed over the whole processor array R. Furthermore, components X and Y are
distributed to disjoint processor subsets.

Fig. 4. The LOCATION attribute

fied processor array section is *reserved* for all objects of that derived type. As a
consequence, all subobjects of such objects are distributed to the specified processor array section. If the LOCATION attribute is omitted, the primary processor
array is associated with the dummy processor array by default.

Assume that a derived type T is parameterized with a processor array Q
as shown in Figure 4. As a consequence, Q becomes the only processor array
accessible within the derived type definition[3]. The dummy processor array Q
is associated with an actual processor array section by means of the LOCATION
attribute. Note that the LOCATION attribute may only be specified within the
declaration of objects of statically distributed derived type.

Structure components which have the DYNAMIC attribute may be associated
with a new distribution by executing a DISTRIBUTE or ALIGN statement or as
the result of a procedure call. Given an array of dynamically distributed derived
type, corresponding components of different array elements may be associated
with different distributions.

3.6 Distribution of Pointers

One important feature of Fortran 90, which for example is very useful for multigrid applications, is that structure components may be dynamically allocated
arrays. Since in Fortran 90 the ALLOCATABLE attribute must not be specified for
a component of a derived type, the POINTER attribute has to be used to declare a structure component that is dynamically allocated. In analogy to ordinary
arrays, array pointers may be associated with a distribution either statically
or dynamically. However, Vienna Fortran 90 allows using statically distributed

---

[3] Different views of the dummy processor array may be provided by using the RESHAPE
function.

```
PROCESSORS R2(10,10)

TYPE GRID
    REAL, DISTRIBUTED(BLOCK,BLOCK), POINTER :: U(:,:)
    REAL, DISTRIBUTED(=U), POINTER          :: F(:,:)
END TYPE GRID

TYPE (GRID) :: MG(10)

ALLOCATE(MG(I)%U(N,N), MG(I)%F(N,N))   ! allocate & distribute i-th grid
```

In this example the derived type GRID consists of two statically distributed array pointers. This kind of data type is useful in multigrid applications where the sizes of the grids U and F are determined at runtime, depending on the grid level.

Fig. 5. Distributed Multigrid Data Structure

pointers (SDPs) only in a restricted form. An SDP must not be the left hand side of a pointer assignment statement. SDPs have been included in Vienna Fortran 90 for two reasons. First, they enable that components of derived types that are dynamically allocated arrays may be distributed (see Figure 5) and second, dynamic memory allocation may be hidden inside of a procedure.

An object that has both the **POINTER** and **DYNAMIC** attribute is called a *dynamically distributed pointer* (DDP). Using DDPs, the multigrid data structure of Figure 5 can be modified in such a way that, depending on the size of the grids on different levels, they are distributed to different processor subsets. By mapping the coarser grids (i.e. the smaller grids) to only a subset of the processors the computation-to-communication ratio and thus the performance may be significantly improved.

A much more powerful feature of Fortran 90 pointers is to use them as aliases for arrays or array sections. An array pointer of rank n can be associated with any array or array section of rank n by means of the pointer assignment. A dynamically distributed pointer may be the alias of more than one distributed array (section). In contrast to SDPs, DDPs may be associated with sections of distributed arrays by means of the pointer assignment statement. Therefore, the distribution associated with a DDP may be changed at run time through the execution of a pointer assignment statement, an **ALLOCATE** statement, a **DISTRIBUTE** or **ALIGN** statement, or as the result of a procedure call. If a DDP is associated with a section of a distributed array in a pointer assignment statement, then it usually will be associated with a new distribution. The mechanisms to determine the distribution of a pointer to an array section are the same as those encountered when an array section is passed to a procedure. A DDP that is currently associated with a statically distributed object must not be associated with a new distribution by means of a **DISTRIBUTE** statement or as the result of a procedure call.

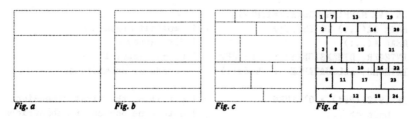

```
PROCESSORS R(6,4)

DISTRIBUTED(MRD(A,(/3,2/),(/2,2/))) :: A(N,N)    ! use mapping procedure
```

This example illustrates a multiple recursive distribution of a matrix according to the mapping procedure of Figure 7. Fig. *a.* and *b.* show the decomposition of the first dimension and Fig. *c.* and *d.* the partition of the second dimension. The final distribution is shown in Fig.d. where the numbers indicate to which processors (with respect to the implicit processor array *$P*) the resulting segments are mapped.

Fig. 6. A user defined distribution

3.7 Mapping Procedures

The Vienna Fortran mechanisms of user defined distribution functions and user defined alignment functions [20] have been unified and generalized by introducing mapping procedures. By means of mapping procedures it is possible to specify arbitrary distributions or alignments. Furthermore, mapping procedures may be used to specify the work distribution of *parallel loops*. The activation of a mapping procedure results either in the computation a distribution or an alignment, or if it is activated in the context of a parallel loop, it determines a mapping of loop iterations to processors. Mapping procedures may have arbitrary arguments as a normal Fortran procedure. However, all the arguments implicitly have the **INTENT(IN)** attribute. A mapping procedure has two implicit arguments, the *from-domain* and the *to-domain* which can be thought of as arrays in the sense of Fortran with the difference that they do not have a type and do not occupy any storage. If a mapping procedure is referenced within a distribution specification, the from-domain is implicitly associated with the index domain of the array to be distributed and the to-domain is associated with the index domain of the processor array to which the distribution refers. If mapping procedures are used to specify alignments, the from-domain is implicitly associated with the index domain of the alignee and the to-domain with the index domain of the alignment source array. Similarly, when a mapping procedure is referenced in the work distribution part of a parallel loop, the from-domain is associated with the index domain of the loop iteration space and the to-domain with the index domain of the specified processor array. Apart from the computation of a data distribution, an alignment or a work distribution, mapping procedures must not produce any side effects. Moreover, mapping procedures

```
RECURSIVE MAPPING MRD(A,PF1,PF2)
   FROM IA(:,:) TO IR(:,:)                    ! implicit arguments
   REAL A(:,:)                                ! data array
   INTEGER, DIMENSION(:) :: PF1,PF2           ! prime factor lists
   INTEGER, ALLOCATABLE  :: bnds(:)           ! bounds of submatrices

   IF (SIZE(PF1) > 0) THEN                     ! partition the first dimension
      bnds => ...                             ! determine bounds of submatrices
      DO I=1, SIZE(bnds)-1
         IA(bnds(I):bnds(I+1),:)    &    ! MAP statement
            MAP(MRD(A(bnds(I):bnds(I+1),:),PF1(2:),PF2)) TO  &
         IR((I-1)*SIZE(IR,1)/PF1(1):I*SIZE(IR,1)/PF1(1),:)
      END DO
   ELSE
      IF (SIZE(PF1) > 0) THEN                  ! partition the second dimension
         bnds => ...                          ! determine bounds of submatrices
         DO I=1, SIZE(bnds)-1
            IA(:,bnds(I):bnds(I+1)) &    ! MAP statement
               MAP (MRD(A(:,bnds(I):bnds(I+1)),PF1,PF2(2:))) TO  &
            IR(:,(I-1)*SIZE(IR,2)/PF2(1):I*SIZE(IR,2)/PF2(1))
         END DO
      ELSE
         IA -> IR                             ! index mapping statement
      END IF
   END IF
END MAPPING MRD
```

This mapping procedure realizes a multiple recursive distribution of a 2-d matrix with respect to a 2-d processor array with $p * q$ processors. Assume that the prime factor decomposition of p and q is given by $p = p_1.p_2....p_r$ and $q = q_1.q_2...q_s$, $r, s \geq 1$. The distribution is carried out in $r + s$ stages as follows. In the first r stages the first dimension of the array is partitioned recursively into p submatrices. In stage 1 the first dimension of IA is partitioned into p_1 parts such that the load is balanced equally among the resulting submatrices (i.e each submatrix contains the same number of non-zero elements). For each of the submatrices the mapping procedure is invoked recursively, and each of the submatrices is decomposed subsequently into p_2 submatrices, and so on. In stages $r + 1$ to $r + s$ the same technique is applied to partitioned the second dimension according to the prime factors contained in $PF2$.

Fig. 7. Multiple recursive distribution

may be recursive and may be passed as arguments to mapping procedures. This feature is in particular very useful to specify pseudo-regular distributions such as *binary* or *multiple recursive distributions* [5, 17] which are often used to achieve good load balancing for sparse matrix computations. Figure 6 visualizes a multiple recursive distribution as proposed in [17] which is defined using the recursive mapping procedure of Figure 7.

4 Procedures

The distribution of statically distributed arrays never changes as the result of a procedure call. Dynamically distributed actual arrays may, however, have a modified distribution after a procedure call if the corresponding dummy array has been redistributed inside the procedure. Whereas this allows to define or modify the distribution of dynamically distributed arrays within procedures, unrestricted use of this feature may seriously complicate the task of the compiler to determine which distributions may reach a particular array reference and thus requires sophisticated interprocedural analysis. Restoration of the original distribution can always be enforced by specifying the RESTORE attribute, either in the dummy argument declaration or with the actual argument at the point of the call.

Dummy arrays may be either distributed explicitly, or they may inherit the distribution from the corresponding actual array. For dummy arrays that inherit the distribution from the actual array a range of possible distributions may be specified in the same way as for dynamically distributed arrays. A call to an internal procedure also may change the distribution of all dynamically distributed arrays that are accessible by host association or by use association as long as they are not associated with a dummy argument. The restrictions of Fortran 90 on entities associated with dummy arguments have been extended in order to cover the distribution of an entity.

Interface blocks of external procedures may be extended with data distribution information and are extremely important for supporting separate compilation. Vienna Fortran 90 requires that the interface of a procedure that has distributed dummy arrays is explicit. Furthermore, procedure local processor array declarations must be specified in an interface.

In order to provide a mechanism for calling sequential procedures from a Vienna Fortran 90 program a procedure may be specified with the keyword LOCAL. This mechanism is especially useful if some sequential standard algorithm should be applied to the local portion of a distributed object, independently on each processor. LOCAL procedures behave like ordinary sequential Fortran procedures[4] and it is assumed that they are executed on a single processor. If a local procedure is executed on a particular processor it may only access data that is owned by that processor. Besides that it must not produce any side effects. More precisely, it must not access or update a global variable or an object that is storage associated with a global variable or a subobject thereof, except through the use of a dummy argument. In Vienna Fortran 90 a call to a local procedures must either appear inside of a FORALL loop or inside another local procedure. If a local procedure is called from a FORALL loop the programmer is required to explicitly specify which processor should execute the procedure. This can be achieved by either appending an ON-clause to the call statement or by providing a work

---

[4] Local procedures also may be coded in any other sequential language like for example C.

distribution specification in a surrounding FORALL loop. It is the responsibility of the programmer to ensure that all the data accessed by a local procedure is exclusively local to the executing processor (i.e it must not be replicated). For this purpose Vienna Fortran 90 provides additional intrinsic functions. For example, the Fortran 90 intrinsic function LBOUND may be used with a processor number as additional argument. In this case it returns the smallest index of the corresponding array that has been mapped to that processor.

5 Parallel Loops

Vienna Fortran 90 provides an explicitly parallel FORALL loop enabling the user to assert that the iterations of a loop are independent and can be executed in parallel. No value written in one iteration of such a loop may be read or written in another iteration, unless special reduction statements are used which permit global operations to be performed. The result of such an operation is not available within the loop. An intrinsic reduction function and intrinsic reduction operations are provided (ADD, MULT, MAX and MIN). The user may define further such operations. Moreover, the user may explicitly specify how the iterations of a FORALL loop should be distributed to the available set of processors by means of an ON-clause.

Forall loops are especially important in the context of irregular applications where large data arrays are accessed indirectly. In such cases the compiler usually cannot determine if the corresponding loops contain loop carried dependencies and thus will fail to parallelize such loops. Forall loops may be regarded as a generalization of the Fortran 90 array assignment since they allow to express assignments to more general array sections than achievable with triplet notation. The only difference of Vienna Fortran 90 FORALL loops to those defined in [20] is that in addition to the *on clause* the work distribution may be specified in much the same way as the distribution of arrays, including the use of user defined mapping procedures. Thus, arbitrary mappings of loop iterations to processors may be specified.

6 Implementation

A number of selected language elements of Vienna Fortran 90 has been integrated in the Vienna Fortran Compilation System (VFCS) [7]. This includes multidimensional block and generalized block distributions, distribution by alignment allowing arbitrary linear alignment functions, and distributions with respect to processor subsets. The VFCS provides advanced interprocedural analysis techniques in order to determine the distribution of dummy arrays that inherit their distribution from actual arrays, and data flow analysis as well as dependence analysis techniques needed for the parallelization of DO-loops. Regular computations which can be analyzed at compile time are parallelized based on the *overlap concept* [11]. New techniques for the parallelization of array assignments involving arbitrary block and cyclic distributions (including linear alignment) which may depend on run-time data are currently implemented [3, 4]. Runtime compilation techniques based on the PARTI primitives [18] are used for the compilation of explicitly parallel FORALL loops with indirect array references. The VFCS currently generates code for several different distributed memory architectures, including the Intel iPSC/860, the Paragon and the Meiko CS-2.

7 Conclusion

We conclude with a brief discussion of the relation of Vienna Fortran 90 and HPF. The HPF language model includes, besides the basic features for data distribution and alignment, the concept of *templates*. Templates, similar to Fortran D decompositions, are basically a named index domain that can be used for specifying alignment between arrays. The data distribution model of HPF is based on a three-level mapping. Arrays are mapped to templates which in turn are mapped to virtual processor grids. Virtual processor grids in turn are mapped to the physical processors. This last mapping, however, is not specified within HPF. HPF assumes that each array is aligned to a template, either explicitly or implicitly. However, this causes problems in the context of allocatable arrays since templates cannot be allocatable. Templates, as a language construct, significantly complicate the semantics of argument transfer at procedure boundaries. In HPF pointers may be the object of a redistribute or realign statement only if they are associated with a whole array, not an array section. The semantics of pointer assignments in the context of distributed arrays is currently undefined. Furthermore, HPF does not provide any support for the distribution of components of derived types. HPF follows Vienna Fortran 90 closely in a number of features. This includes in particular Fortran 90 as the base language, abstract processor arrays, direct distribution and alignment of arrays, distinction between static and dynamic distributions, definition of the procedure interface, in particular inherited and enforced distributions, and FORALL loops (called *independent* loops in HPF).

On the other hand, a number of advanced concepts of Vienna Fortran have *not* been included in HPF. Among them are different processor views, with an explicit specification of the equivalence, the implicit definition of a canonical one-dimensional processor array, distribution of arrays to processor sections, generalized block and indirect distributions, user-defined distribution functions, return of distributions from a procedure call, and distribution of pointers and of objects of derived type. These omissions, in particular the absence of language features for the formulation of arbitrary distribution functions, significantly impairs the applicability of HPF to advanced algorithms using, for example, irregular or adaptive grids.

References

1. S.Benkner, B.Chapman, H.P.Zima. Vienna Fortran 90. In *Proceedings of the Scalable High Performance Computing Conference*, Williamsburg, USA, April 1992.

2. S. Benkner, P. Brezany, H. Zima. Processing Array Statements and Procedure Interfaces in the Prepare High Performance Fortran Compiler. In P.A. Fritszon, editor, *Compiler Construction, Proceedings of the 5th International Conference*, LNCS 786, pages 324-338. Springer-Verlag, April 1994.

3. S.Benkner. Vienna Fortran 90 and its Compilation. Ph.D.Thesis. Technical Report, University of Vienna, Institute for Software Technology and Parallel Systems, September 1994.

4. S.Benkner. Handling Block-Cyclic Distributed Arrays in Vienna Fortran 90. In *Proceedings of the International Conference on Parallel Architectures and Compilation Techniques,*Limassol, Cyprus, June 26-29, 1995, to appear.

5. M.J. Berger and S.H.Bokhari. A Partitioning Strategy for Nonuniform Problems on Multiprocessors. IEEE Trans. Comput., vol 36, no. 5, pp. 570-580, 1987.

6. B. M. Chapman, P. Mehrotra, H. Zima: *Programming in Vienna Fortran*, Scientific Programming, Vol.1, No.1, 1992.

7. B. Chapman, S.Benkner, R.Blasko, P.Brezany, M.Egg, T.Fahringer, M.Gerndt, B.Knaus, P.Kutschera, H.Moritsch, A.Schwald, V.Sipkova, H.Zima. *Vienna Fortran Compilation System. Version 1.0. User's Guide.* Institute for Software Technology and Parallel Systems, University of Vienna, January, 1993.

8. M. Chen and J. Li. Optimizing Fortran 90 programs for data motion on massively parallel systems. TR YALE/DCS/TR-882, Yale University, January 1992.

9. B. Chapman, P. Mehrotra, H. Zima. Extending HPF For Advanced Data Parallel Applications. Technical Report,TR 94-7, University of Vienna, May 1994.

10. G. Fox, S. Hiranandani, K. Kennedy, C. Koelbel, U. Kremer, C. Tseng, and M. Wu. Fortran D language specification. Department of Computer Science Rice COMP TR90079, Rice University, March 1991.

11. H.M. Gerndt, *Updating Distributed Variables in Local Computations,* Concurr ency: Practice and Experience, Vol. 2(3), 171-193 (September 1990)

12. High Performance Fortran Forum. *High Performance Fortran Language Specification. Version 1.0* TR, CRPC-TR92225, Rice University, May 3, 1993.

13. ISO. Fortran 90 Standard, May 1991, ISO/IEC 1539 :1991 (E)

14. P. Mehrotra, J. Van Rosendale. The BLAZE language: A parallel language for scientific programming. *Parallel Computing*, Vol. 5, 339-361, 1987.

15. P. Mehrotra, J. Van Rosendale. Programming Distributed Memory Architectures Using Kali. In A. Nicolau, D. Gelernter, T. Gross, and D. Padua, editors, *Advances in Languages and Compilers for Parallel Processing*, pages 364–384. Pitman/MIT-Press, 1991.

16. D.M. Pase, T. MacDonald, A. Meltzer. MPP Fortran Programming Model. Technical Report, Cray Research, March 1994.

17. L.F. Romero and E.L. Zapata. Data Distributions for Sparse Matrix Vector Multiplication. In *Proceedings of the Fourth International Workshop on Compilers for Parallel Computers*. Delft University of Technology, The Netherlands, 1993

18. J. Saltz, R. Das, R. Ponnusamy, D. Mavriplis, H. Berryman and J. Wu. Parti Procedures for Realistic Loops. In *Proceedings of DMCC6*, Portland, OR, 1991.

19. Thinking Machines Corporation. CM Fortran Reference Manual, Version 5.2. Thinking Machines, Cambridge, MA, September 1989.

20. H. Zima, P. Brezany, B. Chapman, P. Mehrotra, and A. Schwald. Vienna Fortran - a language specification. ICASE Internal Report 21, ICASE, Hampton, VA, 1992.

Programming Abstracts for Synchronization and Communication in Parallel Programs

Anatoly E. Doroshenko

Glushkov Institute of Cybernetics
National Academy of Sciences of Ukraine
Glushkov prosp., 40, Kiev 252187, Ukraine
E-mail: dor@d105.icyb.kiev.ua

Abstract. A class of distributed/shared memory parallel programs with static, race free structure of accesses to shared memory is considered and programming abstracts in the form of regular expressions are proposed as synchronization facilities for these programs. Along with more concurrency these facilities can expose with respect to semaphore-like ones they can be applicable for designing efficient communucation schemes for multilevel distributed/shared memory parallel programs.

1 Introduction

General purpose semaphore-like synchronization facilities are known to be too restrictive to obtain efficient parallel programs, so alternative special purpose tools dedicated for particular cases important for applications are desirable. We consider a class of parallel programs with distibuted primary (local) memory and shared secondary (global) one that have static, race free structure of accesses to shared memory. It means that any pair of data dependent statements, at least one of them modifying shared value, should be always performed in the same order. This class is fairly broad and includes, for instance, all direct and many iterative methods for solution of linear algebraic equation systems. We propose to capture this structure with formal regular expressions and to use them as synchronization and communication tools.

The idea of regular control of synchronizing parallel processes was pioneered in [1] in the form of path expressions but so far it has not been applied for speeding up data exchanges and improving their asynchronism. For these purposes in [3, 4] a class of formal expressions called *forcing expressions* have been introduced by the author and their application for enhancing synchronization and communication features has been shown. It was also proven [4] that semaphore-like facilities are too restrictive to obtain efficient parallel programs in cases of race free programs. In this paper we develop further our approach showing that forcing expressions can decrease synchronization overhead significantly for the class of parallel programs considered. Moreover, using these expressions we show how to produce simple user-based forms of governing data exchanges to improve also communication part of parallel programs efficiency in multilevel memory environment via formal program transformations and systematic elimination of slow memory accesses.

2 A Model of Parallel Programs

We consider a class of parallel programs of large granularity (like as in [6] we call them *macroconveyor programs*), that have distibuted primary (local), shared secondary (global) memory and universal pairwise parallel component communication possibilities.

Macroconveyor program is considered as a tuple $p = (P, K, t, E)$ where $P = \{P_i\}$ is a finite set of sequential *component programs* (modules), K is a set of *components* — logical names of parallel processes, $t : K \to P$ is a (partial) *initialization map* providing intial program configuration, E is a set of *outer array* names. Modules are ordinary sequential programs except parallel procedure call and data exchanges statements. The last are of two kinds: *direct* pairwise exchanges with statements $x- > k1$ (transfering) and $y < -k2$ (accepting) that are executed at components $k2$ and $k1$ respectively, and *external* exchanges through shared memory with statements $x :< -A$ (reading) and $y : - > A$ (writing) where x, y are inner and A is outer array name. Outer arrays establish shared memory of a program and are organised as two-level structures of multidimensional array of *data blocks* that are multidimensional arrays of *data elements*.

Basic parallel facilities are supposed to include explicit parallel components definition and parallel (remote) procedure call. Semantics of macroconveyor program execution establishes simultanious execution of components whose intialization map is definite. Program configuration may vary during execution due to parallel procedure calls of the form PARCALL $F(X1,...,Xn)$, whose semantics means adding a new component to the set of intialized ones, loading module F in it and execution of F given input parameters in parallel with calling module. Modules called with such a parallel call statement are synchronised with PARDO...PAREND statement brackets.

Input and output data are supposed to be in outer memory.

3 Forcing Expressions

The notion of forcing expression introduced by the author [3, 4] can be explained in general terms of algebra of algorithms [5]. Let (P, K, t, E) is a macroconveyor program. For every $k \in K$ define R_k — symbol of reading and W_k — symbol of writing. Let V be a variable set and D a data domain for these variables. A set of partial mappings $B = \{b : V \to D\}$ is called a set of memory states. Assume being known a set of basic operators $Op = \{y : B \to B\}$ with unit operator ε and a set of basic conditions $Co = \{u : B \to \{0, 1\}\}$ that also includes boolean constants $\mathbf{0}$ and $\mathbf{1}$. An algebra of partial transformations Y, generated on Op by means of three operations: $P; Q$ — concatenation ";", $u \to (P \text{ else } Q)$ — branch operation and $while(u, P)$ — iteration, where P, Q are operators and u is condition, is called algebra of operators. An algebra U, generated on Co by means of boolean operations and operation of multiplication by condition Pu that stands for "u after P", is called algebra of conditions. The two-set algebra

$A(Y, U)$ considered as set of operators and conditions closed under operations above is called algebra of algorithms. Each element of algebra $A(Y, U)$ can be represented as regular expression of elements basic operators and basic conditions sets and operations of algebra of algorithms. Regular expressions of algebra of operators Y are called regular programs. Assume also defined the binary operation of parallel reading (P, Q) — commutative and associative operation constructed with regular expressions P and Q that use the reading symbols only.

Let $K(A)$ be a set of components of a race free program that are communicated externally via outer name A. Then the *forcing expression* (FE) is a regular expression $f(A)$, constructed with symbols R_k and W_k , $k \in K(A)$, unit operator and memory conditions by means of regular operations and operation of parallel reading.

The main idea of FE introduction, unlike path expressions [1], is to enforce the order of component accesses to outer memory, that may be known a priory in the case of race free program, and to eliminate indeterminacy for increasing program performance. Execution of race free program whose external exchanges controlled by FE consists in joint iterpretation of component programs and forcing expressions. Read (write) statement execution initialization in component k must correspond interpretation of R_k (W_k) as current symbol of FE otherwise synchronization delay in the component invades. In this context a FE is an inalienable part of the parallel program considered that allows to produce different program behaviours with the same program components due to various FEs. To clarify the significance of the introducing FEs let us consider an example of the following two-component program with components named respectively $k1$ and $k2$ from left to right:

```
for  i:=1  to  n-1 do          for  i:=1  to  n-1 do
     x :<- X(i);                    y :<- Y;
     y := h(x);                     x :=g(y);
     y :-> Y;                       x :-> X(i+1);
end loop;                      end loop;
```

where Y and $X(1 : n)$ are outer arrays. This program executes multiple assignment $X(i + 1) := g(h(X(i)))$, $i = 1, \ldots, n - 1$, if FEs are $f(Y) = while(u, W_{k1};$ $R_{k2})$, $u = (0 < i < n)$, and $f(X((i)) = (v \rightarrow (R_{k1} \ else \ \varepsilon); \ w \rightarrow (W_{k2} \ else \ \varepsilon))$, $v = (0 < i < n)$, $w = (1 < i < n + 1)$ whereas the same program performs recurrent computations $X(i + 1) = g(h(X(i)))$, $i = 1, \ldots, n - 1$, if FEs are $f(X(i)) = (w \rightarrow (W_{k2} \ else \ \varepsilon); v \rightarrow (R_{k1} \ else \ \varepsilon))$. The difference is that in first case the values of $X(i)$, $i = 1, \ldots, n - 1$, should be read before the values of $X(i)$, $i = 2, \ldots, n$, be recomputed and written. In latter case these operations are to be performed in reverse order and computations of components must be executed in fact sequentially.

As an example of forcing expressions application for effective synchronization of external data exchanges let us consider Cholesky factorization problem. We assume input matrix $A = (a_{ij})$ and Cholesky factor $L = (l_{ij})$ to be, for simplicity, dense full $N * N$ symmetric positive definite matrices broken into square blocks $B * B$ so that $n = N/B$ is integer. Define component set as $\{K(i,j) : 1 \leq j < i \leq n\}$ and assume that factorization of (i,j)-block is performed by component $K(i,j)$. A straitforward version of macroconveyor program for solving this problem on p processors is of the master/worker style. A worker module, say, Chol_Fact_Block(i,j) performes factorization of (i,j)-block of matrix having as input data (i,j)-block of input matrix A and (j,k)- and (i,l)-blocks of result matrix L, $1 \leq k < j$, $1 \leq l \leq j$. Given A and L matrices are stored in corresponding outer arrays, the form of master module then depends on synchronization facilities used. Let designate r_{ij}^{jk} a moment of reading the block produced by component $K(j,k)$ in component $K(i,j)$ and w_{ij} - a moment of writing result block into auter array by component $K(i,j)$. Then conditions for correct synchronization can be presented as $w_{ij} < r_{il}^{ij}$, $j < l \leq i$, and $w_{jk} < r_{ij}^{jk}$, $1 \leq k \leq j$. These inequalities (call them specifications) can be implemented in different ways. If wavefronts are defined as $Q_k = \{(i,j) : i + j = const, 1 < i + j \leq 2n\}$, $1 \leq k \leq 2n - 1$, then PARDO...PAREND synchronization is sufficient and master module can be shown as following:

```
master prog Chol_Fact(m,n,A,L)
    {   for k=1 to  2n-1 do
            PARDO;
            for (i,j) in Q do
                PARCALL Chol_Fact_Blocks(i,j,A,L)
            end for;
            PAREND;
        end for;
    }
```

One can see that synchronization is correct as the algorithm above implements even stronger conditions than those needed by specifications, i.e. $K(i,j)$ can begin its processing only after components $K(i-1,j)$ and $K(i,j-1)$ are completed. The algorithm is simple but its efficiency is not high because computations of different fronts can not overlap and different points of the same front provide different workload. If we assume the time needed to factorization of a block of the first column as a time unit then $T_1 = O(n^3/6)$ and $T_{n/2} = O(n^2)$ and the efficiency $e(p) = T_1/pT_p$ is of order $O(1/3)$ in this case.

If wavefronts are organized along columns of components matrix and semaphore-like synchronization is used then a wavefront Q_k, $1 \leq k \leq 2n-1$, includes diagonal component given k is odd and consists of components of the same column but the diagonal one if k is even. Assuming lock and unlock statements are respectivly the first and the last statement of the Chol_Fact_Block module the same master program above (with PARDO...PAREND eliminated) can fit this case. But it does not improve the order of computation time and even decrease the order of efficiency to $O(1/6)$ because of extreme workload dispersion for different points of the same front.

Forcing expressions for this problem are: $f(A_{ij}) = R_{ij}$; and $f(L_{ij}) = W_{ij}$; $(while(u, R_{ij+k}), while(v, R_{li}))$; where $0 < j < i \leq n$, $u = (1 \leq k \leq i - j)$, $v =$

$(i \leq l \leq n)$. They use wavefront organization the same as for semaphores and leave efficiency at the level of order $O(1/3)$ but allows to obtain a variant of program two times faster than previos ones. Of course these theoretical estimations should not mislead. In practice the program is executed on $p < n$ processors that gives $T_p = O((2n^3 - 3n^2p + np^2)/12p)$ and if $p << n$ then multiprocessor efficiency is close to 1. Table 1 below exhibits values of multiprocessor efficiency for the first ten values of the quantity $k = n/p$.

Table 1. Multiprocessor efficiency for FE-synchronization

k	1	2	3	4	5	6	7	8	9	10
e(p)	0.33	0.53	0.64	0.71	0.76	0.79	0.81	0.83	0.85	0.87

In [4] a general statement is argued that FE have more expressive power than semaphor-like facilities and some general implementation mechanism for FE is proposed. Next section shows that FE may be used also to produce simple user-based forms of data exchange speedup in multilevel memory system.

4 External exchange speedup

Exchanges speedup in multilevel memory environment is an important source of parallel programs efficiency enhancement. Basically one can distinguish two approaches there. The first consists in program analysis and transformations to reduce number of accesses to slow (global) memory. Another one is buffering slow memory exchanges in fast (local) memory of multiprocessor system. We propose a *hybrid dedicated* method that instead of general purpose buffering algorithms take into account some "knowledge" of special case catched in forcing expressions. In many important cases transformations are very simple and buffering is low costed.

Following is an example of such forcing expresions application where distributed memory of one or more processors are assigned to buffer pool. Under conditions of large mumber of processors available and limited number of buffered blocks such a usage of processors in this manner would be quite reasonable. Likely situation takes place in band matrix Cholesky factorization. Asuming $2M$ be a bandwidth of matrix so that $m = M/T$ is integer and $m(i) = max(1, i - m)$ modification of previous forcing expressions for this case results in $f(A_{ij}) = R_{ij}$; and $f(L_{ij}) = W_{ij}; u \rightarrow ((while(v, R_{ij+k}), while(w, R_{i+li})) \, else \, (while(v, R_{ij+k}), while(q, R_{i+pi})))$; where $0 < j \leq i < n$, $v = (1 \leq k \leq i - j)$, $w = (0 \leq l \leq j - i + m)$, $u = (0 < j \leq n - m), q = (0 < p \leq n - i)$. The very form of the FEs shows that exchanges with A matrix need not to be buffered because every its block is read only once but L matrix exchanges buffering is desirable because of its multiple reading. It can be shown that buffer volume is not more than $m(m+1)/2$ of matrix blocks and so depends on bandwidth only. Therefore a program with the same buffer volume would perform Cholesky factorization of matrices of any order providing bandwidth of matrix does not exceed any limit.

5 Conclusion

We have considered an application of formal facilities of forcing expressions as programming abstracts to decrease communication and synchronization overhead and improve distributed/shared memory parallel programs efficiency. Forcing expressions are aimed to control parallel processes accesses to shared memory that are to be ordered a priori. It is such a "knowledge" of discipline of exchanges through shared memory that allows to obtain more effective paralllel programs in classes of applications. A method for speeding up external exchanges based on forcing expressions application is also presented. Algorithms of program transformations for our techniques are developed and partially implemented [2, 3] in system software of ES 1766 multiprocessor [6, 7] that consists of up to 256 processors with 1 Mb/processor distributed main memory, shared disc memory and any pairwise communications and yields peak performance of about 500 Mflops. The techniques as we belive are useful not only for macroconveyor but for other architectures too.

References

1. R.H. Campbell, N.A. Habermann, The specification of process synchronization by path expressions. Lect. Notes Comput. Sci., **16** (1974) 89-102.
2. A.E. Doroshenko, Advancing synchronization and communication techniques for distributed/shared memory parallel programs, in: *PARCELLA'94: Proc. VI Int. Workshop on Parallel Processing by Cellular Arrays and Automata, Sept. 20-22, 1994, Potsdam, Germany*, ed. C.Jesshope et al. (Academie Verlag, Berlin, 1994) 131-139.
3. A.E. Doroshenko, A Programming Methodology for Effective Data Exchanges in Macroconveyor Programs, in *Parallel Computing Technologies, Proc. Int. Conf., 7-11 Sept.1991, Novosibirsk, USSR*, ed. N.N.Mirenkov (World Scientific, Singapore, 1991) 330-338.
4. A.E. Doroshenko, A method of external exchanges synchronization in macroconveyor programs, *Cybernetics and System Analysis*, No. 5 (1991) 68-76 (Translated from Russian).
5. A.A.Letichevsky, Algebra of algorithms, data structures and parallel computations, in: *Information Processing 83* (IFIP, Amsterdam, 1983) 895-864.
6. V.S.Mikhalevich, Ju.V.Kapitonova, A.A.Letichevsky, On models of macroconveyer computations, in: *Information Processing 86* (IFIP, Amsterdam, 1986) 975-980.
7. P.Wolcott, S.E.Goodman, High-Speed Computers of the Soviet Union, *Computer*, **21**, No. 9 (1988) 32-41.

A Program Manipulation System for Fine-grained Architectures*

Vladimir A. Evstigneev, Victor N. Kasyanov

A.P.Ershov Institute of Informatics Systems
Siberian Division of Russian Academy of Science
630090, Novosibirsk-90, Russia

E-mail:{eva,kvn}@iis.nsk.su

Abstract. The PROGRESS system being implemented at the Institute of Informatics Systems in Novosibirsk is discussed. The system is intended to support rapid prototyping of compilers for high level languages (e.g. Fortran-77, Modula-2, SISAL) and for a family of architectures exploited fine-grained parallelism. The next goal of the project is to develop an environment for investigation of optimizing and restructuring transformations of programs to be parallelized.

Key words: parallel processing, fine-grain architectures, transformational approach, program restructuring, multifunctional cooperation

1 Introduction

One of the problems of parallel processing is that of a rapid development of a compiler prototype for a new computer. Having such compiler prototype one can begin to exploit the computer, to reveal its merits and demerits, and to evaluate its performance. To achieve this goal, we have begun the project PROGRESS aimed at rapid prototyping of compilers for a family of high-level languages and for a family of architectures exploiting fine-grained parallelism [1].

The next goal that we should like to achieve is to develop an environment for investigation of optimizing and restructuring transformations of the programs to be parallelized. From this point of view, the system under development is also intended to study currently available transformations and to create new ones (in particular, composite transformations involving existing ones) for programs written in high-level languages which are extended by facilities to annotate programs.

We are also planning to use the PROGRESS system as an integrated collection of tools to support the following opportunities:

— to convert a sequential program into a parallel one written in a parallel dialect of the input language,

— to optimize programs at the input language level using various criteria of quality,

* Partially supported by the Russian Foundation for Fundamental Research under Grant 95-07-19269

— to compare versions of the programs with respect to complexity,

— to include most of the capabilities of modern symbolic algebra systems,

— to tune the compilation process upon a given architecture.

2   The PROGRESS system

The PROGRESS system includes the following subsystems:

— *the translating subsystem (TRSS)* which supports conversion of a source program into the basic intermediate form (abstract syntax tree or AST);

— *the intermediate representation subsystem (IRSS)* which supports conversion of the basic program representation into other intermediate forms (program dependence graph, hierarchical task graph, ideograph and so on);

— *the transformation subsystem (TSS)* which supports program transformations and extraction of program properties needed;

— *the retranslating subsystem (RTSS)* which supports conversion of an intermediate program into high-level language program to be pretty printed or visualized;

— *the evaluation subsystem (EVSS)* which supports static program analysis and program run simulation to evaluate program quality and performance;

— *the code generator subsystem (CGSS)* which supports a code generation for a given target computer;

— *the specialization subsystem (SSS)* which supports a design of compiler prototype for a given input language and a given target computer by means of concretizing transformations;

— *the information subsystem (INSS)* and others.

Each subsystem is designed as an abstract data type — through the set of operations supported by this subsystem. Interaction between the subsystems is accomplished by a special interface subsystem.

We assume a compiler prototype being constructed to have several components, $P_1, \ldots, P_k$, where compilation process consists in applying P_1 to source program and, in general, in applying P_j to the result of applying P_{j-1}. Of course, some modifications of input languages, of program transformations implemented in the system or of target architectures may require corresponding modification of one or several subsystems. So, each subsystem should be open to include new features. However, we suppose that many components of compiler prototypes may be constructed from corresponding subsystems of the PROGRESS system on the base of concretizing transformations [2].

3   Input languages and target architectures

We are planning to have both the imperative languages (Fortran 77, Fortran-90, C, Pascal, Modula-2) and the applicative language SISAL [3],[4] as input ones.

It is assumed that source programming languages are extended by the so-called annotations which are formalized comments in the source programs and intended for permitting advices and partially relaxing the limits on the source language. That is, the program manipulation system accepts not only the source program, but also some annotations being directions (guidances) on how to do the transformation. However, annotations are not just pragmas or hints for a manipulation system (e.g., how to better parallelize a sequential program). They can be used to modify the semantics of the source program, but only in a very moderate manner [5].

Our current interests are connected with fine-grained architectures which include VLIW, superscalar, superpipelined and others. The importance of these architectures is connected with the existence of a tendency to offer both kinds of parallelism: coarse-grained and fine-grained ones.

4   Translating subsystem TRSS

The translating subsystem TRSS plays a role of the system manager which organizes and manipulates system components. A program or a program fragment

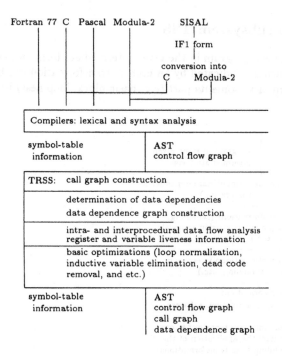

to be investigated (parallelized) is analyzed and transformed by the TRSS into the basic intermediate representation which is used as an input for other subsystems such as the IRSS or the TSS. For support further manipulations, the TRSS performs also the dependency analysis. As a result, we obtain symbol-table and data-dependency information for reference by the IRSS and TSS subsystems.

The TRSS performs also a data flow analysis, builds the call graph and performs intra- and interprocedural analysis. In order to make possible the data dependency analysis the TRSS performs some standard optimizations, e.g. loop normalization, dead code removal, and etc. For processing SISAL programs, the TRSS includes the special tools to convert a SISAL program into the IF1 form and then into the Modula-2 (or C) program.

5   Intermediate representation subsystem IRSS

As an input, the IRSS obtains from the TRSS a program in the form of an abstract syntax tree and a control flow graph, and also an information about a data dependency. The IRSS builds the representation to be required: a) the program dependence graph; b) the hierarchical task graph; c) the ideograph; d) the dependence flow graph; e) the program dependence web and etc.

To achieve this goal the IRSS designs dominator and postdominator trees, finds control dependencies, and determines the execution order of program operators.

6   Transformation subsystem TSS

As an input, the TSS obtains a program in the given intermediate form and executes transformations which are indicated by an user. A transformation can be applied to a whole program or to some its part (e.g. basic block, loop nest) and

symbol-table
information

program in some given
intermediate form

TSS: program transformation without data dependence
checking (the illustration operating)

general-purpose transformations (renaming,
strip mining, common subexpression removal,
strength reduction, etc.)

reordering transformations (loop interchange,
loop collapsing, loop spreading, etc.)

VLIW directed transformations
- optimizations (loop quantization, software
  pipelining, etc)
- percolation scheduling base transformations
- algorithms to control the application of the
  percolation scheduling base transformations
- other global scheduling algorithms
- local scheduling algorithms
- liveness information update

transformed program
(or transformed program graph)

either as a fully automatic process or a user-guided manipulation. The TSS contains a set of built-in transformations and strategies which can be extended by an user. In some cases (e.g. for teaching aim), a source program can be transformed without a program dependencies checking. In general case, a transformation is applied if it is possible.

The TSS includes also the set of fine-grained restructuring transformations for the creation of long instruction words. For example, they are Percolation Scheduling base transformations (Aiken's version of Trace scheduling and Compact Global, resource-constrained version of Percolation Scheduling and others). These methods perform scheduling on the program graph (control flow graph) and provide semantics-preserving transformations for reordering. Percolation Scheduling can be extended by loop unrolling and software pipelining.

7 Fine-grain architecture model

The architecture model of our system presents a family of units. The basic architecture includes several independent functional units, number of memory blocks and number of common data bus interconnecting all the model components.

The Functional Blocks. The functional blocks of our architecture model are similar to the units of RISC and FPS processors. The model includes the following blocks:

- control unit, which executes ALU operations and branches (16-bit integer);
- floating-point units: consist of an adder, multiplier and multifunctional adder-multiplier (38-bit);
- units of memory: consist of block program memory, block data memory, memory of constant and two blocks of register memory.

The all functional blocks and the blocks of memory are connected by common data bus.

The basic instruction word contains more then 10 operations and has length from 64-bit to 1024-bit.

The Basic Machine Instructions and Timing. The basic machine instructions are similar to the instructions of FPS processor, but only they are subset of all operations. We propose the following timing scheme:

- for operations of control unit are required one clock cycle;
- for operations of floating-point units - two or three clock cycles;
- for operations with memory - one (for register memory),two or three clock cycles.

8 Current state and related works

Today many programming tools and environments are being constructed to coordinate the disjoint activities of editing, debugging, and tuning complex applications designed to run on parallel architectures. The DELTA system, Faust, PTOPP, ParaScope and others can be mentioned among them.

Like DELTA [6], our system is a program manipulation one to study optimizing and restructuring algorithms, to design new transformations, to find out transformation application order mostly suited for the given classes of programs and computers. Unlike DELTA and other similar systems, the PROGRESS system uses a number of intermediate representations (such as the abstract syntax tree, the control flow graph, the program dependence graph, etc.) for programs being transformed, manipulates with annotated programs and can be used for the rapid prototyping of parallelizing compilers for different input languages and different target computers.

The initial version of the system manipulates with programs written in the Fortran-77 and Modula-2 languages extended with program annotation facilities and supports data flow analysis and optimizations. For program transformed, it uses such intermediate presentations as an abstract syntax tree, a control flow graph and SSA-form [7].

Multifunctional integration method aimed at solving the compaction problems for fine-grained computers and based on multiple-function multiple-data procedures has been developed. A computer-aided integrator for Fortran programs and a library of multifunctional procedures for the ES-2706 computer with the VLIW architecture have been implemented [8], [9].

Now the next version of the system is under development in which the translating subsystem will include the Fortran-90, C and SISAL languages, the intermediate representation subsystem will be extended on the program dependence graph and IF1, the program transformation subsystem will support restructuring transformations. Moreover, the system will be enriched by an evaluation subsystem.

References

[1] Evstigneev, V., Kasyanov, V.: The PROGRESS program manipulation system; In: Proc. of the International Conf. Parallel Computing Technologies (PaCT'93), Vol.3, Obninsk, 1993, 651 – 656.

[2] Kasyanov, V.N.: Transformational approach to program concretization; Theoretical Computer Science 90,1 (1991), 37 – 46.

[3] Feo, L.T.: SISAL; LLNL, Preprint UCRL-JC-110915, July 1992.

[4] Cann, D.: Retire Fortran? A debate rekindled; Comm. ACM 35, 8 (1992), 81-89.

[5] Kasyanov, V.N.: Tools and techniques of annotated programming; Lecture Notes in Computer Science 477 (1991), 117 – 131.

[6] Padua, D.: The DELTA program manipulation system. Preliminary design; University of Illinois at Urbana-Champaign, CSRD Rep. 880, June 1989.

[7] Software intellectualization and quality / Ed. by V.N.Kasyanov, Novosibirsk, 1994, (in Russian).

[8] Evstigneev, V.: Some peculiarities of the software for the computers with large instruction word; Programmirovanije, 2 (1991), 69 – 80. (In Russian).

[9] Bulysheva, L.: Methods and tools for optimization of computation for processors with VLIW-architectures; Computing Center of Sib. Div. of the RAS, Preprint 975, Novosibirsk, 1993. (In Russian).

Compilation of CDL for Different Target Architectures

Christian Hochberger, Tel.: +49 6151 165312
EMail: hochberg@isa.informatik.th-darmstadt.de

Rolf Hoffmann, Tel.: +49 6151 163611
EMail: hoffmann@isa.informatik.th-darmstadt.de

Stefan Waldschmidt,
EMail: waldsch@isa.informatik.th-darmstadt.de

Fax: +49 6151 165410

Fachgebiet Mikroprogrammierung
Institut für Systemarchitektur, Technische Hochschule Darmstadt
Alexanderstraße 10, D-64283 Darmstadt, Germany

Abstract. Cellular Processing is an attractive and simple massive parallel processing model. To increase its general acceptance and usability it must be supported by a software environment, an efficient simulator and a special language. For this purpose the cellular description language CDL was defined and implemented. With CDL complex cellular algorithms can be described in a concise and readable form. Compilers were developed which generate C–code for the software simulator or a logical design for the CEPRA–8L simulator, which uses field programmable gatearrays to compute the state transition of the cells. An example is presented to show the process of compilation for different target architectures.

1 Introduction

Cellular Processing is based on the processing model of Cellular Automata. All cells obey in parallel to the same local rule, which results in a global transformation of the whole generation. The cells are connected to their adjacent cells only. In the two dimensional case 4 neighbours (von Neumann neighbourhood) or 8 neighbours (Moore neighbourhood) are considered. In the three dimensional case up to 26 neighbours can be taken into consideration.

Cellular Automata with a few bits per state have been studied extensively from the theoretic point of view and are of special interest in physics. Papers on cellular automata and their application in physics are periodically published in the PHYSICA D[1] and COMPLEX SYSTEMS[2].

Typical applications are: crystal growth, biological growth, simulation of digital logic, neuronal switching, electrodynamic fields, diffusion, temperature distributions, movement and collision of particles, lattice gas models, liquid flow, wave optics, Ising systems, image processing, and pattern recognition.

With the new designed language CDL (Cellular Description Language) the cellular algorithms are presented in a concise and readable form. CDL has been proved to be very useful for the description of complex cellular algorithms. One version of the compiler generates C code for the software simulator XCellsim, another version generates a hardware description for field programmable gatearrays which we use in our hardware simulator CEPRA-8L[3].

2 Target Architectures

In the course of the cellular processing project at the Technical University of Darmstadt different architectures for simulators have been investigated. Two of these architectures are presented below.

2.1 Software Simulator

For the evaluation of cellular algorithms we have developed the X11/Motif based simulator XCellsim. Experiments for this simulator consist of three basic parts: the description of the rule, the initial states of the cells in the array and some information about the visualization.

The simulator allows the user to store the cell state in a structured datatype. One of the easiest and most often used visualization concepts is the assignment of colours to cell states. Thus the simulator provides a visualization tool that uses one of the cells components as an index into a colourmap. The cell does not only calculate its state transition but also the corresponding colour index. The user is responsible for the consistency with the range of this colour index and has to supply a table that contains the colour for each index.

The initialization of the cellular field is done with a separate editor. The information for the initialization is stored together with a description of the cell structure. This structure is available for the rule as **struct** in a C header file.

The rule is written in C and is linked with a kernel which controls the simulation. To access neighbours the kernel provides a **neighbour** function. The kernel is capable of calling different rules depending on the position within the cellular field. By this technique special rules for borders and corners can be defined.

2.2 Hardware Simulator

The hardware simulator CEPRA-8L was developed in the Cellular Processing project at the TH Darmstadt. It is a parallel architecture calculating eight cells at a time, using one programmable Logic Cell Array (Xilinx XC3064) per cell. The calculation is supported by pipelined memory fetch and store operations. Fig. 1 gives an overview of the architecture of the simulator.

During the calculation of a state transition the old states of all eight direct neigbours (Moore-neigbourhood) are available. The number of different states per cell is limited to 256 (8 bit). There is no additional memory, neither local nor global, and there are no communication paths between the cells other than the

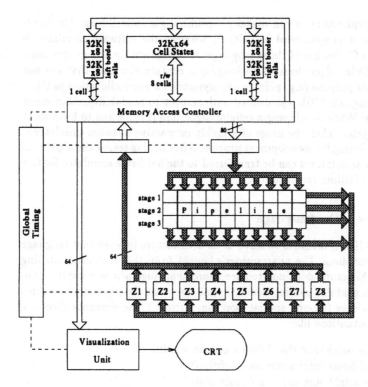

Fig. 1. Overview of the CEPRA–8L simulator

entire cell states. Each programmable Logical Cell Array receives four signals
that indicate whether the actual calculated cell lies on one of the four borders
of the simulation array. Each cell state is used as an index into a colour look-up
table for visualization. CEPRA–8L computes 30 generations of $512 \times 512 \times$
eight bit in a second. In order to obtain this fast simulation speed it is desired
to calculate the state transition in one time step only. For that reason the rules
must are defined as boolean equations without the usage of any registers.

The cell rules can be described in the special hardware description language
LOGiC. The commercial available compiler minimizes the logical design and
translates it into a netlist. This netlist is then mapped onto the Logic Cell
Arrays by the Xilinx design software.

It is the task of the new compiler to translate cellular algorithms written
in the cellular description language CDL to the input language of the LOGiC
system.

3 CDL, a Language for Describing Cellular Automata

Until now cellular algorithms are programmed in simulator dependent special
languages and data structures. Thus the programmer needs special knowledge

of the target architecture, which makes programming a tedious task. The hardware simulator is programmed in LOGiC, whereas the software simulator is programmed in C. Neither of those languages is convenient for the programmer to describe cellular algorithms. Both languages contain elements that are not required for this purpose (e.g. pointer and dynamic memory allocation in C).

The new language CDL was defined with respect to readability, conciseness and portability. While developing a cellular algorithm it is desired to have short turn–around cycles. Thus the usage of a highly interactive software simulator is recommended during the development process. After having tested the algorithm on the software simulator it can be transferred to the hardware simulator for fast execution and realtime visualization.

3.1 Features of the Language

The language CDL is intended to serve as an architecture independant language for cellular algorithms. The programmer's benefit from this is clear: Switching the target architecture does not require more than just a new compiler run. Moreover CDL contains special elements that make the description of complex conditions very easy (groups, special loop constructs). These elements allow the description of situations like:

- Is there any neighbour that fulfils a certain condition?
- Do all neighbours fulfil a certain condition?
- How many neighbours are in a certain state?

CDL does not contain conditional loops, which has two positive sideeffects. (1) It enforces the termination of the rule because it is impossible to write endless loops and (2) it enables the compiler to unroll all statements which is extremely important for the synthesis of hardware. CDL allows the user to describe the cell state as a record of arbitrary types. All common data types are available in CDL (integer, boolean, float, etc.). In addition the user can define new types (enumerations and subranges of integers or enumerations).

The visualization of cellular arrays is often done by assigning colours to cell states or to a set of cell states. A colour definition part is included in CDL for that purpose. Thereby all CDL features can be used in these definitions. Firstly the set of states to which a colour expression applies can be specified using statenames, constants and groups that are already defined for this particular cellular automaton. Secondly the colour expression can be built with components of the cell defining a distribution of colours in a single expression.

3.2 Example

To give an impression of a CDL program we present the Belousov–Zhabotinsky reaction[5]. It does not show all the special features of CDL, but demonstrates some of the problems that have to be handled quite differently on hardware and software simulators.

```
(01) cellular automaton Belousov_Zhabotinsky ;
(02)
(03) const dimension = 2 ;
(04)       distance  = 1 ;
(05)       maxtimer  = 7 ;
(06)       cell      = [0,0];
(07)
(08) type celltype = record
(09)        active : boolean;
(10)        alarm  : boolean;
(11)        timer  : 0..maxtimer;
(12)      end;
(13)
(14) group
(15)   neighbours={[-1,0],[1,0],[0,1],[0,-1],
(16)               [1,1],[-1,1],[1,-1],[-1,-1]};
(17) color
(18)   [0  , 255, 0]         ~    *cell.active and     *cell.alarm;
(19)   [255,  0, 0]          ~    *cell.active and not *cell.alarm;
(20)   [*cell.timer * 255 div maxtimer,0,0]
(21)                         ~ not *cell.active;
(22)
(23) var
(24)   neighbour : celladdress;
(25)
(26) rule
(27) begin
(28)   *cell.active := *cell.timer=0 ;
(29)   *cell.alarm  :=
(30)         num(neighbour in neighbours : *neighbour.active)
(31)                                  in {2,4..8};
(32)   if *cell.active and *cell.alarm and (*cell.timer=0)
(33)     then *cell.timer:=maxtimer
(34)     else
(35)        if *cell.timer!=0 then *cell.timer:=*cell.timer-1;
(36) end;
```

The type celladdress, as used in line (24), is implicitly defined by the compiler from the two constants dimension and distance. They define how many dimensions the model uses and how far the access to other cells reaches. Both constants must be supplied by the programmer. The type celladdress is a record with as much components as the model has dimensions. Each component can have a value between -distance and +distance. Lines (15) and (16) show the celladdresses of all eight Moore neighbours.

4 Transformation into a Software Description

The transformation of a CDL program into an experiment for XCellsim can be divided into three tasks[4]:

- The generation of the cell structure stored in the experiment data.
- The transformation of the rule into a C function. This function is responsible for the calculation of the colour index also.
- The generation of a colour map that corresponds to the indices which the C function computes.

4.1 Generation of the Celltype

The first part can be managed quite easily. Lines (08)–(12) define the structure of the cell. It has three components. The first two are of type boolean. The third is a subrange of integer. To simplify the handling of the components and for reasons of efficiency we do not use bitfields to store booleans. Instead we put boolean components into characters. The subrange type also fits into a variable of type character. The resulting C **struct** will be:

```
struct celltype {
   char   active;
   char   alarm;
   char   timer;
}
```

4.2 Transformation of the Rule into a C Function

The second part can be done by successively transforming each statement into a corresponding C statement. Most of the elements of CDL have a direct counterpart in C. In line (30) one of the constructs (**num**) can be found which take more effort to translate. The meaning of this construct can be explained in the following way:

- all the elements of the group **neighbours** will successively be assigned to the variable **neighbour** as defined in line (15).
- The condition following the colon is evaluated for each assignment.
- The result of the function is the number of evaluations with result **true**. In our example it is the number of neighbours which are active (i.e. their state component **active** is **true**).

The above explanation contains a guideline how the compiler can translate the **num** function into C code. A sequence of **if** statements is generated, each of which having the condition after the colon. But instead of the variable **neighbour** the elements of the group neighbours are used. In case a condition is **true** an internal variable is incremented:

```
internal=0;
if (*[-1,0].active) internal++;
if (*[1,0].active) internal++;
if (*[0,1].active) internal++;
        ⋮
if (*[-1,-1].active) internal++;
result=internal;
```

Other elements of CDL like **one**, **all** or **in** can be translated in a similar way. These statements terminate the calculation of their conditions if the result is determined. The result of the **one** statement is the boolean value, which indicates if at least one of the conditions evaluates to **true**. The iteration is aborted at the first **true** condition. An implementation of a **one** expresion may be (substitute num by one in line (30)):

```
if (*[-1,0].active) result=true
else if (*[1,0].active) result=true
        ⋮
else result=false;
```

The **all** statement aborts the iteration if a condition is **false**. The boolean return value becomes **true** only if all conditions are **true**. Thus an implementation could be:

```
if ( !(*[-1,0].active)) result=false
else if ( !(*[1,0].active)) result=false
        ⋮
else result=true;
```

One property of CDL rules requires some additional attention. Because of the cellular processing model, assignments to the cell state are not visible within a rule until the next generation. There is an intermediate variable that has the same type as the cell. All assignments to the cell state write into this intermediate variable. At the termination of the computation cycle the intermediate cell state is assigned to the cell.

4.3 Generation of the Colourmap

The third part is a little bit difficult, because most systems have a limited number of colours that they can display at the same time. In case the system is capable of displaying a fixed number of colourmap entries, the compiler must check that the colour expressions (line (18)–(21)) do not define more colours than can be displayed at the same time. This can be done by computing all possible values these expressions can have. The compiler builds a tree for each of the expressions. Each of the leaves in this tree is then marked with a range and a step defining the values it can take. These ranges and steps are then merged from the leaves to the root. Simple rules can be defined for every operation that is done at the inner nodes. The range and step that is computed for the root defines the number of possible values for this expression. The function that computes the colourindex can be extracted from these trees too.

5 Transformation into a Hardware Description

Even simulators that are based on specialized hardware are supported. The CEPRA–8L simulator has been choosen as an example during the design phase of CDL.

From the description of the CEPRA–8L hardware for example one may extract several limitations a hardware based simulator has. The most important properties of a hardware simulator are the limited number of cell states and the limitations in the rule complexity. Although floating point numbers are desired and should be included in a cellular language, they are usually not implemented in a specialized hardware simulator because of hardware costs.

5.1 Celltype

In the case of CEPRA–8L the states of the cell must be coded with eight bits. If the **celltype** is a record (as in lines **(08)**–**(12)**) there may be the following trade-off. On one hand, it is more easy to reserve bit groups for the subtypes of this record (one bit for each boolean in lines **(09)**–**(10)** and three bits for the integer subrange in line **(11)**). Usually, this will simplify the logic for the rules, because often the rules access only components of the cell record (e.g. line **(28)**). On the other hand, this may lead to a state coding, where not every of the 2^8 states can be used (e.g. if the integer subrange does not have power of two elements). Enumerating all possible cell states (the powerset of the components) will not waste any of the 256 states, but will increase implementation cost. The CDL compiler decides itself which method to use.

5.2 Variables

The classical synthesis approach uses registers to represent variables. The datapaths between these registers are controlled by a finite state machine. For the CEPRA–8L machine this is not desired, because it would imply the usage of a clock signal. The number of clocks required to complete the calculation would then depend on the data. The varying time could stall the pipeline and slow down the calculation speed.

To simulate CDL variables, they are represented by local signals. Because a new value can be assigned to signals only once, for each assignment new signals must be created.

Consider the following CDL fragment:

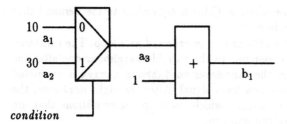

Fig. 2. The implementation of local variables and assignments

```
(01) a:=10;
(02) if condition then a:=30;
(03) b:=a+1;
```

The assignment in line (01) produces the local variable a_1 (Fig. 2). It contains the constant value 10. The assignment in line (02) produces another local variable a_2, which contains the constant value 30. Which of both variables to use in the following program is decided by a multiplexer. It is controlled by the condition of the **if** statement. The result is named a_3 and used as input to an adder, which produces the signal b_1.

5.3 Optimizations

The hardware resources inside a programmable Logical Cell Array are limited. Therefore optimization is necessary. The optimization supported by the LOGiC compiler is good but not sufficient. The CDL compiler already should keep an eye on the complexity of the description. It should not use too many local signals and avoid generating unused code. To reduce implementation cost, early expression and condition evaluation is necessary and was implemented. The compiler evaluates constant expressions during compilation, taking special properites of the operation into consideration. The **or** operation, for example, with one operand being constant **true** is evaluated during compilation and translated into the constant **true**.

Usually a data type is represented by a fixed number of bytes (8 bits) on common computers. To reduce implementation cost, the compiler should use single bits instead of bytes as the smallest unit. In addition, the size of a data type may vary. For example a variable of an integer subrange type, which is divided by two will need one bit less after the division. Therefore it is usefull to know the exact range of possible values for each variable and expression.

5.4 Loops

To simulate the behaviour of a loop, hardware must be generated for each iteration. Conditional loops are not available because their number of iterations can not be determined during compilation. (This is equivalent to the demand that calculation must always terminate.)

The num expression in line (30) can be interpreted as a loop. The constants of the group neighbours are assigned to the variable neighbour one after the other. After each assignment the expression *neighbour.active is evaluated and the result is assigned to a new local signal. After the eight iterations, the eight signals are connected to a logic, which sums up the conditions that are true. The sum is the result of this expression.

5.5 Conditional Statements

The only statement which has a permanent effect is the assignment of a value to a variable or the cell state (e.g. line (28)). For this reason the assignment statement is affected by the corresponding condition. Have a look at line (35). Only if the condition is true, the assignment shall have an effect. Therefore each assignment is implemented as a two–to–one multiplexer, where one input is the old value and the other is the new value. The select signal of this multiplexer is connected to the condition of the surrounding conditional statement. For nested conditonal statements their conditions are combined using the logical and operation. An else part can be realized using the inverted condition and a case statement using different cascaded conditions.

5.6 Colour

The colour definition must be loaded into the CRT controller as a look–up–table . To create this look–up–table during compilation, each possible cell state is associated with the contents of the cell (*[0,0]) and the expressions in the colour definition (lines (20)–(26)) are evaluated.

6 Conclusion

CDL is an implemented language for the concise, readable and portable description of cellular algorithms. One version of the compiler generates C-code for the software-simulator. Another version generates logic equations for the field programmable gate arrays of the CEPRA-8L machine. The logic equations are partly minimized by the compiler and partly by the commercial available design system LOGiC.

Main features of the language are records, unions, groups and the loop construct for testing complex conditions. The language can be used to describe complex cellular algorithms of practical relevance.

Based on the experience with the language we plan to extend the language with features like phase algorithms, moving cells, initialization of the processing field and complex visualizations.

References

1. Physica **D** (1984), **D 34** (1989), **D 45** (1990)
2. Complex Systems, **Vol. 1–7**
3. Hoffmann, R., Völkmann, K.-P., Sobolewski, M.: The Cellular Processing Machine CEPRA-8L, in Parcella 94,179-188, Mathmatical Research Vol. 81, Akademie Verlag 1994 Editors: Jesshope, Jossifov, Wilhelmi
4. Hussain, H.: Integration eines Compilers für die Zellularsprache CDL in das XCellsim–System, Masterthesis Technische Hochschule Darmstadt (1994)
5. Zaikin, A., Zhabotinsky, A.: Nature **225** (1970) 535

Performance Evaluation and Visualization with VISPAT

Anna Hondroudakis[1], Rob Procter[1] and Kesavan Shanmugam[2]

[1] Department of Computer Science, Edinburgh University,
Mayfield Road, Edinburgh, EH9 3JZ, UK
[2] Edinburgh Parallel Computing Centre, Edinburgh University,
Mayfield Road, Edinburgh, EH9 3JZ, UK

Abstract. A tool for performance analysis of parallel programs implemented using the MPI message passing standard is presented. The paper discusses the way information about program execution is gathered, processed and visualized by the graphical front end of the tool. Emphasis is placed on demonstrating how the tool helps the tuner to reduce the volume of data that has to be examined and to relate the behaviour of the program to the source code.

1 Introduction

Programmers who normally write sequential code often encounter major difficulties when applying data and program decomposition techniques to parallel programs. Communication and synchronization issues among usually large numbers of processes increase the amount of effort involved in parallel programming. To counter these problems, program performance visualization and evaluation environments have been developed and have now become crucial tools in parallel program implementation.

One common technique for performance analysis tools is to collect trace data and then visualize it in order to reveal possible causes of poor performance. The program source code is then modified in the light of the analysis. In practice, however, tuning is much more difficult than this brief sketch suggests.

The amount of trace data produced may be very large, particularly in the case of massively parallel systems. For this data to be useful, the tuner needs appropriate tools to process and present it in a comprehensible form. It can often be very difficult to relate the low-level account of program behaviour provided by the trace data to the source code. Compounding this problem is the tendency for parallel programming environments to provide progressively higher-level programming facilities [1]. Whilst this is of great assistance in the design and coding stages of program implementation, it often makes tuning more difficult, with the tuner having to relate low-level events to increasingly abstract program representations.

This paper describes VISPAT [3], a tool for Visualization of Performance Analysis and Tuning of parallel programs as it has evolved to cater for programs using the MPI standard. Numerous examples of such tools already exist [2, 5].

VISPAT's originality lies in the emphasis it gives to source code reference and trace data filtering. The following three sections describe respectively how the trace data is gathered, processed and visualized.

2 Programming Environment

MPI is intended to be the standard message passing interface for parallel application and library programming [4]. It caters for point to point communication between pairs of processes and collective operations between groups of processes. Its more advanced features provide among other things, for the manipulation of process groups and their topological structure. A local implementation of the MPI standard has been developed at the Edinburgh Parallel Computing Centre (EPCC).

MPI programs can be linked with the instrumented version of the MPI library. The resulting executable generates a trace file for each process in the program that can subsequently be processed by the Trace Processing Engine (TPE) and visualized by the front end of VISPAT. Each instrumented MPI function corresponds to a *phase* in the execution of the process calling this function. A user-annotated logical part of the source code is also a phase. Instrumentation can be turned on or off in specific parts of the program so as to perturb the instrumented program as little as possible and to reduce the amount of trace data gathered.

3 Trace Processing Engine

The Trace Processing Engine reads in all the trace files from the processes in the program and analyses them in order to generate the appropriate data structures that are used by the visualization component.

Apart from creating the data structures, TPE has facilities which act as a query mechanism on these data structures. The query mechanism can be used to access the information of the data structures and to drive the visualization displays of VISPAT. The query mechanism also contributes to the extensibility of VISPAT. The information generated by trace data queries can be used (with suitable formatting) by new visualization schemes or by displays incorporated from other performance analysis and visualization tools.

4 Performance Visualization

The design of the visualization component of VISPAT was to a large extent driven by the requirement for source code reference (ref). The control flow of each process's code consists of time-grouped sequences of interesting events, or phases. Groupings can cover many layers of abstraction — e.g., top level phases can consist of a series of sub-phases and so on. There is a one-to-one relationship between the structure of program phases and the structure of the trace files. This

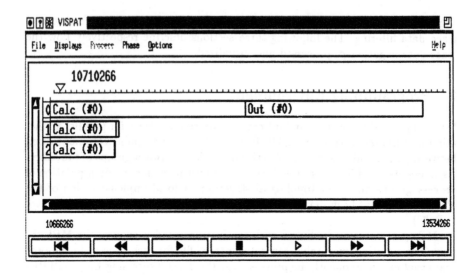

Fig. 1. The Navigation Display

is carried through into VISPAT's data visualization facilities. This is the means by which VISPAT enables the tuner to relate the behaviour of the program to the source code.

In this hierarchical presentation of events and phases, a mechanism to help the tuner identify events of interest and determine what data will be subsequently visualized by the performance displays is important. In particular, the tuner should be able to determine interactively: a region of the trace file (pan over the data); the time grain (zoom in or out of the chosen region); which events will be visible (filter out unwanted events) and, finally, control the level of abstraction (fold or unfold phases).

These requirements were realised in VISPAT through a single user interface mechanism, the Navigation Display (see Figure 1). The Navigation Display determines the context of data visualization. It has a central role because VISPAT's other displays render data only over the time period and parts of the program that are currently visible within it. The Navigation display renders the parallel event histories of the processes in the program. It is a form of Gantt chart where the time line is depicted on the horizontal axis and the set of processes on the vertical axis. When the Navigation Display is used in combination with VISPAT's abstraction mechanisms, this context also provides the means for achieving source code reference.

Apart from the Navigation Display, VISPAT's display set currently includes the Communication Display, the Statistics Display, the Membership Matrix Display and the Profile Display.

The Communication Display presents an animated graphical representation of the communication events in an MPI-based parallel program. The numerous communication events in a parallel program necessitate filterings that reduce the complexity of the communication space. MPI communicators provide the means of separating the communication space since each communicator specifies a communication context for a given communication operation. Communications that happen within one communication context do not interfere with communications in a different context. VISPAT provides multiple instances of the Communication Display, where each instance depicts the communication events within a particular context.

The abstraction achieved above can be extended to allow for filtering over the processes that participate in the communications of particular communicator(s). A list of single-line textual descriptions of each communication event is also provided along with every instance of the Communication Display. The textual description aims to:

- resolve any ambiguities that might be present in the graphical representation,
- provide timing information about the beginning and completion of events and
- supply the tuner with a history list of communication events, so that the current state of the display can be related to previous ones.

5 An Example of the Use of VISPAT

VISPAT has been applied to several performance studies of programs solving a number of the so-called "Cowichan problems" [6]. One of these is the inverted percolation problem. The corresponding program simulates the displacement of one fluid such as oil by another such as water in fractured rock. An NxN matrix is filled with randomly generated numbers representing the resistance of the point to its displacement. During each iteration, the process assigned with a member of the matrix examines the four orthogonal neighbours of this cell and chooses to fill the one with the lowest value. The simulation continues until a certain part of the array is filled or some other condition is satisfied. Figure 2 shows the phase tree for each of the processes in the application.

The program in question is written in C++ and uses MPI for communication. It consists of three distinct phases: input, calculation and output. Each of these phases consists of sub-phases. The Navigation Display in Figure 1 reveals that the calculation (Calc) phase is the dominant execution phase. It also shows that the output (Out) phase takes a lot more time to complete on Process 0 than on any of the rest of the processes. By expanding the phase Out for Process 0 (see the Profile Display in Figure 3), it is clear that its sub-phase Write is responsible for most of the delay observed. This was expected because this process first gathers all the partial results from the rest of the processes and outputs them into a file. The program execution time can be reduced by a factor of ten percent if the result data is output in parallel by every process in the program. Subsequently the tuner can improve the algorithm employed for the calculation of the matrix.

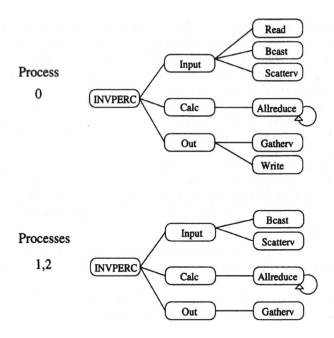

Fig. 2. The phase hierarchy of the inverted percolation program.

6 Conclusions and Future Work

A prototype tuning tool has been implemented which through the concept of hierarchical phases enables the tuner to relate low-level events in trace data to program source code. In VISPAT, there is one-to-one correspondence between the structure of program phases, the structure of trace files and its visualization mechanisms. VISPAT has been extensively evaluated by prospective users and the feedback gained is being used to refine the functionality and improve usability.

Future work will include the extension of VISPAT's query mechanism to include appropriate filters to extract information from trace data convert it to a suitable format for use with other performance analysis and visualization tools.

References

1. Carriero, N., Gelernter, D.: Applications experience with Linda. Proceedings of the ACM Symposium on Parallel Programming (1988).
2. Heath, M. T., Etheridge, J. A.: Visualizing the performance of parallel programs. IEEE Software **8(5)** (1991).
3. Hondroudakis, A., Procter, R.: The design of a tool for parallel program analysis and tuning. IFIP WG10.3 Working Conference on Programming Environments for Massively Parallel and Distributed Systems (1994) 321–332.

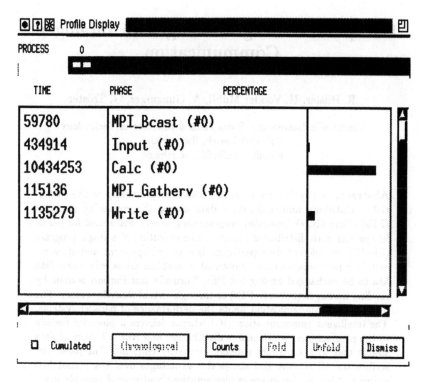

Fig. 3. The Profile Display.

4. Message Passing Interface Forum.: MPI: A Message-Passing Interface Standard (1994).
5. Reed, D. A., Aydt, R. A., Madhyastha, T. M., Noe, R. J., Shields, K. A., Schwarts. B. W.: An overview of the pablo performance analysis environment. Technical report, Department of Computer Science, University of Illinois, Urbana, Illinois 61801 (1992).
6. Wilson, G. V.: Assessing the usability of parallel programming systems: The cowichan problems. IFIP Working Conference on Programming Environments for Massively Parallel Distributed Systems (1994) 183–194.

Dataparallel Programming with Intelligent Communication

R. Hüsler, H. Vonder Mühll, A. Gunzinger, G. Tröster

Electronics Laboratory, Swiss Federal Institute of Technology
CH-8092 Zürich, Switzerland
e-mail: huesler@ife.ee.ethz.ch

Abstract. A key feature in data-parallel programming is the potential to distribute and redistribute data among the processing elements (PEs) efficiently. Dataparallel programming is very well suited for parallel systems with distributed memory. The execution of a single program (SPMD) on different data partitions is easy to implement and often results in a performance close to optimal. A problem arises only when data has to be exchanged among the PEs. Normally distribution is done by sending messages (between PEs) or through virtual shared-memory. The cost for this communication limits the performance of parallel systems. The intelligent communication (IC) scheme delivers a powerful feature to the programmer, which makes distribution and redistribution of data simple and with hardware support extremely efficient. This paper describes the IC scheme and shows the advantages over traditional MP systems. Also two hardware implementations and several possible mappings on MP systems are shown. Performance results give a closer view of the superiority of intelligent communication.

1 Introduction

The increasing need for high processing power led to the design of parallel computers. Due to the lack of dedicated software to program computers with several processing elements (PEs) the use was restricted to a small number of specially trained programmers. As parallel computers became more popular the pressure to the software community was getting stronger. Several new programming paradigms were developed to simplify the use of parallel computers. These paradigms rely on the available communication facilities of parallel computers. They range from message-passing in parallel computers with distributed-memory (implemented as PVM, MPI, P4 ...) to real shared-memory parallel computers with only one single big memory module.

Today the most popular programming scheme for parallel computers is global address-space because the programmer doesn't have to deal with data layout and data distribution, he or she can allocate a block of memory and reference it from any PE. The possibility of having global address-space on parallel computers makes them easy to program but often results in a big loss of performance. The access time for a data reference cannot be evaluated in advance and therefore the actual run-time of an application is unpredictable. The implementation of a global address-space on parallel computers can be done with virtual shared-memory, real shared-memory or a cache-only architecture. The realization in a computer with distributed-memory, called virtual shared-memory (VSM), is very inefficient if realized in software. An access to a remote data has to go through the operating system and over the interconnection network. For every remote access you have a given latency which slows your application down. To overcome this problem latency hiding techniques were developed, but they can only be applied to a small number of applications. Cache-only architectures are often built as distributed-memory computers with special hardware-support for the access of remote data, which reduces the cost for a remote access. Here a remote access is much faster than with virtual shared-memory and by slowing down local accesses all memory references take the same amount of time. In this way architectures with Uniform Memory Access (UMA) are realized. A parallel computer with only one memory module is the other extreme. Bandwidth of the common memory limits the accesses and thus the achievable performance. Accesses to the same memory page have to be sequentialized in case of writing and can be satisfied in parallel for reads. Locking mechanism have to be introduced to protect PEs from manipulating other PEs data. Time where PEs are waiting for data to access increases exponentially with the rising number of PEs.

To get a reasonable performance from parallel computers with global address-space you have to outline your data very carefully and you must have a detailed knowledge of the hardware to use the maximum of data-locality in your application.

Partitioning the data in independent pieces and having them in local memory enables you to achieve good performance results. But as stated earlier, you have to be an expert in analyzing applications and programming parallel computers.

To run a program on a message-passing system you also have to analyze your application with respect to data dependencies. Once you finished this you can distribute the data among the PEs. To redistribute the data on n PEs you have to send at least n messages, which, in best case, can be sent simultaneously. This is an easy task if all data from one PE has to be sent to another PE but more complex if a 2-dimensional array was distributed row-wise and has to be distributed column-wise in the next step. Here the messages have to be received in order or must be assembled by the PE in the right order. This additional task only decreases your system performance.

Intelligent Communication is not relieving you from the task of analyzing your application, but it gives you a powerful and very simple method to distribute and redistribute data among the PEs.

If not otherwise stated shared-memory, virtual shared-memory and cache-only architectures are ignored in the rest of the paper.

2 Intelligent Communication

As described in the introduction the intelligent communication scheme is very powerful for distributing data on distributed-memory parallel computers. This will be demonstrated with a very simple example: Consider having a parallel computer with three PEs and a 2-dimensional array with 9 elements in both dimensions. In a first step the array has to be distributed row-wise and in the second step column-wise as shown in Figure 1. Assume the array comes from a single source.

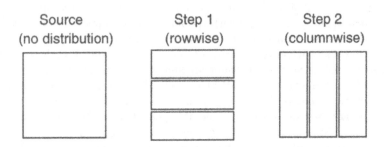

Fig. 1. Desired distributions for the example

Realized with message-passing part 1 of the data is read and sent to PE1, part 2 read and sent to PE2 and so on for the first step. The redistribution for the second step needs even more messages (Figure 2).

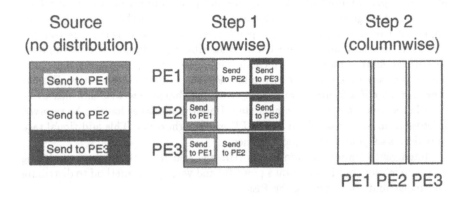

Fig. 2. Messages to be sent for the example

The distribution for the first step can be done with 3 sends. To be ready for the second step 6 messages have to be sent (data which remains on a PE doesn't have to be sent). Every PE receives a message from every other PE. The received messages have to be analyzed before they can be placed in the array if the messages arrive in a random ordering, otherwise they can be placed directly. This means some intelligence for the communication has to be included in the program.

The implementation with intelligent communication has to be done as follows. At the beginning the size and desired distribution of the array is defined. When the data is ready to be distributed the communication controller (CC) starts to read the data from the source and places every value into the memory of the destination PE. The CC reads the values in a well defined order and distributes them. Every PE can receive the whole array or any part of it. To redistribute the data you have to tell the CC how the array is distributed among the PEs and how it will be redistributed. Again as soon as the data is ready the CC reads the data according to the size of the array (figure 3) from the PE having this value in its local memory and writes it to the destination PE. Unlike in MP systems where only values for another PE has to be sent with IC every element of an array goes over the interconnection network. So a value will also be communicated if the sender PE and receiver PE are identical.

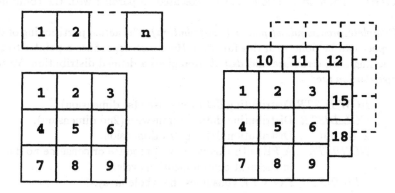

Fig. 3. Ordering of Elements in Arrays

Three functions have to be implemented in order to support the intelligent communication: Init_comm(...), Data_Ready(...) and Wait_data(...).

Init_comm(p_struct, p_ptr, c_ptr, mode): This function initializes the CC with the parameters for the following communication cycle. The parameters are as follows:

p_struct Pointer to the data-structure which defines the
size and distribution of the data.

p_ptr Pointer to the data to be sent (producer data).

c_ptr Pointer to the buffer where the data has to
be copied (consumer data).

mode With this parameter specific hardware-dependent
effects to speedup the communication can be
realized. The value COMM_NORM defines a
standard mode without any hardware-dependencies
(always supported).

Data_Ready(nelements): Defines how many elements of the array are ready
to be sent. ALL_DATA as parameter gives the entire block free.

Wait_data(nelements): With this function the programmer can ask how
much data is already consumed and copied into the consumer buffer. This function blocks until the desired amount of data has arrived. With ALL_DATA as
parameter Wait_data waits for the whole communication cycle to finish.

There are additional functions which do the actual partitioning of the data
space: Complete_prod_window(...) and Complete_cons_window(...). The data-
structure for the partitioning can also be filled manually to realize non-standard
distributions. Between Data_Ready(...) and Wait_data(...) any computation can
be inserted. These instructions will be executed in parallel with the communication.

Complete_prod_window(p_struct, distribution): The actual partitioning of the
data space can be done with this function. Here *p_struct* defines a pointer to the
partitioning data-structure and *distribution* gives a defined distribution. Values
for *distribution* are:

ROW_DISTR Distributing data row-wise (1st dimension).

COL_DISTR Distributing data column-wise (2nd dimension).

Z_DISTR Distribution data in 3rd dimension.

NO_DISTR A PE with this value will produce or consume no data
in the next communication cycle.

ALL_DISTR Every PE consumes the whole array.

Also combinations of ROW_DISTR, COL_DISTR and Z_DISTR are possible.

Complete_cons_window (p_struct, distribution, x, y, z): The same as Com-
plete_prod_window(...) for the partitioning of the consumer data space. With
the parameter x, y and z you can distribute the data with an overlap according
to the dimension.

The communication code of the example program is given below.

... any preprocessing

```
/* initializing p_struct with the size of the array        */
p_struct.dim.x = 9;
p_struct.dim.y = 9;
p_struct.dim.z = 1;
p_struct.elem_size = sizeof(''element of the array'');

/* Define partitioning of the data:                        */
/*      produced from a single source                      */
Complete_prod_window ( &p_struct, NO_DISTR );
/*      consumed row-wise distributed among all PEs         */
/*      (no overlap)                                       */
Complete_cons_window ( &p_struct, ROW_DISTR, 0, 0, 0 );

/* Start the communication cycle for distributing the data */
Init_comm ( &p_struct, p_ptr, c_ptr, COMM_NORM);
Data_ready ( ALL_DATA );  /* Give the calculated data free */
Wait_data ( ALL_DATA );   /* Wait for all data            */
```

... do any calculation

```
/* Define partitioning of the data:                        */
/*      produced row-wise distributed among all PEs         */
Complete_prod_window ( &p_struct, ROW_DISTR );
/*      consumed column-wise distributed among all PEs      */
/*      (no overlap)                                       */
Complete_cons_window ( &p_struct, COL_DISTR, 0, 0, 0 );


/* Start the communication cycle for redistributing the data*/
Init_comm ( &p_struct, p_ptr, c_ptr, COMM_NORM);
Data_ready ( ALL_DATA );  /* Give the calculated data free */
Wait_data ( ALL_DATA );   /* Wait for all data            */
```

... any postprocessing

A general computation and communication cycle is shown in figure 4. The big arrows represent the communication cycles and the thin arrows show which part of the data is computed by the according PE.

Also distributions as shown in figure 5 can be realized easily. The advantage of the IC lies especially in the ease of programming and the potential to support any desired distribution. Low latencies and high communication bandwidth can be achieved by implementing IC in hardware. A disadvantage arises only when two PEs want to exchange data or a message is sent from one PE to another, since the

Fig. 4. General computation and communication cycle

setup time (latency) is higher than in standard MP systems. This disadvantage can be ignored if your application uses mainly distribution of arrays among a big number of the available PEs.

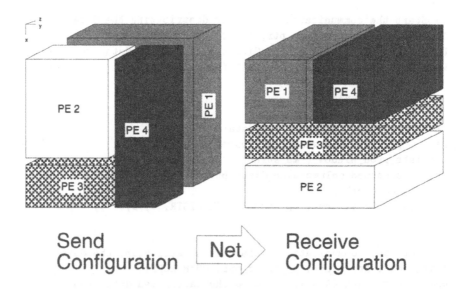

Fig. 5. Possible distribution of a 3-d array

2.1 Hardware Implementations

The following subsections shows two hardware implementations of the intelligent communication scheme. In the first implementation, the MUSIC system, all processing elements are connected in a ring and a distributed communication controller (CC) is realized. The second one, the Alpha7 system, uses a bus as interconnection network and a centralized CC.

The MUSIC System: A Distributed Communication Controller The MUSIC system (MUlti processor System with Intelligent Communication) is a parallel distributed memory architecture based on digital signal processors (Motorola DSP96002). Several systems with up to 63 processing elements are operational. A 63 PE system has a peak performance of 3.8 GFlops, an electrical power consumption of less than 800 W (including forced air cooling) and fits into a 19" rack ([1], [3], [5]).

According to Flynn [2] the MUSIC system can be classified as an MIMD computer. In particular it is programmed as a SPMD (Single Program Multiple Data) machine. The PEs run the same program but on different parts of data. Therefore every PE can execute an other part of the program.

Connected to a host the MUSIC system is used as an attached processor.

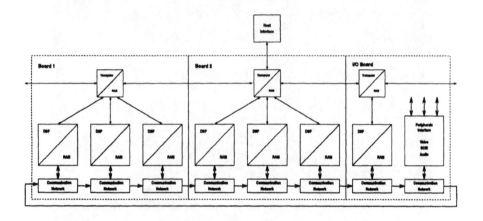

Fig. 6. Architecture of the MUSIC-System

Figure 6 shows the architecture of the MUSIC system with an I/O node. To every PE and to the I/O-node a communication controller has been attached to have direct access to the ring bus. Running the same program on every PE, each individual CC can be configured to realize any desired distribution. Up to 3-dimensional arrays with size of $16384 \times 16384 \times 1024$ can be communicated. This limitation comes from the size of the FPGA (Field Programmable Gate Array) in which the CCs are implemented.

To start a communication every CC must know exactly what part of the data its PE produces and consumes. This information is provided to the CC by the Set_comm(...) instruction. With this instruction all CCs are synchronized before the communication cycle starts. After the synchronization and the Data_Ready(...) of the PE with the first producer data value the communication begins. The CC reads the values from the producer PE and sends them to the next CC in the ring. This CC tests whether the value has to be consumed by its

PE or not and does it likewise. The value is then sent to the next CC. This procedure repeats until the value arrives at the CC from where it was inserted in the ring. There the data will be discarded. That means every data value goes around the ring bus exactly once. After the Wait_Data(...) the PE has all information it needs to continue with the computation.

Fig. 7. Photograph of a MUSIC Board with 3 PEs

The Alpha7 System: A Central Communication Controller The Alpha7 system is a multi-user multi-tasking computer with a complete operating system (OSF/1) so that it can be used as a stand-alone computer. Seven processors (DEC Alpha 21066) are connected through a high speed network on a single board. The Alpha7 system has a peak performance of 1.16 GFlops ([6]).

Figure 8 shows the architecture of the Alpha7 system. PE0 has additional

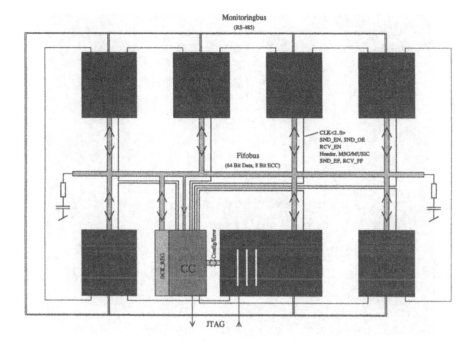

Fig. 8. Architecture of the Alpha7-System

features: A second DRAM bank, a realtime clock and three PCI slots for standard peripheral cards. All PEs are connected with FIFOs to the 72-bit wide high-speed bus. The FIFOs are controlled by the central CC, realized with three FPGAs.

To start an intelligent communication all participating PEs have to place a header in the sender FIFO to signal that they are ready. If the CC sees that all participants have placed a corresponding header in their FIFOs the communication starts. The CC reads the first value of the array from the sender FIFO and writes it to all participating receiver FIFOs. This procedure is repeated until the whole array has been communicated.

Figure 9 shows a photograph of the Alpha7 system.

2.2 Software Implementations

All described software implementations are based on standard message-passing mechanism as PVM or MPI. This allows to have performance results from a big number of machines. The use of PVM or MPI gives a high portability but results in a performance far below peak. The observations are not restricted to SPMD programming. MIMD can also be used but the programmer has to guarantee that in the case of an intelligent communication all computing processes initialize a communication with the same parameters.

Fig. 9. Photograph of the Alpha7 Board

Three different ways are shown to map the IC on a MP architecture. The first mapping uses a distributed CC process attached to every computing process (CP), the second is implemented with one CC process for all the computing processes and the last implementation includes the CC into the computing process.

Distributed Communication Controller Process With a CC process attached to every computing process this mapping realizes the communication mechanism of the MUSIC system in software. Figure 10 gives an overview how the processes are connected together.

As shown in the figure 10 the CCs are connected together as a ring. The CPs communicate among themselves over the attached CC. So an overlap of computation and communication can be realized as in the MUSIC system.

The setup of an intelligent communication and the handling from a programmers point of view is exactly as in the MUSIC system.

With this implementation not all CCs have to participate in a communication cycle. It is possible that some CCs are bypassed for a specific communication. This can be easily realized because the connection between two CCs is not hardwired.

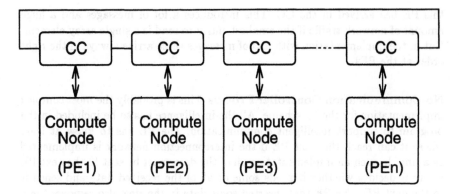

Fig. 10. IC with Distributed CC Process

One Communication Controller Process One communication controller process receives all data from the CPs and sends the parts in the shape of the desired distribution back to the CPs. This mapping reflects the Alpha7 hardware realization.

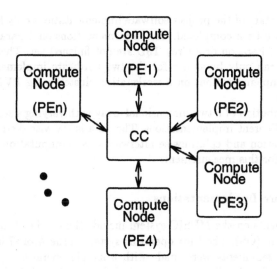

Fig. 11. IC with one CC Process

The central communication controller can be implemented in different ways. It can collect the whole array in its memory and distribute it afterwards, which is very inefficient or send part of the data to the PEs as soon as some data for this PE has arrived in the CC. This introduces a lot of messages and a huge amount of network traffic if the smallest entity to send is a single array element. But in the implementation with lots of messages these arrive always in the right order at the PEs.

No Communication Controller Process This is probably the most complex implementation for the IC scheme. All the intelligence has to be included in the program to support intelligent communication. The PE has to know at least where it can reach the next PE if the interconnection network is implemented as a ring. In such an implementation all of the data must be sent to the next PE where it decides whether it needs some or all of the received data and sends it to the next PE. The PE that inserted some data in the ring also removes them as they arrive. To get rid of the great message traffic it is necessary that all PEs know how to reach all the other PEs. With this knowledge a PE can part its data in pieces which can be sent to individual PEs. This reduces the amount of messages and decreases the time for a communication. A disadvantage is that the messages with parts of the desired data arrive in any order. Data location information have to be append to the messages.

3 Performance Results

At the current state of the project software implementations only for a workstation cluster have been completed. The implementations on a parallel computer such as an Intel Paragon or a Cray T3D are not finished yet. Therefore performance results can only be shown for the two hardware implementations, and the software implementations on a workstation cluster using PVM and socket communication.

The redistribution of a two-dimensional array with varying sizes will be measured for the different implementations. The data is rowwise distributed before the communication and columnwise afterwards. No computation will be done with the data for this measurement.

3.1 Hardware Implementations

The measurements on the MUSIC system include the overhead induced by the operating system (OS). The Unix operating system in the Alpha7 is not running yet so the measurements were made with a simple operating system similar to the MUSIC OS. Applications are compiled on a Digital AlphaStation and downloaded to the Alpha7.

MUSIC System The MUSIC system gives you a setup time of 80 μsec for every intelligent communication with the operating system. The bare hardware is capable to deliver a setup time of 6 μsec. The peak bandwidth to transfer data between the CCs is 20 MByte/sec. Every data element has to circle the communication ring exactly once. Therefore the transfer time increases linearly with the size of the communicated data. The setup and transfer time are nearly independent of the number of processing-elements participating the intelligent communication and the distribution. The total communication time is the sum of the setup time, the transfer time, the time used to fill the communication pipeline and the overhead, which increases linearly with the number of the participating processing elements. Is the distribution different from the measured one, then the overhead can be a dominant factor in the sum

Alpha7 System On the Alpha7 system the setup-time is even shorter, without the operating system, it uses 5 network-cycles (≈ 300 nsec) for a message-passing communication setup. Setting up an intelligent communication uses 10 cycles in general and 4 cycles for every participating processing-element resulting in a total of 38 cycles for the whole board ($\approx 2.4\ \mu$sec). The setup time will increase with an operating system running on the Alpha7. The peak bandwidth on the common bus is 128 MByte/sec which can be sustained if the data from the processing elements is ready to be communicated. The sustanded transfer rate is independent of the number of processing elements. The Unix operating system will enlarge the setup time.

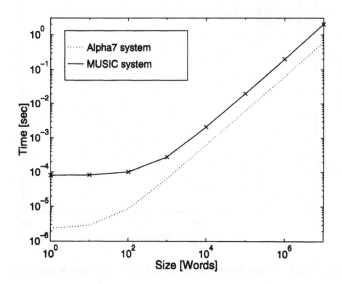

Fig. 12. Communication times measured for the hardware implementations

For both hardware implementations the communication times increase almost linearly with the size of the communicated data. For data sizes bigger than 16 kByte the communication time can be approximated with the network bandwidth and the data size.

The communication time therefore is limited by the setup time for small data sizes and by the network bandwidth for big data sizes.

The mentioned setup- and transfer-times for the hardware implementations can be arbitrary long if the data on one or more processing elements are not ready to be communicated.

3.2 Software Implementations

The described software mappings have been measured on a Sun workstation cluster connected with an ethernet. Because the bandwidth is a major factor in achieving short communication times the measurements have been done on a single workstation and with the network. The measured setup time for a socket communication is 0.8 msec and for PVM 1.3 msec average. The transfer times are tightly coupled with the load of the network.

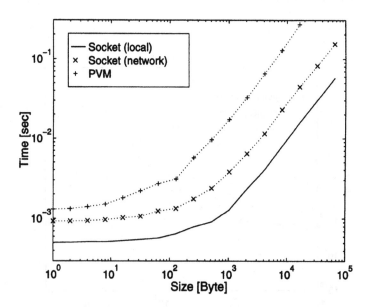

Fig. 13. Transfer times measured for socket and PVM communications

Centralized Communication Controller To realize the intelligent communication with a centralized communication controller (CC) first all data parts from every computation process (CP) must be sent to the communication controller and afterwards the data has to be distributed to all CPs. The centralized CC is the bottleneck in this implementation because all data has to go through one process.

The CC has to receive P messages and send P messages, because the messages are different it is impossible to use broadcast for the sends. The time needed for this procedure is at least 1 setup time for the receive, P setup times for the sends and the time to transfer twice the whole data array. The information how the data is distributed and how it will be can be included in the messages from the CPs.

Distributed Communication Controller The implementation with a distributed communication controller (DCC) is much better than the one with the centralized CC. All independent communication controllers (iCC) form together the DCC. The advantage of the DCC comes from the possibility that all iCCs can communicate with their attached CP in parallel. Also the assembly of the data for the CP can be done simultaneously in the iCCs. An intelligent communication proceeds as follows: All iCCs receive the data from their CP in parallel. Then the data has to be transmitted to the other iCCs what can be done as in the MUSIC system; the iCCs are fully connected or in a ring. For the ring every data part has to go once around and must be discarded at the sender iCC. The best implememtation is a fully connected network, which is feasible for a small number of CPs. With this topology the distribution to the other iCCs can be done with a broadcast. The needed data for a CP will be collected in the corresponding iCC and then sent to the CP.

No Communication Controller Including the communication controller in the CP is the most complicated implementation of the IC scheme on a message-passing system because all CPs have to know at least where and how they can reach the next CP. The interconnection topology can be fully connected or a ring. With this implementation there is no possibility to execute computation and communication parallel. Two ways to send the data to another CP were implemented:

– send the whole data to the next or all CPs
– send only the part of the data, which is needed by the receiver CP

Are the CPs connected in a ring, then all data has to be sent to the next CP. Every CP can do this in parallel whereas P steps are needed to terminate a communication.

If every CP knows how to reach every other CP only the part of the data has to be sent which is needed by the appropriate CP. In this case $P - 1$ messages must be sent from every CP. The total message-count for this implementation is $P \times (P - 1)$ messages of the size N^2/P^2. The received data has to be assembled in each CP.

The following table shows the message-count and the message-sizes for the described implementations:

Implementation	Connection	Message-Count	Message-Size
central CC		$2 \times P$	$\frac{N^2}{P}$
distributed CC	ring	$2 \times P + P^2$	$\frac{N^2}{P}$
	fully connected	$2 \times P + P \times (P-1)$	$\frac{N^2}{P}$
		$2 \times P + P \times (P-1)$	$\frac{N^2}{P^2}$
no CC	ring	P^2	$\frac{N^2}{P}$
	fully connected	$P \times (P-1)$	$\frac{N^2}{P}$
		$P \times (P-1)$	$\frac{N^2}{P^2}$

For every implementation the number of messages can be greater if one CP is able to send part of its data to the CC or another CP. In the extreme a message for every data element will be sent. This results in an enormous traffic on the network and a very poor performance.

With the above table and the communication times for different message sizes the resulting redistribution times can be easily approximated for the mentioned software implementations. It was shown that this approximations are very accurate.

4 Conclusions and Future Work

The Intelligent Communication scheme is a very powerful and easy-to-use mechanism to distribute and redistribute data on a distributed-memory parallel computer. If implemented in hardware there is no way to distribute data faster than with IC. Compared with software implementations on a workstation-cluster the two described hardware implementations are at least 10 times faster, mainly because the distribution work can be done in hardware and processed in parallel with the computing processes. The major drawback of all software implementations is the impossiblity of doing computation and communication in parallel, because the computation and communication process run on the same CPU.

Implementation of the software mappings on parallel computers such as the Intel Paragon will show that the influence of the communication bandwidth, which reduces the performance dramatically on workstation clusters, is very important to achieve good performance results. Also spezialiced communication libraries are available to increase the speed of the communication between processing elements.

Furthermore different distributions will be measured to get a closer view how much computation can be done inside the communication controller to make efficent use of the available network bandwith.

The software mappings will be implemented on the Alpha7 system to have a direct comparison between the hardware and software implementations.

4.1 Acknowledgment

We would like to thank Björn Tiemann and Ivo Hasler for the realization of the Alpha7 prototype and Bernhard Bäumle for the implementation of the operating system for and the measurement on the MUSIC system.

References

1. Bernhard Bäumle. Dokumentation MUSIC Operation System. Institut für Elektronik ETHZ, 1992.
2. M.J. Flynn. Very high-speed computers. Proceedings of the IEEE, Volume 54, pp 1901-1909, Dezember 1966.
3. A. Gunzinger, U. A. Müller, W. Scott, B. Bäumle, P. Kohler, W. Guggenbühl. Architecture and Realization of a Multi Signalprocessor System. In *International Conference On Application Specific Array Processors*. IEEE Computer Society Press, 1992.
4. Ch. W. Kessler (ed). Automatic Parallelization, new Approaches to Code Generation, Data Distribution, and Performance Prediction. Vieweg, Wiesbaden, Germany, 1994.
5. U. A. Müller, B. Bäumle, P. Kohler, A. Gunzinger, W. Guggenbühl. Achieving Supercomputer Performance for Neural Net Simulation with an Array of Digital Signal Processors. IEEE Micro, October 1992.
6. H. Vonder Mühll, B. Tiemann, I. Hasler, E. Hiltebrand, A. Gunzinger, G. Tröster. High Performance Multiprocessor Workstation with Intelligent Communication Network. In *Proceedings of the HPCN Europe 95*, 1995.

Optimization Scheme on Execution of Logic Program in a Dataflow Environment

A. R. Hurson and Byung-Uk Jun

Department of computer Science and Engineering The Pennsylvania State University
University Park, PA 16802 USA

Abstract. We have developed a technique that maps logic programs (database queries) onto a dataflow graph to support static scheduling in a multiprocessor environment [8]. A dataflow graph explicitly shows the execution paths, data dependence, and synchronization points in a query. The scheme attempts to properly group fine grain operations – select and join – into coarser grains as a means to exploit parallelism while minimizing the communication costs. This leads to a higher hardware utilization and performance.

In this paper, we expand the scope of our scheme by using a set of heuristic rules to assign processes to available processors more efficiently. This is made possible by analyzing the probability of success of each branch in the logic program. In a logic program, the early scheduling and execution of some branches with higher probability of failure leads to a higher possibility to eliminate many other branches. On the other hand, early execution of some branches with higher probability of success can lead to a higher hardware utilization. The extended scheme has been simulated, and its performance has been compared against the original model and the traditional parallel execution paradigm of the logic program.

1 Introduction

Although today's computer systems can do number crunching with lightning speed, yet they are incomparably weaker than humans when it comes to knowledge processing. Knowledge processing includes applications such as natural language understanding, planning, machine translation and many other areas normally associated with Artificial Intelligence. Some of the main issues in knowledge processing include the representation of knowledge, the manipulation and maintenance of very large knowledge bases, and the implementation of various reasoning mechanisms. Inherent difficulties in knowledge processing can be traced to the diverse nature of knowledge and ambiguities caused by an incomplete knowledge base.

Because of their underlying data size and ambiguity, knowledge based systems require more complicated techniques and sophisticated analysis than those available in the traditional database management systems (DBMSs). Although traditional DBMSs can effectively manage large amount of data, they have failed to manage the complex semantics of databases effectively. Using a logic program as an advanced query language is an alternative to support these complex applications [4]. A logic program is more suitable to represent and manipulate the large semantic rules found in knowledge base systems [3]. A logic program, usually, in conjunction with the relational data model is used to support the efficient manipulation of large data found in knowledge base applications [11] [18].

It has been shown that, multiprocessing techniques offer performance improvement in the execution of the database queries. These techniques rely mainly on increasing the hardware utilization and decreasing the execution time by exploiting fine grain parallelism embedded in a query [5] [9]. Complexities of the conventional multiprocessing environment, however, have motivated researchers to seek other alternatives for handling concurrent applications. Since 1970s, dataflow paradigm has been recognized as an alternative computational model to support concurrency [12]. The attractiveness of the dataflow concept stems from the fact that dataflow operations are asynchronous in nature. Therefore, the instructions in dataflow do not impose any constraints on sequencing except for the data dependencies contained in the program. In a dataflow computation, the execution of a program can be progressed along various paths simultaneously and hence, inherent parallelism can be exploited more efficiently.

The execution of logic program in a dataflow multiprocessor environment has been addressed in [1] and [14]. However, these efforts did not address the issue of load balancing and scheduling of the logic programs. The scheme proposed in [8] maps a logic program (AND/OR tree) onto a dataflow graph. The parallel execution of the logic program was further improved by partitioning the generated dataflow graph into subgraphs and allocating the resulting subgraphs onto available processors. This paper attempts to expand the scope of our previous work by using a set of heuristic rules and simulates the performance improvement of proposed optimization scheme with various sample programs.

In handling large volume of data, execution time of each basic operation is one of the major factors that should be considered in an allocation policy. The execution time depends on several parameters: size of the data, size of main memory available, page size, and the number of disk accesses. In the current work, the execution time of each node is estimated and statistical parameters are used to calculate the size of the generated data. Such an estimated value along with a simple set of heuristic rules are used to rank and schedule the execution of different dataflow paths.

The logic program and transformation of its AND/OR tree to a dataflow graph are briefly discussed in section 2. This section also describes how a dataflow graph is partitioned into vertical layers as an attempt to balance computation time and communication cost in a multiprocessor platform. The proposed optimization scheme is presented in section 3. Analysis of the proposed model and its simulation are addressed in section 4. Finally, section 5 concludes the paper.

2   Logic Program and Dataflow

2.1   Logic Program

Logic programming is a programming paradigm constructed from the first order logic and powerful enough to facilitate the development of advanced applications. It is mainly used for symbolic processing in areas such as artificial intelligence and data/knowledge base applications, as well as general applications such as compiler writing. The logic programming has grown out of research on resolution inference described by Robinson [16]. Resolution is an inference step required to build a complete inference system for predicate logic in clause form. Applying the rule of resolution into the Horn clauses makes the resolution inference highly suitable for computer implementation. From the language designers point of view, a logic language is a highly structured High Level Language (HLL). Similar to other HLL, the manipulation of data and flow of control are the main concerns in the implementation of the logic programming languages. The basic structure that programs deal with are constants, variables or compound terms [2]. A logic program is a collection of statements which are known to be true. The statements take two forms – *facts* and *rules*. A fact represents a known knowledge. A rule states some relationships that is held for some data. The program is used by posing a query to ask if some other statements are true based on this knowledge.

The logic programming differs from other languages in that it is a single assignment language, i.e., once a variable takes a value in a computation, it keeps that value throughout the computation. If a variable occurs in many places in the program, each occurrence takes the same value at the same time. Evaluation consists of proving the goal statement with an automatic proof procedure and binding the variables of the goal to certain values. An execution step consists of selecting a subgoal from a goal statement, finding a clause with a matching head, and constructing a new goal statement. The component of the system decides which literal in a goal statement to select and with which clause to match it. Upon failed unification, it also has to decide to backtrack to a previous choice point and try another alternative.

Figure 1 shows a logic program named N-Queens as an example program of our discussion, and Figure 2 shows its AND/OR tree representation. Since our main concern to use the logic program is data/knowledge base processing, we have used the structure of N-Queens by modifying the recursive statements in the program into the function calls that searches the base relation, such as 'search R16' in the program. Figure 1 imposes a query 'Queens(8,Q)' which searches for the value 'Q' by retrieving the rules in the program. In Figure 2, the root of the tree represents the query and the leaf nodes represent the actual database relations to be searched. The interior nodes show the intermediate goal statements in the program and they represent the AND (rectangular nodes) and OR (circular nodes) relations, respectively. Arcs among the nodes represent data dependencies within the program. The execution of logic program in a multiprocessor environment requires a parallel execution model which enforces an efficient execution order of the AND/OR branches. In the sequential execution

```
Queens(X2, X1) :-
    poss_rows(X2,X0),
    solve(X0, 0, [], X1).
solve([X7|X6], X5, X4, X3) :-
    X2 is X5+1,
    delete([X7|X6], X1, X0),
    safe(X2, X1, X4),
    search R16.
delete([X3|X2], X1, [X3|X0]) :-
    search R6.
delete([X1|X0], X1, X0).
notthreaten(X4, X3, X2, X1) :-
    X5 is X4+X3, X6 is X2+X1, X5≠X6,
    X7 is X4-X3, X8 is X2-X1, X7≠X8.
```

```
safe(X4, X3, [(X2,X1)|X0]) :-
    notthreaten(X4, X3, X2, X1),
    search R8.
safe(X1, X0, []).
poss_rows(X1, X0) :-
    search R1.
poss_rows(X0, X0).
poss_rows(X3, X2) :-
    X0 is X3-1,
    search R4.

? Queens(8, Q).
```

Fig. 1. An Example of Logic Program.

model – i.e., conventional uniprocessor environment – depth first execution of an AND/OR tree is a reasonable paradigm. However, in a parallel environment, where hardware utilization and higher throughput are of concern, one is required to devise a more sophisticated scheme to execute an AND/OR tree.

There have been various systematic approaches to solve this problem [6] [17] [19]. Most of these techniques are based on the exploitation of OR-parallelism, independent AND-parallelism, and dependent AND-parallelism [20]. The OR-parallelism corresponds to a parallel search of the OR branches in the AND/OR tree, which means several clauses matching a goal are processed concurrently. Independent AND-parallelism occurs when several data independent goals in a clause can be processed simultaneously – no common variables among goals. Dependent AND-parallelism occurs when mutually dependent goals that share common variable(s) are executed in parallel to produce a binding for the variable(s). Parallel execution of dependent AND-parallelism branches are problematic. In such a case, it would be impractical to check the consistency of all combinations of the solutions obtained from each body atom. In addition, the size of the intermediate data generated becomes even more problematic in applications with large amount of data. To reduce the size of the intermediate data and increase the parallelism, an efficient sequence of execution based on the producer/consumer relationship should be developed. On the other hand, rules with OR-parallelism and independent AND-parallelism can be executed in parallel. However, this could easily result in an explosion in the number of activated processes. Therefore, again for practical cases where available resources are restricted, the processes should be activated in a limited manner which improves the performance and increases the hardware utilization. Most of the previous approaches to the parallel execution of logic program have been based on the

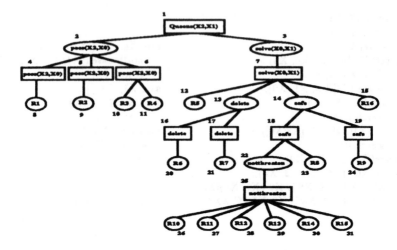

Fig. 2. AND/OR tree representation of Figure 1.

fine grain parallelism. However, by the nature of execution model of logic program – failure of unification and backtracking – the burden of execution time
becomes even greater when the application involves a large amount of data – i.e.,
knowledge base processing. To reduce the unnecessary processes and communication cost, a proper scheduling of the coarser grain parallel processes should be
exploited.

2.2 Graph Transformation

Dataflow techniques have been proposed as an alternative execution model to the
conventional control flow model of computation. Because of the parallel nature
of dataflow computation, execution of logic program in a dataflow multiprocessor environment has been recognized by some researches [1] [14]. However, in
spite of attractive properties of dataflow processing, dataflow researchers should
develop effective schemes for partitioning and allocation of dataflow graphs in
a multiprocessor environment. To take advantage of the dataflow computation
in the execution of logic program, a scheme has been proposed to transform the
AND/OR tree to a dataflow graph [8]. The converted graph: *i*) holds the rich semantics embedded in an AND/OR tree, *ii*) allows the exploitation of parallelism
in a logic program, and *iii*) allows efficient partitioning of the program graph.

The transformation scheme observes the propagation of data value(s) to map
the AND/OR tree to its equivalent dataflow graph. First, a directed AND/OR
tree is generated that shows all possible propagation paths, hence, the execution
orders in a tree (Figure 3). Then the directed AND/OR tree is converted to
a dataflow graph. Two special nodes are introduced to combine partial results
generated by the subgraphs – Intersect and Union nodes that represent the AND
relations and OR relations in the original AND/OR tree, respectively. Finally,

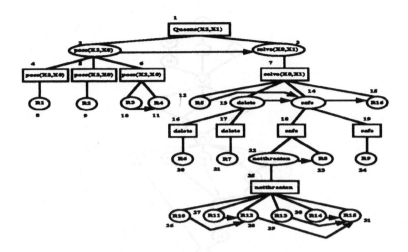

Fig. 3. Directed AND/OR Tree of Figure 2.

to simplify the partitioning and allocation task, an attempt has been made to reduce the complexity of the dataflow graph by removing bookkeeping operational nodes – i.e., AND/OR nodes. The node removal is done by connecting the successor(s) of each deleted node to its ancestor in the dataflow graph. Semantics of the AND/OR nodes are still reflected by the Intersect/Union nodes.

Figure 4 illustrates the converted dataflow graph of the Figure 3. 'S' and 'E' are dummy nodes which represent the start node and the exit node of the graph. The *intersect node* and *union node* are represented by '⋂' and '⋃', respectively. The numbers shown in the Figure 4 represent the node numbers in the AND/OR tree of the Figure 2. Note that Figure 4 shows the execution order and synchronization point of the operations (the leaf nodes and the special nodes). Each node in the dataflow graph can be any computational operation depending on how the predicate has been defined.

Figure 5 shows the symbolic representation of each dataflow node – V_i is the input vector, V_o is the output vector, s is the selectivity factor and R is the cardinality of the underlying relation. For example, in case of a select node, $\sigma_{V_i}(R)$, the input vector represents conditions of the select operation. These conditions could be in conjunctive, disjunctive form generated by the preceding intersect node and/or union node. Attributes of the input vector and output vector are defined in the program as the arguments of the predicate.

2.3 Execution Time and Communication Time

In a multiprocessor environment, one is required to exploit the parallelism as a means to achieve a higher performance. However, due to the limited hardware resources available and the communication overhead, the parallel processes should also be distributed among the available processors efficiently. In the partitioning

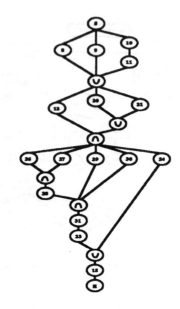

Fig. 4. Dataflow Representation of Figure 3.

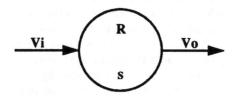

Fig. 5. Symbolic Representation of a dataflow node.

of a program, several issues should be taken into consideration: A partitioning method should maximize the exploitable parallelism – attempt to aggregate processes should not restrict or limit parallelism. In other words, processes that are grouped into a thread should be the parts of a program where little or no exploitable parallelism exists. In addition, the longer the thread length, the smaller the communication cost between processors becomes. This increases the locality and consequently increases the utilization of the resources. In order to realize the efficient partitioning of the program, one is required to estimate the execution time of each process and the communication time between processors.

In our scheme, the execution time of each dataflow nodes and the communication costs will be estimated to exploit efficient partitioning. Using the parameters in Figure 5, the execution time of each node, T_{exe}, is a function of V_i, R, s, and the complexity of the operation. On the other hand, the communication cost, T_{comm}, between the source and the destination nodes is a function of V_o and the communication network. The timing is defined as:

$$T_{exe} = \alpha \times V_i \times R \quad \text{and} \quad T_{comm} = T_{setup} + \tau \times V_o$$

where α is the time required to perform a unit operation, T_{setup} is the mandatory setup time to transmit data, and τ is the communication cost per unit of data. α, T_{setup} and τ are system dependent parameters. V_o is dynamic in nature and a function of the user query, the underlying relation, and the input vector. However, techniques such as the one proposed in [13] can be used to estimate such a parameter:

$$V_o = s \times V_i \times R.$$

2.4 Vertically Layered Allocation

Once the AND/OR tree is converted to the dataflow graph and the execution time of each node is estimated, the dataflow graph is partitioned and allocated to the available processors. Partitioning is the division of an algorithm into procedures, modules and processes. Assignment, on the other hand, refers to the mapping of these units to processors. The ultimate goal is to maximize the inherent concurrency in a program graph by minimizing contention for processing resources. However, the problem is not a trivial one. It has been shown that obtaining an optimal allocation of a graph with precedence is NP-complete [15]. Therefore, heuristic solutions are one of the practical directions to solving the allocation problem.

The *Vertically Layered* (VL) allocation scheme has been proposed which compromises between computation and communication costs [10]. The scheme consists of two separate phases: separation and optimization phase. The basic idea behind the separation phase is to arrange nodes of a dataflow graph into vertical layers such that each vertical layer can be allocated to a processor. This is achieved by distinguishing the critical path of a program and recursively determine the other vertical layers by finding longest directed paths emanating from the nodes which have already been assigned to vertical layers. The estimated execution time of each node is used to determine the longest directed paths. Therefore, the separation phase minimizes contention and inter-processor communication time by assigning each set of serially connected nodes to a single PE. Once the initial phase is completed, the second phase optimizes the final allocation. This is done by considering whether the inter-PE communication overhead offsets the advantage gained by overlapping the execution of two subsets of nodes in separate processing elements.

To apply this phase, the execution time of a new critical path which includes the effects of inter-PE communication costs is determined. If an improvement results, the nodes are combined into a single PE. Since combining two parallel subsets of nodes into a single processing element forces them to be executed sequentially, a new critical path may emerge from the optimization process. This process is repeated in an iterative manner until no improvement in performance can be obtained.

A simulator was developed to evaluate the effectiveness of the VL allocation scheme. Several dataflow graphs with varying degree of complexities were
chosen as the testbed. The simulation results have shown that, in general, the
total execution time decreases as the number of processing elements increases.
Also, in cases where inter-PE communication delays are negligible, the scheme
showed only slight degradation in performance compared to the critical path list
scheme. However, as communication delays increase, the proposed scheme offers
promising performance improvements.

3 Optimization

Two main approaches, namely *static* and *dynamic*, exist for task allocation. In
spite of their differences, the goal of program allocation is to maximize concurrency in a program graph by minimizing contention for processing resources. In
this paper, we propose a hybrid static and dynamic allocation scheme to achieve
higher performance in the execution of logic program. The static allocation is
enforced using a set of heuristics based on the estimated execution time and
the size of output vector of each node. The dynamic allocation is enforced by
observing the actual size of the output vector of each node and possible migration (elimination) of the node(s) or branches during the execution time. In order
to carry out our optimization scheme, three types of relationships among the
serially connected nodes in the dataflow graph are considered:

- Nodes connected based on producer/consumer relationship: In this case, the
  output of a node (producer) is directly consumed by the successor node
  (consumer). Naturally, an empty output vector of the producer node may
  eliminate the consumer node.
- Two or more branches are merged with a union node: If one of input branches
  to the union node generates a non-empty output vector, the input vector of
  succeeding node is non-empty. Thus, the execution of the succeeding node
  is guaranteed unless all the input vectors to the union node are empty.
- Two or more branches are merged with an intersect node: If one of the input
  branches to the intersect node generates an empty output vector, the output
  vector of the intersect node is empty. Thus, the execution of the succeeding
  node can be eliminated.

3.1 Heuristics for Static Allocation

In a shared nothing multiprocessor environment, communication and synchronization among processes are necessary to control the global execution of the
program. Each processor executes its task, and sends the result to the destination processor(s) according to the data dependence among the processes.
Therefore, one is required to introduce a proper control mechanism that guarantees a valid execution. In our scheme, the converted dataflow graph due to its
partial ordering guarantees such a valid execution order. However, in a multiprocessor environment where computation resources are scarce, one has to devise

a scheme that reduces the amount of the computation as well. We propose a set of compile-time heuristics for scheduling of the branches of the converted dataflow graph. The estimated execution time of each path (T_{P_i}) and the size of the output vector (V_{o_i}) are used to prioritize the execution of the paths as a means to manage the resources.

Based on the AND and OR relationships embedded in the definition of the converted dataflow graph – union node or intersect node – the proposed optimization algorithm utilizes two sets of the heuristic rules:
For the AND relation, the algorithm attempts to eliminate as many branches as possible by early scheduling of the ones with higher probability of the failure:

    i) Schedule the branches that have smaller expected execution time,

    ii) Schedule the branches that have smaller expected output vector,

    iii) Schedule the branches that have higher number of the intersect nodes.

For the OR relation, the algorithm attempts to improve the hardware utilization by early scheduling the branches with higher probability of success:

    i) Schedule the branches that have lower estimated execution time,

    ii) Schedule the branches that have higher expected number of the output,

    iii) Schedule the branches that have fewer number of the intersect nodes.

In short, if we consider two paths P_1 and P_2 that are emanating from a node and merged with one of the special nodes, then for branches within:

Intersect Relation

i) If $T_{P_1} \gg T_{P_2}$ then perform path P_2,

ii) If $T_{P_1} \approx T_{P_2}$ then If $V_{o_1} \gg V_{o_2}$ then perform path P_2,

iii) If $V_{o_1} \approx V_{o_2}$ then perform the path that encounters more Intersect operations.

Union Relation

i) If $T_{P_1} \gg T_{P_2}$ then perform path P_2,

ii) If $T_{P_1} \approx T_{P_2}$ then If $V_{o_1} \gg V_{o_2}$ then perform path P_1,

iii) If $V_{o_1} \approx V_{o_2}$ then perform the path that contains fewer Intersect operations.

3.2 Effects on Dynamic Allocation

Performance of the aforementioned static allocation policy can be further improved by considering the issue of dynamic allocation. In this section, an optimization scheme has been presented by observing the propagation of empty output as a means of reducing the amount of computation at run-time. The size of output vector is a function of the user query, the size of relation, selectivity, and the size of input vector (refer to Figure 5). Naturally, a node with a non-empty input vector is executed and an empty output vector is propagated throughout the program graph. Therefore, if a node generates an empty output vector at run-time, propagation of the empty output vector could eliminate some of the branches in the dataflow graph.

As discussed earlier, if one of the input branches to the union node generates a non-empty output vector, the input vector of succeeding node is non-empty. Therefore, the propagation of an empty output vector can be terminated at the union node unless all the input vectors to the union node are empty – if a node generates an empty output vector, the next possible valid execution point is the closest union node. As an example in Figure 4, an empty output vector from node 30 eliminates processing of the next intersect node and node 31 and node 23. This in turn will eliminate node 26, 27, 28, and 29 as well. Thus, the next union node in line has to wait for input from node 24. Interestingly, generation of an empty output vector by node 12 eliminates the whole dataflow graph. Algorithm I shows the sequence of the operations. The run-time scheduling could also drastically improve the resource utilization by reducing the communications among the processors and reducing the processors' operational loads.

Algorithm I (Run-time Scheduling).
BEGIN
If (output is empty) {
        Find next Union node.
        Eliminate processes until the Union node.}
Perform next node.
END

4 Simulation and Results

In handling large knowledge bases, one has to measure the amount of computation in each process and the communication costs among processes. As a result, Vertically Layered allocation scheme [10] has been extended to scale up according to the estimated execution time and communication time of each node. A simulator was developed to evaluate the effectiveness of the proposed scheme. Seven logic programs with varying degrees of complexity were chosen as the testbed. The first program, entitled Queens, is the example utilized throughout this paper (Figure 1). The second and third programs – called EVAL and PARS, respectively – are parts of sample program in Turbo Prolog, namely GeoBase, which is a natural language interface to some geographic knowledge bases. The EVAL and PARS contain 61 and 791 nodes with maximum degree of parallelism of 19 and 53, respectively. Rest of the examples are the benchmark programs that have been used in [7] – Pentominos, Houses, Hanoi, and Knight. Simulator converts the AND/OR tree of a sample program into dataflow graph, partitions it into subgraphs, and allocates the partitions onto the available PEs using the vertically layered allocation scheme extended by the proposed heuristics.

In contrast to the traditional execution of the logic program in a parallel environment, the dataflow execution model of logic program exploits all variations of the AND/OR parallelism simultaneously. As shown in the Figure 6, the dataflow model is superior to the models supporting AND-parallelism and the OR-parallelism alone.

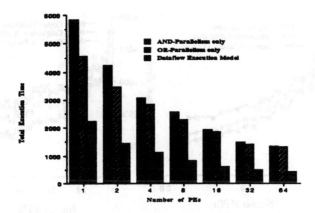

Fig. 6. Performance Improvement of Dataflow Execution Model.

The simulator is designed to measure the effectiveness of the static and dynamic scheduling for various system configurations and network topologies. First, the execution time and communication time for each node in the program graph are estimated. These estimated values are used to partition a dataflow graph into subgraphs and allocate the subgraphs onto available processors using the VL allocation scheme. Finally, the zero output vectors are forced to simulate the run-time scheduling. Note that each point in various curves is an average of 10 independent simulation runs.

Knight and EVAL were chosen as the representative programs. Choice of Knight and EVAL was due to their complexities and their flexibilities in expanding the size of their databases. Figure 7 compares the performance of the extended VL scheme against the original partitioning model. As one can observe, the curves flattened as the number of the processors gets closer to the embedded maximum degree of parallelism. In this simulation study, the mean value for the size of the relations was 100,000, and the selectivity factor ranged from .01% to 1.0%. Finally, the ratio between the unit communication time and the unit operation time was chosen among various system configurations. The result shows the validity and effectiveness of both compile-time and run-time optimization schemes proposed earlier.

Figure 8 depicts percentage improvement in performance of the proposed scheme relative to the original VL allocation scheme. As one can expect, increasing the number of PEs improves the performance. However, regardless of the number of the processors available the proposed optimization scheme offers better performance. The simulator also measures the effectiveness of the proposed schemes with varying size of relations and selectivities. The results have shown that the performance improvement is independent of the size of the relations, but it is directly related to the selectivity factor. Table 1 shows the average percentage improvement in performance with varying selectivity for the sample testbed programs. A lower selectivity leads to a higher possibility of the elim-

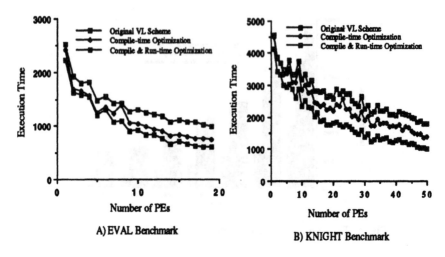

Fig. 7. Execution Time of the Proposed Schemes.

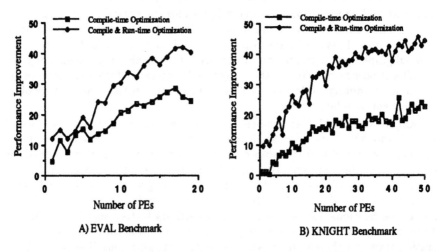

Fig. 8. Performance Improvement compare to Original VL scheme.

ination of some branch(es). Therefore, the performance improvement is higher
when the selectivity factor is lower.

Since our scheme reduces the communication cost among processors by prun-
ing the unnecessary execution of branch(es), the simulator also measures the
performance improvement with various unit communication time. The unit operation time and the selectivity factor have been fixed at 10^{-8} seconds and 0.1%,
respectively, for this simulation run. As shown in Table 2, the performance improvement increases as the unit communication time increases. This is due to the
effect of VL allocation scheme and the reduced communication cost by elimina-

Table 1. Performance Improvement for various Programs with varying selectivities factors

Selectivity	PARS	EVAL	KNIGHT	QUEENS	PENTO	HANOI	HOUSES
0.001	40.0	24.2	32.5	48.7	35.4	23.2	39.6
0.005	34.2	15.7	26.7	30.4	28.5	17.5	29.4
0.010	31.2	12.4	23.8	24.1	22.7	15.3	24.5
0.050	28.7	10.8	19.3	21.6	17.0	13.7	21.9

Table 2. Performance Improvement for various Programs with varying communication speed

Comm.	PARS	EVAL	KNIGHT	QUEENS	PENTO	HANOI	HOUSES
0.0001	12.7	7.8	14.9	5.4	10.6	2.7	6.8
0.0003	16.5	11.6	17.3	8.6	14.2	6.3	10.7
0.0005	19.3	13.3	18.9	10.4	15.9	7.5	12.8
0.0010	23.6	15.3	23.5	12.9	18.3	9.5	15.4
0.0050	31.8	21.5	30.6	17.5	22.6	11.2	19.7

tion of unnecessary nodes that caused by the generation of empty output during the execution of program.

5 Summary and Conclusion

Parallel execution of the logic program and its optimization within the scope of database environment are main interests of this work. The execution of logic program in a multiprocessor environment requires a parallel execution model which enforces an efficient execution order of the AND/OR branches. We have developed a technique to map the coarse grain operations in logic program onto a dataflow graph to support scheduling and allocation of the logic programs in a multiprocessor environment. This was achieved by partitioning the generated dataflow graph into vertical layers and allocating the resulting layers on available processors. This technique was further improved by enhancing the scope of the partitioning scheme by a set of compile-time and run-time optimization rules. A simulator has been developed to measure the effectiveness and feasibility of the proposed optimization scheme. Simulation results indicated the practicality of the proposed scheme in reducing the overall execution time.

References

1. Anurag Acharya, Milind Tambe, and Anoop Gupta, "Implementation of Production Systems on Message-Passing Computers," IEEE Transactions on Parallel and Distributed Systems, vol.3, No.4, July, '92, pp.477-487.

2. Jonas Barklund, and Hakan Millroth, "Integration Complex Data Structures in Prolog," Inter'l Symp. on Logic Programming, '87, pp.415-425.

3. Johann Eder, "Logic and Databases," International Summer School, '92, pp.95-103.

4. Y. Freundlich, "Knowledge Bases and Databases," IEEE Computer, vol.23, no.11, Nov. '90, pp.51-57.

5. Sumit Ganguly, Waqar Hasan, and Ravi Krishnamurthy, "Query Optimization for Parallel Execution," ACM SIGMOD, '92, pp.9-18.

6. G. Gupta and V. S. Costa, "AND-OR Parallelism in Full Prolog with Paged Binding Arrays," Proc. of PARLE, '92, pp.617-632.

7. Gitu Jain, B. Ramkuman, and Jon G. Kuhl, "A Control Strategy Based on Heuristic Techniques for the Parallel Execution of Logic Programs," 8th Inter'l Conf. on Parallel Processing Symposium, '94, pp.311-315.

8. Byung-Uk Jun, A.R. Hurson, and B. Shirazi, "Handling Logic Programs in Multithreaded Dataflow Environment," Second Biennial European Joint Conf. on Engineering Systems Design and Analysis, '94, pp.533-540.

9. Rosana S.G. Lanzelotte, Patrick Valduriez, and Mohamed Zait, "Optimization of Object-Oriented Recursive Queries using Cost-Controlled Strategies," ACM SIGMOD, '92, pp.256-265.

10. B. Lee, A.R. Hurson, and T.Y. Feng, "A Vertically Layered Allocation Scheme for Data Flow Systems," Journal of Parallel and Distributed Computing, vol.11, '91, pp.175-187.

11. Sang-goo Lee, L.J. Henschen, and G.Z. Qadah, "Semantic Query Reformulation in Deductive Databases," 7th Inter'l Conf. on Data Engineering, '91, pp.232-239.

12. B. Lee, and A.R. Hurson, "Dataflow Architectures and Multithreading," IEEE Computer, vol.27, no.8, '94, pp.27-39.

13. M.V. Mannino, P. Chu, and T. Sager, "Statistical Profile Estimation in Database Systems," ACM Computing Surveys, vol.20, no.3, Sep. '88, pp.191-221.

14. Dan Moldovan, Wing Lee, and Changhwa Lin, "SNAP: A Marker-Propagation Architecture for Knowledge Processing," IEEE Transactions on Parallel and Distributed Systems, vol.3, No.4, July, '92, pp.397-410.

15. C.D. Polychronopoulos and U. Banerjee, "Processor Allocation for Horizontal and Vertical Parallelism and Related Speedup Bounds," IEEE transactions on Computer, vol.C-36, no.4, Apr. '87, pp.410-420.

16. J.A. Robinson, "A Machine-Oriented Logic based on the Resolution Principle," Journal of the Association for Computing Machinery, '80, no.12, pp.23-41.

17. S. Taylor, et al., "Logic programming using parallel associative operations," Inter'l Symp. on Logic Programming, '84, pp.58-68.

18. Jeffrey D. Ullman, Principle of Database and Knowledge Base Systems, vol.2, Computer Science Press, 1989.

19. M. J. Wise, "Message-Brokers and Communicating Prolog Processes," 4th Inter'l Conf. on Parallel Architectures and Languages in Europe, '92, pp.535-549.

20. Z. Yuhan, T. Honglei, and X. Li, "AND/OR Parallel Execution of Logic Programs: Exploiting Dependent AND-parallelism," ACM SIGPLAN Notices, vol.28, no.5, '93, pp.19-28.

COVERS - A Tool for the Design of Real-Time Concurrent Systems

A.V. Borshchev[1], Yu.G. Karpov and V.V. Roudakov
Technical Cybernetics Department
St.Petersburg State Technical University
195251 St.Petersburg Russia
E-mail: covers@dcs.stu.spb.su

We give an overview of the existing commercial tools for the design of real-time concurrent systems and propose a list of features the ideal design environment should have. Then the COVERS tool is described. Its underlying abstract model is a derivative of the Timed Transition System. The concrete modelling language is based upon the structural, behavioral and data processing views on the real-time concurrent system. COVERS supports a sequential subset of Statecharts and ANSI C. The formal semantics of the concrete model is presented. We describe a method of testing the real time temporal properties using spy processes, and, briefly, debugging and performance analysis means.

1 Introduction and overview of existing tools

A lot of papers has been written on the importance of using the executable models and the corresponding tools in the design of real-time concurrent systems. However, so far none of the existing tools is being seriously used as a real design instrument. The reasons should be partly clear from a short overview we give below.

The most popular tool is, probably, the **BONeS Designer** [BONeS]. A system under development is described there as a hierarchical data flow diagram. A block is triggered as the data items arrive to its input ports. There are hundreds of standard blocks in the BONeS library, however, an experienced user can try to write an algorithm of the primitive block in C. The types of data items are organized in a hierarchical structure with a sort of limited inheritance. The other basic entities include resources (server-type and quantity-shared), memories and events, each having some standard blocks to work with it. The simulation algorithm is based on the event calendar containing asynchronous events which are scheduled by such blocks as delays. An asynchronous event may cause several instantaneous synchronous events. The probing mechanism is provided to collect statistics.

The main disadvantage of the tool is that the user is forced to express everything in terms of the data flow diagrams. When it comes to the

---

1. Until March, 1996 with Hewlett-Packard Laboratories, Bristol. E-mail: avb@hplb.hpl.hp.com

sequential algorithms or data processing, the model tends to look huge and very unnatural. Further, BONeS tries to provide its own special language for every king of thing, like data types or expressions. This increases the distance between the model and the real object. For instance, the data types in the main hierarchy do not correspond to the data types of C (that is used in other parts of the tool), or any other programming language. The semantics of block diagram also causes inconveniences for the user, who has to care of data losses, "stale" data, racing, etc. caused not by the nature of the system he models. Recently (in version 3.0) the finite state machines were introduced for the block behavior description, however, the way they are implemented leaves much to be desired. Unfortunately, all this moves BONeS towards an eclectic combination of discordant approaches and ideas.

The model in **SES Workbench** [SES] consists of one or several submodels, each represented by a directed graph. The basic elements are *nodes, arcs, transactions* and *resources*. Nodes correspond to a certain stage in the transaction's life: service, delay, allocation or release of resource. Transactions (representing messages, jobs, processes, etc.) travel from node to node along the arcs. Having arrived to a node, transaction is either serviced or, if the node is busy, joins the queue. An arbitrary data structure can be associated with transaction. Among the 24 basic types of nodes in SES Workbench there are resource control nodes, transaction flow control nodes, nodes for work with submodels, and so on. The user can create his own nodes in object-oriented manner and define references to nodes. A transaction arriving at a node is considered as calling a method of a node. The statistic collection is bound to either nodes or transaction categories, for instance: the time interval between two subsequent arrivals of transaction to a particular node, amount of available resources, the time transaction waits in a queue. An assertion can be set at any place, and it will be tested each time a transaction crosses the place. The simulation algorithm is pretty much the same as the one of BONeS.

As one can see, SES Workbench uses the same dataflow diagram concept as BONeS, having, however, less flexibility. The main limitation of SES Workbench is again the absence of natural means for the description of control flow. This leads to an awkward models. For example, in [P92] the network communication object is modelled by a loop of nodes with a special transaction defining the location of control.

Statemate [HLNPPSST90] is based on more modern ideas in the reactive system design. Following the statement that the functional model should be supplemented with the behavioral one, the authors of the tool implemented the Statecharts formalism [H87] - a serious attempt to structurize the behavior description. The functional structure of the system under development is specified as a set of communicating activities with which the Statecharts can be associated. In Statecharts, the states of finite-state machines can be substituted for by a state machine of a new level, or even a set of concurrent state machines. The first option is definitely useful when one describes the different operation modes of the system, or just a reaction on a certain event that is common for a subset of states. Also, more flexibility is added to a description technique by allowing the transitions to cross the hierarchy boundaries. Concurrent parts of the system communicate using the broadcast. The transitions of the state machines are triggered by broadcast signals or timing events. A guard expression and an action can be associated with a transition. In addition to the common simulation tool functionality, Statemate can try to construct the reachability graph of the system behavior and thus analyse the reachability properties. However, this is possible for toy models only.

Among the reasons why the Statemate is not widely used, the main ones, to our mind, are a very restricted communication mechanism having sophisticated semantics, and a poor language for data manipulation.

It is also worth to mention the tool called **Design/CPN** [DCPN]. Its underlying mathematical model is a Petri net overgrown with a huge number of extensions. The transitions can be hierarchically decomposed into new nets, the tokens are coloured, the guard expressions can be associated with transitions. The real time is introduced by assigning delays to transitions and arcs, and timestamping tokens.

Not surprisingly, none of the efficient Petri net analysis techniques can be applied to the resulting object called HCPN, and the main question arising here is: what is reason for using Petri nets then? The only thing available is the construction of the occurrence graph (the graph of reachable markings) according to the HCPN operational semantics, and it is implemented in the tool. Again, for practical systems the occurrence graph is too big. The other problem is the use of Standard ML as the data processing language, which is nice, but too academic.

Summarizing this overview we propose the list of features the ideal real-time concurrent systems development environment should have:

1. Two separate modelling languages: one for the description of the structure of communicating activities and the flow of data between them, and the other one - for the description of behavior of these activities, i.e. the flow of control inside them.

2. Possibility to specify different communication disciplines. At least shared data, synchronous communication and message passing should have easy representation.

3. Simple means to express the basic elements of reactive behavior: the state of waiting for the several alternative events, timeouts and delays.

4. Powerful standard data processing language conveniently embedded into the structure / behavior specification.

5. Hierarchy for both functional structure and behavior description techniques.

6. Possibility to define types of activities and, probably, behavior elements and refer to them.

7. Scalability. The user should be able to define a variable size periodic structure of communicating activities.

8. Rigorous formal semantics for all elements of modelling language. The semantics should clearly define the time model, duration of actions and communications, level of atomicity, simultaneity, nondeterminism.

9. Executability. The ability to obtain any of the possible trajectories of the system behavior.

10. Visualization of the system behavior and "source code" debugging facilities.

11. Requirement specification language covering real time temporal properties of the system. Possibility to verify and/or test these properties.

12. Convenient performance analysis tools.

13. The straightforward translation into the implementation language wherever possible.

The COVERS tool described in this paper is designed to meet most of these requirements.

2 Abstract model

The COVERS underlying model has two levels: abstract model and concrete model. The first one is a mathematical abstraction dealing with fundamental issues of the discrete real-time behavior. It is not directly visible to the user. The concrete model captures such aspects of the system under development as concurrency, data flow, communication, control flow, data processing etc. The user works only in terms of concrete model.

The object used as an abstract model is derived from the Timed Transition System [HMP92] and is called TTS below. It is a tuple

$\langle \Sigma, s^0, T, C, d \rangle$, where

Σ is (possibly, infinite) set of states,
$s^0 \in \Sigma$ is the initial state,
$T \subseteq \{\tau | \tau : \Sigma \to \Sigma \cup \{Null\}\}$ is a finite set of transitions,
$C \subseteq T \times T$ is a conflict relation,
$d : T \to R^{\geq 0}$ is a function assigning a *firing delay* to each transition.

Time in TTS is measured by real numbers. Transitions are defined as functions on the set of states. Transition τ is called *enabled* in the state s if $\tau(s) = s' \neq Null$. A set of all transitions enabled in the state s is denoted by $T(s)$. A transition can be *taken* (can fire) only when it is enabled. Transition firing takes zero time. When τ is taken in the state s, the next state of the system is $\tau(s)$. In between two subsequent transition firings the system state remains the same. The important property of TTS is that transitions in general are not alternative to each other. They can fire independently, and this enables us to model the concurrent systems.

It might happen that between the moment the transition τ becomes enabled and the moment it is taken, the other transitions fire. Some of them may disable τ, the others - do nothing to it, and the third - disable and re-enable it at once. To make distinction between two last cases we introduce the *conflict relation*. The way it works is explained later.

The operational meaning of the TTS is captured by the notion of *computation* - a sequence of *situations* and *steps*:

$$\langle s_0, t_0 \rangle \overset{\tau_0}{\to} \quad \langle s_1, t_1 \rangle \overset{\tau_1}{\to} \dots \to \quad \langle s_i, t_i \rangle \overset{\tau_i}{\to} \dots ,$$

where $s_i \in \Sigma$, $s_0 = s^0$, $t_i \in R^{\geq 0}$, $\forall i : t_i \leq t_{i+1}$ and $\tau_i \in T \cup \{\varepsilon\}$.

The situation $\langle s_i, t_i \rangle$ means that at time t_i the system enters the state s_i. The step τ_i which is taken at t_{i+1} drives the system into the state s_{i+1}. A step can be either the transition firing ($\tau_i \in T$) or the *timed step* denoted by ε. In the following definitions ε is not in conflict with any of the transitions.

Transition $\tau \in T$ *becomes enabled* at the situation $\langle s_i, t_i \rangle$ if $\tau(s_i) \neq Null$ and either $i = 0$ or $\tau(s_{i-1}) = Null$ or $\langle \tau_{i-1}, \tau \rangle \in C$.

Transition $\tau \in T$ *is taken* at the situation $\langle s_i, t_i \rangle$ if $\tau_i = \tau$.

Transition $\tau \in T$ is *continuously enabled* from $\langle s_i, t_i \rangle$ to $\langle s_j, t_j \rangle$, $i \leq j$ if $\forall k : i \leq k \leq j : \tau(s_k) \neq Null$ and $\forall k : i \leq k < j : \langle \tau_k, \tau \rangle \notin C$.

The computation must satisfy the following three conditions.

1. $\forall i$ if $\tau_i \in T$ then $s_{i+1} = \tau_i(s_i)$ and $t_{i+1} = t_i$. Otherwise, if $\tau_i = \varepsilon$ then $s_{i+1} = s_i$ and $t_{i+1} > t_i$. Also, we require that if $\tau_i = \varepsilon$ then $\tau_{i+1} \neq \varepsilon$. This means that a computation consists of alternating *state-changing*

and *time-changing* phases. In a state-changing phase, which takes zero time, several transitions can be taken. In a time-changing phase the time progresses, and the system state remains the same.

2. If $\tau \in T$ is continuously enabled from $\langle s_i, t_i \rangle$ to $\langle s_j, t_j \rangle$, $i \leq j$ then $t_i + d(\tau) \leq t_j$. Thus, any transition can not be continuously enabled longer than is defined by its firing delay. If $d(\tau)$ passes since τ has been enabled, it should be either disabled or taken.

3. If $\tau \in T$ becomes enabled at $\langle s_i, t_i \rangle$, is continuously enabled from $\langle s_i, t_i \rangle$ to $\langle s_j, t_j \rangle$, $i \leq j$, and taken at $\langle s_j, t_j \rangle$, then $t_i + d(\tau) = t_j$. Thus, a transition can not be taken before its firing delay expires.

This definition of computation is, however, not constructive. To be able to build any computation of the TTS we will extend the notion of situation.

A *full situation* is a triple $\langle s, t, r \rangle$, where $\langle s, t \rangle$ is a situation, i.e. a state and a time it has been entered, and $r:T(s) \rightarrow R^{\geq 0}$ is a function assigning a *remaining firing time* (or, simply, *remainder*) to each transition enabled in s.

Obviously (we also can refer the reader to the [AH92]), the full situation fully defines the future behavior of the system. The following algorithm is used in COVERS to obtain the computations of the TTS.

Let $\langle s, t, r \rangle$ be the current full situation, and τ_{next} - the next step.

```
//  initially, remainders are set to the firing delays
⟨s,t,r⟩  =  ⟨s⁰,0,r⁰⟩ ,  where  ∀τ ∈ T(s):r⁰(τ) = d(τ) ;
while( T(s) ≠ ∅ )  {  //  while some transitions are enabled
    r_min  =  min(r(τ)|τ ∈ T(s)) ;  //  we get the minimum remainder
    if(  r_min > 0  )  {  //  if no one is ready to fire
    //  a timed step is made
    τ_next  =  ε ;
    //  and remainders are decreased by r_min
    ⟨s,t,r⟩  =  ⟨s,t + r_min, r⟩ ,  where  ∀τ ∈ T(s):r'(τ) = r(τ) − r_min ;
    }  else  {  //  if someone is ready to fire
    τ_next  =  any  τ ∈ T(s)  such that  r(τ) = 0 ;
    //  the state changes instantaneously
    ⟨s,t,r⟩  =  ⟨τ_next(s),t,r'⟩ ,  where  ∀τ ∈ T(τ_next(s)) :
        //  for the transitions that become enabled
        //  remainders are equal to their firing delay
        r'(τ) = d(τ)  if  τ(s) = Null ∨ ⟨τ_next, τ⟩ ∈ C ,  and
        //  for the transitions that remain enabled
        //  remainders are not changed
        r'(τ) = r(τ)  otherwise;
    }
}
```

The set of all sequences of full situations and steps generated by this algorithm coincides with the set of all possible computations of the TTS, or its *behavior*.

It is interesting to consider the possibility of finite representation of the system behavior. A directed graph with pairs $\langle s, r \rangle$ as vertices and steps τ as arcs could serve as such a representation. Unfortunately, even if the TTS has a finite number of states, the set of reachable pairs $\langle s, r \rangle$ can be infinite. The simplest example is the following TTS: $\Sigma = \{s\}$, $s^0 = s$, $T = \{a, b\}$, $a(s) = b(s) = s$, $C = \emptyset$, $d(a) = \sqrt{2}$ and $d(b) = \sqrt{3}$. Since $\sqrt{2}$ and $\sqrt{3}$ do not have a common multiple, the set of reachable pairs $\langle s, r \rangle$ is infinite. This frustrating result applies generally to all models capable to express this two primitive concurrent cyclic transitions. If we restrict ourselves by considering *rational* firing delays only, the behavior will always have a finite representation. However, it still can be too big to be constructed by a computer, and, moreover, by making such an approximation we can loose some important branches.

Consequently, any verification of real-time concurrent systems based on the construction of all reachable situations is practically impossible. In the paper we mainly concentrate on other analysis methods such as testing of temporal properties.

3 Concrete model

The concrete model, or the modelling language of COVERS is based upon the three views on the system under development: structure, behavior and data processing. From the point of view of functional structure the system is represented by a set of concurrent communicating *processes*. *Extended state machines* (visually being a "sequential" Statecharts [H87]) are used to specify the behavior of processes. All processing of data (sending, reception, testing and modification) is specified in C language.

A *process* is a sequential object driven by the external events like communication with another process or elapsing of the specified amount of time. We assume that there is a global clock in the system, and also that each process is "executed on its own processor".

Three disciplines of process communication are provided by COVERS as basic: synchronous communication (*rendezvous*), asynchronous message passing (*cast*) and *shared variables*. This set was chosen for the following reasons. First, all three types can be frequently met in real-life systems. Second, they are a sort of orthogonal, since it is hard to express one of them in terms of the others. Finally, more sophisticated communication mechanisms can be easily constructed on top of them.

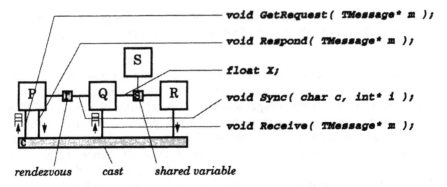

Fig. 1. Structural view on the system under development

An example of structure chart is shown in Fig. 1. Processes P, Q, R and S are connected to the communication objects with *connectors*. A C declaration associated with a connector defines how the process will access the communication object. In case of shared variable it is just a variable declaration, in case of rendezvous or cast it is a function declaration.

Synchronization of two processes, or rendezvous, is similar to the rendezvous of the Ada language. It occurs immediately as soon as both processes are ready, and takes zero time. If one process is ready, and the other is not, the first one has to wait for the partner - see Fig. 2. Bidirectional data exchange can be performed during the rendezvous. The exchange algorithm can be specified by the user in C.

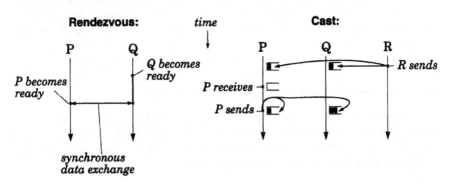

Fig. 2. Synchronous and asynchronous communication

Cast is a message passing mechanism with queuing. It is asynchronous in the sense that the sender can send a message at any time, it does not care whether the receivers are ready. Cast communication objects may connect arbitrary number of processes. A process can be connected to the cast as a sender, as a receiver, or both. Having been sent, the message immediately appears in the input queues of all receivers - see Fig. 2. Having been received by the process, the message is removed from its queue. If the process wants to receive a message, but the queue is empty, it waits. The messages of a particular cast object are of the same C data type.

A process connected to a shared variable can access it at any time. The operation on shared variable performed during a single system step is considered as atomic. An access to a shared variable as well as an act of sending a cast message take zero time.

The behavior of a process is described in terms of *states* and *transitions*. Being in a state, the process is waiting for some external event to occur. The transitions outgoing the state define the set of events the process will react to, and the reaction itself. A transition has three attributes: *guard, event* and *action*. A guard is a Boolean C expression over the process' private variables and variables shared with other processes. All guards of the transitions outgoing the current state are checked "continuously". A transition can only fire when its guard evaluates to TRUE.

Three possible kinds of events can be associated with transitions. The first one is a reception of the cast message, the second - a rendezvous with other process, and the third - elapsing of the specified amount of time (time delay). Syntactically first two kinds look like a call to a corresponding function, and the last one - as an arbitrary C expression of the float type.

Action is a piece of C code describing the process' reaction on the event. It may include the modification of private and shared variables and sending cast messages.

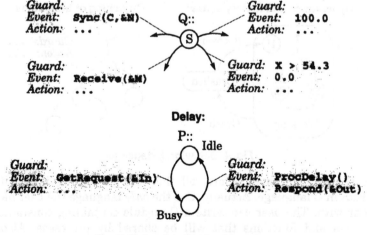

Fig. 3. Behavior. Basic elements

A transition fires instantaneously as soon as the corresponding event is available. If the time delay t is associated with a transition, transition will fire provided the guard is *continuously* TRUE for t time units.

Fig. 3. shows how the COVERS modelling language represents the basic elements of the reactive behavior. The process Q (its external connections are shown in Fig. 1.) in the state S waits for the rendezvous with process P, the cast message from P or R, and for the shared variable X to become greater than 54.3. Note that the waiting for a condition c to become TRUE is specified as a transition with the guard c and zero delay. If none of these events are available within 100.0 time units since Q has entered the state S, the *Timeout* transition is taken. The "pure delay" is shown in the behavior of the process R below. Having received the cast message, R comes to state *Busy*, spends there the time *ProcDelay()*, then sends some message back and returns to *Idle*.

Besides the plain state diagrams, COVERS supports the following Harel's extensions [H87]: hyperstates, history states and branching of transitions. Hyperstate is a compact representation of the group of states having the identical reaction on a particular event. Consider the model of a process with failures in Fig. 4. The hyperstate Working corresponds to the normal operating mode, and in the state *Crashed* the process is crashed. The transition *Crash* may be taken no matter what the process is doing, i.e. in either of the states *S1*, *S2* or *S3*. If after the recovery the process wants to return to the state where its operation has been interrupted, it can be specified by the history pseudo-state. Then, sometimes it is very convenient to change the transition's destination state depending on some condition, for example, on the type of the received message. Conditional pseudo-states and pseudo-transitions (Fig. 4. right) serve for that purpose.

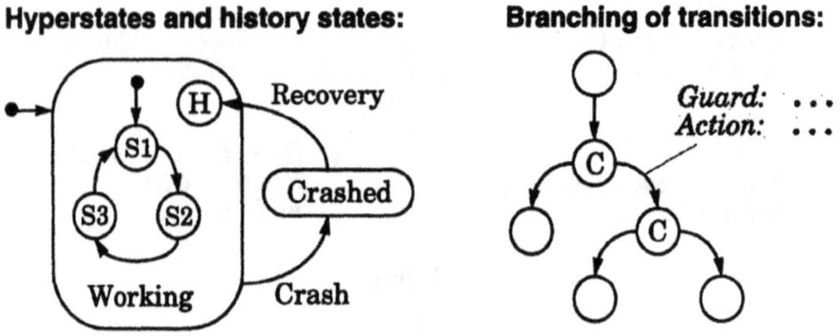

Hyperstates and history states: **Branching of transitions:**

Fig. 4. Behavior. Extensions

As it was mentioned before, all the data processing is specified in COVERS in C language. Actually, C is the *only* language the user has to be familiar with. The user can write a C module containing constants, type definitions and functions that will be shared by processes. Also, each process may have its private C module containing private variables, functions, etc. Of course, there is no function like *main()*, since the control flow is defined by the state diagram of the process. Functions are executed only if they are called during the firing of transitions or checking the transition's guards.

The semantics of the modelling language is defined as follows. The TTS $\langle \Sigma, s^0, T, C, d \rangle$ is built on the basis of the concrete model. In this TTS

Σ contains all possible combinations of three components:
- current states of all processes,
- values of all private and shared variables,
- values of all cast input queues.

s^0 is the TTS initial state, where
- every process is in its initial state,
- private and shared variables are initialized,
- all the cast queues are empty.

T contains one TTS transition for:
- each transition of each process marked with the reception of the cast message. For those TTS states where this transition is not open, or the corresponding queue is empty, the next TTS state is *Null*. Otherwise the next TTS state is obtained by moving the message from the queue to the given private buffer, executing the action of the transition, and moving the process to the new state.
- each pair of transitions of two different processes marked with the matching rendezvous functions. For those TTS states where at least one of the transitions is not open, the next TTS state is *Null*. Otherwise the next TTS state is obtained by executing the data exchange function, executing actions of both transitions, and moving the processes to the new states.
- each transition of each process marked with the time delay. For those TTS states where this transition is not open, the next TTS state is *Null*. Otherwise the next TTS state is obtained by executing the action of the transition, and moving the process to the new state.

C contains all pairs $\langle \tilde{\tau}, \tau \rangle$ of TTS transitions where both $\tilde{\tau}$ and τ include the transitions of one process, and the hierarchy level of the process' transition included in $\tilde{\tau}$ is higher or equal to the hierarchy level of the process' transition included in τ.

d, the firing delay function,
- is 0 for all TTS transitions corresponding to a cast message reception or a to rendezvous.
- for the TTS transitions corresponding to the process' transitions marked with the time delay, is equal to this time delay value.

Now, the semantics of the concrete model is the set of all possible computations of the TTS built according to these rules. It is easy to check that all timing assumptions, and all explanations of the communication mechanisms and state machines we gave are nothing else but just the consequences of this formal semantics. The concrete model now becomes fully executable.

4 Analysis of real time temporal properties

Among the different analysis tools provided by COVERS, one of the most interesting is the capability of testing the real time temporal properties. The general idea is the one proposed in [H92]: the user constructs the "special piece of behavior" tuned to enter the error state whenever the violation of the desired property takes place. This object is executed in parallel with the main system model, it watches everything what happens in the system, but it cannot affect the system behavior. Such objects are called *spies*.

The transition guards in the spy state diagram may refer to every variable, private or shared, to firing of a particular transitions, to rendezvous, etc. The only type of event allowed there is a time delay, or an empty event - instant transition. The way the instant transitions are executed is a bit special. First, the next state of the main system model is obtained, and then the guards of the instant transitions are checked. If some of them evaluate to TRUE, the spy makes a step *synchronously* with the system.

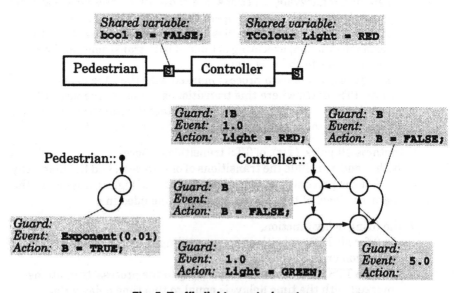

Fig. 5. Traffic lights control system

Let us consider the traffic lights control system example from [HMP92]. The model consists of two processes: the traffic light controller and the Poisson stream of pedestrians - see Fig. 5. The variable *Light* corresponds to the traffic light for the pedestrians. Pedestrians press the button once every 100 seconds, on average. When the button is pressed, the Boolean shared variable B is set to TRUE. If the *Light* is RED and B is set to TRUE, the *Controller* resets B and, in 1 second, shows the GREEN. After a 5 second pause, B is tested again. If it is still FALSE and remains FALSE for 1 second more, the RED light is shown. Otherwise, B is reset and *Controller* repeats the 5 second pause.

In the original paper the following two requirements are put upon the system:

1. Whenever B is TRUE then *Light* is GREEN within 5 seconds for at least 5 seconds.

2. Whenever B has been TRUE for 25 seconds, then *Light* is RED.

1. $\square$ (B $\rightarrow$ $\Diamond_{[0,10]}$ ($\square_{[0,5]}$ (Light==GREEN)))

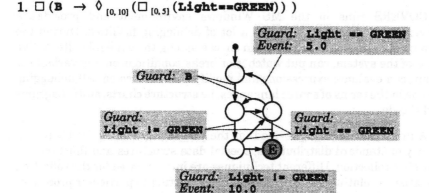

2. $\square$ ($\square_{[0,25]}$!B $\rightarrow$ $\Diamond_{[25,25]}$ (Light==RED))

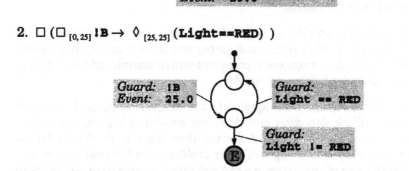

Fig. 6. Spies and temporal formulas expressing the requirements

The corresponding bounded temporal operators notation (see [AH92] for the details) and spies for these requirements are shown in Fig. 6.

When the *B* becomes TRUE, the first spy comes to the state *Check* and tests the *Light*. If it is already GREEN, it comes to the state *Green*, if not - to the state *Red*. If while the spy is in the state *Red*, *Light* does not become GREEN within 10 seconds, or if while it is in the state *Green* the *Light* becomes *Red*, the error state is entered. The second spy is straightforward.

Thus, the spies transform the temporal property into the reachability property, which can be easily tested during the system execution. If we manage to visit all the reachable states of the system model, and spy never enters the error state, the corresponding temporal property holds. But the most important thing about spies is that even if we cannot construct the whole state space, they will still *test* the property along all the simulation runs.

The two spies above were constructed manually. The subclass of the real time temporal properties which can be represented by spies, and the algorithm of spy construction still are to be found.

5 Other functionality of COVERS and conclusion

COVERS runs in the MS Windows environment and provides a convenient and easy GUI. It has a lot of debugging facilities. During the step-by-step execution the user can choose among the available alternative steps of the system, can put watches or break conditions on any variable or event, can evaluate expressions and modify data, and so on. All debugging is done in the terms of source languages, i.e structure charts, state diagrams and C code.

A number of tools is provided for the performance analysis. There is a library of standard distributions, special data structures and functions for statistics collection. Different techniques are implemented for the collection of statistics relating to migrating data and relating to particular processes, states or other static objects.

The user can specify a type of process, can organize processes hierarchically, and, what is the most important issue, can specify an array or any other periodic structures of processes and communication objects, the size of the structure being a parameter.

So far, COVERS has been applied to the analysis of several multicast protocols, deadlock detection and deadlock avoidance algorithms for the distributed databases, distributed election algorithms for the fault-tolerant systems, real-time scheduling and other problems. Unfortunately, because of the limited size of the paper, we can not afford to give here any of these interesting case studies.

References

[AH92] R. Alur and T.A. Henzinger. *Logics and Models of Real Time. A Survey*. LNCS, 1992.

[BONeS] *BONeS Designer. Modelling Reference Guide. Version 2.6*. Comdisco Systems, a business unit of Cadence Design Systems, Inc. USA, 1993.

[DCPN] *Design / CPN. A Reference Manual. Version 1.75*. Meta Software Corporation, USA, 1991.

[H87] D. Harel. *Statecharts: A Visual Formalism for Complex Systems*. Science of Computer Programming, Vol. 8, No. 3, June 1987, pp 231-274.

[HLNPPSST90] D. Harel, H. Lachover, A. Naamad, A. Pnueli, M. Politi, R. Sherman, A. Shtull-Trauring and M. Trakhtenbrot. *STATEMATE: A Working Environment for the Development of Complex Reactive Systems*. IEEE Transactions on Software Engineering, Vol. 16, No. 4, April 1990, pp 403-414.

[HMP92] T.A. Henzinger, Z. Manna and A. Pnueli. *Timed Transition Systems*. Technical Report TR 92-1263, Department of Computer Science, Cornell University, January 1992.

[P92] A.S. Palmer. *An Illustration of Data Resources + Transaction Modelling as Applied to a Simple Network Problem*. Scientific and Engineering Software Inc., USA, March 1992.

[SES] *SES Workbench. User's manual*. Release 2.1. Scientific and Engineering Software Inc., USA, 1992.

Status and Prospect of ZM4 / SIMPLE / PEPP: An Event-oriented Evaluation Environment for Parallel and Distributed Programs

Rainer Klar and Peter Dauphin
Universität Erlangen-Nürnberg, IMMD VII
Martensstr. 3, D-91058 Erlangen
email: klar@informatik.uni-erlangen.de
url: http://www7.informatik.uni-erlangen.de/tree/IMMD-VII/Research/Groups/MMB/

Abstract

Debugging and performance evaluation of parallel and distributed programs can be facilitated by tools which consider a parallel program in terms of the dynamic flow of significant events and of their interaction.

This paper describes the current state of an evaluation environment, consisting of event-oriented tools which enable the programmer to exactly assess the functional behavior and the performance of parallel and distributed programs. The evaluation environment combines tools for event-driven hardware/software monitoring, event trace analysis, and modeling. It is peculiar to this environment that it closely integrates modeling, monitoring, and event trace analysis and establishes correct causal relationships between events of interest.

1. Introduction

Users and operators of parallel and distributed systems often find it very difficult to exploit the immense computing power at their disposal. Writing and debugging parallel programs which use the underlying hardware in an efficient way proves to be a difficult task even for specialists. There is typically not enough insight into the internals of the hardware, the system software and their alternating effect with the user program. Bugs are hard to locate and tuning, which depends on a detailed knowledge of such factors as idle times, race conditions or access conflicts, is often not done systematically but by using ad-hoc methods. To analyze the functional behavior and the performance of a parallel program it is not enough to employ summarizing methods such as profiling and accounting. Methods and tools which reveal the program's dynamic behavior and the concurrency of its tasks are needed to handle these issues.

Monitoring. Event-driven monitoring has proved to be a well-suited technique for understanding and analyzing the dynamics of parallel programs running on a parallel or distributed system. It can be done by hardware, software or hybrid monitoring. We prefer hybrid monitoring which combines advantages of both hardware monitoring (small interference) and software monitoring (source-related, i.e. problem-oriented event description).

Event trace analysis. In the eighties Ferrari argued that *"the study of performance evaluation as an independent subject has sometimes caused researchers in the area to lose contact with reality"* [4]. Our contribution to meet this challenge are tools for event-driven monitoring of real world programs, and especially, a comfortable set of analysis tools for arbitrarily formatted event traces. Its comfort is based on its universality and on using source-related identifiers in the representation of results. Comfortable analysis tools pave the way for making monitoring a matter of course in the software design cycle.

Modeling. The analysis of parallel programs should not be limited to observing those programs which have been actually implemented for an underlying distributed architecture. Many questions can be solved more easily and more efficiently by setting up a model of the program and the machine, varying parameters in the model to predict the performance of the program under various circumstances.

Integration of methods. There is a great potential to integrate event-based models and event-driven monitoring since both methods are based on the same abstraction (the event) of the dynamic behavior of the program under study. Models of the program help to prepare measurements by defining events systematically and they support event trace evaluation by defining evaluation scenarios. Automatically instrumenting the program using model defined events guarantees that there is the same set of events in the model and in the measured trace. This allows to check the consistency between the model and the event trace, validating either the trace or the model.

2. Events and their Causal Relationship

Events. We regard an event as an atomic instantaneous action. In the context of monitoring it is reasonable to define an event as a timeless state transition taking place when program execution passes a point of interest, called 'potential event'. Practically, a 'potential event' is implemented as an additional 'monitoring instruction' which remains latent as long as it is only inserted in a program to be measured. Only passing a 'potential event', i.e. executing a 'monitoring instruction' really produces an event. Each measured event is characterized by a token which indicates which 'potential event' has been passed, a time stamp which indicates at what point of time the respective 'potential event' has been passed, and parameters describing the context in which the event occurred. The measured overall dynamic program behavior is represented by one or many (parallelly) recorded event traces.

Causality. Events in a single process on a single processor are sequentially ordered and it is obvious that events which are causally effective on others must precede the latter. However, causal relations between events in a multi-process environment with many processors are no longer easy to define. For establishing a causal order between events in a multi-process environment it is economical to begin with neglecting all obvious causal relations, i.e. those in one sequentially executed process, and to first concentrate on points in the parallel program where communication between processes takes place. Regarding just these points as 'potential events' leads to event traces which span a skeleton of the causal interdependence structure of the dynamic behavior of the parallel program. All later, more detailed event analysis and their ordering can rely on this skeleton.

Two different methods for finding out which causal order exists between monitored events have been developed:

a) Hardware monitoring with globally valid precise time stamps. This method works for all communication mechanisms (via message passing and via shared variables).

b) An ordering method based on the accuracy of the decentral clocks and on known causal relationships, e.g. communications. This method works only for communication via message passing.

3. An Integrated Evaluation Environment

3.1. Monitoring (ZM4)

Event-driven monitoring is the only monitoring method (in contrast to time-driven monitoring) suitable for clarifying program analysis [5] and for gaining insight into the dynamic behavior of a parallel program. The definition of events depends on the applied monitoring technique. There are three monitoring techniques: hardware, software and hybrid monitoring. Using *hardware monitoring*, the event definition and recognition can be difficult and complex. A potential event is defined as a bit pattern on a processor bus or in a register. It becomes an event when it is detected by the probes and detection circuitry of a hardware monitor. In this case it is difficult to relate the recorded signals to the monitored program, i.e. to find a source-related, i.e. problem-oriented reference. Using *software* or *hybrid monitoring*, the potential events are defined by inserting monitoring instructions at certain points in the program under investigation (*program instrumentation*). These instructions write event tokens into a reserved memory area of the monitored system (software monitoring), or to a hardware system interface which is accessible for a hardware monitor (hybrid monitoring). In defining events by program instrumentation, each monitored event token can be clearly assigned to a point in the program; this provides a source-related reference. Thus, the evaluation of the event trace can be done on the program level which is familiar to the program designer. As hybrid monitoring combines source-related event specification with a small interference with the usual object system's behavior, it is our favorite monitoring technique.

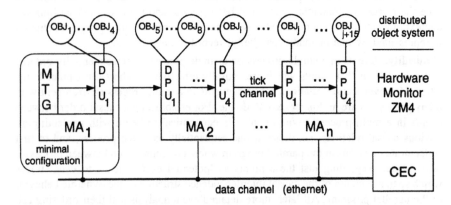

Figure 1: Distributed architecture of the hardware monitor ZM4

The distributed hardware monitor ZM4, see Fig.1, for event-driven monitoring is scalable (open number of monitor agents MA) and can be adapted to arbitrary object systems (the system on which the program under study is running), [7, 8, 2]. ZM4 can monitor several processors even if they are spatially distributed (LAN distance). It has a high-precision global clock (accuracy of 100ns) which allows to coherently monitor several nodes of the object system by assigning globally valid time stamps to measured events. This provides sufficient precision for establishing a global view and correct causal relations in any of today's parallel and distributed systems. The monitor agents MA are AT-compatible PCs equipped with special hardware boards for timing (monitor tick generator MTG) and monitoring (dedicated probe unit DPU). Each monitor agent produces an event trace. All measured event traces are sent to the central evaluation computer CEC which evaluates them off-line.

3.2. Trace Evaluation (SIMPLE)

SIMPLE (*S*ource related *I*ntegrated *M*ultiprocessor and -computer *P*erformance evaluation, visualization, and mode*L*ing *E*nvironment) is an event trace analysis system which is completely independent of the monitor system ZM4. However, being able to evaluate arbitrarily formatted event traces, it matches the needs of analyzing ZM4 traces [2]. SIMPLE is designed as a software package which comprises independent tools that are all based on a new kind of event trace access: the trace format is described in a trace description language (TDL) and evaluation tools access the event trace through a standardized interface (POET).

SIMPLE uses a general logical structure of measured data (event trace), see fig.2 as a basis for making measurement and trace evaluation independent of each other. The general logical event trace structure is conceived as an abstract data type with standardized access methods, see fig.3.

TDL (*T*race *D*escription *L*anguage): the language TDL is designed for a problem-oriented description of event traces. It clearly and naturally reflects the fundamental structure of an event trace. The compilation of a TDL description into a corresponding binary *access key file* has the advantage that syntactic and semantic correctness is checked once and before evaluation.

POET (*P*roblem *O*riented *E*vent *T*race Interface): the POET library is a monitor-independent function interface which enables the user to access

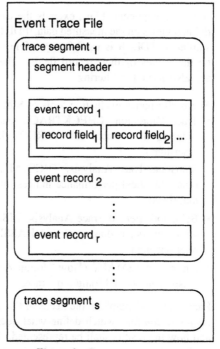

Figure 2: Event trace structure

measured data stored in event trace files in a problem-oriented manner. In order to be able to access and decode the differently structured measured data, the POET functions use the access key file which contains a complete description of formats and properties of the measured data.

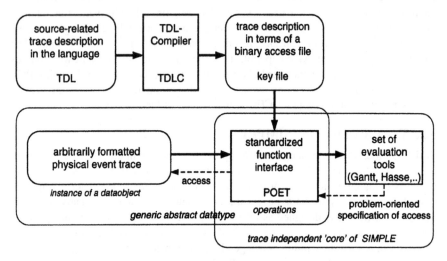

Figure 3: POET and TDL as a base for the trace analysis system SIMPLE

A third component, FDL, extends the capabilities of TDL/POET by allowing user-defined views on the measured data. FDL (*Filter Description Language*) is an approach similar to TDL. It is used for specifying rules for filtering event records depending on the values of their record fields. The source-related identifiers of the TDL file are also used for filtering.

The performance evaluation tools of SIMPLE cover the following evaluation areas:
• Trace Validation: CHECKTRACE (check for completeness and correct temporal ordering of a trace) and VARUS (check for the validity of problem-oriented assertions).
• Statistical Trace Analysis: TRCSTAT (computation of frequencies, durations and other statistical performance indices) and FACT (find activities and compute their durations).
• Behavior-oriented Trace Analysis: LIST (readable trace protocols), GANTT (drawing time-state diagrams) and HASSE (drawing diagrams reflecting the causal relationships).
• Animation: SMART (*Slow Motion Animated Review of Traces*) and VISIMON (Visualization of Monitored Traces).

Each tool is adaptable to the needs of the application under investigation via so-called *configuration files* which define what questions shall be answered by the evaluation and how the results shall be represented. These configuration files enable SIMPLE to perform the evaluation in an application-specific way without loosing its universality.

As an example of a typical performance evaluation with SIMPLE, we regard the representation of a communication between two processes called Initiator and Responder, via the INRES protocol [9]. Fig. 4 shows a part of the Initiator's time-state-diagram. The Initiator starts in state 'disconnected' and changes into state 'waiting' after having sent a connection request signal. It waits until the receipt of the Responder's connection confirm, then changing into state 'connected'. While connected the Initiator sends data, causing it again to change into state 'waiting' where it remains until the receipt of the Responder's acknowledgment.

The Gantt diagram shows all state transitions in their functional and temporal order. The duration of all activities are expressed over a common time axis.

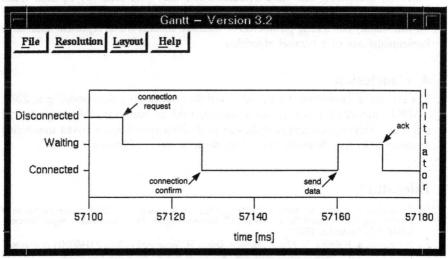

Figure 4: Gantt diagram of an observation of the INRES protocol

3.3. Graph Models and Integration of Modeling and Monitoring (PEPP)

Stochastic graph models are used for predicting the performance of a parallel algorithm. Nodes represent program tasks and arcs precedence relations between program tasks.

The modeling tool PEPP (*Performance Evaluation of Parallel Programs*) supports the generation and evaluation of stochastic graph models [1]. PEPP contains a powerful set of evaluation tools ranging from exact methods to approximation methods. Most of these tools allow to specifying arbitrary run time distributions for modeled activities. At the moment the following evaluation tools are available: SPASS (Series Parallel Structures Solver), state space analysis, de-approximation [11], and bounding techniques [6].

Stochastic graph models also play an important role in the context of 'Trace Evaluation'. They can be seen as one essential in a triplet of interdependent performance evaluation methods: *models*, *monitors*, and *trace evaluation* which are integrated to one comprehensive evaluation environment for parallel and distributed programs.

There exists a modeling toolset which uses stochastic graph models as an integral part for supporting:

- model-driven monitoring (i.e. model-driven instrumentation (AICOS) [10], model-driven configuration of hardware monitors, etc.),
- model-driven validation, i.e. consistency check between measured event traces and the underlying graph model,
- model-driven event trace evaluation (assignment of source-related identifiers and generation of TDL files, generation of SIMPLE configuration files for application-specific performance evaluation, etc.) [3].

However, monitoring and trace evaluation not only gain profit by models. Also stochastic graph models take advantage of measurement in using evaluated results for realistically calibrating parameters of modified models which represent alternative implementations of a parallel algorithm.

4. Conclusion

The evaluation environment for parallel and distributed programs consisting of ZM4, SIMPLE and PEPP has been succesfully applied in many research and industrial projects. Ongoing research is dedicated to develop specification-driven monitoring based on SDL specifications and a description of points of interest via MSCs.

Literature

[1] P. Dauphin, F. Hartleb, M. Kienow, V. Mertsiotakis, and A. Quick. PEPP: Performance Evaluation of Parallel Programs — User's Guide – Version 3.3. Technical Report 17/93, Universität Erlangen–Nürnberg, IMMD VII, September 1993.

[2] P. Dauphin, R. Hofmann, R. Klar, B. Mohr, A. Quick, M. Siegle, and F. Sötz. ZM4/SIMPLE: a General Approach to Performance–Measurement and –Evaluation of Distributed Systems. In T.L. Casavant and M. Singhal, editors, *Readings in Distributed Computing Systems*, chapter 6, pages 286–309. IEEE Computer Society Press, Los Alamitos, California, Jan 1994. ISBN 0-8186-3032-9.

[3] P. Dauphin and V. Mertsiotakis. MENTOR — a Model Based Event Trace Evaluation Support System. In *Tools and Posters Proc. of the 7th Int. Conf. on Modelling Techniques and Tools for Computer Performance Evaluation*, Vienna, Austria, May, 3rd – 6th 1994.

[4] D. Ferrari. Considerations on the Insularity of Performance Evaluation. *IEEE Transactions on Software Engineering*, SE–12(6):678–683, June 1986.

[5] D. Ferrari, G. Serazzi, and A. Zeigner. *Measurement and Tuning of Computer Systems*. Prentice Hall, Inc., Englewood Cliffs, 1983.

[6] F. Hartleb and V. Mertsiotakis. Bounds for the Mean Runtime of Parallel Programs. In R. Pooley and J. Hillston, editors, *Proceedings of the Sixth International Conference on Modelling Techniques and Tools for Computer Performance Evaluation*, pages 197–210, Edinburgh, 1992.

[7] R. Hofmann. The Distributed Hardware Monitor ZM4 and Its Interface to MEMSY. In A. Bode and M. Dal Cin, editors, *Parallel Computer Architectures: Theory, Hardware, Software, Applications*, pages 66–79. Springer Lecture LNCS 732, Berlin et al., March 1993.

[8] R. Hofmann, R. Klar, B. Mohr, A. Quick, and M. Siegle. Distributed Performance Monitoring: Methods, Tools, and Applications. *IEEE Transactions on Parallel and Distributed Systems*, 5(6):585–598, June 1994.

[9] Dieter Hogrefe. *Estelle, LOTOS und SDL*. Springer, Berlin, 1989.

[10] A. Quick. A New Approach to Behavior Analysis of Parallel Programs Based on Monitoring. In G.R. Joubert, D. Trystram, and F.J. Peters, editors, *ParCo '93: Conference on Parallel Computing, Proc. of the Int'l Conference, Grenoble, France, 7–10 September 1993*. Advances in Parallel Computing, North-Holland, 1993.

[11] F. Sötz. A Method for Performance Prediction of Parallel Programs. In H. Burkhart, editor, *CONPAR 90–VAPP IV, Joint International Conference on Vector and Parallel Processing. Proceedings*, pages 98–107, Zürich, Switzerland, September 1990. Springer–Verlag, Berlin, LNCS 457.

The Separating Decomposition of Discrete Fourier Transform and Vectorization of its Calculation

O.V. Klimova

Institute of Engineering Science,
Ural Branch of the Russian Academy of Science,
91 Pervomayskaya St., 620219 Ekaterinburg, Russia

Abstract. The transfer to the parallel calculations gives new possibilities for digital signal processing. However, for the realization of these possibilities, it is necessary to use efficiently high-speed parallel processors and vector computers. For that one needs algorithms orientated on parallel calculating procedures. We propose the method of the separating decomposition of discrete Fourier transform (DFT) orientated to the creation of the DFT algorithms with a flexible structure characterized by the parametrical adjustability to different forms of parallel processing. We consider the recursive vector DFT algorithms based on the separating decomposition of DFT in which both the algorithm of the standard fast Fourier transform (FFT) and the mixed-radix FFT algorithm can be used. The proposed algorithms are characterized by the natural succession of the samples of both the input signal and its spectrum and provide the effective application of the vector arithmetic instructions in DFT calculations with a wide range of lengths.

1 Introduction

The discrete Fourier transform (DFT) is one of the basic operations of digital signal processing. Therefore, the algorithms of its calculations have been developing intensively, since the fast Fourier transform (FFT) was created. The inevitability of the transition to parallel calculations, obvious now, requires new calculating procedures. The conventional fast algorithms do not allow one to use the possibilities of parallel processors and vector computers in full measure. However, the great calculating efficiency of these algorithms stimulates the search of methods for their adaptation to parallel processing.

The existing solutions for this problem [1-4] were obtained through the investigation into the structure of the selected algorithm which was transformed to the vector or parallel form. The immediate vectorization of the FFT scalar algorithm results in very short vectors not permitting to use vector arithmetic efficiently. The algorithms described in works [1-3] solve the problem of increasing the length of the vector being handled, but in every case it is reached by means of additional operations connected with the selection of the required data block from memory at every stage of the calculation. Besides, such algorithms are often worked out for the architecture of concrete vector computers. The solution suggested by Agarwal and Cooley [4] provides the simple addressing of data and allows one to use vector lengths, constant or close to each other, within every step of vector algorithms. Their method for the vectorization of DFT is based on the use of the mixed-radix FFT algorithm. The vector algorithm of DFT is characterized by the concrete factorization of the input sequence length $N = N_1 \times N_2 \times \ldots \times N_p$ and requires the digit-reversed rearrangement of input array elements accompanied by the following operations for every multiplier N:

- loading of r vector registers by vectors with the length equal to N/r, where r is multiplier N;
- multiplication of (r-1) vectors by the vectors of rotating multipliers;
- calculation of r-point DFT of these vectors.

It is necessary to have structurally flexible algorithms for the efficient use of functional possibilities of high-speed parallel processors and vector computers. By this property of the algorithm we mean the possibility of its parametrical adjustability for efficient realization not only within one class of architectures, but also within different kinds of architectures. To create such DFT algorithms, one is to work out the mechanism of their flexible adaptation to the possibilities of modern computers.

In this work we suggest the method of separating decomposition oriented to create structurally flexible DFT algorithms. The method allows one:

- to decompose DFT into independent components, the sum of which gives the sought DFT;
- to vectorize the calculation efficiently;
- to combine different kinds of parallel processing;
- to control algorithm parameters with the purpose of adjusting them efficiently for the architecture to be used.

2 The Separating Decomposition of DFT

To perform the DFT separating decomposition

$$S(q) = \sum_{t=0}^{N-1} x(t)W_N^{tq} \ , \tag{1}$$

where

$$W_N = e^{-2\pi i/N},$$

we factor the number N as follows: $N = h_0 \times N_1 = N_0$. Then we can present t in the following form:
$$t = j + t_1 N_1,$$
where
$$t_1 = 0, \ldots, h_0 - 1 \quad \text{and} \quad j = 0, \ldots, N_1 - 1.$$

Further we use function [5]

$$x^*(t) = \begin{cases} x(t), & t = t_1 N_1 \\ 0, & t \neq t_1 N_1 \end{cases} \tag{2}$$

given within $[0, h-1]$ by the function $x(t)$. We do it as follows. By the function $x(t)$, within $[0, h-1]$, we give the functions $x_j^*(t)$ by the formula:

$$x_j^*(t) = \begin{cases} x(t+j), & t = t_1 N_1 \\ 0, & t \neq t_1 N_1 \end{cases}, \quad j = 0, \ldots, N_1 - 1.$$

Then, if $x_j(t) = x(t+j)$, we can determine $x_j^*(t)$ by formula (2). By means of the $x_j^*(t)$ function, the $x(t)$ function can be taken in the following form:

$$x(t) = \sum_{j=0}^{N_1-1} x_j^*(t-j) . \tag{3}$$

Equation (3) gives the decomposition of the $x(t)$ signal. Using eq.(3) in (1)

$$S(q) = \sum_{t=0}^{N-1} \sum_{j=0}^{N_1-1} x_j^*(t-j) W_N^{tq},$$

we obtain the DFT separating decomposition:

$$S(q) = \sum_{j=0}^{N_1-1} W^{jq} \sum_{t=0}^{N-1} x_j^*(t) W_N^{tq} = \sum_{j=0}^{N_1-1} W^{jq} S_j^*(q) = \sum_{j=0}^{N_1-1} S_j(q) , \tag{4}$$

where

$$S_j^*(q) = \sum_{t=0}^{N-1} x_j^*(t) W_N^{tq}, \quad S_j(q) = S_j^*(q) W^{jq}.$$

3 DFT Algorithms with a Flexible Structure

On the basis of equation (4) it is possible to obtain the flexible structure of DFT if one takes q as $q = q_1 + ph_0$, $q_1 = 0, \ldots, h_0 - 1$, $p = 0, \ldots, N_1 - 1$ and applies formula (2):

$$S_{q_1}(ph_0) = S(q_1 + ph_0) = \sum_{j=0}^{N_1-1} W_{N_1}^{jp} W_N^{jq_1} \sum_{t_1=0}^{h_0-1} x_j(t_1) W_{h_0}^{t_1 q_1} . \tag{5}$$

Such a design admits both vector and parallel processing of input data.

In the vector algorithm raised by the above mentioned formula the input sequence $x(t)$ can be written as h_0 vector registers with the length N_1 in the natural succession. The vectors undergo h_0-point DFT, $(h_0 - 1)$ samples of which are multiplied by the vectors of rotating multipliers. Further, from the obtained vector sequence, one forms vectors with the length h_0 and they undergo N_1-point DFT. Unlike the vectorization method suggested by Agarwal and Cooley, the samples of the input signal enter the algorithms in the natural succession, and multiplications by the rotating multipliers follow immediately after h_0-point DFT. The samples of the spectrum are formed in the natural succession too.

Formula (5) also implies the possibility of parallel calculation and the combination of different principles of parallel processing. Actually, in accordance with formula (5), the calculational procedure can be presented as N_1 parallel h_0-point DFT which must be subjected to N_1-point-vector DFT after $(N_1 - 1)$ from them are multiplied by the vectors of rotating multipliers.

Both calculational schemes can be combined in one DFT algorithm. For example, for $N = 1024$ and decomposition $N = 256 \times 4$ the following variant of the DFT algorithm can be suggested. One calculates 4 of 256-point DFT in parallel, three of them are multiplied by the vectors of the rotating multipliers, after that 4-point-vector DFT is performed . Every 256-point DFT is performed by the vector scheme of calculation based on the idea of the separating decomposition of DFT. The general principles of such algorithm creation will be formulated bellow. If the decomposition $256 = 2 \times 128$ is chosen, then one can work with the vectors which are 128 long during the whole calculation of the 1024-point DFT.

So, we can adjust the DFT algorithm to different architectures and use their calculational possibilities more efficiently selecting different variants of the decomposition of the input sequence length and combining different calculational schemes in one algorithm.

If the length of the input sequence N can be presented as $N = h_0 \times h_1 \times \ldots \times h_{k-1} \times N_k$, then the separating decomposition of the input signal and its DFT can be applied iteratively in every i-th step of the calculation, $i = 0, ..., k - 1$ for input sequences consisting of N_i samples:

$$
\begin{aligned}
N_0 &= h_0 \times N_1 \\
N_1 &= h_1 \times N_2 \\
\ldots & \qquad \ldots \\
N_{k-1} &= h_{k-1} \times N_k.
\end{aligned}
$$

At the same time the vector with the length N/N_i $(i = 0, ..., k - 1)$ is the sample or the point of the input sequence of the i-th step, and the decomposition of the input sequence is vectorial, as well as DFT for the i-th step $(i = 1, ..., k - 1)$. The input sequence of the i-th step consists of N_i samples, written in the natural succession. Every l-th sample of the i-th step is formed of l-th samples of h_{i-1} vectors of the (i-1)-th step, $l = 0, ..., N_i - 1$. One can provide the maximal and constant vector length and use also one and the same variant of the fast DFT algorithm selecting the factoring of the number N in the proper way . For example, for $N = 2^k$, we obtain the k-step vector algorithm selecting the 2-point DFT as a basic calculational module. In each of these steps the 2-point DFT is performed for vectors with the length 2^{k-1}. The samples of spectrum at the exit of the algorithm are formed in the natural succession.

The presented algorithms may be used for the efficient DFT calculation with a wide range of lengths by the vector computers. In fact, the flexible algorithm structure allows to process both short and long successions adjusting algorithm parameters to specific vector realization. This adjustment may be carried out by means of formulars (2) - (5). These formulars provide for both composition and decomposition of the $x(t)$ signal with the subsequent processing by the proposed algorithms.

4 Conclusion

Thus, the DFT separating decomposition of the signal $x(t)$, as well as the vector DFT separating decomposition allow one to create DFT algorithms with a flexible structure oriented to both parallel and vector realization. These algorithms use vector arithmetic efficiently, provide simple data addressing, and allow one to adjust the calculation of DFT to the corresponding architecture of computers.

References

1. Pease M.C.: An adaptation of the fast Fourier transform for parallel processing. J. Assoc. Comput. Mach. **15** (1968) 253-264
2. Korn D.G., J. Lambiotte, Jr.: Computing the fast Fourier transform on a vector computer. Math. Comput. **33** (1979) 977-992
3. Petersen W.P.: Vector Fortran for numerical problems on CRAY-1. Commun. Assoc. Comput. Mach. **26** (1983) 1008-1021
4. Agarwal R.C., Cooley J.W.: Vectorized mixed radix discrete Fourier transform algorithms. Proc. of the IEEE. **75** (1987) 1283-1292
5. Klimova O.V.: Parallel architecture of the arbitrary-length convolution processor with the use of Rader number transforms. Izv. AN Tekhn. kibernet. (Russia). **2** (1994) 183-191

PFSLib — A Parallel File System for Workstation Clusters*

Thomas Ludwig, Stefan Lamberts

Technische Universität München
Institut für Informatik
Lehrstuhl für Rechnertechnik und Rechnerorganisation
D-80290 München, Germany
e-mail: {ludwig|lamberts}@informatik.tu-muenchen.de

Abstract. In this paper, we dicuss the the design and implementation of the PFSLib library wich offers the functionality of Intel's parallel file system PFS. It is intended to be used with parallel programming environments like PVM, P4, and NXLib on workstation clusters. We also present preliminary performance results of PFSLib in comparison to NFS.

1 Introduction

Since the early days of parallel computing one of the main problems was how to handle the I/O traffic between nodes of a parallel computer and the hard disks. First solutions where all output was exclusively handled by a host computer produced a severe I/O bottleneck, especially when writing results from numerical calculations to disk. As a consequence, vendors like Intel and nCUBE produced dedicated I/O subsystems for their parallel computers, which are able to perform parallel I/O operations concurrently on a set of disks. During the last years calculating of computationally intensive applications was no longer restricted to parallel computers only. Many programming environments like PVM [9], P4 [2], and NXLib [8] provide means to run these programs also on workstation clusters. However, up to now there are hardly any high performance I/O libraries available to support these environments. This would not only be necessary for handling calculation results, but also to integrate mechanisms of load balancing and fault tolerance based on cyclic checkpointing techniques. A main problem for designers of I/O libraries is that the user requirements are not well studied and understood. Therefore, most existing approaches like PIOUS [7] or the MPI-I/O draft [3] concentrate on open user interfaces. They claim to be flexible and to be adaptable to future requirements.

In 1993 the parallel processing group at the Chair of Computer Technology and Computer Organization at Munich University of Technology developed an emulator for the Intel Paragon supercomputer. The library NXLib allows to run early software development phases on a workstation cluster and to switch to the real machine for final production runs only. The user interface of the emulator currently comprises only the message passing and process management routines. The new library PFSLib adds the functionality of the Intel parallel file system to this emulator. The design and implementation of this parallel I/O-library is driven by the following considerations:

---

* This project was partially funded by a research grant from Intel Corporation

1. Feedback from NXLib users showed that there is a need for such an extension as they would also like to develop applications on a workstation cluster which use parallel file I/O calls.
2. Having a complete emulator makes it feasible to run real world supercomputer applications on clusters and to investigate and study use of I/O functions and the efficiency of various concepts.
3. We are currently adapting the performance analysis tool PATOP to NXLib. A fully featured version of PATOP [1] will be capable to examine I/O performance and bottlenecks on workstation clusters.

After a short summary of related work we will give an overview on the PFSLib user interface and some design and implementation aspects and show some performance results. For a more detailed description please refer to [6]. The last paragraph will concentrate on the future of the Paragon emulator in total.

2 Related Work

Available results related to the design and implementation of PFSLib can be subdivided into three categories:

- Operating system integrated approaches for remote I/O handling for workstation clusters (e.g. NFS, AFS, DFS).
- Existing approaches for parallel I/O for workstation clusters (e.g. PIOUS).
- Definitions of user interfaces for parallel I/O (e.g. MPI-I/O, Intel PFS [5], IBM Vesta [4]).

An existing approach for a parallel I/O system (PIOUS) for workstation clusters was presented in 1993 by Moyer and Sunderam. PIOUS supports process groups on a heterogeneous cluster in accessing common data on disk drives. The first version of PIOUS tries to cover the following issues:

- Independence of the underlying file system and the transport mechanisms to allow portability to other systems. PIOUS only requires reliable data transfer mechanisms between cooperating workstations.
- Execution of operations is asynchronous to use full parallelism of a system.
- Files are stored in a distributed manner to guarantee scalability.
- Integrated control of parallelism and mechanisms for fault tolerance. Fault tolerance is achieved by replicating data on several disks.
- Currently, there is no knowledge available about an optimal structure of such a file system. Therefore, PIOUS has a flexible design that allows to modify the user interface and the internal data structures to some extend.

As for the definition of user interfaces for parallel I/O subsystems it is not yet clear, which concepts have to be integrated. Available interfaces offer different I/O modes, i.e. well defined ways how processes participating in parallel I/O access parts of a file. The usual read and write calls are enhanced by additional parameters, e.g. to provide blocking and nonblocking services. With MPI-I/O it was suggested to treat I/O as a special kind of message passing. However, by adhering to the syntax of message passing calls an I/O library can only be used with one individual message passing library. PFSLib provides much more flexibility in that point.

3   User Interface of PFSLib

The user interface of PFSLib is in most parts identical to that of the Intel parallel file system PFS. This is dictated by the primary design goal of creating a Paragon emulator which provides source code compatibility to application programmers. However, several restrictions had to be made due to the different architectural concepts of clusters. Furthermore, in the first phase we do not consider any enhancements of this user interface. The main concepts of parallel I/O concern file access patterns and the semantics of read and write calls.

File access patterns are selected by specifying one of five I/O modes, which can be set, queried, and changed by using library calls (obviously all processes involved in accesses to a specific file must use identical I/O modes).

M_UNIX provides each process with its own file pointer and it is the programmer's responsibility to perform reasonable read and write calls. All read/write requests are served inpendently.

M_LOG provides a single file pointer for all processes. Each I/O operation modifies the file pointer of all processes. Thus, this mode is preferable to write log-files to disk.

M_SYNC provides a single file pointer for all processes. The operations are ordered by the logical number of the calling process. Thus, all processes have to perform the same sequence of calls. This mode can be used to write ordered lists or checkpoint informations to disk.

M_RECORD is similar to M_SYNC but gives each process its own virtual file pointer. The data is read or written in records of equal size. Consequently, all processes have to stick to the same sequence of calls but they are no longer synchronized when actually performing them.

M_GLOBAL provides read accesses in a broadcast manner, where all processes read the same data. Write accesses will write the data of only one arbitrary process to the file. This mode is appropriate to efficiently read large input files in parallel.

The concept of reading and writing to parallel files follows the principle of message passing between processes. However, there is no syntactical or semantical dependency with the NX message passing calls. This is a prerequisite for PFSLib to be usable with other programming environments.

Read and write calls exist in two variations: as blocking and as nonblocking calls. With blocking calls the data is already read or written when the call returns whereas with nonblocking calls the user has to check for completion of the call. In addition to reading and writing sequences of bytes the user interface supports the same operations for scattered data structures.

Additionally, the user interface comprises various calls for opening and closing and for advanced management of files.

4 Design and Implementation Aspects

One of our main goals in the design of PFSLib is to be independent of the programming environment used by the programmer. PFSLib will work together with major environments like PVM, MPI [10], and NXLib. Neither do we rely on any semantical information from the environment nor is PFSLib based on a specific message passing subsystem. Two issues have to be covered to achieve this: 1.) Processes which implicitly form a group by accessing the same file are ordered by their identifiers to ensure correct semantics for M_SYNC and M_RECORD mode. 2.) To be independent of the message passing system PFSLib uses the remote procedure call mechanisms provided by the UNIX operating system. Finally, the complete functionality can be accessed via a C and a Fortran user interface.

The current implementation of PFSLib has a centralized server for managing file access and does not yet incorporate mechanisms to distribute single files to several disks. The design aspects of this version cover the following issues:

Internal states of server and clients. As opposed to NFS the PFSLib server is not stateless. Its activities depend for several modes on the sequence of read and write requests transferred by the processes (clients) to the server. In the current implementation the server keeps information on both connected clients as well as open files.

File access strategy. Currently, the server handles all read and write operations. Hence, file systems with and without NFS support can be treated identically. If the amount of data exceeds a configurable threshold the server forks a so-called IO-server which handles the file access. In case of an asynchronous operation the client process forks and the child process carries out the file access. Unix IPC shared memory is used for the data transfer between client and its child process in read calls.

Course of operation. 1.) The client checks whether the operation accesses a file controlled by PFSLib or a Unix file. If the file is a Unix file the appropriate standard library call will be executed and the call returns. 2.) In case of a PFSLib file the client increases the RPC timeout if the operation is synchronizing. This is necessary because the answer of the sever might be delayed until all other processes issued the same operation. 3.) The client sends a RPC request to the server. 4.) The server carries out several security and parameter checks. 5.) The server handles the request and sends the result back to the client. 6.) The client analyzes the response and the call returns.

Client synchronization. In the case of synchronizing calls (e.g. in M_SYNC mode) the call can not be completed unless all participating processes performed that call. Hence, the server delays the completion of the corresponding remote procedure calls.

5 Performance Results

In Table 1 we show the time for Unix I/O operations accessing a remote file via NFS and synchronous PFSLib I/O operations in mode M_UNIX for different number of processes.

The values are the average of 100 operations measured during normal working hours. For the NFS measurements we made sure, that the read operations result in reading from the remote machine and not from the local NFS cache.

Note the almost linear slowdown of the operation for a large amount of data in read operations for NFS and PFSLib . We believe that this is because of the competition for disk accesses and can be solved by distributing the file over several workstations.

Writing to NFS more than 0.5 MBytes with four processes and more than 128 kBytes with eight processes caused the call to return with a timeout error. Thus, a parallel use of NFS file systems is limited to a small number of processes accessing one file without modification of NFS parameters. In contrast to that, writing large amount of data from many processes with PFSLib gets increasingly slower but is still possible.

Table 1. Time for read and write operations in seconds

No.	NFS						PFSLib					
of	read()			write()			cread()			cwrite()		
Proc.	256B	32kB	1MB	256B	32kB	1MB	256B	32kB	1MB	256B	32kB	1MB
1	0.015	0.05	1.3	0.05	0.17	8.4	0.011	0.19	2.3	0.02	0.14	2.7
2	0.019	0.07	1.8	0.08	0.25	10.3	0.014	0.27	3.5	0.02	0.30	3.4
4	0.041	0.27	4.6	0.16	1.2	X	0.025,	0.67	5.3	0.03	0.63	5.6
8	0.038	0.37	7.7	0.25	7.5	X	0.035	1.45	12.2	0.07	1.5	29.5

Figure 1 shows the time needed for the operations in a log-log-scale as a function of the amount of data read or written for four processes. PFSLib write operations are faster than NFS operations for almost an order of magnitude. Read operations with PFSLib take about the same time as NFS operations for small and large amount of data. For medium sized (4-32 kByte) read operations NFS is faster. Currently, we are investigating this behavior in order to improve PFSLib at this point.

6 Future Work

In the future we will improve the efficiency of PFSLib by modifying some of the internal concepts of implementation. Our main goal is to achieve scalability. Hence, we will introduce a concept of distributed servers which will access files distributed over several workstations in parallel. Furthermore, we will enhance the user interface in order to study the usefulness of different access modes.

References

1. H.J. Beier, T. Bemmerl, A. Bode, et al. TOPSYS — Tools for Parallel Systems. SFB-Bericht 342/9/90 A, SFB 0342, Technische Universität München, 80290 München, Germany, January 1990.

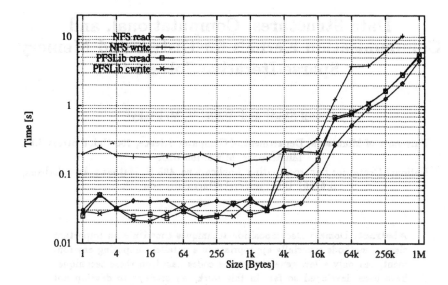

Fig. 1. Time for read and write operations with four processes

2. R.M. Butler and E.L. Lusk. Monitors, messages, and clusters: The p4 parallel programming system. *Parallel Computing*, 20(4):547–564, April 1994.
3. P. Corbett, D. Feitelson, Y. Hsu, et al. MPI-IO: A parallel i/o interface for MPI version 0.3. NAS Technical Report NAS-95-002, NASA Ames Research Center, Moffett Field, CA 94035-1000, USA, January 1995.
4. P. Corbett, D. Feitelson, J.-P. Prost, and S. Johnson Baylor. Parallel access to files in the Vesta file system. In *Proc. Supercomputing '93*, pages 472–481. IEEE Computer Society Press, November 1993.
5. Intel Corporation, Supercomputer Systems Division, Beaverton, Oregon. *Paragon User's Guide*, 312 489-003 edition, June 1994.
6. S. Lamberts, T. Ludwig, C. Röder, and A. Bode. PFSLib — A file system for parallel programming environments. SFB-Bericht, SFB 0342, Technische Universität München, 80290 München, Germany, 1995. To be published in summer.
7. S.A. Moyer and V.S. Sunderam. PIOUS: An architecture for parallel i/o in distributed computing environments. In *Workshop on Cluster Computing*, Tallahassee, FL, USA, December 1993. Florida State University.
8. G. Stellner, A. Bode, S. Lamberts, and T. Ludwig. Developing application for multicomputer systems on workstations. In W. Gentzsch and U. Harms, editors, *High-Performance Computing and Networking, International Conference and Exhibition, Volume II*, number 797 in LNCS, pages 286–292. Springer, April 1994.
9. V.S. Sunderam, G.A. Geist, J. Dongarra, and R. Manchek. The PVM concurrent computing system: Evolution, experiences and trends. *Parallel Computing*, 20(4):531–545, April 1994.
10. D.W. Walker. The design of a standard message passing interface for distributed memory concurrent computers. *Parallel Computing*, 20(4):657–673, April 1994.

Data Structures, Computational, and Communication Kernels for Distributed Memory Sparse Iterative Solvers *

Yousef Saad[1] and Andrei V. Malevsky[2]

[1] University of Minnesota, Department of Computer Science, 200 Union Street S.E., Minneapolis, MN 55455 USA
[2] National Center for Supercomputing Applications, 405 N. Mathews Ave., Urbana, Il 61801 USA; malevsky@ncsa.uiuc.edu ***

Abstract. Domain Decomposition techniques constitute an important class of methods especially appropriate in a parallel computing environment, but only a few general purpose codes based on these techniques have been developed so far. In this work, we attempt to develop not only algorithms but also software libraries and tools to help in the parallel implementation of such techniques. These algorithms and tools form P-SPARSLIB, a library of distributed sparse iterative solvers.

1 Introduction

Domain decomposition (DD) has emerged as a quite general and convenient paradigm for solving partial differential equations on parallel computers. Typically, a domain is partitioned into several sub-domains and some technique is used to recover the global solution by a succession of solutions of independent subproblems associated with the subdomains. Each processor handles one or several subdomains in the partition and then the partial solutions are combined, typically over several iterations, to deliver an approximation to the global system.

Flexibility is critical in a general purpose DD implementation. A general purpose DD library must be able to accommodate various data structures, iterative solvers, preconditioners, and be easily adaptable to different computer architectures. There is always a trade-off between flexibility and performance. As a consequence, it is important to tune the functions that are the most critical to obtaining good performance to a particular environment. We need to isolate these routines to be able to adjust them to changes in computer architecture and programming environment. Thus, a desirable design feature of a general purpose library is a hierarchical structure. All the functional routines (iterative solvers and preconditioners) must not depend on data structures and message-passing specifics, but rely on a lower level set of kernels dealing with these issues.

---

* Work supported by ARPA under grant number NIST 60NANB2D1272
*** New address (effective June 1, 1995): Centre de Recherche en Calcul Appliqué, 5160, boul. Décarie, bureau 400, Montréal (Québec) H3X 2H9, Canada

We have employed a 'reverse communication mechanism' in order to bypass the need of particular data structures in the functional routines. We have also tried to make the code as machine-independent as possible to keep the bulk of the routines reusable if an architecture or a message-passing paradigm changes. We have not embraced any of the proposed message-passing standards such as PVM [2] or MPI [3] throughout the code. Instead, we have isolated the communications routines in order to be able to port them with minor efforts and to utilize the native libraries and other vendor-supplied software and hardware solutions. We have assembled the communications routines in a toolkit which together with the basis sparse linear algebra routines (BLAS-1) serves as the ground level of the library.

2 Implementation of Krylov subspace algorithms

The computational requirements of the various conjugate gradient like algorithms that have been developed are essentially identical. The GMRES algorithm was introduced in [4] for solving general sparse nonsymmetric linear systems. Here, we would like to illustrate the implementation of these methods with only one such technique, namely the Flexible variant of the GMRES algorithm (FGMRES) [5]. The FGMRES allows the preconditioner to vary from step to step. In our context, we would like to be able to use any secondary iterative procedure as a preconditioner, a feature which is quite helpful in DD methods or in any parallel computing implementation. In the simplest case, if a a block-Jacobi iteration is used as a preconditioner (additive Schwarz), in which the blocks correspond to the different subdomains, then we solve each system associated with a subdomain by an iterative process. In the standard 'non-flexible' techniques, these inner solutions must be 'exact' or highly accurate in each subdomain. With FGMRES and other flexible techniques this does not have to be the case. FGMRES even allows the inner preconditioning steps to be completely asynchronous, a feature which may help minimize communication and synchronization costs in a parallel approach.

To further enhance flexibility, we found it extremely helpful to include an additional feature referred to as a 'reverse communication mechanism' whose goal is to avoid passing data structures to the iterative solver [1]. The passing of a matrix can an be a heavy burden on the programmer since it is nearly impossible to find a data structure that will be suitable for all possible cases. The solution is not to pass the matrices in any form. Whenever a matrix-by-vector product or a preconditioning operation is needed, we can simply exit the subroutine and have the subroutine caller perform the desired operation. The calling program should call the iterative routine again, after placing the result of the matrix-vector operation in one of the vector arguments of the subroutine. Reverse communication enhances the flexibility of the FGMRES routine enormously. For example, when changing preconditioners, we may iterate on a coarse mesh and do the necessary interpolations to get the result at a given step and then iterate on the fine mesh in the following step. This can be done without having to pass any data regarding the matrix or the preconditioner to the FGMRES accelerator. Since the matrix-by-vector multiplication has been taken away from the body of FGMRES routine, the only communication routine it calls is the distributed dot product of two vectors. The rest of operations can be done independently and require no synchronization.

3 Distributed matrix-by-vector multiplication

A matrix-by-vector multiplication is usually the most expensive part of an iterative solver, and its performance defines the overall speed of the scheme. In this section, we describe the formats of data structures used for the distributed matrix-by-vector multiplication. These formats are intended to optimize interprocessor communications and allow an overlap between computations and communications. The proposed communication formats only assume that the matrix is distributed row-wise among the processors, but do not specify the local storage mode.

Assume that we have a convenient partitioning of the domain. We call a node *internal* to a processor i holding a subset V_i if it is connected only to the elements of V_i. The *local interface nodes* are connected to elements of other subsets. The *external interface nodes* are the nodes which belong to the other processors but are connected to the elements of V_i. All these three categories of nodes must be accomodated in a local data structure in order to perform a matrix-by-vector multiplication.

The first step in setting up the local data-structure prior to executing an iterative algorithm for a distributed sparse matrix is to have each processor determine the set of all other processors with which it must exchange information when performing matrix-vector products. We will refer to the label of a given processor in which a copy of the (same) code is executed on each processor as myproc. In this phase, myproc will also determine its external interface nodes, or the nodes which belong to the neighboring processors and are coupled with the local interface nodes of that processor. When performing a matrix-by-vector product, neighboring processors must exchange values of their adjacent interface nodes. In order to perform this data exchange operation efficiently, it is important to group these nodes processor by processor. Two arrays are used for this purpose, one called ix which lists the nodes as indicated above and a pointer array ipr which points to the beginning of the list for proc(i). At the end of the preprocessing step each processor myproc must have the following information.

1. nproc – The number of processors holding adjacent subdomains.
2. proc(1:nproc) – List of the nproc adjacent processors.
3. ix – The list of local interface nodes.
4. ipr – The pointer to the beginning of the list in array ix of each of nproc neighboring processors.

In order to perform a matrix-by-vector product with a distributed matrix, we need to multiply the matrix consisting of rows that are local to a given processor by a distributed vector. Some components of the vector will be local, but some components (the external interface variables) must be moved to the current processor from the adjacent processors. Let A_{loc} be the local matrix, i.e., the (rectangular) matrix consisting of all the rows that are mapped to myproc. We will call B_{loc} the 'diagonal block' of A_{loc}, or the submatrix of A_{loc} whose nonzero elements a_{ij} are such j is a local variable. Note that B_{loc} is a square matrix of size $nloc \times nloc$ where $nloc$ is the number of unknowns residing on myproc. Similarly, we will call B_{ext} the 'off-diagonal' block, i.e., the submatrix of A_{loc} whose nonzero elements a_{ij} are such that j is not a local variable. It is important to reorder A_{loc} in such a way to have all the internal nodes followed by the interface nodes. The advantage of this order is that we can iterate with interface points only, in a Schur complement type approach. Once the interface points have converged we can back-substitute to obtain the other local variables.

To perform a matrix-vector product, one needs:

1. multiply the diagonal block B_{loc} by the local variables;
2. bring in the external variables (components of the distributed vector at the external interface nodes);
3. multiply the off-diagonal block B_{ext} by these external variables and add the result to that obtained from the first multiplication.

Note that the steps 1 and 2 can be performed simultaneously. A processor can be multiplying B_{loc} by the local variables while waiting for the external variables to be received.

The following code section illustrates this approach.

```
call MSG_bdx_send(nloc,x,y,nproc,proc,ix,ipr,ptrn)
call amux(nloc,x,y,aloc,jaloc,ialoc)
call MSG_bdx_receive(nloc,x,y,nproc,proc,ix,ipr,ptrn)
nrow = nloc - nbnd + 1
call amux1(nrow,x,y(nbnd),aloc,jaloc,ialoc(nloc+1))
```

In the above code segment, MSG_bdx_send and MSG_bdx_receive are the interface data exchange routines, amux and amux1 are the local sparse matrix-by-vector multiplication routines. In the above example, nbnd is the pointer to the start of the interface nodes and aloc, jaloc, ialoc are the data structures for the two matrices B_{loc} and B_{ext} stored together. The call to amux performs the operation $y := B_{loc} x_{loc}$. The call to amux1 performs $y := y + B_{ext} x_{ext}$. Notice that the data for the matrix B_{ext} is simply appended to that of B_{loc}, a standard technique used for storing a succession of sparse matrices. The B_{ext} matrix acts only on the subvector of x of the length $nrow = nloc - nbnd + 1$ which starts at the location $nbnd$.

4 Message-passing tools

Operations with matrices and vectors on the distributed-memory architectures require data exchange between the processors. There are only two operations within the body of a solver which employ inter-processor communications, the date exchange between the boundaries of subdomains and distributed dot product of two vectors. These two procedures require close attention in order to maintain good performance. The boundary exchange and distributed dot product routines together with auxiliary routines form the message-passing toolkit. We have implemented three versions of the toolkit, the CM5-CMMD version, CRAY-T3D version, and PVM version.

In order to perform the boundary exchange efficiently, we have exploited two important features of message-passing, the asynchronous message-passing capabilities and redundancy of communications. The asynchronous message-passing means that a processor can send data into the network and continue to perform some work without waiting for the data to actually arrive to the destination. In the above code segment, **MSG_bdx_send** sends the interface data out. The interface information is needed only for the second matrix-by-vector multiplication. The first multiplication involves only internal nodes, and therefore is done while waiting for the interface data to arrive. The call to **MSG_bdx_receive** ensures that all the inter-processor communications have been completed prior to the matrix-by-vector multiplication for the interface nodes.

The date exchange between the boundaries of subdomains often follows a repeated pattern. The redundancy can be exploited in some cases. The parameter **ptrn** passed to **MSG_bdx_send** specifies a communication pattern to use. First, **MSG_bdx_send** creates a communication channel specified by **ptrn**. The processors exchange the addresses of their send/receive buffers, length and type of message. Each subsequent call to **MSG_bdx_send** with the same **ptrn** utilizes the corresponding channel. In the CM-5 version, we have employed the virtual channels functions provided in CMMD, the CM-5 message-passing library, which allow direct link between processors and minimize the handshaking overhead involved in point-to-point message passing. Once a pattern is established, the processors can communicate without extra handshakes, and the latency decreases from 85 microsec (point-to-point communication) to 30-35 microsec (virtual channel). In the CRAY-T3D version, the receiving processor initially sends the address where the interface data must be put to the sender. At each subsequent call to **MSG_bdx_send**, the sender knows a location in the receiver's memory to place the data. The advantages of establishing communication channels originate from the features specific to message-passing libraries, and there is no general recipe for programming the channel functions.

The dot product belongs to a family of operations known as 'global reductions' where the data are gathered from the processors, combined following a certain rule, and then broadcast back to the processors. The best strategy for global reductions depends on a network topology. Many parallel computer manufacturers are starting to provide hardware and software support for performing global reduction operations efficiently. For instance, the reductions are performed on the CM-5 by a separate low-bandwidth and low-latency network. Global reductions are included in the MPI standard [3] and in the CRAY-T3D message-passing library (SHMEM). However, the global reductions must be coded employing the point-to-point communications for the PVM version. The dot product requires only a single number to be gathered from all the processors after they perform the reduction on a local vector, and a network latency rather than a bandwidth controls the performance of it.

5 Summary

We have implemented the above concepts in a software library for parallel sparse matrix computations, P-SPARSLIB. It consists of the accelerators (GMRES, FGMRES, CG, etc.), preprocessing tools, preconditioning routines, and message-passing tools. The accelerators and preconditioners constitute the functional layer of the library. These modules are completely machine-independent and work in both distributed and shared-memory environment. The message-passing tools with the local BLAS-1 routines form the lowest level of the library. The message-passing toolkit consists of the boundary information exchange routine, distributed dot product, send/receive routines used at the preprocessing stage, and some auxiliary functions such as timers and machine configuration inquiries.

Matrix-by-vector multiplications and preconditioning operations are usually the most time-consuming parts of an iterative solver. In addition to the cost of inter-processor communication, a sparse distributed matrix-by-vector product involves more expensive local operations, characterized by indirect addressing which lead to unfavorable local communication to computation ratio. We have tested the distributed matrix-by-vector product kernel for the CRAY-T3D, CM5 (SPARC2 processors), and CM5E (SPARC10 processors) and found that the local BLAS-1 routines predominantly control performance of the library. The communication overhead for all three machines was rather moderate, and did not exceed 10% for all the cases tested. Any improvements of local arithmetic computation rates, e.g., via the use of vendor-supplied, optimized BLAS-1 routines, may lead to significant gains in the performance of P-SPARSLIB.

References

1. Ashby, S. F., and M. Seager: A proposed standard for iterative linear solvers. Technical report, Lawrence Livermore National Laboratory (1990).
2. Beguelin, A., J. Dongarra, A. Geist, R. Manchek, K. Moore, and V. Sunderam: Tools for heterogeneous network computing, In: Proceedings of the 6th SIAM Conference on Parallel Processing for Scientific Computing, SIAM, Philadelphia, (1993) 854-862.
3. Gropp, W., E. Lusk, and A. Skjellum: Using MPI: Portable Parallel Programming with the Message-Passing Interface, MIT Press, 328 pp., 1994.
4. Saad, Y., and M. H. Schultz: GMRES: a generalised minimal residual algorithm for solving nonsymmetric linear systems. SIAM J. Sci. Statist. Comput. 7 (1986) 856-869.
5. Saad, Y.: A flexible inner-outer preconditioned GMRES algorithm. SIAM J. Sci. Statist. Comput. 14 (1993) 461-469.

PARMA : A Multiattribute File Structure for Parallel Database Machines

Atilla Özerdim[1], M.Osman Ünalır[1], Oğuz Dikenelli[1], and Esen Ozkarahan[2]

[1] Ege University, Department of Computer Engineering,
35100 Bornova/Izmir, Turkey
{ozerdim,unaliro,dikenelli}@staff.ege.edu.tr

[2] Dokuz Eylül University, Department of Computer Engineering,
35100 Bornova/Izmir, Turkey
miseoz@vm.ege.edu.tr

Abstract. Parallel database systems have gained major interest in high performance information processing. In the first place, these systems require efficient declustering approaches to partition each relation and to allocate them to the parallel architecture. However, the low level maintenance and the execution of database operations in parallel have to be considered together with declustering. In this paper, a new parallel multiattribute file structure, namely PARMA, is proposed. PARMA is a two-level hierarchical distributed directory structure which combines the features of DYOP and grid files. PARMA preserves integrity of the declustered subsets of the grid file so that interquery and intraquery parallelism can be consistently maintained. Also, the internal structure of PARMA provides a basis for efficient algorithms regarding both data and communication intensive database operations such as join and reorganization.

1 Introduction

Over the past decades parallel database systems have gained much interest due to data-intensive applications. The relatively low cost of off-the-shelf processors, primary and secondary storage devices, and the possibility of the execution of database operations in parallel make the design of parallel DBMSs feasible.

Parallel databases exploit the parallelism of multiprocessor systems to achieve high performance, high throughput, and high availability for multiuser database systems. The virtue of parallel databases lies not only in the fact that they can accommodate terrabytes of information but also in their ability to exploit interquery and intraquery parallelism. By using intricate declustering schemes, the data is partitioned across several disk units and the locality of a given query region is distributed across these units so that the search for qualifying tuples is concurrently performed by independent processors on independent disks.

The kind of architectures for parallel databases can be classified as shared-memory, shared-disk, and shared-nothing. Shared-memory and shared-disk systems suffer from performance degradation due to access conflicts as the number of nodes in the system is increased. Because of limited scalability, they can not be used in building massively parallel systems. Studies have shown that shared-nothing systems

259

are the most viable solution for high-end systems [18] since there is no extendibility problem. On the other hand, shared-nothing architectures require much more attention in load balancing which can be achieved by proper declustering.

Declustering of relations is the first step towards parallelization. For proper declustering, a mechanism is needed to partition the relation horizontally over the parallel architecture so that optimal performance in accessing the relation in accordance with its access statistics is achieved. Declustering is studied extensively in the literature [3], [5], [9], [12], [13]. Declustering can be based on a single attribute or a combination of attributes (i.e. multiattribute declustering). Single attribute declustering schemes (hashing, range partitioning, round-robin partitioning) have the main disadvantage that access to a non-partitioning attribute can not be executed in parallel. Multiattribute partitioning schemes solve this problem by using spatial data structures and dividing the data space into subregions where each subregion can be handled by a different processor.

If the existing multiattribute file structures are analyzed, it can be seen that their design was basically concerned with efficiency and dynamism of the directory on a single processor. In addition to efficient resource usage and dynamism, declustering a relation over a shared-nothing architecture requires that each dataset be maintained in a physically independent, but logically coherent way.

In this study, we propose a new parallel multiattribute file structure which which implements the dynamism of a grid file on a parallel shared-nothing architecture and supports topology dependent declustering scheme set forth in [7]. The rest of the paper is organized as follows. In Section 2, we summarize the existing multiattribute file structures and analyze their pecularities with respect to their ability to fit parallel database operations. In Section 3, we propose a new parallel multiattribute file structure, PARMA, and present its software architecture and internal structure in Section 4. Section 5 concludes with simulation results for the performance of PARMA.

2 Review of Existing Multiattribute File Structures

The increasing applications of databases and integrated information systems has been a motivation for the development of file structures specifically suited to multiattribute based access. A single key attribute file structure can be envisioned as a set of 1-tuples, consisting of an instance of the key attribute, ordered along a linear, 1-dimensional space. Other attributes are attached to the 1-tuple and do not have an effect on the ordering of the tuples

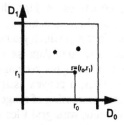

Fig. 1. A two dimensional example of a n-dimensional multiattribute file.

File processing in contemporary information systems requires file structures that allow efficient access to records, based on the value of any one of its attributes or a combination thereof. In an abstract sense, this can be achieved by extending the idea of ordered tuples in a 1-dimensional space, which is presented above, to n dimensions. The n key attributes of the multiattribute file are represented by a n-tuple defining the coordinates of a n-dimensional hyperspace as shown in Fig. 1.

2.1 Spatial Data Structures

The multidimensional representation of multiattribute files leads to dynamic spatial data structures. Dynamic spatial data structures and the associated algorithms are based on some partitioning of the space into regions with the property that the data encompassed by one region fits on a single disk page of capacity c. A directory mechanism is employed for maintaining the partitioning points along each dimension and the assignment of disk pages to regions.

The task of the grid directory is to assign grid blocks to disk pages. A grid directory consists of a dynamic collection of data structures whose elements (pointers to data pages) are in one to one correspondence with the grid blocks of the partition. During the operation of a grid file system, the underlying partition of the space may need to be modified in response to the splitting of a grid block or merging of two adjacent blocks. When the assignment of grid blocks to pages changes, an update of the directory is needed.

A grid partitioning scheme can be obtained by imposing non-overlapping regions over n-dimensional space. The policies involved in the partitioning scheme make it possible to design different file structures with different dynamic behaviours. In the remainder of this section, we focus on some of the existing file structures.

2.2 Grid File

The grid file, proposed in [14], is one of the first multiattribute file structures. Grid files partition a data space into a grid structure by introducing several non-uniformly spaced intervals over each dimension. Such a grid may be viewed as a n-dimensional array. Cells or elements in the grid are defined by identifying their index along each dimension where each grid element points to a disk page. Several grid elements can point to the same disk page if their total size (number of tuples contained) is less than the capacity of a page. A directory is maintained in order to determine the physical location of each grid element.

From the perspective of single node architectures, the grid file combines the advantages of many other file structures. A high disk utilization of 70 percent, combined with insensitivity to data skew, is achieved on a single processor system. The two-disk-access principle is supported which guarantees fast access to individual records, irrespective of relation size and data skew. The nonuniformly spaced intervals over a given dimension define hyper rectangles that stretch across the full range of every other dimension. Thus, a convex assignment of grid blocks to data pages is obtained allowing efficient processing of range queries.

A problem, from our point of view, with grid files arises in case of data skew. A non uniform data distribution causes a certain region of the value domain to be highly populated with respect to other regions. In a scale based grid file [8], the partitioning of the densely populated region of a dimension is more fine grained, in contrast to coarse grained partitioning of sparsely populated regions. This phenomenon does not only result in an exponential growth of the directory, but also may hurt the efficiency of load balancing. Thus, we are motivated to consider interpolation based file structures among which DYOP is an example.

2.3 DYnamic and Order Preserving (DYOP) File Structure

DYOP is an interpolation based grid file [15] with the main property being that the dimensions are partitioned in uniform intervals and in a cyclic manner. The directory mechanism of DYOP has a multilayered structure where the bottom layer constitutes the representation of the actual data. In a similar fashion, the upper level directory information of DYOP is envisioned as data and is also maintained as a DYOP file. An overflow of a disk page due to repeated insertion of data triggers the split of all linear scales on the candidate split axis so that the number of intervals on every dimension is always a power of two. Disk utilization is efficient due to a mechanism which combines the buddy regions and assigns them to the same page.

The directory mechanism of DYOP employs a set of mathematical equations based on binary arithmetic, exploiting a regularity due to the cyclic splitting policy. However, this policy does not make any assumptions on the access frequencies of the attributes individually. Access frequencies of attributes, on the other hand, play an important role if workload balancing is to be considered. Obviously, if a dimension with high access frequency is split less, the level of parallelism for the queries accessing this attribute degrades the overall system performance. Moreover, if a dimension with smaller access frequency is split more than necessary, the directory size grows redundantly resulting in high memory consumption and extra communication cost while executing any database operation in a parallel environment. The PARMA mechanism extends the DYOP methodologies in such a way that it supports any split policy based on the access frequencies or on any other criteria.

A common property of all the reviewed multiattribute file structures is that they have been designed for maintaining data on a single-node machine. The main concern of their design has been the efficient execution of a transaction and efficient resource utilization of the hardware. Although these goals are still valid in essence, we have to change our point of interest to how to achieve these goals on a parallel architecture. PARMA tries to address this problem.

3 PARallel MultiAttribute File Structure: PARMA

The proposed parallel multiattribute file structure is designed to combine the features of DYOP and grid files on a parallel system. PARMA is a two-level hierarchical directory structure which supports declustering and the parallel execution of database operations. The main objective of PARMA is to come up with a file system that efficiently supports the integrity and dynamism of parallel database operations on a shared-nothing architecture.

The task of the first level directory in PARMA, called Global View Integrator-GVI, is to maintain the logical integrity of subgrids coherently into a global logical grid file. Given a parallel database operation, the first level directory identifies the related subgrids and processors which possibly are subject to the operation. The second level directory maintains the physical mapping of each subgrid region to disk pages. Every processor has its own second-level directory which is used for the local subgrid. This one-to-one association is depicted in Fig. 2.

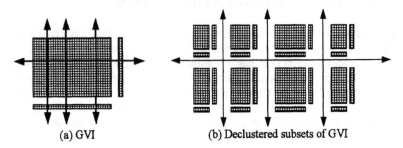

        (a) GVI   (b) Declustered subsets of GVI

Fig. 2. The Structure of PARMA.

In the literature, there have been several studies which use grid file structure as a basis for declustering. However, these studies did not consider declustering in conjunction with efficient execution of parallel database operations. For example, Coordinate Modulo Declustering-CMD [13] only considers the efficient execution of range queries on a parallel architecture. Indeed, CMD achieves a high disk access concurrency while executing range queries. However, the coordinate transformation function (CTF) used in CMD provides a mapping of regions to processors which is not efficient for data intensive operations like join and reorganization. This is due to the fact that the regions mapped to a processor do not form a convex area within the space. Thus, during the reorganization process, all the regions dispersed over the architecture have to be reapplied to CTF which results in redundant operations.

PARMA comes up with a file system which does not only consider declustering but also the dynamism of database operations in a parallel environment. In general, any declustering approach uses a grid-like file structure which serves as a global view to decluster a relation over the parallel system. However, after declustering is completed, parallel operations can be executed more efficiently if the declustered subsets of the relation are maintained in coherence with the global view. In this sense, PARMA can be considered as an integrity preserving parallel grid file since the structure of each subgrid is preserved after declustering.

In PARMA, the GVI resides in a kind of host processor. GVI structure contains information about the declustering points which define the boundaries of the subgrids. Each declustered subset is mapped to a parallel system node where it is physically maintained as a subgrid. From a local file structure point of view, each subgrid is an independent grid file which is integrated with the other subgrids through GVI.

Before we proceed with the discussion of declustering and PARMA dynamism, it would be appropriate to explain the basic concepts and terminology of PARMA.

3.1 PARMA: Concepts and Terminology

Both the GVI and the declustered subsets of PARMA are point-based spatial data structures. The data space is a n-dimensional hyperspace where each dimension d_i represents the respective domain, D_i, of the ith attribute of relation R. The domain of each attribute is independent of the data type it represents and is transformed and normalized into the form $D_i:[0,1)$. Therefore, the data space set, ds, is the cartesian product of the domains, ds={D_0 x D_1 x ... x D_{n-1}}.

A tuple, t, is an element of ds, t∈ds, t=($r_0,r_1,...,r_{n-1}$) where r_i is the value of attribute i. An ordered sequence of domain value points, called split points, along dimension i defines a linear scale such that $ls_i = \langle sp_{i,0}, sp_{i,1},...,sp_{i,gs_i-1} \rangle$ where $sp_{i,j}$ is the jth split point and gs_i is the number of grid split points on dimension i. Note that this sequence is a linear ordering .

The data space can be seen as divided into hyper slices where each slice is the region between two hyperplanes that are orthogonal to two consecutive split points of a given dimension. Hence, a $slice_{i,j}$, the jth slice of dimension i, is a subset of ds such that it contains those tuples whose i^{th} attribute values are in the range [$sp_{i,j},sp_{i,j+1}$), i.e., $slice_{i,j}$ = {t | t∈ds ∧ $sp_{i,j} \le r_i < sp_{i,j+1}$}.

The cardinality of $slice_{i,j}$, card($slice_{i,j}$), is referred to as slice size. The sequence sc_i holds the slice sizes of dimension i, in the form $sc_i = \langle card(slice_{i,0}), card(slice_{i,1}),...,card(slice_{i,gs_i-1}) \rangle$. The sequence sc_i is also a linear ordering.

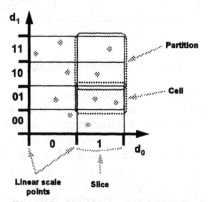

Fig. 3. Basic grid concepts of PARMA.

The data space can be envisioned as a collection of hyper rectangular grid regions called cells. A cell is bounded by two consecutive hyper planes along each dimension. By using the slice indices, it is possible to set up a coordinate system for arranging the cells within the data space. Thus, any given cell can be addressed uniquely as cell($c_0, c_1,...,c_{n-1}$) where c_i is the slice index of the cell on dimension i. In this respect, a cell is an atomic element of the data set, representing a 'unit of space.' All the concepts introduced so far are represented pictorially in Fig. 3 for a two-dimensional grid.

3.2 PARMA: Declustering Support

Declustering can be defined as the allocation of grid cells to the parallel architecture. In the literature, there has been extensive work on devising declustering strategies [3], [4], [5], [7] which aim to distribute cells such that the load is as balanced as possible. All these strategies approach the problem from a different perspective and, therefore, differ in the basic philosophy of their mapping functions that allocates cells to processors.

One such approach, which we also have adopted in our studies, is called blocking [10]. The idea of blocking is to group the grid into hyper rectangular blocks, as depicted in Fig. 4. These blocks are made up of collection of cells whose boundaries are determined by imposing intervals over the grid dimensions which may span several slices. Every block (i.e., the grid cells within the block) is then assigned to a parallel system node as in Fig. 2.

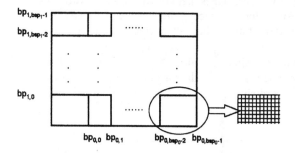

Fig. 4. The structure of blocking.

A block structure is obtained by superimposing a second level grid, *Blocking Grid*, over a given grid structure, *Base Grid*, in which the former is typically more coarse grained than the base grid. To differentiate the associated terminology of the two structures, we refer to an element of a base grid linear scale as *slice*, and to the element of blocking grid linear scale as *range*. For each dimension, an ordered sequence of block split points, $bs_i = \langle bp_{i,0}, bp_{i,1},..., bp_{i,bsp_i-1} \rangle$, is maintained where bsp_i is the number of block split points on dimension i. Similar to ls_i, it can be proven that bs_i is also a linear ordering. Therefore, it is possible to index each range by an integer number.

Based on this ordering, a block can be addressed, similar to the way a cell is addressed, by its range indices as block(b_0, b_1,...,b_{n-1}) where b_i is the index of the range on dimension i.

For efficient query execution, a workload model is used to determine the number of processors, P, which is also called degree of declustering [2], by making use of some statistical information of a typical query set [7], [9], or simulation [3]. In [7], we used an analytical model to determine number of ranges (i.e., bsp_i-1) for each dimension of a given relation that can optimally execute a query with predicates involving that dimension. This model uses CPU, disk, and network overheads, the access frequencies, and the expected number of tuples to be retrieved by a query accessing the dimension in question.

If the foregoing multiattribute declustering strategies are analyzed to identify their common properties, it would be clear that all these strategies distribute grid cells over the parallel architecture so that each node contains approximately the same number of cells. However, each cell may contain different number of tuples because of non uniform data distribution. In contrast, an efficient declustering approach has to consider cell sizes during declustering.

An efficient blocking mechanism which takes into account the cell sizes rather than the number of cells, called BLOCKER, is introduced in [7]. The Blocker has a heuristic which uses the grid file structure described so far and the optimum number of processors over which the grid will be blocked as input. The number of processors has to be a power of two since blocking maps the declustered subgrids to a hypercube topology. The heuristic finds block split points in such a way that the range between two consecutive block split points shares the load equally with the other ranges on the same dimension. The necessary and sufficient information required to proceed by the Blocker algorithm are the slice cardinalities with respect to every dimension. For a detailed discussion of Blocker, see [7].

3.3 PARMA: Parallelism Support

The most striking property of PARMA is that database operations requiring high block interactions can be executed in parallel. Besides providing a global view, GVI supports parallelism by directing queries to the related processors. Intraquery parallelism is achieved by determining the processors which may contain qualifying tuples and performing the query within the processors in parallel. On the other hand, interquery parallelism is based on the idea of utilizing the processors which are not involved in the execution of a query, query-A, to execute another query, query-B. The ideal objective is to maximize disk access concurrency by dispersing the independent queries over the architecture. Hence, the global directory is responsible for supporting parallelism as well as for the integrity of subgrids from a global perspective.

The reorganization process necessitates the transfer of many data blocks among multiple disk units of the shared-nothing architecture. If we look at the existing database systems, reorganization is performed by reshuffling of the entire database without taking advantage of the already balanced parts of the data. However, with GVI, reorganization is simply the repositioning of the block split point(s) which means transfer of some cells constituting slice(s) among neighboring processors. Since our blocking assigns neigboring blocks to neigboring processors of the architecture, the transfer of cells is done between neighboring processors without interprocessor interference. The attachment/detachment of cells to/from the subgrids is straightforward due to the coherency of subgrids with the global view as shown in Fig. 2. Therefore, PARMA provides a file mechanism consistent with the underlying architecture resulting in efficient parallelization of communication intensive operations.

4 PARMA: Software Architecture and Internals

The PARMA file system and the related algorithms have been devised with the hypercube as the core model. This particular parallel hardware model has the nice property that it can be effectively mapped to other models [17] such as mesh, ring, or star topology. Any software designed for one of these models can be mapped to a hypercube without structural modifications or loss of efficiency. This justifies our adoption of the hypercube model as well as of its terminology in the subsequent sections. For a more detailed discussion about the rationale behind using the hypercube topology, see [7].

The architecture of the proposed query engine software, which implements PARMA, logically resembles a multilayer kind of the well-known Farmer-Worker parallel programming model. Fig. 5 outlines the relationship between the software modules and the execution path of a query in PARMA.

At the top of the hierarchy is a master process, which is unique for every grid file (i.e., relation), responsible for interquery parallelism and for the integrity of the subgrids. The master process is maintained in the host processor. This process acts as a 'body of high-level decision making' for the parallel execution of queries and is responsible for user interaction, optimization, and parallelization of database operations for which it maintains the GVI. Queries coming from user applications (ad-hoc or batch) are piped to the master process where they are transformed into a data-flow graph for parallelization. The data-flow graph nodes communicate via messages.

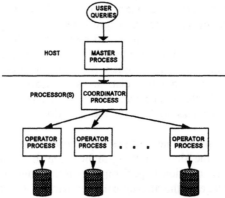

Fig. 5. The execution path of a query in PARMA.

The master process creates a coordinator process for every query so that intraquery parallelism is achieved. The maximum number of coordinator processes allowed is referred to as *multiprogramming level* (MPLEVEL) [2]. The master process selects a node processor for the creation of the coordinator process such that two coordinator processes supervising a query on the same relation do not exist at the same node, if possible. The reason for this policy is to separate the communication path between the coordinator and the subgrids related to the query as much as possible. The coordinator process supervises the execution of the query by activating the related operator processes, by collecting the answers and passing the result back to the master process.

The operator processes, which constitute the bottom layer of the architecture, carry out the query on the subgrid residing on their respective local disks.

4.1 Global View Integrator - GVI

The GVI consists of three sets of n-dimensional arrays. The first set of n-dimensional array holds the split point sequences which define the grid linear scale for each dimension, $LS = \{ls_0, ls_1,...,ls_{n-1}\}$. Similarly, the second sequence of n-dimensional array maintains the block split point sequences, $BS = \{bs_0, bs_1,...,bs_{n-1}\}$. Finally, the third n-dimensional array, $SC = \{sc_0, sc_1,...,sc_{n-1}\}$, holds the cardinality of each slice (i.e. slice size) with respect to all dimensions. Note that all the three multidimensional arrays are representations of LS, BS and SC, each of which is a 'set of sequences' since the elements ls_i, bs_i, and cs_i, respectively, are sequences with cardinalities equal to the number of slices (or ranges) on dimension i.

The multidimensional arrays are sufficient for the master process to perform a point-and-shoot operation to identify the slice and the range indices of a tuple, and to address the processor of a given data point in a query as well, as making run-time decisions like reorganization.

The elements of LS are used for determining the slice indices, i.e., cell coordinates, into which a given tuple or data point falls. Note that we use the terms tuple and data point interchangeably in this concept since a tuple is a $(1 \times n)$ vector defining a point in the n-dimensional space. Assuming a tuple $t=(r_0,r_1,...,r_{n-1})$, a slice index is easily determined by comparing r_i with the linear scale points $ls_i = \langle sp_{i,0}, sp_{i,1},...,sp_{i,gs_i-1} \rangle$. Similarly, by using the BS set, the block coordinate can be determined. Each attribute of t, r_i, is compared with the elements of $bs_i = \langle bp_{i,0}, bp_{i,1},..., bp_{i,bsp_i-1} \rangle$ and the index of the interval containing r_i is taken as the ith coordinate.

Range Queries

It is possible to perform range queries by using the multi dimensional arrays described above. Given a range query, rq, the qualifying tuples within the query region of rq are $\sigma_{rq} = \{t \in ds \mid \forall i, \alpha_i \leq r_i \leq \beta_i\}$. That is, a range query defines a hyper rectangular region within the data space by specifying the lower and upper limits on each dimension, (α_i, β_i), of the query region.

The first step in performing a range query is to identify the block coordinates of the corner points of the hyper rectangular query region. To do so, all lateral end points, (α_i, β_i), are converted to the corresponding range indices, (v_i, o_i), by looking up their indices in the bs_i ordered sequence. All the ranges containing the lateral end points and those in between, if any, are involved in the query and may contain candidate tuples. Repeating the same reasoning for the other dimensions, we end up with a coarse grained area defined over the block grid that minimally covers the query region of the base grid. These ideas are illustrated in Fig. 6.

Once the blocks involved in the query are determined, a coordinator process is set up for the query. The coordinator forwards the query predicates to the nodes associated with each block where the actual search is performed by the operator processes.

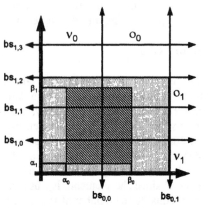

Fig. 6. Range query region and the processor blocks involved.

Insertion and Deletion

The proposed GVI controlled by the master process makes it possible for an insertion or deletion operation to be carried out directly by the interaction of the master process and operator processes. If a tuple is specified for insertion or deletion, its slice and block coordinates are determined as described in the previous sections. The tuple is then forwarded to the processor where it is physically stored for insertion. In case of deletion, only the key attribute values of the tuple to be deleted are forwarded. While the necessary modifications to the local grid directories are done by the operator processes, the master process updates the corresponding slice size information entries, sc_i, of the GVI synchronously.

In the simplest case, the size information of those slices which involve the tuple has to be incremented or decremented, respectively, in order to reflect the insertion or deletion operation. A more complicated case arises when the insertion/deletion operation triggers a page split/collapse on the corresponding processor's local disk. In that case, the master process decides on the axis of split and modifies its directory by introducing a new split point. Then, all the processors which will be affected from the split are informed and upon which they modify their local subgrids where the actual splitting procedure takes place and report their local slice sizes back to the master process. The deletion operation is carried out in a similar manner with the difference that two adjacent slices are merged into one thus removing the corresponding element from the array. This mechanism guarantees that the slices of the local grids are compatible with those of the global grid thus achieving file system integrity.

Reorganization

The declustering procedure ensures that the workload of the relation is evenly balanced over the parallel system nodes. However, in a nondeterministic environment, the successive and random insertion and deletion of tuples will certainly modify the density pattern of the data space thus changing the load of the processors. Eventually, the relation has to be reorganized to restore the load balance.

We classify reorganization into two categories, namely, bounded and unbounded. Bounded reorganization is performed when dataload balance changes but the number of processors may stay the same. In this case, the blocker algorithm is applied and the new block split points are determined. Unbounded reorganization, on the other hand, is applied when workload balance degrades and the number of optimal processors have to be recomputed using the cost model referenced in Section 3.2. Unbounded reorganization has the extra step of allocating a set of new processors, or releasing some of the allocated ones. Otherwise, the two kinds of reorganization are carried out in the same fashion.

The master process has the additional task of monitoring the transactions and operations on the relation and collects statistical information regarding system performance, which is then used to make inferences about the system load. If it is inferred that workload or dataload has degraded, reorganization is triggered and performed by the host processor. Given the current state of a grid file, which is stored in GVI, the host processor runs the Blocker algorithm described briefly in Section 3.2. Using the slice sizes, sc_i, the Blocker algorithm determines the new block split points.

From the GVI perspective, unbounded reorganization means moving a block split point, from $bs_{i,j}=b$ to $bs_{i,j}=b'$, where the interval $[b,b']$ is called the *transition interval*. This requires that the tuples in the transition interval, $\{r \in ds \mid b \leq r_i \leq b' \wedge b < b'\}$ are moved to the left block (or, the tuples r with $\{r \in ds \mid b' \leq r_i \leq b \wedge b' < b\}$ are moved to the right block.) For $b=b'$, no transferring of tuples is necessary. In case of unbounded reorganization, a new block split point is introduced between two existing ones, which means the tuples on either side are moved to their respective blocks, or a block split point is removed, which means that the tuples on either side are moved to the combined block. After the operator processes are informed of the new block split points, only the tuples whose block coordinates have changed, i.e., tuples in transition interval, are transferred to their new nodes.

4.2 The Local Grids

The declustered partitions of the relation, i.e., local grids, are maintained physically in the node processors. Each local grid is itself a grid file and is independent of the way the grid cells are mapped to local disk pages. In order to preserve the integrity of local grids with respect to the global structure, a local n-dimensional linear scale array (a sequence of split points for each dimension) is maintained which is an exact copy of the linear scales of GVI corresponding to the area covered by the processor block.

Since reorganization is an expensive operation in terms of I/O and communication cost, PARMA introduces the concept of *mass migration* at the lower level directory. The idea is that, in order to minimize I/O cost for the processors involved, the tuples should be moved blockwise (Fig. 7), preserving the way grid cells are mapped to pages before and after reorganization. At the same time, tuples outside the transition interval should remain untouched, i.e., the cell-to-page mapping should be preserved. In terms of the local grid file structure, this means that when slices are detached from the source grid or attached to the destination grid, the cells should be moved together with the pages they are assigned to and minimal amount of page filtering should be performed.

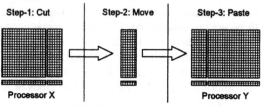

Fig. 7. Mass migration.

The idea of mass migration is also useful during parallel join where the declustered subsets of a relation have to be moved among processors to be joined with another relation. In [1] and [16], several grid based join algorithms are discussed in more detail. A theorethical analysis of a grid based parallel join is presented in [6].

5 Performance Analysis

In order to demonstrate the effectiveness of PARMA, we have developed the 'Parallel Grid Simulator' using the iPSC/2 Hypercube Simulator environment which runs on an Alpha workstation. We have conducted several experiments with different data distributions generated with respect to Zipf function [19].

First, we compared the page utilizations of relations. We generated several DYOP files having the cardinalities of 50000, 100000 and 200000 and data distribution of each file is varied as skewed, moderately skewed, and uniform. We have taken DYOP file structure as a reference to evaluate the performance of PARMA. With the original DYOP file allocated on a single processor, it was observed that the page utilization averaged around 70% except for a slight decrease for the skewed cases, as tabulated in Table-1.

Table 1. Page utilization of DYOP on a single processor.

Degree of Declustering: 1			
Relation Cardinality	50K	100K	200K
Skewed	68%	68%	70%
Moderately Skewed	70%	70%	70%
Uniform	70%	70%	70%

Table-2 shows the average page utilizations of PARMA over 4 and 16 processors. The results suggest that page utilizations tend to decrease for the skewed cases. The reason of this phenomenon is that for non uniform data distributions, some regions of the DYOP file are more densely populated. Therefore, greater number of cells around scarcely populated regions, compared to densely populated regions, are assigned to the same page. Thus, it is more likely that a block split divides a page containing larger number of cells resulting in a slight decrease in average page utilization. This conforms with the observation that page utilizations decrease further when the number of processors (i.e., number of block splits) are increased.

Table 2. Page utilization of PARMA distributed on 4 and 16 processors.

Degree of Declustering:	4			16		
Relation Cardinality	50K	100K	200K	50K	100K	200K
Skewed	67%	67%	69%	64%	65%	68%
Moderately Skewed	70%	69%	69%	70%	67%	68%
Uniform	70%	70%	70%	70%	70%	70%

For uniform data distributions, page utilization is insensitive to relation cardinality and to number of processors over which the grid is distributed using PARMA.

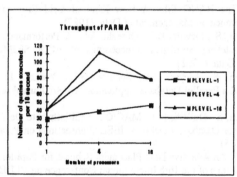

Fig. 8. Throughput of PARMA for uniform range queries.

The second part of the experiment aimed to prove the effectiveness of PARMA in terms of declustering and parallelism support. We observed the throughput of the system by generating a relation of cardinality 100000 and executing a series of uniform range queries with different declustering and multiprogramming levels. Throughput is measured as the number of range queries executed in 10 seconds.

The cost model referenced in Section 3.2 had determined the optimum number of processors to be 4. Actually, throughput can be observed to be improved for multiprogramming levels greater than 1. When MPLEVEL equals 1, there is no interquery parallelism and the throughput linearly and marginally improves with degree of declustering. When even interquery parallelism is exploited by increasing the multiprogramming level, peak throughput is obtained with degree of declustering being equal to 4, which is consistent with the prediction of the cost model.

As can be seen from the results of the page utilization and throughput experiments, the PARMA file system and its related software architecture is capable of performing parallel database operations on a shared-nothing system very efficiently.

References

1. Becker, L., Hinrichs, K., Finke, U.: A New Algorithm for Computing Joins with Grid Files. Proceedings of IEEE Data Engineering Conference. (1993)
2. Boral, H. et. al: Prototyping Bubba: A Highly Parallel Database System. IEEE Transactions on Knowledge and Data Engineering. (1990) 2(1)
3. Copeland, G., Alexander, W., Buoghter, E., Keller, T: Data Placement in Bubba. Proceedings of the ACM SIGMOD Conference on Management of Data. Chicago (1988)
4. Dewitt, D.J., et. al.: The GAMMA Database Machine Project. IEEE Transactions on Knowledge and Data Engineering. (1990) 2(1)
5. Dikenelli, O., Ozkarahan, E.A.: Data Partitioning and Allocation Strategies For Parallel Database Operations. Proceedings of the International Conference On Parallel Computing Technologies. Obninsk-RUSSIA (1993)
6. Dikenelli, O., Ünalır, G., Zincir, A.N., Ozkarahan, E.A.: A Multidimensional Parallel Join Algorithm For Shared-Nothing Systems. Proceedings of The Ninth International Symposium on Computer and Information Science. Antalya-TURKEY (1994)
7. Dikenelli, O., Ünalır, M.O., Özerdim., A., Ozkarahan., E.A.: A Load Balancing Approach for Parallel Database Machines. IEEE 3rd Euromicro Workshop on Parallel and Distributed Processing. Sanremo-ITALY (1995)
8. Freeston, M.: The BANG File: A New Kind of Grid File. Proceedings of ACM SIGMOD Conference on Management of Data. (1987)
9. Ghandeharizadeh, S., Dewitt, D.J., Qureshi, W.: A Performance Analysis of Multi-Attribute Declustering Strategies, Proceedings of ACM SIGMOD Conference on Management of Data. (1992)
10. Ghandeharizadeh, S., Meyer, R.R, Schultz, G.L., Yackel, J.: Optimal Balanced Assignments and a Parallel Database Application. ORSA Journal on Computing. (1993) 5(2)
11. Ghandeharizadeh, S., DeWitt, D.J.: MAGIC:A Multiattribute Declustering Mechanism for Multiprocessor Database Machines. IEEE Transactions on Parallel and Distributed Systems. 1994 5(5)
12. Hua, A., Lee, C.: An Adaptive Data Placement Scheme for Parallel Database Computer Systems. Proceedings of the 16th International Conference on VLDB. (1990)
13. Li, J., Srivastava, J., Rotem, D.: CMD:A Multidimensional Declustering Method for Parallel Database Systems. Proceedings of the 18th International Conference on VLDB. (1992)
14. Nievergelt, J., Hinterberger, H. and Sevcik, K. C.: The Grid File: An Adaptible Symmetric Multikey File Structure. ACM Transactions on Database Systems. 1984 9(1)
15. Ozkarahan, E.A., and Ouksel, M.: Dynamic and Order Preserving Data Partitioning for Database Machines. Proceedings of the 18th International Conference on VLDB. 1985 358-368
16. Ozkarahan, E.A., Bozsahin, H.C.: Join Strategies using Data Space Partitioning. New Generation Computing. (1988) 6(1)
17. Saad, Y., Schultz, M.H.: Topological Properties of Hypercube. IEEE Transactions on Computers (1988) 37(7)
18. Valduriez, P.: Parallel Database Systems: Open Problems and New Issues. Journal of Distributed and Parallel Databases. (1993) 1(2)
19. Wolf, J.L., Yu, P.S., Turek, J., Dias, D.M.: A Parallel Hash Join Algorithm for Managing Data Skew. IEEE Transactions on Parallel and Distributed Systems. (1993) 4(12)

T++ : an Object-Oriented Language to Express Task and Data Parallelism on Multi-SIMD Computers

Marc Michel PIC, Hassane ESSAFI, Marc VIALA and Laurent NICOLAS

LETI (CEA – Technologies Avancées)
DEIN – CE/S F91191 Gif-sur-Yvette Cedex.
phone : (+33) (1) 69 08 53 35
mpic@chouette.saclay.cea.fr

Abstract. In this paper we introduce T++ : a parallel language with object-oriented features designed for Multi-SIMD parallel computers. We propose a new approach to express simultaneously task and data parallelism. We describe the advantages of an object-oriented approach and what kind of semantics we choose to structure our task-data-parallelism. Finally, we explain how to implement it efficiently on a proprietary Multi-SIMD architecture : the SYMPHONIE concept.

Keywords : task-parallelism, data-parallelism, massively parallel systems, language constructs, semantics, Multi-SIMD computers, scientific computing.

1 T++ project : Introduction

The goal of this project is to design an high-level language for Multi-SIMD computers. A Multi-SIMD architecture is a compound machine of several (heterogeneous or homogeneous) SIMD computers. We call each SIMD architecture a *node*. Each node has its own Control Unit, and so could execute its own program. Each node consists of one or more *Processing Elements* (PEs)[1]. In the first part we introduce SYMPHONIE, a Multi-SIMD architecture designed in our laboratory for Real-Time Image Processing and High-Performance Physics Simulations. In the second part, we describe the high-level language T++ based on C++, which allows us to program such architectures using an extension of the data-parallel paradigm. We retain the philosophy of array programming languages, to which we add tools to express multitasking. These tools consist of arrays of tasks. Each task array defines a set of operations to be executed concurrently on a parallel data array. In the third part, we explain the implementation techniques we use to prepare a compiler for this language.

---

[1] MIMD computers are included in this description and our language could be used to program them, but it is designed more specifically for architectures with a number of PEs larger than the number of nodes.

2 The SYMPHONIE Computer

2.1 Description

SYMPHONIE is a Multi-SIMD computer where each SIMD node is a linear array processor. **SYMPHONIE** is conceived especially for image processing but matrix computation applications can be performed efficiently. Each node contains from 32 up to 1024 PEs managed by one Control Unit. Each PE consists mainly of 32 bits processor, a coprocessor dedicated to memory address computation, a floating point accelerator and a communication module. The SIMD nodes are connected using asynchronous intercommunication system. The same system (patented by CEA-LETI) is also used at the SIMD level to perform irregular communication between the PEs[CEJK92]. This system is necessary to SIMD structure for Image Processing. It is designed by the LETI (CEA) for Real-Time Image Processing. It follows the family of SYMPATI SIMD computers designed by CEA-LETI in collaboration with IRIT (University of Toulouse) and produced by Centralp.

2.2 Performances

Performances of SYMPHONIE have been evaluated on specific image processing codes. Its performance for 4 nodes of 1024 PEs is 160 GigaOPS. Table 1 illustrates the performances of one node of 128 processors (one VME card) :

Table 1. Performances of SYMPHONIE

Operations on (256×256) images	Time (in ms)
Hough Transform	2.2
Histogram Equalization	0.3
Labelling	2.5

3 Main Concepts

3.1 A Language for Task and Data Parallelism

Our motivation for the concept of T++ is to extend the data-parallelism paradigm to manage simultaneously the task parallelism.

The main point in the philosophy of this language is that Multi-SIMD computers can be considered as MIMD computers at large scale and as SIMD computers locally. Moreover our language divides the ambivalence of those architectures into two concepts of programmation : the first concept is dedicated to the SIMD level (i. e., the data-parallel one), and the second is dedicated to the MIMD level (i. e., the task parallelism one). Two classes of objects are linked to these concepts : parallel objects (**Tensors**) and parallel operators (**Operators**). Although this general philosophy is close to that of languages like Fortran-M[FC92] and it is linked with High Performance Fortran[IFC94] or HPC++[HPC94] (based on compositional programming[CK92a][CK92b]), the kind of language is different. The trick of our language is to connect strongly these two concepts through those two objects.

T++ defines parallel objects which are :

1. elementary object : **local arrays of data**. **Tensors** are tables of N dimensions put on a single SIMD node;
2. composite object : **global arrays of data**. **MTensors** group several tables of data distributed on several nodes;
3. elementary object : **local operators**. **Operators** manipulate parallel tables of data on a single SIMD node;
4. composite object : **global operators**. **MOperators** manipulate group of parallel objects distributed on several nodes;
5. and meta-operations which allow us to build new composite operators from elementary ones or from other composite ones.

Tensors contain all the useful information about the data mapping on a node and technical information like virtualization, ... The elementary Operators cover all the functionalities of a Data-Parallel C[PH91] (like point-to-point arithmetic and logic operations) and more. With meta-operation it is possible to define irregular **MOperators** which will have different actions over the various nodes of the architecture.

Let's take an example : in a data-parallel C, we can write C = A + B to express addition of two matrices.

In our Task and Data parallel language we would like to express :

$$
\begin{pmatrix}
a_{11} + b_{11} & a_{12} + b_{12} & a_{13}\%b_{13} \\
a_{21} \times b & a_{22} \times b_{22} & g(a_{23}, b_{23}) \\
a_{31} \times b & f(a_{32}, b_{32}) & a_{33} - b_{33}
\end{pmatrix}
$$

$$
= \begin{pmatrix}
a_{11}a_{12}a_{13} \\
a_{21}a_{22}a_{23} \\
a_{31}a_{32}a_{33}
\end{pmatrix} . \begin{pmatrix}
+ & + & \% \\
\times & \times & .g. \\
\times & .f. & -
\end{pmatrix} . \begin{pmatrix}
b_{11}b_{12}b_{13} \\
b_{21}b_{22}b_{23} \\
b_{31}b_{32}b_{33}
\end{pmatrix}
$$

with C = A.O.B; where O is the matrix of operations.

3.2 An Object-Oriented Language for Supple Hardware

Object-oriented languages facilitate the construction of such a compiler. Aside from the internal qualities of highly structured languages, we can class the advantages of object-oriented programming for our goal as follows :

1. classes allow us to prepare dynamic mapping of data and simplify memory allocations;
2. overload of functions and operators enhances the coherency of the syntax;
3. encapsulation connects strongly, on each node, parallel data and methods to process it;
4. inheritance simplifies the creation of generic methods which operate on every node.

The black box effect of Objects is well-suited to extend the implementation of T++ to new architectures and increases its portability.

We choose to base our language on C++ due to its widespread use in the world of computer science and programmers, and to its qualities for real-time computation and even for scientific applications [Don91]. Moreover C++ brings us a skeleton to build T++ ; we try to keep as far as possible the internal coherency of its rules in the conception of T++.

4 Description of the Syntax

4.1 The Parallel Tensors

Primary Objects Tensors. Using the object encapsulation, we include : a) the geometric description of the variable, and b) the description of its implementation in the parallel memories, in the basic object —called Tensor—. Information available on Tensors is divided into two parts. A "structure" part contains the characteristics of the tensor, like its rank (number of dimensions), its size in each dimension, and information on the type of its elements. The second part contains pointers to data in parallel memory and data mapping description. Methods —functions dedicated to the manipulations of objects— are encapsulated (cf. Fig. 1).

However a Tensor does not need to be completely declared, either to exist or to be manipulated. In this last case the results of the manipulation will force the structure.

The general declaration of Tensoris[2] :

$$\texttt{Tensor}\, var\ [(\, structure[, data\_pointer\ ])\,];$$

but a Tensor can also be declared from another :

$$\texttt{Tensor}\, var1\ =\ var2;\ \ /*\ \text{structure of}\ var1\ \text{is a}$$
$$\text{copy of}\ var2\text{'s one.}\ */$$

---

[2] the following typewriting conventions are used :

1. **teletype font** for T++ code.
2. *italic font* for symbolic names to be replaced.
3. and the [to note something optional].

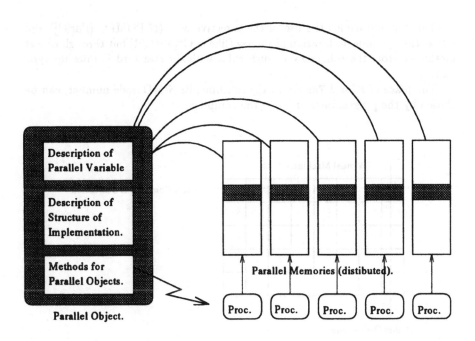

An Encapsulated Parallel Object containing :

> - description of the variable.
> - description of the data in the parallel machine.
> - functions to operate on those data.

Fig. 1. Encapsulation mechanism.

No shape is needed outside of atomic operations. We include all information necessary to the control of parallel objects in themselves, at the level of a single operation, thus atomizing the control. Local rules resolve the differences between the shapes and avoid the use of a "with" statement : `A = B + C;` where the shape of B could be different from that of C. The geometry to use for the computation is directly determined by a *type–rule* as follows :

Let us call *Geometrical-Type* the shape of a Tensor. We say that two Tensors of same shape have the same *Geometrical-Type*.

1. In case of statement like in *Geometrical-Type 1 = Geometrical-Type 2*,
   (a) if the *Geometrical-Type 1* is defined, the *Geometrical-Type* used to compute is type 2 but the result is casted to type 1.
   (b) if *Geometrical-Type 1* is not defined, it will be implicitly casted to type 2.
2. The *Geometrical-Type* of an operation between two Tensors of different *Geometrical-Types* is the biggest, if (and only if) one is included in the other. If it is not the case the operation is **illegal**.

This method avoids the use of the directive with (cf POMPC [Par92]) and allows the dynamic declaration of shapes (like in C*[TMC91] but through object methods). Note the coherency of such rules with the standard C rules for type casting.

The place of a local **Tensor** in the machine, its SIMD node number, can be chosen by the programmer or let to the compiler.

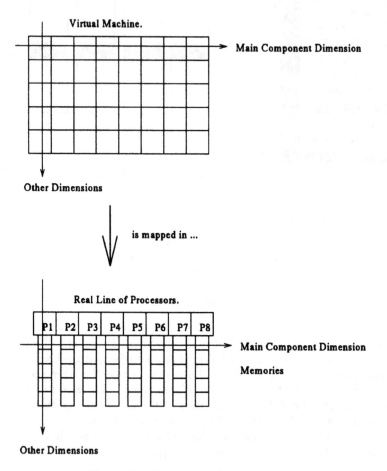

Fig. 2. One-Dimensional MCD Paradigm.

Parallel Data Mapping on a Node. From the previous discussion, we have the ability to include the description of the physical implementation of the data in the object itself. We want to map data of various shapes and structures efficiently —which need to allow some control to the user—, but on the other hand we want to avoid too much complexity to the user. So we adopt a hierarchical mechanism of complexity in programming. In High Performance FORTRAN (HPF) such a mechanism is available through the align directive. We propose another paradigm to achieve this goal : at the first level of complexity only one physical dimension is used as a template of the data transfer. In opposition to HPF, the alignment of data is not produced by immersion of the variables' space in the template's space but by identification of a common dimension. Other virtual dimensions are stored perpendicularly as shown in Fig. 2.

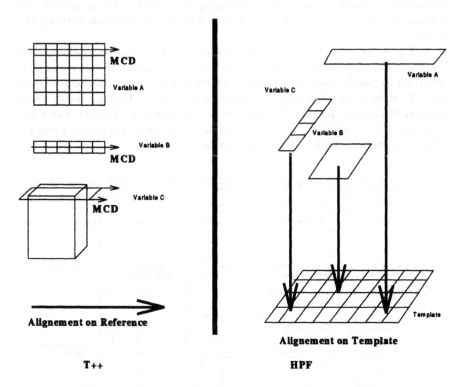

Fig. 3. Comparison of alignement between T++ and HPF.

Main Component Paradigm (MCD) : User manipulates tensors of rank N. With each tensor is associated a reference dimension. A reference dimension is also associated with the machine architecture. All those references are aligned at each step of the program (cf Fig. 3). If communications are not limited to this reference dimension —called the Main Component Direction—, exchange of dimensions are accomplished by transpositions. This is very expensive on grid or cubic architectures, but very well-suited to the SYMPATI-2 structure with its line of processor and its helicoidal mapping of data[PB71][DJL88][Lee88]. The level of the paradigm used depends on the machine, and the Main Component Direction can be replaced by a Main Component Plane or Hyperplane, when the architecture requires 2D or 3D communications to improve the efficiency. The portability of the code is not affected by this point because higher dimensions can always be folded up by virtualization.

Composite Objects : MTensors. With the introduction of objects containing both the geometry and the information pointing on the data in the computer, we are free to conceive composite objects with heterogeneous components. Sophisticated constructions are available, leading us to a natural solution to express data-parallel operations on Multi-SIMD computers. Those objects are the link between the SIMD mode used on each node and the MIMD mode between the nodes.

In Fig. 4, we point out an example of what could be done on a Multi-SIMD computer with heterogeneous data to be processed : simultaneously a similar operation (a parallel addition) could be executed on various topologies of data using local methods (functions encapsulated in objects) through independant pointers managed in parallel. The method for the parallel addition on a tree and on a cube will be different, but if the pointer of the method is on the adequate one, the operation could be done simultaneously.

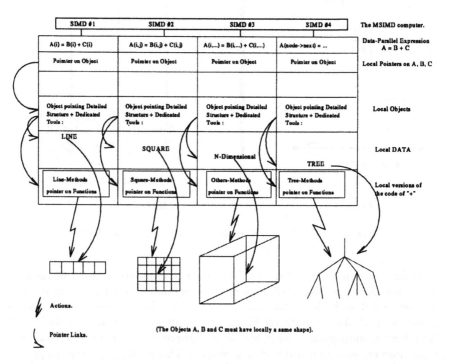

Fig. 4. Example of use of a Multi-SIMD computer in a Data-Parallel mode.

The declaration of a **MTensor** needs a virtual machine representation. This representation codes the topology of the SIMD nodes. In the case of SYM-

PHONIE, representation is a vector, but most sophisticated representation could be imagined such as matrices (virtually for SYMPHONIE or physically for future computers).

$$\text{MTensor } \textit{variable\_name[(number\_of\_virtual\_nodes)]};$$

In a MTensor we can place as many Tensors as the number of virtual nodes defined.

$$MTensor\_name = \text{inst\_MTensoR}(\textit{Tensor table[number\_of\_virtual\_nodes]}) ;$$

This kind of composition and more complex manipulations of data can also be achieved through the common tools for data and operators (see Sect. 4.3 on Meta-Operations).

Once an elementary operation like an addition on several SIMD architectures is defined, the same operation on the compound Multi-SIMD computer is defined by inheritance of the corresponding class properties from the various Tensors to the composite MTensor.

4.2 The Parallel Operators

Primary Objects Operators. Operators are the elementary operations described in the last section. One Operator describes the operation to do on one node of PEs. Usual scalar operations (arithmetic and logic) are extended to parallel functionnality on each node. Overloads of usual C operators are defined.

$$\begin{pmatrix} c_{11}c_{12}c_{13} \\ c_{21}c_{22}c_{23} \\ c_{31}c_{32}c_{33} \end{pmatrix} = \begin{pmatrix} a_{11}a_{12}a_{13} \\ a_{21}a_{22}a_{23} \\ a_{31}a_{32}a_{33} \end{pmatrix} + \begin{pmatrix} b_{11}b_{12}b_{13} \\ b_{21}b_{22}b_{23} \\ b_{31}b_{32}b_{33} \end{pmatrix}$$

could be noted : C = A + B;

More complex operations can be used through a functionnal notation or through an operator-like notation if they need only one or two arguments. Operator is used to declare such parallel operators.

Operator *operator_name(methods, arg1, arg2, ...)*

where *methods* is a pointer to a table of functions to apply, and *args* describe the type of the arguments.

To use it, the functionnal notation is :

operator_name(arg1, arg2, ...)

and the operator-like one[3] :

arg1. operator_name. arg2

---

[3] in fact this notation is preprocessed by the first lex-yacc step of the T++ compiler and transformed in the functionnal notation.

Composite Objects MOperators. We have seen in Sect. 4.1 how to define a regular operation to be applied on all the sub-tables of a **MTensor**. Now we present how to define an irregular operation, in order to use the Multi-SIMD abilities of the architecture.

The main idea is to declare a table of operations (a vector in the case of SYMPHONIE, but more complex tables like matrices could be used in future implementations). We present in Fig. 5 an exemple of operations :

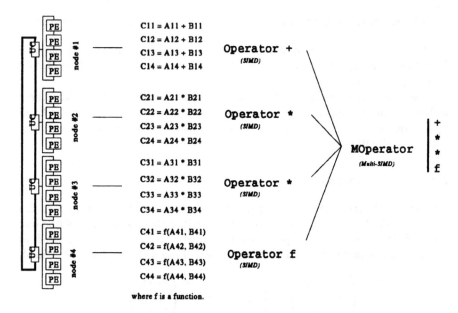

where f is a function.

Fig. 5. Parallel Operator : table of operations.

We declare the Multi-SIMD parallel objects as follows :

MOperator operator_name/(number_of_virtual_nodes)/;

Operators are kind of functions :

$$O(a, b, c);$$

but as **Operators**, binary **MOperators** can be denoted : $c = a.O.b$; and some direct overloads like $c = a + b$; are included in the language constructs.

In T++, the example of Fig. 5 could be written :

declaration.
MOperator O(4);
MTensor A,B,C;
construction of MOperator, see section 9.

```
O = plus.c.mult.c.mult.c.f;
```
construction of MTensor, see section 9.
```
A = A_node1.c.A_node2.c.A_node3.c.A_node4;
B = B_node1.c.B_node2.c.B_node3.c.B_node4;
```
operation.
```
C = A.O.B;
```

For operators with more than two arguments, or with various number of arguments, the construction is identical, with "null" arguments to replace the void ones.

4.3 The Meta-Operations

The syntax of the Meta-Operations which allow manipulation of the **Operators** is divided into two parts. The first part groups the spatial meta-operations, (which modify the shape or the order or replace the contents of the operators vector) and act only inside the boundaries of a synchronization barrier. The second part groups meta-operations which compose sequentially vector's elements and modify the place of synchronization barriers. The parenthesis in the following rules could be seen as a materialization of the synchronization. Only the first class of meta-operations can be use to build **MTensors** from **Tensors**.

Spatial Meta-Operations :

1. concatenation : $(++).c.(\times \times) = (++\times \times)$
2. expansion : $(+).e.(3) = (+++)$
3. reduction : $(+ \times /).r.(2) = (Null \times Null)$
4. permutation : $(++\times /).e.(1\,3\,4\,2) = (+/+\times)$
5. replace : $(Null + Null\ Null).r.(\times \times \times \times) = (\times + \times \times)$

Time Meta-Operation :

1. sequentialization : $(++++).s.(\times \times \times \times) = (+.s.\times\ +.s.\times\ +.s.\times\ +.s.\times)$
   where : $+.s. \times (a,b,c) \equiv (a+b) \times c$

But the Meta-Operations (the spatial ones) also allow us to manipulate directly the data-parallel objects. The rules are the same. A concatenation could replace the **inst_Tensor**() function :

if $A = \begin{pmatrix} TensoR\_\alpha\_on\_node\_1 \\ TensoR\_\beta\_on\_node\_2 \end{pmatrix}$

and $B = \begin{pmatrix} TensoR\_\gamma\_on\_node\_3 \\ TensoR\_\delta\_on\_node\_4 \end{pmatrix}$

The statement : **MTensorC = MTensorA . c . MTensorB;**

will produce : $C = \begin{pmatrix} TensoR\_\alpha\_on\_node1 \\ TensoR\_\beta\_on\_node\_2 \\ TensoR\_\gamma\_on\_node\_3 \\ TensoR\_\delta\_on\_node\_4 \end{pmatrix}$

5 Example of Simple Application : The Wavelet Transform.

The Wavelet Transform (WT) is a powerful tool for signal and image processing[Mal89b] [Mal89a]. It is a time-frequency representation like the Fourier Transform (FT). In contrast to the FT, the WT allows us to study the spatial location of the frequencies in a signal. The "Algorithme à Trous"[MHP88] [Dut89] is an algorithm to implement the Wavelet Transform on computers. It needs only filter convolution and image shrinking. Thus it is quite adapted to be implemented on parallel computers.

Filters convolutions needed in this model or in general sub-band coding[EG77] [Gal83] can be of different lengths and of different precisions (so of different types) for the approximations and the details parts of the decomposition.

We sum up the algorithm in Fig. 6.

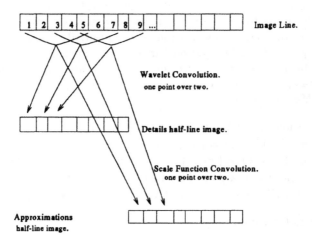

Fig. 6. Wavelet filter convolution and decimation.

On SIMD computers, the natural way to parallelize this algorithm is to associate one virtual processor with each pixel of the image, or with a group of pixels[HE92] [MP93]. With Multi-SIMD computers we can use the parallelism between the scale filtering function and the wavelet filtering function at each step of the computation.

```
/* declarations of objects and functions. */
    Tensor A = original image;
    Tensor G = approximation filter.
    Tensor H = detail filter.
    Operator Detail(      *short_filter(),
                          Tensor Result_Image,
                          Tensor Image,
                          Tensor Filter);
/* short_filter is the method to compute with short precision the small filter */
```

```
Operator Approximation(*long_filter(),
                       Tensor Result_Image,
                       Tensor Image,
                       Tensor Filter);
/* long_filter is the method to compute with long precision the large filter */

/* declarations of Multi-SIMD Objects on a 2-nodes machine. */
    MTensor I(2);
    MTensor R1 = I; /* R will receive the intermediate image. */
    MTensor R2 = I.s.I; /* R will receive the result image. */
    MTensor F(2);
    MOperator WT1(2), WT2(2);

/* Code. */

/* horizontal filtering. */
    WT1 = Detail.c.Approximation;
    I = A.c.A;
    F = G.c.H;
    R1 = I.WT1.F;

/* vertical filtering. */
    WT2 = (Detail.s.Approximation).c.(Detail.s.Approximation);
    F = (G.s.H).c.(G.s.H);
    R2 = R1.WT2.F;

/* end of the code. */
```

The Best-Basis Algorithm[Wic90] is an extension of the Wavelet Transform mainly used for Image Compression. The elementary process is the same (two-filters convolution and shrinking), but there is a recursive use of it in order to decompose both details and approximations. In this model at each step new task parallelism can be found : after the first step four sub-images need to be processed simultaneously which correspond to four tasks, sixteen sub-tasks can be extracted after the second step, and so on...

6 Implementation of T++

To implement T++ on our SYMPHONIE Multi-SIMD computer, we consider two parts in the code :

1. locally optimizable codes : we select small instructions streams, which are to be executed on a node that we call *Sections*. We split them into two parts, one to be executed on the Control Unit of a node, one to be executed on the Processing Elements. Two compilators adapted from GNU CC to our CU and PE, produce the different machine language codes. A library is built with those codes for each source code. We call it the source-dependent library. The *Sections* in the source code are replaced by calls to functions of this library.

2. globaly optimizable codes : Overloads of C++ operators, Objects Classes, Object-oriented features like inheritance are used to convert **Tensors, MTensors, Operators**, and **MOperators** in calls to an intermediate library called VM-SIMD (for Virtual Multi-SIMD). This library calls the functions of the source-dependent library.

The advantage of this technique is to enhance the portability of the code : Classical sequential C compilers (like GNU CC[Sta94]) are used to produce the local machine language code, High-level processing is insured by C++ tools regardless of the machine and the only machine-dependent part of the compilation is in the VMSIMD library. VMSIMD constitutes a model of a Multi-SIMD machine, hence giving rise to its name. In order to port T++ on a new computer with a different architecture only this last part needs to be changed.

7 Conclusion

Programming a Multi-SIMD computer efficiently needs various techniques. Different approaches can be used to program it. It can be considered as a MIMD machine if the grain of a program is large, or as a SIMD machine if the grain is fine. Also, to achieve real efficiency one needs to be able to extract both data-parallelism and task-parallelism from the program. A high-level language for this kind of computers must allow one to express both of them.

We propose in T++ to use object-oriented properties to gain expressivity and to build a common semantics both for the data-parallelism and for the task-parallelism. The paradigm of array programming languages, frequently used to express the data-parallelism, is used here to introduce arrays of operators which represent the different tasks to be executed. Implementation of T++ over C++ and over a intermediate model of virtual Multi-SIMD architecture insures its portability on various computers.

In conclusion, we believe that high-level languages which express both task and data parallelism in a coherent way will be fruitful to program future Multi-SIMD computers and possibly generic MIMD computers, and that object-oriented languages are well-suited to achieve this goal and insure coherency.

References

[CK92a] K. M. Chandy and C. Kesselman. The cc++ language definition. Technical Report Caltech-CS-TR-92-02, California Institue of Technology, 1992.

[CK92b] K. M. Chandy and C. Kesselman. The derivation of compositional programs. In *Joint International Conference and Symposium on Logic Programming.* MIT Press, 1992.

[DJL88] H. Essafi D. Juvin, J.L. Basille and J.Y. Latil. Sympati 2, a 1.5 d processor array for image application. In J.L. Lacoume A. Chehikian N.Martin and J. Malbos, editors, *Signal Processing IV : Theories and Applications.* Elsevier Science Publishers B.V. (North-Holland), 1988.

[Don91] T. Mac Donald. C for numerical computing. *J. of Supercomputing*, 5, 1991.

[Dut89] P. Dutilleux. *An implementation of the algorithme à trous to compute wavelet transform.* Springer-Verlag, 1989.

[EG77] D. Esteban and C. Galand. Application of quadraqture mirror filters to split band voice coding systems. In *International Conference on Acoustic, Speech and Signal Processing*, pages 191–195, Washington, USA, May 1977.

[FC92]   I. Foster and K.M. Chandy. Fortran m : A language for modular parallel programming. *J. Parallel and Distributed Computing*, 1992. (to appear), Preprint MCS-P327-0992.

[Gal83]   C. Galand. *Codage en sous-bandes : théorie et application à la compression numérique du signal de la parole*. PhD thesis, Université de Nice - France, March 1983.

[HE92]   M. Pic H. Essafi. Application of parallel computing to wavelet transform. In *International Conference on Wavelets and Applications*, Toulouse, 1992.

[HPC94]   Hpc++, extreme computing. Technical report, California Institute of Technology and CICA, University of Indiana, 1994. http://www.cica.indiana.edu/extreme/hpc++/index.html.

[IFC94]   B. Avalani I. Foster, M. Xu and A. Choudhary. A compilation system that integrates high performance fortran and fortran m. In *Scalable High Peformance Computing Conf*. IEEE Computer Science Press, 1994. (to appear).

[Lee88]   D. Lee. Scrambled storage for parallel memory systems. In *Internat. Symp. Comput. Architecture*, 1988.

[Mal89a]   S. G. Mallat. Multifrequency channel decompositions of images and wavelet models. *IEEE Trans. on Acoustics, Speech and Signal Processing*, 37(12):2091–2110, 1989.

[Mal89b]   S. G. Mallat. A theory for multiresolution signal decomposition: The wavelet representation. *IEEE Trans. on Pattern Analysis and Machine Inte lligence*, 11(7):674–693, 1989.

[MHP88]   Morlet J. M. Holschneider, Krondland-Martinet R. and Tchamitchian P. The *algorithme à trous.*, May 1988.

[MP93]   D. Juvin M. Pic, H. Essafi. Wavelet transform on parallel simd architectures. In *Visual Information Processing II*, volume 1961 of *SPIE Proceedings*, Orlando, 1993. SPIE.

[Par92]   N. Paris. Definition of pompc. Technical Report LIENS – 92 – 5-bis, Ecole Normale Supérieure, 1992.

[PB71]   D.J. Kuck P. Budnik. the organization and use of parallel memories. *IEEE Trans. Comput.*, C-20, 1971.

[PH91]   M.J. Quinn P.J. Hatcher. *Data-Parallel Programming on MIMD computers*. M.I.T. Press, Cambridge (Massachusetts), 1991.

[Sta94]   R. Stallman. Using and porting gnu cc. Technical report, GNU is Not Un*x, 1994.

[TCK92]   D. Juvin T. Colette, H. Essafi and J. Kaiser. Sympati x : A simd computer performing the low and intermediate levels of image processing. In *PARLE*, June 1992.

[TMC91]   C* programming guide. Technical report, Thinking Machines Corporation, 1991.

[Wic90]   M.V. Wickerhauser. Picture compression by best-basis sub-band coding. Technical report, Yale University, New Haven, Connecticut, 1990.

mEDA-2: An Extension of PVM*

Vladimir Vlassov**, Hallo Ahmed and Lars-Erik Thorelli

Royal Institute of Technology, Electrum 204, S-164 40 Kista, Sweden

Abstract. This article presents mEDA-2, an extension to PVM which provides Virtual Shared Memory, VSM, for inter-task communication and synchronization. mEDA-2 consists of functions to access VSM and a daemon to manage parallel program termination. Access to VSM is based on the semantics of the EDA model. The aim of developing mEDA-2 was to facilitate construction of parallel programs in PVM by providing a unified approach to message passing and shared memory models.

1 Introduction

Over the past decade, several Parallel Programming Environments, PPEs, were developed to facilitate efficient design and implementation of parallel applications. One of the widely used environments for heterogeneous parallel computing is the Parallel Virtual Machine, PVM [1], which permits the construction of a virtual multiprocessor from networks of computers. PVM, like the majority of PPEs, is not based on a parallel language, instead it uses conventional sequential languages with library extensions to provide dynamic configuration, process control, communication and synchronization of parallel processes. Most modern PPEs support the distributed memory programming model and are based on message passing [2]. An alternative is the shared memory model which is characterised by its ease of programming.

In this article we present mEDA-2, an extension library for PVM which provides a Virtual Shared Memory, VSM, capability and consequently increases PVM's expressive power and ease of programming.

2 PVM Communication and Synchronization Techniques

A PVM parallel program is a dynamic set of sequential tasks [1]. Each task can spawn instances of another task or itself, which are called its children. A task running on PVM obtains a unique identifier, tid, which can be used to define a branch in the program and as a destination address for message passing.

The PVM communication model involves asynchronous tagged message sending and both non-blocking and blocking tagged message receiving. A message is

---

* This work is partially supported by the Swedish National Board for Industrial Development, NUTEK (contract No. 93-3084).
** On leave from the State Electrotechnical University, St.Petersburg, 197376, Russia. The author is supported by a scholarship from the Wenner-Gren Center.

stored before sending or after receiving in a send or receive buffer, respectively. The user has the possibility to create a number of buffers and manipulate them.

The PVM library contains three main functions for sending a message:

1. *pvm_send*, sends a tagged message to a particular task.
2. *pvm_mcast*, multicasts a tagged message to a set of tasks.
3. *pvm_bcast*, broadcasts a tagged message to all members of a task group.

Each of the sending functions is non-blocking and asynchronous, i.e. does not require an acknowledgement. PVM guarantees strong time ordering of messages directed to the same task. A PVM task is responsible for consuming the messages directed to it. The blocking receive function, *pvm_recv*, blocks the calling process until a matching message arrives. The non-blocking receive functions, *pvm_nrecv* or *pvm_probe*, immediately return an empty buffer value if the matching message has not arrived. Each function has two arguments: *tid* and *tag*. The receive function waits for a message from a task specified by *tid* or from any task (if $tid = -1$). The receive function can accept a message with a tag matching that specified by the user or with any tag (if $tag = -1$).

Using the above communication actions, a PVM program can support a number of data-driven synchronization schemes, such as exclusive producer-consumer relationships, data streams, group barrier synchronization, etc.

3   The EDA Multiprocessing Model

EDA is a multiprocessing framework, which provides a unified approach to communication and synchronization using distributed shared memory [3, 4, 5, 6, 7, 8, 9]. Our first implementation of EDA was built on top of PVM to support distributed multithreaded computations on the level of C-functions [8]. EDA was also used as a basis for developing a distributed knowledge based environment, called rNUT [9]. A formal description of EDA can be found in [7].

An EDA program is presented by a dataflow graph whose nodes denote objects or actors, each containing data and a sequential thread of control. In mEDA-2 objects are realized as PVM tasks. Arcs connecting EDA objects indicate their communication and synchronization requirements in terms of the shared variables. Shared variables can be used by several objects and are distributed between them. Each shared variable may be in one of two states: *full* (containing data) or *empty*. A shared variable can be accessed using synchronization rules defined in terms of *fetch* and *store* operations. EDA recognizes four kinds of operations:

1. *x*-operations, for accessing critical regions in mutual exclusion and supporting synchronous producer-consumer relationships.
2. *s*-operations, for supporting asynchronous producer-consumer relationships.
3. *i*-operations, for synchronizing single writer and multiple readers and OR-parallelism.
4. *u*-operations, for supporting asynchronous access to shared memory.

X-fetch and x-store operations are blocking, synchronous and alternating. An x-store to an empty shared variable succeeds if the location is empty, changing its state to full. Otherwise the operation is enqueued until the variable is emptied by extracting its value with a fetch operation. An x-fetch destructively reads (extract) data from a full shared variable changing its state to empty, otherwise, the x-fetch request is enqueued until the variable becomes full.

S-fetch and s-store operations facilitate stream communication between objects. An s-store is supported by a buffering mechanism, therefore it always succeeds and the executing object continues without suspension. If the variable is already full, the value is buffered until the variable is emptied. An s-fetch operation on a full variable extracts its value to local object memory.

An i-store operation is non-blocking, and an i-store to a full variable is ignored. An i-fetch operation copies data from a full shared variable to local object memory and leaves the shared variable intact. An i-fetch operation from an empty variable enqueues the request on that variable and the executing object is suspended until the variable becomes full.

U-fetch and u-store operations do not require memory access synchronization. A u-store updates the value of a shared variable and a u-fetch copies the value from a shared variable to local memory.

Successful extraction of a value from a full shared variable by x-fetch or s-fetch allows the first pending x-store or s-store request to resume. A successful store operation allows the first pending x-fetch, s-fetch or all pending i-fetch requests to resume.

4 Overview of mEDA-2

mEDA-2 is an extension of PVM and consists of two parts: the mEDA daemon and the mEDA library. The main function of the daemon is to manage parallel program termination. The mEDA library provides functions for accessing the Virtual Shared Memory.

4.1 Virtual Shared Memory

Virtual Shared Memory is a dynamic set of shared variables, used for inter-task communication and synchronization. Data is stored in a shared variable in the form of a message packed in a PVM send buffer. Access to VSM is based on the semantics of the EDA model. Shared variables are not declared, instead they are created dynamically by the store function, *eda_store*, and destroyed by the fetch-extract function, *eda_fetch* (x-fetch or s-fetch operation).

VSM is distributed among PVM tasks. Each variable is addressed by two components: a task identifier, *tid*, and a variable identifier, *vid*. The VSM addressing scheme assumes that each PVM task has a hash table, with a fixed size, ts. During access to a shared variable, mEDA functions calculate the hash value: $hv = vid\%ts$, which is used as an entry index to the table. Each component of the hash table is a pointer to a dynamic list of shared variables with the same *hv*. Each variable has a *vid* and a value field. The latter is used to store the identifier of a PVM buffer which contains the packed data. An empty virtual shared variable either does not exist or it has an identifier *vid* ≤ 0. A virtual shared variable is emptied when mEDA frees the PVM buffer associated with the variable and resets its value to 0 or terminates it (compression of VSM).

4.2 Virtual Shared Memory Access

The mEDA library provides the following functions to access VSM:
eda_store(int op, int *tids, int n, int vid, char *m, int size)
   eda_fetch(int op, int tid, int vid, char **m, int *size)
   eda_prefetch(int op, int tid_from, int vid_from, int *tids, int n, int vid_to)
In all functions, argument *op* defines one of four types of shared memory accesses: *EdaX*, *EdaS*, *EdaI* or *EdaU*, corresponding to *x*-, *s*-, *i*- or *u*-operations of EDA.

The function *eda_store* is used to store data to shared variables specified by the same *vid* and located in a number of tasks. It takes the following actions:

1. Construct a store request by packing to the PVM send buffer the operation code (*op*), a shared variable identifier (*vid*), and the data pointed to by *m*. The size of packed data is defined by *size*.
2. Multicast the store request to *n* PVM tasks, specified by *tids*.
3. If *op* is *EdaX*, then computation is suspended until *n* acknowledgments arrive from *n* destination tasks. However, at this stage the calling task can perform any VSM requests directed to it. Other operations, such as *s*-, *i*- and *u*-store, are non-blocking, i.e. do not require an acknowledgment.

The function *eda_fetch* is used to fetch data from a shared variable to local memory. It takes the following actions:

1. Construct a fetch request by packing *op* and *vid*.
2. Send the fetch request to a PVM task specified by *tid*.
3. Computation is suspended until a reply arrives from destination. Parameters *m* and *size* return a pointer and the size of the unpacked data, respectively. If the received message contains an empty value (i.e. an *s*-fetch or *u*-fetch from an empty variable) then *m* and *size* return *NULL* and 0, respectively.

The non-blocking function *eda_prefetch* generates a request to prefetch data from a shared variable to shared variables with the same *vid* in other tasks.

A task can serve VSM requests directed to it only when its computation is suspended. If a shared variable is unaccessible, the request is enqueued until it becomes accessible by a matching VSM operation.

4.3 The Termination Problem

The mEDA daemon insures the synchronous exit of all tasks which use VSM to avoid deadlock while accessing shared variables distributed among them. The termination problem is solved through barrier synchronization for VSM users.

The function *eda_spawn* starts any number of instances of a task as VSM users. During spawning, the parent task sends the tids of its children to the mEDA daemon and also to each newly spawned child in order to register them as VSM users and to notify the children about their siblings. Each child is responsible to get this information using the function *eda_inpvm*. To exit a group of VSM users, a task calls the function *eda_exit* which generates an exit request to the mEDA daemon. The task requesting to exit is suspended until an exit permission is received. At this stage the task does not perform any computation, however, it can still serve remote VSM requests from other tasks.

The daemon uses a semaphore to support an exit barrier. When the parent task notifies the daemon about its children, the semaphore is incremented by the number of spawned tasks. When a VSM user is either terminated or has sent an exit request, the semaphore is decremented. When the semaphore becomes zero, the daemon broadcasts exit permission to all VSM users and exits itself.

4.4 Performance of mEDA-2

mEDA-2 was verified by implementing several parallel applications on a network of workstations. One of these applications is a two-dimensional Laplace equation solver with Dirichlet boundary conditions, which is formulated as:

$$\nabla^2 \Phi = \frac{\partial^2 \Phi}{\partial x^2} + \frac{\partial^2 \Phi}{\partial y^2} = 0 \tag{1}$$

To solve this equation using the Jacobi method, the surface is partitioned into an n by n grid whose elements represent the initial state of Φ. A new value of Φ can be calculated using:

$$\Phi_{x,y} = 0,25(\Phi_{x-1,y} + \Phi_{x,y-1} + \Phi_{x+1,y} + \Phi_{x,y+1}) \tag{2}$$

An mEDA program to solve this equation is constructed from two types of tasks: *partition* and *collector*. The collector starts first and spawns m partitions $m \leq n$. Each partition calculates n/m columns of matrix Φ and sends a result to the collector using *s*-store operations. The collector fetchs the final results and sends them to the output. On each iteration, the partitions exchange their boundary columns using *s*-store and *x*-fetch operations. Figure 1 shows the processing time of the program as a function of the number of hosts, where each partition is processed on a separate host. In these experiments, the size of matrix Φ is 1024 x 1024 floating point numbers and the number of iterations is 100.

5 Conclusions and Future Work

We have introduced mEDA-2, an extension of the PVM environment, to provide flexible and efficient mechanisms for inter-task communication and synchronization by means of Virtual Shared Memory. VSM is a set of shared variables in which data is stored as packed PVM messages. VSM is distributed among PVM

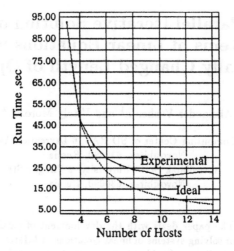

Fig. 1. Run times of the Dirichlet problem

tasks and has two addressing levels: a task identifier and a variable identifier. An access to VSM is based on store and fetch operations defined in the EDA model. These operations can be used in matching pairs or in different combinations. Our plans include the testing of mEDA-2 on real multiprocessors and the development of real-time mechanisms for mEDA.

References

1. A Geist, A., et al.: PVM3 User's Guide and Reference Manual. ORNL/TM-12187. Oak Ridge National Lab. (1994)
2. McBryan, O.A.: An Overview of Message Passing Environments. Parallel Computing. **20** (1994) 417-444
3. Wu, H.: Extension of Data-Flow Principles for Multiprocessing. TRITA-TCS-9004 (Ph D thesis). KTH, Stockholm. (1990)
4. Milewski, J., Wu, H., Thorelli, L-E.: Specification of EDA0: An Extended Dataflow Actor model. Tech. Rep. TRITA-TCS-EDA-9208-R. KTH, Stockholm. (1992)
5. Wu, H., Milewski, J., Thorelli, L-E.: Sharing Data in an Actor Model. Proc. 1992 Int. Conf. on Parallel and Distributed Systems. Taiwan. (1992) 245-250
6. Wu, H., Thorelli, L-E., Milewski, J.: A Parallel Programming Model for Distributed Real-Time Computing. Proc. Int. Workshop on Mechatronic Computer Systems for Perception and Action. Halmstad. (1993) 301-308
7. Thorelli, L-E.: The EDA Multiprocessing Model. Tech. Rep. TRITA-IT-R 94:28. KTH, Stockholm. (1994)
8. Vlassov, V., Thorelli, L-E., Ahmed, H.: Multi-EDA: A Programming Environment for Parallel Computations. Tech. Rep. TRITA-IT-R 94:29. KTH, Stockholm. (1994)
9. Vlassov, V., Tyugu, E., Addibpour, M.: Distributed Programming Toolkit for NUT. Tech. Rep. TRITA-IT-R 94:34. KTH, Stockholm. (1994)

Parallel Iterative Solution of Systems of Linear Equations with Dynamically Changed Length of Operands [*]

Alexander Vazhenin[1] and Vitaly Morozov[2]

[1] Computing Center of SD RAS, 6 Lavrentiev Ave.,
Novosibirsk, 630090, Russia
[2] Novosibirsk State University, 2 Pirogov Str.,
Novosibirsk, 630090, Russia

Abstract. The paper deals with the development of parallel iterative algorithms for solving systems of linear equations in MIMD architecture. The problem is discussed taking into account factors, defining both the time and the accuracy of solution. The new parallel algorithm is described implementing the multistep refinement of results. The speedup is achieved using small operand length at early stages of solution. The results are presented of some numerical experiments executed in a multitransputer system.

1 Introduction

An efficient way to achieve high accuracy of the results of computations is to increase the capacity of operands. The best results in terms of the problem solution rate and effectiveness of memory using can be reached when a computer system provides for dynamic capacity control and parallel data processing.

The developments of current VLSI technology and computer science allow the design of parallel systems functioning with varying operand length. This led to computer systems solving problems at an accuracy given before calculations or an accuracy provided by system resources and known to the user after the computation terminates [1, 2, 3, 4].

In most known systems, the speedup of problem solution is ensured by synchronous execution of operations for all parts of super-long operands or by pipelining of these operations. In other words, a sequential computer with programmable word length is realized by means of a parallel system.

In the approach proposed in [2, 4], the speedup is achieved also by parallel processing of super-long operands themself, similar to the traditional processing in parallel systems. This allows to use the efficient parallel algorithms. An example of such approach is the SPARTH-processor which is implemented within the basic fine-graned SIMD architecture and oriented for solving problems containing many vector and matrix operations. Comparison with known dedicated

---

[*] This research was supported by a Russian Foundation for Basic Research grant No.95-01-01350a

programming systems for high-precision computations on sequential computers shows that SPARTH-processor ensures the similar accuracy of results. Moreover, this accuracy is achived in this case simultaneously for numerous data sets in corresponding processing elements of massively parallel system.

Solving of many scientific and applied problems requires numerical solution of systems of linear equations [5]. The present paper deals with the development of parallel iterative algorithms for solving of systems of linear equations in MIMD architecture. The goal of this work is to port thr SPARTH-tecnology into the MIMD parallel systems, and to estimate possibilites of these systems for high accuracy processing with dynamically changed length of operand.

In Section 2 this problem is discussed taking into account factors, defining both the time and the accuracy of solution. In Section 3 a new parallel iterative algorithm is described implementing the multistage refinement of results, and the dynamic control of operand length. In Section 4 the results are presented of some numerical experiments obtained in a multitransputer system.

2 Theoretical background

2.1 General iterative scheme

Given a system of linear equations

$$\mathbf{A}X = F \tag{1}$$

with a nonsingular matrix $\mathbf{A}$. Generally, the iterative solution of (1) can be represented as a sequence of vectors $X^{(1)}, X^{(2)}, \ldots, X^{(k)}$ obtained by recurrent formula

$$X^{(k)} = X^{(k-1)} + \mathbf{H}^{(\mathbf{k})}(F - \mathbf{A}X^{(k-1)}), \tag{2}$$

where $\mathbf{H}^{(0)}, \mathbf{H}^{(1)}, \ldots$ is a sequence of matrices defining the type of the concrete iterative method, and $X^{(0)}$ is an initial approximation.

The well-known iterative method is the Jacoby's algorithm

$$X^k = \mathbf{B}X^{k-1} + G, \tag{3}$$

where the matrix $\mathbf{B}$ and vector G are formed by

$$\mathbf{B} = \begin{pmatrix} 0 & -\frac{a_{12}}{a_{11}} & \cdots & -\frac{a_{1n}}{a_{11}} \\ -\frac{a_{21}}{a_{22}} & 0 & \cdots & -\frac{a_{2n}}{a_{22}} \\ \cdots & \cdots & \cdots & \cdots \\ -\frac{a_{n1}}{a_{nn}} & -\frac{a_{2n}}{a_{nn}} & \cdots & 0 \end{pmatrix} \qquad G = \begin{pmatrix} \frac{f_1}{a_{11}} \\ \frac{f_2}{a_{22}} \\ \cdots \\ \frac{f_n}{a_{nn}} \end{pmatrix} \tag{4}$$

The theorems below define the convergence and evaluation of accuracy for this method [5, 6].

Theorem 1. *If $||B|| < 1$ then the system (1) has an unique solution, and the iterative scheme (3) converges to this solution.* ☐

Theorem 2. *Let $X^k = \mathbf{B}X^{k-1} + G$ be the iterative process, $\tilde{X}$ be an accurate solution, and $Y^k = X^k - \tilde{X}$. If $||X^k - X^{k-1}|| \le \varepsilon$ then $||Y^k|| \le \frac{\rho}{1-\rho}\varepsilon$, where $\rho = ||B||$.* ☐

The iterative scheme (3) can have either a convergent or nonconvergent character depending on properties of $\mathbf{A}$. In the second case, it is necessary to execute some additional transformations of $\mathbf{B}$ supporting the solution stability. It can be done directly during the implementation of (3) by analyzing of $||X^k - X^{k-1}||$ at each iteration. If this remainder was increased then the correction of $\mathbf{B}$ is executed.

The basis for another approach is a provisional estimation of $\mathbf{A}$ according to Theorem 1, and the transformation of $\mathbf{B}$ if the convergence condition was not satisfied. In this case, the iterative solution is more regular. This is convenient for parallelizing of method (3). Note also, that this procedure can be removed if properties of $\mathbf{A}$ were known a priori.

The procedure called *scaling* can be used to transform $\mathbf{B}$ [6]. It contains the following stages:

1. Forming an equivalent system $\mathbf{A}^*\mathbf{A}X = \mathbf{A}^*F$, where $\mathbf{A}^*\mathbf{A} = \bar{\mathbf{A}}$ is a symmetrical positive defined matrix.

2. Computing the norm $\mu = ||\bar{\mathbf{A}}||_1$.

3. Let $\mathbf{B} = \left(\mathbf{E} - \frac{2}{\mu}\bar{\mathbf{A}}\right)$, and $G = \frac{2}{\mu}\mathbf{A}^*F$.

Therefore, the general scheme of iterative solution can be presented by the following steps:

Step 1. Forming the matrix $\mathbf{B}$ and vector G according to (4).

Step 2. Calculation of $||\mathbf{B}||_1$;

Step 3. If $||\mathbf{B}||_1 \ge 1$ then implement the *scaling* procedure.

Step 4. Set an initial approximation of X^0.

Step 5. Implementing the iterative solution.

    5.1. $X^{k-1} \longleftarrow X^k$.

    5.2. Obtaining new approximation X^k by (3).

    5.3. Computing $\alpha = ||X^k - X^{k-1}||$.

    5.4. If $\alpha > \varepsilon$ then go to 5.1.

Step 6. End of solution.

2.2 Improving convergence of iterative methods

Let us consider the problem of an error evaluation of iterative algorithms.

If X' is an approximate solution of equation (1), and $\tilde{X}$ is an accurate result, then the solution error can be expressed as:

$$||X' - \tilde{X}|| = ||\mathbf{A}^{-1}(\mathbf{A}X' - F)|| \le ||\mathbf{A}^{-1}|| \cdot ||\mathbf{A}X' - F||. \tag{5}$$

The calculation of $||\mathbf{A}^{-1}||$ is computation intensive. Therefore, the practical utilization of (5) is rarely used.

A simple way named δ^2-*method* was described in [7]. Let V^k be a practical error of an approximation X^k approaching to X. If

$$\lim_{k \to \infty} \frac{||V^k - (X^k - X)||}{||X^k - X||} = 0,$$

then $||V^k|| \sim ||X^k - \tilde{X}||$.

Let $\lambda_1, \lambda_2, \cdots, \lambda_i, \cdots, \lambda_m$ be eigenvalues of $\mathbf{B}$, and $1 > |\lambda_1| > |\lambda_2| \geq \lambda_3 \geq \cdots \geq |\lambda_m|$. Let us assume that

$$\lambda^{(k)} = \frac{(X^k - X^{k-1}, X^k - X^{k-1})}{(X^{k-1} - X^{k-2}, X^k - X^{k-1})}. \tag{6}$$

Then

$$V^k = \frac{X^k - X^{k-1}}{1 - (\lambda_1^{(k)})^{-1}}, \tag{7}$$

where $||V^k|| = |c_1| \cdot |\lambda_1|^k + O(|\lambda_2|^k)$.

The time of solution of equation (1) can be decreased using results of evaluation of V^k. To do that, it is necessary to add the results of the last iteration to the error values V^k obtained by δ^2-method.

2.3 Dynamically changed length of operands

The convergence of iterative methods may be also improved by reducing rounding errors [4]. The decrease of these errors is achieved by means of using multiprecision arithmetic which allows for accurate arithmetic calculations at each iteration. In some cases, an application of a dynamically changed length of operands supports the reduction of the total solution time because of assuming the processing of only significant bits of operands needed for exact implementation of concrete arithmetic operation.

The suggested fast algorithm with multistep refinement of results is illustrated in Fig.1. The speedup is achieved by using of small operand length at early stages of computations. In other words, *rough* approximations of results are calculated at first. Then, they are improved by switching to next capacity limits. In this case, the parameter determining the required precision is a vector $E = \{\varepsilon_1, \varepsilon_2, \cdot, \varepsilon_j, \cdots, \varepsilon_l\}$. Each ε_j defines the accuracy at corresponding capacity limit. When the condition of terminating of current computation step is reached, the computing system is switched to next capacity limit, and computations are implemented with a new ε_j.

A similar approach was used in [4] for effective iterative solving of the equation (1) in fine-grained massively parallel SIMD-systems. In the next Sections we will show the possibility to port this algorithm to a multitransputer MIMD system.

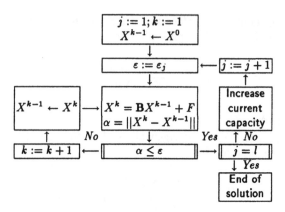

Fig. 1. Multistage iterative sheme

3   Peculiarities of MIMD iterative algorithm

To a programmer, an SIMD (single instruction stream, multiple data stream) computer can be viewed as a single processor directing the activities of a number of arithmetical and logical processing units, each capable of fetching and manipulating its own local data. In any time unit a single operation is in the same state of execution on multiple processing units, each manipulating different data. Hence this programming model is called *synchronous*. This can allow for the efficient control of dynamically changed length of operands [4].

In contrast, a MIMD (multiple instruction stream, multiple data stream) computer allows for concurrent execution of multiple instruction stream, each manipulating its own data. It is possible for each processor in a MIMD computer to execute an unique program, but it is far more common for each processor to execute the same program. This is known as SPMD (single program, multiple data stream) programming. Although the processors may coordinate with each other at synchronization points, the MIMD and SPMD programming models are called *asynchronous*, because between the synchronization points each processor executes instructions at its own pace.

The multitransputer architecture is based on the *message passing* technology. To communicate with other processors, a sender have to form a data block called *message* and send it to a receiver. The receiver can also transmit messages to its neighbors supporting communications between remote processors. For computations with dynamically changed length of operands, it is necessary to implement the additional synchronization to control the capacity value for all processors as well as for selected groups of ones.

To explain the parallel iterative algorithm we will use the following definitions:

1. The parallel system contains $m + 1$ transputers. m transputers will be named *workers*. Each of them implements the same program.

2. One of the transputers will be named *root*. It forms the tasks and manages calculations in workers.

3. Each worker has an unique number and implements the calculations of a part of X^k. To do this, it has to place the full vector X^{k-1}, $\frac{n}{m}$ rows of **B** and $\frac{n}{m}$ elements of G.

4. After each iteration, all parts of X^k are concentrated in the root.

In Fig.2 a description of parallel MIMD algorithm is presented. Is was developed taking into account all the mentioned ways of the solution optimization: preliminary analysis of the features of initial system, scaling procedure, δ^2-method, and dynamically changed length of operands.

The following procedures were developed to implement this algorithm:

set_current_capacity(J) - forms and sends from root to workers the integer vector $J(l)$ containing values of capacity;

get_current_capacity(J) - receives vector $J(l)$;

current_capacity(j) - switches the current capacity to value $J(j)$;

send_parameters - sends integer constants to workers;

receive_parameters - receives integer constants from root or neighbors;

resend_parameters - transmits integer constants from current worker to other neighbors;

send_to_worker - sends data to worker;

send_to_root - sends data to root;

receive_from_worker - receives data from worker;

receive_from_root - receives data from root;

resend_to_worker - transmits data from root to workers;

resend_to_root - transmits data from worker to root.

The variable *dobs* defines parameters needed to calculate error by (6). The variable *flag* is used to point the necessity of switching the capacity values, or the termination of sending procedures. Vector Y is a part of X^k computing in the current worker.

The synchronization of the capacity value is implemented for each iteration. After testing the condition $\alpha > \varepsilon$, the root defines the necessity of changing the operand length. Each worker implements the switching to next capacity limit (if it is necessary) before each iteration.

The parallelization of the algorithm is made by means of pipelining of computations in such a way that the transputers should not wait each other. This is obtained due to the concurrent implementation of the analysis of the results of current iteration (in the root), and the computing of the next iteration (in the workers).

4 Numerical experiments

The proposed algorithm was realized in a multitransputer system including five T800 transputers, and IBM PC/AT computer as a host. The programming language was C-3L.

300

Step	Root	Worker
1	Forming $\mathbf{B}$ and $\mathbf{G}$ If $\|\mathbf{B}\|_1 \geq 1$ then Scaling_proc();	Initializing the transputer

2	$j := 0;\ n_1 := \frac{n}{m};\ \varepsilon := \mathbf{E}[j];$
	set_current_capacity($\mathbf{J}$);
	current_capacity(j);
		$j := 0;$
		get_current_capacity($\mathbf{J}$);
		current_capacity(j);

3 3a	$flag := 0;$
	
	for $i = 1$ to m
	  send_parameters($2, n_1, flag$);
	$flag := -1;$
	send_parameters($2, n_1, flag$);
	3b for $i = 1$ to m
	  send_to_worker(i,
	  $\mathbf{B}[(i-1)*n_1][0], \mathbf{G}[(i-1)*n_1]$));
		$flag := -1;\ n\_worker = 0;$
		receive_parameters($2, n_1, i$);
		repeat
		  resend_parameters($2, n_1, i$);
		  $n\_worker := n\_worker + 1;$
		until $i = flag;$
		for $i = 2$ to n_worker
		  resend_to_worker($i, \mathbf{B}, \mathbf{G}$);
		receive_from_root($i, \mathbf{B}, \mathbf{G}$);

4	$X^{k-1} \leftarrow X^0;\ iterations := 0;$
	for $i = 1$ to m
	  send_to_worker($i, \mathbf{X}^{k-1}$);
		for $i = 2$ to n_worker
		  resend_to_worker($\mathbf{X}^{k-1}, flag$);
		receive_from_root($\mathbf{X}^{k-1}, flag$);

5	$flag := 0;$
	repeat
	  for $i = 1$ to m
	  receive_from_worker(i,
	    $\mathbf{X}^k[(i-1)*n_1], dobs$);
	  for $i = 1$ to m
	    send_to_worker($\mathbf{X}^k, flag$);
	  Products to execute δ^2-method;
	  Computing $\mathbf{V}^k$ and $\alpha = \|\mathbf{V}^k\|_1;$
	  $iterations := iterations + 1;$
	  If $\alpha > \varepsilon$ then
	  $\mathbf{X}^{k-2} \leftarrow \mathbf{X}^{k-1};\ \mathbf{X}^{k-1} \leftarrow \mathbf{X}^k;\ flag = 0;$
	  else
	    $flag := 1;\ j := j + 1;$
	    If $j < l$ then
	    $\varepsilon := \mathbf{E}[j];$ current_capacity(j);
	until $j = l;$
		repeat
		  Computing $\mathbf{Y}$; Computing $dobs$;
		  $\mathbf{X}^{k-2} \leftarrow \mathbf{X}^{k-1};$
		  send_to_root($n\_worker, \mathbf{Y}, dobs$);
		  for $i = 2$ to n_worker
		    resend_to_root($i, \mathbf{Y}, dobs$);
		  for $i = 2$ to n_worker
		    resend_to_worker($i, \mathbf{X}^{k-1}, flag$);
		    receive_from_root($i, \mathbf{X}^{k-1}, flag$);
		  If $flag = 1$ then
		    $j := j + 1;$
		    If $j < l$ then
		      current_capacity(j);
		until $j > l;$

6	End of solution	

Fig. 2. Parallel algorithm for a multitransputer system

Fig.3 shows the results of measurements of execution time for a system defined by

$$\begin{cases} 2x_1 - x_2 = 1 \\ -x_1 + 2x_2 - x_3 = 0 \\ \dots\dots\dots\dots\dots \\ -x_{n-2} + 2x_{n-1} - x_n = 0 \\ -x_{n-1} + 2x_n = 1 \end{cases} \tag{8}$$

which has the accurate solution $X = \{1, 1, \cdots, 1\}$. Testing was implemented for double-precision floating-point numbers, $X^0 = \{0, 0, \cdots, 0\}$, and $\varepsilon = 0.0001$.

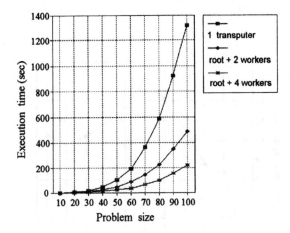

Fig. 3.

In Fig.4 are shown the results of evaluating the relative speedup. They were calculated by $S = \frac{T_1}{T_p}$, where T_1 is the execution time for one transputer, and T_p is the time needed for parallel implementation. Note, that computations in four transputers were made using δ^2-method. As shown in Fig.3 and Fig.4, this approach makes possible to reduce significantly the time of iterative solution for systems of this kind.

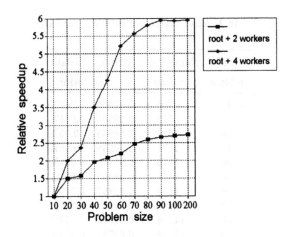

Fig. 4.

Fig.5 shows the speedup evaluations obtained by the dynamically changed length of 'operands. Computations were implemented for a system (8) at two capacity limits: $\varepsilon_1 = 0.01$ (single precision) and $\varepsilon_2 = 0.0001$ (double precision). As shown in Fig.5, this technique provides for the average speedup value about 1.5 times.

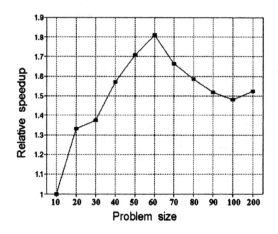

Fig. 5. Speedup for dynamic capacity

The solution time can vary depending on the ratio between ε_i and the length of operands. However, the accuracy of the results was stable, at least during the experiments (See Tables 1 and 2).

Table 1. Error evaluation for fixed capacity

Size of problem	Number of iterations	Result	Relative error
10	193	0.99957	0.043%
20	735	0.99967	0.036%
30	1528	0.99950	0.05%
40	2579	0.99935	0.065%
50	3876	0.99919	0.081%
60	5411	0.99903	0.097%
70	7176	0.99887	0.113%
80	9166	0.99871	0.129%
90	11374	0.99855	0.145%
100	12824	0.99785	0.215%

Table 2. Error evaluation for dynamic capacity

Size of problem	Number of iterations		Result	Relative error
	$\varepsilon_1 = 0.01$	$\varepsilon_2 = 0.0001$		
10	103	97	0.99973	0.027%
20	325	344	0.99934	0.066%
30	636	761	0.99906	0.094%
40	1012	1327	0.99870	0.130%
50	1456	2060	0.99842	0.158%
60	1940	2945	0.99832	0.168%
70	2886	3995	0.99778	0.222%
80	3044	5197	0.99739	0.261%
90	3665	6562	0.99714	0.286%
100	4277	8083	0.99679	0.321%

5 Conclusion

In this paper, we have shown the possibilities of organization of effective parallel computations with dynamically changed length of operands in MIMD computers. In the proposed approach, speedup can be reached not only for multidigital numbers but also for usual floating-point numbers of a single and double precision format.

The problem of the initial capacity of operands is very important, because its wrong selection can significantly change the features of the initial system and break the convergence of iterative process.

References

1. Buell, D., Ward, R.: A multiprecise integer arithmetic package. The Journal of Supercomputing. **3** No 2 (1989) 89-107
2. Vazhenin, A., Mirenkov, N.: SCORE: Scientific Computers for Overcoming Rounding Errors. PARALLEL COMPUTING: Trends and Applications. North-Holland (1994) 347-354
3. Aguliar, M.F., Duprat, J.: Towards a high precision massively parallel computer. Proc. of PARLE'94 Conference. Lect. Not. in Comp. Sci. Springer-Verlag. Berlin **817** (1994) 73-84
4. Vazhenin, A.P.: Efficient high-accuracy computations in massively parallel systems. Proc. of the Workshop on Parallel Scientific Computing (PARA'94-L). Lect. Not. in Comp. Sci. Berlin, Springer-Verlag **879** (1994) 505-519
5. Rice, J.R.: Matrix Computations and Mathematical Software. McGraw-Hill Book Company, New York (1981)
6. Fadeev, D.C., Fadeeva, V.N.: Computational Methods of Linear Algebra. FISMAT-GIS, Moscow, (1963)
7. Bakhvalov, N.S., Zhidkov, N.P., Kobelkov, G.M.: Numerical Methods. Nauka, Moscow, (1987)

Parallelization of Computer Code MASTAC Three-Dimensional Finite Elements Method Implementing

M.Royak, E.Shurina, Yu.Soloveichik
Novosibirsk State Technical University, K.Marx
pr.20,630092,Novosibirsk,Russia
E-mail: videnis@nstu.nsk.su
V.Malyshkin
Computer Center Russian Academy of Sciences,
Lavrentiev pr.6,630090,Novosibirsk,Russia.
E-mail: malysh@comcen.nsk.su

Abstract. The special features of MASTAC algorithms and the way of MASTAC parallelization are considered.

1.Introduction.

The special features of computer code MASTAC for non-linear three-dimensional magnitostatic field calculations and abilities of its parallelization are considered. Computer code MASTAC is implemented on IBM-compatible computers using C++ and FORTRAN-77 programming languages. MASTAC has been used to calculate magnetic field for wigglers, curvilinear dipole magnets of positrons accumulator-cooler, direct current electric machines with high magnetic concentration degree. All these tasks are characterized by complex three-dimensional geometry with curvilinear surfaces that divides parts of construction with different physical properties.

MASTAC has comfortable graphic preprocessor and provides magnitostatic fields' calculation in complex three-dimensional constructions with high accuracy. All these properties make MASTAC very attractive for researchers who use such calculation for analyzing and creating complex technical constructions. Parallelization of MASTAC calculation procedures at high efficiency workstation computers gives researchers an ability to solve many problems of complex technical constructions designing optimization and analysis.

2. Basic Features of Computer Code MASTAC.

Three-dimensional magnitostatic problem solving method implemented in MASTAC uses two scalar potentials [1]: total in magnetic material and reduced in the rest of the region with current sources. Computer code TOSCA [2] is one of the widespread computer codes that are oriented on similar problem class. The application area of computer code TOSCA and computer code MASTAC is practically the same: calculations in electroengeneering, calculations of the particles' accelerator, permanent magnet hexapole, etc.

Computer code MASTAC has high efficient tools for three-dimensional mesh describing and related abilities to increase calculation accuracy (using special tools for effective local node condensing in separate construction part). MASTAC contains graphic subsystem for current coils describing that permits build different complexity degree current coils (contained curvilinear axis, with altered form of section, etc) very easy.

Magnitostatic problem solving procedure of MASTAC contains the following steps:

1) tetrahedron mesh building in calculation area and current coils describing;

2) magnetic induction calculation created by current coils in homogeneous medium and calculation of the potential difference at the boundary between total and reduced potentials;

3) finite element system of linear algebraic equations (SLAE) generation;

4) finite element SLAE solving;

5) magnetic field characteristic calculation using two scalar potentials values.

Let's analyze calculation expenditure and parallelization possibility of these steps.

2.1. Three-dimensional Mesh Building.

The step of tetrahedron mesh building and current coils describing is distinguished by large amount of operator work with MASTAC preprocessor. Calculation expenditure for this step is insignificant and parallelization of calculations is not reasonable.

The process of irregular tetrahedron mesh building is automated in computer code MASTAC. This process uses the reproduced surface procedure [3] that implemented as follows. The base section contained arbitrary polygonal macroelements are formed. The macroelement boundaries may be line segments or arcs with given number of internal nodes and given coefficient of their condensing. These boundaries can be internal or external boundaries of the calculation area and additional fictive boundaries that are determined specially to control of finite element mesh node generation on the base section. Figure 1 displays the fragment of base section triangular mesh for curvilinear dipole magnet.

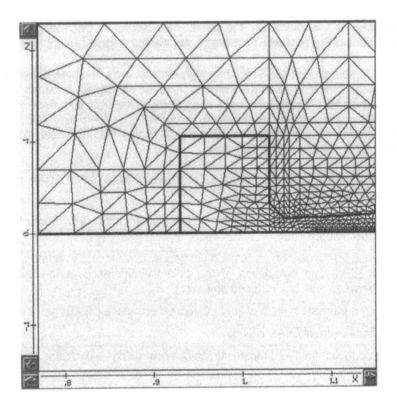

Figure 1 Curvilinear dipole magnet base section triangular mesh
fragment

For base section reproduction stage the facilities to form specified surface for description of modeling object's internal three-dimensional boundaries
are developed. These facilities are based on three-dimensional moving of
section nodes' group. On the one hand, they give an ability to set local spacing
change in three-dimensional mesh. On the other hand, these facilities can be
helpful to avoid unnecessary node condensing, when calculation area contains
bodies, essentially enlarged (or compressed) along the direction of reproducing. Figure 2 shows the section of curvilinear dipole magnet by plane contained the curvilinear axis of surface reproducing.

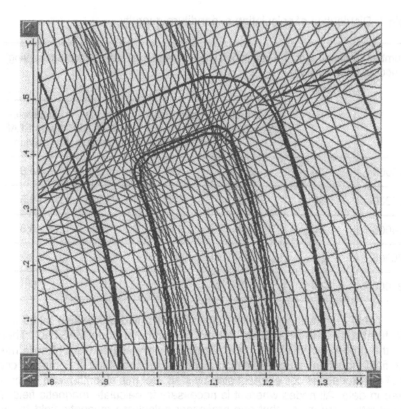

Figure 2. Curvilinear dipole magnet section contained reproducing axis

2.2. Calculations of Induction and Potential Difference.

Second step consists of two different calculation procedures. The first procedure is a calculation of magnetic field induction from current coils. Calculation expenditure of this procedure depends on current coil difficulty and nodes' quantity on the boundary of potential discontinuity. Those expenditures may be a great part of total calculation expenditures in many types of practical problems. Calculation expenditures quantity characteristics are given in table 1.

Table 1: Distribution of calculation expenditure quantity.

Number of nodes	Number of non-linearity iteration	Calculation time (% from total time of problem solving)			
		current coils processing	potential difference calculation	finite element SLAE generation	finite element SLAE solving
16000	26	26	6.5	16.9	50.6
30000	26	21.4	8.9	23.25	46.5
64000	25	22.2	5.5	26	46.3
70000	26	21	6.1	21.7	51.2
85000	26	17.5	5.6	18.9	58

Table 1 shows that current coils magnetic field processing takes up to 26% from total time of problem solving by computer code MASTAC. Therefore, the problem of this step parallelization is very actual. Current coils magnetic field induction value calculation algorithm implemented in computer code MASTAC processes coil element step by step. So, this algorithm can be parallelized in data. All nodes where it is necessary to calculate magnetic field are divided into n groups so that one processor calculates magnetic field for one group of nodes.

The main expenditures for potential difference calculations (up to 9% of total time of calculation) are expenditures for solving of SLAE got by minimization of functional from difference between current coils magnetic field density and total potential gradient on boundary of potential disconnecting. SLAE is solved by conjugate gradient method with preconditioning by simple diagonal dividing. Parallelization of this procedure can be done by parallelization of matrix by vector and vector by scalar multiplication and scalar product calculations.

2.3. Finite Element Equation System Generation.

The step of finite element equation system generation is second by the calculation expenditure and it takes up to 26% from total time of magnetic field calculation. Row-wise format [4] is used to store finite element SLAE. SLAE is generated by processing of all finite element mesh tetrahedrons. Local matrix is built for each tetrahedron, then this local matrix is put down to global matrix. The main input data for generation process is array of mesh nodes coordinates and total potential value in these nodes (for non-linearity processing) and array of tetrahedron vertex numbers. Finite element matrix is stored as matrix structure (two integer arrays) and real arrays of diagonal and non-zero non-diagonal elements (separate storage of diagonal and non-diagonal elements permits to decrease structure volume).

Tetrahedrons' array is divided into n groups for finite element SLAE parallelization. Each group is processed independently at one of the processors. One tetrahedron group processing depends on only small part of initial data (nodes' vertex coordinates and total potential value in this vertex) and only small part of matrix structure. Since tetrahedron mesh building is based on the method of reproduced sections in computer code MASTAC, it is convenient to group tetrahedrons, that fills up space between two fixed reproduced sections. It is necessary to define (n+1) fixed reproduced sections. Data array overlapping will be a little in this case and it can be processed easily. Really, nodes coordinate arrays and total potential value arrays are overlapped only for (n-1) fixed sections. Structure pointers' array, matrix diagonal elements' array and right part vector have the same overlapping. But non-zero non-diagonal elements' array and array of corresponding column numbers (from matrix structure) are not overlapped (because of separate store of matrix diagonal and non-zero non-diagonal elements in MASTAC). Finite element SLAE generation parallelization allows to reach linear acceleration.

2.4. Finite Element Equation System Solving.

Finite element equation system solving step is the most significant in calculation expenditures. This step takes up to 58% of total time of calculations (as shown in table 1). Conjugate gradient method with preconditioning is used for SLAE solving. Two types of preconditioning are implemented in computer code MASTAC: 1) SLAE matrix is transformed by multiplying of left and right parts by diagonal matrix $D^{-1/2}$ (matrix D consists of global matrix diagonal elements); 2) incomplete Choleski decomposition (ICD) [5]. Calculation time is expended only on matrix by vector multiplying procedure at first type of preconditioning. Process of SLAE solving parallelization can be built very easy in this case. Matrix is divided into n fragments (such as at SLAE generation step) and one matrix fragment is multiplied by corresponding vector elements on each processor. Data overlappings are minimum because of small overlapping of matrix structure row pointer elements array and corresponding vector elements. The elements from large arrays of non-zero non-diagonal elements and corresponding column's numbers (from matrix structure) are not overlapped. Forward and back substitutions for preconditioning matrix are necessary when ICD method is used. Forward and back substitution calculation expenditures are comparable with matrix by vector multiplication. For forward (or back) substitution procedure some unknown values that be determined before in the same procedure are used. Therefore, parallelization of finite element SLAE solving with ICD preconditioning method becomes difficult. Parallelization of procedure of finite element SLAE solving with ICD is purposefulness for tasks where ICD allows to decrease calculations time in compare with diagonal preconditioning. This situation is met rarely in area of magnitostatic problems solving.

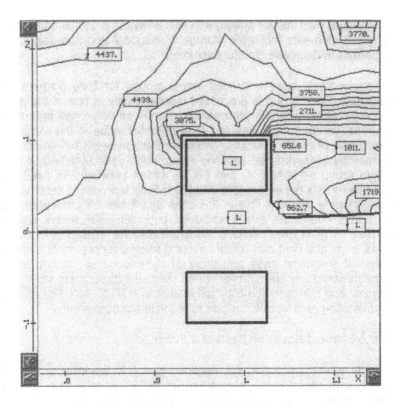

Figure 3 Magnetic permeability coefficient isolines.

The post-processor MASTAC allows to take out magnetic permeability, three components of magnetic induction, magnetic induction module in arbitrary cross-section of construction in form of graphs, color maps and isolines. Figure 3 illustrates graph of magnetic induction module in base section on axis x. Figure 4 illustrates the map of magnetic permeability isolines in base section of curvilinear dipole magnet.

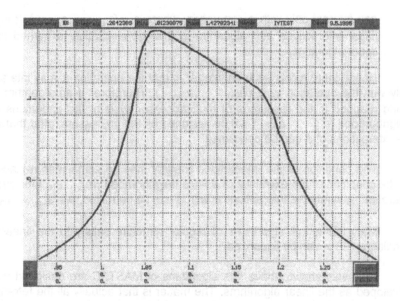

Figure 4 Magnet induction module distribution.

3. Method of MASTAC Parallelization.

The method of linearized mass computation [6,7] is planed to be used in implementation of the parallel version of MASTAC. This method has been developed on the basis of the theory of the parallel program synthesis [8]. It was embodied in the language and parallel programming system (PPS) Inya [9]. Inya is an extension of Fortran or C languages with additional facilities for specification of the system of interacting processes. Generally, the mass computation is defined in Inya as a system of interacting processes. Each executing process dynamically locks out the necessary resources (processor element, memory, etc.), PPS provides tuning of the processes system on the available resources of the specific multiprocessor and effective execution of parallel program without deadlocks.

Method imposes some restrictions on the structures of multiprocessor system and on the of interprocesses communications. In particular, Inya supports the execution of the linear algorithms only. The conditions of algorithm linearity are formulated as follows:

1) All the operations of the algorithm should be linearly ordered. Operation here denotes a computation step, in parallel program it is an execution of a certain procedure or of a subroutine with its specific input data.

2) In chosen linear ordering all interactions must be linear, e.g., if a_i and a_j operations interact, then $j=i+b_k$, $k=1,2,...,n,$ b_k , n are the integer constants. Therefore an integer constant m exists and any operation a_i

can interact only with a_j operation, where $a_j \in \{a_{i-m} , ..., a_{i+m} \}$. It is a linear interactions and algorithm in this representation is named the linear algorithm.

Hence there exists such an integer m that the operation a_i may interact only with the operation a_j, $a_j \in \{a_{i-m} , ..., a_{i+m} \}$. Therefore if an algorithm is being mapped in the resources of multiprocessor system, the operations of neighborhood $\{a_{i-m} , ..., a_{i+m} \}$ will be assigned on the processors, after that all the interactions of a_i can be performed.

The condition of the interactions linearity may be sometimes replaced by the condition of the existence of a finite neighborhood $\{a_{i-m}, ..., a_{i+m}\}$ for each operation a_i where the interactions a_i with a_j can be permitted, $a_j \in \{a_{i-m}, ..., a_{i+m}\}$.

Many numerical algorithms of regular structure satisfy to the linearity conditions 1-2 or can be linearized.

As it was shown above, the algorithms of MASTAC are designed and developed as the linear algorithms. The matter is that actually all the tetrahedrons are numbered layer by layer (layers of tetrahedrons between the adjacent plains). It provides immediately the linearity of all the MASTAC algorithms. It means, they can be parallelized and represented with Inya facilities for parallel computation representation.

PARSYTEC multiprocessor (8 PowerPC as the nodes, 80MHz, each processor element has 8Mb of main memory) is planed to be used as a platform. New parallel version of MASTAC should be accessible in 1996.

REFERENCES

1) J.Simkin and C.W.Trowbridge. Three dimensional nonlinear electromagnetic field computations using scalar potentials; Proceedings of the IEEE, vol.127, no.6, p.p.368-374, 1980.

2) TOSCA, GFUN, CARMEN, ELECTRA, BIM2D, OPERA and PE2D User Manuals. Vector Fields Ltd., 24 Bankside, Kidlington, Oxford OX51JE, 1988.

3) E.P.Shurina, J.G.Soloveitchik, M.E.Royak.Three-dimensional fields modelling on irregular mesh using finite element method ; Proceedings of the First Asian Computational fluid dynamics Conference, vol.3, p.p.1125-1127, Hong-Kong, 1995.

4) S.Pissanetzky. Sparse Matrix Technology; Academic Press Inc., London Ltd., 1984.

5) J.M.Ortega. Introduction to Parallel and Vector Solution of Linear Systems, Plenum Press, New York,1988.

6) V.E.Malyshkin. Linearized Mass Computation.-In Proceedings of PaCT-91 International Conference (Novosibirsk, USSR, 1991), pp. 339 - 353. Published by World Scientific, Singapore.

7) V.E.Malyshkin. Organization of Parallel Computations on Large-Block Multiprocessor Systems. - Programmirovanie, No.4, 1991,.(In Russian)

8) V.A.Valkovskii,V.E.Malyshkin. Synthesis of Parallel Programs and Systems on the Basis of Computational Models. - Nauka, Novosibirsk, 1988, 128p. (In Russian).

9) V.A.Anisimov, V.E.Malyshkin. Assemble Parallel Programming System INIA. - In Proceedings of PaCT-91 International Conference (Novosibirsk, USSR, 1991), 316-324. Published by World Scientific, Singapore.

New Trends in Simulation of Distributed Shared Memory Architectures

Luis Barriga and Rassul Ayani

Royal Institute of Technology, Dept. of Teleinformatics
S-16440 Kista, Sweden

Abstract. In this paper we review several issues related to simulation of modern distributed shared memory architectures: workload selection and characterization, processor-memory interaction, memory simulation and simulation efficiency. These issues are discussed in the context of several modern architecture simulation workbenches. Various efficient simulation techniques are presented. In particular, we discuss the feasibility of parallel discrete event simulation techniques and argue that this is a promising approach for efficient simulation of parallel computer architectures.

1 Introduction

Multiple Instruction Multiple Data computer architectures with distributed memory are broadly classified into message-passing and shared-memory multiprocessors. At a low level both classes have similar layout - a network of interconnected nodes where a node consists of processor, cache, local memory and network interface. Communication between nodes is achieved via messages. The difference between these classes is that their architectural units are specifically designed to efficiently support the corresponding programming model —message-passing or shared memory. During the last years intensive research has been conducted to investigate distributed shared memory (DSM) multiprocessors and integrated architectures [11,14].

Computer architects use several methods to assist the design process. Analytical modeling is very hard to employ for complex architectures. Building the target machine in hardware is an expensive and non-flexible approach. Emulation uses off-the-shelf reconfigurable hardware to emulate different designs [2,20]. Simulation has been the preferable approach since it is flexible and can provide any desired level of detail, but at the cost of a considerable amount of computing resources. Therefore, efficient techniques are indispensable for high-performance simulation.

Throughout this paper we will use the following terminology. The *target* architecture is the multiprocessor to be simulated. The *host* is the computer where simulation is performed. Simulation results are metrics that describe the performance of the *target*. Simulation performance is mainly expressed by *simulation time*.

The rest of this paper is organized as follows. Section 2 reviews some workloads used for performance evaluation. Section 3 describes processor-memory interaction and several techniques for efficient memory simulation. The performance of some modern workbenches is reviewed in Section 4. Section 5 summarizes the paper.

2   Workload Issues

Representative workloads must exhibit the characteristics of those parallel applications which are expected to be executed on parallel machines: degree of parallelism, data granularity, operating system activity, working set, locality, computation-to-communication ratio, degree of sharing, etc. *Synthetic* workloads are mathematical models that describe program behavior. *Traces* are workloads obtained by monitoring an architecture and recording events of interest such as instructions or memory references. *Real programs* are also used as workloads. Simulation that uses synthetic-, trace- or program workloads is called distribution-, trace- or program-driven simulation respectively.

Synthetic- and trace workloads have been extensively used to assist the design of new processors or memory hierarchies. Synthetic workloads are attractive since their characteristics can be controlled via parameters. For example, a recent work proposed and validated a synthetic model for generating uniprocessor memory traces that had similar characteristics as real traces [24]. This model has the drawback that trace generation is very slow [1]. To our knowledge there has not been any satisfactory analytical models for multiprocessor traces.

Trace-driven simulation is also attractive since most events and their timestamps are already recorded in the trace simplifying the simulation process. However, this approach is prone to misuse. Several issues must be carefully considered when using traces [10]. Since traces are strongly dependent on the architecture where they are generated they can only be used to study such an architecture. Moreover, parallel programs are in general non-deterministic, and therefore a certain trace represents only one execution path. Another pragmatic problem is that traces demand vast amounts of secondary storage making trace-driven simulation highly I/O intensive [1].

Program-driven simulation does not suffer from the limitations named above. Selecting a representative suite of parallel programs for benchmarking has been discussed in the computer community with no formal agreement yet. Workloads are categorized into real-world applications, kernels and loops. Real-world applications include computational-, I/O- and system activities. Kernels are computational phases which are often encountered in real-world applications. Loops are even smaller phases which are commonly found in kernels. Which of these workloads to use depends on the purpose of study. At early stages of computer design the focus is on the architectural impact of kernels or loops. Thus, other factors such as multiprogramming, operating system, virtual memory, network capacity are not considered since they add too much complexity to the simulation leading to longer execution times and complicated output analysis.

One of the most popular benchmark suites is the Stanford ParaLlel Applications for SHared memory multiprocessors SPLASH [23]. This suite comprises applications which are commonly used in engineering and scientific problems. SPLASH has been employed in numerous multiprocessor performance studies. Consequently, several workload characteristics are well understood thus streamlining the validation and verification processes. The main drawbacks of this suite is that it only represents a subset of the whole range of parallel applications which are expected to be executed on multiprocessors. A recent study shows that the architectural impact of commercial workloads greatly differs from that of technical/scientific workloads [18].

3 Memory Simulation

Computer architecture simulators include a target instruction-set interpreter. This facility can be implemented by writing one procedure per target instruction. This approach is known as instruction-driven architecture simulation (IDS). Efficient techniques for fast instruction interpretation has become a hot topic due to the rapid development of new processor designs. This requires backward- or cross-compatibility. Modern techniques compile target instructions to host instructions [6]. Alternatively, target code is translated to an intermediate format which can be easily interpreted [3,16]. Translation (compilation) can be done statically or dynamically. Dynamic translation is more convenient since most binary workloads are large; they use only a fraction of the code and the instruction set, and they rely on dynamic libraries. Binary compilation techniques are highly sophisticated and have shown good performance by reducing the number of host instructions to 2-50 per target instruction depending on the desired level of accuracy and the closeness between host and target instruction sets.

Accurate processor simulation of new instruction-sets is not considered an issue for several multiprocessor studies. To speed up processor simulation several simulators use binary workloads containing instructions from the same instruction set as the host architecture. Thus, blocks of target instructions can be directly executed on the host under the control of the simulation kernel. This approach is called Execution-driven simulation (ExDS). Since target and host processors may not have the same performance, the simulator has to take care of a correct count of target processor cycles. Besides, memory accesses must be observed by the simulator and therefore the control flow must be passed to the simulator upon a memory access.

3.1 Processor-Memory Interaction

Memory access detection can be done statically (by the programmer or by the compiler) or dynamically (at run time via software or hardware mechanisms).The common approach is to augment the source code to return control to the simulator either when an important event is encountered or after a certain number of cycles has passed. This technique has been employed by simulators such as Tango [8], Proteus [4], RPPT [7] and WWT [21]. The host operating system kernel can also be adapted to cause a trap on certain events [25]. If specialized hardware is available on the host the detection can be done at run time by trapping to the simulator when an important event is about to happen [21].

Although ExDS is faster than IDS it is not as general for simulating non-conventional instruction-sets. IDS is also more flexible since it can be adapted to track events of interest: register level transfers, accesses to local/shared memory, network and cache transactions, and system-level events. IDS also has the advantage that it does not require changes to the source code. By contrast, augmentation in ExDS has the drawback that it dilates the source code affecting the space and time characteristics of a workload which can potentially affect the simulation results. ExDS applies special techniques to correct this problem.

3.2 Simulation of the Memory Subsystem

Simulation experience show that the simulation time is dominated by memory simulation [4,5,8]. The number of different memory-related events is much larger than when simulating a processor at the register-transfer level. A simple processor-induced event such as a shared memory access can spawn numerous events in the first-/second-level cache, memory directory and other caches. The number of memory-related events increases with more detailed memory simulators as for example SimOS [12] and SimICS [17] that incorporate simulation of the Memory Management Unit (MMU).

For specific memory-related studies, when accurate processor simulation is not an issue, trace-driven memory simulation can be the viable approach under the limitations discussed in Section 2. On a multiprocessor host these traces can be processed in parallel since a trace consist of subtraces generated by separate processors. This approach was originally employed to evaluate cache coherence protocols [15]. To achieve good speedup it was required to preprocess the traces so that conditional events were converted to unconditional ones. This was mandatory to reduce synchronization during simulation.

Parallel Discrete Event Simulation (PDES) [9] can be used to reduce simulation time in program-driven simulation. Target processors can be simulated as a set of concurrent asynchronous Logical Processes (LPs). Each LP maintains its own local (virtual) time to indicate how far this particular target processor has come in virtual time. To avoid violating the causality constraint LPs must synchronize for global events such as an access to a shared variable. There are two general synchronizations mechanism *conservative* and *optimistic*. In the conservative scheme it is ensured that the causality constraint is not violated before an event is processed. This requires that LPs keep static or dynamic system-knowledge about other LPs' intentions [19]. In the optimistic scheme events are processed and if at some later stage it is discovered that the causality constraint has been violated the system is rolled back to a previous safe state [13]. The WWT simulator [21] uses a conservative approach. To our knowledge no attempt has been done in applying the optimistic approach to program-driven simulation.

4 Simulation Performance

Slowdown, the main metric to measure the performance, is defined as the ratio T_s/T_h where T_s is the real time to execute a workload on the simulated target architecture; and T_h is the real time to execute the workload directly on the host. Note that the slowdown is highly dependent on the workload and the level of simulation detail.

The first version of Tango [8] reported slowdowns of 700-18000. The low performance was due to using expensive UNIX processes and operating system primitives. Its successor, Tango Lite [10], based on user-level threads improved the performance reducing the slowdowns to 10 -150. Proteus [4] exhibited slowdowns of 35-100 comparable to that of Tango Lite. CacheMire [5] reported slowdowns of 100-5000 mainly due to the IDS approach and more detailed simulations. Note that Tango and Proteus require workload preprocessing based on specialized techniques whereas CacheMire does not.

For parallel simulators the slowdown is dependent on the number of processors.

Besides, speedup is used to show how efficient the parallel simulation technique is. The WWT [21] showed slowdowns of 50-187, and ran 9-150 times faster than Tango. WWT was also benchmarked using two scaling models [22]. Under the constant problem size model WWT's execution time decreased linearly whereas under the memory constrained model this time increased slowly.

5 Summary and Conclusions

Computer architects use simulation to assist the design of high-performance distributed shared memory multiprocessors. Simulation using real representative programs as workloads is the preferable approach for such studies. However, there is no standard workload suite for performance evaluation purposes. Accurate processor simulation is not considered an issue since the total simulation time is dominated by memory simulation. Most techniques employed so far are basically sequential. One consequence of this is that researchers are seriously limited in the design space they can investigate. To speed up processor- and memory simulation various efficient simulation techniques have been presented. Some researchers have used the parallel discrete event conservative simulation schemes to reduce the execution time of architecture simulators. However, the reported results demonstrate limited success. The application of more advanced schemes is still an open research topic.

Acknowledgments. This research is part of a research project on Advanced Simulation Techniques and Tools financed by the Swedish National Board for Industrial and Technical Development (NUTEK) under contract number 93-3319. Thanks to Nader Baguerzadesh from the University of California at Irvine, Andrzej Ciepielewski from Carlstedt Elektronik AB, and Babak Falsafi from the University of Wisconsin-Madison for reading a draft of this paper and suggesting valuable improvements.

References

1. L. Barriga and R. Ayani. Parallel Cache Simulation on Multiprocessor Workstations. In Proceedings of the International Conference in Parallel Processing, Illinois, Aug. 1993.
2. L. Barrozo, S. Iman, J. Jeong, K. Öner, K. Ramamurthy, and M. Dubois. RPM: A Rapid Prototyping Engine for Multiprocessor Systems. IEEE Computer, pages 26–34, Feb. 1995.
3. R. Bedichek. Some Efficient Architecture Simulation Techniques. In Proceedings of the Winter USENIX Conference, pages 53–63, January 1990.
4. E. Brewer, C. Dellarocas, A. Colbrook, and W. E. Weihl. PROTEUS: A High Performance Parallel-Architecture Simulator. Technical Report MIT/LCS/TR-516, Laboratory for Computer Science, Massachusetts Institute of Technology, September 1991.
5. M. Brorsson, F. Dahlgren, H. Nilsson, and P. Stenström. The CacheMire Test Bench - A Flexible and Effective Approach for Simulation of Multiprocessors. In Proceedings of the 26th Annual Simulation Symposium, pages 41–49, March 1993.
6. B. Cmelik and D. Keppel. Shade: A Fast Instruction-Set Simulator for Execution Profiling. In Proceedings of the ACM Sigmetrics Conf. on Measurement & Modeling of Computer Systems, pages 128–137, May 1994.
7. R. Covington, S. Dwarkadas, J. Jump, S. Madala, and J. Sinclair. Efficient Simulation of Computer Systems. International Journal in Computer Simulation, 1(1):31–58, June 1991.

8. H. Davis, S. Goldschmidt, and J. Hennessy. Multiprocessor Simulation and Tracing Using Tango. In Proceedings of the International Conference on Parallel Processing, pages II99–II107, August 1991.

9. R. M. Fujimoto. Parallel discrete event simulation. Communications of the ACM, 33(10):30–53, October 1990.

10. R. Goldschmidt and J. Hennessy. The Accuracy of Trace-Driven Simulations of Multiprocessors. In Proceedings of the ACM Sigmetrics Conf. on Measurement & Modeling of Computer Systems, volume 21(1), pages 146–157, May 1993.

11. J. Heinlein, K. Gharachorloo, S. Dresser, and A. Gupta. Integration of Message Passing and Shared Memory in the Stanford FLASH Multiprocessor. In Proceedings of the 6th International Conference on Architectural Support for Programming Languages and Operating Systems (ASPLOS), pages 38–50, October 1994.

12. S. Herrod, E. Witchel, M. Rosenblum, and A. Gupta. Fast and Accurate Multiprocessor Simulation: The SimOS Approach. To appear in IEEE Parallel and Distributed Technology, Fall 1995.

13. D. R. Jefferson. Virtual time. ACM Transactions on Programming Languages and Systems, 7(3):404–425, July 1985.

14. D. Kranz, K. Johnson, A. Agarwal, J. Kubiatowicz, and B.-H. Lim. Integrating Message-Passing and Shared-Memory: Early Experience. In Proceedings of the 4th Symposium on Principles and Practices of Parallel Programming, pages 54–63, May 1993.

15. Y.-B. Lin, J.-L. Baer, and E. Lazowska. Tailoring a Parallel Trace-Driven Simulation Technique to Specific Multiprocessor Cache Coherence Protocols. In Proceedings of the SCS Multiconference on Distributed Simulation, pages 185–190, March 1989.

16. P. Magnusson. A Design for Efficient Simulation of a Multiprocessor. In Proceedings of the Int. Workshop on Modeling, Analysis and Simulation of Computer and Telecommunication Systems (MASCOTS), pages 69–78, January 1993.

17. P. Magnusson. Efficient Memory Simulation in SimICS. In Proceedings of the 28th Annual Simulation Symposium, March 1995.

18. A. M. G. Maynard, C. M. Donelly, and B. R. Olszewski. Contrasting Characteristics and Cache Performance of Technical and Multi-User Commercial Workloads. In Proceedings of the Sixth International Conference on Architectural Support for Programming Languages and Operating Systems (ASPLOS), pages 145–156, October 1994.

19. J. Misra. Distributed-discrete event simulation. ACM Computing Surveys, 18(1):39–65, March 1986.

20. H. Muller, P. Stallard, D. Warren, and S. Raina. Parallel Evaluation of a Parallel Architecture by Means of Calibrated Emulation. In Proceedings of the 8th International Parallel Processing Symposium, pages 260–267, April 1994.

21. S. K. Reinhardt, M. D. Hill et.al. The Wisconsin Wind Tunnel: Virtual Prototyping of Parallel Computers. In Proceedings of the ACM Sigmetrics Conf. on Measurement & Modeling of Computer Systems, volume 21, pages 48–60, May 1993.

22. J. P. Singh, J. Hennesy, and A. Gupta. Scaling Parallel Programs for Multiprocessors: Methodology and Examples. IEEE Computer, 26(7):42–50, July 1993.

23. J. P. Singh, W.-D. Weber, and A. Gupta. SPLASH: Stanford Parallel Applications for Shared-Memory. Computer Architecture News, 20(1):5–44, March 1993.

24. D. Thiebaut, J. Wolf, and H. Stone. Synthetic Traces for Trace-Driven Simulation of Cache Memories. IEEE Transactions on Computers, pages 388–410, April 1992.

25. R. Uhlig, D. Nagle, T. Mudge, and S. Sechrest. Kernel-based Memory Simulation. In Proceedings of the ACM Sigmetrics Conference on Measurement & Modeling of Computer Systems, volume 22(1), pages 286–287, May 1994.

Standard Microprocessors versus Custom Processing Elements for Massively Parallel Architectures

Daniel Etiemble and Cécile Germain

LRI CNRS-Université Paris Sud
91 405 Orsay Cedex, France
{cecile,de}@lri.fr

Abstract. Choosing a standard microprocessor or a custom processing element as CPU of a massively parallel architecture has major impact on the hardware and software costs. The standard microprocessors have a high performance/cost ratio, but the associated cache hierarchy leads to completely reconsider the programming of the applications that have been developed for vector supercomputers. Low hardware cost is associated to a high software development cost. New approaches, as multi-threaded architectures, have low software costs, but expensive hardware costs.

1 Introduction

The CM-2 as a SIMD machine, the CM-5 [3] as a MIMD machine, have marked the emergence of massively parallel machines as practical solutions for the "Grand Challenge" of high end computing. Parallel and massively parallel architectures seem the only practical way to overcome the limits of vector supercomputers, both in term of computational capabilities and of memory costs. The high performance market is quickly moving. A lot of new MIMD machines have appeared: Intel Paragon, IBM SP1 and SP2 [8], Cray T3D [5], KSR1 [6] and 2, etc. Some vendors have failed (TMC, KSR).

The MIMD architectures have different execution models: some use a distributed memory model (Paragon, SP1-2), other ones use a shared memory model (T3D). Several programming models are currently used: data parallelism, concurrent tasks, message passing; the difficulties to normalise High Performance Fortran as a well accepted standard show that a unique parallel programming model is still a dream. Most of the typical users of high performance machines are fond of vector programming and look very reluctant to move to parallel programming.

In this paper, we discuss the trends in the newcoming architectures of parallel machines by considering a fundamental architectural choice: using "off the shelves" high performance microprocessors, or designing specific processing elements, customised to deal with the high latency of remote data accesses. The consequences of the choice are examined according to two criteria: hardware costs and programming models, which means software costs.

2 Vector Processors and Microprocessors

2.1 The Vector Supercomputers

Vector supercomputers are still the mostly used high performance machines. They are based on a relatively small number of vector processors. Vectorisation techniques are well known and the associated software tools are largely used. These tools are machine independent (the vector register length is only significant architectural parameter). The parallelism that is exploited is coarse grain concurrent tasks, which is the most common and popular parallel paradigm. Most of the big applications that are currently used in QCD, fluids mechanics, thermodynamic, ... have been developed according to this programming model. Programmers see a common memory, with a single address space, and they don't have to deal with optimisations according to a memory hierarchy, which is a key issue with parallel machine using standard microprocessors. When the problem size is not too large for the vector supercomputers, these machines are also the most efficient ones: the sustained to peak performance ratio is far better than the corresponding ratio for massively parallel MIMD machines.

Vector supercomputers have several drawbacks. The most important one is probably the memory cost: they use SRAM modules, which cost about 8 times more than the corresponding DRAM modules. For the Cray C916/16 machine, the cost of memory banks + interconnection system is about 75% of the machine cost. The scalability of these machines is difficult to achieve. Except when there are bank-conflicts, the memory access time is constant, which is more and more difficult to achieve when the number of vector processors increases: The Cray YMP8 has 8 processors and 256 memory banks ; the Cray YMP C916 has 16 processors and 1024 banks; the last one, the T90, has 32 processors and 4096 banks! The vector processors are also custom ones, which means expensive ones, compared to the low cost of standard microprocessors.

The situation for vector supercomputers can be summarised in the following way: they cannot achieve the TeraFlop performance; their main drawback is hardware cost; software developments are easy, because the programming model is simple and well known by a large community of users, and a lot of programming tools are available.

2.2 Memory Cost and CPU Choice

The only way to reduce memory cost is well know: the main memory must use DRAM chips. DRAM size is multiplied by 4 every 3 years for a constant price/performance ratio. But there is a growing mismatch between CPU cycle time and DRAM access and cycle times: the DRAM access time decrease is only 18% per year, to be compared to the 50% performance increase of the CPU chips.

For massively parallel architectures, the problem is complicated by the large memory size. Either for logically distributed memories or for logically shared memory, the memory is physically distributed. The memory access includes the interconnection network latency when accessing remote memories. Reducing or hiding memory latencies is thus the key issue for massively parallel architectures.

The CPU choice is fundamental because it induces the technique which can be used to manage memory latencies. A low cost CPU means a standard microprocessor, which has one or several level of caches. A *memory hierarchy* is then the natural choice, even if it can be implemented according to several execution models. Innovative techniques such as decoupled architectures or multi-threaded architectures can be used to reduce or hide memory latency, but they imply several custom units for decoupled architectures, or a custom multi-threaded processor, and consequently an increased hardware cost compared to machines using standard CPUs. We will illustrate the two terms of the alternative by considering some currently used parallel machines with standard CPUs, and a new machine based multi-threading (the Tera machine).

3 Standard Microprocessor Based Massively Parallel Architectures

3.1 Standard Microprocessors and Cache Hierarchy

Several massively parallel machines use standard 32 or 64 bit microprocessor: i860XP for Intel Paragon, Power and PowerPC architectures for IBM SP1-2, Alpha chips for Cray T3 , MIPS RISC chips for SGI, HP-PA chips for Convex parallel machines . The CM-5 and CM-5 E machines using Sparc or SuperSparc chips constitute a special case, as vector coprocessors are associated to the Sparc technology. We will discuss this case later.

Using standard microprocessors has several advantages. The CPUs, which have been developed for the high volume market of PCs and workstations, are cheap and exhibit high performance, both for integer and floating point (FP) computations (except for the Sparc and SuperSparc FP performance). Most of them can use the performance improvements associated with each new implementation of the architecture.

All the recent implementations of these architectures are superscalar. The actual instruction throughput depends on many significant architectural features: number of different integer units, FP units, load/store units, levels of branch prediction and speculative execution, cache size and structure (including write policy), etc. Code optimisation must consider both the internal microparallelism associated to the superscalar implementation, the cache behavior and the data access patterns that are typical of scientific computations.

Most of the recent microprocessors have special features to insure cache coherency in a multiprocessor context. The MESI protocol, or a slight variation of this protocol is used with bus snooping. The hardware implementation of high performance multiprocessors is relatively easy. A typical example is the Power Challenge SGI approach [10] to parallel computing for scientific applications: the POWERpath-2 interleaved bus, with 1.2GB/s sustained 'bandwidth, allows the connection of up to 36 R4400 chips or 18 R8000 chips to build high performance multiprocessors. They can be connected by high speed links to form a cluster of multiprocessors. Convex approach also uses a cluster of multiprocessors [4].

3.2 Massive Parallelism and Memory Hierarchy

Many different options are possible to design massively parallel architectures from these standard CPU chips. They differ both by the execution model, (distributed memory or distributed shared memory) and the interconnection network between the CPUs.

IBM SP1 and SP2 is based on the distributed memory model, where each CPU has it own address space, and a multistage interconnection network. Message passing is the fundamental programming model. Cray T3D is based on the shared memory model, but limits cache coherency problems by assigning a single memory location to shared variables. The coherency problem is thus limited to the CPU on-chip cache and the corresponding external local memory hierarchy.

Non-Uniform Memory Access architectures, as Stanford DASH [9], or Cache Only Memory Architectures, as implemented on KSR-1 and 2 machines are two other different ways to implement a distributed shared memory with physically distributed memory. The cache coherency is either implemented by a mix of hardware and software (DASH) or only by hardware (KSR).

Distributed memory architectures are more suitable for the data parallel programming model (SPMD) or for message passing. Distributed shared memory architectures use the task parallelism. Both have to deal with the presence of caches. Cache means the coherency problems. But it also mean that the actual performance strongly depends on the cache behavior, i.e. on data locality. Many examples [2] shows that developing parallel applications for a distributed shared memory system could be far easier and faster than for a message-passing system. But, in any case, the effort to reduce the gap between sustained and peak performance needs to consider and improve data locality and cache performance. The issue is even more important for developers of compilers for data parallel languages (HPF). If compiler optimisations don't consider the cache problems, the corresponding performance could be very disappointing.

3.3 "Specialised" Standard Microprocessors?

Before considering the impact of custom CPU, it is valuable to examine two special cases. The CM-5 machine has custom vector processors, that are used as coprocessors of the SPARC processor. For economical reasons, the coprocessor technology doesn't improve so fast as processor technology. When TMC replaced the SPARC processor in the CM5 by the SuperSparc in the CM5-E, they kept the same vector processor and the performance only improved by 25% on Linpack 1000×1000 (TPP). This must be compared to the 100% improve when IBM replaced Power1 chips by Power2 chips when moving from SP1 to SP2.

Another more significant example is the MIPS R8000 chip. This chip has been designed for supercomputing purposes. The most significant feature is that the on-chip data cache is reserved for integer data. The FP data bypass the on-chip cache. The design has considered the typical low locality of FP data in numerical applications. FP data accesses from external cache have a 5-cycle latency, but using pipelined SRAMs for tag and data, the R8000's external cache can service two 64-bit loads every cycle. Data and instruction queues help hiding the five-cycle latency. Standard microprocessors designed for supercomputing are thus possible. Once again, the key point is economical. Is there a sufficient market demand for these processors to be profitable? The announced R10000 MIPS chip, which is a general purpose one, will have better figures for SpecFP than the R8000, which means that R8000 will be strictly restricted to high end computing applications, where data locality is low.

4 The Custom Hardware Based Massively Parallel Architectures

The multi-thread approach has been considered for many years, within many projects (HEP, Horizon, MASA, Alewife, etc.). The Tera architecture [1] is derived from that of Horizon. The Tera processor is a custom multi-threaded processor. It implements up to 128 different instruction streams, each one having one 64-bit Stream Status Word, 32 64-bit General Registers and 8 64-bit Target Registers. On each clock cycle, the processor can switch from one stream to another one if the current stream cannot execute because of memory latency, data dependency, etc. The Tera processor has several other features that we don't discuss there. A Tera machine with p processors has an 3-D toroidal mesh with $p^{3/2}$ nodes, with resource nodes (p processors, $2p$ data memory units, p I/O cache units and p I/O processors) and the remaining nodes devoted to communications. Data can be located in any memory unit, without any need for data locality because the large number of streams allows to hide the memory latency which can reach 70 clock cycles.

The other significant point is that 128 streams mean 4096 general registers and 1024 target registers, which is important to compare in both quantity and function to vector registers or words of cache in other architectures. The large number of registers and the fast stream switching allow this architecture to easily emulate the vector processors, without needing SRAMs. The multi-threaded architectures are known to be able to exploit heterogeneous parallelism, both fine grain, medium grain and coarse grain. The programming effort is relatively small. According to results with operational compilers and the machine simulator presented by Tera company at Supercomputing 1994, the performance are very promising. For the NAS Parallel Benchmark Integer Sort, the performance relative to a Cray Y-MP1 is 8.07 for a Tera machine (1 PE) versus 0.97 for a Cray T3D (16 PEs), 2.29 for IBM SP-2 (8 PEs) and 3.44 for a Cray C-90 (1PE). For the NAS Conjugate Gradient, the corresponding figures are respectively 2.07, 0.80, 2.43 and 3.36. According to these figures, the Tera processor is slightly less efficient than the C-90 processor on vectorized code (NAS CG), but outperforms the C-90 processor on scalar code (NAS IS). It is roughly equivalent to a SP-2 (8 PEs) and 2 times more performant than a T3-D (16 PEs) on vectorized code. For scalar code, the advantage is multiplied by 4 compared to parallel machines. These results must still be confirmed on real hardware. High level performance can be expected with a reduced software effort. But the price of this type of machine will start in the 10 M$ range (16 processors and16 GBytes of memory).

5 Remarks to Conclude

Most of the high end scientific applications have been developed on vector supercomputers, which have two basic features: they use coarse grain parallelism with a single address space and there is no memory hierarchy. The present limits of vector supercomputers in term of price and performance rise a significant economical problem for users of high end scientific applications. Must they move towards massively parallel machines based on standard microprocessors? Or must they move towards machines that have been specially designed for the high end scientific applications, with specific hardware.

In one case, the hardware cost is relatively small, starting in the 1M$ range, but the major problem is to program again the application and to consider efficiently the impact of the memory hierarchy: the software development cost is the key issue. In the other case, the software development cost is relatively small, but the hardware cost is significant. There is an associate economical question: is the market of high end computing large enough to allow specialised manufacturers to be profitable?

References

1. R. Alverson et al. The Tera Computer System. In *1990 Int. Conf. on Supercomputing*, 1990
2. F. Baskett and J. L. Hennessy. Microprocessors- from the desktops to supercomputer. July 1993.
3. CM-5 Technical Summary. 1993
4. Convex Exemplar Scalable Parallel Processing System, System Overview, 1994.
5. CRAY T3D Technical summary. 1993
6. S. Franck, H. Burkhart III, J. Rothnie. The KSR1: Bridging the gap between shared memory and MPPs. In *Proc. Compcon 1993*, pp 285-294
7. J-L Hennessy, D. Patterson. Computer Architecture - A quantitative approach. Morgan Kaufmann Publishers, 1990
8. IBM POWER Parallel Technology Briefing: Interconnection Technologies for High Performance Computing.
9. D. Lenoski, J. Laudon, K. Gharachorloo, and J. Hennessy. The Stanford DASH Multiprocessor. *IEEE Computer*, 25(3), March 1992.
10. SILICON GRAPHICS. Symmetric Multiprocessing Systems. Technical Report, 1993.

Further Pipelining and Multithreading to Improve RISC Processor Speed. A Proposed Architecture and Simulation Results

Bernard Goossens and Duc Thang Vu

IBP-LITP, Université Paris 7 Denis Diderot, 2 place Jussieu
75251 Paris cedex 05, France
email: bg@litp.ibp.fr, vu@litp.ibp.fr

Abstract. This paper presents a new pipeline architecture which should improve both the number of Cycles Per Instruction (CPI) and the cycle width. The pipe stage critical path, imposed by the 64 bits integer unit, has been cut in half by data slicing and pipelining the Arithmetic and Logic Unit (ALU). Moreover, because this proposed pipeline stages division should impose a very long latency for CPU external accesses, a multithreading structure has been included. Up to four threads may be simultaneously run with a no delay context switch. Thus, multithreading is mainly used as a latency hiding technique for external accesses and internal dependencies. In order to estimate the real benefit of the construct, a simulator has been built. Simulation results show the impact of pipeline improvements without multithreading (between 24% and 32% according to cache size) and with it (from 56% to 65% with four threads and same caches).

1 The Three RISC Generations

Processor efficiency *Peff* is given by the following (and now famous) equation:

$$Peff = CPI * cycle * number\_of\_instructions \qquad (1)$$

The *CPI* term in (1) has been improved in two steps: from Complex Instruction Set Computers (CISC) to Reduced Instruction Set Computers (RISC) and from RISC to superscalar. The evolution of the *cycle* term follows the evolution of RISC processors themselves. It can be decomposed in three successive steps corresponding to improvements in the pipeline organization.

The first so-called RISC processor, namely RISC-I [13], had a two stages pipeline: instruction fetch and register file read for the first stage, ALU computation and register file write for the second one. ALU could be used by three different types of instructions: register ones, load/stores and Program Counter (PC) relative branches. In the two latter cases, the ALU computed an address. In case of a load/store, a third cycle was needed to perform the memory access, fetch being suspended. In case of a branch, the target address was only known after a one cycle delay. However, the pipeline was not suspended in such a case and the instruction following the branch in memory, namely the delay instruction, was normally fetched and executed.

The two pipeline stages were speed-balanced because in the early 80's, a 32 bits ALU in nMOS technology had a speed comparable to a Dynamic Random Access Memory (DRAM) external access.

The next year appeared the MIPS processor [8]. It had two separate memory accesses for instructions and data and the pipeline included a special stage for data external accesses. By this mean, in contrast with RISC-I, every instruction would require the same time to be computed and no fetch suspension would occur during load/stores. The MIPS pipeline is said to have five stages but it merely corresponds to three stages, each stage being subdivided in two halves. The first half does the fetch with a ready address and simultaneously increments PC. The second half decodes the received instruction and reads the operands from the register file. This ends the first stage. The second stage uses the same ALU twice. During the first half, it computes a memory address, either for load/store or for PC-relative branch. Second half serves either for result computation (interregister instruction) or to store a datum (store instruction). Third stage first half achieves load and register file write. Second half is not used.

MIPS and RISC-I are the first step (DRAM) in pipeline evolution. In both cases, the pipeline division is based on the fact that external access and ALU computation take the same time. Both processors can also be considered underpipelined [10] with each stage including a register file access in addition to its main operation (ALU or memory access).

The second step is represented by the two industrial versions of the RISC and MIPS prototypes: the SPARC [12] and the MIPS R2000 [11]. The main innovation lies in the apparition of a Static RAM (SRAM) cache between the processor and the DRAM memory. This was imposed by the fact that processor speed had been more improved than DRAM speed, requiring more than a CPU cycle to perform an access (in fact, an instruction cache had already been provided in the first MIPS prototype). However, this had no impact on the pipeline because the SRAM speed still allowed a single cycle fetch. Thus, the only improvement in the pipeline design resided in the separation of the register file read from fetch stage and register file write from execute stage. This had a drawback: the execute stage was then no more adjacent to the fetch one. Computing branch target address through the ALU would impose a 2 cycles delay for control flow instructions. To keep the delay to a single cycle, an address adder was provided in the decode stage. In these designs, the cycle width had been improved a little but was still fixed by the external access time, close from the 32 bits ALU time.

The third step came when it was possible to include caches in the processor chip as in the MIPS R4000 [3] and in the Alpha 21064 [4]. Then, fetching, loading and storing no more needed an external access and could be done much faster. In the same time, the data width extended from 32 bits to 64 bits, imposing a 64 bits ALU. The computing stage became the most critical one.

2 Further Improvements in Pipeline Design

The generation to come could further improve pipeline critical path by data slicing and pipelining the ALU and the next address compute operator. In [6] we have shown how integer arithmetic operations (addition, multiplication and division) can be sliced, by operating on 16 bits data slices. For example, a 64 bits addition can be computed through four pipeline stages, each containing a 16 bits adder, providing a 50% speed improvement compared to a 64 bits adder[1].

Figure 1 shows a 7 stages pipeline (*ic* stands for instruction cache read, *itag* for instruction cache tag check, *dc* and *dtag* have the same meaning for data cache, *rf rd* is the register file read stage, *rf wr* the register file write one and *exec* the ALU stage). Loads have a 3 cycles latency (from *rf rd* to *dtag*) and conditional branches must be predicted during *itag* stage. A bad prediction is detected during *exec* stage and annuls 2 instructions (the ones in *ic* and *itag* stages). This pipeline is derived from what can be found in actual superpipelined processors like the MIPS R4000 or the DEC 21064 if we leave apart the superscalar features.

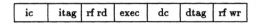

Fig. 1. A seven stages pipeline

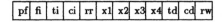

Fig. 2. A twelve stages pipeline with a sliced ALU

Figure 2 shows what such a pipeline would become after ALU and next address compute operator slicing. This 12 stages pipeline gives load a 6 cycles latency and bad prediction branches annul 6 instructions. These stages are described below:

1. Prepare fetch address (*pf* on Fig. 2)
   Fetch address preparation is handled out of fetch stage to shorten fetch operation. The address is obtained via a by-pass selection of the previous incremented fetch address not yet registered in PC, and PC itself. PC register,

---

[1] In the same manner, a multiplication step operator giving a 8*64 bits result and a radix 16 division step operator have been proposed. The three operators are based on the same four stages pipeline, each stage critical path being limited to the crossing of a 16 bits adder.

however modified every cycle, is written only at the end of last pipeline stage, as are all the registers. This simplifies instruction cancellation and restart after load miss and bad branch prediction. The *pf* stage latched output is fetch address.

2. Fetch and compute next address lower part (*fi* on Fig. 2)

   Fetching means addressing the internal instruction cache with the lower part of the fetch address. This lower part has been prepared during *pf* stage. In parallel with instruction cache access, fetch address lower part is incremented. The incremented value is by-passed to the *pf* stage. In the same time, fetch address upper part is prepared through by-passing. The *fi* stage latched outputs are the next address lower part, the prepared upper part address and the set of tags and data extracted from the cache.

3. Translate the virtual address into a physical one and compute next address upper part (*ti* on Fig. 2)

   This involves an access to a Translate Lookaside Buffer (TLB), with a search of full fetch address. Only the upper part of the address is changed by the translation. In parallel, it is incremented and by-passed to the *fi* stage. The *ti* stage latched outputs are the next address upper part and either the physical address or a Memory Management Unit (MMU) miss indication.

4. Check the instruction cache tags (*ci* on Fig. 2)

   Cache tags check compares the tags output after *fi* stage to the physical address upper part output from *ti* stage. The *ci* stage latched output is either the fetched instruction or a cache miss indication.

5. Read the instruction operands 16 lower bits from register file (*rr* on Fig. 2)

   This stage decodes the fetched instruction. Unlike traditional pipelines, operands are not read in one shot for data dependency reasons. The latched outputs are the by-passed operands slices.

6. Compute result 16 lower bits and read operands bits [31:16] from register file (*x1* on Fig. 2)

7. Compute result bits [31:16], read operands bits [47:32] from register file and access data cache (for load/store instructions) (*x2* on Fig. 2)

   Data cache is addressed with the lower part of the computed virtual address, which is identical to the physical one. The outputs are the tags and data cached in the addressed set.

8. Compute result bits [47:32] and read operands bits [63:48] from register file (*x3* on Fig. 2)

9. Compute result bits [63:48] (*x4* on Fig. 2)

10. Translate the data virtual address into a physical one (for load/store instructions) (*td* on Fig. 2)

    This involves an access to the TLB, with a comparison of the computed address to each entry. The output is either the physical address or a MMU miss indication.

11. Check the data cache tags (for load/store operations) (*cd* on Fig. 2)

    Cache tags check compares the tags output from stage *x2* to the physical address output. This stage output is either the data read (load instruction) or a write enable (store instruction) or a data cache miss indication.

12. Write result in register file or in data cache. Update PC and other special registers (rw on Fig. 2)

Result is written in one shot to allow precise interrupt handling. This implies a propagation of result slices from the stage they are output to the write back stage.

In every stage, each operation propagation delay is kept lower than a 16 bits adder one. This is the case for the PC-slices incrementers. This is also the case for internal cache access (mainly an address decoding), tag check (equality comparator), MMU translation (also equality comparators) and register file read and write. By-pass mechanism must also be carefully designed: it is built with a cascade of multiplexers, passing the latched results. The last multiplexer is the only one in the critical path, passing the only unlatched result computed during the same cycle. This concerns all the registers, including PC.

3 Improvement Impact on Processor Cycle: Simulation Results

However such an improvement in actual pipelines should allow a 50% speed increase as expected at the beginning of Sect. 2, the real benefit is limitated by the penalty imposed to the processor in case of cache misses. This penalty should be more important for the proposed architecture because the speed difference between the processor and the SRAM secondary cache is increased. The extension of the pipeline also increases loads and control flow instructions latencies which should further reduce the gain.

In order to give an accurate estimation of the real improvement, and hints to fine tune the pipeline (reduce the number of lost cycles), we have built a simulator. The simulation process is based on random drawings of the instruction flow. Different instruction types have been distinguished to take care of external accesses latency and of idle cycles induced by loads and jumps latencies. Their distribution has been choosen according to [9]: 25% of loads, 13% of stores, 14% of conditional branch instructions, 2% of other control flow instructions and 46% of miscellaneous instructions. Each load has been charged a two cycles penalty in the 7 stages reference pipeline (Fig. 1) and a four cycles penalty in the 12 stages proposed pipeline (Fig. 2) (we have considered that on the average, 2/3 of the delay slots were filled with No OPeration instructions (NOP); this estimated rate is not based on any measure).

The simulation parameters include the instruction and data internal caches sizes, given in Table 1 in Kilo Bytes (KB), the external bus size and the external unified cache size. Another important parameter is the SRAM/CPU speed ratio. It has been fixed to 6 for the proposed processor and to 3 for the reference one (the reference ratio corresponds to 15ns SRAM linked to a 5ns CPU like the DEC 21064).

The miss rates for caches have been taken from [9] and appear in Table 2.

Table 1. Memory hierarchy parameters used in the simulator

Cache size	Int. cache size (KB)	Ext. cache size (KB)	Ext. bus size (bits)
small	16+16	512	64
medium	32+32	1024	64
large	64+64	2048	128
very large	128+128	4096	128

Table 2. Cache miss rates applied to the simulations

Cache size	Instruction cache	Data cache	External cache
small	0.036	0.053	0.0072
medium	0.022	0.040	0.0045
large	0.014	0.028	0.0039
very large	0.010	0.021	0.0022

Simulation results shown on Table 3 are based on runs of 10000 instructions. It has been checked that larger runs do not change results due to the uniformity of the random drawings. It should be noticed that the cycles in the 12 stages case are half of the ones in the 7 stages case. This is why Table 3 third column shows the ratio 6 raw results and in parenthesis the ratio 3 scaled results.

Table 3. Number of cycles to run 10000 instructions

Cache size	7 stages, ratio 3	12 stages, ratio 6	Improvement
small	31202	46192 (23096)	26%
medium	25732	39064 (19532)	24%
large	19156	26752 (13376)	30%
very large	17665	23899 (11950)	32%

The simulations results show, as expected, that the most part of pipeline improvements is cancelled out by external accesses and dependency latencies. Even if caches and buses are highly enlarged, the CPI remains high.

4 Branch and Load Latencies in a Highly Pipelined Processor

Loads and control flow instructions are long latency and frequent operations. For these two reasons, they must be especially adapted to deep pipelines.

Control flow instructions can be separated in two types: PC-relative and absolute. PC-relative branches have always represented a hardware complication: they need an adder to be performed. In our proposal, this adder would have to be sliced as the ALU is. Then, next instruction address would not be complete before the end of stage $x1$ (fetch followed by a four slices addition), delaying cache tag check until this moment. Late cache miss detection is not favorable since it leads to the annulment of more instructions.

PC-relative branches have been invented for two purposes: give a relocatable property to the code and more compactly encode immediate target address. The first purpose is no more actual since the MMU ensures code relocation through memory paging. The second purpose is becoming less important because the instruction operation code (opcode) width is increasing: in a 16 bits opcode, operation type and branch condition encoding leave very little space for target immediate address. This field may not be interpreted as an absolute address. In a 32 bits opcode, target address is still too small to be considered absolute. But in a 64 bits opcode, an at least 48 bits target absolute address may be encoded. The price is an enlarged instruction codification but the benefit is a simplified hardware with a one cycle delay unconditional branch.

In the proposed pipeline, branching is always absolute and handled in two stages. First, the branch opcode is fetched during fi stage. Then, a pre-decoding is done during ti stage so that any break in the instruction flow will be effective after a one cycle delay.

In case of a conditional branch, the opcode will contain a prediction bit: go on with target instruction for backward conditional branch and do not branch for a forward target (a prediction bit is needed since absolute target field in the opcode does not directly indicate if the target point follows or precedes the branch instruction; with a relative displacement, this can be deduced from the field sign bit; anyway, this prediction technique should be efficient because loop branching instructions opcodes give a correct prediction for each loop but the last one; for *if then else* statements, prediction hit is enhanced if the rare case is placed in the *else* part). In case a false prediction is made, falsely fetched instructions will be annulled (at most 6: see Fig. 3; prediction check is done during the last ALU stage and delay instruction is not annulled).

Indirect jumps may need an ALU operation to provide target address. In order to keep branching delay to one cycle, the target address preparation will have to be done in a preceding inter-register instruction. The address preparation and the indirect jump will have to be separated by at least 6 cycles (see Fig. 4; a 64 bits target address will be obtained at the end of fourth ALU stage; in a 7 stages pipeline like the one on Fig. 1, only 2 separation cycles would be needed; a 6 cycles delay is not a handicap since indirect jumps are unfrequent instructions). The target address is read from a source register during ti stage, requiring a special read port. It is by-passed to the pf stage (a selection is made between the fi incrementer output -no branch- and the ti target address output -branch- based on prediction bit; see Fig. 5). Return from subroutine is a special case of indirect jump. It will be handled the same way.

Load instructions have a longer latency in the 12 stages pipeline than in the 7 stages one, due to the more stages between the register file read stage and the data load stage. Loaded datum may be by-passed to register file read stage after

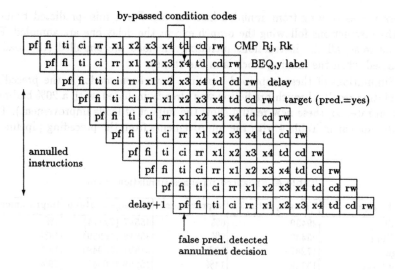

Fig. 3. Conditional branch

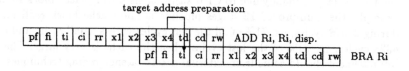

Fig. 4. Indirect branch

data cache tag has been checked. This is a very long latency (6 cycles for the 12 stages pipeline and 3 cycles for the 7 stages one) for a so frequent instruction type: if it is considered that 25% of the executed instructions are loads, it means that groups of loads should occur at least every 10 cycles. This leaves very few instructions that may be inserted in the loads delays. It is better to allow loaded datum by-passing as soon as it has been read from cache, even though a miss would be later detected. The data cache must then have a direct organization so that there is a single word and tag output. The load latency is now given by the distance between the register file read stage rr and the data cache read stage $x2$, i.e. 2 cycles only. However, instructions might have to be annulled each time a miss is detected. But, because load hits are more frequent than load misses, it is still an improvement.

As we have said in Sect. 2, to handle annulments, the PC register is written at the end of the last pipeline stage, as are the other registers. A by-pass mechanism provides the temporarily incremented value to the following fetch cycles. It also filters values coming from annulled instructions. For a miss-predicted branch, all the instructions following the branch except the delay one are annulled. For a load miss, all the instructions including the load are annulled (the load is restarted when the missing block is in the cache).

Simulations of these improved pipelines have been made (in the preceding simulation results, branch prediction was already included, with a 20% bad prediction rate; so, these new results show the impact of loads improvement). The results appear in Table 4 with the improvements from the preceding pipelines.

Table 4. Enhanced pipelines simulation results

Cache size	7 stages, ratio 3	Improvement	12 stages, ratio 6	Improvement
small	29430	6%	45547 (22774)	1%
medium	23439	9%	33918 (16959)	13%
large	17287	10%	21897 (10949)	18%
very large	15769	11%	19268 (9634)	19%

More detailed results explain why the improvement cannot be important: the lost cycles are mainly due to CPU suspensions during cache block refill. For example, the unimproved 12 stages pipeline is idle (cache block refill latency) during 25578 cycles, i.e. 71% of all the lost cycles with a small cache and during 4323 cycles, i.e. 31% of the lost cycles when the cache is very large. The main improvement should come from external access latency hiding techniques.

5   Multithreading as a CPI Improving Technique: External Access Latency Hiding

In order to hide external access latency, one can use at least two techniques: multithreading and anticipation. Anticipation is essentially a software technique because a good anticipation of cache loads, whether for instructions or data, is program dependent. Multithreading in constrast is mainly a hardware problem. A multithreaded processor runs more than one thread in pseudo-simultaneity. To do so, it is provided with several register files and program counters. The pipeline is shared.

The described multithreaded computers may be separated in two types: every cycle, no delay context switch (HEP like [14], [7]) and suspending event context switch (APRIL and SPARCLE like [1], [2]). In HEP, the pipeline may not contain more than one instruction per thread. The consequence is that a reasonable efficiency may be obtained only when enough threads are available, at least as many as pipeline stages. In APRIL and SPARCLE, the pipeline may not contain instructions from more than one thread. Thus, it must be emptied upon each context switch: the lengthier the pipeline, the more the suspension cycles.

Moreover, because internal caches are still small today, suspending events (cache misses) should be quite frequent.

Our proposal is in between HEP and SPARCLE. The pipeline will contain instructions from ready threads. If only one thread is ready, the processor will perform as SPARCLE and as a single threaded processor. If many threads are ready, one will be selected for fetch.

The maximum number of threads has been limitated to 4. The reason is that if more than one thread is often suspended at a time, this probably means that the suspension time is more important than the mean time between two suspensions. Then, progressively all the threads but one will be suspended. This situation being not favorable, it is better to build the processor and its memory hierarchy so that an external access lasts less than the mean time between two suspensions. In such a case, two threads are enough to hide latencies. However its probability should be low, two close suspensions may concern the two threads. A third one would then be useful. This other thread may also be convenient to reduce the dependencies between instructions. One more thread may give a little more flexibility.

Each thread slot in the processor may be in one of four states: empty slot, ready thread, suspended thread (cache block refill) or long latency operation in progress (load or conditional branch).

PC by-pass mechanism is provided for each thread so that four prepared fetch values are latched at the end of pf stage. In order to keep cache and MMU accesses simple, only one fetch may occur per cycle. The selection of the fetching thread is done during pf stage. A configuration of four output enable bits is formed and latched. These bits are used at the beginning of fi stage to enable one fetch latched value among the four to address the instruction cache. If no thread is ready, no fetch takes place. The selection process is based on a round robbin priority, leaving away from the selection the suspended threads stopped by a cache miss and the empty slots. Between a ready thread and a thread running a long latency operation, the first one is selected. This feature has the advantage to interleave other ready threads when a load or a conditional branch is being run, so that in case of a late load miss or bad prediction detection less annulments will occur.

An instruction cache miss is detected during ci stage. The thread is marked suspended until the cache controller achieves the missing cache block load. The falsely fetched instruction must be annulled. If successive instructions of the same thread have yet been fetched (at most 3 in fi, ti and ci stages while the missed instruction is in its rr stage), they are also annulled. The execution of the thread restarts from the missing instruction as soon as it is available (notice that the suspended thread's PC will not be updated neither by the missing instruction nor by the annulled ones).

In case of a data cache miss caused by a load instruction, the cache controller performs the load while the processor keeps running other ready threads. Because the thread is suspended during this operation, its register file is no more in use. Nevertheless, the CPU is not suspended so that writing in the register file is still possible. Thus, the cache controller may procede to the register write and terminate the load, which need not be restarted. Moreover, successive instructions that have been fetched before the miss was detected, as long as they are independent from the load, may be continued. In a single thread processor, the compiler would have to reorganize the code and possibly insert NOPs to force independency. In a multithreaded CPU, it is better to rely on threads interleaving to ensure independency. Thus, the compiler never inserts NOPs and can no more guarantee independency. In such a case, the hardware inserts the NOPs (SPARC like internal NOP opcode) only when needed, i.e. when no other thread is in the ready state and next instruction is a dependent one. This is why, since the load has a two cycles latency, the two slots following it surely contain independent instructions (naturally independent, inserted NOP or belonging to another thread). They may procede, even though the thread is suspended. Annulments concern at most 8 instructions but surely less than that, thanks to threads interleaving.

Control flow breaks must also be adapted to the multithreaded case. The reason is that we cannot be sure that the delay instruction will be run one cycle after the control flow instruction (an instruction of another thread may be inserted in between). The instruction type and prediction bits are pre-decoded during ti stage and form the break bit (break bit is asserted if and only if opcode type is control flow and opcode prediction bit is asserted). The target address is latched at the end of the ti stage. The break bit and the target address are forwarded all along the pipeline and registered at the end of the rw stage. A by-pass mechanism (see Fig. 5) provides the target address and the branch decision to the fi stage, which passes either the incremented fetch address or the target address to the pf stage, according to the by-passed break bit. Figure 5 low part shows how fetch address is by-passed when threads are interleaved in the pipeline. The by-passed latched value is either the latched incremented one (no branch) or the latched target address (branch). If the delay instruction is itself a branch instruction with an asserted branch prediction bit, it will reassert break bit. Otherwise, break bit will be cleared as any non control flow instruction does.

We have adapted the simulator to the multithreaded architecture with a varying number of threads from 1 to 4. The simulation results are given in Table 5. For the simulations it has been considered that threads use disjoined memory areas. Thus, caches are shared and miss rates are fixed according to the share size. Runs were still limited to 10000 instructions, i.e. for 4 threads, roughly 2500 each. Table 6 shows the improvements in performance, due to multithreading (m percentage column: comparison between the 12 stages pipeline result in Table 4 and the results from Table 5) and to both multithreading and ALU slicing ($m+s$ percentage column: comparison between Table 4 seven stages pipeline results and Table 5 results). We can see that even though cache size is increased, multithreading keeps paying. A second result that can be deduced from the two tables is that the most part of the multithreading improvement is due to the adding of a single second thread.

Detailed results are presented in Table 7. In each cell, the values are the

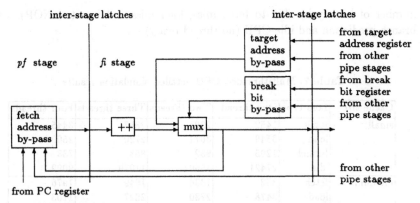

By-pass condition: same thread, not annulled, break bit on for branch by-pass
By-pass priority: leftmost stage has highest priority, register file has lowest

ti PC latch by-pass: same thread, not annulled, highest priority

pf	fi	ti	ci	rr	x1	x2	x3	x4	td	cd	rw	thread i
	pf	fi	ti	ci	rr	x1	x2	x3	x4	td	cd	rw	thread j
		pf	fi	ti	ci	rr	x1	x2	x3	x4	td	cd	rw	thread k
			pf	fi	ti	ci	rr	x1	x2	x3	x4	td	cd	rw	thread i

Fig. 5. PC and branch address by-pass mechanism

Table 5. Multithreaded CPU simulation results

Cache size	One thread	Two threads	Three threads	Four threads
small	43637	31915	27554	25787
medium	33157	23664	19810	17830
large	21400	15136	12976	12130
very large	19068	13971	11960	11197

Table 6. Multithreading performance improvement over monothreading

Cache size	One thread		Two threads		Three threads		Four threads	
	m	m+s	m	m+s	m	m+s	m	m+s
small	4%	26%	30%	46%	40%	53%	43%	56%
medium	2%	29%	30%	50%	42%	58%	47%	62%
large	2%	38%	31%	56%	41%	62%	45%	65%
very large	1%	40%	27%	56%	38%	62%	42%	64%

number of lost cycles due to fetch miss, load miss and inserted NOPs, bad branch prediction and idle CPU (no thread ready).

Table 7. Multithreaded CPU detailed simulation results

Cache size	Loss type	One thread	Two threads	Three threads	Four threads
small	fetch	1452	2301	2887	3445
	load	3549	3071	2720	2500
	branch	1205	932	858	733
	idle	27421	15601	11079	9099
medium	fetch	852	1334	1649	1976
	load	3478	2780	2227	1703
	branch	1259	939	741	649
	idle	17558	8599	5183	3492
large	fetch	552	687	803	947
	load	3278	2161	1250	638
	branch	1290	866	569	326
	idle	6270	1412	344	209
very large	fetch	400	447	434	517
	load	3046	1940	875	389
	branch	1280	825	496	236
	idle	4332	749	145	45

6 Shared Pipeline: Improvement to Further Reduce the CPI

Dependency situations can be further reduced through pipeline sharing. For this purpose, we separate the pipeline in two parts (see Fig. 6). Stage pf to stage ci form the fetch part, producing checked and ready to be run opcodes. Stage rr to stage rw constitute the run part, consuming opcodes. These opcodes are stored at the tail of one among four First In First Out structures (FIFO) (one per thread). The ci stage serves for the run part as the pf stage does for the fetch part: a selection occurs among the ready threads to choose the FIFO head entry that will enter the rr stage for run. This mechanism ensures that when a fetch miss is detected, however no new opcode is registered in any FIFO, if at least one is not empty, its head entry will enter the run part instead of a bubble. Moreover, annulments in case of a fetch miss will no more correspond to idle cycles if the ready opcodes stock is not empty.

In addition to the opcodes coming from the fetch part, the FIFO may receive ready to be run opcodes from the run part after a load miss. Among the 8 annulled instructions, five of them are in the run part from rr to $x4$ stage. All those belonging to the same thread re-enter its FIFO.

Each FIFO has 5 places. Each stage keeps track of the FIFO entry number where the opcode it takes care of resides. When a load miss occurs, the head

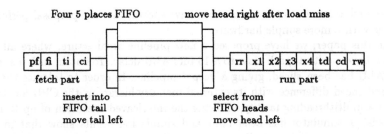

Fig. 6. Two parts pipeline

pointer is updated with the oldest FIFO entry number by-passed, corresponding to the annulled instruction next to the load (the pointer moves backward of at most 5 positions). In the same time, the tail pointer gets the old head pointer value. Instructions of the same thread in the pipeline fetch part are also annulled. For bad branch predictions, the annulled instructions will not be restarted and they are not inserted in the FIFO. Finally, a thread with a full FIFO does not compete for fetch selection. A last simulation has been made and the results appear in Table 8, with the number of cycles ($nbc.$) needed to run 10000 instructions and the improvement ($imp.$) with the non separated pipeline. Two reasons explain the improvement values obtained: first, by increasing the caches sizes, we decrease the number of misses and also the number of restorable lost cycles due to fetch annulments and the number of FIFO inserted opcodes after load annulments; second, less annulled opcodes are inserted in the FIFO when the number of threads is increased, because thread interleaving is forced while a load is in progress.

Table 8. Two parts pipeline simulation results

Cache size	One thread		Two threads		Three threads		Four threads	
	nbc.	imp.	nbc.	imp.	nbc.	imp.	nbc.	imp.
small	39220	10%	27867	13%	24297	12%	21589	16%
medium	29015	12%	21672	8%	17674	11%	16069	10%
large	18507	14%	13437	11%	11922	8%	11574	5%
very large	16119	15%	12381	11%	11324	5%	10950	2%

7 Conclusion

In [5], we have proposed another multithreaded architecture. This proposal differs in many ways: firstly, by the simulation results not available in [5]; secondly, in the architecture. As the simulations have shown, the new proposal performs better with a more simple hardware.

In this paper, we have proposed a new pipeline architecture, where all the stages have a critical path close to a 16 bits ALU delay. To obtain such a speed, the ALU has been sliced, giving a deeper pipeline. In order to tolerate the increased speed difference with its external memory hierarchy, the CPU has been given a multithreading facility, allowing the interleaved execution of up to four threads. A simulator has been built and simulation results show that multithreading is essential to really improve performance through superpipelining, whatever the internal cache size is.

Extending the proposed pipeline to a Very Large Instruction Word (VLIW) structure is possible, but the regularity of the pipeline division must not be broken. In a certain sense, to build an efficient VLIW or superscalar processor, first build an efficient superpipelined processor as was done for the DEC 21064.

Such a processor can also serve as the main building block in a multiprocessor. Multithreading helps to tolerate external communications latency and should perform well in a Cache Only Memory Architecture (COMA).

References

1. A. Agarwal, B.H. Lim, D. Kranz and J. Kubiatowicz: APRIL a processor architecture for multiprocessing. Proceedings of the 17th AISCA, 1990
2. A. Agarwal, J. Kubiatowicz, B Kranz, B.H. Lim, D. Yeung, G. D'Souza, M. Parkin: SPARCLE: an evolutionary processor design for large scale multiprocessor. IEEE Micro, june 1993
3. A. Bashteen, I. Lui, J. Mullan: A superpipeline approach to the MIPS architecture. IEEE, 1991
4. Digital Equipment Corporation: Alpha architecture reference manual. DEC, 1992
5. B. Goossens and M. Akil: MT a multithreaded 64 bits RISC CPU. Proceedings of PaCT-93, Obninsk 1993
6. B. Goossens and D.T. Vu: Data slicing arithmetic operators. Real numbers and computers, St. Etienne, april 1995
7. R.H. Halstead and T. Fujita: MASA, a multithreaded processor architecture for parallel symbolic computing. Proceedings of the 15th AISCA, 1988
8. J.L. Hennessy, N. Jouppi, F. Baskett, A. Strong, T. Gross, C. Rewen and J. Gill: The MIPS machine. Proceedings of COMPCON, feb. 1982
9. J.L. Hennessy and D.A. Patterson: Computer architecture. A quantitative approach. Morgan Kaufmann, 1990
10. N.P. Jouppi, D.W. Wall: Available instruction level parallelism for superscalar and superpipelined machines. Proceedings of the 3rd ASPLOS, april 1989
11. G. Kane: MIPS R2000 RISC architecture. Prentice Hall, 1986
12. N. Namjero, A. Agarwal: Implementing SPARC: A high performance 32 bits RISC microprocessor. SUN microsystems, 1988
13. D.A. Patterson, C.H. Sequin: RISC-I: a reduced instruction set VLSI computer. Proceedings of the 8th AISCA, 1981
14. B.J. Smith: Architecture and applications of the HEP multiprocessor computer system. SPIE proceedings, 1981

The Massively Parallel Computer System MBC-100

Zabrodin A.V.[1] and Levin V.K.[2] and Korneev V.V.[2]

[1] Keldysh Institute of Applied Mathematics
4,Miusskaya sq.,125047,Moscow,RUSSIA
tel:(095) 2518869
[2] SRI KVANT, 15,4-th Likhachevsky Lane,
125438,Moscow,RUSSIA
tel: (095)1534700
fax: (095)1539584
e-mail: korneev@kwant.mipt.su

1 Introduction

The present report contains the basic concepts of the project of the supercomputer family with the highest model performance being 100 GFLOPS and with the possibility of increasing the performance up to 1 TFLOPS.

The family of supercomputers is intended to solve the most sophisticated problems requiring high performance and enlarged memory size of a computer system. At present, there exists a number of problems having both scientific and practical significance, and to solve them one should have the speed of tens and thousands of GFLOPS.

The goal of this project is to design a family of high- peformance computer systems and workstations using imported qtransputers and microprocessors. The development of the above computer system will make it possible to solve, within Russia, a wide range of key problems of high performance computer systems creation and application with little expenses and in a short time and will stimulate the development of the Russian hardware. Besides, the direct solution of the actual applied problems in this case is combined with new perspective developments in computer technologies and programming.

In the course of realizing this project the following problems will be solved:

- the raise (for the order of magnitude) of the present level of computer systems performance: the prognoses performance of the computer system under consideration in the maximal configuration makes 100 GFLOPS with the possibility of increasing it for up to 1 TFLOPS;

- the realization of the remote access to a multiprocessor system which will provide a number of scientific and industrial institutions with calculating resources of the maximal performance;

- the designing of the portable (mobile) software providing the efficient usages, easy programming and the continuity of applied programs for highly parallel computer systems;

- the creation of computer technology foundations for computers with parallel structure, the technology comprising: parallel techniques, algorithms and programs for solving applied problems; the software support of applied programs; the techniques of storage and processing great data scopes; visualization of the n-dimensional calculations results;

- providing of solving three-dimensional problems of continuum mechanics, which is a principally new stage in the sphere of numerical simulation and will allow us to solve problems which are too difficult to be solved now, for instance, simulation of processes in nuclear reactions, ecological forecasting, etc.;

- stimulation of the Russian hardware development due to the accumulation of experience and using highly parallel systems on the basis of high-performance microprocessors.

2 Basic software and hardware concepts

Elaborating the requirements upon the models of the super-computer family we have analyzed specific applied problems from the following subject areas:

- the three-dimensional nonstationary gas dynamics;
- the two-dimensional nonstationary gas dynamics with the account of heat conduction;
- the theory of control, navigation and differential games;
- aerodynamics of flying vehicles;
- nonlinear, nonstationary processes of radiation particles transfer, taking into account their interaction with the environment;
- neutron physics: complex calculation of nuclear reactors, analysis of their security, protection from penetrating radiation.

On the basis of the analysis of the above problems the main requirements upon the software/ hardware realization of the super- computer family models could be formulated:

1. A user should have efficient possibility to divide the whole scope of work into processes. This does not exclude the automatization elements for a whole process, a user wishing it to be so.

2. The processes may be generated in the course of calculation. The possibility of dynamic loading of processes is necessary.

3. As a rule, there is one or several host processor elements which control a process of task running. The exchange of common data is performed via these processor elements. It is advisable that such a processor element should have large memory size.

4. Processor elements should have the possibility to exchange both on the basis of the address principle (relatively small) and within the logic topology (the great bulk of the exchange).

5. It is known that message exchange graphs which realize both address exchanges and within the logic topology, unlike the physical one, have the acceptable speed (as compared to the theoretically possible one) for message lengths exceeding 500- 1000 bytes. At the same time, the analysis of the problems under consideration shows that the average message length during exchange equals, as a rule, at least hundreds of bytes. Due to this we may consider the

program routing to be the basic tool, and not to require hardware realization of a user's topology; it suffices to minimize the maximal and average lengths of paths among processor elements. The removal of these requirements makes the hardware and software support much cheaper and reduces the terms of their realization.

6. It is necessary to have the possibility of asynchronous interprocessor message exchanges .

The main computer resource of all the models of the super-computer family is a parallel processor with the MIMD- architecture. In the course of designing such a processor it is necessary to provide the balance, for a given class of tasks, of such parameters as: the processing speed in a node, the internode data transmission rate, the capacity and speed of memory, and the input/output rate.

The analysis of the nowadays market of commercially available microprocessors leads to an actually simple choice of i860, or, more specifically, its modification i860XP, to be the node processor.

For the selected processor and for an assigned class of tasks to be solved one should determine the necessary internode data transmission rate. The class of tasks to be solved is characterized be their structuring degree which implies a number of operations in a node per a computer word (ordinary or double one) arriving from the neighbouring nodes. It is obvious, that to completely load the node processor the structuring degree should at least equal the ratio of the processing rate in the node to the internode data transmission rate.

For the processor i860 the relation is as follows: the internode data transmission rate for the full loading of the processor should be at least 30/S, where S is the task structuring degree. Thus, while processing 64-bit floating point numbers, the upper bound of the internode data transmission rate in the system under consideration makes 240 Mbps. The designing of the communication interface (the system device) providing such data transmission rate may only be realized on the basis of a custom-built specialized LSI manufactured abroad. The cost of such LSI prototype makes approximately $ 100.000, the designing time is 1-1.5 years, a single LSI in a small lot costs about $ 300.

The alternatives to the communication interface with less transmission rates, but realized in much less time and for much less cost are: the use of commercially available transputers of INMOS and Texas Instrument, and the development of communication interfaces on the basis of Russian gate- array chips with the layout design rules of 2.5-1.5 MKM. The communication interface on the basis of transputers of the families T4 and T8 provides the internode transmission rate of about 20 Mbps for the cost of about $ 400. In this case the task structuring degree for the full loading of the processor should equal at least 96. The interface on the basis of TMS320C40 provides the internode transmission rate of 20 Mbps for the cost of about $ 800. The task structuring degree for the full loading of the processor should be at least 12.

The version of the communication interface based on Russian gate-array chips should provide full loading of the processor for the intermediate task structuring degree of 12-96. Within the present project we consider three variants of realizing a system interface on the basis of the T-805 transputer, the microprocessor TMSS320C40 and a Russian gate - array chip.

The architecture of the super- computer provides the possibility to increase the computing power without changing the system software. This technology is supported both by the unification of system constructive elements and electric parameters of nodes, and by the unification of the corresponding software.

3   The main results of applied programming

Numerical problems to be solved nowadays are characterized by great complexity and strict requirements upon the accuracy of results, especially in case they are used in fundamental researches or in technical design systems for specific articles.

The analysis of complexity of typical problems from the above spheres, due to the requirement to obtain results with guaranteed accuracy, shows that to solve them in admissible time one should have computers with the performance of tens of milliards flops [1]. These requirements correspond to the modern standards and will increase with the course of time. Such great necessity of performance are mainly due to the following reasons.

First, the problems to be solved grow more complicated in the course of technological progress.

Second, the requirements grow more strict upon the trustworthiness and completeness of mathematical models, their being adequate to the physical essence of the processes and phenomena being investigated. These circumstances, in particular, make it necessary to use complete models and not simple ones. The latter makes the numerical experiment much more complicated since the complexity of numerical problems increases faster than their dimension[2,3].

Third, it is necessary to obtain the guaranteed correct result when the initial continuous model becomes discrete. The transfer from the initial differential (infinite- dimensional) model to the discrete (finite- dimensional) one inevitably displays the approximation errors. Their manifestation means not only the quantitative differences of the approximated numerical solution from the sought- for differential one, but possible distortion of the evolution picture of the approximated solution as compared to the accurate one.

Let us illustrate the above with typical examples. The processes taking place:

- while cumulating energy to realize the thermonuclear reaction;
- during the motion (single or group) of aircrafts;
- during the evolution of global atmospheric phenomena, and many others contain the elements of unstability in their behavior.

While constructing numerical methods with the use of finite-difference representation of the initial differential equations due to the approximation error (leading to the "numerical (mathematical) viscosity"), the behavior of the numerical solution may be distorted. Therefore, as a rule, when using insufficiently detailed numerical grids we have "redundant stability" in the behavior of the approximated solution, which is not adequate to the accurate one. In numerical calculations of unstable or neutral solutions the "redundant stability" distorts its true behavior and makes the results of the mathematical experiment inadequate to those of the physical one. This circumstance greatly hampers simulation in the numerical experiment of small- scale phenomena, i.e. the important details of the sought- for mode behavior. This inadequacy may be practically avoided only by repeating the calculations on a sequence of condensing grids. This makes the calculations much more cumbersome, and it must be taken into account when grounding the requirements to computers[3,4].

The main difficulty in using multiprocessor systems when solving the above and some other problems is to obtain actual performance close to the peak one while increasing a number of processor elements in the multiprocessor. Below we consider how the above problems take into account the structural peculiarities of specific numerical algorithms in order to raise the paralleling efficiency. Below find the arguments common for the paralleling of algorithms of the above problems.

Preparing parallel programs becomes essentially simpler if the MIMD circuit lies in the basis of constructing a multiprocessor system. This makes it possible to distribute among various groups of processor elements the program blocks which may be executed simultaneously (large- scale paralleling). Large-scale construction of a program is typical for the most of algorithms to solve complicated numerical problems.

Partition by physical processes is the basic form of large-scale paralleling. As a rule, when constructing numerical algorithms for solving problems, in which numerous physical factors should be taken into account, the technique of "partition by physical processes" is used. In this case the forming of the mathematical model by physical processes is realized by means of sequential correction at the time stage of the solution vector, taking into account each subsequent physical factor. The possibility to perform such a correction by several factors simultaneously provides the partition of calculations by physical processes.

It is significant that the information exchange among processor elements be realized simultaneously with performing arithmetic operations, perhaps with some delay which does not depend on the number of processor elements. The most of multiprocessor systems (MBC-100 among them) have only distributed memory as RAM. Therefore, when determining its size it is important to take into account the necessity of additional memory resource for buffering messages. In the course of constructing a processor element for MBC-100 the performance of numerical operations and exchange functions have different hardware. This makes it possible to simplify the construction of the message transfer system in the multiprocessor, and to optimize the efficiency of multiprocessor system functioning when increasing the number of processor elements. There exist other types of paralleling, besides the large- scale one. Let us consider "geometric paralleling". Note that it may be especially efficient when solving multi- dimensional problems, when , see above, high performance of computers is especially needed. Unlike large-scale paralleling, the so- called geometric one implies mass parallelism when performing calculations. Such paralleling is realized especially simply and efficiently if a numerical algorithm is constructed on the basis of local dependence of a totality of numerical values on the initial data. The explicit techniques of calculation for regular calculation grids may serve an example. In this case as "grids" we mean not only the construction of quantization in a geometric space, but, for instance, the quantization by spectral parameters of radiation, or by other independent variables. Most of sequential algorithms with good reputation are constructed on the combination of explicit dependence of calculated values on the initial data, and on the partial dependence of the sought- for ones(explicitly- implicit techniques).This techniques realized in the method of variable directions for solving multi-dimensional problems may serve an example of such algorithms [22]. The paralleling of calculations in such algorithms may also be performed with satisfactory efficiency. The paralleling of implicit algorithms, when the procedure of obtaining the sought- for values only implies the solving of systems of equations with larger dimension, is more complicated. In these cases there, too, exist paralleling techniques - obtaining the solutions of systems of algebraic equations. However, it turns out to be more efficient to modify the initial numerical algorithm keeping the advantages of the implicit technique, but realizing the explicit dependence of the sought-for values, which can easily be partitioned [10,11].

Actual numerical algorithms used to solve complicated applied problems are much more sophisticated than the techniques considered above. When passing from the initial differential (infinite-dimensional) mathematical model to the numerical discrete (finite- dimensional) one it is necessary, besides approximation and stability, to fulfill the conditions providing an adequate presentation in the finite- dimensional approximation of the solution of the initial differential problem. Let us call the fulfillment of these conditions an adaptation of numerical algorithms [2,3].

The concept of adaptability implies the possibility, while solving any specific problem, to take into account the singularities of the behavior of the solution. These singularities are revealed in the course of numerical construction of the solution. This is done to raise the accuracy of the finite- dimensional approximation and to obtain the accurate numerical solution with its true evolution (see above). Let us illustrate the procedure by the examples of constructing numerical algorithms for solving multi- dimensional problems of gas dynamics. Certainly, this is true for wider classes of equations, for instance, for the quasi-linear ones. The structure of solutions of gas dynamics equations is characterized by smooth domains and discontinuities separating them. In the former ones differential equations are being solved. For the latter there exist several types of discontinuities for which the corresponding relations should be held connecting the values on different sides. If we neglect this while constructing numerical algorithms, we may obtain incorrect numerical result, though the formal conditions - approximation and stability - were held [3]. Therefore, the essence of constructing self- adapting numerical algorithms for the gas dynamics problems means taking into account and pointing out the main discontinuities. This allows us to realize the approximation of the accurate solution, adequate to its actual smoothness. Therefore, in the course of paralleling such algorithms one has to take into account their structure - the multiblock arrangement of each specific problem and the "geometric parallelism" typical for finite- difference techniques. In this case one should bear in mind that the multi-block arrangement itself may vary in the course of calculations, since the discontinuities singled out during calculation may be modified with the evolution of the solution in time and, therefore, the pattern of links changes.

Let us not go deep into the details of constructing numerical algorithms for solving various classes of the gas dynamics problems. Note that while constructing the family of MBC-100 we managed to work out the tradeoff between the constancy and adjustability of links providing efficient enough mapping of quasiregular algorithms structures upon the architecture of the samples of the family.

Below see the results of the solved gas dynamics problems that confirm this statement.

4 Solving the problems of calculating the aircraft aerodynamics

Different variants of calculating the supersonic flow along existing aircrafts of complicated shape were performed. Determined were the basic aerodynamic parameters and investigated were the singularities of flow fields close to control blocks, air intakes and other elements of an aircraft. Held were multivariant calculations of aerodynamic optimization of aircraft fuselage being designed[23,24]. The peculiarity of such calculations is to obtain reliable dependencies of altering aerodynamic parameters upon the variation of external lines. A system of Euler non- stationary equations was taken to be the basis of the mathematical model.The stationary solution was calculated for assigned initial and boundary conditions for various values of time until it stopped to change. The method of calculation is based on the combination of two algorithms: the method of numerical integration by time of a system of non- stationary equations, and the method of numerical integration by one of spatial variables of a system of stationary equations [5]. The typical volume of numerical operations to calculate one variant is estimated to make 10**9 arithmetic operations [4].

Besides flow along individual aircrafts, numerically studied were group motion taking into account aerodynamic interaction. Such calculations were realized due to the use of created samples of MBC-100 of Gflops performance.

The averaged data of the efficiency of parallel realization of the program complex used are presented in Table 1. These results show that the realized computer approach to solve aerodynamics problems allows one to obtain high efficiency of paralleling due to correct balance of loading processor elements of a multicomputer.

5 Solving the problems of two dimensional nonstationary gas dynamics taking into account nonlinear heat transfer

The actual scientific technological problems that can be solved within the two dimensional model of the heat conductive gas dynamics are the following ones:

- the problems of investigating the compression of structures to obtain high density of energy, for instance, the targets of controlled thermonuclear reaction.

- the problems of calculating explosions for the development of many technological constructions and for the development and operation of oil and gas condensate fields [25].

- the problems of calculating technological processes concerning heat and mass transfer.

The above problems are very cumbersome in calculations and to solve them one should have high performance computers. However, the algorithms of solving these problems admit, as a rule, high degree of paralleling, and the use of multiprocessor system in this case is very promising.

The construction of numerical algorithms for such evolution problems correspond to the conventional technique: splitting by physical processes at each numerical step in time. The peculiarity of the method considered below is the splitting which, after the sequential calculation of gas dynamics and then heat transfer, provides, in general, the fulfillment of conservation laws corresponding to the setup of the problem as a whole, i.e. without the splitting into these parts. This provides, for the finite difference approximation, the adequacy of the accurate and approximated setups of the problems.

The peculiarities of constructing algorithms for solving gas dynamics problems have been discussed above.

Now we consider the constructing a numerical technique of calculating heat transfer. As a rule, when solving the problems of heat transfer the implicit calculation techniques are used. The paralleling of such techniques has been discussed above. In both these approaches the paralleling is possible, though somewhat difficult.

Note that one of the main conditions of the efficient realization of parallel calculations is the adequacy of the computer's architecture and the structure of an algorithm used. Therefore, for parallel calculation it is often advantageous to construct new algorithms instead of adjusting the existing ones. So we did in the present case. The developed technique (it got the name of local iterations [26,27]) by its structure is identical to the explicit one, but allows one to perform calculations without restriction upon the value of time step, which is characteristic for the explicit technique. For the spatial quantization of the heat conductivity operator local approximation of the solution by polynomials is used. The algorithms are constructed by the values of the solution on grid patterns. Then we perform the substitution of polynomials into the integral relation determining the solution. Two layer quantization is used by time variable. The transfer to a new time layer is realized by the explicit iteration technique with the Chebyshev set of parameters. Such a structure of an algorithm preserves the local structure of links obtained during spatial quantization.

Below we present the data describing the numerical labour content of the algorithm. Let the characteristic number of nodes in a grid be 10^4, then the amount of numerical work per a numerical node makes approximately 10^4. For the typical number of steps in time the total amount of calculations makes 10^{12}. The averaged data on the efficiency of parallel realization of the developed program complex are presented in Table 2. Note that these results testifying to high enough efficiency of paralleling were obtained after studying the optimal combination of large scale and geometric paralleling.

6 Neutron-physical problems of calculating nuclear reactors

For neutron-physical calculations of nuclear reactors a complex of applied programs REACTOR was developed. It is operated on a PC [12,13]. The complex comprises multigroup diffusion approximation of the neutron transfer equation, which is widely used to analyze the criticality, to calculate a group of reactors, to obtain the preliminary approximation to calculate more accurate approximations, etc. The setup of problems may be performed in one-, two- and three-dimensional geometries. Therefore this model was selected first of all to be set up at the samples of MBC-100. The paralleling of the algorithm of solving a neutron-physical problem is realized both by means of large scale decomposition of calculated domains and with the use of geometric parallelism.

In case the problem is set up in the three-dimensional geometry, the most labour-consuming is the solution of the diffusion equation in each of the groups for determining a flow of neutrons. The quantization of the corresponding differential operator is constructed on a finite difference grid, and to obtain group flows the iteration technique of pointwise sequential upper relaxation (SOR) is used [14]. The paralleling of the solution of this system of equations is realized by means of decomposition of numerical domain into layers along the axis of oz (the vertical axis of the reactor's assembly). Each of the layers consists of a number of calculated planes ($z = const$) and is processed on its group of processor elements. The information exchange is performed by the obtained values of flows at the boundaries of layers. The technique, where the calculation of planes is performed in all the processor elements simultaneously in the directions off the upper and lower boundaries of the reactor towards its central plane, turned out to be efficient. For such an arrangement of paralleling there are blocks of a numerical algorithm which are somewhat difficult to partition. They are: the calculation of the eigenvalue of time constant of neutron multiplication by the obtained distribution of flows (K_{eff}), and the verification of the criterion of the end of calculations. It turned out possible to perform the latter simultaneously

with the calculation of current iteration in its processor element. In this case
the additional numerical operations which are the result of extra iteration are
compensated due to the removal of one of unparalleled sectors of the program.
After a number of modifications the obtained efficiency of parallel calculation
realization is presented in Table 3. These results, though satisfactory, are considered to be preliminary, and there exist possibilities to raise the paralleling
efficiency with the increase of a number of processor elements.

7 Problems of simulating processes of radiation excitation of electromagnetic fields

Efficient methods of solving multi-dimensional equations of electrodynamics
can only be developed with the account of peculiarities of solutions' structure
of such problems [15] . They include, first, the significantly different scales
of processes both in space and in time. In particular, with the generation of
electromagnetic fields there arise the propagating boundary layers whose characteristic spatial and time parameters are four-five orders of magnitude smaller
than the size of the domain being calculated. In these problems, as in the gas
dynamics problems considered above, the numerical algorithms should necessarily be adapted to structural peculiarities of solutions, for instance, to point
out the main discontinuities, the adjust grids taking into account appearance
of solution domains with larger gradients.

When constructing a numerical solution in such problems it is necessary
to perform great amount of numerical work. Therefore it is necessary to use
multiprocessor computers in this case.

The initial sequential algorithm of numerical integration is constructed on
the basis of decomposition by spatial variables of the differential operator in
Maxwell equations. This allows one to represent the initial domain of solution
(t is time, r is radius, f is a polar angle) in the form of a set of planes t, r
($f = f_i, i = 1, \cdots$).

The solution is obtained at a subsequent time layer by some technique which
is explicit in each plane t, r (of the "travelling calculation" type) and implicit
by the variable f. The domain of the solution at each time step is located
within $0 < r < r_{max}$. For $r = r_{max}$ the external boundary condition is imposed.
Such a structure of numerical algorithm determines the "local' dependence
of the sought-for solutions upon those obtained in the nearest points of the
grid in each of the planes t, r. This makes it possible to partition calculations
with the minimal changes of the initial algorithm. Paralleling is realized by
partitioning the numerical domain into subdomains which are spherical layers
by the variable r, each of them being calculated by one processor element.
Information exchange between them is realized via the values of the sought-for
variables at the grid points, adjacent to the partition boundary. The number
of processor elements and, hence, the number of layers is a parameter whose
selection determines the optimization of paralleling. The obtained results are
presented in Table 4.

They confirm high efficiency of paralleling the calculations within the approach used. It should be noted that these results are to a great extent determined by homogeneity of numerical formulae and the simplicity of boundary conditions. The obtained results give us the hope that the approach of using parallel algorithms when solving the problems of electrodynamics will turn out to be efficient enough.

8 The problems of nonlinear, nonstationary particle and radiation transfer taking into account their interaction with environment

For the mathematical simulation of processes mentioned in the title and typical for the plasma physics the SND methods were developed and the complex of programs to realize it for various types of computers with the sequential information processing [16]. The obtained system of integral differential equations which describes these processes is very complicated, and we will not go into details. Note that when constructing a numerical model the technique of "splitting by physical processes" was used, see above. The algorithm of calculating each physical process is based on the finite difference approximation of the corresponding differential operator and is performed by the step-by-step transfer by the time variable. The solution of the corresponding systems of finite difference equations on a grid is realized by the explicit or implicit technique, the type of the initial operator being taken into account. The results of solving some basic problems of nonlinear, non-stationary particle and radiation transfer, taking into account their interaction with the environment, are presented in Tables 5,6. As follows from the tables, with the increase of the processor elements number soon enough there arises the situation when the paralleling efficiency considerably lowers. Besides the reasons mentioned above, it is possible that this is due to the reduction of numerical work upon a processor element with the increase of their number.

9 The problems of decoding and simulation of spatial structures of biomacromolecules

Biochemical properties of such biological macromolecules as proteins and nuclein acids (DNA, RNA) are to a greater extent determined by their spatial configuration than by their chemical composition. To obtain the spatial structure of these molecules is one of the fundamental problems of molecular biology. Lately, computer techniques of investigation gained great popularity.

Most of the computer methods of obtaining spatial structures of biomolecules are based on the search of global or local minimums of biomolecules free energy (the free energy of biomolecules is determined by its spatial shape and the initial structure). The main difficulties one comes across is a great amount of calculations which rapidly increases with the growth of a molecule, and a large number of local minimums among which it is necessary to select that corresponding to the actual spatial configuration. The approach being described was developed in papers [17,18] and implies the construction and use of models of processes of appearance and growth of biomolecules in a live cell (the simulation of the step-by-step growth of a chain with the simultaneous spatial reconstruction of its structure). Within this approach the simulation of structure forming processes during sequential growth, on the one hand, results in the significant decrease of the number of appearing locally stable configurations, and, on the other hand, it turned out to be more economical from the viewpoint of numerical work. Nowadays this approach is widely recognized. However, in Russia, due to the absence of the corresponding computer means, the calculations on the structure decoding may be conducted but within certain limits. The samples of MBC-100 of Gflops performance being created, the possibility of realizing the calculation was analyzed. It turned out that the developed mathematical models of describing structure forming admit efficient paralleling. This made it possible to perform calculations on the samples of MBC- 100. Let us estimate the amount of numerical calculations when realizing this mathematical model. Let M be a number of nucleotides in a molecular chain ($M = 10^3 \div 10^4$). The time of calculating a new structure t_e grows linearly with the length of the chain. The time spent to item-by-item examination of possible structures at one step $ns = KM^2$. Hence the total time spent at the step $t_t = t_e \times ns = KM^3$. If we use a system with N processors, then the time of calculations is reduced by N, but there arise losses concerning the data transfer among the processors. Thus, the total time of calculations in the parallel algorithm may be estimated to be $t_p = \frac{KM^3}{N} + K^2 M N$. If we put the paralleling efficiency to be $E = \frac{t_p}{t_t}$, then we obtain $E = Y_n + \frac{K^2 N}{M^2}$. It is clear that with the growth of the molecular chain (M) the efficiency tends to $\frac{1}{N}$, i.e. to the maximal theoretically possible. Therefore, in the case of the proposed approach it is advantageous to simulate structure forming of long molecules at parallel systems. This is correlated with the fact that the structure of just long molecules is most difficult to be decoded by other techniques. The measured (averaged by a considerable number of variants) paralleling efficiency at 16 processor elements makes $E = \frac{1}{12}$ (instead of the maximal one equal to $\frac{1}{16}$).

The created program complex to investigate the process of structure forming of biological macromolecules was adapted for the samples of MBC-100 and is nowadays used to investigate the important class of molecules, the so-called RNA-ferments.

Table 1. The problems of aerodynamics

N	1	3	7	11
K	100	97.7	81.7	77.

Table 2. The problem of two-dimensional gas dynamics
**   with heat transfer.**

N	1	4	8	12	16	20	24
K	100	95.	93.8	89.2	86.3	85.	81.2

Table 3. Neutron-physical problems.

N	1	2	4	8	16
K	100	96.4	96.7	85.9	49.8

Table 4. The problems of electrodynamics in eigentime.

N	1	2	4	8
K	100	98.	97.	93.

Table 5. The problem of calculating a thermal wave
**   via the ionization of plasma particles by electrons.**

N	1	3	4	6	8	12
K	100	59.	48.	36.	34.	30.

Table 6. The problem of calculating the interaction of laser
**   radiation with target substance.**

N	1	3	4	6	8	12
K	100	49.	41.	36.	29.	20.

Denotations

$K = \frac{t_1}{(t_N N)} 100\%$, where

t_1 is the time of solving the problem at one processor;

t_N is the time of solving the problem at N processors;

N is the number of processors.

References

1. A.N.Andrianov, K.I.Babenko, A.V.Zabrodin, I.B.Zadykhailo, E.I.Kotov, A.N.Myamlin, N.V.Podderyugina, L.A.Pozdnyakov. On the structure of a computer to solve flow problems. Complex approach to design. Moscow, Nauka, 1985, "Vychislitel'nye processy i sistemy", vyp. 2, pp. 13-62, ed. G.I.Marchuk.

2. Theoretical Foundations and Design of Numerical Algorithms of the Mathematical Physics Problems. Moscow, Nauka, 1979. Ed. K.I.Babenko.

3. A.V.Zabrodin, I.D.Sofronov, N.N.Chentsov. Adaptive difference techniques of mathematical simulation of non- stationary gas - dynamics flows (Review). Voprosy atomnoi nauki i tekhniki. Series: Methods and Programs of numerical solution of the mathematical physics problems. 1988, vyp. 4, pp. 3-22.

4. A.V.Zabrodin. On the problems of numerical silumation of gas-dynamics flows with complex structure, pp. 18-32. Konstruirovanije algorytmov i reshenije zadach matematicheskoi fiziki. Sbornik nauchnykh trudov, Keldysh Institute for Applied mathematics, 1987.

5. G.P.Voskresenskij, A.V.Zabrodin. The problems of numerical simulation of the supersonic spatial flow and the problems of mapping algorithms upon the computer architecture. Preprint N 83, Moscow, Keldysh Institute of Applied Mathematics, 1986.

6. A.V.Zabrodin, A.N.Myamlin, E.I.Kotov, L.A.Pozdnyakov. The structure of the array computer system CMC-14, and the concept of creating a number of computers on common basis. Preprint N 134, Keldysh Institute of Applied Mathematics, 1990.

7. I.N.Bukreev, A.V.Zabrodin, V.K.Levin.Computer systems with mass paralleling: state of affairs and perspectives. vestnik Rossijskogo obshchestva informatiki i vychislitel'noj tekhniki, N 3, 1994. Moscow, VIMI.

8. A.Yu.Gridin, B.G.Efimov, A.V.Zabrodin et al. Calculation and experimental investiggation of supersonic flow of a dulled body with a needle in the presence of electric charge in its front part. Preprint N 19. Moscow, Keldysh Institute of Applied Mathematics, 1995.

9. M.D.Brodetskij, L.G.Vasenyov, E.K.Derunov, A.V.Zabrodin et al. Specific character and perspectives of using multiprocessor supercomputers in the calculation and experimental investigation of complex gas-dynamics flows. Teplofizika i aeromekhanika, SO RAN, 1995 (to appear).

10. A.V.Gusev, V.T.Zhukov, A.V.Zabrodin, A.O.Latsis, A.E.Lutskij, I.L.Petrushenkov, L.A.Pozdnyakov, O.B.Feodoritova. Solving the problems of gas dynamics and aerodynamics on parallel computers. Voprosy atomnoj nauki i tekhniki, Series: Mathematical simulation of physical processes. Vyp. 2, 1993, pp. 44-54.

11. V.T.Zhukov, A.V.Zabrodin, O.B.Feodoritova. A method of solving two-dimensional equations of the heat-transfer gas in the domains of complicated shape. ZhVM i MF, Moscow, t.33, 1993.

12. A.V.Voronkov, M.V.Maslennikov. On a mathemtical model of neutron-physical processes in the nuclear reactor. Sbornik "Sovremennye problemy matematicheskoij fiziki i vychislitel'noj matematiki. Moscow, Nauka, 1982.

13. Reactor Program System For Neutron Physical Calculation. Advances in Mathematics, Computation and Reactor Physics, Pittsburg, PA, USA, 1991.

14. A.N.Chebeskov, I.V.Krivitskij, G.V.Matveev, Y.N.Miranivich, A.V.Voronkov, E.P.Sychugova, A.D.Knipe. Low reactivity sodium-void benchmark study in an

angular heterogeneous assembly. International Topical Meeting, Obninsk, Russia, October 3-7, 1994.

15. G.D.Vasil'kov, M.E.Zhukovskij, V.P.Zagonov, E.G.Lukjanova. Creation of parallel algorithms to numerically solve the electrodynamics problems in eigentime. Preprint N 87, Keldysh Institute of Applied Mathematics, 1994.

16. G.V..Dolgolyova. Methods of calculating the motion of a bi-temperature radiating gas. Voprosy atomnoi nauki i tekhniki. Series: Methods and programs of numerical solving of the mathematical physics problems, 1983, vyp. 2(13), pp. 29-33.

17. N.I.Kozlov, B.I.Kugushev. Doklady Akademii Nauk, 1992, t.324, N 1, pp. 200-205.

18. B.I.Kugushev, N.N.Kozlov. Computer simulation of structurizing properties of plus- and minus - chains of DNA encoding SSp RNA and t RNA Doklady Akademii Nauk, t.33, N 1 (Biochemistry, Biophysics, Molecular Biology).

19. V.L.Gasilov, N.N.Krasovskij, Yu.S.Osipov. The problem of raising accuracy of moving objects navigation. Trudy Vsesoyuznoj shkoly po problemam matematicheskogo obespecheniya i arkhitektury bortovykh vychislitel'nykh sistem. Tashkent, 1988.

20. V.L.Gasilov, A.P.Kukushkin. Simulation of a controlled Lagrangian system on a parallel computer net. Tezisy dokladov konferentsii "Transputer systems and their applications". Domodedovo, 1994.

21. V.L.Gasilov, V.B.Kostousov. The identification of a moving object problem on the basis of processing the picture of the external information field. Izvestiya RAN. Technicheskaya kibernetika N 3, 1994.

22. N.N.Yanenko. The method of fractional steps of solving multidimensional problems of mathematical physics. Novosibirsk, Nauka, 1967.

23. A.I.Blinov, A.V.Gusev, A.E.Lutskij, I.L.Petrushenkov. Numerical investigations of the effect of a supersonic transport aircraft composition upon its aerodynamic parameters. Preprint N 105, Keldysh Institute of Applied Mathematics, 1990.

24. A.V.Gusev, A.E.Lutskij, I.L.Petrushenkov. Application of multiprocessor systems in aerodynamic designing of aircraft. voprosy atomnoi nauki i tekhniki. Series: Mathematical simulation of physical processes. 1992, vyp. 3, pp. 11-14.

25. E.I.Zababakhin, I.E.Zababakhin. Phenomena of unbounded cumulation. Moscow, Nauka, 1988.

26. V.O.Lokutsievskij, O.V.Lokutsievskij. Application of Chebyshev parameters for the numerical solution of some evolutionary problems. Preprint N 99. Moscow, Keldysh Institute of Applied Mathematics, 1988.

27. V.T.Zhukov. Difference techniques of local iterations for parabolic equations. Preprint N 183, Keldysh Institute of Applied Mathematics, 1986.

DFS-SuperMPx: Low-cost Parallel Processing System for Machine Vision and Image Processing

Vason P. Srini

Data Flux Systems Inc.
30 Kameha Way, Box. 141
Dillon Beach, CA 94929
Tele: 510-527-7183

ABSTRACT

The architecture of a low-cost hosted MIMD parallel processing system containing parallel processor chips interconnected by a hierarchy of crossbars is described. The parallel processing system is attached to the system bus of the host and uses the operating system and programming environment of the host. Each parallel processor chip contains 64 processors. The processors in a chip are simple in their architecture and structured so that data streams can be processed efficiently using dataflow semantics. A static dataflow model of computation is assumed for programming the chip. Arithmetic, logical, multiply, conditional branch, and select instructions are supported. Each processor has a 16-bit data path and a microcontroller. The processors in a chip are clustered for reducing data communication latency time. Eight processors are grouped into a cluster and there are eight clusters in a chip. Segmented and switched buses are used for intra and inter cluster communication in a chip. A global bus is provided for supplying instructions to the processors during program setup and to communicate the status of the processors during program execution. Two global buses are provided for data transfer between the external memory or I/O devices and the data memories of the processors. Each chip has two ports with 16 bits of data, 16 bits for processor address, and control signals for connecting to other chips using a hierarchical crossbar interconnection network. The interconnection network is based on a 16 X 16 crossbar chip with 32 ports (16 paths) capable of connecting 16 processor chips or 15 processor chips and a second level of crossbar chip. With two levels of crossbar chips it is possible to connect 225 parallel processor chips and achieve one Teraop in a shoebox sized system. The applications selected for the parallel processing system are image processing, machine vision, video compression and decompression, and 3-D imaging.

1. Introduction

Reconfigurable hardware elements such as Xilinx's SRAM based FPGAs have pretty much replaced SSI and MSI level TTL logic chips in the hardware of computer and communications systems. In a similar manner, reconfigurable parallel processor chips are proposed as a replacement for many of the ASIC chips in the computer and communication systems and the implementation of DSP algorithms in image processing, multimedia data communication, video compression and decompression, and 3-D medical imaging. The flexibility and programmability provided by these low-cost parallel processor chips can offset some of the performance gains obtained by expensive ASIC chips. Rapid prototyping of application specific systems can be carried out using these parallel processor chips.

This paper describes the architecture of a low-cost parallel processing system that can be used as an accelerator for image processing, realtime video compression and decompression, and machine vision applications. The parallel processing system is a hosted MIMD system containing parallel processor chips interconnected by a hierarchy of crossbars. The parallel processing system is attached to a workstation (host). The host operating system and programming environments are used to program the parallel processing system. The parallel processing system has a 32-bit address space (byte addressed) called pixel space and a 32-bit instruction address space (byte addressed). Each frame of a shot, a scene, or a sequence occupies a part of the pixel space. The algorithm for manipulating the pixels uses a part of the instruction address space. All addresses are physical addresses in the parallel processing system. A single application can run on the parallel system at any particular time. Multiple applications are supported by partitioning the pixel and instruction address spaces and using software to reconfigure the system and load the desired pixel and instruction spaces. The function of the parallel processing system is to manipulate the data in the pixel space according to the programs specified by the users and deliver the results.

A block diagram of the parallel processing system with interface to a SPARCstation host is shown in Figure 1. The system comprises two modules, an interface module and a parallel processing subsystem module. The interface module decodes NTSC/PAL analog video and digitizes pixels, supplies digitized pixel data to the parallel processing subsystem module, receives digitized pixel data from the parallel processing subsystem module, encodes digital data to NTSC/PAL format, and supports data communication with the SBus of SPARCstation. The SPARCstation and the SBus can be replaced by a Pentium based PC and PCI bus using appropriate bus interface chips.

The parallel processing subsystem module contains parallel processor chips, instruction and data buses, and crossbar chips forming the interconnection network. A hierarchical crossbar with 32 ports (16 paths) in each crossbar chip is selected because of the low-latency and high bandwidth communication of data. With two levels of crossbar chips it is possible to connect 225 parallel processor chips in a subsystem module.

Each low-cost parallel processor chip (LPC) contains 64 processors. The processors in a chip are simple in their architecture compared to a RISC processor such as MIPS-R3000. Arithmetic, logical, multiply, conditional branch, select, and deliver result instructions are supported. Each processor has a 16-bit data path and a microcontroller. The 16-bit data path is motivated by the 16-bit YCrCb color space for digitized pixels. A small instruction memory allowing 16 single word instructions to be stored, a small data buffer with capacity for 128 words (16 bits per word), and internal registers are also contained in a processor. Each processor also has a 16-bit identifier and a 16-bit processor identifier (PID) register. A maximum of 64 K processors is planned for the system. The processors in an LPC are designed so that data streams can be processed efficiently using dataflow semantics. An instruction is executed when its operands are ready.

The processors in a chip are clustered for reducing data communication latency time. Eight processors are grouped into a cluster and there are eight clusters in a chip. Segmented and switched buses are used for intra and inter cluster communication in a chip. A 16-bit global bus (GIS) is provided for supplying instructions to the processors during program setup and to communicate the status of the processors during program execution. All the LPCs forming a parallel processing system are connected to GIS. Two 16-bit global buses (GD1 and GD2) are provided for data transfers between an external memory or video I/O devices and the data memories of the processors. All the LPCs are also connected to GD1 and GD2. All three buses are also interfaced to the system bus of the host allowing data communication between the LPCs or video I/O devices and the host.

Each LPC has two ports for connecting to other LPCs using a crossbar interconnection network. Each port has 16 bits for data, 16 bits for processor address, and control signals. Interface logic for crossbar connection setup and address filtering is

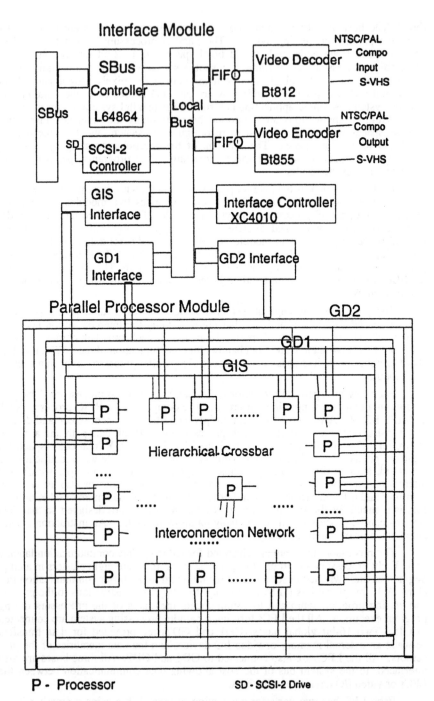

Figure 1   Block Diagram of the Parallel System

included as a part of the two ports. The crossbar network is based on a 16 X 16 crossbar chip with 32 ports. Each processor uses two ports to connect to a crossbar chip. If only 16 LPCs are used in a system then a single crossbar chip in enough to form the interconnection network. A hierarchy of crossbars is needed to connect more than 16 LPCs. Using a two level tree with 16 crossbar chips it is possible to connect 225 LPCs in a system.

A static dataflow model of computation is used for programming the parallel processing system. Many algorithms in image processing, machine vision, and video compression can be expressed using the dataflow graphs. The nodes in a dataflow graph representing an image processing algorithm are clustered to form an intermediate dataflow graph with coarse grained nodes. The coarse grained nodes are assigned to the processors in an LPC. The arcs in dataflow graphs carry tokens in a stream. The arcs are represented by the input and output registers in the processors and the interconnection between the processors. Synchronization is done in hardware using the dataflow semantics. If operands are available to an operation and results can be forwarded then the operation is done. Otherwise, the operation is in a pending state until resources become available. This simple approach makes programming easier.

The intended applications of the parallel processing system are in image processing, machine vision, video compression and decompression, and 3-D imaging. Most of these applications require operations to be performed on a stream of data coming from a video camera, digitizing CAT scanners, or digitizing X-ray units. There is also locality of data in the computations since algorithms such as filtering, convolution, and transforms depend on von Neumann (four neighbor) or Moore (eight neighbors) neighborhoods. To accommodate a large class of applications, a flexible interconnection network such as the crossbar is used for connecting the LPCs.

The LPC and a crossbar chip (16 X 16) form the core of the systems architecture. The processing element of an LPC is described in Section 2. The interconnection networks used in an LPC to support the communication between 64 processors in a chip is described in Section 3. The system level interconnection network using crossbars is described in Section 4. The interface between the parallel processing system and the host is discussed in Section 5. The programming environment for the parallel processing system is described in Section 6 using the X window system and the Ptolemy framework of University of California, Berkeley. Some of the implementation issues and other uses of LPC are included in Section 7. Related research activities at other places in the development of parallel DSPs is discussed in Section 8.

2. Architecture of a Processor in LPC

The low-cost parallel processor chip (LPC) contains 64 identical processors with a 16-bit data path. The 16-bit data path was chosen to support 16-bit color images and motion video in YCrCb format, audio coding and decoding, and 3-D medical image processing. The operations present in image processing, video processing, and 3-D imaging algorithms are gathered to form operator statistics. By using a 10% rule, architecture support for different operations such as add/sub, shift, comparisons, multiply, and multiply accumulate are determined. The relationships between different operations in the algorithms are determined to form interconnect statistics. The type of control structure required for each algorithm is also determined. Some examples are pipeline, loop, and multiway branches. Control statistics for the algorithms are gathered. The sampling rates used in the different algorithms are gathered to determine I/O statistics. The computation rates for the different algorithms are calculated using the total number of operations and the clock rate. The above statistics are used to determine the components of the processor and the instruction set. The design tools used are Alchemy instruction set generator [1] to determine the instructions needed in a processor, and Hyper Synthesis and Analysis system [234] to estimate area, power, and performance of potential chip implementations. A block diagram of the LPC is shown in Figure 2. The three global buses, GIS, GD1, and GD2 are shown connecting the processors. Each cluster of processors has cluster buses for communicating data between the processors. The details of the processor architecture are described in this section.

The processor architecture uses dataflow semantics for the execution of instructions [5] since most DSP algorithms have a natural dataflow representation. This observation has been used by Array Microsystems [67] in the chip set design for video compression. Array Microsystems has crafted an image compression coprocessor (ICC) and a motion estimation coprocessor (MEC) that combines limited programmability and high performance for the compression and decompression of JPEG, MPEG, and H.261 video standards. The ICC uses a data flow architecture. The data flow control unit passes instructions and data over a 96-bit global bus. All of the subprocessors of the chip can potentially operate in parallel. The ICC can do forward and inverse DCT, adaptive quantization control, and other functions. The MEC executes custom motion estimation algorithms. The resources on the chip allows two levels of motion estimation searches on full screen images. There are several other DSP algorithms that have been efficiently implemented using dataflow architectures.

General purpose dataflow architectures have been proposed by many groups [5]. However, the performance of these architectures have been limited by communication overhead and by the copying semantics when parts of a data structure are to be updated or by the mechanisms needed to support reference count checking. We avoid the above problems by focusing on DSP applications, image processing, video compression and decompression, and 3-D imaging. The data types allowed are streams of integer, unsigned numbers, fixed point numbers, and strings. We extend the dataflow model of computation by including memory for keeping state information. With this extension it is possible to assign a sequence of instructions (a subgraph of a dataflow graph) to a processor and keep intermediate results in registers or memory and thus reduce communication between processors. In DSP applications, data is in the form of streams and the processors execute the operations assigned to them on the elements of the data stream. A static communication channel between processors representing the arcs in a dataflow graph is sufficient to send and receive data streams between subgraphs. This is supported by buses connecting a processor to its neighbors, buses for receiving and sending data to video and image I/O devices, and buses for receiving programs and sending processor status.

Programmability of the processor requires changing the communication channels between processors and contents of instruction memory so that different DSP algorithms can be executed. Interconnection networks that support reconfiguring the communication channels between processors is used to achieve this. A collection of programmable segmented buses is used for this. A static reconfiguration scheme is supported to reduce the complexity of the interconnection network control. The block diagram of a processor is shown in Figure 3.

The number and types of functional units, number of registers in the register file, instruction size, instruction memory size, data memory size, communication channels to a processor, and controller for the processor are determined based on the analysis of algorithms. Each processor uses a 16-bit word and has one ALU, a register file with 8 registers, an instruction memory for storing 16 words, a data memory with 128 words, and communication units for sending and receiving data from three global buses, GIS, GD1, and GD2. The register file is provided for communicating data between processors and to store frequently used data or constants. In addition, there are internal registers for supporting the instruction set architecture (ISA). These internal registers are available to system programs and not application programs. Each processor has an identification number (PID) register and a processor status word (PSW) register that are 16 bits long. PID values are given at setup time by

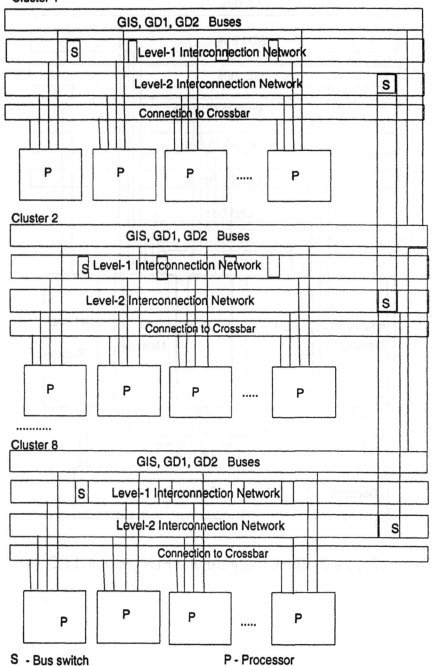

Figure 2 Block Diagram of LPC   with 64 Processors

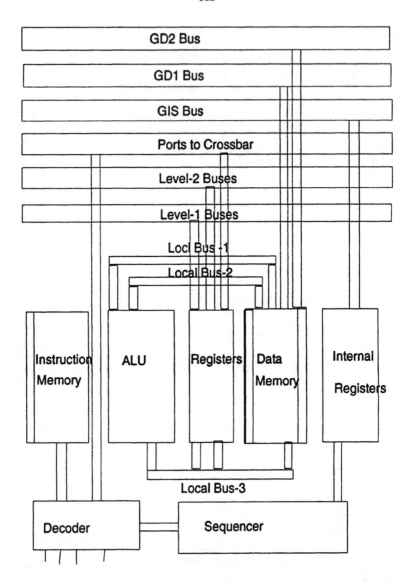

Figure 3 Block Diagram of a Processor in LPC

software and can be reassigned by software during reconfiguration to put out of commission faulty processors. There are two 32-bit registers specifying the starting address of the pixel address space assigned to the data memory of the processor (DCBR) and the starting address of the instruction address space assigned to the processor (ICBR). The number of words to be captured in the data memory (NDR - 7 bits), and the number of instructions to be captured in the instruction memory (NIR - 4 bits) are specified in the registers NDR and NIR. The data memory has four banks with 32 words in each to support applications with a maximum of four algorithms each taking not more than 16 words in the instruction address space. The current bank register (CBR) contains the bank number for the active bank. Each bank corresponds to a context. An application can have four different algorithms and the data belonging to the four algorithms can reside simultaneously in the processors using the four contexts.

Most of the instructions are 16 bits long and there are four formats corresponding to ALU operations, conditionals, register file oriented operations and internal data forwarding to other processors. Data delivery to other LPCs over the interconnection network and loading data from other LPCs are supported by two words long instructions (32 bits). The fields of the ALU operations instructions are opcode (4 bits), context (2 bits), source1 operand offset (5 bits) in data memory, and source2/destination operand offset (5 bits) in data memory. The fields of the conditional instructions are opcode (4 bits), conditions to check for (3 bits), relative or absolute (1 bit), target2 address (4 bits), and target3 address (4 bits). The instructions for data forwarding to other processors in the same chip have the following fields: opcode (4 bits), cluster number (3 bits), processor number in a cluster (3 bits), and offset to data memory (5 bits) where data is to be placed. Loading data from other LPCs and delivering data to other LPCs is performed using instructions that are two words long. One word is taken up by the 16-bit PID for the processor from where data is to be loaded or the processor to which data is to be delivered. The fields of the second word are: opcode (4 bits), offset to data memory (5 bits), context (2 bits), and offset to data memory (5 bits) of the sending (receiving) processor.

The controller for each processor has a sequencer, a program counter, logic for receiving and sending data over buses, and initializing the processor on power up and during reconfiguration..

3. LPC Level Interconnection Network

The chip level interconnection network provides connection between the 64 processors on a chip and the interface to the external environment for doing I/O, program loading, and status communication. Since interconnects are area and power intensive, it is important to keep them simple. The nature of DSP algorithms implies a static connection between nodes in a dataflow graph. This can be achieved by point to point connections. However, programmability dictates changing the connections between processors when a different algorithm is to be implemented on the parallel processing system. What is needed is a configurable point to point connection between processors.

Chen [8] has analyzed a class of DSP algorithms and counted the connectivity of different operations in each algorithm. The results show that point to point connections are dominant (70%) and connections from a single source to two destinations (1:2) occur 15% of the time. The algorithms discussed in this paper are analyzed to determine the 1:n connectivity where $1 <= n < 6$ and m:1 connectivity, here $1 <= m < 4$. The results of the analysis show that the number of connections needed between processors is two to four..

The interconnection network used in the LPC is a collection of segmented-switched buses for data communication between processors. In addition, a global bus

(GIS) is provided for supplying instructions to the processors during program setup and to communicate status of the processors during program execution. Two global buses (GD1 and GD2) are also provided for data transfer between the external environment (I/O) and the data memories of the processors. A two level cluster based interconnection network is used for data communication between 64 processors. Each group of eight processors in the chip is treated as a cluster and the connections between these processors is called level-1 network. The eight clusters in a chip are connected by level-2 network. The level-1 network has four buses with eight segments in each bus. The programmable switches are set during setup time and retain the setting until changed. The switches are not expected to be changed often and hence power consumption will not be a problem. Although switched buses have been proposed by other researchers [9] for DSP architectures, the design and implementation proposed in this work uses area efficient approaches. Another difference is that I/O and instruction communication are accomplished by using global buses. The width of the buses are 16 bits. The level-2 interconnection network has four buses with eight segments, one per cluster. Each segment can be used to communicate data to processors in a cluster or to other clusters using one or more switches.

Some of the results from the design and fabrication of PADDI-1 [8] and PADDI-II [10] are used in the design of the interconnection networks and switches. Area efficient switch cells are designed for connecting or disconnecting bus segments. Routing the buses are done using a separate metal layer. Based on the experience with the routing of 11 buses that are 32-bits wide in a commercial quality Prolog microprocessor [11], we expect to have the level-1 and level-2 interconnection networks and the global buses routed on two metal layers using 0.5 micron technology and a die size of 16 mm X 16 mm.

4. Crossbar Interconnection Network

A key component of the low-cost parallel processing system is the interconnection network between LPCs. To support a large number of LPCs in a parallel system, a hierarchical crossbar network is selected to provide high bandwidth communication between parallel processor chips. To implement the interconnection network, a 16 X 16 crossbar chip with low latency is designed.

Bandwidth and latency of an interconnection network are two significant factors that influence the performance of a parallel system. For example, doubling the data path width between the processors can potentially double the data available to a processor for a load instruction. This may result in fewer loads and increase performance. Reducing the latency in the interconnection network reduces the data movement time, which may in turn improve the effectiveness of the system. Our goal is to design an interconnection network that will be inexpensive and fast. Since the communication pattern between processors is known at compile time for DSP applications and they do not change randomly on a cycle by cycle basis, efficient crossbar switch designs are possible. The crossbar selected for use in the parallel systems is a 16 X 16 crossbar. The crossbar can connect 16 processors using 16 paths (32 ports). Each path is 16 bits wide. The crossbar has low latency, i.e., 10 ns of delay using a 0.5 micron static CMOS technology. The switch setup of the crossbar takes 16 basic cycles to load the 16 address control registers. The details of the crossbar are described below.

Although crossbars have been in use in computer systems [121314], they do not meet our bandwidth and latency requirements. The crossbar switch connections are static and do not permit changing them dynamically. A dynamic crossbar with low latency for changing switch settings is needed. A crossbar chip for connecting 16 processors has been developed [15]. The switch connection in the crossbar can change every cycle based on requests from the processors. Such crossbar switches are useful in general purpose multiprocessor systems.

In this work, a crossbar switch that can be efficiently implemented using CMOS VLSI technology is presented. Since the connections of the crossbar need not change every cycle due to he nature of DSP applications, an area efficient design is possible. The crossbar design has five components: decoder, arbiter, crosspoint matrix, input drivers, and output drivers. The design details of each component are now described. The decoder receives a 4-bit destination processor address and a request signal from each of the 16 input ports. These addresses are stored in decode registers if there are no conflicts i.e. two processors are not wanting to communicate with the same processor. In the event of a conflict, the addresses are stored in a buffer and processed by the arbiter. The arbiter selects one of the processors for communication on an output port at any time. To prevent a single processor from holding up a destination processor while others are waiting for the same processor, a fairness scheme is introduced in arbitration.

The crosspoint matrix component connects the 16 processors to each other using 256 switches. Each switch is a combinational logic block comprising a four input NAND gate and a tri-state driver connected to a bus. 16 of these switches are connected to a bus forming a 16-to-1 multiplexer. The signals entering the crossbar from the processors are directed to various components using drivers. The read, write, address, and data signals are sent using drivers. These signals first go to output pads and are then connected to the processors. The connection between the ports of the crossbar can be setup in a few cycles. The connection is retained until reconfigured.

5. Host Interface

The interface between the parallel processing system and the host computer comprises the interface module shown in Figure 1 and device driver programs. The parallel processing system is treated as an SBus device by the SPARCstation host running Unix operating system. Each SBus device gets 32 MBytes of address space in the Unix process address space. The pixel address space and the instruction address space of the parallel processing system has to be mapped to this 32 MBytes of SBus address space when communicating with the host.

The video data from cameras, VCRs, Laser Disks, TV tuners, and Cable receivers enter the interface module through the video decoder input. The analog data is converted to YCrCb color space, digitized, and supplied to a FIFO by the video decoder. The initial design uses a Bt812 chip and filters to do the video decoding. The digitized data is put on the local bus using a FIFO and supplied to the parallel processor module using the GD1 and GD2 bus interfaces. The interface controller generates the necessary pixel space addresses based on the line number in a field and the number of a field in a shot. The digitized video data can be optionally stored in a disk or a RAID system using the SCSI-2 controller. The instructions for the parallel processing system are supplied by the host using the SBus. This data is communicated from the SBus to the local bus using the SBus controller and to the GIS bus using the interface controller.

Processed data from the parallel processor module can be stored in disk or supplied to a video encoder for displaying on a TV monitor or recorded in a VCR. The initial design for the video encoder uses a Brook Tree Bt855 chip and reconstruction filters. The interface controller is responsible for setting up the control registers of the video encoder, video decoder, SBus controller, bus interfaces, and the LPCs. The storing of incoming images or processed images without using the host's disk drives and SBus is supported by the SCSI-2 controller connected to the local bus. The interface controller manages the simultaneous transfer of data to the disk drives connected to the SCSI-2 controller and the GD1 and GD2 buses of the parallel processing system. The interface takes up one SBus card (7.5 mm X 12.5 mm).

6. Programming Environment

The programming environment for the parallel processing system is divided into two parts, applications programming and systems programming. It runs on the host using the file system and the X windowing system. Since most of the DSP applications can be expressed in dataflow like graphs, a graphical user interface (GUI) that supports block diagram descriptions is desired. The University of California, Berkeley (UCB) has developed a framework for simulation, modeling, and code generation, called Ptolemy [1617], with a GUI that supports block diagram descriptions. The blocks in the diagram are represented by C++ programs describing their functionality. The block diagram can be simulated by running the C++ models under the Ptolemy environment. By replacing the functionality by a code generation module in the C++ programs, Ptolemy can generate code for the blocks in C or the assembly language of a parallel processor. The generated assembly language code code can be run on the parallel processor. The Ptolemy framework is used to develop DSP applications and generate code for the parallel processing system. An LPC domain is under development for Ptolemy to generate code for the parallel processing system based on LPCs. The Ptolemy system runs on the host and the generated code will be loaded to the processors in the parallel processing system using the interface module.

The systems programming environment is the Unix system of the host, C programming language, assembler and loader for the parallel processing system, a reconfiguration routine and a diagnostic routine. The parallel system can be initialized and diagnosed using the diagnostic routine. It can be reconfigured by deactivating faulty processors in the clusters of LPCs using the reconfiguration routine.

7. Implementation Issues

Some of the challenges in implementing the architecture of the parallel processing system using VLSI chips is described in this section. The 64 processor LPC requires a minimum of four layers of metal to support the many buses of the architecture. Level-1 and Level-2 segmented buses are routed in one layer of metal. The global buses are routed using one layer of metal. The port connections and local buses are routed on one layer of metal. To reduce the power dissipation in the bus wires, the data dependent logic swing internal bus architecture proposed by Hitachi researchers [18] is used. The CMOS level logic swings is replaced by a reduced swing based on the number of bits in a bus. Area efficient multiported register files and data memory are needed in each processor. The goal is to keep the die area needed for a processor under 2 X 2 sq. mm using 0.5 micron CMOS process. The estimated area for an LPC is 16 X 16 sq. mm and power dissipation is 2 watts using 3V power supply. The estimated speed for the LPC is 80 MHz and performance is 5.12 GOPS.

The crossbar chip is expected to need more than 1000 pins to connect 16 processors. The pinout problem will be handled by using ball grid area packages and area pads in the design. The availability of multiple layers of metal is expected to help the routing of the data buses through the chip. The estimated area for the chip is 14 mm X 14 mm using 0.5 micron CMOS technology.

A modular approach will be used in building the parallel processing system. The mother board will contain a row of sixteen 300 pin (split into two 150 pin groups) connectors, a crossbar chip, and wiring that connects the crossbar ports on the connectors to the crossbar chip. An ISA size PC board containing 15 LPCs, one crossbar chip, and bus drivers can be connected to each of the 16 connectors on the mother board. A maximum of 15 such boards can be connected on a mother board. The 16-th board is a crossbar interface unit that has an external cable connector for joining the mother board to the next level of crossbar chips. The ISA sized boards of the parallel processing system have connectors at the bottom that allow connections to GD1, GD2, GIS buses and two ports of a crossbar. It is estimated that a 20 cm X

15 cm X 40 cm card cage will house the mother board, 15 processor boards, one crossbar interface unit, power supply, and a cooling fan. One such card cage will have the peak performance of one Teraop and has the memory to process in realtime a frame of HDTV.

LPCs can also be placed on the mother board of PCs to implement dedicated applications such as image enhancement and manipulation (e.g. Adobe's Photoshop program), desktop conferencing, composite edge detection, motion video compression and decompression, and 3-D image processing. PC and workstation hosted parallel processing systems are useful in industrial environments such as the monitoring of robot activities in factories, desktop conferencing among foremen and production staff in plants, medical imaging, training, maintenance of equipment with expert advice from remote sites, education, and presentations.

8. Related Research

The parallel processing system described in this paper uses some of the features and ideas that have been proven in other processors. Sky Computer's Skychannel and Shamrock-II modules based on Intel's i860 XR processors and Mercury Computer's parallel processor are two other systems that use crossbar chips to achieve interconnection between processors. The cluster size in the case of Sky is four VLSI processors. The processors used are capable of doing single and double precision floating point calculations and are expensive. Mercury uses a similar scheme. The difference between Sky and Mercury is in the size of the crossbars they use. Skychannel is a packet bus, where data flows as packets. The data packets move at a rate of 320 MBytes/second. The bus uses a split transaction scheme so that processor chips connected to it can operate independently without holding each other up.

The architecture of the processor in LPC uses some of the ideas from PADDI-I [8] and PADDI-II [10]. PADDI-II chip contains 48 processors, two levels of interconnection network, and supports a dataflow like model of computation for digital signal processing (DSP) algorithms. It uses 16-bit buses. It does not support memory for saving state information in the processor.

A DSP chip executes a sequence of instructions of a DSP algorithm. Once a DSP's instruction memory is loaded and started with a data stream, it continues execution until the data stream is finished or a signal is sent to load a new program in the instruction memory. The controller for a DSP can be quite simple compared to a general purpose microprocessor. The parallel processor chip has a very simple controller compared to commercially available DSP's such as TMS 320C40, MC56001, MC96000, and WE DSP32C.

Adaptive Solutions' CNAPS-1064 [19] is a parallel processor in a chip. It contains 64 processors operating in the SIMD mode. Although it can be used for implementing Neural nets, it does not have the communication bandwidth and flexible control to implement some of the image processing, video compression/decompression, and other DSP algorithms.

Three chip sets with parallel processing capability have been in the market for more than a year to do video compression and image processing. They are IIT's vision processor (VP) and vision controller (VC) [20], AT&T's MPEG encoder and decoder [21222324], and Array Microsystems' chip set [67]. C-Cube's CL450 MPEG chip [25] is another chip for video compression but it is not efficient for many complex DSP algorithms.

The IIT's VP contains a SIMD processor, a RISC processor, a command processor, an I/O state machine, 4K word microcode ROM, and memory units. The SIMD processor is effective in the parallel execution of discrete cosine transform (DCT) and its inverse. A macroblock (four luma and two chroma - Cr and Cb blocks) can be processed by the SIMD processor. The MPEG and the H.261

standards use the DCT. The microcode for the JPEG, MPEG, and H.261 standards are stored in the ROM. In addition, special microcode can be supported in external SRAM. By changing the microcode different compression standards can be implemented.

The AT&T's MPEG / H.261 encoder chip contains a SIMD processor with six engines for operating on a macroblock, a quantization processor (QP), host interface (HBI), motion estimator (ME), memory management and algorithm flow control unit (MMAFC), variable length encoder (VLE), videobus interface (VBI), global controller (GC), and FIFOs. Since the chip is targeted for MPEG / H.261 and the control is implemented in hardware and ROM, it is difficult to program the chip for other standards. The AT&T's MPEG / H.261 decoder chip also contains a SIMD processor for doing inverse DCT, a 16-bit RISC processor for assembling run-length coded coefficients into DCT difference blocks and to do other functions, variable length decoder, memory controller, host interface, a 6K X 32-bit ROM, and FIFOs.

Array Microsystems has crafted an image compression coprocessor (ICC) and a motion estimation coprocessor (MEC) that combines limited programmability and high performance for the compression and decompression of JPEG, MPEG, and H.261 standards. Some of the details of ICC and MEC have been described earlier.

Texas Instruments has developed a high speed multimedia video processor (MVP) chip, called TMS 320C80 [26], containing four parallel DSPs, a RISC processor, a crossbar switch, and multiple banks of memory shared by the processors. The chip contains more than four million transistors and has a peak performance of 2 GOPS. It is fabricated using a 0.5 micron CMOS process and expected to sell for $400.

9. Acknowledgement

The discussions with Jan Rabaey, Alfred Yeung, and Arthur Abnous on the details of PADDI-II, and the work with Nelson Chow and Stas Frumkin on the SBus interface board are acknowledged.

References

1. B. K. Holmer and B. M. Pangrle, "Hardware/Software Codesign Using Automated Instruction Set Design and Processor Synthesis," *International Workshop on Hardware-Software Co-Design*, Cambridge, MA, Oct., 1993.

2. J. M. Rabaey, C. Chu, P. Hoang, and M. Potkonjak, "Fast Prototyping of Datapath-Intensive Architectures," *IEEE Design & Test of Computers*, pp. 40 -51, June, 1991.

3. R. Mehra and J. M. Rabaey, "High Level Power Estimation and Exploration," *International Workshop on Low Power Design*, 1994.

4. J. M. Rabaey, "DSP Specification Using the Silage Language," *HYPER: Selected Papers, University of California*, Berkeley, CA 94720, 1993.

5. V. P. Srini, "An Architectural Comparison of Dataflow Systems," *IEEE Computer*, pp. 68-88, March 1986.

6. D. Bursky, "Image-Processing Chip Set Handles Full-Motion Video," *Electronic Design*, pp. 117 - 120, May 3, 1993.

7. Array, "Videoflow, The Magic Behind Multimedia," *Array Microsystems, Product Brochure*, Colorado Springs, CO, July 1993.

8. D. C. Chen, "Programmable Arithmetic Devices for High Speed Digital Signal Processing," *Electronic Research Laboratory, Memorandum No. UCB/ERL M92/49, University of California*, Berkeley, CA 94720, May 14, 1992.

9. M. H. Sunwoo and J. K. Aggarwal, "Flexibly Coupled Multiprocessors for Image Processing," *1988 Intl. Conf. on Parallel Processing*, St. Charles, IL, Aug. 1988.

10. A. K. W. Yeung and J. M. Rabaey, "A Data-Driven Architecture for Rapid Prototyping of High Throughput DSP Algorithms," *VLSI Signal Processing V, Edited by K. Yao, R. Jain, W. Przytula, J. Rabaey, IEEE New York*, pp. 225 - 234, New York, 1992.

11. V. P. Srini, J. V. Tam, T. M. Nguyen, Y. N. Patt, A. M. Despain, M. Moll, and D. Ellsworth, "A CMOS Chip for Prolog," *Proceedings of the International Conference on Computer Design*, pp. 605 - 610, Rye Town, New York, Oct. 1987.

12. Burroughs Corporation, *Burroughs B6700 Reference Manual*, Detroit, Michigan, 1969.

13. W.A. Wulf and C.G. Bell, "C.mmp - A Multi Miniprocessor," *Proceedings of the AFIPS Fall Joint Computer Conference*, Montvale, New Jersey, 1972.

14. W.A. Wulf and S.P. Harbison, "Reflections in a Pool of Processors," *Proceedings of the AFIPS Fall Joint Computer Conference*, Montvale, New Jersey, 1978.

15. V. P. Srini, "Bit-sliced Cross-connect Chip Having a Tree Topology of Arbitration Cells for Connecting Memory Modules to Processors in A Multiprocessor System," *U.S. Patent No. 5,053,942*, October1, 1991.

16. E. A. Lee and D. G. Messerschmitt, "An Overview of the Ptolemy Project," *Technical Report, University of California, EE Dept.*, Berkeley, CA, June, 1992.

17. J. Buck, S. Ha, E. A. Lee, and D. G. Messerschmitt, "Ptolemy: A Framework for Simulating and Prototyping Heterogeneous Systems," *International Journal of Computer Simulation, Special Issue on Simulation software Development*, 1992.

18. M. Hiraki and et al, "Data-Dependent Logic Swing Internal Bus Architecture for Ultralow-Power LSI's," *IEEE Journal of Solid-State Circuits*, vol. 30, no. 4, pp. 397 - 402, April, 1995.

19. AdaptiveSolutions, "CNAPS-1064 Digital Parallel Processor," *Adaptive Solutions Inc. Product Brochure*, Beaverton, OR 97006, Jan. 1994.

20. IIT, "IIT Vision Processor," *IIT VP Data Sheet*, Santa Clara, CA, Nov. 1992.

21. B. D. Ackland and et al, "A Video-Codec Chip Set for Multimedia Applications," *AT&T Technical Journal*, pp. 50 - 66, Jan./Feb. 1993.

22. R. Aravind and et al, "Image and Video Coding Standards," *AT&T Technical Journal*, pp. 67 - 89, Jan./Feb. 1993.

23. S. K. Rao and et al, "A Real-Time P*64/MPEG Video Encoder Chip," *IEEE Solid-State Circuits Conference*, pp. 32 - 33, San Francisco, Feb. 1993.

24. D. Brinthaupt, "A Video Decoder for H.261 Video Teleconferencing and MPEG Stored Interactive Video Applications," *IEEE Solid-State Circuits Conference*, pp. 34 - 35, San Francisco, Feb. 1993.

25. S. Bose, S. Purcell, and T. Chiang, "A Single Chip Multistandard Video Codec," *Symposium Record, Hot Chips V*, Stanford, CA, Aug. 1993.

26. D. Bursky, "Parallelism Pushes DSP Throughput," *Electronic Design*, pp. 151 - 154, March 21, 1994.

Architectural Issues of Distributed Workflow Management Systems

Christoph Bußler, Stefan Jablonski, Thomas Kirsche,
Hans Schuster, Hartmut Wedekind

Dept. of Computer Sciences VI (Database Systems),
University of Erlangen,
Martensstraße 3,
D-91058 Erlangen, Germany

Abstract. A specific task of distributed and parallel Information Systems is workflow management. In particular, workflow management systems execute business processes that run on top of distributed and parallel Information Systems. Parallelism is due to performance requirements and involves data and applications that are spread across a heterogeneous, distributed computing environment. Heterogeneity and distribution of the underlying computing infrastructure should be made transparent in order to alleviate programming and use. We introduce an implementation architecture for workflow management systems that meets best these requirements. Scalability (through transparent parallelism) and transparency with respect to distribution and heterogeneity are the major characteristics of this architecture. A generic client/server class library in an object-oriented environment demonstrates the feasibility of the approach.

1 Introduction

In the area of business process reengineering, technologies for the execution of business processes are needed that can be adjusted flexibly and dynamically to the rapidly changing structure of business processes. Due to their distributed and parallel nature they are enacted by distributed and parallel Information Systems. *Workflow management* (WFM) is aimed at the automation of business processes. We call the executable image of a business process *workflow*. According to [McBl91] *workflow management systems* (WFMS) are characterized as

> "proactive computer systems which manage flow of work among participants, according to a defined procedure consisting of a number of tasks. They coordinate users and systems participants, together with the appropriate data resources [...]. The coordination involves passing tasks from participant to participant in correct sequence, ensuring that all fulfil their required contributions [...]."

Some typical elements of workflows are described in this citation. The example depicted in Fig. 1 gives an idea of how the aspects show up in workflow specifications. From the *functional viewpoint*, the workflows being executed are "Travel Claim Processing", "Submit Travel Claim", "Approve Travel Claim", and "Reimburse Client". The latter three are refinements of the overall travel claim process. Nesting workflows within the workflow "Travel Claim Processing" means that they implement the composite workflow. The ordering between workflows is specified by arrows indicating a *behavioral aspect*. *Organizationally*, the persons who should execute the workflows are attached to the workflows (e.g. client, manager). Data elements being passed between workflows are travel claim (TC) data in this example. Thus, the TCs form the *informational perspective*. Both workflows "Submit Travel Claim" and "Approve Travel Claim" point to the application "Travel Claim System"; the workflow "Reimburse Client" points to the application "Finance Booking System". When executing one of these workflows, the application pointed to is called. Obviously, all workflows can be arbitrarily distributed. Sect. 2 provides a more detailed discussion of the aspects briefly explained here.

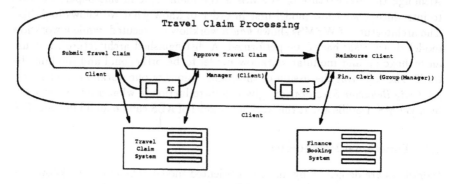

Fig. 1. Travel Claim Processing

WFM comprises of many different tasks which are orchestrated by the (kernel of the) WFMS [BuJa93]: workflows ready for execution have to be determined using control flow structures; human or non-human agents have to be selected for executing the workflows; data needed for workflow execution must be provided; finally, applications – including legacy applications – are called to perform a function.

Workflows are executed in complex enterprises. Therefore, WFMSs are characterized by the following infrastructural requirements and facts:

- WFMSs are large scale systems. They have to handle huge numbers of workflow types, instances, users, departments, etc.
- According to the distribution of an enterprise a WFMS is a distributed application by itself.
- The hard- and software infrastructure of an enterprise will be heterogeneous; however, a WFMS must cover up this heterogeneity.

- WFMSs have to integrate newly written and legacy applications.
- WFMSs are active systems. They drive the execution of workflows by notifying agents about outstanding tasks.
- WFMSs are a basis for collaborative work. They coordinate cooperating agents during the execution of workflows.

These characteristics have to be considered in the architecture of a WFMS. It will turn out that the main architectural issues of WFMS are *transparency* with respect to hard- and software heterogeneity, hard- and software distribution, varying size of the system, and different services supported. A client/server architecture is very suitable for achieving this goal. In this paper, we detail the client/server architecture of a WFMS.

2 Workflow Modeling in Workflow Management Systems

Although the architecture of WFMSs is the main topic in this paper, we have to introduce a workflow model first in order to know what workflows look like. The architecture of WFMSs shows *how* a workflow is executed, while a workflow model shows *what* has to be performed. A distinguished architecture must use an orthogonal and modular workflow model to be orthogonal and modular by itself. The following discussion of the ramifications of our workflow model ABS (*Activity Behavior Specification*) gives an introduction in what has to be enacted by a WFMS. Details about the workflow model of ABS can be found in [BuJa94].

2.1 Functional Perspective

Workflows are described by an object-oriented model. Therefore, workflows are object types and their fundamental features are represented by data variables and methods. A workflow represents a functional unit (cf. Fig. 1). Workflows are either elementary or composite; composite workflows reference further workflows (called subworkflows) so that nesting of workflows occurs. Elementary workflows invoke applications which are separately modeled as object types. Applications represent an executable image, like a program or a server routine. Workflows are specified in a modular way such that they can be reused in different contexts i.e. by different workflows. A workflow is called by its name along with a predefined set of values for the interface variables. Inside of a workflow, only variables local to that workflow can be referenced (scoping rule). Local policy variables may be needed to specify notification and policies (see Sect. 2.3). The most important method of a workflow is *execute()*. Usually, the interface parameters of a workflow describe the calling parameters for this function.

2.2 Behavioral Perspective

For composite workflows the execution sequence of their subworkflows is determined by dependencies between the subworkflows This defines the control flow among subworkflows. Two major types of control flow are distinguished [Jabl93]. *Prescriptive types* of control flow are *serial, alternative*, and *parallel execution*. They bear the usual semantics. We use the following notation, whereby it is assumed that a superworkflow A comprises of two subworkflows B and C. Descriptive control flow among B and C is expressed by the following constructs:

- serial: $\rightarrow (B; C)$
- alternative: $if(cond(); B; C)$
- parallel: $\| (B; C)$

To enhance the clearness of a specification complex dependencies should be represented by only few constructs. Therefore, we introduce three descriptive control constructs:

- deadline: $\ll (B; C)$
- delay: $\gg (C; B)$
- existence: $\Rightarrow (B; C)$

In order to obtain even more complex control flow specifications, the six primitives introduced above can also be nested by replacing a workflow placeholder with another control construct.

The set of prescriptive and descriptive control flow constructs introduced so far make up a decent basis for the definition of additional problem-specific control flow constructs. Further constructs may be desired for the specification of workflows in dedicated application environments. This implies that the component which implements the behavioral aspect must cope with the introduction of new, even more complex constructs. Thus, it must be implemented in a very modular way in order to support the required extensibility.

2.3 Organizational Perspective

While workflows are being executed, *policies* are evaluated. This is called *policy resolution* [BuJa93]. Policies determine who has to authorize a particular workflow or who must execute a particular application. Instead of pointing to a single user, policies sometimes indicate that a set of users is required to authorize or execute a workflow. As stated above, *user* is not limited to a human being but can be a NC-machine, a program server, and the like. Therefore, we use *agent* synonymously with *user*.

Policies capture the organizational context. Because of the architectural scope of this paper, we present a subset of the organizational elements only. The basic elements are *user* and *role*. Additional organizational elements are groups, departments, projects, and the like. A role groups users by common properties (e.g. same capabilities or behavior) in organizations often by functions they can fulfill (e.g. "manager" or "secretary"). Since an agent is capable of performing several functions, a user might be able to play several roles. According to Fig. 1, a person must be a group manager if he has to approve a travel claim; he must act as a client if he wants to start his own travel claim.

Users are notified about work to be done through a component called *Notification*. This component inserts tasks into the agents' *worklists* that contain outstanding work.

Given a description of an organization, the policies for a particular workflow can be specified. A common policy is to declare a list of roles and/or users who have to authorize and/or execute a workflow. In addition, the notification method is described for each user/role and workflow (e.g. e-mail). Usually more than one user is notified about work to be done (e.g. all users who can play a certain role are informed). However, not all users are supposed to execute the workflow. A sample policy might specify that only one user, the first and the "fastest", should execute. All other users must be prevented from doing the same job. This coordination and book-keeping is one of the main tasks of the policy resolution component.

3 Fundamentals of the ABS Architecture

This section reveals basic requirements towards an WFMS architecture (Sect. 3.1). It also shows why these requirements are best met by a client/server architecture (Sect. 3.2). Sect. 3.3 presents an overview on our WFMS architecture called ABS (according to the name of the workflow model). This architecture follows the classification of aspects of the ABS workflow model introduced in Sect. 1.

3.1 General Considerations

WFM is performed in highly heterogeneous and distributed environments like big enterprises. This leads to high diversity with respect to hard- and software. In contrast to this, a WFMS has to be homogenous from the users' point of view: a user deals with a *transparent* common interface to workflows despite of the distribution and heterogeneity of the underlying computing environment. Internally, the WFMS takes advantage of the computing infrastructure, for example by using distribution to raise performance and availability.

Another important issue arises from the organizational and operational area in which a WFMS is embedded. A WFMS has to deal with a varying and often huge number of agents and business processes. Thus, either dozens and thousands of workflow instances must potentially run in parallel without loss of performance. Furthermore, the numbers of users, roles, and other organizational stuff also vary over a large scale. Therefore, WFMSs have to be *scalable*.

Additionally, the implementation complexity increases as a result of the variety of internal services. As outlined in Sect. 2, many different tasks have to be accomplished by a WFMS: workflows have to be initiated, agents have to be notified and coordinated, applications have to be integrated, etc. Due to these requirements, the ABS WFMS cannot be implemented as a monolithic system. Such an architecture would limit scalability (usually achieved through configuration and restructuring which is hard to accomplish for monolithic systems).

Besides, it is very cumbersome to extend or manipulate monolithic architectures in distributed, heterogeneous computing environments. Additionally, supporting a variety of WFM services makes this task even more difficult. However, client/server models [Andr91], [Tane92], [GrRe93] support the required features in a seamless manner (cf. Sect. 3.2). For these reasons we prefer a client/server architecture for ABS.

In Fig. 2, a conceptual view on the architecture of a WFMS is depicted. Three architectural layers are distinguished. The bottom layer is built up by the operating/communication system and the system hardware. This layer supports processes, threads, RPC mechanisms, etc. The middle layer is constituted by Executables (Sect. 4.2). Executables define client/server pairs that provide the basis for the implementation of the WFMS execution engine. They offer elementary system services like an abstract "call mechanism" that hides heterogeneity and distribution of the underlying layer (cf. Sect. 4.2). The top layer in Fig. 2 represents the WFMS execution engine, i.e. the various WFMS services that are implemented. The fundamental interface to the user of the WFMS (services) is constituted by workflows. The top layer hides implementation details like number of servers that implement a specific service (i.e. it provides scalability) or variety of WFMS services. The user of the WFMS exclusively deals with the execution of workflows and is not aware of the complexity of the WFMS.

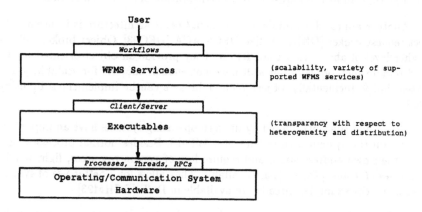

Fig. 2. Application environment for WFMSs

3.2 Client/Server Paradigm

In its abstract form, a client/server relationship consists of two parties. An application program (*the client*) wants a certain function to be performed but is itself unable to do so, and another program (*the server*) offers the desired function. Clients and servers support *stubs* (following the RPC term because of its similarity) that provide communication ports. A client program can request the execution of a function at a server site by engaging its stub to send this request to a server stub which in turn delegates it to its server program. After the server call terminates, the server sends the result back to the client.

The specifications of client/server models facilitate many variations: after issuing a request a client may be blocked until the result is provided (synchronous request); alternatively, client and server can work in parallel (asynchronous request). Both server and client can be at the same site. Servers providing the same function can be replicated. No assumptions on a particular client/server model are made in the ABS WFMS architecture.

A common mechanism for the implementation of client server models is the remote procedure call (RPC, [Tane92]). RPCs provide a procedural interface for the client to access server functions and hide the location of servers at calling time. Nevertheless, the implementor would need to know exactly about synchronous or asynchronous calling modes. RPCs are well suited for the implementation of distributed services in heterogeneous environments. There are different implementations of RPCs, e.g. SUN RPC [Corb91] or DCE RPC [BGHM93]. Both provide synchronous and asynchronous call mechanisms. Transparent server replication that is vital for WFMS with respect to scalability and extensibility is not directly supported by them. However, DCE offers rudimentary services that allow the hard-coded implementation of server replication.

Another approach to implement a client/server architecture is to use an object request broker [DHHN91] like DEC's ACA [DEC93]. Object brokers offer a higher level of abstraction than RPCs. They provide an object-oriented model and remote method calls but still have not enough support for scalability and extensibility. Incidentally, object request brokers can be implemented by using RPCs.

Processing concepts offered by modern operating systems have an important impact on the system architecture of a WFMS. Besides normal processes that have their own address space and require lots of system resources, light weight processes (*threads*, [Tane92]) are available. They allow for a better use of system resources. For example, threads are available in DCE [BGHM93].

Full scalability is only achievable when implementation mechanisms like RPC or threads are transparent on the WFMS level. In such a case, implementations can be transparently replaced by more efficient ones if they do not meet performance requirements. For example, an inadequate single server implementation can be substituted by a replicated server implementation.

In order to achieve scalability and transparency with respect to distribution and heterogeneity in the ABS architecture, we implement the ABS client/server model as an abstract data type. All implementation details are encapsulated in that abstract data type. For the implementation, an object-oriented approach is taken [Meye88]. Specifically, the inheritance and overloading mechanisms of the object-oriented paradigm are very suitable for our needs.

3.3 Overview on the Architecture

The focus of this paper are functional, behavioral, and organizational aspects of WFMS. Four main tasks have to be accomplished in the ABS WFMS:

- workflows must be executed according to a control flow specification.
- agents eligible to execute workflows must be determined (policy resolution).
- agents determined to execute workflows must be notified.
- work coming due for agents must be managed in worklists.

Fig. 3 shows the four logical components that implement the four tasks. The components are attributed "logical" since a real system can have more than one instance of each component at the same time. For example, there are many worklists in existence since each agent is typically associated with one worklist.

The *WFMS kernel* implements the functional and behavioral aspects. It is responsible to execute workflows, i.e. to instantiate them, to execute them, and to keep track of their status. Besides management interfaces for installing workflow types or status reporting (which are not dealt with in this paper), the kernel offers an *execute()* interface which starts workflows or subworkflows within a workflow.

The *policy engine* implements the organizational aspect, specifically the subtask policy resolution. Since more than one operation can be invoked on a workflow (e.g. start, stop, resume), the policy engine computes for each operation of a workflow a set of eligible agents. Even for a single workflow, these sets can be different (e.g. a clerk can *execute* a workflow, whereas the manager of the clerk can *stop* it). To trigger its computation, the policy engine offers the *resolve()* interface. Since the computation depends also on the status of a workflow or the workload of agents, the policy engine has two *inform* interfaces: *inform_status()* tells about status change of a workflow; *inform_request()* reports an agent request for workflow execution. These interfaces enable the policy engine to react to busy agents so as to not overload them.

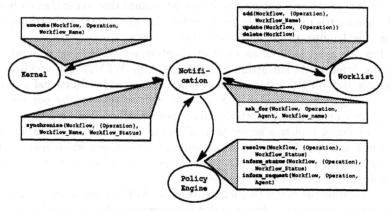

Fig. 3. Logical ABS Architecture

A *worklist* reveals the workflows to be executed to an agent. It acts as the interface between an agent and a WFMS. All workflows the agent is responsible for are listed. Through the interfaces *add()*, *delete()*, and *update()*, workflows can be added, deleted or their status changed. When an agent starts workflow execution, the worklist object forwards such a request to *notification* using the *ask_for()* interface.

Notification acts as a switchboard between the components of the architecture. With respect to the worklist, notification notifies eligible agents of workflows ready to be executed. Notification receives the workflows ready for execution from the kernel through the *synchronize()* interface. For each workflow ready for execution, notification consults the policy engine through the *resolve()* interface to find out which worklists the workflow has to be added to. Furthermore, notification forwards to the kernel requests of an agent to execute a workflow. Notification receives such a request through its *ask_for()* interface. Subsequently, it calls the *execute()* interface of the kernel as well as the *inform_request()* interface of the policy engine for informing about an agent's intention to execute a workflow. This information is necessary to control policies (cf. Sect. 2.3)

4   The ABS Architecture

This section provides an overview on the implementation of the ABS WFMS. First, the general aspects concerning the implementation of the ABS WFMS are elaborated. This leads to the definition of an abstract programming model that provides a logical client/server architecture. Using this model we present the characteristic parts of the ABS WFMS. The ABS WFMS is implemented in C++.

4.1   Implementation of the ABS Client/Server Architecture

In Sect. 3 the requirements for the ABS WFMS were discussed. A WFMS must make use of a distributed computing environment in order to be adaptable to the large scale of workflow requirements. It was determined that a client/server based implementation is most suitable. In this subsection the general ABS architecture of Fig. 3 is detailed, i.e. its implementation is shown.

After the application of an abstract client/server model, Fig. 4 shows the complete implementation architecture of the ABS WFMS. The architecture represents the WFMS service layer of Fig. 2. It provides functional extensibility through strict modularity. Scalability will be achieved by our specific client/server implementation which is discussed broadly in Sect. 4.2. Each component of Fig. 4 depicts a server that offers the functions introduced in Sect. 3.3. Additionally, each component comprises of some clients which enable communication with servers located in other components. All services are generally available to all other system components.

Fig. 4 reveals two major characteristics of the ABS implementation. The first characteristic is that each client worklist is implemented by one worklist component which contains one worklist server. All worklist servers are of the same data

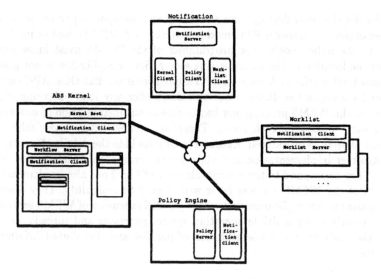

Fig. 4. Implementation of the ABS Client/Server Architecture

type. Worklist servers are passive, i.e. they do not proactively ask notification for work to do. Instead notification informs the worklist servers about work to do. Alternatively, notification could be passive and the worklist servers actively inquire work from notification. This implementation variant bears at least two disadvantages: the management of outstanding work becomes more difficult because notification has to keep track of the whole worklist information; moreover, polling by the worklist servers would be necessary which is very expensive.

The second characteristic of the ABS architecture is that the ABS kernel consists of a set of workflow servers. Instead of a single server ABS kernel, the workflow structure itself is used to constitute the kernel. That is, each workflow is implemented as a separate server within the kernel. The ABS kernel itself is a dedicated parent workflow, called *kernel root*. All other top level workflows available in the WFMS are subworkflows of this parent workflow and are always ready for execution. As a consequence, the ABS kernel is a set of nested workflow servers. It is important to note that workflow servers and operating system processes are independent with respect to their numbers of instances.

The ABS WFMS servers do not imply any operating system process structure. In Sect. 4.2 different client/server classes are presented that implement the kernel in one or more operating system processes or in threads.

4.2 Implementation of Executable Objects

Scalability and transparency towards hardware and software heterogeneity and distribution are very important goals of the ABS implementation (Sect. 3). A client/server architecture is the first step towards these objectives. Using a particular client/server implementation (e.g. RPCs) increases implementation dependencies that may destroy both scalability and transparency in the worst case. For example, if a classical RPC mechanism like SUN RPC is used to implement calls to the policy engine the programmer of the WFMS must know exactly about the location of the policy engine server. Server replication is not possible without further efforts. Advanced RPC implementations like DCE RPC can hide server location and replication but still don't offer any load balancing mechanism, i.e. the WFMS programmer has to care about instantiation of new servers and about workload of each server. Therefore, an abstraction layer, called *Executable Objects*, is introduced. Executable Objects hide the details of a particular client/server implementation and allow for the transparent distribution of objects. They correspond to the Executable layer of Fig. 2 but also implement some aspects of the WFMS services layer with regard to scalability. They allow for transparent server replication and enable parallel execution of WFMS services by transparently using multiple operating system processes and threads, i.e. they form the basis for the implementation of parallel and distributed Information Systems.

Base Object Classes For the implementation of the Executable layer (Fig. 2) we use abstract data types. They provide well defined interfaces and hide implementation details by encapsulation.

```
class Executable
{
        call (exec_method, parameter);
        is_ready ();
        wait ();
        get_result ();
};
```

Fig. 5. Characteristic parts of Executable Base Objects

To provide a most flexible architecture with respect to the heterogeneity of WFMS environments and further modifications, we introduce a class *Executable* (Fig. 5). This class provides an abstraction from hardware and software heterogeneity by providing a unique interface that offers general call semantics for client/server models. For this reason the four methods depicted in Fig. 5 are introduced. A server call to *exec_method* is initiated by the *call()* method of the Executable Object. For example, if notification wants to call the *resolve()* interface of the policy engine the request will be denoted *call(RESOLVE, ...)*, i.e. the function to be performed has to be encoded. This is done by a simple mapping mechanism. *is_ready()* informs about the completion of a server call; *wait()* blocks until the server call completes; and *get_result()* provides its result. This interface offers a general asynchronous calling model that contains synchronous calls as a special case. If a client/server pair uses synchronous calls, *call()* will block until the request completes. Afterwards *is_ready()* will return true and the result may be picked up. In the case of "real" asynchronous calls *call()* will not block.

Each client/server pair is represented by two abstract data types. Client and server objects are members of a class derived from the abstract class *Executable*. In order to reuse implemented classes, we propose the Executable Base Object classes *Executable_S* and *Executable_C*, derived from class *Executable*. They implement the application-independent functionality of a client/server model and may be only used for derivation.

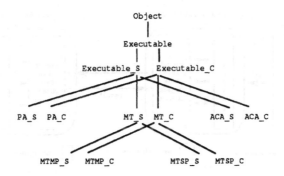

Fig. 6. Example class hierarchy for Executable Base Objects

Fig. 6 shows a possible class hierarchy for Executable Base Object classes, i.e. a number of client/server models. Each client/server model consists of a pair of classes denoted as *<name>_S* for the server object class and *<name>_C* for the client object class:

- *Executable_S* and *Executable_C* are abstract classes for servers and clients. They do not implement a concrete client/server model but they define the interface to all client/server pairs captured in our model.
- *PA_S* and *PA_C* implement pseudo asynchronous Executable Objects.
- *MT_S* and *MT_C* are classes for client/server models that use multi threading.
- *MTMP_S* and *MTMP_C* (multi threading, multi process) use multi server facility in addition to the threading facilities of the *MT* classes.
- *MTSP_S* and *MTSP_C* (multi threading, single process) offers multi threading in a single operating system process.
- *ACA_S* and *ACA_C* provide ACA-based client/server communication.

The *MT*, *MTMP*, and *MTSP* classes combine functionality as provided by DCE [BGHM93]. While the *MTMP* class supports a multi server facility, *MTSP* offers no server replication. Further client/server models may be added.

For the WFMS on top of Executable Objects the actual client/server model is transparent because it only has to deal with the interfaces of the *Executable_S* and

Executable_C classes. Their internal structure is encapsulated in these classes. Additionally, scalability with respect to increased workload is provided, because *MTSP* can be transparently switched to *MTMP* which offers server replication, for example.

Implementing Client/Server Applications on Top of Executable Base Object Classes Executable Base Object classes are an abstraction of a particular client/server implementation. In the following we show how client/server applications can be obtained by derivation from Executable Base Objects.

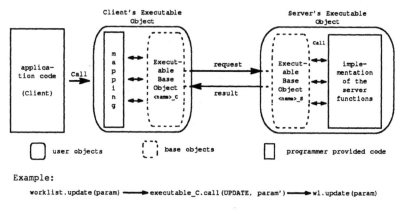

Example:

worklist.update(param) ⟶ executable_C.call(UPDATE, param') ⟶ wl.update(param)

Fig. 7. Implementing client/server models with Executable Objects

A derived server and client class object is shown in Fig. 7. A call through an application program (e.g. *worklist.update(param)*) is transformed by mapping mechanisms to a call to the Executable Object of the client (*executable_C.call(UPDATE, param')*). The base object sends the request to a corresponding server object. This one calls the proper function of the server object (*wl.update(param)*). Hence, the client object has to fulfill two tasks. The first task serves the *call()* interface (cf. Fig. 5) of the Executable Base Object. The method name and parameters are encoded according to the Executable Base Objects. The second task transmits the request to the server object.

The server object decodes the message and maps it to the appropriate method call. Afterwards, the result is sent back to the client object. The client object forwards it to the application. The communication channel used and other implementation details on the server side corresponding to the application-dependent part of the client/server model are completely transparent to the implementor of the client application. He only uses the interface depicted in Fig. 5. Under the assumption that a proper mapping is provided (Fig. 7), methods of objects implemented by client/server can be called in exactly the same way as methods of local objects. For example, neither the client nor the server programmer has to know about the existence of multiple servers. This is hidden by the Executable Base Objects. After invocation of the *call()* method of the client base object it chooses a suitable server by itself. The programmer doesn't need to care about this mechanism that is internal to the client base class object. Additionally, parallel execution may be reached on the client side by using base objects that support "real" asynchronous calls.

Executable Base Objects perform the communication part both on the client and the server side. The client's mapping has to be done by front-end code included in the object derived from an Executable Base Object. It hides the interface shown in Fig. 5 and provides an application-specific interface. For example, consider the worklist component of Fig. 3. They offer the methods *add()*, *delete()*, and *update()*. A worklist is implemented as a client/server pair of Executable Objects. Because Executable Base Objects have only the interface of Fig. 5, a client object of a worklist is derived from the Executable Base Object. Its methods are implemented on top of the interface of the base object. If the client/server model is changed, only a new client object is derived from the proper Executable Base Object.

A server object can also be derived from an Executable Base Object. Parallel execution is established by server objects that offer multiple activities like *MTSP* or *MTMP*. The server implementation determines the interface of the server object. In contrast, in an implementation based on DCE a server object registers at the DCE service but does not offer any methods besides a constructor and a destructor. The server functions are triggered internally by DCE. At creation time, a server object initializes the mapping. As a consequence, modifications of the client/server model are not fully transparent at the server side. Modification is unavoidable because the server programmer has to know if a server itself will be responsible for all activities after creation or if activities are managed by some system services (e.g. ACA), for instance. In the first case, the server programmer has to be concerned with the proper calling of the server methods. In the second case, the creation call of the server objects will not return as long as the server is running and control flow is handled by some system services.

5 Conclusion

The benefits of workflow management systems include controlling business processes in an enterprise. Due to the distribution, heterogeneity, and complexity of these processes, a central supervisory instance is inflexible against extensions and resource-devastating, if implementation is obtainable at all. A distributed, scalable architecture is therefore of paramount importance for utilization and success of WFMSs as the implementation platform for parallel and distributed Information Systems.

The client/server paradigm is most flexible against load balancing, service replication, and naming transparency. Furthermore, the basic RPC technique as a particular client/server implementation has found its way into many vendor's products. High level facilities like Digital's ACA are commercially available. Hence, an implementation of WFMSs based on these services is a promising approach to get WFMSs operational in "real" environments. For reasons of transparency and scalability, however, an additional layer is necessary to abstract from of the concrete service (Executable Objects).

In this paper, a client/server architecture for the ABS WFMS was detailed. The client/server calling mode is not limited to the interaction among ABS's four main components (kernel, worklists, policy engine, and notification) but also applies to the kernel structure itself and can be extended to further WFMS services not discussed here [BuJa94].

Acknowledgements

The authors would like to thank Glenn Maxey for his help in making this paper more readable.

References

[Andr91]   Andrews, G.R.: Paradigms for Process Interaction in Distributed Programs. ACM Computing Surveys, 23(1), 1991, pp. 49-90

[BGHM93]   Bever, M.; Geihs, K.; Heuser, L.; Mühlhäuser, M.; Schill, A.: Distributed Systems, OSF DCE, and Beyond. In: Schill, A.: Proc. DCE - The OSF Distributed Computing Environment, International DCE Workshop, Karlsruhe, 1993, pp. 1-20

[BuJa93]   Bussler, C.; Jablonski, S.: Process Modeling and Execution in Workflow Management Systems. In: Proc. 3rd International Workshop on Information Technologies and Systems (WITS), Orlando, FL, 1993

[BuJa94]   Bussler, C.; Jablonski, S.: An Approach to Integrate Workflow Modeling and Organization Modeling in an Enterprise. In: IEEE Third Workshop on Enabling Technologies: Infrastructure for Collaborative Enterprises (WET ICE), Morgan Town, West Virginia, April 1994

[Corb91]   Corbin, J.R.: The Art of Distributed Applications. Springer Verlag, Berlin, 1991

[DEC93]   Digital Equipment Corp.: DEC ACA Services. ULTRIX Online Documentation Library, Aug., 1992

[DHHN91]   Digital Equipment Corp.; Hewlett-Packard Co.; HyperDesk Corp.; NCR Corp.; Object Design Inc.; SunSoft, Inc.: The Common Object Request Broker: Architecture and Specification. Revision 1.1, Dec. 1991, OMG Document Number 91.12.1

[GrRe93]   Gray, J.; Reuter, A.: Transaction Processing: Concepts and Techniques. Morgan Kaufmann Publishers, San Mateo, 1993

[Jabl93]   Jablonski, S.: Transaction Support for Activity Management. In: Proc. Workshop on High Performance Transaction Processing Systems, Asilomar, CA, September 1993

[McBl91]   McCarthy, J.C.; Bluestein, W.M.: The Computing Strategy Report: Workflow's Progress. Forrester Research Inc., Cambridge, Mass., Oct. 1991

[Meye88]   Meyer, B.: Object Oriented Software Construction. Prentice-Hall, New York, 1988

[Tane92]   Tanenbaum, A.S.: Modern Operating Systems. Prentice Hall, Englewood Cliffs, 1992

Parallelization of the Solution of 3D Navier-Stokes Equations for Fluid Flow in a Cavity with Moving Covers

Oleg Bessonov[1], Valery Brailovskaya[2], Vadim Polezhaev[1], Bernard Roux[3]

[1] Institute for Problems in Mechanics of Russian Academy of Sciences,
101, Vernadsky ave., 117526 Moscow, Russia
[2] Institute of Applied Physics of Russian Academy of Sciences,
46, Ulianov str., 603600 Nizhni Novgorod, Russia
[3] Institut de Mécanique des Fluides, 1, rue Honnorat, 13003 Marseille, France

Abstract. This paper describes the numerical method of solution of 3D Navier-Stokes equations in a regular domain and direct method of parallelization of solution for distributed-memory computers. A vorticity-vector-potential formulation and Finite Difference method of solution are chosen, using fractional step ADI method for vorticity equation and Fourier method for Poisson equation. Special attention is paid to single-processor optimization of the algorithm. Parallelization technology is given in detail, with speedup and efficiency levels achieved for 2 and 4 processors. Numerical results are presented for different geometries and Reynolds numbers.

1   Introduction

Numerical investigation of 3D incompressible viscous flow in a lid-driven cavity is a well-known test problem for comparison of numerical methods and evaluation of their performance. Some experimental and simulated results have been published on this problem. Most famous of them are the detailed experimental study of Koseff, Street [1] and a publication of GAMM workshop [2] with the results of numerical simulations obtained by several research teams.

Another direction of research has been devoted to investigation of shear flow in channels and cavities with oppositely moving covers (see [3], [4] for 2D channels). Systematic studies of 2D flow in cavities with different height-length (H/L) ratios have been carried out in [5], [6]. However, for high Reynolds numbers such flows should be essentially three-dimensional.

The present work concerns both directions mentioned, with a parallelized implementation of the algorithm on a multiprocessor computer. The main objectives of the work are:

- to develop simple and economical method for investigation of unsteady laminar flow of incompressible fluid in a cavity with moving covers;
- to design and implement method of parallelization of solution for distributed-memory parallel computer;

- to obtain numerical results for lid-driven cavity and verify them in comparison with related published data;
- to investigate shear flow in a cavity with oppositely moving covers.

Note, that the results of previous 3D research have been obtained using expensive supercomputers, mainly CRAY Y-MP [2]. In contrast, this work represents an efficient implementation of a 3D algorithm for a medium class parallel computer, Intel iPSC/860. The implementation is machine-independent and can be easily adapted for any other distributed-memory computer.

2 Numerical Method

2.1 Mathematical Formulation

A vorticity-vector-potential form of Navier-Stokes equations is chosen for the numerical solution of a non-steady 3D viscous incompressible flow.

The governing equations are written in conservative form:

$$\frac{\partial \omega}{\partial t} - \nabla \times (\mathbf{V} \times \omega) = \frac{1}{\text{Re}} \nabla^2 \omega \tag{1}$$

$$\nabla^2 \psi = -\omega \tag{2}$$

where ω and ψ denote the vorticity and the vector potential respectively, both defined through the velocity $\mathbf{V}$:

$$\omega = \nabla \times \mathbf{V} \tag{3}$$

$$\mathbf{V} = \nabla \times \psi , \quad \nabla \cdot \psi = 0 \tag{4}$$

The vorticity-vector-potential formulation is practically equivalent to the vorticity-velocity form [7] with the advantage that the velocity field identically satisfies the incompressibility condition $\nabla \cdot \mathbf{V} = 0$.

No slip boundary conditions are imposed for the velocity. Boundary conditions for tangential (ψ_{T_1} and ψ_{T_2}) and normal (ψ_n) components of the vector potential are defined as in [8]:

$$\psi_{T_1} = 0 , \quad \psi_{T_2} = 0 , \quad \frac{\partial \psi_n}{\partial n} = 0 \tag{5}$$

Special boundary conditions for the vorticity are derived from the following equation, to be satisfied near the boundaries:

$$\nabla^2 \mathbf{V} = -\nabla \times \omega \tag{6}$$

Equation (6) is identical to (2) and represents the velocity equation for vorticity-velocity formulation.

2.2 Spatial Discretization

The finite difference method with discretization of a parallelepipedic region on a 3D regular non-staggered grid is used (Fig. 1, left). The grid is uniform in directions X and Y and non-uniform in the direction Z, with the greatest clustering of grid points near the top and bottom walls. Symmetry conditions of the computational domain are not applied.

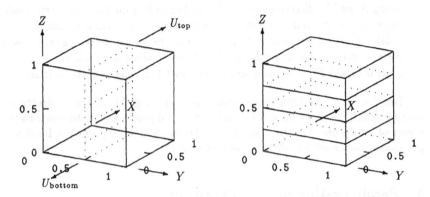

Fig. 1. Computational domain (left) and its decomposition for parallelization (right)

The convective terms of vorticity equations are approximated by 2-nd order upstream-biased differences (modified QUICK scheme [9], [10]). For other terms of governing equations, 2-nd order centered differences are used.

2.3 Solution of Vorticity Equation

A fractional step Alternating-Direction-Implicit (ADI) method with a stabilization correction [2] is adopted to solve the vorticity transport equation (1) providing a 2-nd order time accurate scheme. The method for the solution of each vorticity-component equation $\frac{\partial \omega}{\partial t} = A\omega - \Phi$ is based on the splitting of the finite difference operator $A = (L_x + L_y + L_z)$.

The algorithm for computing ω at time $k + 1$ consists of 3 fractional steps:

$$\left(L_x - \frac{2}{\Delta t}\right)\omega^{k+\frac{1}{3}} = -\left(L_x + 2L_y + 2L_z + \frac{2}{\Delta t}\right)\omega^k + 2\Phi \qquad (7)$$

$$\left(L_y - \frac{2}{\Delta t}\right)\omega^{k+\frac{2}{3}} = L_y\omega^k - \frac{2}{\Delta t}\omega^{k+\frac{1}{3}} \qquad (8)$$

$$\left(L_z - \frac{2}{\Delta t}\right)\omega^{k+1} = L_z\omega^k - \frac{2}{\Delta t}\omega^{k+\frac{2}{3}} \qquad (9)$$

With chosen spatial discretization, operators $L1$, $L2$, $L3$ are 3-diagonal; therefore the solution of each fractional step for every component of the vorticity field involves the solution of a 2D set of independent 3-diagonal linear systems.

2.4 Solution of Vector-Potential Equation

For the solution of Poisson equations for the vector potential (2), the Fourier method is chosen [11]. The algorithm of solution of equation for every component of the vector potential comprises the following steps:

- a 2D Fast Fourier Transform (FFT) is applied to every (X, Y) plane of the computational domain. The 2D transform consists of two 1D transforms, along X and Y directions respectively. Depending on the boundary conditions for a particular component, sine or cosine transform is chosen;
- a 2D set of independent 3-diagonal linear systems is solved. Every linear system corresponds to a column of grid points along Z direction;
- a 2D inverse FFT is applied again to every (X, Y) plane of the domain.

The Fourier method imposes a requirement on the grid in X and Y directions: spacing should be uniform, and the number of grid points should be equal to the power of 2 plus one. On the other hand, this method is very efficient itself and possesses a potential for efficient parallelization.

3 Parallelization of the Algorithm

3.1 Single-Processor Optimization

Let us consider single-processor optimization requirements as a necessary preliminary stage to the parallelization. For the efficient execution of programs on modern superscalar RISC microprocessors, some constraints are imposed:

- arrays should be processed with unit stride, that is first dimension for multi-dimensional arrays (in FORTRAN) should be processed first;
- unnecessary memory accesses and indirect addressings should be avoided;
- frequent division operations should be replaced with multiplications by inverse values; arrays of inverse values should be prepared in advance to replace arrays of divisors.

Besides the direct effect of such limitations on the execution speed, following these rules makes a program more suitable for vectorization and for additional optimization by smart compilers.

The most important constraint is the unit-stride requirement. To follow it, some stages of the algorithm need a transformation. Let the 1-st dimension of arrays correspond to the direction X, the 2-nd — to Y, and the 3-rd — to Z. Then different steps of the algorithm should be implemented by the following way, depending on the direction of the run in the original formulation:

- all calculations of ADI and Fourier methods, that run along X axis, already satisfy this requirement;

- sweeps of ADI method along Y axis are executed simultaneously for all values of X (in a plane $Z = $ const); i.e., a front of computations ($Y = $ const) moves in Y direction with an internal loop in X direction along the front (Fig. 2, left). Coefficients and right-hand-side (RHS) values of 3-diagonal systems solved are kept in 2-dimensional arrays;
- FFT transforms in Y direction are implemented similarly;
- sweeps of ADI and Fourier methods along Z axis are executed simultaneously for all values of X and Y in the domain; i.e., a frontal plane of computations ($Z = $ const) moves in Z direction, with internal loops in X and Y directions within the plane (Fig. 2, right). Coefficients and RHS values of 3-diagonal systems solved are kept in 3-dimensional arrays.

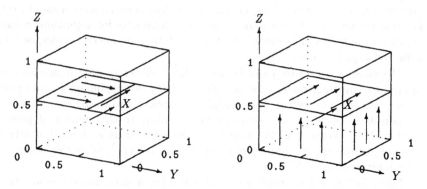

Fig. 2. Front of computations (left) and frontal plane of computations (right)

These transformations along with other optimizations have increased the execution speed more than 2 times comparing to the "natural" form of the algorithm (for Intel i860 RISC processor). Also, the algorithm became prepared to the form suitable for the following parallelization.

3.2 General Considerations and Constraints of Parallelization

The present work considers the parallelization of the algorithm for distributed memory multiprocessor (MIMD) computers. Modern parallel computers of this class are built upon high performance superscalar RISC microprocessors and represent the most efficient instrument for solution of time-consuming fluid dynamics problems from the point of view of price-performance ratio. Comparing to the shared memory class of multiprocessor computers, distributed memory machines are usually much less expensive (for the same peak performance level and total memory size) and can be expanded to configurations containing tens or hundreds of processors.

However, organization of such computers as a set of independent processors (nodes) with local memories, interconnected by relatively slow communication channels, requires application of special approaches to parallelization, generally excluding usage of automatic parallelization tools and compilers. Basic criterion of efficient parallelization as an ability to reduce the time necessary for communications between nodes, below the computation time. Often, the communication time should be an order of magnitude lower than the computation time; this depends on the exchange mode (synchronous or asynchronous) and on the transfer block size.

Consider the characteristics of an Intel iPSC/860 computer consisting of 8 to 128 processors (i860, 40 MHz) each with 16 MBytes of memory. For double-precision calculations, average computation speed of one processor is of the order of 10 million floating point operations per second (MFLOPS), while communication speed is about 2 MBytes/sec., or ~ 0.25 million words per second. Since every arithmetic operation requires 2 or 3 operands, total data rate for computations is about 2 orders of magnitude higher than communication speed limit. For this reason, the efficient parallelization is impossible for algorithms requiring either the access to common (or adjacent) data from different nodes, or total data exchange between nodes.

Therefore, an algorithm can be parallelized efficiently only if independent branches in different nodes process different data, exchanging only small parts of the data when necessary. For example, it is possible when 3D computational domain is decomposed into subdomains (according to the number of processors) with an exchange of 2D boundary planes (or areas with small overlap), because in this case the number of computations is $O(N^3)$ while the amount of communications is $O(N^2)$.

Note, that similar approach is desirable also for modern shared memory (and "virtual shared memory") computers with a big number of processors, since the transfer rate for shared or remote data is still much less than the processing rate.

3.3 Description of the Parallelization

For the parallelization of the algorithm on the distributed memory MIMD computer, the computational parallelepipedic domain is decomposed in Z direction into the number of subdomain corresponding to the number of processors (Fig. 1, right). The subdomains are overlapped for providing calculations of derivatives and exchange of data between processors. Overlap level is equal to 2; i.e., in every node's memory one adjacent plane of points from each neighbour node is stored in addition to internal grid points (see Fig. 4 as an example).

Now consider the parallelization of every step of the algorithm.

ADI Runs along X and Y. All calculations of ADI method, that run along X and Y axes, don't depend on the order of processing in Z direction and are performed in parallel (independently, on different nodes). The implementation is similar to the single-processor case. On the completion of the step, adjacent nodes exchange boundary planes of grid points.

FFT Runs along X and Y. FFT in X and Y directions are produced by the same way. Following data exchanges are not required in this case.

Solution of 3-diagonal Systems in Z Direction. Calculations in Z direction for ADI and Fourier methods are not independent on the order of processing and can't be parallelized easily. They involve the solution of a 2D set of independent 3-diagonal linear systems (each being split between all processors), and a traditional sweep procedure (Gauss elimination) is not applicable.

There exist several methods of parallelization of the solution of 3-diagonal systems. The most convenient of them is Johnsson's (or single-width separator) method [12], [13]. The idea of the method is illustrated in Fig. 3:

- elimination of subdiagonal elements is performed independently in different nodes, with the fill-in of left-side columns;
- elimination of superdiagonal elements is performed independently in different nodes, with the fill-in of right-side columns;
- now every node contains a N-shaped matrix, where elements marked as big ● form a reduced distributed 3-diagonal system; these elements are then transferred to some node for the solution. The system is solved, and then the results are transferred back;
- back-substitution is performed independently in different nodes.

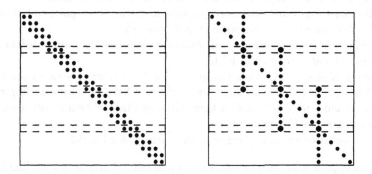

Fig. 3. Illustration of Johnsson's method of solution of 3-diagonal system

Johnsson's method represents a general case of parallelization of the solution. In order to reduce the number of data exchanges, a modified method has been derived, similar to the two-way parallel partition method described in [14]. For the number of processors $P = 2$, it is equivalent to the twisted factorization method (Fig. 4, left):

- subdiagonal elements are eliminated in the 1-st node, superdiagonal elements are eliminated in the 2-nd node;

- data exchanges are performed between nodes (2 exchanges are required), and then a 2×2 linear system in the center of the matrix is solved independently in both nodes;
- back-substitution is performed independently also.

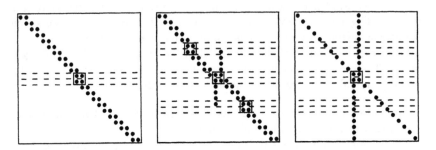

Fig. 4. Illustration of two-way method of parallelization for 2 and 4 processors

For the number of processors $P = 4$, the similar idea is applied recursively (Fig. 4, central and right):

- subdiagonal or superdiagonal elements are eliminated in the 1-st/2-nd and the 3-rd/4-th pairs of nodes, with the fill-in of some columns;
- data exchanges are performed between nodes in every pair, and then two 2×2 linear systems are solved (Fig. 4, central);
- remaining superdiagonal or subdiagonal elements are eliminated in both pairs of nodes, with some fill-in;
- now a X-shaped matrix is formed, with a 2×2 linear system in the center (Fig. 4, right); data exchanges are performed between corresponding nodes (2-nd and 3-rd), the system is then solved and the solution is sent to another set of 2 nodes (1-st and 4-th);
- back-substitution is performed independently in all nodes.

This approach avoids the solution of a reduced 3-diagonal system distributed between different processors. In order to reduce the number of communications, a duplication of some computations is applied in adjacent nodes (e.g. in the solution of 2×2 linear systems). As a result, for 4 nodes the solution requires only 5 data exchanges.

This method can be extended for a greater number of nodes by applying additional levels of recursion. Like Johnsson's method, it is stable for diagonal-dominant matrices.

Since a 2D set of independent 3-diagonal linear systems is solved simultaneously, processing of any equation in the system corresponds to a frontal plane of computations, and any single data exchange corresponds to an exchange of 2D arrays between nodes.

3.4 Parallelization Results

The method of parallelization described here has been implemented on Intel iPSC/860 distributed memory computer for 2 and 4 processors. Speedup and efficiency results of parallelization are presented in Table 1 for different grid sizes.

Table 1. Speedup and efficiency of parallelization (note the superlinear speedup due to cache effects)

	2 processors		4 processors	
Problem size	Speedup	Efficiency	Speedup	Efficiency
$33 \times 33 \times 42$	1.95	97.7%	3.09	77.3%
$65 \times 65 \times 50$	2.05	102.6%	3.33	83.3%
$65 \times 65 \times 98$			3.4	85%

For the problem size $65 \times 65 \times 98$ the results are based on the estimated execution time for 1 processor because the size of the program exceeds in this case the memory size of a single node. For the largest problem size $65 \times 129 \times 94$ speedup results are not applicable because the program requires 60 MBytes of memory and is therefore implemented only for 4-processor configuration.

For some problem sizes a superlinear speedup can be seen for 2-processor implementation. This is possible because after the distribution of program data between 2 nodes sizes of some arrays fall below particular hardware limitations (data cache size, translation buffer size etc.) and locality properties of the program are then improved.

As expected, the parallelization efficiency increases with the increasing of the problem size. For the largest configuration measured ($65 \times 65 \times 98$) the total loss of efficiency is about 15% and is caused by 2 main reasons:

- 6% — communication delays due to the synchronous mode of data transfers;
- 9% — algorithmic overhead due to the increased amount of computational work in the solution of 3-diagonal systems, as well as due to some disbalance between the number of operations in innermost (2-nd/3-rd) and outermost (1-st/4-th) nodes.

This level of parallelization efficiency is reasonable for such class of parallel computers with relatively fast processors and relatively slow communication channels. The implementation is machine-independent, its communication routines can be easily adapted to any communication protocol. Currently, 2 variants of the routines exist:

- with iPSC communication library, for Intel iPSC/860 computer;
- with Parallel Virtual Machine (PVM) library, which is standard for parallel computers and has been installed on most platforms.

4 Numerical Results

A numerical investigation has been provided for different geometries of cavity and different Reynolds numbers.

The results for lid-driven cubic cavity for Re = 400, Re = 1000 and Re = 2000 for a steady state solution are in a good qualitative and quantitative agreement with the results from [7]. In the case of Re = 3200 the fluid flow is essentially unsteady, with the formation of longitudal Taylor-Görtler-like (TGL) vortices near the downstream wall of the cavity (Fig. 5). These vortices are very unstable and migrate with time. The results are very similar to that of presented in [10].

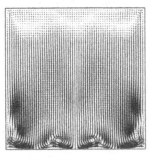

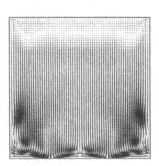

T=50   T=100

Fig. 5. Flow pattern in the plane $x = 0.766$ in cubic domain, Re = 3200

A more interesting flow behavior can be found for a cavity with spanwise aspect ratio 3 : 1 (cavity size $1 \times 3 \times 1$), Re = 3200 (Fig. 6). Here, there are several pairs of TGL vortices of different size. Figure 7 visualizes the evolution of TGL vortices, representing a set of successive pictures with a time interval $\Delta T = 1$ (only bottom part of cross-section is presented for every moment of time). It is seen that TGL vortices are very time-dependent and display non-periodic movement. These results complement well the results presented by several research teams on the GAMM workshop held in Paris in June, 1991 [2].

Other results have been obtained for a shear flow in a "flat" cavity (cavity size $1 \times 1 \times 0.1$) with oppositely moving covers. For Re = 1000 (Fig. 8) the flow is almost steady, with a few weak longitudal vortices. A very unsteady and irregular behavior can be seen for Re = 5000 (Fig. 9) at $T = 10$, and the flow picture becomes even more complicated later. Note, that for both regimes the velocity field represented on transversal cross-sections ($X = 1/2$, $X = 7/8$, $X = 15/16$) has a scale factor 4 times higher than that on longitudal cross-sections ($Y = 1/2$, $Y = 1/16$).

Finally, Fig. 10 represents the flow in a lid-driven cavity of size $1 \times 1 \times 2$ for Re = 5000, at $T = 100$. Despite the high Reynolds number, the flow behavior is rather simple in this case and displays a slow movement with time.

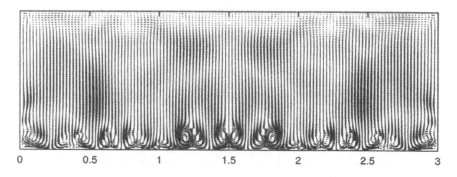

Fig. 6. Flow pattern in a cavity $1 \times 3 \times 1$, plane $x = 0.766$, $T = 50$

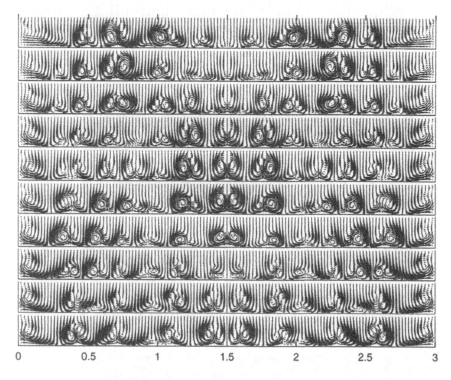

Fig. 7. Evolution of Taylor-Görtler-like vortices, plane $x = 0.766$ (from top to bottom, $T = 46 \div 55$, $\Delta T = 1$)

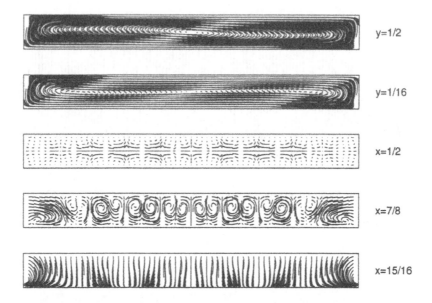

Fig. 8. Flow in a cavity with oppositely moving covers, $H/L = 0.1$, Re $= 1000$

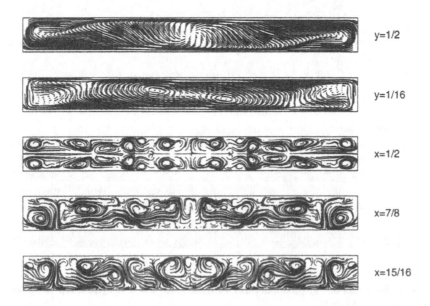

Fig. 9. Flow in a cavity with oppositely moving covers, $H/L = 0.1$, Re $= 5000$

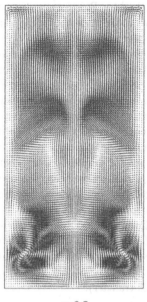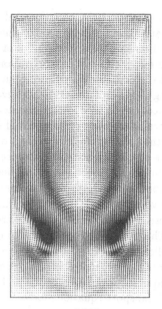

x=0.5   x=0.766

Fig. 10. Flow in a lid-driven cavity with $H/L = 2$, Re $= 5000$

5 Computational Cost and Performance

The program for numerical time-dependent simulation of a fluid flow in a lid-driven cavity of size $1 \times 3 \times 1$, for Re $= 3200$, has the following characteristics on Intel iPSC/860 computer:

- number of processors used: $P = 4$;
- grid size: $65 \times 129 \times 94$;
- program memory size: 60 MBytes;
- number of degrees of freedom :4.7 millions;
- spatial steps: $h_x = \frac{1}{64}$, $h_y = \frac{3}{128}$, $h_z = \frac{1}{256} \div \frac{1}{64}$;
- time step :0.0156;
- elapsed time to obtain solution up to $T = 200$: 110 hours;
- elapsed time per time step : 30.6 sec.;
- time per time step per grid point : 3.9×10^{-5} sec.;
- fraction of processor time spent on a solution of Poisson equation: 30%.

6 Conclusion

A vorticity-vector-potential formulation of Navier-Stokes equations and a Finite Difference method of solution have been chosen, using fractional step ADI method for vorticity equation and Fourier method for Poisson equation. Particular attention has been paid on the development of reliable quadratic upstream-biased scheme for discretization of convective terms.

Direct method of parallelization has been developed oriented on the achievement of good efficiency for computers with relatively slow communication links, giving as a result the efficiency level of about 98% for 2 processors and 85% for 4 processors on iPSC/860 computer. This approach to parallelization ensures the algebraical identity of parallelized implementation to the sequential one. Therefore the solution doesn't depend on convergence properties of the algorithm as in the case of iterative domain-decomposition methods.

Numerical investigation has been carried out for different cavity geometries and for different Reynolds numbers. Interesting results have been obtained about the evolution of TGL vortices, and also about the fluid flow in cavities with oppositely moving covers for different H/L ratios.

The work will be continued in the direction of improving the efficiency of parallelization, adapting to different parallel computers (IBM SP-2, Parsytec PowerXplorer), increasing the number of processors, and further enhancement of physical formulation of the problem (by coupling the Navier-Stokes equation with transport equations for heat and/or mass transfer).

References

1. J.R. Koseff, R.L. Street. The lid-driven cavity flow: A synthesis of qualitative and quantitative observations. J. Fluids Engin., **106**, 390–398, 1984.

2. Numerical Simulation of 3-D Incompressible Unsteady Viscous Laminar Flows: A GAMM Workshop / ed. by M. Deville et al. Notes on Numerical Fluid Mechanics, **36**, Vieweg, 1992.

3. V.A. Romanov. Stability of plane parallel Couette flow. Doklady Akademii Nauk SSSR, **196**, No. 5, 1971.

4. B.L. Rozhdestvensky, I.I. Simakin, M.I. Stoinov. Simulation of turbulent Couette flow in a flat channel. Preprint of the Institute of Applied Mathematics, Academy of Sciences of USSR, **106**, 1987.

5. H.W. Ryu, D.I. Lee. Numerical study of viscous flow in rectangular cavities with translating top and bottom walls. Proceedings of the Third Pacific Chemical Engineering Congress, Seoul, Korea, 1983.

6. S.A. Baranov, V.A. Brailovskaya, V.R. Kogan, L.V. Feoktistova. Numerical investigation of fluid flows in a plane and volume cavity. Proceedings of X Congress in Mechanics, Paris, 1991.

7. G. Guj, F. Stella. A vorticity-velocity method for the numerical solution of 3D incompressible flows. J. Comput. Phys., **106**, 286–298, 1993.

8. P.J. Roache. Computational Fluid Dynamics. Albuquerque, Hermosa Publishers, 1976.

9. C.J. Freitas, R.L. Street, A.N. Findikakis, J.R. Koseff. Numerical simulation of three-dimensional flow in a cavity. Int. J. Num. Meth. Fl., **5**, 561–575, 1985.

10. C.Y. Perng, R.L. Street. Three-dimensional unsteady flow simulations: Alternative strategies for a volume-averaged calculations. Int. J. Num. Meth. Fl., **9**, 341–362, 1989.

11. R.W. Hockney. A fast direct solution of Poisson's equation using Fourier analysis. J. Assoc. Comput. Math., **12**, 95-113, 1965.
12. J.M. Ortega. Introduction to Parallel and Vector Solution of Linear Systems. Plenum Press, 1988.
13. L. Johnsson. Solving narrow banded systems on ensemble architectures. ACM Trans. Math. Software, **11**, 1985.
14. C. Walshaw, S.J. Farr. A two-way parallel partition method for solving tridiagonal systems. University of Leeds, U.K., School of Computer Studies Research Report Series, Report 93.25, 1993.

Distributing Search and Knowledge using a Coordination Language

P.Ciancarini[1] and P.Mancini[2]

[1] University of Bologna - Italy E-mail:cianca@cs.unibo.it
[2] Scuola Normale Superiore - Pisa - Italy

1 Introduction

Modern general-purpose networked systems make available higher and higher computing power at cheaper prices, and this encourages the development of CPU-bound programs which exploit the new high-performance computing hardware. Chess-playing programs are CPU-bound, but they are also difficult to parallelize. In fact, to build a strong parallel chess program is much more difficult than building a strong sequential chess program, because there are many special problems introduced by parallelism: most heuristics developed to improve the performance of the alphabeta algorithm do not scale well to distributed implementations [10].

The new technology of *coordination languages* [2] offers new approaches to the construction of parallel programs using general purpose high performance systems. In this paper we explore its application in the field of distributed search and knowledge.

We have built a number of distributed chess programs using the coordination language Linda and a widespread hardware architecture, i.e., a network of general-purpose workstations (SUN Sparc 1). The programs are based on software architectures which range from master-worker to more complex structures involving several types of agents with different knowledge. We made many experiments that show that the software architecture has a strong influence on the (playing) performance of programs.

Our main working hypotheses were based on the researches by J.Schaeffer on the analysis of chess knowledge in numeric evaluation functions [9] and on the parallelization of search in the ParaPhoenix program running over a network of workstations [17]. These works, and others [19], show that parallel search cannot gain too much advantage from several networked processors when it is supported by complex domain-oriented heuristics; thus, it is necessary to find alternative methods for exploiting the computing power potentially offered by modern networks. Our approach, based on coordination of distributed knowledge, seems to offer new hopes for economically improving the playing strength of current programs.

2 Parallel search

The alphabeta algorithm is the basis of most playing programs that search game trees. One could expect that multiprocessors and multicomputers are helpful in building stronger programs based on brute-force search, since more computing power is available. However, it is well known that the efficient parallelization of alphabeta is a difficult problem. Several different ways to parallelism in chess playing programs have been explored; a short survey is found in [8]. The main methods are:

1. Parallel aspiration search [6]: the alphabeta window is partitioned in a number of contiguous segments, that are used by different processors to explore the same game tree; this is a form of OR-parallelism.

2. Parallel evaluation by special hardware; *e.g.*, HITECH uses parallel hardware for move generation [3], whereas Deep Thought [5] uses special hardware for evaluating positions in parallel.

3. Mapping the search space on the processors' set by a hash function: this is advantageous if the search space contains several duplicate states; *e.g.*, [18] describes how the whole search space of some chess endings was mapped on a Connection Machine.

4. Parallel search of a split game tree: the game tree is decomposed assigning its nodes to different processes which perform separate searches.

The last method is the most widely studied and used. For instance, in [10] several search algorithms were described and compared; other experiments with different algorithms are described in [11].

The main problem in searching a game tree by a splitting method is to decide when the association between a subtree and a process should be established. Usually, it makes no sense to allocate subtrees to processes before search starts, because it is necessary to know the whole tree, and moreover the alphabeta algorithm property of cutting subtrees makes useless the visit of some of them. It is impossible to determine a priori the identity of these subtrees and then to obtain at run-time a uniform load distribution.

At search time we usually have the following scenery: some "lucky" processes complete search before others (*e.g.*, because of better cuts) and will remain idle. Every solution for avoiding idleness must be dynamic, *i.e.*, it must provide mechanisms able, during the search, to reassign to idle processes subtrees already assigned to overloaded processes. Therefore, a classification of splitting methods in static and dynamic is not really meaningful, because actually the only plausible solution is dynamic. On the other hand, it makes sense to distinguish different approaches according to the time they establish nodes where it will occur a splitting.

A splitting node is one at which it is established the generation of a parallel search task, *i.e.*, where some of its subtrees are visited by processes different from its explorer. A *static* splitting algorithm decides all the splitting nodes before the search starts; a *dynamic* algorithm decides some splitting nodes only during the search.

3 Parallel search on a network of workstations

High-level parallel programming languages are gaining momentum, because they simplify the task of building software for the novel architectures with several processors. Parallel search algorithms are good tests for these new languages [1, 7].

Parallel search algorithms have been programmed in several languages; for instance, in [15] we find an algorithm based on semaphore primitives; in [13] the Orca language was used. We have used Linda, a coordination language that consists of a small set of parallel programming primitives that can be added to any sequential language [2].

Linda is based on the tuple space, an abstractly shared data structure. The tuple space can be used in a way similar to an agenda that coordinates tasks assigned to processes: tuples representing parallel tasks are grabbed by idle processes; this architecture has good load balancing properties [12].

In Linda, primitive **eval** allows process spawning: this is the basis for parallel execution. There are several possible software architectures that can all be programmed in Linda; one of the most useful is the master-worker model [12]. According to this model tasks created during the parallel evaluation of a program are dynamically distributed among processors.

The parallel program should be structured as follows:

- a master process generates tasks and coordinates the collection of solutions;
- several identical worker processes pick and execute tasks and return task results to the master; when a task is terminated, a new task can be chosen;
- in the tuple space there are two main kinds of tuples: active tuples for tasks (we call this multiset the agenda), and passive tuples that represent task results.

In the master-worker model of search based on splitting the supervisor of a node is a master process that coordinates several explorers as workers. This is simple to model statically: in the program shown below only the root is a splitting node.

```
int master_main(int n_worker,int depth)
{
position *root,*successor;
int nmoves,minimax,i,master(),worker();
for (i=0;i<n_worker;i++)
   eval ("worker",worker(depth));  /* create n workers */
while (!end())
   {
   load_new_position (&root); /* a new game tree */
   nmoves=genmoves(root,&successor);
   if (nmoves==0)    /* no search to do? */
     return(evaluate(root));
   out("root",*root); /* put new tree in agenda */
   out("sync",n_worker);
   for (i=0;i<n_worker;i++)
     out("job",NEW_POSITION); /* new job */
   in("sync",0); /* master continues only after all workers are ready */
   minimax=master(n_worker,nmoves,depth,successor);/* search */
   in("root",*root);  /* delete visited tree */
   }
for (i=0;i<n_worker;i++)
   {
   out("job",QUIT);  /* end of task */
```

```
      in("worker", 0);  /* delete worker */
      }
return (0);
}


int master(int n_worker,int nmoves)
{
int nmoves,local_score,subtree,free,best;
local_score=-INFINITE;  /* initialize local score */
out("score", local_score);  /* initialize global score */
free = n_worker;
subtree = 1;
while ((subtree <= nmoves) || (free<n_worker))
        /* loop terminates when job done */
    if ((subtree <= nmoves) && (free>0))
    /* more tasks in agenda and a worker is idle? */
  { out("job",subtree); /* insert search task in agenda */
    free--;
    subtree++;
  }
    else     /* wait completion of a task */
    {
    in("result",?value,?r_subtree);  /* get result */
    if (value>local_score)  /* improved score? */
                { local_score=value;      /* local update of score */
                  in ("score",?int);
                  out("score",local_score); /* global update of score */
                  best=r_subtree;
        }
    free++;}
 in("score",?int); /* to avoid interference with next search */
 return (local_score);
}
```

Creating and terminating an active tuple for each task is an expensive activity
in Network Linda, thus we have defined a general worker structure that can survive
the end of a task and can be specialized when it is necessary.

```
int worker(int depth)
{
 position *root,*successor,*tree_pointer;
 int nmoves,subtree,score,value,job_type,quit,s;
 quit=false;
 while(!quit)
  {
   in("job",?job_type);
   switch(job_type)
```

```
    {
      case QUIT:  /* terminate */
        quit=true;
        break;
      case NEW_POSITION: /* new game tree */
        in("position",?*root);
        in("sync",?s);
        out("sync",s-1);
        nmoves=genmoves(root,&successor);
        break;
      default: /* sequential alphabeta */
        subtree=job_type;
        tree_pointer=successor+subtree-1;
        makemove(tree_pointer);
        rd("score",?score);  /* update local score */
        value=-alphabeta(tree_pointer,-INFINITE,-score,depth);
        out("result",value,subtree);
        undomove(tree_pointer);
        break;
      }
    }
  return(0);
}
```

We have developed and measured the performance of several distributed programs all based on the master-worker coordination architecture algorithm [4]. The most important value we measured is the time to search a game tree. For sequential versions, this is defined as the interval between the root invocation of alphabeta and its termination (we actually measure CPU time used for such an evaluation). For the parallel versions, we let the master to measure time between the distribution of the root node and the collection of its minimax value (for such an evaluation we used real time; the network was used during unloaded hours).

For all programs we have systematically measured the speedup S up to 11 processors. We have seen that the theoretically optimum speedup S=N with N processors is impossible to reach for the following reasons:

- communication overhead, given by messages between processors;
- search overhead, given by duplication of subtree evaluation;
- synchronisation overhead, given by bad load balancing.

The most annoying problem is the strong coupling among these overheads: if we tried to reduce one, we got always an increase in another one. Thus, we searched for a tradeoff among the overheads. Our results say that the best results are given by PVSplit combined either with score sharing or with dynamic distribution [4].

Our results can easily be compared with results obtained by other researchers. For instance, in [11] a speedup of 3.66 with 5 workstations is reported; such a measure was obtained with a depth of 7 plies on the same test suite; with a shallower depth (5 plies) we got a speedup of 3.49 (3.75 with score sharing). In [17] a speedup of 4.78 with 7 processors, depth of 7 plies was obtained for DPVSplit; we got a speedup of 4.54 (depth = 5 plies). These results seem to say that the use of the Linda programming model does not introduce any special overhead for this class of programs.

On the other hand, we got bad comparison results for algorithms based on dynamic distribution of search. However, the problem seems to be the hardware architecture, not the programming environment; in fact, we found the following results in literature.

The paper [13] reports that the program Oracol, based on dynamic splitting and written in Orca, gets a maximum speedup of 5.5 on a multiprocessor with shared memory and 10 processors. Instead, the paper [14] presents a dynamic algorithm based on the concept "young brothers wait", that is a strategy to coordinate idle workers. On a transputer with 256 processors, the authors report a speedup of 126 (depth 8 plies).

These results suggest that dynamic splitting algorithms can offer good performances, but only on shared memory or on massive parallel systems where communication and fine-grain parallelism are cheap. It would be interesting to test our general dynamic splitting algorithm on these architectures.

4 A new coordinated architecture

In [16, 17] Schaeffer described other experiments for parallelizing alphabeta searches. His results showed that on a network of workstations parallel alphabeta algorithms do not scale well over 10 processors. Our results confirm what was found by Schaeffer, even if we used a different software platform: parallel version of alphabeta cannot use effectively more than 7-8 networked processors. If alphabeta search is not able to exploit more processors, maybe using knowledge in a different way we can do better.

In order to take advantage of a greater number of processors we have explored the idea of *distributed knowledge,* i.e., of chess programs composed of several independent processes having different knowledge on the game. We have tested several knowledge distributions, that allow to build several different advisors. Then we have built a coordinator-decider process, which uses a selection policy to choose a move among those suggested by the advisors; we have tested several selection policies as well.

The basic idea is to have several independent evaluators (we call such processes "advisors") which use different knowledge on the game. The approach we have followed to generate the advisors consists of "splitting" the evaluation function of GNUChess to develop several players each having a simplified and different evaluation function. We call this "distributing knowledge", because it amounts to have several cooperating agents with different knowledge on the same domain.

We expected the following advantages of the new approach to parallelization with respect to the classic one:

- with several independent searches each embedding different knowledge we can collect more "good" candidate moves with respect to parallel alphabeta methods, that only return one move to play;
- most searches could reach a deeper exploration of the game tree with respect to their sequential prototype, being based on simpler evaluation functions.

We have developed in Linda a basic program that acts as coordinator of sequential advisors embedding simplified evaluating functions.

What follows is such a coordination program, that works as a master that distributes jobs to a number of workers:

```
void master (int n_instances,int *functions)
{
 int my_function, quit, instance;
 move *moves, move_selected, mv;
 statistics *search_data, stats;
 my_function = functions[0]; /*master gets its evaluation function */
 for (instance=1;instance<n_instances;instance++)
   /* create workers and give them their evaluation functions */
   eval("instance",worker(instance,functions[instance]));
 NewGame (); /* GnuChess function to initialize game */
 /* some data structures are dynamically allocated */
 memory_alloc(n_instances,&moves,&search_data);
 quit=false;
 while (quit)
    {
    if (side_to_move()==PARALLEL_PLAYER) /* whose move? */
       { /* all workers have to work */
       for (i=1;i<=n_instances;i++) out ("job",i,DO_SEARCH);
/* even master works */
       moves[0]=SelectMove (my_function, &search_data[0])
/* collect suggestions from workers */
       for (instance=1;instance<=n_instances;instance++)
         { in("instance_move",?instance,?mv,?stats);
           moves[instance]=mv;
           search_data[instance]=stats;
         }
       move_selected=policy(move,search_data);
        /* apply selection policy */
       }
      else  /* get move from enemy */
        move_selected=other_player_search();
        MakeMove (move_selected); /* update game state */
        if (quit=end_gamep())  /* end of game? */
           for (instance=1;instance<n_instances;instance++)
              out ("job",instance,QUIT);
         else  /* workers update their state */
           { out("move_selected",move_selected);
             out("sincr",n_instances-1);
             for (instance=1;instance<n_instances;instance++)
             out("job",instance,DO_MOVE);
             in("sincr,0); /* synchronize master and workers */
```

```
            inp("move_selected",move_selected);
        }
    }
for (i=1;i<n_instances;i++) /* workers terminate correctly */
    in("instance",0);
return ();
}
```

A worker in this case is an independent agent that searches a position and returns a candidate move.

```
int worker (int identifier,int my_function)
{
int job,quit,s;
move mv;
statistics stats;
NewGame ();
quit=false;
while (!quit)
    { in("job",identifier,?job); /* receive job */
      switch (job);
{case DO_SEARCH:
    /* sequential evaluation of current position */
    mv=SelectMove (my_function, &stats)
    out("instance_move",identifier,mv,stats);
    break;
  case DO_MOVE:
    rd ("move_selected",?mv);
    MakeMove (mv); /* update game state */
    in ("sincr",?s);
    out ("sincr",s-1);
    break;
  case QUIT:
    quit=true;
    break;
  default:
    break;
    }
  }
return (0);
}
```

Using such a master-worker skeleton, we have built several chess-playing programs based on distributed knowledge; they differ in

- the number of independent instances they include (from a minimum of 3 to a maximum of 6);
- the approach to the distribution of knowledge terms;

– the selection algorithm used to choose a move among the candidates computed by the workers.

Our method for distributing knowledge works as follows: given an evaluation function P that is a polynomial including n knowledge terms t_i, then we can build several functions derived from P simply using different subsets of knowledge terms. For instance, analyzing the evaluation function of GNUChess, we find eight knowledge terms. Combining in all possible ways these knowledge terms, we could build 256 different composite players, but we did not test all possible combinations. We have kept low the number of instances for each composite player, including in all combinations those knowledge terms that according to Schaeffer are most important, and that in our hopes could contribute most to the generation of a list of good candidate moves; for instance, material was always included.

The selection algorithm can be based on several policies; we have developed a classification of possible selection policies:

– *selection based on the best independent minimax value.* Each instance suggests a move and its minimax value, and the selection algorithm uses also the minimax values to make its choice. The underlying hypothesis is that all evaluation functions have the same zero value for a totally balanced position and express the same quantitative advantage if they return the same value.

– *selection based on the search depth.* Weights used in deciding the move could be a function of the search depth reached by each player. Usually each instance will be allotted the same search time, but the maximum search depth they reach is different. However, this policy penalizes most complex evaluation functions, that normally will be an obstacle to deeper searches.

– *Selection based on a selective search of the game tree using only suggested moves.* Another approach consists of using all the moves suggested by the different instances to restart a brute force search with a full evaluation function. We have the problem of balancing the time used for the first phase of distributed evaluation against the second phase of brute force search. This approach seems useful to recognize bad moves, but it seems less able to differentiate among almost equivalent moves.

The results we got are not simple to evaluate; however, some features are quite clear:

– 75% of parallel players is stronger than GNUChess; this is an encouraging result because it shows that knowledge distribution can improve playing strength;

– among successful players, most won 20-games tournaments against GNUChess with scores like 13-7 and even 14-6, a result that in Elo terms gives a difference of 150-200 points using from 5 to 7 workstations only; this also is encouraging, because results for programs based on parallel search say that we need at least 10 workstations to have a comparable improvement [4];

– in general, players based on more instances play worst; possibly this shows a problem in either the use of selection heuristic or the choice of the combination of evaluating functions;

- balanced knowledge looks better than other distribution policies: it seems the approach that balances better the different kinds of knowledge;
- move choice based on weighted selection looks better than democratic majority, except for players based on incremental distribution of knowledge. This anomaly is possibly due to a wrong choice of weights which privileges weaker instances.

These results were encouraging, but not conclusive. Too many design choices were arbitrary: ordering of heuristics, distribution policies, selection policies, limitation in length of games, use of simplified programs (*e.g.*, no opening book, no hash table).

5 Conclusions

We have compared a number of distributed chess-playing programs based on different coordination architectures. We used Linda to develop two basic coordination structures, one for distributing search and one for distributing knowledge.

We claim that the approach based on knowledge distribution and coordination was successful because we had good results in two kinds of experiments:

1. tests on 500 middle game positions; sequential GNUChess and most simpler instances had a max solution ratio of about 20%. However, the impressive data is that more than 50% of the positions was solved by at least one instance! These data per se do not help in developing the best combination of agents, but at least they show that there is room for research and experimentation.
2. tournaments of 20 games between sequential GNUChess and the distributed players; some distributed players won their tournaments with clear advantages. We have found an interesting "anomaly": distributed players built of more agents are not always stronger than players built with a smaller number of agents.

Acknowledgements. This paper was partly founded by ESPRIT BRA Project 9102 *Coordination*, and by the Italian CNR Comitato Scienze e Tecnologia dell'Informazione.

References

1. H. Bal. Heuristic search in PARLOG using replicated worker style parallelism. *Future Generation Computer Systems*, 6:303–315, 1991.
2. N. Carriero and D. Gelernter. *How to Write Parallel Programs: A First Course*. MIT Press, Cambridge, MA, 1990.
3. C.Ebeling. *All the Right Moves: A VLSI Architecture for Chess*. MIT Press, 1986.
4. P. Ciancarini. A Comparison of Parallel Search Algorithms based on Tree Splitting. Technical Report UBLCS-94-14, Comp. Science Laboratory, Università di Bologna, Italy, May 1994.
5. F.Hsu. *Large scale parallelization of alpha-beta search: an algorithmic and architectural study with computer chess*. PhD thesis, Carnegie Mellon University, Pittsburgh, PA, Feb 1990.
6. G.Baudet. *The Design and Analysis of Algorithms for Asynchronous Multiprocessors*. PhD thesis, Carnegie-Mellon Univ., Apr 1978.
7. H.Bal. A comparative study of five parallel programming languages. *Future Generation Computer Systems*, 8:121–135, 1992.

8. H.Bal and R.vanRenesse. A summary of parallel alpha-beta search results. *Journal of the Int. Computer Chess Association*, pages 146–149, Sept 1986.

9. J.Schaeffer. *Experiments in search and knowledge*. PhD thesis, University of Alberta, Edmonton, Canada, Jul 1986.

10. T. Marsland and M. Campbell. Parallel search of strongly ordered game trees. *ACM Computing Surveys*, 14(4):533–551, 1982.

11. T. Marsland, M. Olafsson, and J.Schaeffer. Multiprocessor tree-search experiments. In *Advances in Computer Chess 4*, pages 37–51. Pergamon Press, 1986.

12. N.Carriero, D.Gelernter, T.Mattson, and A.Sherman. The Linda Alternative to Message-passing Systems. *Parallel Computing*, 20:633–655, 1994.

13. R.Elias. Oracol, A Chess Problem Solver in Orca. Master's thesis, Dept. of Mathematics and Computer Science, Vrije Universiteit, Amsterdam, 1990.

14. R.Feldmann, P.Mysliwietz, and B.Monien. Experiments with a fully-distributed chess program. In J. VanDenHerik and V. Allis, editors, *Heuristic Programming in AI*, pages 72–87. Ellis Horwood, 1992.

15. S.Akl, D.Barnard, and R.Doran. Design, analysis, and implementation of a parallel tree search algorithm. *IEEE Trans. on Pattern Analysis and Machine Intelligence*, 4(2):192–203, 1982.

16. J. Schaeffer. Experiments in distributed game-tree searching. Technical report, University of Alberta, Edmonton, Canada, Jan 1987.

17. J. Schaeffer. Distributed game-tree searching. *Journal of Parallel and Distributed Computing*, 6:90–114, 1989.

18. L. Stiller. Group graphs and computational symmetry on massively parallel architecture. *The Journal of Supercomputing*, 5:99–117, 1991.

19. T.Marsland, T. Breitkreutz, and S. Sutphen. A network multiprocessor for experiments in parallelism. *Concurrency: Practice and Experience*, 3(3):203–219, 1991.

Design and Evaluation of a Multi-threaded Architecture for Parallel Graph Reduction

Francis CAUDAL, Bernard LECUSSAN

ONERA-CERT/DERI
av. E. BELIN, BP 4025, 31055 TOULOUSE CEDEX, FRANCE.
Tel: 62-25-25-90
e-mail : {caudal,lecussan}@cert.fr

Abstract:

Main limitations of distributed memory machines involving thousands of processors, deal with network latencies for remote data and/or programs accesses. In this paper we present multithreading techniques for parallel graph reduction model that can tolerate latencies of thousands of cycles by dynamically creating a set of threads. Efficiency is achieved by introducing fast context switch, non preemptive threads and comparative long run-lenght threads (thousand of cycles). Conventional multithreaded techniques deals with statically defined threads (at compile time) and dynamically or statically scheduling.of the work to be performed. Parallel graph reduction is an attractive model because of its simplicity and inherently distributed nature : parallelism is introduced by parallel evaluation of function parameters corresponding to dynamically created set of threads. The single assignment feature and the absence of side effect, since the internal representation of programs remains purely functional, overcomes the difficulties of synchronized accesses to shared data and scheduling of parallel activities.

1 INTRODUCTION

A distributed parallel machine consists of a large number of processor elements, each of which has an execution unit and a local memory. Futhermore, experiences have shown that shared memory machines are easier to program than distributed memory machines, because global addressing space permits parallelization independent of memory data location. In such a multiprocessor architecture, one of the most important design issue is the latency problem which is caused by remote data access and remote procedure invocation. The performance of a distributed program strongly depends on the ratio of processing to communication time, because small activities require more communication. In order to achieve efficient execution in a parallel machine, the processor element must perform high speed context switch among medium-grain concurrent threads of computation. Therefore, the granularity must be sufficiently large to limit the number of thread switches.

The graph reduction execution model offers a solution for parallel processing in a natural way. A program is represented as a graph, each node representing functional expression terms [HAM 91]. Program execution consists in rewriting non reduced expressions (redex) into their reduced form, following a set of rules. Computation is done when no more rules can be applied : this reduced form is the final representation of the initial program. The rewriting mechanism is done in a destructive way but in single assignment mode: the content of a node is replaced by the computed value. In this way, shared sub-expressions are reduced only once and parallelism is introduced by parallel evaluation of function arguments. The single assignment feature and the absence of side effect -since the internal representation of the program remains purely functional- allows to overcome the difficulties of synchronised accesses to shared data and of the distribution of parallel computations.

Program execution could be implemented using three models: 1) control flow model in which execution control is depending on the execution of the program instruction list; 2) data flow model in which computation is done when data will be computed; with both models, instructions and data are explicity splitted; 3) reduction model doesn't make difference between data and instructions: everything is expression; program (data and code) and its result are the same object in different representations.

Parallelism is introduced by parallel evaluation of function parameters; a method, built on combinatory logic, consist in removing all bounded variables using specific operators, named combinators. The graph reduction consists in executing combinator definitions to recompose the original expression.

In this paper we will present the design of a multi-threaded abstract architecture to execute a combinatory code; parallel threads are generated by the combinatory graph reduction mechanism and the granularity of computation can be dynamic : lightweight threads are computed sequentially and compute intensive threads are distributed to other processors using different algorithms (random, least loaded ...). This abstract model has been implemented on an Intel Paragon computer in order to evaluate the efficiency of the multithread concept for parallel graph reduction of functional programs.

2 THE EXECUTION MODEL

The source language is a purely fonctional language that includes higher order functions, implicit curryfication of functions, the possibility of strictness annotations and the form "processus" to express explicit parallelism. The full description of the language is presented in [CC 91].

The machine language code definition is based on a set of indexed combinators. The basic combinators are defined below :

. identity :
$Ix \rightarrow x$
. displacement :
$M_n e_1 e_2 \dots e_n \rightarrow e_1 e_n e_2 \dots e_{n-1}, n \geq 3$
. copy and displacement :
$W_n e_1 e_2 \dots e_n \rightarrow e_1 e_n e_2 \dots e_{n-1} e_n, n \geq 2$
. kill :
$K_n e_1 e_2 \dots e_n \rightarrow e_1 e_2 \dots e_{n-1}, n \geq 2$

. creation of application nodes :
$B_n\ e_1\ e_2\ ...\ e_n\ ->e_1\ (e_2\ e_n), n\geq 3$
. recursivity :
$Y\ f\ ->\ f(Y\ f)$

For more optimization, some additional combinators are used :

. application node creation :
$N_n\ e_1\ e_2\ ...\ e_n\ ->e_1\ (e_2\ e_n)\ e_3\ ...\ e_{n-1}, n\geq 3$
. copy and creation :
$Q_n\ e_1\ e_2\ ...\ e_n\ ->e_1\ (e_2\ e_n)\ e_3\ ...\ e_{n-1}, n\geq 3$
. swap :
$S_n\ e_1\ e_2\ ...\ e_n\ ->e_1\ e_n\ e_3\ ...\ e_{n-1}\ e_2, n\geq 3$

Indices show the range of the combinators, that is the number of arguments involved in the associated rewriting rule. These arguments are needed to trigger combinator execution. Basically, the aim of the rewriting rules is just to move the arguments within an execution stack. The basic abstraction algorithm, given in [MARS 89], shows the starting point of the compilation.

We have demonstrated that the length of an expression (expressed throught the number of atoms) in the object code does not exceed twice the length of the corresponding source code in source program. In fact, most of the time, we have founded an expansion rate close to one.

3 THREADS DEFINITION

Multithreading seems to be an interesting technique for tolerating high latency in multiprocessor systems. Previous multithreading research has been motivated by tolerating memory latency, building an efficient pipeline with no data dependencies and overlapping cache defaults. As threads are statically defined, the cost of multithreading is closely related to the number of threads needed, the size of the register file, the scheduling complexity and the cycles lost to context switching overhead. In distributed multiprocessor systems multithreading can be the mean to tolerate network latency; support for multiple contexts and fast context switching permit high latency operations, such as message sending and receiving, to be overlapped with computation.

While the idea of using multiple hardware context per processor for a distributed multiprocessor it itself not new, we believe multithreading is well adapted to parallel graph reduction and simple to implement. First of all, we can define long run-lengths of threads (thousand of cycles) corresponding to the combinator or operator execution which allow local data accesses during the thread computation. In fact, operands are previously loaded in the local stack grouping all data needed inside one message. Then, threads are dynamically created and there are no fixed set of register file for each threads. All threads share a common address space on each processor with dynamic allocation of contexts with varying sizes.

As the execution model remains purely fonctional, thread activation can be done out of order ; so, there are no scheduling policies to resume a suspended thread on message arrival. The Church Rosser theorem indicate that, if the result of the computation exists, any way taken to reduce the graph reaches the solution; therefore, it seems that some ways could be more efficient than others. It would be an interesting research topic to try to find the better way to reduce the graph and evaluate the scheduling cost for that. Right now we have considered that such a scheduling algorithm could take too many processor cycles.

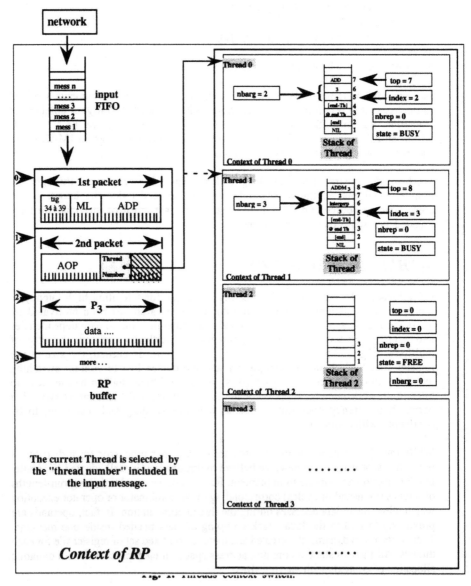

The current Thread is selected by the "thread number" included in the input message.

Fig. 1. Threads context switch.

The creation of a thread is triggered by the arrival of a message of the following type :
<thread-creation, address sub-graph root,arg_n ... arg_1,fct>.
At the end of a thread, the result of the sub-graph reduction is written in memory using the following message :
<result-writing, address node root, reduced result>

and the target node switches from "non-reduced" to "reduced" state. Once the emission of the message is over, the thread is freed, in puting the "stat" variable of the thread context to "free".

4 ABSTRACT MACHINE DEFINITION

As a result of the mechanisms induced by the source language and the parallel graph reduction model, we can elaborate a basic description of a parallel virtual machine (Fig. 2). Processes apply reductions rules to the nodes of the graph. The strategy for process creation is mainly demand-driven with some features of the data-driven approach in order to increase parallelism.

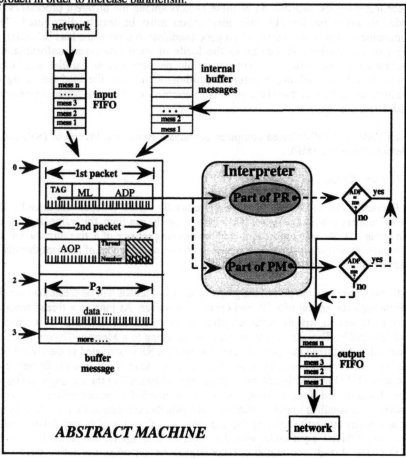

Fig. 2. Abstract machine definition.

A tag on each node is provided for synchronisation of memory accesses, in order to prevent that more than one process reduces the same node at the same time. Processes and nodes are separate entities and relationship between them must be defined. In a multithreading implementation processes are identified to threads. An efficient organization consists in associating one thread to many cells to increase the number of local references and the run-lenght of thread.

The communication latency time, that is to say the time between the emission of a request and the reception of the associated response, can be rather long. For a full use of the processor resources, the latency can be hided by the activation of one another thread consisting in reading the input file message to find the new thread number.

A thread swap occurs each time a response is being awaited. An activated thread cannot be interrupted until it reachs a point to send a message in order to keep busy the internal pipe-line of the processor.

The dynamic aspect of the thread creation and the memory cell creation implies a mechanism for the distribution of these objects among the different processors. In order to avoid bottlenecks, this mechanism must be totally distributed. The communication network seems to be a good candidate to support the load balancing of the parallel machine in managing the loads of each processor; unfortunately, programming the network is not accessible on commercial parallel machines; currently we are studying different algorithms to manage the load balancing of memory allocation and thread creation. The presented results in this paper are obtained with a random algorithm.

Each node of the distributed computer contains a Reduction Processor (RP) and a Memory Processor (MP).

4.1 The Reduction Processor (RP)

A Reduction Processor (RP) must therefore handle several independant threads. The thread number is a parameter set when generating the run-time; this value depends on the cache size, the stack utilization and the working set size of active threads; we are currently investigating methods for finding an optimum number of resident threads in each RP for different processor type.

A thread must carry out part of the graph reduction. Threads will be created within the RP through the arrival of a "thread creation" message. As long as a thread remains active, it has at his disposal all the resources of the RP and it is strictly uninterruptible. Threads activation is made according to a Message-Driven mode. It means that the thread currently executed within the RP is activated at the arrival of a message which was bound to it. At first, this message is put into the in-buffer of the RP (a FIFO waiting list of messages); then, when reading the message, the target thread is activated (for each message, the thread number is located inside the second packet). The handling of every other message (whether it is bound for the active thread or any other) that arrives during the execution of a thread is of course delayed, until the current thread is put aside; until that time, the message remain stored into the in-buffer. The thread commutation (see Fig. 1) occurs when the active thread has finished the reduction of the sub-graph it is committed to, or when it must communicate with the outside (sending a request toward the Memory Processor (MP) for reading a node, for instance) . Another thread is then activated through the reading of the following message from the in-buffer. This commutation of threads allows to hide the communication latency of remote accesses with a context switching cost of 20 processor cycles.

The elapsed time between the execution of the last instruction of a thread and the execution of the first instruction of the following thread is the commutation time. This time corresponds to the load of the target thread number which is used as an index to point to its local work context. Neither a state save, nor any context loading, is made during the commutation; remark that threads are self scheduled as redex could be reduced out of order, so any present thread in the processor can be activated without scheduling algorithm penalties.

A thread is represented by the content of its execution stack. The top of the stack contains a function code which will be applying to the various elements of the stack. The computations inside a thread will be represented by some reduction rules . The number of messages awaited by the same thread is practically always equal to one, except in the very case of the emission of several messages devoted to the incrementation of reference counters.

The RP contains a table of contexts to handle properly the execution of the threads (see Fig. 3). Each thread has its own execution context represented by the set of variables that a thread uses during its whole life :

-> A context will describe *the state of a thread* (two possible states) and will contain successively various threads one after the other. The "stat" variable indicates whether the thread is "free" or "busy".

-> *A static evaluation stack* containing part of the graph to be reduced. As we will use a static array to embody the stack, we also use a *"top"* variable to contain the top of the stack value. The operator (or the combinator) on top of the stack will point out the stack element to be handled (unary or binary operator). An *"index"* variable is introduced to handle more than one element of the stack. An element inside the stack is always located according to the top of the stack.

-> The *"nbarg"* variable contains the number of arguments of the current local evaluation.

-> The *"nbrep"* variable represents the number of acknowledge messages awaited by the thread.

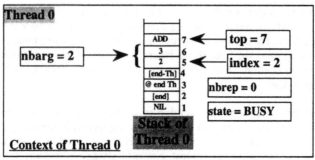

Fig. 3. Resources of threads.

4.2 *Memory Processor (MP)*

The memory management is absolutely transparent for the user. Memory nodes are of two kinds: application nodes (application of a function to an argument) and "cons" nodes (data structures construction). Each cell has two data fields : For application nodes, the right field contains the function and the argument is located in the left field. For "cons" nodes, the right field is the "cdr" and the left field is the "car".

Each memory node has a "*stat*" field which shows the state of the cell during its active life. A cell has a life cycle corresponding to the successive states (see Fig. 4) : "free", "non-reduced", "under-reduction", "reduced" and again "free". Garbage collection is done by means of a reference counter that stores the number of references to a node, from processes and from nodes.

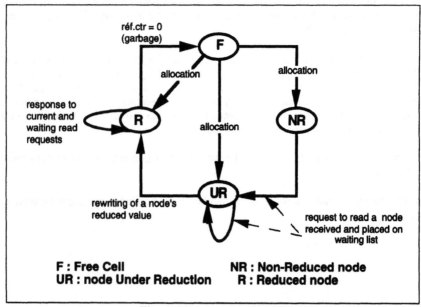

Fig. 4. Memory cell life cycle.

During its active life, a memory cell passes through different states:

"free"
"cons"
"non-reduced"
"reduced"
"ready"
"under-reduction"

A distributed parallel computer is made of nodes supporting reduction processor, memory processor and communication primitives. The implementation of previously described processors form a run-time loaded on each node of the multiprocessor. We study performance of the parallel computer as a function of several parameters such as the number of contexts, the context switch overhead, the latency of the network and the run-length (number of cycles) between context switches. The main result obtained with an Intel Paragon computer is the multithreading efficiency : we have defined a simple benchmark program (Fig. 5) which generate a large number of parallel threads with different size of the run-length; the operator OP has been redefined to allow modification of the computation granularity. Detailed results are given in section 5.

$$(letrec\ ((\ f\ (lambda\ (n)\ (declare\ (strict\ n))$$
$$(if\ (eq0\ n)\ 1$$
$$(if\ (eqn\ n\ 1)\ 1$$
$$(OP\ (f\ (sub1\ n))\ (f\ (sub\ n\ 2\ ))))))))$$

Fig. 5. Parallel generation of threads.

4.3 Communication

We are now going to draw a detailed description of the messages used. Messages constitute the interface between a thread and the memory. There exist two types of messages, those which have a particular target ("on address messages"), and those without address ("on load messages"). Let's point out these last ones which will be routed "on load", that is to say they will be sent to the processor being considered as the least loaded.

A message contains the address of a target processor. A message is made of four byte packets represented in Fig. 6 :

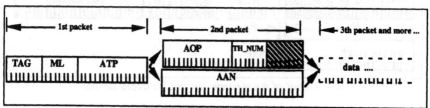

Fig. 6. General format of messages.

The first packet has always the useful informations defined for the routing "on load" or "on address" :

. **Tag of routing** (TAG): type of message.
. **Message Length** (ML): number of packets of four bytes included in the message.
. **Address of the Target Processor** (ATP): All the messages have a target address. The size of this field is two bytes. So 65535 processors could be addressed.

Some messages have only one packet (for example : initialisation of the physical memory), but most of the messages have more than one packet. The second packet contains informations used to exchange data between RP and MP. This second packet doesn't contain the same information according to the message code (TAG).

-> In the first case : the packet contains two informations (two fields : AOP and TH_NUM) :

. **Address of Origin Processor** (AOP): for getting an answer to a reading request, for example, a processor must put its address in this field.
. **Thread Number** (TH_NUM) : a Reduction Processor contains many active threads.

-> In the second case : the second packet contains only one field.

. **Address of Acceded Node** (AAN) : cell address to write the result (four bytes)

Some messages contain a various number of packets for data transfert.

Let us give two examples of messages, assuming that P_i is ith packet included in the message.

     1 - example of an "on load message" :

       - request for thread creation : in this case, a Memory Processor sends a request for thread creation to a Reduction Processor. The format of this message is described in Fig. 7 .

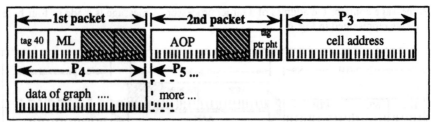

Fig. 7. Format of the message "request for thread creation".

2 - example of an "on address message" :

       - request for reading a node : it's a thread that send the target cell in the local memory. The format of this message is showed in Fig. 8.

Fig. 8. Format of the message "request for reading a node".

5 RESULTS

In this section we present some general results obtained with a multiprocessor Intel Paragon. We have written a simple program in which we can statically define the run-length of each thread without cache misses; we want to examine the behavior of the program on the parallel machine depending on the number of nodes and the number of threads per nodes. These results give an overall idea of the multithreading technique efficiency for hiding long communication latency in a multiprocessor. They also show the effect of thread granularity and maximum number of threads defined on each processor.

Let T the execution time of f previously defined, C the overall communication cost and G the number of processor cycles taken to compute OP. We have :

$$T = C + G*tc$$

where tc is the processor cycle time.

Since computation is message driven, the value of C contains the network communication cost and the processor idle time when the input buffer is empty.

Table 1 shows the results for a eight nodes configuration of the parallel machine under different levels of multithreading and different run-lenght; table 2 to table 4 are for 16, 32 and 41 nodes configuration. For these tests we use a random algorithm for thread creation or memory allocation invoked by "on load" messages. Althought the run time could be tuned to obtain better performance, our goal is to evaluate the impact of dynamic creation of threads on the parallel machine performance.

Table 1 : computation on 8 processors.

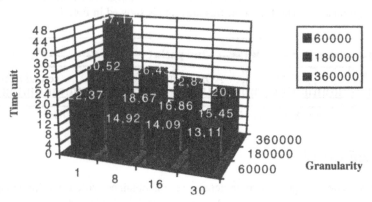

Table 2 : computation on 16 processors.

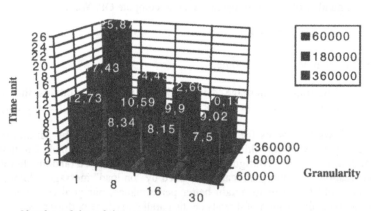

Table 3 : computation on 32 processors.

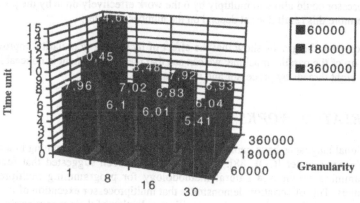

Table 4 : computation on 41 processors.

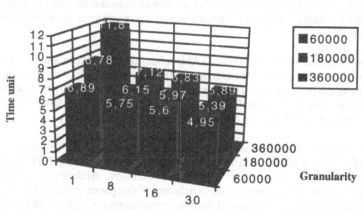

On each diagram we can see that increasing the number of threads to 30 threads the execution time decreases in a range from 1.5 to 2.3 depending on the value of G. We note that the same execution time was obtained for G=60,000 with one thread and for G=360,000 with 16 threads; we can interpret this result as implementing 16 threads by processor could allow to multiply by 6 the work effectively done by the processor. Furthermore this result does'nt depend on the number of nodes.

As expected, the graphs show that the effect of increasing granularity improves the speed-up of the parallel machine; we can see that the improvement is noticeable from one to eight threads by processor and marginal up to eight.

6 RELATED WORKS

Functional languages have gained attention as vehicles for programming in a concise and elegant manner [GOL 88]. In addition, it has been suggested that functional programming provides a natural methodology for programming multiprocessor computers. This dissertation demonstrates that multiprocessor execution of functional programs is faisible, and results in a signifiant reduction of their execution times.

A Lisp-based approach is attractive for parallel computing since Lisp languages and systems assume significant clerical burdens, such as storage management [HAL 88].

Parallel graph reduction is an attractive implementation for functional programming languages because of its simplicity and inherently distributed nature. [JON 89]. This paper outlines some of the issues raised by parallel compiled graph reduction, and presents an approach adopted for the parallel machine, GRIP.

The Spineless Tagless G-Machine is an abstract machine designed to support higher-order functional languages. Presentation of the machine is done into three parts in [JON 92].

The Threaded Abstract Machine (TAM) refines dataflow execution models to address the critical constraints that modern parallel architectures place on the compilation of general-purpose parallel programming languages. TAM defines a self-scheduled machine language of parallel threads, which provides a path from data-flow-graph program representations to conventional control flow [TAM 93].

*T is a multithreaded massivelly parallel architecture [NIK92] which is the latest evolution of dynamic dataflow architectures, starting with the MIT Tagged-Token Dataflow architecture, the Manchester Dataflow Architecture and the LAU Architecture of our group. In the conclusion of this paper, authors state that "the real challenge is to provide general purpose programming models in which applications can have much more dynamic structure"... " A very promising approach is to start with declarative languages where the compiler can effortlessly extract large amount of fine grain parallelism".

7 CONCLUSIONS

The concepts of multi-threaded architecture, common shared-address memory space, dynamic invocation of parallel threads and fast context switch are the key issues to implement efficiently parallel graph reduction model on a wide range of parallel computers.

In our approach the source language as well as the intermediate language are purely functional; therefore the number of parallel threads is quite greater than the number of nodes in the parallel architecture. Each node is then allowed to have sufficient threads ready to execute in order to hide the network latency and no scheduling policies are needed to resume a suspended thread on message arrival. But, this mode of "message driven" computation implies that the network bandwith requirements are high for all applications. Multithreading with medium-run threads addresses this problem and for most applications seems to reduce the bandwidth to acceptable levels.

We have studied performance as a function of several parameters such as the number of threads per processor, the run length of each thread, the latency of the network and the context switch overhead; it is not obvious to separate each parameter in order to evaluate their contribution to the efficiency of the parallel machine.

We are currently doing more in-depth evaluation of our parallel graph reduction model implemented on conventional parallel architectures in order to optimize the current implementation.

8 ACKNOWLEDGEMENTS

We would like to thank Hugues LEROY from INRIA/IRISA for allowing us to use the Intel Paragon machine for gathering the data for this paper. We also wish to thank Guy Durrieu and Michel Cubero-Castan for their contributions to the presented work.

9 REFERENCES

[CC 91]   E.COUSIN, C.COUSTET,
MaRS_Lisp : User Manual V1.0,
Document interne ONERA-CERT-DERI, June 1991.

[MARS 89]   A. CONTESSA, E. COUSIN, C.COUSTET, M. CUBERO-CASTAN, G.DURRIEU, B. LECUSSAN, M. LEMAITRE,P. NG,
MaRS, a combinator graph reduction multi-processor,
ONERA/CERT/DERI, Parallel Architectures andLanguages Europe, Eindhoven, The Netherlands, Proceedings, VOL. 1, June 1989.

[GOL 88]   Benjamin F. GOLDBERG,
Multiprocessor Execution of Functional Programs,
Research report yaleu/dcs/rr-618, Department of Computer Science, Yale University, April 1988.

[HAL 88]   Robert H. HALSTEAD,
New Ideas in Parallel Lisp : Language Design, Implementation, and Programming Tools,
In T. Ito and R. H. Halstead, editors, *Parallel Lisp : Language and systems,* volume 441 of *Lecture Notes in Computer Science,* pages 2-57, Sendai, Japan, June 5-8, 1988, Springer, Berlin.

[HAM 91]   K.HAMMOND, S.PEYTON JONES,
Profiling Scheduling strategies on the GRIP parallel reducer,
Proc 4th Intl Workshop on Parallel Implementation of Functional Languages; Kuchen H and Loogen R (Eds) ; RWTH,
Aachen 1992.

[JON 89]   S.L. PEYTON JONES, C. CLACK, and J. SALKID,
High-Performance Parallel Graph Reduction,
In E. Odijk, M. Rem, and J.-C. Syre, editors, PARLE '89, *Parallel Architectures and Lanquages Europe, Volume I : Parallel Architectures, volume 365 of Lecture Notes in Computer Science,* pages 193-206, Eindhoven, The Netherlands,
June 12-16, 1989, Springer, Berlin.

[JON 92]   S.L. PEYTON JONES,
Implemented Lazy Functional Languages on Stock Hardware : The Spineless Tagless G-machine,
Journal of Functional Programming, 2(2):127-202,
April 1992.

[TAM 93]   D. E. CULLER, S.GOLDSTEIN, K. ERIK SCHAUSER, and T. VON EICKEN,
TAM - A Compiler Controlled Threaded Abstract Machine,
Journal of Parallel and Distributed Computing, pages 347-370, 1993.

[NIK 92]   R.S. NIKHIL, G.M. PAPADOPOULOS, ARVIND
*T : A multithreaded massively parallel architecture
ISCA'92 Pages 156-167, 1992

Implementation of the Multigrid Method for Solving the Boundary-Value Problems for the Poisson and Helmholtz Equations on the Massively Parallel Computers*

Mamedova I.G.

Computing Centre of the Russian Academy of Sciences
Russia, 117967, Moscow, Vavilova, 40

Abstract. The parallelization of multigrid method for solving some boundary-value problems is under consideration. The parallel algorithms for the solution of the problems concerned have been implemented on the massively parallel computer PARSYTEC. The suggested approach is proved to be efficient.

1 Introduction

With the aim of designing high-efficiency methods of numerical solutions of the first boundary-value problem for a Stokes-type system with a small parameter ϵ new iterative methods with uncomplete and complete boundary-condition splitting were worked out and investigated in [1, 2, 3]. As pointed out in those paper well known difficulties derived by the presence of a pressure and continuity equation in the system (especially in three-dimensional problems) arise on solving the problem numerically. In such a manner it is sure to be the matter of great importance to develop iterative methods which would make it possible to get the boundary-value problems related to velocity and pressure separately at each iterative step.

The iterative methods considered in there have essentially important feature. Those techniques give opportunities of splitting the boundary conditions at each step of the procedure; in this way two separate problems to be solved appear: the Neumann problem for a pressure and Dirichlet-Neumann vector problem for values of velocity if uncomplete splitting takes place or Dirichlet scalar problems (for each component of velocity for the Helmholtz equation) if complete splitting does.

For implementing numerically the methods with boundary-condition splitting for the singularly perturbed Stokes-type systems those auxiliary problems are approximated by the finite-element method with bilinear elements and solved by means of the multigrid method [4] with usual operations of projection and interpolation [5].

* Research supported by the Russia Fundamental Research Fund, Grant No. 95-01-00630 & No. 93-01-00606

Implementation of the multigrid methods on parallel machines seemed to be rather complicated and associated with many difficulties due to the heavy hierarchy and also due to the icrease of mesh-size of the calculation grid on performing of a V-cycle of the multigrid method forward and, the decrease of mesh-size on performing a V-cycle backward.

Our aim was to implement the methods concerned with regard to the field of the problems which are spoken about here on a massively parallel computer PARSYTEC with a rectangular mesh topology, which enables us not only to speedup the algorithms, but also to enlarge the size of the matrix representing the solution.

Two possibilities for solving the problems on such kind of computers have been tried depending on data distribution scheme. The first one assumes the row-oriented distribution of matrix elements across the processors. It is supported by linear topology of processor connection. The second one assumes the rectangular grid distribution, defined by assigning certain matrix elements to a cetain processor in the network of $Q \times R$ processors. Both of them have been dealt with, which enables to compare them. The speed-up and the efficiency of concurrent calculations were found quite high for row-oriented distribution, and not rather high for grid distribution. It is certain to be explained by the necessity of column-oriented communications between processors in the latter case (note, that implementations in C programming language have been experimented).

2 Outline of the Algorithm

The purpose of this section is to present an outline of the based on the multigrid method parallel algorithms solving the problems discussed here. It makes sense to consider one of those algorithms, for example, the Neumann problem for a pressure, just to simplify the discussion. What is going to be said in regard to the Neumann problem also holds in all respects for the Dirichlet scalar problem and Dirichlet- Neumann vector problem.

The algorithm consist of the parallel composition of $p = Q \times R$ processes, denoted by $(s,t), 0 \leq s < Q, 0 \leq t < R$, each executing on one processor, denoted by (s,t). Each processor has a local memory. The processors use a rectangular mesh communication network to pass messages between them. Two processors(s,t) and (s',t'), $0 \leq s < Q, 0 \leq t < R$, are able to communicate if and only if $\|s-s'\|+\|t-t'\| = 1$. For our purposes it seems to be more convenient to consider (as in [2]) the Neumann problem in two-dimensional space for the Helmholtz equation not with a small parameter but with a parameter μ that can be large.

$$-\Delta u + \mu^2 u = F \quad in \quad \Omega$$
$$\frac{\partial u}{\partial n} = g \bigg|_{\Gamma},$$

When $\mu=0$ the Poisson equation takes place. In the two-dimensional case the problem is approximated by the finite-element scheme.

The main stages of the multigrid method developed to solve the finite-element scheme appearing here are the procedures of over relaxation (with according relaxation parameter) which is taken as a smoother on each grid level obtained, projection of residual to the grid with twice as much mesh-size and interpolation ; multiple execution of those stages make up a V-cycle of the multigrid method. It is important to note here that the transition to the rect-angular mesh grid with twice as much mesh-size would result in redistribution of the matrix.

In generally, the data distribution for the problems solved on the basis of multigrid methods cannot be chosen freely because the data are already distributed as a result of previous calculations, and the cost of redistribution would be higher than the cost of the algorithm itself, leading to extra infor-mation exchange between processors, which is, naturally, not desired. To avoid those unnecessary data exchange the new allocation of matrix elements should be done followed the scheme given in Fig. 1.

Fig. 1. *The allocation of the distributed matrix with regard to any of the matrix dimensions*

The matrix U, the values of which are either approximations to the solution or corrections in grid nodes is distributed across the processors by assigning the element $u_{ij}, 0 \leq i < N, 0 \leq j < M$, to process $(s,t) = (2^l i/(N/Q), 2^l j/(M/R))$, where $l \geq 0$ is the grid level of a V-cycle.

Each processor performs the part $([n_1..n_2],[m_1..m_2])$, $0 \leq n_1, n_2 \leq N, 0 \leq m_1, m_2 \leq M$, of the original matrix of size $N \times M$ independently. And the boundary points of the processors are the only ones in which information from the neighbours are necessary for continuing the calculation. Data communica-tions take place before each stage of the multigrid method. Due to the fact that the amount of information being sent through the processors to one another is turned out not to be much it does not essentially affect efficiency of the parallel algorithm.

It is worth noting here that there is also the necessity of data exchange at the stage of overrelaxation. As a matter of fact, due to the finite-element scheme accepted for this stage. the new values of the matrix elements in the boundary points of processors at the overrelaxation stage are defined from either boundary conditions (in the first or the last processors) or by using information from neighbour points. To reduce the data exchange at the stage of overrelaxation the nodes of the grid are handled in "checker-board"-type order. Fig. 2 illustrates this sequence of calculations.

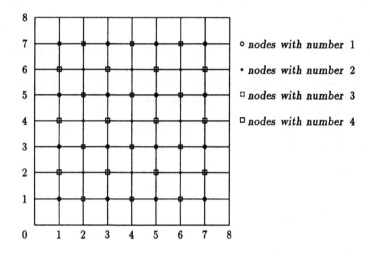

Fig. 2.

At the first step of the overrelaxation the nodes with numbers "1" are handled concurrently over the processors, then the nodes marked "2","3" and "4" in turn. Every time when changing the node type the new values of the nodes calculated previously are used. As each process does not possesses all the necessary values of matrix elements u_{ij}, which have to be updated, this phase require communications between processors as mentioned above. For example, if the nodes with number "2" are being calculated and the row with even number is the first to be updated in the processor, the nodes with the numbers "1" and "3" are those that should be received by the processor before computations in nodes with number "1" start.

An ordering for grid nodes is important because it allows us to achieve maximal parallelization of the overrelaxation stage.

3 Experimental Results on Parallel Calculations

The algorithms for solving the Dirichlet problem, the Neumann problem and the Dirichlet-Neumann problem have been implemented in the programming language C and executes on a rectangular mesh of INMOS T800 transputers - PARSYTEC parallel system and also on a pipeline of processors. Timing results were obtained for a pipeline composed by $p =4$, 8, 16, 32, 64 processors and for square matrices of order up to $N \times M = 2048 \times 2048$. Each processor possesses a local memory of 4Mb, allowing the storage of 448×256 matrix per processor. All computations are done in double precision (64bits) and from 4 to 6 operations of projection and interpolation of a V-cycle are performed.

Table 1. Timing (in sec) of the solution of the Dirichlet problem with a velocity matrix of $N \times M$ order on a pipeline of p transputers

$N \times M$	$p = 1$ seq	$p = 4$	$p = 8$	$p = 16$	$p = 32$	$p = 64$
128×128	8.56	2.44	1.40	0.89	0.68	
256×256	34.5	9.01	4.72	2.59	1.53	1.12
448×256	60.6	15.5	7.98	4.21	2.34	1.52
1024×1024				35.4	18.0	9.41
2048×2048						35.8

Table 1 shows the time $T_p(N, M)$ of the parallel algorithms for solving the problems under consideration, running on a pipeline of p processors. The time $T_p(N, M)$ is a monotounas decreasing function of p for a fixed matrix order $N \times M$. It is the case for two other problems under discussion.

Tables 2, 3, 4 illustrate the efficiency of parallel algorithms for solving the Dirichlet problem, the Neumann problem and Dirichlet-Neumann problem accordingly.The efficiencies are shown for various matrix order n and m and for a fixed number of processors. The measure of efficiency is

$$E_p(N, M) = \frac{T_{seq}(N, M)}{p T_p(N, M)}$$

where T_{seq} is the time taken by the problem being solved by a sequential algorithm on a single transputer. $p T_p(N, M)$ is the time which is obtained for the problem solving a parallel algorithm on p processors. As it is clear from the tables for the small size matrices the values of efficiency are small.It happens due to the load imbalance of processors in the inner grid levels and the increase of the data exchange expences. It is not the case for the matrices of large size.

Table 2. The Efficiency of parallel algorithm for solving the Dirichlet problem for various velocity matrix order

$N \times M$	$p = 4$	$p = 8$	$p = 16$	$p = 32$	$p = 64$
128×128	0.66	0.76	0.60	0.39	
256×256	0.96	0.91	0.83	0.70	0.48
448×256	0.98	0.95	0.90	0.81	0.62
1024×1024			0.97	0.96	0.91
2048×2048					0.96

Table 3. The Efficiency of parallel algorithm for solving the Neumann problem for a pressure

$N \times M$	$p = 4$	$p = 8$	$p = 16$	$p = 32$	$p = 64$
128×128	0.88	0.84	0.77	0.65	0.48
256×256	0.90	0.88	0.85	0.79	0.68
448×256	0.91	0.90	0.88	0.84	0.77
1024×1024			0.89	0.87	0.85
2048×2048					0.87

Table 4. The Efficiency of parallel algorithm for solving the Dirichlet-Neumann problem

$N \times M$	$p = 4$	$p = 8$	$p = 16$	$p = 32$	$p = 64$
128×128	0.90	0.87	0.81	0.70	0.48
256×256	0.93	0.92	0.90	0.86	0.77
1024×1024			0.94	0.93	0.91
2048×2048					0.93

In order to be able to estimate the real performance of parallelizing procedure it make a sense to draw attention to the following ideas. The results obtained in the serial computations for a matrix of size 256×256 on one processor show that the runtime taken by six levels of a V-cycle is 34.5s, while in concurrent computations with the grid 2048×2048 the run time is 35.8s. As far as the amount of calculations in the latter case is 64 times as much than in the former case, so the coefficient of parallelizing according to our estimations is not less than

$$\frac{34.5}{35.8} \approx 0.96$$

The coefficients of efficiency of the parallel algorithm shown in the tables above are calculated on the basis of this ideas.

References

1. Pal'tsev B.V. On fast iterative methods with boundary-condition splitting for a multidimensional system of Stokes-type system. Periodic "flows" between parallel walls. Russian Acad. Sci. Dokl. Math.,Moscow, V.325, N.5, 1992, p.925-932.
2. Pal'tsev B.V. On fast iterative methods with uncomplete boundary-condition splitting for a multidimensional singularly perturbed Stokes-type system. Mat.Sbornik, V.185, N.4, 1994, p.101-150.

3. Pal'tsev B.V. On fast iterative methods with complete boundary-condition splitting for a multidimensional singularly perturbed Stokes-type system. Mat.Sbornic, V.185, N.9, 1994, p.109-138.
4. Fedorenko R.P. Relaxation method of the solution of difference schemes for elliptical equations. J. Comp. math. Math. Phys. V.1, N. 5, 1961, p.922-927.
5. Mc.Cormick S.F. Multigrid methods for varitional problems. SIAM J.Numer. Anal., V.19, N.5, 1982, p.924-929.
6. Serebriacov V.A., Bezdushny A.N., Belov C.G. SYNAPS/3-an extention of C for scientific computations. Proc. SMS TPE, Sept. 19-23,1994, Moscow.

Parallel Seismic Data Processing Method for MEMSY Multiprocessor System [*]

A.Kremlev[1] , O.Monakhov[1] , T.Thiel[2]

[1] Computing Centre, Sibirian Division of Russian Academy of Science,
Pr. Lavrentiev 6, Novosibirsk, 630090, Russia,
e-mail: {kremlev,monakhov}@comcen.nsk.su
[2] University of Erlangen-Nurnberg, IMMD, Martensstrasse 1/3,
D 91058 Erlangen, Germany,
e-mail: thiel@informatik.uni-erlangen.de

1 Introduction

The results of testing of seismic data parallel processing by Wave analogy of the Common Depth Point (WCDP) method on multiprocessor pyramidal architecture MEMSY System are presented.

2 WCDP method

The WCDP method [1] stands out among other prestack migration methods as being based on the strict mathematical solution of the inverse scattering problem in Born's approximation on multifold data.

Let $U(\bar{\rho}, \bar{\rho}_0, t)$ be a reflected signal detected at the point $\bar{\rho}_0 = \{x_0, y_0, 0\}$ after shooting at the point $\bar{\rho} = \{x, y, 0\}$. This function is satisfied by the following equation

$$\Delta U - \frac{1}{c^2}[1 + a(\bar{r})]U_{tt} = -4\pi\delta(\bar{r} - \bar{\rho}_0)\delta(t)$$

with zero initial conditions $U_{t<0} = 0$ and the emission boundary condition. The problem is to find the function $a(\bar{r})$, which describes an inhomogeneities inclusion from the scattering waves $U(\bar{\rho}, \bar{\rho}_0, t)$, which are known on the plane $z = 0$ for different shoot and receiver positions. These data are redundant and are to be used in order to suppress nonregular noise-waves and to assure statistical reliability of the result. The formula

$$\alpha(\bar{r}) = \frac{1}{N} \int\limits_0^{\Omega} \frac{d\omega}{2\pi} \int \frac{d\bar{\kappa}}{(2\pi)^2} \frac{d\bar{\kappa}_0}{(2\pi)^2} [\Phi(\bar{r}, \bar{\kappa}, \bar{\kappa}_0, \omega) \times \omega(\bar{\kappa}, \bar{\kappa}_0, \omega) + c.c],$$

gives local average of function through the volume with the scale $\lambda = 2\pi\Omega/c$ and meets these demands. Here N is a multifold parameter, Ω - is highest

* This work is supported by RFBR projects N94-05-17073, N94-00-00682

frequency supplied by a recording system, $w(\bar{\kappa}, \bar{\kappa}_0, \omega)$ - is the reflected wave spectrum,

$$\Phi(\bar{r}, \bar{\kappa}, \bar{\kappa}_0, \omega) = \frac{1}{\omega}\left(\frac{\omega^2}{c^2} + \bar{\kappa}\bar{\kappa}_0 + \sqrt{\frac{\omega^2}{c^2} - \kappa^2}\sqrt{\frac{\omega^2}{c^2} - \kappa_0^2}\right)^{\frac{1}{2}} \times$$

$$\times \exp\left[i(\bar{\kappa} + \bar{\kappa}_0)\bar{\rho} - iz\left(\sqrt{\frac{\omega^2}{c^2} - \kappa^2} + \sqrt{\frac{\omega^2}{c^2} - \kappa_0^2}\right)\right] \times$$

$$\times \theta\left(\frac{\omega^2}{c^2} - \kappa^2\right) \times \theta\left(\frac{\omega^2}{c^2} - \kappa_0^2\right),$$

where $\bar{r} = \{\bar{\rho}, z\}$ and $\theta(x)$ is the Heaviside function.

The WCDP processing algorithm, which is based on these formulas, has two main features. The first is that an elementary object is "point" inclusion, which is the source of the secondary diffracted waves. Common depth square being an elementary object for CDP method, is built from these "point" diffractors. The second feature is that the accumulation of useful signals, due to the input data redundancy, allows noise suppression and velocity analysis.

3 MEMSY - pyramidal multiprocessor system

MEMSY (Modular Expandable Multiprocessor System) [2] is an experimental multiprocessor system with a scalable architecture based on locally shared memory between a set of adjacent nodes and other communication media. The MEMSY system continues the line of systems which have been built at the University of Erlangen - Nurnberg (Germany) using distributed shared-memory and pyramidal topology.

The MEMSY structure consists of two planes with 4 nodes in the upper plane and 16 processor nodes in the lower plane. In each plane the processor nodes form a rectangular grid. Each node has a shared - memory module, which is shared with its four neighbouring nodes. Each grid is closed to a torus. One processing element of the upper plane has access to the shared memory of the four nodes directly below it, thereby forming a small pyramid.

The MEMSY consists of the following functional units: 20 processor nodes, one shared-memory module (communication memory - 4 Mbytes) at each node, the interconnection network between processor nodes and communication memories, a special optical bus (FDDI net) connecting all nodes and a global disk memory (1,57 Gbytes). Each node of the MEMSY consists of four processors $MC88000$ with 25 Mflops performance , 32 Mbytes local memory and 500 Mbytes local disk memory.

The programming model of the MEMSY was designed to give direct access to the real structure and the power of the system. The application programmer can use a variety of different mechanisms for communication and coordination defined as a set of system library calls which can be called from C and

$C++$ languages. There are the following mechanisms for communication and coordination: shared communication memory between neighbouring nodes, message passing mechanisms, semaphores and spinlocks, FDDI net for fast transfer of high volume data. The operating system of MEMSY (MEMSOS) is based on Unix adapted to the parallel hardware. The multitasking/multiuser feature of Unix and traditional I/O library calls for local and global data storage are supported. The MEMSOS allows different applications (single user parallel program) to run simultaneously and shields from one another.

4 Parallel algorithm and experimental results

The time-frequency integral in the formula of the WCDP method can be separated into parts, which can then be calculated one at a time. A master - slave model was chosen and the message technique was used to implement parallel computation for the $2D$ case [3]. The master process prepares the data for all slaves and write them to hard disk. Then the master sends message to slaves to read a certain portion of the data and to start calculations. Having received the message that any slave has finished his work, the master sends his permission to add this portion of the result to hard disk and waits for the reply that it is done.

CPU user_time and system_time were measured for master and slave processes versus node numbers. The results are presented in the table. It shows that master user_time and system_time are constant, while slave user_time decreases inversely proportionally to node numbers.

Table.

Node numbers	1	4	8	16	20
master user_time	466	463	463	465	462
master system_time	15	15	16	18	17
slave user_time	21311	6775	2889	1382	1061
slave system_time	1	1	1	1	1
slave speed_up	1	3.145	7.377	15.42	20.08

An example of seismic stack in Okhotsk Sea Derugin Basin, which was calculated by this technique, is presented on Fig.1.

Our results show that MEMSY architecture is well suitable for pre-stack migration WCDP method of processing seismic data.

5 Acknowledgments

We would like to thank Prof. H.Wedekind for supporting this work.

WCDP-STACK 1991.104 <DYNGU L300>

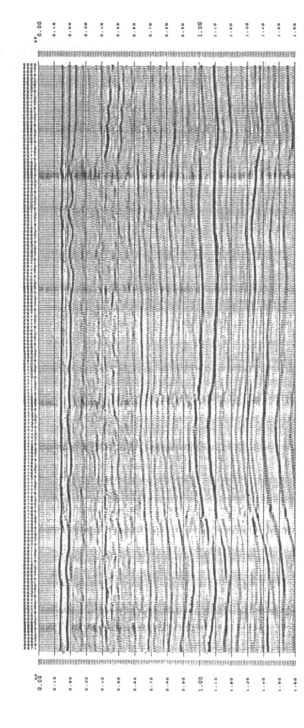

Fig. 1. Seismic section in the Okhotsk Sea Derugin Basin

References

1. A.N.Kremlev: About inverse wave scattering problem. - Dokl. AN SSSR, vol. 281, No 6, (1985) 1349-1351.
2. F.Hofman, M.Dal Cin, A.Grygier, H.Hessenauer, U.Hildebrand, C.-U.Linster, T.Thiel, S.Turowski: MEMSY: a modular expandable multiprocessor system. - Technical report. University of Erlangen-Nurnberg, 1992, 18p.
3. O.G.Monakhov: Organization of the distributed resource control in computer systems with programmable structure. - Programmirovanie, No.2, (1984) 75-83.

Hardware and Software Platform for Information Processing

Esen Ozkarahan

Dokuz Eylul University
Dept. of Computer Engineering
Bornova, Izmir, Turkey

Abstract. In view of the limitations of the classical uniprocessor architecture and of the characteristics of contemporary information processing which may involve multi-media objects, a hardware software platform is defined over parallel processing. Such a platform possesses a system architecture which combines parallel algorithms, parallel data structures, parallel processors, and an efficient input output architecture. Our research that uses this platform in the implementation of a multi-media information system and its methodology are outlined.

Keywords: Shared nothing architecture, parallel database algorithms, multimedia information system, multidimensional and order preserving data partitioning, load balancing

1. INTRODUCTION
1.1 Architecture

To this date the limitations of the classical centralized Von Neumann type uniprocessor architecture have become well known. These limitations are manifested as "processor" and "I/O" bottlenecks [8] arising from the fact that huge amounts of data must be processed by a single cpu located away from the data source which can be reached by a limited I/O bandwidth.

To overcome these limitations two types of parallel processor architectures have emerged. These are the "shared memory" and "distributed memory" or also known as "shared nothing" systems as depicted in Figures 1(a) and 1(b), respectively.

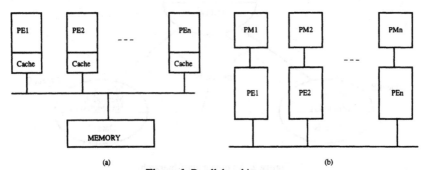

Figure 1. Parallel architectures

The shared memory parallel architecture of Figure 1(a) has the usual upscalability and memory coherence problems even though it is conceptually easier to program. Considering the fact that in information processing large volumes of data are searched even for a small answer, the shared memory parallelism could create "memory bottleneck" due to memory contention among parallel processors racing to access parts of memory for parallel processing.

In view of the foregoing problems, the shared nothing parallel architecture emerges as the desirable choice for parallel architecture. It offers the features of low cost, availability, scalability, and therefore, the potential for high performance information processing.

1.2 Features of Information Processing

Information processing has the following basic characteristics:
- associative search and retrieval
- set-oriented processing
- formatted as well as unformatted data structures
- relational algebra operations and string search capability
- object-oriented database

Almost all search and retrieval requests in all areas of computer science, and certainly in information processing, involves associative reference which consequently calls for associative search and retrieval. In other words, the user presents a variable and requests the values corresponding to it (i.e., belonging to the same data class) that satisfy a predicate. The opposite to associative reference would be to request retrieval of storage addresses rather than the values of that variable.

In order to implement associative search the storage contents must be exhaustively searched for all data sets and predicates must be evaluated according to set theoretic operators.

Information processing today involves information from multiple media such as facts (relations), text, audio, and images. Most of these information sources involves unformatted data. Such data structures require different search operators such as string searching, audio and image recognition, analysis, and matching besides relational algebra.

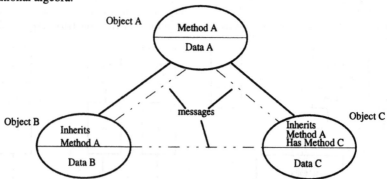

Figure 2. An object class hierarchy

The multimedia based information processing must be object oriented because abstract data types and complex objects are involved for modeling multimedia data types and classes. Figure 2 represents an object class hierarchy between a generic object A and descendant objects B and C. B and C inherit the characteristics (methods) of their ancestor, besides having their own, and objects communicate via messages.

As an example, object A can be a robot and objects B and C can be its arms. All parts of the robot obey the operation directed to them so that arm movements must be in unison with the main control (method A) and the robot in its entirety must operate in synchronization by exchanging sensor and control signals (messages) among its parts.

1.3 Hardware and Software Platform

In view of the foregoing discussion we must define a suitable hardware and software platform for efficient system performance. We will present this platform (or framework) according to its system architecture, our research activity that is carried out within this framework, and the methodology of our implementations. Due to the generality of the problems tackled we believe that this framework can provide a useful reference to the researchers in the same field.

2. SYSTEM ARCHITECTURE FOR INFORMATION PROCESSING

Shared nothing parallel architectures are being produced with respect to various interconnection structures and they are usually directly exploitable by numeric algorithms for the simple reason that such algorithms are computation intensive and require basic interconnections such as the nearest neighbor topology of the mesh architecture. However, we have come to realize up to this point that information processing has certain requirements to achieve high performance. A definition of this computer system architecture was made [10] earlier, and it is still valid. This system architecture is based on:
- hardware architecture
- software system
- data and storage structures
- algorithms

Unlike numeric processing, where parallel systems can almost directly be used, in information processing, which is mostly of nonnumeric in nature, the parallel hardware architecture must be a starting point in building a suitable system architecture. With respect to the four features listed above the hardware architecture must be a shared nothing parallel processing system due to the reasons discussed in Section 1.1.

The software system must be capable of executing relational algebra operations, string searching, and support representation and retrieval of audio and images. The system must be object oriented, due to the reason discussed in Section 1.2, and therefore, support a server model. In information system applications, large number of object instances are involved. Each object consists of data, methods, and messages (i.e., server = object = data + methods + messages).

Therefore, a server processes an object and as such it should be modeled by a machine possessing memory, states, and instructions. This can be realized by an automaton or simply by a processing unit. At this point we can see the direct applicability of the shared nothing distributed memory architecture to the server model. The shared nothing system communicates via message passing, just like the message based communication of an object oriented system.

Data or storage structures in both formatted and unformatted databases must be partitionable for the very simple reason that information processing involves huge amounts of data and the search effort must be shared by multiple processors, hence parallelism. Each processor must search its own data hence the distributed memory architecture. Inter processor communication must be minimized, hence ideally one processor must search one partition and inter partition communication must be minimized, hence nonoverlapping, disjoint data partitioning. As can be seen, we can mesh the parts of the system architecture into a well blended overall architecture.

The search and processing algorithms for all components of the multimedia information system must be parallel algorithms that must avoid useless iterations and/or wasteful I/O (i.e., be of linear complexity). Figure 3 depicts the concept of system architecture for information processing.

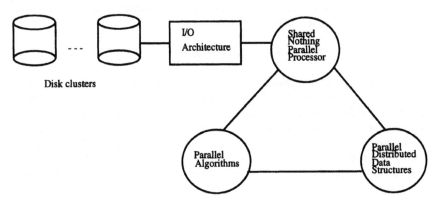

Figure 3. System architecture for information processing

In geometry three points define a plane and in our context the hardware-software platform for information processing is defined by the triangular arrangement of system components that mesh well with each other, namely the shared nothing parallel processor architecture, the parallel or partitioned data structure, and the parallel algorithms. As can be seen in the figure, to provide the proper I/O bandwidth required by database searching we must include an efficient I/O architecture in the system architecture. The I/O architecture can consist of disk clusters, search filters, and intelligent I/O controllers.

3. RESEARCH ACTIVITY

Our main application in the information processing area is multimedia database representation and information retrieval. Such an undertaking entails

- the realization of a relational database
- support of object oriented information representation, storage, and retrieval
- text storage and retrieval
- implementation of querying facility for multimedia
- multimedia search engine

The multimedia search engine operates in the following three consecutive search steps [11]

- associative search
- semantic search
- media specific search

The associative search involves query analysis, keyword extraction, and search space narrowing by performing parallel signature block or clustered database searching. In the following methodology section we will present some details of the techniques discussed here.

Semantic search receives the database scope determined by associative search and performs query processing using the multimedia query processor. Query processing is executed according to the model base equivalent of the multimedia database. Figure 4 shows an example multimedia document of a health database. As can be seen, this document involves all four dimensions of multimedia information namely, facts (e.g., PHYSICIAN), texts (i.e., WRITTEN TEXT),, audio (e.g., VOICE COMMENTS), and image (e.g., LIVER SCAN, LIVER BODY, GALL BLADDER, and COMMON BILE).

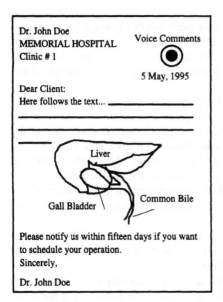

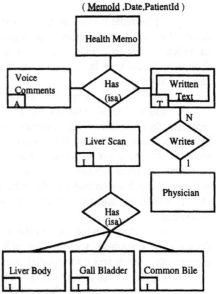

Figure 5.

Figure 4. A multimedia document

Conceptual model of the multimedia document

As technology does not permit us to conduct complex audio and image retrieval directly on that media, we convert the multimedia database into its model base equivalent expressed by a conceptual data model. Figure 5 shows the model base equivalent of Figure 4 expressed in terms of the E^2/R conceptual model [4,9].

The user queries are expressed on the conceptual representation, that is, the model base, and the search engine operates on the object oriented and relational database equivalent of the model base.

In terms of the object server model, the queries expressed on the conceptual schema graph determine the execution hierarchy, i.e., the class hierarchy, of the corresponding objects together with their communication structure in the search process that takes place within the parallel system architecture.

4. METHODOLOGY

4.1 Data Partitioning

In this section we present the methodology for implementing the building blocks of the parallel system platform. These blocks involve

- data partitioning of
  - unformatted data
  - formatted data
- allocation and balancing of database over the parallel search processor
- parallel search algorithms

Unformatted data consists of text documents besides bitmaps for image and digitized audio. Text documents are represented by a set of keywords extracted from an index vocabulary which is turn extracted from the body of text files. Each document would then be described by the keywords it contains. For example if our keyword vocabulary is

{architecture, compute(r), design, logic, message, network}

and if DOC-i contains the terms *{compute, logic, network}* then we can represent that document with a binary vector of length 6, i.e., the cardinality of the index vocabulary, <0,1,0,1,0,1> where zeros indicate absence and ones indicate presence of the corresponding keyword in the document. Alternatively, we can represent the same document with a signature block which can be constructed by superimposing the hash codes of the individual keywords present in the document e.g., 000111 which is a signature block, and for our convenience, we may regard that also as a vector.

Accordingly, whichever of the representations we use, we would have a large database of document vectors. For efficient searching of this database we must partition this vector space for parallel searching.

Figure 6(a) shows a signature vector database of 20 vectors partitioned with respect to the Extended Prefix Method (EMP) [5] using a zero count of 2 in the prefix key. According to EPM, the partition key lenghts and partition sizes vary. In Figure 6(b), however, Floating Key Method (FKM) produces prefix keys of fixed length with more uniform partition distribution.

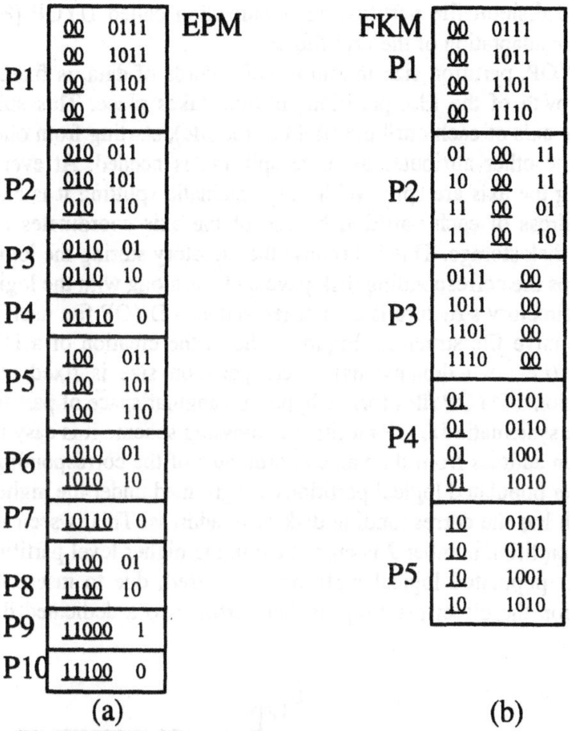

Figure 6. Signature partitioning where Pi's indicate partition numbers

If the vector space corresponds to document representations, as shown earlier with the example of DOC-i, then that vector space can be partitioned into document clusters. The algorithms we use is called Cover Coefficient Based Clustering methodology [1] which is a seed based clustering algorithm. Considering the document vector space, a 1 x n document vector would be represented by a point in that space. Figure 7 is a representative example of a cluster from a clustered document database. In the figure the bullet indicates the seed document, x's indicate individual documents and $\underline{x}$ represents the centroid vector (i.e., the cluster representative or the average vector) of the cluster.

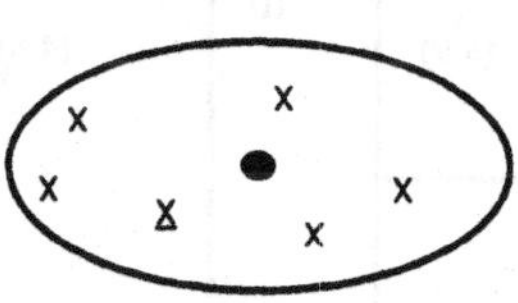

Figure 7. A document cluster consisting of six documents

Both Figure 6 and Figure 7 show us partitioned data sets for unformatted data. Each of these data sets can be allocated to a processor of the parallel processing system to be searched in parallel.

In the partitioning of the formatted data which is the file space of the relations corresponding to objects of the multimedia database we use a multidimensional (i.e., all fields of the records are part of the partition key), order preserving, and disjoint file partitioning organization called DYOP [8]. DYOP is a more systematic adaptation of the grid file [6].

In DYOP, partition size in number of records of data, is fixed and as insertions cause growth of the file, partition splitting takes place. This splitting is done along the value axis of each attribute (field of the file), starting from one attribute and cycling over the other attributes as more splitting is needed. At every split all the partitions along the axis are split. With this systematic splitting it is easy to compute the logical address of each partition by use of the axis coordinates and access the partition from disk storage. This is because the directory storing the logical address of a partition keeps the corresponding disk page address along with the logical address.

The directory structure is also organized as a DYOP file itself, resulting in a multilevel recursive file structure. Figure 8 shows the creation of a DYOP file with two attributes (i.e., two dimensions) where partition size is fixed at two records. Higher dimensional DYOP files form a hyper rectangular space of partitions.

In the systematic DYOP partition addressing scheme it is easy to compute the logical partition address from the value coordinates of the corresponding data record. However, under populated logical partitions are grouped under the higher level logical partition which has the corresponding disk page address. This is seen in Figure 8 (d) where logical partition number 2 is embedded in the higher level partition 0. It is only when an under populated logical partition is released, due to insertion, as an independent partition the direct mapping of that partition to a dedicated disk page takes place.

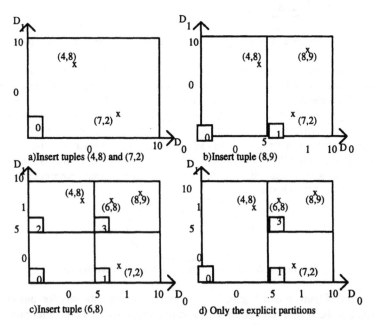

Figure 8. Creation of a DYOP file

4.2 Allocation and Balancing

Allocation of the partitions of formatted or unformatted data to a parallel processing system can be made in various ways where partition per processor based allocation being the first strategy that comes to mind. However, there are various other issues to consider, such as the following, that may complicate the picture.

    (a). 100 % utilization of parallel processors

    (b). utilizing only the optimally required number of processors

    (c). mismatch between the optimally required and the available number of parallel processors

    (d). minimizing interprocessor communication

    (e). achieving a balanced record count among the processors

Contrary to the common sense thinking of running as many as parallel horses to pull a cart, our experience has shown us that utilizing 100 % of the parallel processing power (item (a)) does not always yield the optimal result. The reason for this is certain overhead such as of load balancing and communication structure and also of activation of high number of processors, especially in the case of relatively small dataloads. Therefore, the sensible thing to do is to determine the required number of parallel processors with respect to a given dataload as well as workload (item (b)). To do this, simulation or analytical modeling can be used.

In cases where there is disparity between the available number of processors and the required number (item (c)) some sacrifice from the inherent parallelism of the processing algorithm must be made by overloading the available processors with tasks to be run serially and/or by cutting down on the number of parallel data dimensions e.g., instead of running all 3 attributes of a DYOP file in the hyperspace one may have to reduce it to a 2 dimensional file where the finer partitions of the former would be aggregated within coarser partitions.

With respect to item (d) we can mention two extreme approaches to data allocation to a parallel processing system. The first one is to deal the records of the data file as play cards to the processors of the parallel system in round robin fashion without regard to data ordering until all records are allocated. The second approach is to use data partitioning. And, as in DYOP, with order preserving data partitioning the data partitions would be disjoint hence the need for interpartition, and therefore interprocessor communication, would be minimized. In cases where some local activity, such as in the cases of partition splits and collapses, necessitates communication of neighboring partitions we must also observe partition adjacency. If this is not observed we may create interpartition communication overhead from random points in the processor farm. We have addressed this adjacency problem in our load balancing system [3], a short description of it will follow later in the discussion related with Figure 10.

Before we tackle the issue of item (e) let us discuss data allocation and balancing in general. In some studies where records are dealt among parallel processors as play cards in round robin fashion without regard to ordering, the load balance may deteriorate over time, and hence some load balancing data traffic would be necessary to fully utilize parallelism. Our experience has shown that the overhead of such balancing becomes an overwhelming portion of the total processing time, especially as number of processors becomes large.

448

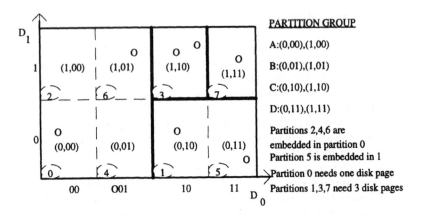

Figure 9. A DYOP file for allocation example, Os indicate records

The foregoing discussion brings us to the alternative of using data partitioning, such as DYOP. We had two implementations of data allocation using DYOP. The first one [12] is a straightforward address mapping of DYOP partition groups into processors whose addresses are determined from the bits of the corresponding partition coordinate addresses. This mapping is followed by a load sharing of processor contents until all processors contain balanced number of records. As an example, we can show the mapping of the DYOP file partitions to a hypercube processor system. Using Figure 9, assume the first dimension D_0 is to be processed for a join or selection and hence partition allocation is made over that dimension. Every value interval, corresponding to a partition interval, defines a partition group and all the partitions in that interval converging over all the other dimensions are contained in it. In Figure 9 four partition groups A through D are shown together with the partitions they contain. In the allocation (i.e., mapping) of partitions to hypercube processors (we will explain our rationale of using the hypercube shortly) we concatenate the leading bits of the partition coordinates to obtain the corresponding hypercube node address as shown below.

Partition Group	Hypercube Address	In Hypercube of Degree 3	
A: (0,00)	00	000	
(1,00)	10	010	
B: (0,01)	00 *	000	→ 100
(1,01)	10 *	010	→ 110
C: (0,10)	01	001	
(1,10)	11	011	
D: (0,11)	01 *	001	→ 101
(1,11)	11 *	011	→ 111

As can be seen in this mapping, partition groups A,B and C,D are mapped on the same processors initially. Because this is undesirable for full parallelism a further distribution operation spreads partition groups B and D (whose hypercube addresses are marked by asterisks) to hypercube nodes 4,6 and 5,7, respectively.

As an alternative to mapping DYOP partitions to parallel processors hashed distribution based on the values of the file dimension can also be used. However, every time this operation is needed, the hashing overhead has to be paid for distributing the data represented by the hash codes to their respective processors. Also, if the application shifts to another file dimension, then hashing has to be repeated for the values in that dimension. In the DYOP or grid file, however, the file is maintained partitioned with respect to all the file dimensions (i.e., fields or attributes) eliminating any partitioning overhead.

Our most recent data allocation and balancing strategy [3,7] performs a blocking operation over the DYOP file. In this way, the following are achieved.
- the blocks created preserves the characteristics of DYOP
- the number of blocks created is made to match the total number of available processors, or the optimally required number of processors as determined analytically from the workload characteristics
- the blocks are created in such a way as to achieve load balance among the parallel processors--we will demonstrate this shortly.

In the blocking, a DYOP like partitioning structure is imposed upon the existing DYOP file. The grid partition space of DYOP file is considered as the data space and splits are performed over this space as many times as is necessary to produce blocks equal to the number of processors. Whereas the contents of DYOP partitions are records (tuples) the contents of the blocks of this splitting are partitions of the DYOP file. Furthermore, whereas the splits of the DYOP file level are performed at mid range points, the splits of blocking are performed at the points dividing the total record count along the split axis to equal parts as much as possible.

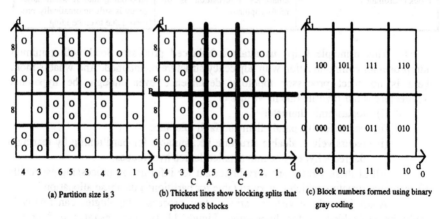

(a) Partition size is 3

(b) Thickest lines show blocking splits that produced 8 blocks

(c) Block numbers formed using binary gray coding

Figure 10. Blocking of DYOP partitions

Figure 10 demonstrates an example of blocking. In Figure 10 (a) we see a DYOP file that has been split five times in total, 3 times along d_0 and twice along dimension d_1. The bullets in the figure show records. The directory corresponding to this file would hold the coordinate addresses instead of the records, and additionally, it would keep the total record (tuple) count along each partition interval e.g., 4 records along d_0 in the first partition from the left; 6 records in total along d_1 in the first partition from the bottom.

In Figure 10 (b) we see the superimposed blocking. The file had to be allocated to 8 processors hence 8 blocks would have to be created. This is done with a total of 3 (2^3=8) splits, twice along d_0 and once along d_1, shown as A,B,C at the split points. However, as can be seen while the splits were made, the record count information of Figure 10 (a) was used. Therefore, the blocking split shown at A was made at the point with 13 (7+6) records to the left and 15 (8+7) records to the right. The second split blocked partitions 14 to 14 along d_1, and finally the split at Cs did the final splits of 13 and 15 records. The resulting structure produced 8 blocks with total record counts of 4,3,3,3,4,4,3,4 which demonstrates the load balancing achieved.

Figure 10 (c) shows the addressing of the blocks obtained. In the figure we see that the blocking intervals (ranges) along the coordinates are numbered with respect to binary gray coding, and the address of each block is formed by concatenating high to low coordinates in left to right order. In this way, the resulting block addresses preserve neighborhood hence adjacency structure. That is, going from block 000 to its neighbors 100 or 001 there is a hamming distance of 1 (i.e., only one bit is toggled in the source address).

At this point we can present an important aspect of our system platform. And that is the adaptation of the following principle in our partitioning, load balancing, and processor allocation:

Maintain data adjacency structure by gray code numbering of block coordinates	Directly map this structure over a hypercube structure where adjacency information is directly captured	Use hypercube processor architecture or any other topology embedding into it where adjacency is still automatically preserved due to embedding

This principle helps us attain a balanced processor load with minimum interprocessor communication with adjacency structure maintained. And what is more, there is no strict processor topology dependence even though the hypercube architecture is our favorite due its virtues of

(i) logarithmic diameter

(ii) cost effective parallelism and fault tolerance

(iii) recursively scaleable structure i.e., suitable for partitioning by tearing a degree n hypercube into smaller degree hypercubes

All of these virtues are very important for information processing especially the recursive structure which is very suitable for partitioned database allocation.

Apart from these virtues various other processor topologies can relatively easily be embedded in the hypercube. Figure 11 (a) demonstrates a degree 3 hypercube and Figure 11 (b) shows an eight element ring and a 2 × 2 mesh topology embeddings into it. As can be observed from the resulting processor addresses, the adjacency structure is always maintained.

4.3. Parallel Algorithms

Given relations R(D0,D1) and S(D0,D1) their join with respect to D0 attribute

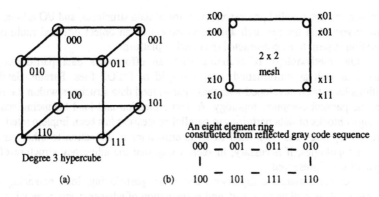

Figure 11. Hypercube and some embeddings

$$R \ JOIN_{R.D0=S.D0} \ S$$

can be parallelized in our system platform [2]. However, before we go that far let us review the sequential algorithm for join. In join we have two relations R and S and usually they differ in size and we call them small and large relations. Let us assume S is the small relation.

The join processing is a subset of the Cartesian product of the two sets (relations) being joined. Therefore, the following nested join algorithm is a well known sequential algorithm.

```
repeat i=1
    repeat j=1
        if R_i.D0 = S_j.D0 then do
            begin
            t=join(R_i,S_j)
            output (t)
            end
            j=j+1
    until j=m
    i=i+1
until i=n
```

This algorithm has a complexity of mxn. With the partitioned data organization such as DYOP, this complexity can be linearized by range partitioning both R and S relations and joining them along D0 dimensions. Assuming that R relation is that in Figure 8 and S relation is that in Figure 9, then we would process their join by pairing the compatible partition groups, along D0, which would be assigned in a such a way that each partition group pair would reside on the same processor node or subcube within the hypercube. Joins of compatible partition group pairs would be run in parallel. In this way, we not only linearize the join complexity (since a partition group is compared with only its compatible group in the other relation), but also achieve speed up due to parallel processing.

5. CONCLUSION

We have presented the concepts of the hardware and software platform for parallel information processing. Such a platform involves a system architecture consisting of parallel algorithms, parallel processors, partitioned data structures, and I/O arhitecture. We are involved in the research and development of an object oriented multimedia information system to be constructed over such a platform.

Our methodology of realizing such an effort uses data partitioning of formatted as well as unformatted data, and grid or DYOP files. Parallel database algorithms have been developed with these partitioned data structures within the basic hypercube parallel computer topology. A data allocation and load balancing scheme that assigns blocks of data partitions to parallel processors has been implemented. The hypercube topology has been used as an intermediary in allocation to other parallel processor topologies, if necessary, in such a way that the adjacency structure of the data partitions is preserved.

Our performance comparisons show that partitioning, load balancing with respect to work as well as data load, and preservation of adjacency structure wins over schemes that do not exploit these desirable features in their system platform.

6. REFERENCES

[1]   Can, F. & Ozkarahan, E.A. (1990). Concepts and Effectiveness of the Cover Coefficient Based Clustering Methodology for Text Databases. *ACM Transactions on Database Systems*, 15 (4), 483-517.

[2]   Dikenelli, O. & Ozkarahan, E. (1993). Data Partitioning and Allocation Strategies for Parallel Database Operations. *Proc. of Intl. Conf. on Parallel Computing Technologies (PACT93)*, Obninsk, Russia, 2, 271-290.

[3]   Dikenelli, O., Unalir, O., Ozerdim, A. & Ozkarahan, E. (1995). A Load Balancing Approach for Parallel Database Machines, *Proc. of Third IEEE Euromicro Workshop on Parallel and Distributed Processing*, San Remo, Italy.

[4]   Dogac, A., Ozkarahan, E.A. & Chen, P.P. (1989). An Integrity System for a Relational Database Architecture. *Proc. of Eight Intl. Conf. on Entity Relationship Approach*, Toronto, Canada, 294-308.

[5]   Lee, D.L. & Leng, C. (1989). Partitioned Signature Files: Design Issues and Performance Evaluation. *ACM Transactions on Information Systems*, 7 (2), 158-180.

[6]   Nievergelt, J., Hintberger, H. and Sevcik, K.C. (1984). The Grid File: An Adaptable Multikey File Structure. *ACM Transactions on Database Systems*, 9 (1). 38-71.

[7]   Ozerdim, A., Unalir, O., Dikenelli, O. & Ozkarahan, E. (1995). PARMA: A Multiattribute File Structure for Parallel Database Machines", *Proc. of Intl. Conf. on Parallel Computing Technologies (PACT95)*, St. Petersburg, Russia.

[8]   Ozkarahan, E. (1986). *Database Machines and Database Management*. Englewood Cliffs, N.J: Prentice-Hall Inc.

[9]   Ozkarahan, E. (1990). *Database Management:Concepts, Design, and Practice*. Englewood Cliffs, N.J: Prentice-Hall Inc.

[10] Ozkarahan, E. (1991). System Architecture for Information Processing. *Information Processing and Management*, 31 (1), -.

[11] Ozkarahan, E. (1995). Multimedia Document Representation and Retrieval. *Information Processing and Management*, 27 (4), 347-370.

[12] Penaloza, M. & Ozkarahan, E. (1992). Parallel Algorithms for Executing Join on Cube Connected Multicomputers. *Proc. of Eight Intl. Conf. on Data Engineering*, Phoenix, AZ, 20-27.

Numerical Simulation
of Reacting Mixing Layer
with a Parallel Implementation

Edgard Kessy, Alexei Stoukov and Dany Vandromme

LMFN, INSA, URA-CNRS 230-CORIA
BP 118, 76134 Mont Saint Aignan CEDEX, France

Abstract. This work concerns the parallelization of an explicit algorithm for the simulation of compressible reacting gas flows, applied to supersonic mixing layers.

The reacting Navier-Stokes equations are caracterized by three tightly coupled physical phenomena, i.e. the convection, diffusion and chemical source terms. To compute the chemical source terms, full complex chemistry is used. By considering the elapsed time for solving the problem, the numerical treatment of the chemical source terms takes about 75% of the total execution time.

The main goal of the present work is to reduce the relative cost of chemical source terms calculation and also to optimize the global cost of the procedure resolution by the use of parallel computation.

1 Choice of Parallel Approach

On parallel architectures, independent computations are executed simultaneously. To achieve this goal, the algorithm is divided into several independent tasks. All tasks can be executed simultaneously and communicate with each other during the execution.

Two different types of parallel methodologies exist: data-parallelism and control parallelism [14]. The first approach relies on the fact that each processor performs at a given time the same instruction on different data. This approach exploits the great potential of massively-parallel computers, SIMD (Single Instruction Multiple Data) architectures [11].

In the control-parallelism approach, the computational problem is divided into a number of more-or-less independent tasks, with different processors performing different tasks in parallel. This approach is adapted to multi-processor computers, MIMD (Multiple Instruction Multiple Data) architectures [1].

In order to use MIMD computers very efficiently, the granularity of tasks should be as large as possible. In CFD the space decomposition of the computational domain is the most efficient technique in order to increase the granularity of tasks for MIMD architectures [5]. This technique (the so-called multi-domain

---

* This work took a large benefit of discussions with Yves Escaig (Mechanical Engineering Laboratory, INSA of Rouen)

technique) consists in partitioning the computational domain into a number of blocks, and to distribute blocks onto different processors [4]. However, there is still a problem to maintain a well balanced decomposition.

The choice of the adopted parallel approach is influenced by the numerical algorithm. However, one can notice that data-parallel and control-parallel approaches can both be combined [12]. By considering that in most reacting flows, reacting and non-reacting zones occur simultaneously, the computation of chemical source terms can be restricted to the main reactive region. Thus a decomposition efficient for pure hydrodynamical problem becomes unefficient when the reacting zones dimension differ greatly between blocks. In such a way the standard multi-block technique is no longer well suited for the reacting flow. In this paper, a classical multi-block technique is used for convective and diffusive terms, whereas SPMD (Single Program Multiple Data) approach is employed for chemical source terms.

2 Flow configuration, physical, chemical and mathematical model

Figure 1 shows the physical model considered in the present study. It consists of two chemically active hydrogen and air streams with different streamwise velocities. In this work the spatial mixing of reacting streams has been simulated in a two-dimensional domain. The static pressure at the inlet side is the same for both streams. To prescribe the inlet conditions the self similar solution of the compressible mixing layer [9] is used at the inlet with a vorticity thickness equal to 0.05 of the transverse length.

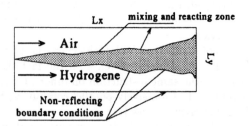

Fig. 1. Flow configuration

The flow evolution is governed by the unsteady compressible Navier-Stokes equations coupled with the energy and species transport equations. These equations are written in two-dimensional form as:

$$\frac{\partial U}{\partial t} + \frac{\partial F(U)}{\partial x} + \frac{\partial G(U)}{\partial y} = S(U) \tag{1}$$

where the variable vector, the convective and diffusive fluxes and source terms are defined respectively by:

$$U = \begin{pmatrix} \rho_1 \\ \vdots \\ \rho_{nsp} \\ \rho u \\ \rho v \\ \rho e_t \end{pmatrix}$$

$$F = F_c + F_v = \begin{pmatrix} \rho_1 u \\ \vdots \\ \rho_{nsp} u \\ \rho u u + p \\ \rho u v \\ (\rho e_t + p)u \end{pmatrix} - \begin{pmatrix} \sigma_{Y_1 x} \\ \vdots \\ \sigma_{Y_{nsp} x} \\ \sigma_{xx} \\ \sigma_{xy} \\ \sigma_{xx} u + \sigma_{xy} v - q_x \end{pmatrix}$$

$$G = G_c + G_v = \begin{pmatrix} \rho_1 v \\ \vdots \\ \rho_{nsp} v \\ \rho v u \\ \rho v v + p \\ (\rho e_t + p)v \end{pmatrix} - \begin{pmatrix} \sigma_{Y_1 y} \\ \vdots \\ \sigma_{Y_{nsp} y} \\ \sigma_{xy} \\ \sigma_{yy} \\ \sigma_{xy} u + \sigma_{yy} v - q_y \end{pmatrix}$$

$$S = \begin{pmatrix} \dot{\rho} \\ \vdots \\ \dot{\rho}_{nsp} \\ 0 \\ 0 \\ \sum_{j=1}^{N_r} Q_{r_j} \dot{w}_{r_j} \end{pmatrix}$$

$$\sigma_{Y_k x} = D_k \frac{\partial Y_k}{\partial x} \qquad\qquad \sigma_{Y_k y} = D_k \frac{\partial Y_k}{\partial y}$$

$$\sigma_{xx} = \mu\left(\frac{4}{3}\frac{\partial u}{\partial x} - \frac{2}{3}\frac{\partial v}{\partial y}\right) \qquad \sigma_{yy} = \mu\left(\frac{4}{3}\frac{\partial v}{\partial y} - \frac{2}{3}\frac{\partial u}{\partial x}\right)$$

$$\sigma_{xy} = \mu\left(\frac{\partial u}{\partial y} + \frac{\partial v}{\partial x}\right)$$

$$q_x = -\lambda\frac{\partial T}{\partial x} - \sum_{k=1}^{nsp} h_k \sigma_{Y_k x} \qquad q_y = -\lambda\frac{\partial T}{\partial y} - \sum_{k=1}^{nsp} h_k \sigma_{Y_k y}$$

The chemical kinetics equations are represented by:

$$\sum_{k=1}^{nsp} a_{kr} X_{kr} \Longleftrightarrow \sum_{k=1}^{nsp} b_{kr} X_{kr} \tag{2}$$

where X_{kr} represents one mole of species k, a_{kr} and b_{kr} are integral stoichiometric coefficients for reaction r. The rate of changes due to r^{th} chemical reaction is

$$\dot{w}_r = K_{fr}\prod_k (\frac{\rho_k}{W_k})^{a_{kr}} - K_{br}\prod_k (\frac{\rho_m}{W_k})^{b_{kr}} \tag{3}$$

where K_{fr} and K_{br} come from a generalized Arrhenius form.

In this work the hydrogen-air combustion kinetics is taken as the detailed mechanism proposed in [7]. The concentrations of H_2, O_2, OH, H_2O, H, O, HO_2, H_2O_2 and N_2 species evolve according to a 37 chemical reactions scheme.

To describe the complex properties of molecular diffusion and thermal conduction the appropriate modules of CHEMKIN-II package [6] were incorporated into the code. The values of enthalpies of formation and specific heats of species are obtained with the JANAF tables [13].

Spatial instability of hydrogen-air mixing zone is generated by disturbing the inlet velocity profile. In this work, the initially incompressible disturbances are imposed only on the longitudinal velocity component at the point of maximum of inlet vorticity profile. The disturbances introduced are $U' = A\cos(\omega t)$, where A is the magnitude equal to 0.5% of the inlet velocity taken at the point of the maximum vorticity. The ω is the circular frequency of oscillation and is chosen from the linear stability analysis results [9].

3 Numerical Algorithm

The equation (1) is solved with fractional-step approach, also called the time-step splitting [15].

$$U^{n+2} = \Psi^{1/2}L_x L_y \Psi L_y L_x \Psi^{1/2} \tag{4}$$

where:

$$L_x : \ \frac{\partial U}{\partial t} + \frac{\partial F(U)}{\partial x} = 0, \ L_y : \ \frac{\partial U}{\partial t} + \frac{\partial G(U)}{\partial y} = 0, \ \Psi : \ \frac{\partial U}{\partial t} = S(U)$$

Let us denote δU_c and δU_v the increments of vector U which are due to convection and diffusion respectively. The overall increment of U is then obtained as their sum:

$$\delta U = \delta U_c + \delta U_v \tag{5}$$

The numerical scheme is written here for one-dimensional inviscid part of equation (1). Following [16, 17, 8] the numerical solution for second-order upwind TVD (total variation diminishing) scheme is :

$$\delta U_{c_i}^n = -\lambda\big(F_{c_{i+1/2}}^n - F_{c_{i-1/2}}^n\big) \tag{6}$$

where $\lambda = \Delta t/\Delta x$, $F_{c_{i\pm1/2}}$ is a numerical flux vector, which is expressed for a non-MUSCL approach as

$$F_{c_{i+1/2}} = \frac{1}{2}\big(F_{c_i} + F_{c_{i+1}} + R_{i+1/2}\Phi_{i+1/2}\big) \tag{7}$$

Here $R_{i+1/2}$ is a right-eigenvector matrix of the Jacobian $A = \partial F/\partial U$, constructed for an approximate Riemann solver at the point between U_j and U_{j+1} using the generalized Roe average [10, 8]. Characteristic speeds $\alpha^l_{i+1/2}$ correspond to the elements of vector $R^{-1}_{i+1/2}(U_{i+1} - U_i)$ where $R^{-1}_{i+1/2}$ is a left-eigenvector matrix of the Jacobian A, of which diagonal elements are denoted as $a^l_{i+1/2}$ and the elements $\phi^l_{i+1/2}$ of vector $\Phi_{i+1/2}$ are

$$\phi^l_{i+1/2} = \sigma(a^l_{i+1/2})(g^l_{i+1} + g^l_i) - \psi(a^l_{i+1/2} + \gamma^l_{i+1/2})\alpha^l_{i+1/2} \qquad (8)$$

where

$$\gamma^l_{i+1/2} = \sigma(a^l_{i+1/2}) \begin{cases} (g^l_{i+1} + g^l_i)/\alpha^l_{i+1/2} & \text{if } \alpha^l_{i+1/2} \neq 0 \\ 0 & \text{if } \alpha^l_{i+1/2} = 0 \end{cases} \qquad (9)$$

$$g^l_i = (\alpha^l_{i+1/2}\alpha^l_{i-1/2} + |\alpha^l_{i+1/2}\alpha^l_{i-1/2}|)/(\alpha^l_{i+1/2} + \alpha^l_{i-1/2}) \qquad (10)$$

and

$$\sigma(z) = \frac{1}{2}(\phi(z) - \lambda z^2) \qquad (11)$$

The increment of vector U due to viscous/diffusion fluxes is obtained by the central difference approximation:

$$\delta U_{v_i} = \frac{\lambda}{2}\left(F_{v_{i+1/2}} - F_{v_{i-1/2}}\right) \qquad (12)$$

where, for example for species k

$$F_{v_{i+1/2}} = D_{k_{i+1/2}}\frac{Y_{k_{i+1}} - Y_{k_i}}{\Delta x_{i+1/2}} \qquad (13)$$

To compute the operator Ψ three different algotithms (CHEM [2], EULSIM [3], LSODE [6]) have been tested. The most accurate results have been obtained with EULSIM scheme which is, however, the most demanding of CPU time.

4 Parallelization

For the splitting of a computational domain into N blocks having the same number of mesh nodes, the calculations are performed according (4).

4.1 Hydrodynamics Part Parallelization

Operators L_x and L_y are found with the standard multi-blocks technique, where each processor unit treats a single block. Here the computational domain may be splitted in arbitrarly, the decomposition being dependent of the particular flow geometry. Numerical scheme employs five-point discretisation. Herefore to find L_x at i-th point, the values at points set (i-2,i-1,i,i+1,i+2) are needed. It means that every neighbouring blocks should have four common mesh nodes. An example of such decomposition is shown on Fig.2 for two adjacent blocks.

Having computed L_x or L_y operator, the neighbouring blocks 1 and 2 are linked up in a following manner:

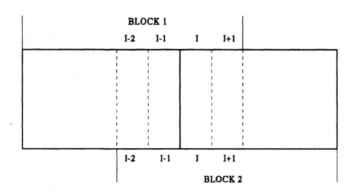

Fig. 2. Linking up of the neighbouring blocks

the columns $I - 2$ and $I - 1$ of the block 1 become those $I - 2$ and $I - 1$ of
the block 2;
the colums I and $I + 1$ of the block 2 become those I and $I + 1$ of the block
1.

In such a manner we need only the communications between the processors
treating the adjacent blocks.

4.2 Parallelization of Chemical Source Terms Computation

To reduce the computer time, the chemical source terms are calculated only on
the mesh nodes where the chemical reactions take place in "reactive" regions.
Size of that regione may differ greatly from one block to another, so the domain
decomposition with equal number of grid points may be highly ineffective. This
is the case, for example, for the simulations of reactive mixing layer, triple flames,
jets etc. Evidently the overall computations rate (and cost) will be determined
with the time needed to treat a block with the largest reactive subzone. Thus
we need to equalize the number of "reacting" points for each processor. In the
beginning the very simple master-slave *algorithm A* is employed with this aim.

Slaves:
  • to distinguish the reactive region in its own block
  • to rearrange the data as vectors:
There are 11 scalar variables (9 species, temperature and internal energy)
on which the source terms depend. Their spatial distributions may be rear-
ranged as 11 vectors of NP_{ibl} length, where NP_{ibl} is number of grid points
in reactive subzone.
  • to send these vectors to the master.

Master:
  • to receive the data from the slaves, and to assemble them into a single

  vector of length $NP = \sum_{ibl=1}^{N_{block}} NP_{ibl}$

- to split that vector on the equal parts
- to send them back to the slaves.

Slaves:

- to get the redistributed data from master
- to calculate the Ψ operator connected with source terms and modify the data
- to send the modified data to master.

Master:

- to get the modified data from the slaves
- to partition them back to their original blocks
- to send them to the slaves.

Slaves:

- to receive the vectorized data from master
- to translate them into the spatial distributions.

This algorithm assures equal load for each slave-processor. However the tests performed showed the time of master-slave transactions being prohibitively great. This is because of large number of communications and large amount of data to transfer.

To avoid the abundant data exchange the algorithm above has been modified. Instead of exchanging all the scalar field now only the number of points to proceed with has to be sent to master by slaves. Master should discriminate between over- and unloaded slaves, which then make the direct data exchange to equalize the burden. The resulting *algorithm B* may be represented as:

Slaves:

- to determine the reactive region
- to rearrange the data as the vectors
- to send to master a number of points in which the chemical source terms should be calculated.

Master:

- to get these numbers for each blocks
- to determine the relative load of each slave and the numbers of data points to be exchanged between them
- to send the orders for data transfer.

Slaves:

- to get the master's orders and to perform corresponding transactions: to get the additional scalar values sets for unloaded processor-slave or to send them for overloaded one. If the load is near the mean one there is no data transfer. One can see that there is no longer double slave-master-slave transaction and only part of data has to be communicated in comparison with A algorithm.
- to compute Ψ operator
- to send back the modified scalar values to the corresponding slave
- to rearrange the data back to the spatial distributions.

5   Results

All the calculations have been performed with cluster of 12 Silicon Graphics
SGI workstations. An effectiveness of the parallelization method has been tested
upon the modelling of supersonic mixing layer with and without chemistry.

5.1   Modelling of Inert Mixing Layer

In this case the equal load of each processor is obtained simply with the equal
partitionning of the computational domain. Multi-block decomposition linking
up on the boundaries do not introduce any numerical disturbance in comparison with the usual single block calculation, no matter how the domain has been
splitted. However, for the computational mesh of $N_x * N_y = 200 * 100$ nodes,
decomposition along x-axe main flow direction appeared to be much more effective. It can be explained with that resulting blocks of $200/Nbl *100$ allow to
take all the advantages of cache memory. Therefore all the computations have
been performed with the decomposition along x-direction.

Time efficiency is illustrated on Fig.3. The difference between the gain in
CPU time and that in elapsed (i.e. real user time) is due to the non-neglidgible
communication time between the processors. Although the time of computations
is decreased with successive increases of block number, communications time
becomes exceedingly large. As a result we obtain some efficiency threshold in
effective user time.

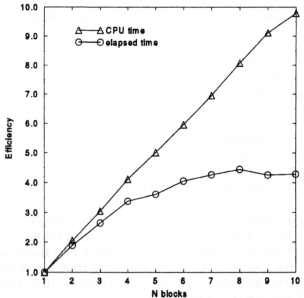

Fig. 3. Relative time reduction in comparison with consecutive simulation for inert
mixing layer

5.2 Reactive Mixing Layer

As it was mentioned above, chemical source terms are most CPU-time-demanding. Usually they consume more than 75% of overall CPU time. So, any progress in their parallelization is rather crucial, and one can expect that improved efficiency would be more significant than for non-reacting case.

On Fig.4 the results are presented for hydrogen-air mixing layer with real complex chemistry. It is worth to note that relative CPU time gain is rather independent of the algorithm implementation. However, the relative gain in CPU time is: greater than in non-reacting case even with standard multi-block technique. An implementation of equalizing algorithm B results to 30% improvement.

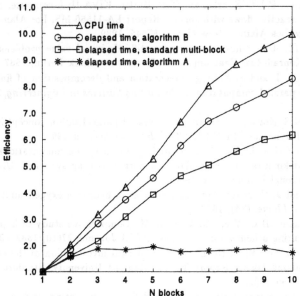

Fig. 4. Relative time reduction in comparison with consecutive simulation for reacting mixing layer

One should note that the longer the time consumed by chemical kinetics calculations is and the stronger the variations in reacting zones dimensions in different blocks are the greater the profit of a procedure like algorithm B would be. At the same time algorithm A reveals a performance even worse than standard multi-block technique.

6 Conclusion

In the present work a combined MIMD-SPMD algorithm is proposed for the problems with complex reaction zone structure. The performances of this algorithm has been tested for the simulation of hydrogen-air supersonic mixing layer. It yields a significant time saving with respect to the ordinary multi-block technique. Nevertheless the chemical source term treatment has not reached the expected efficiency. Therefore, it will be considered in the future to perform that part on a SIMD machine included in the PVM cluster.

References

1. R. Aggarwal, P. Henriksen, R. Keunings, D. Vanderstraeten, and O. Zone. Numerical simulation of non-newtonian flow on MIMD parallel computers. In Hirch, editor, *Computational Fluid Dynamics'92*, pages 1139–1146, 1992.

2. A.A. Amsden, P.J. O'Rourke, and T.D. Butler. KIVA-II: A computer program for chemically reactive flows with sprays. Report LA-11560-MS, Los Alamos National Laboratory, Los Alamos, New-Mexico 87545, 1989.

3. P. Deuflhard. Uniqueness theorems for stiff ode initial value problems. Preprint SC-87-3, Konrad-Zuse-Zentrum fuer Informationstechnik Berlin, 1987.

4. St. Doltsinis, I. and S. Nolting. Generation and decomposition of finite element models for parallel computations. *Computing Systems in Engineering*, 2(5/6):427–449, 1991.

5. H. Friz and S. Nolting. Towadrs an integrated parallelization concept in computational fluid dynamics. In *ERCOFTAC Bulletin*, october 1993.

6. R.J. Kee and J.A. Miller. A structured approach to the computational modeling of chemical kinetics and molecular transport in flowing systems. SAND86-8841, Sandia National Laboratories, 1986.

7. U. Maas and J. Warnatz. Ignition processes in hydrogen-oxygen mixtures. *Combustion and Flame*, (74), 1988.

8. J.L. Montagne, H.C. Yee, and Vinokur M. Comparative study of high-resolution shock-capturing schemes for a real gas. *AIAA Journal*, 27(10):1332–1346, 1989.

9. O.H. Planche and W.C. Reynolds. A numerical investigation of the compressible reacting mixing layer. Report TF-56, Stanford University, Stanford, California 94305, October 1992.

10. P.L. Roe. Some contribution to the modelling of discontinuous flows. In American Mathematical Society, editor, *Lectures in Applied Mathematics*, pages 163–194, Providence, RI, 1985.

11. M.L. Sawley. Control- and data-parallel methodologies for flow calculations. In *Supercomputing Europe'93*, Ultrecht, February 1993. Royal Dutch Fairs.

12. M.L. Sawley and J.K. Tegner. A data parallel approach to multiblock flow computations. *International Journal For Numerical Methods in Fluids*, 19:707–721, 1994.

13. D.R. Stull and Prophet H. JANAF thermochemical tables, second edition. NSRDS-NBS 37, U.S. Department of Commerce/National Bureau of Standards, June 1971.

14. D. Vandromme, L. Vervisch, J. Reveillon, Y. Escaig, and T. Yesse. Parallel treatment of CFD related problems. In preparation, 1994.

15. N. N. Yanenko. *The method of fractional steps*. New York, Springer Verlag edition, 1971.

16. H.C. Yee. Construction of explicit and implicit symmetric TVD schemes and their applications. *Journal of Computational Physics*, 68:151–179, 1987.

17. H.C. Yee. A class of high-resolution explicit and implicit shock-capturing methods. Computational fluid dynamics, march 1989, rhode-st-genèse, belgium, Von Karman Institute for fluid dynamics, Lecture Series 1989-04, 1989.

Parallel Computing in Russia

Ya.I. Fet[1] and D.A. Pospelov[2]

[1] Computing Center, Siberian Division of the
Russian Academy of Sciences, Novosibirsk, Russia
e-mail: fet@comcen.nsk.su
[2] Computing Center of the
Russian Academy of Sciences, Moscow, Russia
e-mail: pospelov@sms.ccas.msk.su

1 Introduction

In various periods of the history of science, Russia presented to the world prominent, original works in mathematics and other fields of exact sciences. This concerns as well the comparatively young computer science.

The history of computers and computer science in Russia abounds in contradictions. From the very beginning of the foundation of computer science, the leading Russian scientists made a valuable contribution to the development of numerical mathematics, mathematical logic, linear programming, theory of automata, etc. They originated new trends in computer hardware and software, particularly concerning the parallel paradigms. Notable were also the research in cellular arrays, formal methods of design and analysis of digital devices, computer aided design of computers, etc.

The early works of Mikhail Gavrilov should be mentioned on application of Boolean algebra to the design of digital circuits. These works have been made simultaneously and independently from Claude Shannon. A very important role in the development of the theory of automata and of logical design in Russia played the famous "Schools" organized by Gavrilov.

Fundamental research in logic and theory of automata has been done in the late 50s and early 60s by Boris Trakhtenbrot and Victor Glushkov.

In the early research of Andrey Lyapunov, Yuri Yanov, and Andrey Ershov have been laid the theoretical foundations of programming as such, as well as of automation of programming, and of parallel programming.

Unfortunately, the poor Russian technology and incompetence of Soviet management, left Russia persistently behind the West in building and using computers.

There exists a number of papers on the history of Soviet computers (see, for instance, [1-4]). As a rule, these papers are restricted to the description and analysis of production models and families of computers, compiled from official Soviet sources. An interesting survey on Russian research in programming has been published by Andrey Ershov [5]. Some information concerning the period of late 80s is contained in a special issue of the "Communications of the ACM" [6]. Recently, two interesting books by Boris Malinovsky have been published in Kiev, presenting some important pages of the history of Soviet computers [7,8].

Of course, each of the mentioned surveys concerns the subject of computer performance. However, one can hardly find there any specific information on the state and the development of parallel computing in Russia. Meanwhile, Russian scientists seem to have made a valuable and original contribution to this important field of computer science. These investigations are practically unknown in the West.

Generally, the Russian research in computer science can be divided into five fields: 1. Theory of Automata. 2. Parallel Programming. 3. Parallel Computing Systems. 4. Distributed Processing. 5. Artificial Intelligence. In the present survey, most attention will be paid to the second, third, and fourth of the mentioned topics.

It should be noted that the content of this paper reflects, in the first place, the authors' point of view. Besides, it does not pretend to be exhaustive.

Historically, several centers of computer science and technology have appeared in Russia, the main of these being Moscow, Leningrad, Kiev, Minsk, Novosibirsk. The Siberian Scientific Center, created near the city of Novosibirsk in the late 50s, also known as "Academgorodok" ("Academic Village"), was conceived from the beginning, as a complex Cybernetic Center, where the applied research in different areas would be supported by the leading development of mathematics and computer science. During the 60s and 70s, in the Academic Village have been working such distinguished scientists as Sergey Sobolev, Leonid Kantorovich, Alexey Lyapunov, Andrey Ershov, and others.

In the beginning of the 60s, we have had in Novosibirsk only some models of first-generation computers of Soviet production. Later, in 1968, the comparatively powerful second-generation BESM-6 appeared, with the peak performance of 1 MFlops. It was clear to all of us that the clock frequency has a definite limit of increasing, while the requirements to the performance will ever be rising. Hence, the only way to the future high-performance computers had to be in parallel computation, in parallel systems.

In retrospect, we can state that, without exaggeration, beginning from a certain moment, the Russian research in parallel computing became concentrated in Siberia.

2 Parallel Programming

2.1 Large-block Programming System

A valuable contribution to the formation of ideas of parallel programming and parallel computations has been made by Leonid Kantorovich, a noted Russian mathematician and economist, Nobel laureate. As early as in 1949 he practically used what we would now call a "multiprocessing system" made of a large number of punched card tabulating machines, to compute simultaneously tables of Bessel functions for all integer values of indices from 0 to 120.

One of the earliest researches in massively parallel processing was due to Leonid Kantorovich who described in 1957 the so-called "large-block programming system" [9]. He suggested to consider as basic objects operated by the system ordered sets called *quantities* (such as vectors, matrices, etc.), a single number being the simplest quantity, called an *element*. Some special operations on quantities were introduced: *arithmetical* operations as extensions of usual arithmetic on any element of the quantity, and *geometrical* operations which do not change the values of quantities but only transform their structures.

Later on, some of the ideas of the large-block approach were developed further in such programming languages as APL, PL/1, Algol-68, etc. Recently, the need for efficient use of highly parallel systems led to the appearance of "data parallel programming" which has much similarity with Kantorovich's large-block approach.

2.2 Graph Structure of Parallel Programs

In early 60s in the Power Engineering Institute (Moscow) was started, under the leadership of Dimitri Pospelov, research of creating models for description of structures of complicated programs and, particularly, for selection of those program branches which could be executed independently and concurrently. In 1966 the first publications appeared concerning these models called *level-parallel forms* (LPF). The LPF language, allowing for formalization of most important issues in the field of parallel computing, has been widely used in the USSR by researchers working in this field.

The level-parallel form is a graph the verteces of which are identified with the segments of the program subject to parallelizing while the arcs correspond to the functional dependences between the segments and the communications between the processes. A typology of LPFs has been developed based on the topology of corresponding graphs, and the requirements to the segmentation of the initial program were formulated ensuring effective execution of LPFs in parallel computing systems consisting of identical or different computers [10].

The notion of LPF led to the correct statement of the problem of optimizing the distribution of a program in a multiprocessor system with a given number of computers, as well as to the search for an optimal configuration of the system executing a given LPF [10,11].

2.3 Network Structure of Computational Processes. Wave Algorithms

The inefficiency of programs written beforehand motivated the search for such means of description of algorithms which could explicitly contain all possibilities of parallel execution of the future program. Several versions of specific languages for the description of parallel features of algorithms have been suggested. One of the most interesting was the *computational models language* proposed in the late 60s by Enn Tyugu [12].

Tyugu treated a computational model as a network the nodes of which correspond to some functional modules, while the edges characterize the interconnections between these modules reflecting possible ways of organization of computations. The final version of the program to be realized (either in sequential or in parallel form) is derived from the model by means of appropriate logical inference.

Based on these models, conceptual programming languages have been constructed the main feature of which is the presence of *semantic memory* intended for storing *concepts* of a given application domain. This memory is accessed by the system during compilation [13].

Computational models were extended by data structures, in particular arrays, to develop the theory of parallel program synthesis and pragmatic approach to designing of functional programming system oriented to parallel execution of generated programs [14].

The computational models turned the attention of specialists in parallel programming to the possibility of exploiting more elaborate semantic networks, in order to specify the variety of alternatives of execution of the computational process. Further investigations in this field led to the design of a *wave model* of computations in semantic networks, where the proper computing is substituted by procedures of pattern matching and logical inference well-known in artificial intelligence. The pattern matching became basic procedures in the VOLNA-0 language [15], ensuering highest possible parallelising.

Later on, various powerful parallel logical inference procedures in semantic networks have been designed [16]. The research in models of parallel computing based on semantic networks led also to the design of a high-performance computing system, under an international project PAMIR [17].

2.4 Models of Collective Behaviour in Organizing Parallel Processes

A unique direction in the theory of parallel processes is associated with the ideas of *collective behaviour of automata* promoted by Mikhail Tsetlin and his followers beginning from the late 50s. These works outran more then by 30 years the Western research in *multiagence systems*. In the frame of the theory of collective behaviour of automata, many problems of functioning of distributed computing systems without centralized control have been stated and solved.

If the system exploits at times synchronization, than the range of problems of decentralized control reduces to the classical problem of *spreading of signals in a chain of shots*. This problem, formulated for the first time by J.Myhill, found its efficient solution in the works of Victor Varshavsky and his followers [18]. The latest results on this subject are contained in [19].

If, however, the distributed system operates in a completely asynchronous mode, than the models of collective behaviour ensure efficient control algorithms overperforming to a considerable extent the known "notice board" procedure [20].

The technique of collective behaviour allowed to create a theory of aperiodic automata able to master numerous hard problems in organizing parallel computations, in particular, the *arbitrage problem* [21].

In [22] fundamental conceptions are stated of the theory of asynchronous parallel processes.

2.5   Parallel High-Accuracy Computations

The main cause of inaccuracy in computer calculations is known to be the rounding errors. The necessity of rounding is attributed to the fixed and relatively low word length of operands in most computers.

In the end of the 80s Alexander Vazhenin (Novosibirsk) developed a virtual vector processor for implementation of high accuracy arithmetic called SPARTH (Super-precision Parallel ARiTHmetic) [23].

In SPARTH, high accuracy is achieved by the use of ultra-high length of operands, as well as by dynamic control of their capacity in the course of computations. This technique allows for elimination of rounding errors. The overall high performance of the SPARTH-processor is due to concurrent processing of multiple operands.

An example of this approach is the implementation of SPARTH-processor within a basic fine-grained SIMD architecture oriented at solving problems containing many vector and matrix operations [24]. A number of new parallel algorithms was developed for solving problems of linear algebra. Comparison with known dedicated programming systems for high-precision computations in sequential computers shows that the SPARTH-processor ensures similar accuracy of results. Moreover, this accuracy is achieved in this case simultaneously for numerous data sets in corresponding processing elements of a massively parallel system.

3   Parallel Computing Systems

3.1   Vector Pipeline Processor AM

In 1960, Leonid Kantorovich proposed a conception of *attached units*. The analysis of quantities and operations of Kantorovich's large-block programming system enables one to define some typical forms of processing, and to formulate the requirements to various specialized devices for concurrent execution of massive operations.

In the early 60s at the Institute of Mathematics (Novosibirsk) a project had been developed under Kantorovich's direction of an attached unit called *Arithmetic Machine* (AM) [25] intended primarily for speeding up the solution of problems of linear algebra and linear programming. Accordingly, vector operations were emphasized in its design.

The main principles used in the AM computer were as follows:

1) Exhaustive use of the number flow obtainable from the main memory of the host computer by direct access;

2) Organizing of a continuous number flow with simultaneous processing in a special high-speed arithmetic unit;

3) Use of special features of data (numeric vectors of large dimensions) and those of the basic operators (the main one being the inner product of vectors) in order to get very high processing speed.

In the arithmetic unit of the AM, a four-stage pipeline was implemented with four levels of buffer registers [26]. To coordinate the functioning of all the pipeline stages, it was necessary to ensure a working speed of the accumulator considerably exceeding the abilities of logic elements available at that time. Thus, a novel powerful multiple-input carry-save adder was developed, which made possible processing of six digits of the multiplier at each cycle, ensuring the necessary speed [27].

A pilot AM computer has been built and was operating at the Computing Center of the Academy of Sciences in Novosibirsk. This computer was one of the first pipeline processors, and thus a prototype of modern vector supercomputers.

3.2 Homogeneous Computing Systems

In 1962, Edward Yevreinov suggested the concept of a *Universal parallel Computing System with programmable structure* (UCS) [28]. The main principles of UCSs were: the basic element of UCS is a general purpose computer (Elementary Machine, EM); the UCS has an homogeneous structure, that is, it consists of identical, equally connected EMs; the number of EMs in the system can be changed; the instruction set, memory size and word length of an EM can also be changed.

It was also proposed to distinguish the UCSs according to their topology: one-, two-, and multi- dimensional; according to the type of exchange between EMs: parallel, sequential, and parallel-sequential; according to the spatial arrangement of EMs: concentrated and distributed.

In the Yevreinov's concept two levels of organization of parallel computing systems were considered: the *macrostructural*, which has just been briefly described, and the *microstructural*, concerning the inner structure of elementary machines, where an homogeneous approach was again proposed, based on Homogeneous Computing Media (see Section 4.1).

Several projects of homogeneous parallel computing systems have been undertaken in Russia in the late 60s - early 70s, under the direction of E.Yevreinov, namely, Minsk-222, Summa, Minimax.

3.3 Multiprocessors with Programmable Architecture

At the end of 70s, Anatoly Kaliaev in Taganrog proposed the conception of multiprocessor systems with programmable architecture. In these systems the interconnection between the processors is accomplished by programming of special *commutation structures* which can be reconstructed in the course of system operation.

In accordance with Kaliaev's conception, the node processors of parallel system have as well a programmable structure and can be configured for execution of large operators (elementary functions, matrix computations, differentiation, FFT, etc.).

These ideas were used in Taganrog Research Institute of Multiprocessor Computing Systems for implementation of a number of experimental, as well as industrial general-purpose and problem-oriented parallel computers.

The foundations of the theory of programmable architecture systems were formulated in [29,30].

One of the intersting developments of the ideas just described was the research of neurolike networks for adaptive robot control [31].

3.4 SIMD Computer PS-2000

In the middle of 70s, in the Moscow Institute of Control Problems, under the direction of Ivery Prangishvili and Sergey Vilenkin, a high-performance SIMD system called PS-2000 (Parallel System 2000) has been designed [32]. This system could be extended from 8 up to 64 PEs (in eight-PE blocks). Each PE had a local memory of 16k 24-bit words and a 24-bit ALU. Each PE was connected with two nearest neighbours and could communicate with them independently from the other PEs. Besides, all the PEs were connected into a ring network; at any moment, only one PE could transfer data into the ring bus while an arbitrary number of specified PEs could receive data from the bus.

These features, together with the priority chain and the activity control made the PS-2000 an associative processor capable of efficient solving of various non-numerical problems.

The serial production of PS-2000 was organized in early 80s at the Severodonetsk Computer Plant (Ukraine).

The experience in solving on the PS-2000 of different problems of geophysics, nuclear physics, aerodynamics, etc. demonstrated a gain of 1 or 2 orders in performance, against the general-purpose computers of that times.

3.5 High-Performance Heterogeneous System "SIBERIA"

In the end of 80s the "Siberia" project was developed at the Computing Center of the Academy of Sciences in Novosibirsk [33]. This project carried out under the direction of Nikolay Mirenkov was one of the first working high-performance systems of heterogeneous architecture. The system was built from completed large modules (on-the-shelf computers). The design of such systems was especially important in Russia at that time when Soviet research laboratories, universities and enterprises had no adequate high-performance computers.

The "Siberia" system consisted of modules assembled into a single installation by the principle of extensibility. The modules were grouped into several subsystems. The central part was a multimachine subsystem including three Soviet ES-1066 (IBM-370 compatible) mainframes. In addition to its main function of general-purpose data processing, this subsystem acted as a host computer for vector-pipeline, vector-parallel, and associative subsystems.

The vector-pipeline subsystem was a set of Bulgarian processors ES-2706 (AP-190L compatible). This subsystem enabled pipelined, macro-pipelined and parallel data processing. The vector-parallel subsystem consisted of Russian PS computers (see Section 3.4). The associative subsystem was a Staran-like computer which enabled the use of various operations on vertical bit-slices.

Several novel programming tools had been designed for the "Siberia" system, aimed to the echievement of maximum parallelism.

3.6 Combined Architecture Systems

The *combined architecture* [34] is a cooperation of a highly parallel host computer with a set of specialized processors. In this architecture, solving of any problem is considered as interaction of several processes, so that execution of each process is delegated to a specialized subsystem, most efficient in implementation of this process. The subsystems are controlled in such a way that their balanced operation might be ensured, and special complementing features of subsystems might be best exploited.

In the combined architecture, the main working load of the processing is delegated to the coprocessors, or *hardware modules* (HMs). Hence, extremely high demands should be made to the performance of each HM. It means that special care is needed in selection of the structures of HMs. In order to ensure an appropriate choice of sets of HMs for different combined architecture systems, a classification was suggested [35] based on the specific "technologies" of processing, *processing types*, necessary for efficient execution of the most labor-intensive procedures involved in the implementation of a problem.

This classification allowed to assume that the variety of processing types involved in machine realization of a broad range of applications is not too large.

The conception of combined architectures provides for design of a family of efficient *concentrated* heterogeneous systems which, in contrast to the existing *distributed* heterogeneous systems does not need for high-bandwidth communication networks, and does not suffer from the delays arising in these networks at the data transfer.

4 Distributed Computing in Cellular Structures

4.1 Homogeneous Computing Media

This important concept was introduced in 1962 by Edward Yevreinov [36]. The *homogeneous computing medium* (HCM) is a logical network consisting of identical and identically interconnected cells. Usually square cells are considered, each connected with its four nearest neighbours. The square form of the element is essential from the viewpoint of complete utilization of the chip area, though the cells can also be triangles or hexagons.

The main idea of computing media is embedding of arbitrary automata into a planar homogeneous cellular structure.

The cell should be a universal one, i.e. it should be configurable to the implementation of each elementary logical function from some complete basis (for instance, AND, OR, NOT), the memory element function, and interconnection functions ensuring construction of arbitrary graphs from accordingly configured chains of cells.

The main properties of the HCM are homogeneity, local interaction, universality of the cells, possibility of setting each cell to implementation of any function from the chosen complete set.

According to Yevreinov, the HCM should be manufactured in a single technological process, like some "computing tissue", getting the required "pattern" at the last stage of production, by means of appropriate configuring.

It is clear now that, as early as the 60s, Yevreinov foresaw the trends of development of parallel computing systems and the potentialities of future VLSI. The early ideas of Yevreinov (as well as of Daniel Slotnick in the USA) by far anticipated the present state of computer science and outlined most of the fundamental problems of development of high-performance computing systems.

4.2 Parallel Substitution Systems

A specific approach to distributed (cellular) computations called *parallel substitution algorithm* (PSA) was suggested in [37]. It represents an abstract automata model providing for a concise mapping of distributed computational process into cellular arrays.

In [38], the problems of interpretation of PSA by networks of automata have been presented in detail.

The parallel substitution system deals with so-called *cellular spaces*, that is, sets of identical cells (automata). To each cell, at each moment (cycle), two values are related: the unique *name* of the cell, and the *state* of the cell, a variable essentially expressing the processed data. A finite set of cells forms a word, or a *configuration*. Each configiration runs through different states in binary alphabet. Data processing in this system is specified by listing the *substitutions* corresponding to the chosen algorithm.

It has been proved that these systems are algorithmically complete. Based on the PSA theory, a variety of techniques were developed for designing algorithmic-oriented cellular VLSI and optical architectures [39].

4.3 Design and Analysis of Systolic Arrays

The systolic arrays take a special place among the modern high-performance parallel data processing architectures. On the one hand, they present an outcome of the development of known ideas of Edward Yevreinov. On the other hand, in the systolic approach, the advantages of these models have been successfully combined by H.T.Kung with the fruitful principle of pipelining the data streams.

Each processing element of a systolic matrix is pumping through itself the data, while performing some prescribed fragments of an appropriate computational process. Thus, in some cases systolic processing could achieve theoretical limits of performance.

An important research in the field of systolic processing has been made by Stanislav Sedukhin (Novosibirsk). He developed a formal method of synthesis and analysis of systolic algorithms and structures based on initial specification of the algorithm given as a system of linear recurrent equations [40]. This method allows for systematic synthesis of *all* equivalent systolic structures admissible for a VLSI implementation with certain constraints. This method was used as a basis for an interactive automated design system S4CAD [41]. Based on these method and system, a number of systolic structures for VLSI implementation were obtained, optimal for solving problems of linear algebra, digital signal processing, graph theory, etc.

We would like to note here that up to the present the great potential possibilities of systolic devices are not sufficiently used in practice, because of difficulties in organizing appropriate powerful data streams. One approach to overcoming this problem is the combined architecture described in Section 3.6.

4.4 Distributed Functional Structures

Most of the cellular automata models (including Yevreinov's HCM) are universal. They can realize arbitrary functions and algorithms, and the synthesis of necessary logical structures proceeds using classical automata theory techniques. Unfortunately, most specific functions will incur time and hardware redundancy when implemented in this way.

Specialized homogeneous structures, which immediately map algorithms into circuits, represent an alternative to the universal ones. In these structures, the given algorithm is simulated by signal propagation through a specialized logical net. A classical example of such structure is the content-addressed, or associative memory with its special basic operation of "equality search". Other specialized structures realizing other basic operations hawe emerged as well. In 1971 Yakov Fet in Novosibirsk proposed a specialized cellular array, called α-structure, with basic operation of "extremum search" [42]. Later on, numerous arrays have been designed implementing various basic operations (threshold searches, nearest neighbour searches, compression, etc.). Arrays of this type have been called *Distributed Functional structures* (DF-structures) [43].

An important feature of the DF-structures is their multifunctionality. Thus, an α-structure can be efficiently used not only for extremum selection, but also as an associative memory, a programmable logic array, an interconnection network, etc.

The conception of DF-structures allows for design of efficient parallel accelerators for diverse computer architectures. Indeed, the modern technology allows to implement distributed functional arrays of sufficient size, which can become a new type of VLSI product, *cellular microprocessors*.

5 Conclusion

Due to restricted size of the paper we needed to limit our overview to short summaries of the above topics. However, there are other Russian works in the field of parallel computing which we would like also distinguish.

The examples of such works are the investigations in parallel asynchronous computing processes made by Vadim Kotov and Alexander Narin'yani in the late 60s [44], the reconfigurable SIMD system designed by Mikhail Kartsev in the beginning of 70s [45], the research on networks of automata by Arkady Makarevsky [46], the works of Victor Malyshkin in methods of program linearization for their efficient parallel execution [47], the project MARS carried out at the Novosibirsk Computing Center in the middle of 80s by Vadim Kotov and his colleagues [6], the work by Vladimir Torgashov et al. on the design of recursive computing systems with dynamically changing structure [48], and many others.

References

1. Davis N.C. and Goodman S.E. The Soviet block's Unified System of computers. Computing Surveys, 1978, Vol.10, No.2, pp.93-122.
2. Wolkott P. and Goodman S.E. High-speed computers of the Soviet Union. Computer, 1988, Vol.21, No.9, pp.32-41.
3. Goodman S.E. The information technologies and Soviet society: problems and prospects. IEEE Trans. on Syst., Man, and Cybern., 1987, Vol. SMC-17, No.4, pp.529-552.
4. Judy R.W. and Clough R.W. Soviet computing in 1980s. -In: Advances in Computing (M.Yovits, ed.), 1989, Vol.29, pp.251-330.
5. Ershov A.P. A history of computing in the USSR. Datamation, 1975, Vol.21, No.6, pp.80-88.
6. Communications of the ACM, 1991, Vol.34, No.6.
7. Malinovsky B.N. Academician S.Lebedev, Kiev, Naukova Dumka, 1992. (In Russian).
8. Malinovsky B.N. Academician V.Glushkov. Kiev, Naukova Dumka, 1993. (In Russian).
9. Kantorovich L.V. On a system of mathematical symbols, convenient for computer operations. Dokl. Acad. Nauk SSSR, 1957, Vol.113, pp.738-741. (In Russian).
10. Pospelov D.A. Introduction to the Theory of Computing Systems. Soviet Radio Publ., Moscow, 1972. (In Russian).
11. Pashkeev S.D. Principles of Multiprogramming for Specialized Computing Systems. Soviet Radio Publ., Moscow, 1972. (In Russian).
12. Tyugu E. Solving problems on computational models. Journal of comp. math. and math. phys., 1970, Vol.10, No.5, pp.716-733. (In Russian).
13. Tyugu E. Knowledge-Based Programming. Addison-Wesley, New York, 1988.
14. Valkovskii V.A., Malyshkin V.E. Parallel Program Synthesis on the Basis of Computational Model. Nauka Publ., Novosibirsk, 1988. (In Russian).
15. Sapaty P.S. VOLNA-0 language as a basis of navigation in knowledge bases on semantic networks. Trans. of the USSR Acad. Sci., Series: Engineering Cybernetics, 1986, No.5, pp.198-210. (In Russian).

16. Vagin V.N. Deduction and Generalization in Decision-Making Systems. Nauka Publ., Moscow, 1988. (In Russian).

17. Vagin V.N., Zakharov V.N., Pospelov D.A., Sapaty P.S., Uvarova T.G., and Khoroshevsky V.F. Project PAMIR. Trans. of the USSR Acad. Sci., Series: Engineering Cybernetics, 1988, No.2, pp.161-170. (In Russian).

18. Varshavsky V.I. Collective Behaviour of Automata. Nauka Publ., Moscow, 1973. (In Russian).

19. Varshavsky V.I., Pospelov D.A. The Orchestra is Playing Without Conductor. Reflections on the evolution of some engineering systems and their control. Nauka Publ., Moscow, 1984. (In Russian).

20. Pospelov D.A., Eivazov A.R. Decentralized computing systems. Trans. of the USSR Acad. Sci., Series: Engineering Cybernetics, 1968, No.5, pp.107-114. (In Russian).

21. Aperiodic Automata. (V.Varshavsky, ed.). Nauka Publ., Moscow, 1976. (In Russian).

22. Automata Control of Asynchronous Processes in Computers and Discrete Systems. (V.Varshavsky, ed.). Nauka Publ., Moscow, 1986. (In Russian).

23. Vazhenin A.P. Hardware and algorithmic support of high accuracy computations in vertical processing systems. Proc. of Int. Conf. "Parallel Computing Technologies (PaCT-93)", Obninsk, Russia, 1993, Vol.1, pp.149-161.

24. Vazhenin A.P. Efficient high-accuracy computations in massively parallel systems. Proc. of the First Int. Workshop on Parallel Scientific Computing (PARA'94-L), Lingby, Denmark, 1994, pp.505-519. (LNCS, Vol.879).

25. Kantorovich L.V. and Fet Ya.I. Computing system comprising a universal digital computer and a small digital computer. USSR Inventor's Certificate No.172567, 1963. (In Russian).

26. Kantorovich L.V., Fet Ya.I., and Ilovayski I.V. Arithmetic unit of a digital computer. USSR Inventor's Certificate No.209032, 1965. (In Russian).

27. Kantorovich L.V., Fet Ya.I., and Ilovayski I.V. Adder for concurrent addition of several binary summands. USSR Inventor's Certificate No.188151, 1965. (In Russian).

28. Yevreinov E.V. and Kosarev Yu.G. High-Performance Homogeneous Universal Computing Systems. Nauka Publ., Novosibirsk, 1966. (In Russian).

29. Kaliaev A.V. Homogeneous Commutation Register Structures. Soviet Radio, Moscow, 1978. (In Russian).

30. Kaliaev A.V. Multiprocessor Systems with Programmable Architecture. Soviet Radio, Moscow, 1984. (In Russian).

31. Kaliaev I.A. Homogeneous neurolike structures for optimization variation problems solving. - In: Proc. of the 5th Int. Conf. "Parallel Architectures and Languages Europe (PARLE'93)", Munich, Germany, 1993, pp.438-451. (LNCS, Vol.694).

32. Prangishvili I.V., Vilenkin S.Ya., and Medvedev I.L. Parallel Computer Systems with Common Control. Energoizdat, Moscow, 1983.

33. Mirenkov N.N. The Siberian approach for an open-system high-performance computing architecture. Computing and Control Engineering Journal, 1992, Vol.3, No.3, pp.137-142.

34. Vazhenin A.P., Sedukhin S.G., Fet Ya.I. High-performance computing systems of combined architecture. Proc. of Int. Conf. "Parallel Computing Technologies (PaCT-91)", Novosibirsk, Russia, (N.N. Mirenkov, ed.), World Scientific Publ., Singapore, 1991, pp. 246-257.

35. Fet Ya.I. and Vazhenin A.P. Heterogeneous processing: a combined approach, Proc. of the First Int. Workshop on Parallel Scientific Computing (PARA'94-L), Lingby, Denmark, 1994, pp. 194-206. (LNCS, Vol.879).

36. Yevreinov E.V. On the microstructure of the elementary machines of a computing system. "Computing Systems", Inst. of Math. of Sib. Div. of USSR Acad. Sci. 1962, Vol.4, pp.3-28. (In Russian).

37. Kornev Yu.N., Piskunov S.V., and Sergeev S.N. Algorithms of general substitutions and their interpretation in automata networks and homogeneous machines. Trans. of the USSR Acad. Sci., Series: Engineering Cybernetics, 1971, No.6, pp.131-142. (In Russian).

38. Parallel Microprogramming Methods (O.L.Bandman, ed.). Nauka Publ., Novosibirsk, 1981. (In Russian).

39. Achasova S.M., Bandman O.L., Markova V.P., and Piskunov S.V. Parallel Substitution Algorithm: Theory and Design. World Scientific Publ., Singapore, 1994.

40. Sedukhin S.G. Design and analysis of systolic algorithms and structures. Programmirovanie, 1991, No.2, pp.20-40. (In Russian).

41. Sedukhin S.G. and Sedukhin I.S. An interactive graphic CAD tool for the synthesis and analysis of VLSI systolic structures. Proc. of Int. Conf. "Parallel Computing Technologies (PaCT-93)", Obninsk, Russia, 1993, Vol.1, pp.163-175.

42. Fet Ya.I. Data Sorting Device. USSR Inventor's Sertificate No.424141, 1971 (In Russian).

43. Fet Ya.I. Parallel Processing in Cellular Arrays. Research Studies Press, Ltd., Taunton, UK, 1995.

44. Kotov V.E. and Narin'yani A.S. Asynchronous processes over shared memory. Kybernetika, 1966, No.3, pp.64-71.

45. Kartsev M.A. The M-10 computer. Dokl. Acad. Nauk SSSR, 1979, Vol.245, pp.309-312. (In Russian).

46. Makarevsky A.Ya. Realization of Discrete Control Devices in Homogeneous Media. Inst. of Control Problems, Moscow, 1970.

47. Malyshkin V.E. Linearized mass computation. Proc. of Int. Conf. "Parallel Computing Technologies (PaCT-91)", Novosibirsk, Russia, (N.N. Mirenkov, ed.), World Scientific Publ., Singapore, 1991, pp. 339-353.

48. Torgashov V.A. and Plyusnin V.U. Dynamic architecture computers (DAC). Proc of Int. Conf. "Parallel Computing Technologies (PaCT-93)", Obninsk, Russia, 1993, Vol.1, pp.25-29.

Early Approaches to Parallel Processing: Increasing performance and dependability

Wolfgang Händler

Universität Erlangen-Nürnberg, IMMD
Martensstr. 3, D-91058 Erlangen.
email: haendler@informatik.uni-erlangen.de

Abstract

Early ideas, developments and investigations regarding Parallel Computing (or Parallel Processing) in Europe are enumerated without a claim for completeness. Beyond it the term ' early' is according to a subjective rating limited to activities till the end of the seventieth. Recent developments like the Transputer - Technology, Industrial - Production lines like Convex, Parsytech etc. are not considered in this contribution.

1. Introduction

From the early beginning of mankind the question was, whether a work can be done by doing several activities at the same time and in what sequence it can be done, if a doing in parallel will result in a conflict. Doing something in parallel (or at the same time) means in general, that a construction can be completed in a time which is shorter than in a sequential order. So it is with shipbuilding. Before we can do anything else we have to lay down the keel. Thereafter we can fix the ribs and only then we can weld the skin on the frame. Finally the launching may be initiated[1] only after having carefully done all intermediate steps before. Sometimes the laws of an admissible order of activities are violated and a bridge under construction crashes down.

In the case of computing appropriate considerations bring up particular theorems. On the one hand the computation must be unique with respect to the result and on the other hand the result has often to be computed in a minimal time, which demands for parallel processing as much as possible. Parallel Processing in several levels, including Pipelining results in an extraordinary performance as well as it is possible in general, to make a system most dependant. Regarding the evaluation of performance there was sometimes confusion. In the context of Amdahl's Law one can state that other more realistic considerations take place meanwhile. A bus driver knows that the efficiency and amortization of his bus is not secured if he always has only one or two passengers. In contrary he has to care for a full or nearly full utilization. Similar considerations are valid in computing.

---

1. The only exceptions are dugouts (canoes) and the so-called Liberty-Ships during world-War II where the floating body is made from a whole unique piece (The Liberty-Ships were poured during the war from concrete as an unique piece.).

2. Going softly into parallelism

The difference in time between handwritten computing and machine computing was so significant about the fourties and fifties that sometimes it seemed not necessary to the pioneers to accelerate the speed of the early computers. Slogans like - "who should read what we can print out in a short time?" - seemed to be severe arguments.[2] In the context of Weather-Forecast and in the context of Real-Time computing nevertheless came up the demand for much higher speed. So it was the endeavour already to execute many things in parallel, wherever this did not result in conflicts.

This initiated a period, where soft parallelism was introduced. Wherever possible an operation was started, before former operations have ended. At the end of this evolution several operations took place overlapping each other, whenever this was possible without a conflict. This soft overlappping parallelism did not alter the attitudes of users or programmers. The control of operations happened in a manner, which was given by the algorithms as defined by the usual programming semantics.

In this period the essential speed-up of computers came along with the pure speed-up of the switching circuitry and to a smaller additional part with the soft parallelism as described before. In order to give figures: between 1950 and 1975 the performance of computers increased by a factor of 10^5. 10^3 of this factor were gained by switching circuitry, while the 10^2 were due to soft-parallel overlapping (comp. [1]). Finally Input-Output-devices were driven independently from the central processor, bringing up another speed-up in the overall performance. Looking slightly ahead with respect to I/O the user or programmer could help to run the computer more economically with a minimum of waiting time or dead periods.

This presentation cannot pay attention to all approaches of soft-parallelism. Nevertheless one approach of the soft-parallelism-era may be considered as significant: the word-parallelism. Computers since the fifties belong mostly to a class which were at that time called simply Parallel Computers. Nevertheless this notation is not correct from a point of view we have now - nearly 40 years later. Rather all possibilities with respect to parallel processing were investigated during this period of evolution. So we have to define whatever we mean with parallelism.

In this context we should remark that word-parallelism, as just described, belongs to soft parallelism, since it is not necessary, to alter the attitudes of programming compared with the same business in utilizing computers which are working bit by bit serially with respect to the wordlength. Word-parallelism was suggested by the insight that working on parallel words the gain in speed is significant. At the same time the control of an operation becomes easier than in the case of serial processing. It is only to spend a certain amount of more hardware regarding the carry, which has to be pro-

---

2. Evidently this is not true, since - for instance - a bank has to send all its clients an individual statement.

cessed in a very short time. This problem nevertheless found a couple of good solutions at that time. The user never became aware the transition to parallel-word processing beside the fact that the performance was nearly n-times faster, if n was the word-length (in bit).

At the end of the evolution regarding soft-parallelism a computer became standard which in many respects has something from computers of the class STRETCH, LARC and ATLAS [2]. These three computers represent the result exhausting many possibilities in soft parallelism. About 1960 this was "State of the art" (comp. also: CD 6600 below).

The forementioned "soft parallelism" is described here to a certain extent, in order to make "Parallel Computing" more evident as distinct from Soft Parallel Processing just described. Parallel Computing is rather a matter of knowledge of the programmer, for which the computer architect offers pipelines, a multitude of Arithmetic and Logic Units (ALUs) and/or a multitude of Processors (ALUs with a Control).[3]

The Telefunken-Team in Backnang, later in Konstanz a.B., created beginning in 1957 a production line of computers TR 4 and TR 440, which was typical for this era of exploited soft parallelism [3]. In this context was also developed an interesting concept for microprogramming. The idea was described in 1960 by F.R. Güntsch and W. Händler [6] (fig. 1). A 'musical' notation allowed the Telefunken - Team an easy

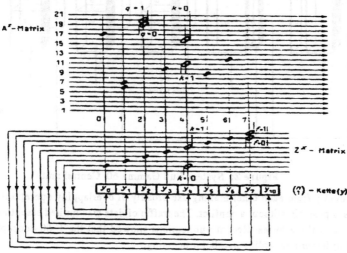

Figure 1: Microprogramming - one Instruction, Instruction planes are composed to a rectangular block in 3 dimensions.

---

3. A Processor is capable to interprete programs or programm parts (tasks), while an ALU cannot.

handling of the tool. Microprogramming was originally created by M. Wilkes in 1951 [4], extensively utilized by H. Billing in 1955 [5] and found its industrial counterpart in TR 4 in the era of discrete elements. The industrial solution in transparent diode matrices (H. Voigt) resembled in a musical notation (as mentioned above), where 'chord' means a parallel execution of some microoperations (called a microinstruction) while 'melody' describes a sequence of microinstructions configuring a machine - instruction (or microprogram). Loops and branching were characterized by an appropriate notation and were realized by additional diodes. This Version proved out to be very useful for exploiting just soft parallelism.

A very early approach in 1958 was also the BULL GAMMA 60-Computer [7]. Instead of a single ALU   Bull allocated between 2 Buses several independent units like comparison units, logic units, arithmetic units, magnetic drums and coding (or recoding) units (Fig. 2). All these units potentially had their own control and could process in-

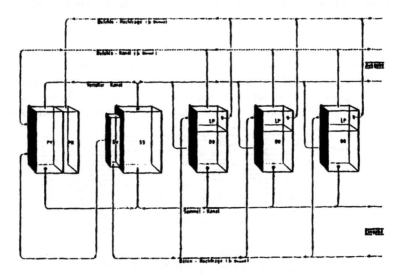

Figure 2: System Bull Gamma 60. Central unit.

dependently from each other making use broadly of overlapping operations as much as this is possible without a conflict. The traffic of data was limited essentially by the capacity of the 2 buses. Recent publications showed that the Γ 60-concept was far ahead of its time regarding parallel processing.

A typical example of exhausting soft parallelism can be seen in the successful CD 6600 (Fig. 3), where all possibilities of soft parallelism were utilized (Fig. 4) in several levels (I/O-Units, 10-I/O-Processors (including independent memories), central memory, numerous Registers, 10 Instruction Exec.-Units; comp. [2]).

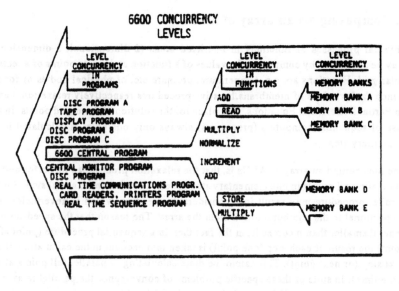

Figure 3: System CD 6600. Independent I/O-Control processors and independent execution of Arithmetic and Logic Units.

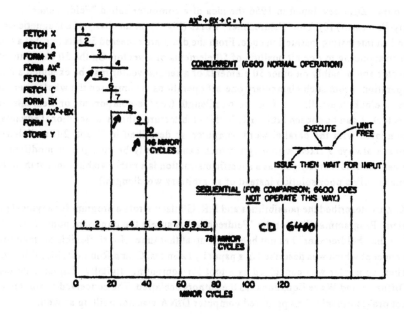

Figure 4: Timing chart. Overlapping execution and purely Non-overlapping in the Central Unit.

3. Computing via an array of ALUs

Physical processes or functions in restricted areas (2-dimensional, 3-dimensional) may be calculated by computing the values of a function at discrete points of a rectangular grid. Functions are e.g. temperature, pressure etc. of physical bodies or for instance dz deviations of membrans. Iterative procedures respectively relaxation, based on Partial Differential Equations, take place for the solution at these grid points. In the case of sequential computers (processors) always only one point is calculated in an elementary step.

The idea behind an array of ALUs is, that the relaxation process can be performed by calculating all points in one elementary step for one iteration (relaxation) step. Such a parallel procedure may result in a considerable speed-up which is nevertheless not proportional to the number n of ALUs in the array. The reason that the speed-up is in general smaller than n comes from the fact that in a sequential procedure (point after point) the result of each step (one point) is taken into account in the calculation of the next step (or next point). This cannot be done calculating in parallel (all points at the same time). In spite of these specific problems of convergence the parallel relaxation (or parallel array process) brings along a considerable advantage over sequential strategies.

Konrad Zuse developed in 1956 the idea of a computer called "Feldrechner" (or Array-Processor) [8]. The "Feldrechner" works (Fig. 5) on the basis of a magnetic drum and an interesting instruction code. From the drum are accessed 50 bits (e.g.) at a time, corresponding to one bit position of 50 elements of a vector. On the 50 elements of a vector and possibly on other 50 elements of a second vector may be executed a basic operation. From such elementary one-bit-operations is composed the whole operation in l clock intervals - if l is the wordlength (for the components or elements of a vector). l can be chosen arbitrarily in this architecture - this is an additional advantage compared with the parallel-word computer, as described in Chapt. 2.(Parallel-word means always a fixed wordlength which cannot easily be changed or modified. At most 'double wordlength' as a specific instruction is a rather viable concept then. But this is only a poor solution instead of an arbitrary wordlength.).

K. Zuse described the possibilities and F.R. Güntsch wrote a program for a typical problem. Programmability for the "Feldrechner" is surely the important point. Nevertheless the "Feldrechner" has not been built up at that time. Not so flexible seemed to be a concept which was described in a paper by Leondes, C. and Rubinoff, M. [9] in 1952. Their computer was conceived as a tool for computing digitally "Laplace, Poisson, Diffusion and Wave Equations" as the authors declaired. The conceived computer was not programmable. The proposed computer DINA was not built up as well.

In 1962 also scientists with Yevreinov began to work on interesting bit-oriented algorithms, well suited to array - processing of an advanced sort [13]. Particularly in the era of integrated circuits the algorithms permitted an extremely fast execution of a class of functions.

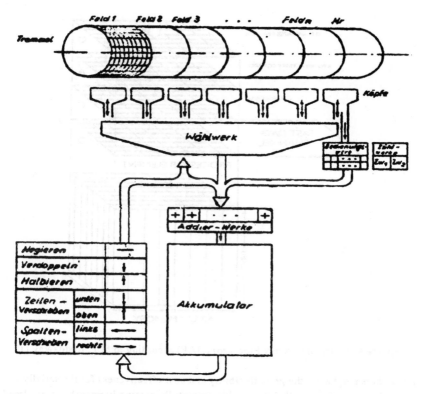

Figure 5: Zuse's idea of an "Feldrechenmaschine".
Many equal operations at the same time, e.g. on components of vectors.

Stewart F. Reddaway (Great Br.) built up in the seventies the DAP (Distributed Array processor) [10]. This was the first operable Array Processor in Europe (Fig. 6). The DAP became later an optional part of the General Purpose Computer ICL 2900. For instance the DAP-Memory could be used also as a memory block of ICL 2900. Equipped with a DAP-modul, the ICL 2900 can work with a rectangular array (field) of one-bit-ALUs. In an array of 32 × 32 bit the DAP operates for instance in an elementary time on 1024 bits according to the (unique) program, centrally interpreted and individually executed then on each ALU. In such a way for instance a physical rectangular space can be calculated. Apparently the hardware extension limits the maximal space which can be included in one calculation step. How fine the grid has to be chosen with respect to the real space depends on the application. According to the need the physical space is brought in a certain number of 'pieces' to the array computer. A flexibility in this context (relation betw. Physical Space and ALU-Space) is called scalability. A certain lost arises if the boundary of the physical space is jagged. The ALUs outside the boundary have to be deactived. They do not take part in the calculation. Evidently these quiet or dead ALUs will diminish the overall performance. All array processors (Zuse, Reddaway) are working in this way.

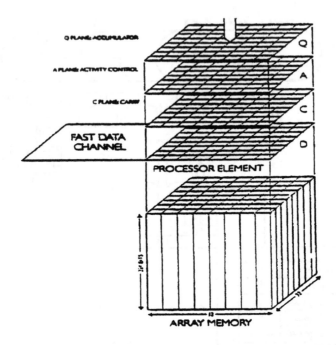

Figure 6: Distributed Array Processor (DAP) according to St.F. Reddaway [10]

All authors emphasize the great flexibility and cost-effectiveness for the serially working ALU (sometimes called P.E. in this context: Processing Element). It was already mentioned that an Array Processor allows an arbitrary wordlength (according to the need of precision).

In 1974, Händler [11] combined the properties of an Array Processor and of a standard processors in one unique processor (Fig. 7). This processor had two operation modes: "horizontal processing" and: "vertical processing". While "horizontal processing" is the conventional mode to compute on machine-words (32 bit for instance), multiplying them, comparing them etc., "vertical processing" is extensively what we described in the context of Zuse's and Reddaway's ideas. One restriction is that the multiplicity of the Array-Processor-Mode (or "vertical processing") is limited to 32 (or 64) according to the usual machine-wordlength. Compared with K. Zuse's Feldrechenmaschine it is rather satisfying the more one can expect that 64 bit wordlength will become standard. Even 64 is nevertheless a low number. Therefore "Vertical Processing" was integrated in Multiprocessors (compare Chapter 5). It was shown how the concept can be combined with considerations of fault tolerant computing [12].

With respect to the conventional mode (horizontal mode) a 'Vertical Processor' is exactly the processor which is usually known as the von Neumann-processor. With respect to the vertical mode we have to add some operations we know from Array Pro-

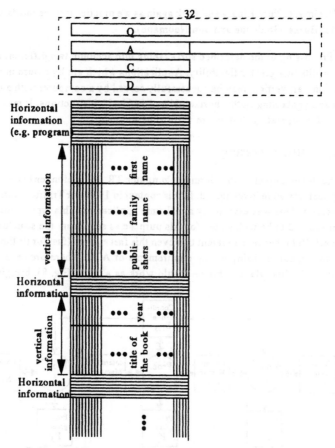

Figure 7: Vertical Processing via conventional processors according to
W. Händler [11, 14]

cessing. This can easily be done by utilizing a microprogramming device. Microprogrammability was the basis of a combined structure which was derived from today's standard-processors by adding Vertical Instructions (Array Processing Instructions). In this way it was possible to make experiments with three different off-the-shelf processors. The experience with Vertical Processing was quite satisfying. The experiments were nevertheless not extended to fault-tolerant Multiprocessors (compare above). A. Bode has carefully investigated and measured the performance regarding vertical processing. Compared with conventional (horizontal) processing there is a considerable speed up, sometimes up to 70 evidently dependent upon the type of application [14].

The extraordinary speedup comes from the point, that the number of instruction fetches in vertical processing is extremely low among all accesses. However it is necessary to convert and to reorder numbers (or other data) into vertical numbers and later back again.Regarding a certain time penalty it can be compared with the known conversion Decimal to Pure Binary and back again as we practice it since the days of Princeton [15] (Burks, Goldstine and von Neumann).

Vertical Processing of the described sort - taking into account two different operation modes - results in a greater flexibility. Applications which are by nature in part horizontal and in part vertical may be successfully solved by a computer with a mixed instruction set, containing both - horizontal and vertical - instructions. It may be noted that parts of an operating system are vertical by nature.

4. Early multiprocessing

During the development of the German Computer TR 4 (Telefunken) since 1957 several applications were investigated. In this context in 1959 Air Traffic Control (ATC) was envisaged. This was essentially a real-time application. This typical soft-parallel computer seemed to be well suited for this purpose as seen from the structure and instruction set. But it became apparent that even this fast system (fast for its time of design) was not capable to bring up the requirements of ATC. Therefore several TR 4 - Processors - at a first glance: three - should work as a team (Fig. 8), bringing up the

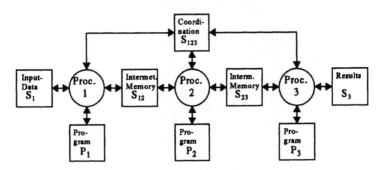

Figure 8: Teamwork of Processors:
Basic Idea for mastering Air Traffic Control (ATC).

necessary performance [16]. The load-sharing in this team had to take into account mainly:

1. Cleaning or smoothing incoming environment data.
2. Collision avoiding procedures.
3. Graphical representation of the ATC - Situation (for ATC-personal and for pilots).

Later the necessity for an additional activity became apparent:

4. Emergency handling and preventive maintenance.

This causes us to enlarge the 'team' by an additional processor. Processors have to communicate with each other. Therefore different kinds of coupling them together were investigated. The most efficient one was that processors share an intermediate memory.

In standard cases three processors worked according to 1. - 3. and a respective fourth processor was diagnosed by a preventive maintenance procedure. After a certain period the roles of the processors were cyclically interchanged. The availability of this 'team' would have been very high, as it is necessary just in the case of ATC. Nevertheless the system was never built up. Two Telefunken TR 4 were delivered to the Center of ATC in Germany mainly for training purposes.

A publication in 1973 [17] describes this concept 'Macro-Pipelining' more in detail and compares it with an other proposed solution of the ATC - Problem by the STAR-AN - Array Processor, which was described in a publication shortly before. Both papers offer an idea of a manifold of possible solutions with respect to parallel processing.

In the case of Macropipelining (fig. 9) all data flow from processor 1or 2 (first col-

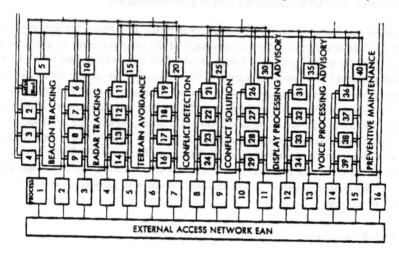

Figure 9: Full-size ATC-System. Proposal for Macropipelining left to right and Parallelism with many processors [17]

umn), specialized on activity *a* to processor 3 or 4 (second column) specialized on activity *b*, etc., etc. As proposed in the paper of 1973 [17], the multiprocessor made use on the one hand of a whole field of smaller processors for increasing the overall performance and on the other hand for maximizing the availability by substituting defect processors in emergency cases. For this latter possibility one has to provide a certain redundance regarding the number of processors and connections.

It is worth to note that since 1966 a couple of interesting multiprocessors or at least systems well suited to multiprocessing were built up in the countries, which were called at that time socialist countries. Examples are MINSK 222 by E.V. Yevreinov, BESM - 6 by S. Lebedev and e.g. ELBRUS (multiprocessor) by S. Burtsev. The file of approaches from the former socialistic countries may be nevertheless not complete [18].

So it is with other European approaches, which partially did not sufficiently come to the knowledge of the public. Telefunken Konstanz (F.R. Güntsch) and the University of Hannover[4] (W. Händler) developed in the mid-sixties for instance with their staff a concept called 'BIENE' (Bee - according to the idea of a colony of bees) [19], where a multitude of processors, memory units, and I/0 - units were connected via a crossbar switch. The units had some standard-wordlengths according to the need of the respective application. The investigations of hardware and software problems offered interesting results. In later developments crossbar - switches were avoided because of their cost (proportional to n^2, where n is the number of units).

The system was never built up completely coming into an era where Telefunken as a daughter of AEG ran in a hard crisis. Nevertheless the Erlangen multiprocessor construction kit 'DIRMU' [20] (Distributed Reconfigurable Multiprocessor) shows some of the ideas of 'BIENE', mainly the idea of a construction kit.

The challenge remained the NP-problem how to match the inherent problem structure with the infrastructure (connection topology) of the multiprocessor in question. In most cases the programmer was forced to introduce improvisions and to utilize his phantasy instead of a suited software tool or analysis. For this reason the acceptance of early multiprocessors in Computing Centers remained very low. No languages for help in multiprocessing and mainly no 'parallel thinking' existed in the late sixties and in the seventies. It proved out to be a matter of mentality whether the computer community accepted the new possibilities of parallelism. The majority of people in the scene was educated in the world of pure von Neumann-Structures, FORTRAN, ALGOL and e.g. Turing which essentially are sequential in their nature. So it was not quite easy at that time to convince people that the utilization of parallel processing offers many advantages.

5. Fundamentals

Designing in Parallel Processing is considerably supported by the theoretical work of Carl Adam Petri, Bonn. Petri created in 1962 a tool for analysing functionalism and in particular concurrent operations, which was later called: "Petri - Nets" [22]. The Automata Theory needs a huge number of nodes and edges to characterize very simple cases, so that it seems to be impropriate for solving practical problems in design. Petri Nets in contrary allow a concise description of functional behaviour and in particular concurrency and interdependence, of functional components. The description itself happens with a minimum of elements in the graph.

The functionalism in Neural Nets was considered in a cooperation of the Institute for Physiology and Biocybernetics (W.D. Keidel) [23] with the Institute of Mathematical Machines and Dataprocessing (W. Händler) at the University of Erlangen-Nuremberg. Starting 1968 with a schema of Data-Processing in human beings (W.D. Keidel) simi-

---

4. at that time correctly cited: Technische Hochschule Hannover

larities as well as dissimilarities with respect to computer structures were investigated. The project DORA (Data-Processing in Organisms and Computer Architecture), sponsored by the German Federal Ministry for Research and Technology[5], reflects a lot of insight in the problems and proved out to be suggestive with respect to the multiprocessor concept EGPA (and to successors DIRMU and MEMSY, compare Sect. 6). The conic shapes of Neural Nets (W.D. Keidel) - for incoming as well as for outcoming data - are reflected by the structure of the EGPA-family, which is shaped as a pyramid (compare the sect. 6).

The predominant shape of an organism is - as we pointed out - the conic (Fig 10).

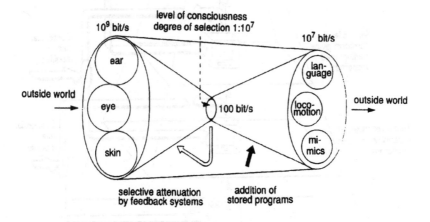

Figure 10: Organism , a schematic and quantitative evaluation.

Nevertheless investigations of global Operating Systems, of some Utility Programs and applications like Pattern Recognition (fig. 11) provoke also a conic or pyramidal structure for multiprocessors. So it was quite natural to choose a (discrete) pyramid for the EGPA-System, which comes very close to a conic shape.[6]

The author apologizes that it is not possible in the frame work of this paper to pay tribute to the theoretical work of Dijkstra (Critical Regions etc.), Hoare and Hansen (Conditional Critical regions etc.) to parallel processing. The same note is valid to an early publication of Karp and Miller.

---

5. Today's name

6. Other institutions all over the world came to similar results. But only in 1986 a NATO-Advanced Research Workshop on Pyramidal Systems took place in Maratea, Italy.

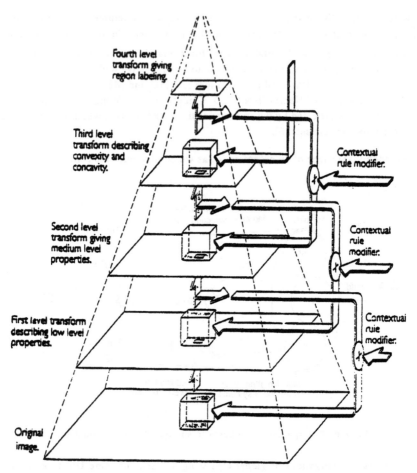

Fourth level transform giving region labeling.

Third level transform describing convexity and concavity.

Second level transform giving medium level properties.

First level transform describing low level properties.

Original image.

Contextual rule modifier.

Contextual rule modifier.

Contextual rule modifier.

Figure 11: Hierarchical structure relating information representation
and operations in pattern recognition (classification)
Material of CONTEXTVISION AB, Stockholm

6. Size-independent Multiprocessors

As we pointed out in Sect. 5 EGPA[7] [21] was designed since this proved out to be the most favourable structure for a General Purpose Multiprocessor Family (fig. 12).A processor (*P*) has always access to a number of memory units (*M*) and a *M* reversely can be accessed by several *P*s. The access is controlled by a multiport which is a part of the memory unit *M*. Only one *P* can access a *M* in an elementary intervall. This is

---

7. <u>E</u>rlangen - <u>G</u>eneral - <u>P</u>urpose - <u>A</u>rchitecture (or <u>A</u>rray)

nevertheless a most efficient procedure for a communication. Some variants of multi-access were investigated.

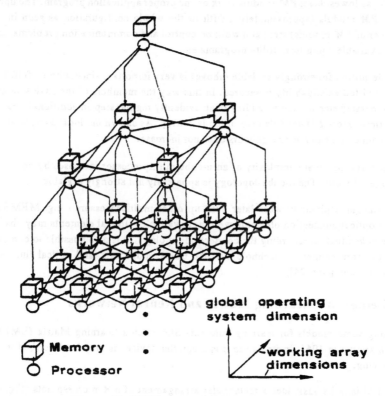

global operating
system dimension

◻ Memory
○ Processor

working array
dimensions

Figure 12: EGPA-System. Family of pyramids.

The pyramid in the sense of discrete Processor-Memory-Moduls (*PM*-Moduls) is at the same time size-independent[8] and with increasing size the local complexity does not increase. One can state:

"A system is strongly scalable if the performance can be enlarged monotonicly and infinitely without changing its technology and topology".

The local complexity is defined as the number of connections of a *PM*-modul to its neighbours[9]. In EGPA-pyramids this number never exceeds 9.

---

8. The term 'size-independent' is used here since it was called in that way in early publications in the context of EGPA. Later this property was generally called 'scalable' or 'scalable hardware structure'.

9. A *P* is always connected (has access) to a *M* via a multiport (fig.). A *P* has not an access to an upper *M* for reliable OS-Systems.

The lowest level *PM*-moduls have apparently each only 5 such connections - to the *M*s of their four neighbours (in directions N , E , W , S) and to their respective local *M*. These lowest level *PM*-moduls work on the proper application program. The upper level *PM*-moduls (approximately a fifth of the whole configuration as seen in the number of *PM*-moduls) store and work on control and communication problems, making available compilers, utility programs etc.

The definition for strongly scalable (above) is very important since with its fulfilling an unlimited extendability is secured. In this way the members of the EGPA-family are generated step be step by adding in an evidently regular step an additional array of four times more *PM*-moduls than in the last array. As shown the local complexity of *PM*-connections to their neighbours does not increase.

In contrary the local complexity of an n-cube-multiprocessor increases by one if we enlarge n by one. The n-cube-topology is apparently not strongly scalable.

At Erlangen University were later built up other multiprocessors - e.g. MEMSY , when optical connection elements were not available. Optical elements may change the whole situation regarding the connection topology. It is also possible to combine two or more connection-technologies like buses, multiports, and optical lines and switches (compare [24]).

7. Steinbuch's Learning Matrix and Neural Networks

Among some models for learning automata Steinbuch's Learning Matrix (LM) became known in 1961. In its nature it is a parallel device, as may be described in the following.

The LM is in its basic idea a rectangular arrangement of n × m crosspoints (Fig. 13)

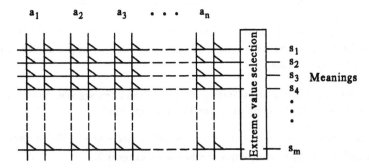

Figure 13: Learning Matrix according to K. Steinbuch [25]. Educated Phase:
A vector of Attributes (a_i) is applied to the vertical wires and
the meaning s_k is selected (one from m) by a peak decision.

with n vertical and m horizontal lines. The n vertical lines (or wires) are input lines (or wires) where binary attributes a_1 , a_2 , ... a_n are applied, which characterize an object.

The m horizontal lines correspond to m meanings s_1, s_2, ... s_m, which - after a teaching process - may be differentiated by the LM. During the teaching process, where men offer typical objects by the presentation of their attributes as a vector $(a_1, a_2, ... a_n)$. At the same time the meaning s_k (one horizontal wire) is activated. At the crosspoints are marked those coincidences where both wires are activated by "Ones". In these cases a weight is increased or decreased according to a given learning law. In the case of non-correspondence of signals the weight is diminished against it.

A detail has to be mentioned in order to be correct. The attributes are applied - each one - by double wires a_i and $\bar{a}_i$ as pairs 01 or 10. This symmetrical (twofold) arrangement is necessary, since otherwise the LM would fail. In the simplest case increasing or decreasing of the weights is realized by modifying accordingly the electrical conductances connecting the wires at the (double) crosspoints.

The LM-device answers reversely - after a certain training period, where the m objects are sufficiently often offered - with an activation of the respective line s_k (one line). This happens by a summation of the attributes - multiplied by the weights at that time - and a selection of the peak value of all rows.

The 2^n possible vectors $(a_1, a_2, ... a_n)$ or events configure a n-cube with 2^n vertices.

In nontrivial cases is $m \ll 2^n$ and the n-cube is partitioned in m sets of vertices. Events (vectors) of the same meaning (s_k) will occupy neighboured (or connected) vertices of one such set. In general vectors of the same meaning show a certain limited Hamming-distance from each other. The system (LM) answers accordingly.

The LM has similar properties as Rosenblatt's Perceptron [26]. It shows an adaptive behaviour, i.e. it follows certain fashionable streams which come up with the time. In other words: the LM collects experiences with the stream of presented objects even in the educated phase. The partition on the n-cube changes accordingly.

The Learning Matrix as well as the Perceptron are in their essence predecessors of more general neural networks which are highly parallel as natural neural networks. It does not make to much sense to simulate them sequentially.

Literature

[1]   Hockney, R.W. and C.R. Jesshope: Parallel Computers 2, Architecture, Programming and Algorithms; Adam Hilger, Bristol and Philadelphia 1988

[2]   Bell, G. and A. Newell: Computer Structures: Readings and Examples; Mc. Graw-Hill, New York, St. Louis, San Francisco etc. 1971

[3]   Material, edited by Telefunken or AEG-Telefunken, e.g. Digital-Rechenanlage TR 4, 1959,
      TR 4 Datenverarbeitungssystem, Automation in Verwaltung und Industrie

[4]   Wilkes, M.: The best way to design an automatic calculation machine
      Manchester University 1951 (Dissertation)

[5] Billing, H. und W. Hopmann: Mikroprogrammsteuerwerk Elektronische Rund-
     schau 9 (1955) 349-353

[6] Güntsch, F.R. und W. Händler: Zur systematischen Behandlung von modernen
     Steuerungsaufgaben in digitalen Rechenanlagen Zs. Angewandte Mathematik
     40 (1960) T 39 - T 44 (in German) or:
     Güntsch, F.R. and W. Händler: Zur Simultanarbeit bei Digitalrechnern
     Elektronische Rechenanlagen 2 (1960) 117-128 (in German)

[7] Smotherman, M. and G. Renard:[10] Architecture and Performance of the Bull
     Gamma 60
     Tumlin, T.J.; M. Smotherman: An Evaluation of the Design of the Gamma 60;
     in: 3ème Colloque Histoire de l'Informatique (Sophia Antipolis, France, 13-15
     Octobre 1993)
     and Material, edited by Compagnie des Machines Bull

[8] Zuse, K.: Die Feldrechenmaschine; MTW-Mitteilungen V/4 (1958)
     (on a patent application from 1956)

[9] Leondes, C. and M. Rubinoff: DINA a digital analyser for Laplace, Poisson, dif-
     fusion an wave equations; AIEE Transact. Communic. and Electronics 71 (1952)
     303-309

[10] Reddaway, St.F.: DAP , a Distributed Array Processor; 1st Annual Symposium
     on Computer Architecture, IEEE/ACM Florida 1973

[11] Händler, W.: Unconventional Computation by Conventional Equipment, Arbeit-
     sberichte des IMMD der Univ. Erlangen-Nürnberg, Bd 7, Nr. 2, Mai 1974, auch
     NATO-DEFENCE RESEARCH GROUP SEMINAR Design and Evaluation of
     Information Systems, 23.-26.04.1974, Athen

[12] Händler, W.: A Multiprocessor Working as a Fault-Tolerant Cellular Automat-
     ion, Computing 48, 5-20 (1992), Springer-Verlag 1992

[13] According to a note from Y.I. Fet, Novosibirsk

[14] Albert, B. and A. Bode: Microprogrammed associative Instructions: Results and
     Analysis of a Case Study in vertical migration: Proceedings Micro 16 (1983)
     115-121 ACM/IEEE

[15] Burks, A.W., H.H. Goldstine, J. von Neumann: Preliminary discussion of the lo-
     gical design of an electronic computing instrument (1946 distributed in a type-
     written form). Reproduced in: Randell, B. (ed.) The origins of digital computers,
     Springer-Verlag (1973) 371-385

[16] Material, notes and figures of F.R. Güntsch and W. Händler, comp. also [3]

[17] Händler, W.: The concept of macro-pipelining with high-availability; Elektroni-
     sche Rechenanlagen 15 (1973) 269-274

[18] comp. e.g.: Ershov, A.P. and M.R. Shura-Bura: The early development of pro-
     gramming in the USSR; in: Metropolis, N., J. Howlett and Gian-Carlo Rota: A
     history of computing in the twentieth century; Academic Press New York, Lon-
     don, Toronto etc. 1980. Beyond it I got references from Dr. Doroshenko, Kiev
     and Dr. Y.I. Fet, Novosibirsk.

---

10. I owe the reference to these papers to Dr. Mounier-Kuhn, Paris

[19] Händler, W., R. Klar, W. Rasche, H.J. Schneider, P.P. Spies, R. Vollmar: BIE-NE, Gedanken zu einem neuen Rechnersystem; Arbeitsblätter d. Lehrstuhls für Elektronische Rechnenanlagen der T.H. Hannover 1965 (internal report)

[20] Händler, W., H. Rohrer: Gedanken zu einem Rechner-Baukasten-System (Thoughts on a computer construction kit); Elektronische Rechenanlagen 22 (1980) 3-13 or: Händler, W., E. Maehle and K. Wirl: The DIRMU Testbed for High-Performance Multiprocessor Configurations; Proceedings of the first International Conference on Supercomputing Systeme, Dec, 16-20, 1985 St. Petersburg, FL.

[21] Händler, W., F. Hofmann and H.J. Schneider: A General Purpose Array with a broad Spectrum of Applications; Computer Architecture, Workshop of the GI, Erlangen, May 22-23, 1975 W. Händler (edit.) Springer-Verlag Berlin, Heidelberg, New York 1976

[22] Petri, C.A.: Kommunikation mit Automaten; Bonn 1962 (Dissertation) (Communication with Automata)

[23] Keidel, W.D.: Informationsverarbeitung (Information Processing) in: Kurzgefaßtes Lehrbuch der Physiologie, W.D. Keidel (edit.); Georg Thieme Verlag Stuttgart 1970

[24] Ikedo, T. and N. Mirenkov: AIZU-Supercomputer: A reality problem engine Technical Report 93-2/1-016, Department of Computer Software. The University of AIZU. Aizu-Wakamatsu City 1993 (cited, since the idea of a pyramid structure remained alive, comp. [21]).

[25] Steinbuch, K.: Die Lernmatrix; Kybernetik 1 (1961) 36-45

[26] Rosenblatt, F.: The Perceptron. A Probability Model for Information Storage and Organization in the Brain; Psycholog. Rev. 65 (1958) 386-408

Author Index

S. Achasova, 1
A. Adamovich, 127
G. Agibalov, 7
H. Ahmed, 288
G. Alekseev, 94
A. Anisimov, 16
R. Ayani, 314
O. Bandman, 21
L. Barriga, 314
S. Benkner, 142
O. Bessonov, 385
A. Bianchi, 36
A. Borshchev, 219
V. Brailovskaya, 385
C. Bussler, 370
A. Bystrov, 94
F. Caudal, 411
T. Churina, 94
P. Ciancarini, 400
S. Coluccini, 36
P. Dauphin, 234
P. Degano, 36
O. Dikenelli, 258
A. Doroshenko, 157
H. Essafi, 273
D. Etiemble, 320
V. Evstigneev, 163
Y. Fet, 464
F. Gasperoni, 51
C. Germain, 320
B. Goossens, 326
A. Gunzinger, 186
W. Händler, 477
P. Hartmann, 57
C. Hochberger, 169
R. Hoffmann, 169
A. Hondroudakis, 180
R. Hüsler, 186
A. Hurson, 204
S. Jablonski, 370
B.-U. Jun, 204
Y. Karpov, 219

V. Kasyanov, 163
E. Kessy, 453
T. Kirsche, 370
R. Klar, 234
O. Klimova, 241
V. Korneev, 341
A. Kremlev, 434
M. Kupriyanova, 117
S. Lamberts, 246
B. Lecussan, 411
V. Levin, 341
T. Ludwig, 246
A. Malevsky, 252
V. Malyshkin, 304
I. Mamedova, 427
P. Mancini, 400
V. Markova, 70
O. Monakhov, 434
V. Morozov, 294
S. Mylnikov, 94
A. Nepomniaschaya, 85
V. Nepomniaschy, 94
L. Nicolas, 273
A. Özerdim, 258
E. Okunishnikova, 94
E. Ozkarahan, 258, 439
M. Pic, 273
S. Piskunov, 70
V. Polezhaev, 386
D. Pospelov, 464
C. Priami, 36
R. Procter, 180
V. Roudakov, 219
B. Roux, 385
M. Royak, 304
Y. Saad, 252
B. Schnor, 109
H. Schuster, 370
U. Schwiegelshohn, 51
K. Shanmugam, 180
E. Shurina, 304
Y. Soloveichik, 304

V. Srini, 356
A. Stoukov, 453
T. Thiel, 434
L.-E. Thorelli, 288
G. Tröster, 186
J. Turek, 51
M. Ünalir, 258
D. Vandromme, 453
A. Vazhenin, 294
G. Vesselovski, 117
M. Viala, 273
V. Vlassov, 288
H. Vonder Mühll, 146
D. Vu, 326
S. Waldschmidt, 169
H. Wedekind, 370
A. Zabrodin, 341

Lecture Notes in Computer Science

For information about Vols. 1–899

please contact your bookseller or Springer-Verlag

Vol. 900: E. W. Mayr, C. Puech (Eds.), STACS 95. Proceedings, 1995. XIII, 654 pages. 1995.

Vol. 901: R. Kumar, T. Kropf (Eds.), Theorem Provers in Circuit Design. Proceedings, 1994. VIII, 303 pages. 1995.

Vol. 902: M. Dezani-Ciancaglini, G. Plotkin (Eds.), Typed Lambda Calculi and Applications. Proceedings, 1995. VIII, 443 pages. 1995.

Vol. 903: E. W. Mayr, G. Schmidt, G. Tinhofer (Eds.), Graph-Theoretic Concepts in Computer Science. Proceedings, 1994. IX, 414 pages. 1995.

Vol. 904: P. Vitányi (Ed.), Computational Learning Theory. EuroCOLT'95. Proceedings, 1995. XVII, 415 pages. 1995. (Subseries LNAI).

Vol. 905: N. Ayache (Ed.), Computer Vision, Virtual Reality and Robotics in Medicine. Proceedings, 1995. XIV,

Vol. 906: E. Astesiano, G. Reggio, A. Tarlecki (Eds.), Recent Trends in Data Type Specification. Proceedings, 1995. VIII, 523 pages. 1995.

Vol. 907: T. Ito, A. Yonezawa (Eds.), Theory and Practice of Parallel Programming. Proceedings, 1995. VIII, 485 pages. 1995.

Vol. 908: J. R. Rao Extensions of the UNITY Methodology: Compositionality, Fairness and Probability in Parallelism. XI, 178 pages. 1995.

Vol. 909: H. Comon, J.-P. Jouannaud (Eds.), Term Rewriting. Proceedings, 1993. VIII, 221 pages. 1995.

Vol. 910: A. Podelski (Ed.), Constraint Programming: Basics and Trends. Proceedings, 1995. XI, 315 pages. 1995.

Vol. 911: R. Baeza-Yates, E. Goles, P. V. Poblete (Eds.), LATIN '95: Theoretical Informatics. Proceedings, 1995. IX, 525 pages. 1995.

Vol. 912: N. Lavrac, S. Wrobel (Eds.), Machine Learning: ECML – 95. Proceedings, 1995. XI, 370 pages. 1995. (Subseries LNAI).

Vol. 913: W. Schäfer (Ed.), Software Process Technology. Proceedings, 1995. IX, 261 pages. 1995.

Vol. 914: J. Hsiang (Ed.), Rewriting Techniques and Applications. Proceedings, 1995. XII, 473 pages. 1995.

Vol. 915: P. D. Mosses, M. Nielsen, M. I. Schwartzbach (Eds.), TAPSOFT '95: Theory and Practice of Software Development. Proceedings, 1995. XV, 810 pages. 1995.

Vol. 916: N. R. Adam, B. K. Bhargava, Y. Yesha (Eds.), Digital Libraries. Proceedings, 1994. XIII, 321 pages. 1995.

Vol. 917: J. Pieprzyk, R. Safavi-Naini (Eds.), Advances in Cryptology - ASIACRYPT '94. Proceedings, 1994. XII, 431 pages. 1995.

Vol. 918: P. Baumgartner, R. Hähnle, J. Posegga (Eds.), Theorem Proving with Analytic Tableaux and Related Methods. Proceedings, 1995. X, 352 pages. 1995. (Subseries LNAI).

Vol. 919: B. Hertzberger, G. Serazzi (Eds.), High-Performance Computing and Networking. Proceedings, 1995. XXIV, 957 pages. 1995.

Vol. 920: E. Balas, J. Clausen (Eds.), Integer Programming and Combinatorial Optimization. Proceedings, 1995. IX, 436 pages. 1995.

Vol. 921: L. C. Guillou, J.-J. Quisquater (Eds.), Advances in Cryptology – EUROCRYPT '95. Proceedings, 1995. XIV, 417 pages. 1995.

Vol. 922: H. Dörr, Efficient Graph Rewriting and Its Implementation. IX, 266 pages. 1995.

Vol. 923: M. Meyer (Ed.), Constraint Processing. IV, 289 pages. 1995.

Vol. 924: P. Ciancarini, O. Nierstrasz, A. Yonezawa (Eds.), Object-Based Models and Languages for Concurrent Systems. Proceedings, 1994. VII, 193 pages. 1995.

Vol. 925: J. Jeuring, E. Meijer (Eds.), Advanced Functional Programming. Proceedings, 1995. VII, 331 pages. 1995.

Vol. 926: P. Nesi (Ed.), Objective Software Quality. Proceedings, 1995. VIII, 249 pages. 1995.

Vol. 927: J. Dix, L. Moniz Pereira, T. C. Przymusinski (Eds.), Non-Monotonic Extensions of Logic Programming. Proceedings, 1994. IX, 229 pages. 1995. (Subseries LNAI).

Vol. 928: V.W. Marek, A. Nerode, M. Truszczynski (Eds.), Logic Programming and Nonmonotonic Reasoning. Proceedings, 1995. VIII, 417 pages. 1995. (Subseries LNAI).

Vol. 929: F. Morán, A. Moreno, J.J. Merelo, P. Chacón (Eds.), Advances in Artificial Life. Proceedings, 1995. XIII, 960 pages. 1995 (Subseries LNAI).

Vol. 930: J. Mira, F. Sandoval (Eds.), From Natural to Artificial Neural Computation. Proceedings, 1995. XVIII, 1150 pages. 1995.

Vol. 931: P.J. Braspenning, F. Thuijsman, A.J.M.M. Weijters (Eds.), Artificial Neural Networks. IX, 295 pages. 1995.

Vol. 932: J. Iivari, K. Lyytinen, M. Rossi (Eds.), Advanced Information Systems Engineering. Proceedings, 1995. XI, 388 pages. 1995.

Vol. 933: L. Pacholski, J. Tiuryn (Eds.), Computer Science Logic. Proceedings, 1994. IX, 543 pages. 1995.

Vol. 934: P. Barahona, M. Stefanelli, J. Wyatt (Eds.), Artificial Intelligence in Medicine. Proceedings, 1995. XI, 449 pages. 1995. (Subseries LNAI).

Vol. 935: G. De Michelis, M. Diaz (Eds.), Application and Theory of Petri Nets 1995. Proceedings, 1995. VIII, 511 pages. 1995.

Vol. 936: V.S. Alagar, M. Nivat (Eds.), Algebraic Methodology and Software Technology. Proceedings, 1995. XIV, 591 pages. 1995.

Vol. 937: Z. Galil, E. Ukkonen (Eds.), Combinatorial Pattern Matching. Proceedings, 1995. VIII, 409 pages. 1995.

Vol. 938: K.P. Birman, F. Mattern, A. Schiper (Eds.), Theory and Practice in Distributed Systems. Proceedings,1994. X, 263 pages. 1995.

Vol. 939: P. Wolper (Ed.), Computer Aided Verification. Proceedings, 1995. X, 451 pages. 1995.

Vol. 940: C. Goble, J. Keane (Eds.), Advances in Databases. Proceedings, 1995. X, 277 pages. 1995.

Vol. 941: M. Cadoli, Tractable Reasoning in Artificial Intelligence. XVII, 247 pages. 1995. (Subseries LNAI).

Vol. 942: G. Böckle, Exploitation of Fine-Grain Parallelism. IX, 188 pages. 1995.

Vol. 943: W. Klas, M. Schrefl, Metaclasses and Their Application. IX, 201 pages. 1995.

Vol. 944: Z. Fülöp, F. Gécseg (Eds.), Automata, Languages and Programming. Proceedings, 1995. XIII, 686 pages. 1995.

Vol. 945: B. Bouchon-Meunier, R.R. Yager, L.A. Zadeh (Eds.), Advances in Intelligent Computing - IPMU '94. Proceedings, 1994. XII, 628 pages.1995.

Vol. 946: C. Froidevaux, J. Kohlas (Eds.), Symbolic and Quantitative Approaches to Reasoning and Uncertainty. Proceedings, 1995. X, 420 pages. 1995. (Subseries LNAI).

Vol. 947: B. Möller (Ed.), Mathematics of Program Construction. Proceedings, 1995. VIII, 472 pages. 1995.

Vol. 948: G. Cohen, M. Giusti, T. Mora (Eds.), Applied Algebra, Algebraic Algorithms and Error-Correcting Codes. Proceedings, 1995. XI, 485 pages. 1995.

Vol. 949: D.G. Feitelson, L. Rudolph (Eds.), Job Scheduling Strategies for Parallel Processing. Proceedings, 1995. VIII, 361 pages. 1995.

Vol. 950: A. De Santis (Ed.), Advances in Cryptology - EUROCRYPT '94. Proceedings, 1994. XIII, 473 pages. 1995.

Vol. 951: M.J. Egenhofer, J.R. Herring (Eds.), Advances in Spatial Databases. Proceedings, 1995. XI, 405 pages. 1995.

Vol. 952: W. Olthoff (Ed.), ECOOP '95 - Object-Oriented Programming. Proceedings, 1995. XI, 471 pages. 1995.

Vol. 953: D. Pitt, D.E. Rydeheard, P. Johnstone (Eds.), Category Theory and Computer Science. Proceedings, 1995. VII, 252 pages. 1995.

Vol. 954: G. Ellis, R. Levinson, W. Rich. J.F. Sowa (Eds.), Conceptual Structures: Applications, Implementation and Theory. Proceedings, 1995. IX, 353 pages. 1995. (Subseries LNAI).

VOL. 955: S.G. Akl, F. Dehne, J.-R. Sack, N. Santoro (Eds.), Algorithms and Data Structures. Proceedings, 1995. IX, 519 pages. 1995.

Vol. 956: X. Yao (Ed.), Progress in Evolutionary Computation. Proceedings, 1993, 1994. VIII, 314 pages. 1995. (Subseries LNAI).

Vol. 957: C. Castelfranchi, J.-P. Müller (Eds.), From Reaction to Cognition. Proceedings, 1993. VI, 252 pages. 1995. (Subseries LNAI).

Vol. 958: J. Calmet, J.A. Campbell (Eds.), Integrating Symbolic Mathematical Computation and Artificial Intelligence. Proceedings, 1994. X, 275 pages. 1995.

Vol. 959: D.-Z. Du, M. Li (Eds.), Computing and Combinatorics. Proceedings, 1995. XIII, 654 pages. 1995.

Vol. 960: D. Leivant (Ed.), Logic and Computational Complexity. Proceedings, 1994. VIII, 514 pages. 1995.

Vol. 961: K.P. Jantke, S. Lange (Eds.), Algorithmic Learning for Knowledge-Based Systems. X, 511 pages. 1995. (Subseries LNAI).

Vol. 962: I. Lee, S.A. Smolka (Eds.), CONCUR '95: Concurrency Theory. Proceedings, 1995. X, 547 pages. 1995.

Vol. 963: D. Coppersmith (Ed.), Advances in Cryptology -CRYPTO '95. Proceedings, 1995. XII, 467 pages. 1995.

Vol. 964: V. Malyshkin (Ed.), Parallel Computing Technologies. Proceedings, 1995. XII, 497 pages. 1995.

Vol. 965: H. Reichel (Ed.), Fundamentals of Computation Theory. Proceedings, 1995. IX, 433 pages. 1995.

Vol. 966: S. Haridi, K. Ali, P. Magnusson (Eds.), EURO-PAR '95: Parallel Processing. Proceedings, 1995. XV, 734 pages. 1995.

Vol. 967: J.P. Bowen, M.G. Hinchey (Eds.), ZUM '95: The Z Formal Specification Notation. Proceedings, 1995. XI, 571 pages. 1995.

Vol. 969: J. Wiedermann, P. Hájek (Eds.), Mathematical Foundations of Computer Science 1995. Proceedings, 1995. XIII, 588 pages. 1995.

Vol. 970: V. Hlaváč, R. Šára (Eds.), Computer Analysis of Images and Patterns. Proceedings, 1995. XVIII, 960 pages. 1995.

Vol. 971: T.E. Schubert, P.J. Windley, J. Alves-Foss (Eds.), Higher Order Logic Theorem Proving and Its Applications. Proceedings, 1995. VIII, 400 pages. 1995.

Vol. 972: J.-M. Hélary, M. Raynal (Eds.), Distributed Algorithms. Proceedings, 1995. XI, 333 pages. 1995.

Vol. 973: H.H. Adelsberger, J. Lažanský, V. Mařík (Eds.), Information Management in Computer Integrated Manufacturing. IX, 665 pages. 1995.

Vol. 974: C. Braccini, L. DeFloriani, G. Vernazza (Eds.), Image Analysis and Processing. Proceedings, 1995. XIX, 757 pages. 1995.

Vol. 975: W. Moore, W. Luk (Eds.), Field-Programming Logic and Applications. Proceedings, 1995. XI, 448 pages. 1995.

Vol. 978: N. Revell, A M. Tjoa (Eds.), Database and Expert Systems Applications. Proceedings, 1995. XV, 654 pages. 1995.